T0183345

Lecture Notes in Artificial Intelligence   12037

Subseries of Lecture Notes in Computer Science

Paulo Quaresma · Renata Vieira ·
Sandra Aluísio · Helena Moniz ·
Fernando Batista · Teresa Gonçalves (Eds.)

Computational Processing of the Portuguese Language

14th International Conference, PROPOR 2020
Evora, Portugal, March 2–4, 2020
Proceedings

 Springer

Editors
Paulo Quaresma 🄓
University of Évora
Evora, Portugal

Renata Vieira 🄓
University of Évora
Evora, Portugal

Sandra Aluísio 🄓
University of São Paulo
São Carlos, Brazil

Helena Moniz 🄓
University of Lisbon
Lisbon, Portugal

Fernando Batista 🄓
INESC-ID/ISCTE-IUL
Lisbon, Portugal

Teresa Gonçalves 🄓
University of Évora
Evora, Portugal

ISSN 0302-9743   ISSN 1611-3349 (electronic)
Lecture Notes in Artificial Intelligence
ISBN 978-3-030-41504-4   ISBN 978-3-030-41505-1 (eBook)
https://doi.org/10.1007/978-3-030-41505-1

LNCS Sublibrary: SL7 – Artificial Intelligence

Preface

This volume presents the 14th edition of the International Conference on the Computational Processing of Portuguese (PROPOR 2020). The conference was held at the Colégio do Espírito Santo, Universidade de Évora, in Évora, Portugal, during March 2–4, 2020. Although the conference is in its 14th edition, it is celebrating the maturity of 27 years of existence, since it has been predominantly a biannual event. In that route it returns to Évora after 21 years.

PROPOR is the main scientific meeting in the area of language and speech technologies for Portuguese and on the basic and applied research issues related to this language. The meeting is a very rich forum for researchers dedicated to the computational processing of Portuguese, promoting the exchange of experiences in the development of methodologies, language resources, tools, applications, and innovative projects. It is also a meeting for the reception of new members to the community, represented mainly by the students in the field. A total of 70 submissions were received for the main event, involving 233 authors from many countries worldwide, such as Portugal, Brazil, Spain, Macau, the UK, Norway, Nepal, India, Germany, and China.

This volume presents 36 full and 5 short papers, selected from 70 submissions, which reflects an acceptance rate of 51% for full papers and 58% overall. Each paper was reviewed by 3 reviewers from a total of 48 academic institutions and companies. The papers are organized thematically and include the most recent developments in speech processing, resources and evaluation, semantics, natural language processing tasks, multilinguality, and applications. This year, reflecting the technological presence of the area in everyday life, the topic with the largest number of submissions and acceptance was natural language applications.

For 2020 our selected team of invited speakers represented the worldwide importance of this area, not only in the academy but also in very well-established companies. They are:

- João Graça, Co-founder and CTO of Unbabel
- Fernando Pereira, VP and Engineering Fellow at Google
- Cícero dos Santos, Research Scientist at Amazon
- Isabel Trancoso, Senior Researcher at Spoken Language Systems Lab, INESC-ID

In this edition we also had four workshops, regarding the following topics: relations of natural language with the digital humanities, technologies for language acquisition, language corpora availability, and tools and resources for paraphrasing. The proceedings of the workshops are not included in this volume, as the organizers of each workshop arranged them separately. The event also includes a contest for best dissertation and thesis, a tutorial, and a session for systems demonstration.

Our sincere thanks to every person and institution involved in the complex organization of this event, especially to the members of the Program Committee of the main event, the dissertations contest and the associated workshops, the invited speakers, and the general organization staff. We are also grateful to the agencies and organizations that supported and promoted the event.

January 2020

Paulo Quaresma
Renata Vieira
Sandra Aluísio
Helena Moniz
Fernando Batista
Teresa Gonçalves

Organization

General Chairs

Paulo Quaresma   Universidade de Évora, Portugal
Renata Vieira   Universidade de Évora, Portugal

Program Chairs

Sandra Aluísio   University of São Paulo, Brazil
Helena Moniz   INESC-ID/FLUL, Universidade de Lisboa, Portugal

Editorial Chairs

Fernando Batista   INESC-ID and ISCTE-IUL, Portugal
Teresa Gonçalves   Universidade de Évora, Portugal

Demo Chairs

José Saias   Universidade de Évora, Portugal
Vládia Pinheiro   University of Fortaleza, Brazil

Best MSc/MA and PhD Dissertation Award Chair

Pablo Gamallo   University of Santiago de Compostela, Spain

Workshops and Tutorials Chairs

André Adami   Universidade de Caxias do Sul, Brazil
Irene Rodrigues   Universidade de Évora, Portugal

Local Organization Committee

Madhu Agrawal   Universidade de Évora, Portugal
Roy Bayot   Universidade de Évora, Portugal
José Duarte   Universidade de Évora, Portugal
Nuno Miranda   Universidade de Évora, Portugal
Prakash Poudyal   Universidade de Évora, Portugal
João Sequeira   Universidade de Évora, Portugal
Hua Yang   Universidade de Évora, Portugal

Steering Committee

André Adami	Universidade de Caxias do Sul, Brazil
Amália Mendes	Centro de Linguística da Universidade de Lisboa, Portugal
Paulo Quaresma	Universidade de Évora, Portugal
João Silva	Universidade de Lisboa, Portugal
Aline Villavicencio	Institute of Informatics, Federal University of Rio Grande do Sul, Brazil, and The University of Sheffield, UK

Program Committee

Alberto Abad	IST/INESC-ID, Portugal
André Adami	Universidade de Caxias do Sul, Brazil
Sandra Aluisio	University of São Paulo, Brazil
João Balsa	Universidade de Lisboa, Portugal
Jorge Baptista	University of Algarve, and L2F-Spoken Language Lab, INESC-ID Lisboa, Portugal
Plinio Barbosa	University of Campinas, Brazil
Anabela Barreiro	INESC-ID, Portugal
Fernando Batista	INESC-ID and ISCTE-IUL, Portugal
Luciana Benotti	Universidad Nacional de Cordoba, Argentina
Maria Bocorny Finatto	UFRGS, Brazil
António Branco	Universidade de Lisboa, Portugal
Nuno C. Marques	DI – FCT/UNL, Portugal
Vera Cabarrão	FLUL/CLUL, Universidade de Lisboa, and INESC-ID, Portugal
Sara Candeias	Microsoft, Portugal
Helena Caseli	Federal University of São Carlos, Brazil
Luísa Coheur	IST/INESC-ID Lisboa, Portugal
Berthold Crysmann	CNRS, France
Valeria de Paiva	Samsung Research America, USA, and University of Birmingham, UK
José de Souza	eBay Inc., USA
Ariani Di Felippo	Universidade Federal de São Carlos, Brazil
Gaël Dias	Normandie University, France
Brett Drury	Scicrop, Brazil
Magali Duran	University of São Paulo, Brazil
Isabel Falé	Universidade Aberta/CLUL, Portugal
Valeria Feltrim	Universidade Estadual de Maringá, Brazil
Marcelo Finger	University of São Paulo, Brazil
Erick Fonseca	Instituto de Telecomunicações, Portugal
Claudia Freitas	PUC-Rio, Brazil
Erick Galani Maziero	Universidade de Lavras, Brazil
Pablo Gamallo	University of Santiago de Compostela, Spain

Teresa Gonçalves	Universidade de Évora, Portugal
Leandro Henrique	Embrapa, Brazil
Mário J. Silva	IST/INESC-ID, Universidade de Lisboa, Portugal
Arnaldo Cândido Junior	UTFPR, Brazil
Fabio Kepler	Unbabel, Portugal
Eric Laporte	Université Paris-Est Marne-la-Vallée, France
Ana Leal	University of Macau, Macau
Nuno Mamede	IST/INESC-ID Lisboa, Portugal
Palmira Marrafa	Universidade de Lisboa, Portugal
David Martins de Matos	Universidade de Lisboa, Portugal
Ana Isabel Mata	Universidade de Lisboa, Portugal
Amália Mendes	Centro de Linguística da Universidade de Lisboa, Portugal
Helena Moniz	L2F/INESC-ID, Portugal
Nelson Neto	Universidade Federal do Pará, Brazil
Hugo Gonçalo Oliveira	CISUC, University of Coimbra, Portugal
Ivandre Paraboni	University of São Paulo, Brazil
Thiago Pardo	University of São Paulo, Brazil
Carla Parra Escartín	Unbabel, Portugal
Fernando Perdigao	IT, Portugal
Prakash Poudyal	Kathmandu University, Nepal
Carlos Prolo	UFRN, Brazil
Paulo Quaresma	Universidade de Évora, Portugal
Violeta Quental	PUC-Rio, Brazil
Alexandre Rademaker	IBM Research Brazil and EMAp/FGV, Brazil
Carlos Ramisch	Aix Marseille University, France
Eraldo Rezende Fernandes	FACOM/UFMS, Brazil
Ricardo Ribeiro	INESC ID Lisboa/ISCTE-IUL, Portugal
Vitor Rocio	Universidade Aberta, Portugal
Irene Rodrigues	Universidade de Évora, Portugal
Norton Roman	USP, Brazil
José Saias	Universidade de Évora, Portugal
Diana Santos	University of Oslo, Norway
Carolina Scarton	The University of Sheffield, UK
Evandro Seron Ruiz	University of São Paulo, Brazil
Antonio Serralheiro	INESC-ID and Academia Militar, Portugal
Christopher Shulby	DefinedCrowd, Portugal
João Silva	Universidade de Lisboa, Portugal
Alberto Simões	2AI Lab-IPCA, Portugal
Augusto Soares da Silva	Universidade Católica Portuguesa, Portugal
Rubén Solera-Ureña	Spoken Language Systems Laboratory, INESC-ID Lisboa, Portugal
Marcos Treviso	Instituto de Telecomunicações/Instituto Superior Técnico, Portugal
Luis Felipe Uebel	Samsung Instituto de Desenvolvimento para a Informática da Amazônia (SIDIA), Brazil

Oto Vale	Universidade Federal de São Carlos, Brazil
Renata Vieira	PUCRS, Brazil
Aline Villavicencio	Institute of Informatics, Federal University of Rio Grande do Sul, Brazil, and The University of Sheffield, UK
Maria Volpe Nunes	USP, Brazil
Rodrigo Wilkens	University of Strasbourg, France
Marcos Zampieri	Rochester Institute of Technology, USA
Leonardo Zilio	CTS, University of Surrey, UK

Additional Reviewers

Danielle Caled
Nathan Hartmann
João Rodrigues

Contents

Semantics

Natural Language Processing Tasks

Speech Processing

Towards Automatic Determination of Critical Gestures for European Portuguese Sounds

Samuel Silva[1(✉)], Conceição Cunha[2], António Teixeira[1], Arun Joseph[3], and Jens Frahm[3]

[1] DETI/IEETA, University of Aveiro, Aveiro, Portugal
{sss,ajst}@ua.pt
[2] IPS, LMU Munich, Munich, Germany
[3] Max-Planck-Institut für Biophysikalische Chemie, Göttingen, Germany

Abstract. Technologies, such as electromagnetic midsagittal articulography (EMA) and real-time magnetic resonance (RT-MRI), can contribute to improve our understanding of the static and dynamic aspects of speech, namely by providing information regarding which articulators are essential (critical) in producing specific sounds and how (gestures). Previous work has successfully demonstrated the possibility to determine critical articulators considering vocal tract data obtained from RT-MRI. However, these works have adopted a conservative approach by considering vocal tract representations analogous to the flash points obtained with EMA data, i.e., landmarks fixed over the articulators, e.g., tongue. To move towards a data-driven method able to determine gestural scores, e.g., driving articulatory speech synthesis, one important step is to move into a representation aligned with Articulatory Phonology and Task Dynamics. This article advances towards this goal by exploring critical articulators determination considering a vocal tract representation aligned with this framework is adopted and presents first results considering 50 Hz RTMRI data for two speakers of European Portuguese.

Keywords: Critical articulator · Speech production model · Data-driven approach · Real-time magnetic resonance

1 Introduction

Our knowledge regarding how the many different sounds of world's languages are articulated is still fragmentary, limiting performance of artificial systems aiming to closely simulate human speech production, articulatory synthesis, audio-visual synthesis, applications for language teaching and speech therapy. Knowledge is particularly limited for the temporal organization, coarticulation and dynamic aspects.

As descriptions based in static configurations of the articulators have limitations, in the last 30 years, speech production research has concentrated in the

© Springer Nature Switzerland AG 2020
P. Quaresma et al. (Eds.): PROPOR 2020, LNAI 12037, pp. 3–12, 2020.
https://doi.org/10.1007/978-3-030-41505-1_1

inclusion of dynamic aspects of human articulation in the definition of abstract sounds. In the framework of Articulatory Phonology [3,8,9] – very representative of such efforts –, speech sounds have been described by tempo-spacial trajectories (gestures) of the vocal tract articulator(s) responsible for their production. For example, the bilabial stop /p/ is mostly described by the closing and opening movement of both lips. Each basic sound of a language will have a small set of gestures that need to be produced, which we can designate as critical gestures, by extension of the critical articulators concept. In turn, these concepts are reflected in the Task Dynamics framework [23] supporting, e.g., articulatory speech synthesis [28].

However, in spoken language speech sounds are not sequential nor isolated, but sequences of consonants and vowels are produced in a temporally overlapping way with coarticulatory differences in timing being language specific and varying according to syllable type (simplex, complex), syllable position (Marin and Pouplier [15] for timing in English, Cunha [6] for EP) and many other factors.

Because of the coarticulation with adjacent sounds, other articulators that are not relevant (i.e., not critical) for the production of the analysed sound can be activated. In this regard, not critical articulators applies to all gestures which are not actively involved in a specific articulation (e.g. a bilabial gestures for /p/), but show anticipatory movement influenced by the following vowel.

Some articulatory based phonological descriptions of speech sounds appeared for different languages with increased access to direct measures of vowel tract inspection as electro-magnetic articulography (EMA) or magnetic resonance imaging (MRI). For EP there are some segmental descriptions using EMA [17] and MRI (static and real time, e.g. [16]) and some work on onset coordination using EMA [5,6]. Also an initial description of EP adopting the Articulatory Phonology framework was proposed [17]. However, these descriptions analysed a reduced set of images or participants and need to be revised and improved.

Recent advances in the collection and processing of real-time MRI [24] are promising to improve existing descriptions, but the huge amounts of collected data are only manageable by proposing automatic data-driven approaches. In these scenarios, where huge amounts of data need to be tackled (e.g., RTMRI, EMA), the community has made an effort to contribute with methods to extract and analyse features of interest [2,4,14,26,27] and, regarding articulator criticality, several authors have proposed data-driven methods, e.g., [1,11,13,20,21,25]. In particular, the statistical method proposed by Jackson and Singampali [11] considers the position of the EMA pellets as representative of the articulators, selects data samples, at the midpoint of each phone, and computes several statistics concerning: (1) the whole articulator data (the grand statistics), used to build the models for each articulator; and (2) the data for each phone (phone statistics). The critical articulators, for each phone, are determined by analysing the distances between the grand and phone probability distributions.

Previous work [29,30] extended these computational methods [10,11], to determine the critical articulators for EP phones from real-time MRI data at 14 and 50 fps. While these works demonstrate the applicability of the methods to MRI data, and present (albeit preliminary) interesting results, they are conservative in the adopted vocal tract variables, since they consider landmarks positioned over the vocal tract, replicating the positions of the EMA pellets, to enable an overall validation of the applicability of the method to novel data by comparison with the results presented by Jackson and Singampali [11]. Therefore, as asserted in [30], one of the aspects requiring further attention concerns how the method would behave for a different set of variables of the vocal tract addressing, e.g., constrictions.

To pursue this topic, this work presents first results for critical articulator determination considering a representation of the vocal tract aligned with the Task Dynamics framework [8].

The remainder of this document is organized as follows: Sect. 2 describes the main aspects of the adopted methods; Sect. 3 presents and discusses the results obtained for the consideration of Task Dynamics variables to determine the critical articulators from RT-MRI data; finally, Sect. 4, highlights the main contributions of this work and proposes routes for future endeavors.

2   Methods

Realtime MRI acquisition was performed at the Max Planck Institute for Biophysical Chemistry, Göttingen, Germany, using a 3T Siemens Magnetom Prisma Fit MRI System with high performance gradients (Max ampl = 80 mT/m; slew rate = 200 T/m/s) at 50 fps. Synchronized audio was recorded using an optical microphone (Dual Channel-FOMRI, Optoacoustics, Or Yehuda, Israel), fixed on the head coil. All volunteers provided informed written consent, were compensated for their participation, and none reported language, speech or hearing problems.

The analysed materials include carrier sentences in two prosodic conditions and alternating the verb as follows: (diga ('Say'); ouvi ('I heard'); leio ('I read')) as in 'Diga pato, diga pato baixinho' ('Say duck, Say duck gently'). The target words consisted of lexical words containing all oral [i, e, E, a, O, o, u, 6] nasal vowels [6 , e , i , o , u] and some lexical diphthongs. The sentences were presented from a computer screen in randomized order with 3 repetitions. So far, this corpus has been recorded from sixteen native speakers (8m, 8f) of EP and the work presented here tests the methods on two of the male speakers.

Data and Articulators Selection—The RT-MRI sequences were processed considering the method presented in [26] to extract the vocal tract profiles. Table 1 shows the phones considered for analysis. Taking into account that different sounds have a different progression, over time, the frame considered to represent the vocal tract configuration was selected from the annotated interval using slightly different criteria, as explained in Table 1. For instance, for /p/, the frame with the minimum inter-lip distance was selected.

Similarly to Silva et al. [30], and considering the dynamic nature of nasal vowels [7,16,18,32], we wanted to have an insight regarding if, for different stages, the determination of the critical articulators would yield some differences.

Table 1. Summary of the criteria used for selecting the representative frame for particular phones (left) and of the computed statistics for each landmark and corresponding notation as in [11] (right).

phone (SAMPA)	criterion
oral vowels 6, a, e, E, i, o, O, u	midpoint
nasal vowels 6˜, e˜, i˜, o˜, u˜	three classes were created, taking the first, middle, and final frames
nasal consonants m, n	[m], frame with minimum inter-lip distance; [n], midpoint
stops p, b, k, d, g, t	[p] and [b], frame with minimum inter-lip distance; [k],[d], [g] and [t], midpoint
sibilants s	midpoint

Grand stats	Not.	Comment
grand mean	M	all selected frames
grand variance	Σ	all selected frames
total sample size	N	Spk 8458: 896; Spk 8460: 486
corr. matrix	R^*	keeping statistically significant and strong correlations ($r_{ij} > 0.2$ and $\alpha = 0.05$)

Phone stats	Not.	Comment
mean	μ^ϕ	frames selected for each phone
variance	Σ^ϕ	frames selected for each phone
sample size	v^ϕ	variable among phones
corr. matrix	R^ϕ	not attending to significance and module

To this end, each nasal vowel was included as three "pseudo-phones", represented by the beginning, middle and final frame of the annotated interval and named, respectively, [vowel]_B, [vowel]_M and [vowel].

Differently from the original application of the method to EMA [11] and subsequent extension to RT-MRI [30] data, for this work the considered variables are not landmarks over the vocal tract, but tract variables aligned with Task Dynamics [3,8]. Apart from the velum, which is represented by a pair of (x, y) coordinates (see [30]), the tongue tip (TT) and tongue body (TB) constrictions are expressed by their degree and location, and the lips by their aperture and protrusion.

Identification of Critical Articulators—Critical articulator determination starts by the computation of the grand statistics, characterizing the distribution of the configuration, for each articulator, along the whole data; and the phone statistics, representing the distribution of articulator properties, for each phone, considering the data selection. Table 1, to the right, summarizes the different statistics computed to initialize the method, adopting the notation as in Jackson and Singampali [11].

Critical articulator identification was performed taking articulator properties (e.g., x and y positions for the velum; or d, degree and l, location, for the constrictions) independently – the 1D case – for example, TBd for the constriction degree at the tongue body, or combining them – the 2D case.

The 1D correlation matrices for the articulators (e.g., considering TBl and TTd, etc.), given the size of our data set, was computed considering correntropy, as proposed in Rao et al. [22]. Bivariate correlations (i.e, taking both properties of each articulator together) were computed through canonical correlation analysis [11,12]. For the grand correlation matrices, adopting the criteria proposed in [11], only statistically significant ($\alpha = 0.05$) correlation values above 0.2 were kept, reducing the remaining ones to zero.

The computed data statistics were used to initialize the critical articulator analysis method and 1D and 2D analysis was performed, for each speaker, returning a list of critical articulators per phone. Additionally, we wanted to assess how the method would work by gathering the data for both speakers in a "normalized" speaker. To that effect, we normalized the articulator data, for each speaker, based on the variation ranges, for each property, computed over the entire corpus, and considered this gathered data as a new speaker following a similar analysis methodology. For each speaker, we opted to define a stopping threshold, Θ_C, as low as to enable each of the phones to have, at least, one critical articulator. Naturally, this resulted in the inclusion of less important articulators for some of the phones, but, in our experience, this would also reveal some results for phones with less data, as was the case of /m/ or /v/.

3   Results and Discussion

Table 2, on the left, shows the 1D correlation matrix for the different tract variable components, for the two speakers. Overall, three sets of mild correlated components appear: lip protrusion and aperture; TB constriction degree and location; and velar x and y coordinates (strong correlation). Speaker 8460 also presents a mild correlation of TB constriction location with the TT constriction degree and lip protrusion. On the right, Table 2 shows the canonical correlation [11,12] computed among articulators and as with the 1D correlation, speaker 8460 presents mild correlations for one of the dimensions of the mentioned articulator pairs.

Regarding the determination of critical articulators, Table 3 presents the results obtained for each speaker (columns 8458 and 8460) and for the full normalized data (column ALL). It is important to note that the order in which the articulators appear is meaningful, starting from the one more strongly detected as critical. Additionally, on the rightmost column, the table provides the characterization of EP sounds based on the principle of articulatory phonology as reported by Oliveira [17].

3.1   Discussion

Regarding the 1D correlation, the Task Dynamics variables are, overall, more decorrelated than what was observed in previous approaches considering landmarks over the vocal tract (e.g., see Silva et al. [30]). Apart from the (expected) strong correlation between velar coordinates, the mild/weak correlation observed for the lips (protrusion vs aperture) and tongue body constriction (location vs degree) are, probably, due to a bias introduced by the characteristics of the considered corpus. In this respect, the matrix for speaker 8460 exhibits, additionally, a correlation between TTCd and TBCl, which is probably due to a lack of phones, in the corpus, emphasizing the independence of the TT towards the

Table 2. To the left, 1D correlations among different articulator dimensions, for both speakers; on the right, canonical correlations among different articulators.

8458	LIPSa	LIPSp	TTCd	TTCl	TBCd	TBCl	Vy	Vx
LIPSa	1.00	0.59	0.26	0.28	0.00	0.00	0.00	0.00
LIPSp	0.59	1.00	0.36	0.00	0.00	0.00	0.00	0.00
TTCd	0.26	0.36	1.00	0.37	0.00	0.37	0.00	0.00
TTCl	0.28	0.00	0.37	1.00	0.29	0.27	0.30	0.34
TBCd	0.00	0.00	0.00	0.29	1.00	0.58	0.31	0.23
TBCl	0.00	0.00	0.37	0.27	0.58	1.00	0.00	0.00
Vy	0.00	0.00	0.00	0.30	0.31	0.00	1.00	0.88
Vx	0.00	0.00	0.00	0.34	0.23	0.00	0.88	1.00
8460	**LIPSa**	**LIPSp**	**TTCd**	**TTCl**	**TBCd**	**TBCl**	**Vy**	**Vx**
LIPSa	1.00	0.69	0.43	0.00	0.23	0.40	0.00	0.00
LIPSp	0.69	1.00	0.64	0.00	0.00	0.61	0.00	0.00
TTCd	0.43	0.64	1.00	0.00	0.23	0.61	0.00	0.00
TTCl	0.00	0.00	0.00	1.00	0.39	0.35	0.00	0.00
TBCd	0.23	0.00	0.23	0.39	1.00	0.45	0.00	0.00
TBCl	0.40	0.61	0.61	0.35	0.45	1.00	0.00	0.00
Vy	0.00	0.00	0.00	0.00	0.00	0.00	1.00	0.97
Vx	0.00	0.00	0.00	0.00	0.00	0.00	0.97	1.00

	8458		8460	
$\rho_{LIPS,TTC}$	0.38	0.00	0.64	0.00
$\rho_{LIPS,TBC}$	0.00	0.00	0.64	0.21
$\rho_{LIPS,V}$	0.24	0.00	0.00	0.00
$\rho_{TTC,TBC}$	0.40	0.26	0.66	0.27
$\rho_{TTC,V}$	0.40	0.00	0.20	0.00
$\rho_{TBC,V}$	0.34	0.00	0.27	0.00

TB, e.g., lateral /l/. Regarding the additional correlations appearing for speaker 8460, also for the canonical correlations, while the hypothesis that these might be a result of articulatory idiosyncrasy cannot be disregarded, they are probably a result of the smaller sample size when compared to speaker 8458.

Regarding the critical articulators determined for each phone, please note that the analysis was performed considering a conservative stopping threshold, Θ_C, to avoid the appearance of phones without, at least, one critical articulator. Therefore, the results should mostly be interpreted considering their order, i.e., those articulators presented last, particularly for those phones which list the four, should not be given as much value as those presented first, and for phones with a shorter list. Overall, and considering that the corpus is prone to strong coarticulation effects, the obtained results are mostly in accordance with descriptions considering Articulatory Phonology [17].

The TB is determined as the most critical articulator, for most vowels, in accordance to the descriptions available in the literature. The appearance of V in a more prominent position for oral vowels, rather than nasal vowels, is aligned with previous outcomes of the method [11,29,30]. This is probably due to a more stable position of V at the middle of oral vowels (the selected frame) than at the different stages selected for the nasal vowels for which it appears, mostly, in the fourth place, eventually due to the adopted conservative stopping criteria, to avoid phones without any reported critical articulator. It is also relevant to note that, for instance, if some of the nasal vowels are preceded by a nasal consonant it affects velum position during the initial phase of the vowel, which will have an incomplete movement towards closure [31]. This might explain why V does not appear as critical in the first frame (_B) of most nasal vowels (typically referred as the oral stage [19]) since the velum is not in a stable position. While L correctly appears, with some prominence, for /u/ and its nasal congenere, the appearance of this articulator for other vowels, probably due to the limitations of the corpus, does not allow any conclusion, in this regard.

Table 3. Critical articulator identification for a list of phones present in the analysed corpus, considering each speaker (columns 8458 and 8460), gathering the normalized data for both speakers (ALL). The rightmost column presents the phone characterization as reported by Oliveira [17]. For the nasal vowels, the B and M suffixes identify the first and middle frame of the vowel interval, respectively, and the row with no suffix the last (maximum velar aperture) frame.

ph	spk 8458	spk 8460	spk ALL	Oliveira [17]
6	B V T L	V L T B	V B T	B
a	T B L	T V B	T	B
e	B T V L	B T	B V	B
E	B V L T	B L V T	B T L V	B
i	B T L V	B V T L	B V	B
o	V B L T	T	V B L	B L
O	B T V L	V B T L	B T V	B L
u	B L T	L B V T	L B V	B L
6~B	T V L	T B L V	T	—
6~M	T	B T L V	T	—
6~	L	L B V T	L B T V	B V
e~B	B L T	L	L	—
e~M	L B T V	L B T	L	—
e~	L B T V	L B	L V	B V
i~B	B V L T	B L T V	B V	—
i~M	B L T V	B L V T	B V	—
i~	B L T V	B V L T	B V	B V
o~B	B L T	B T L V	B T L	—
o~M	B L T V	B L T V	B T V	—
o~	L B T V	V B L	V T	B L V
u~B	B T L	L B T	L B T V	—
u~M	B L T V	L B T	L B T V	—
u~	B L T V	L B V	L B T V	B L V
d	T B L V	T L B	T V	T V
g	B T V L	L V B T	B V	B V
p	L T	V T	L T	L V
b	L B T	V L B T	L V	L V
v	V B L T	V B L	B V	L V
t	T B L	B T L	B	T V
k	V B L T	B V T L	V B	B V
m	L V T	L B V	V L B	L V
n	B T L V	V B L T	B V	T V
r	T B L V	B T V	B T	T
s	T L B V	V T L B	T B V	T B V
M	V	V	V	V

Constrictions at: L : Lips T : Tongue Tip B : Tongue Body V : Velum

Regarding consonants, for /d/, /t/, /s/ and /r/, as expected, T is identified as the most critical articulator. For bilabials, /p/, /b/ and /m/ correctly present L as the most critical articulator, but this does not happen for /v/, although the expected prominence of V appears. For /m/, V also appears, along with L, as expected. For /p/, unexpectedly, the tongue tip appears as critical, for both speakers, probably due to coarticulatory reasons. For /k/, V and TB are identified as the most critical articulators. Finally, M, which denotes the nasal tail, makes sense to have V as critical.

By gathering the normalized data, for both speakers, in speaker ALL, the method provided lists that are, overall, more succinct, cleaner, and closer to the expected outcomes, when compared to the literature [17], even considering the very simple data normalization performed. This seems to point out that the amount of considered data has a practical effect on the outcomes. While this is expectable, it seems to have a stronger impact than in previous approaches using more variables [30].

4   Conclusions

This article shows evidence that a vocal tract representation aligned with the Task Dynamics framework is compatible with a data-driven method for critical articulator determination from RT-MRI data of the vocal tract. The results, obtained by fully automatic analysis, considering data from two speakers, show data which resonates on previous literature for the criticality of articulators for EP phones. One notable aspect observed is that the amount of considered data samples seems to play an even more crucial role when adopting the Task Dynamics variables when compared with previous work [30], which adopted a representation using three variables for the tongue and two for the upper and lower lips, separately.

Considering the body of work exploring this data-driven method for determining critical articulators [11,29,30] and the contributions provided here, showing the methods' applicability considering a set of vocal tract variables aligned with Task Dynamics, the main aspects that need to be addressed, in the future, are the size and phonetic richness of the considered data sample, including a larger quantity of data samples, and covering more speakers and EP phones.

Acknowledgements. This work is partially funded by the German Federal Ministry of Education and Research (BMBF, with the project 'Synchronic variability and change in European Portuguese'), by IEETA Research Unit funding (UID/CEC/00127/2019), by Portugal 2020 under the Competitiveness and Internationalization Operational Program, and the European Regional Development Fund through project SOCA – Smart Open Campus (CENTRO-01–0145-FEDER-000010) and project MEMNON (POCI-01-0145-FEDER-028976). We thank all the participants for their time and voice and Philip Hoole for the scripts for noise suppression.

References

1. Ananthakrishnan, G., Engwall, O.: Important regions in the articulator trajectory. In: Proceedings of the ISSP, Strasbourg, France, pp. 305–308 (2008)
2. Black, M.P., et al.: Automated evaluation of non-native English pronunciation quality: combining knowledge-and data-driven features at multiple time scales. In: Proceedings of the INTERSPEECH, pp. 493–497 (2015)
3. Browman, C.P., Goldstein, L.: Some notes on syllable structure in articulatory phonology. Phonetica 45(2–4), 140–155 (1988)
4. Chao, Q.: Data-driven approaches to articulatory speech processing. Ph.D. thesis, University of California, Merced (2011)
5. Cunha, C.: Die Organisation von Konsonantenclustern und CVC-Sequenzen in zwei portugiesischen Varietäten. Ph.D. thesis, LMU (2012)
6. Cunha, C.: Portuguese lexical clusters and CVC sequences in speech perception and production. Phonetica 72(2–3), 138–161 (2015)
7. Feng, G., Castelli, E.: Some acoustic features of nasal and nasalized vowels: a target for vowel nasalization. J. Acoust. Soc. Am. 99(6), 3694–3706 (1996)
8. Goldstein, L., Byrd, D., Saltzman, E.: The role of vocal tract gestural action units in understanding the evolution of phonology. In: Arbib, M.A. (ed.) Action to Language via the Mirror Neuron System, pp. 215–249. Cambridge University Press, Cambridge (2006)
9. Hall, N.: Articulatory phonology. Lang. Linguist. Compass 4(9), 818–830 (2010). https://doi.org/10.1111/j.1749-818X.2010.00236.x
10. Jackson, P.J., Singampalli, V.D.: Statistical identification of critical, dependent and redundant articulators. J. Acoust. Soc. Am. 123(5), 3321 (2008). https://doi.org/10.1121/1.2933798
11. Jackson, P.J., Singampalli, V.D.: Statistical identification of articulation constraints in the production of speech. Speech Commun. 51(8), 695–710 (2009). https://doi.org/10.1016/j.specom.2009.03.007
12. Johnson, R.A., Wichern, D.W.: Applied Multivariate Statistical Analysis, 6th edn. Pearson Prentice Hall, Upper Saddle River (2007)
13. Kim, J., Toutios, A., Lee, S., Narayanan, S.S.: A kinematic study of critical and non-critical articulators in emotional speech production. J. Acoust. Soc. Am. 137(3), 1411–1429 (2015). https://doi.org/10.1121/1.4908284
14. Lammert, A.C., Proctor, M.I., Narayanan, S.S., et al.: Data-driven analysis of realtime vocal tract MRI using correlated image regions. In: Proceedings of the INTERSPEECH, pp. 1572–1575 (2010)
15. Marin, S., Pouplier, M.: Temporal organization of complex onsets and codas in American English: testing the predictions of a gestural coupling model. Mot. Control 14(3), 380–407 (2010)
16. Martins, P., Oliveira, C., Silva, S., Teixeira, A.: Velar movement in European Portuguese nasal vowels. In: Proceedings of the IberSPEECH, pp. 231–240 (2012)
17. Oliveira, C.: From grapheme to gesture. Linguistic contributions for an articulatory based text-to-speech system. Ph.D. thesis, University of Aveiro (2009)
18. Oliveira, C., Teixeira, A.: On gestures timing in European Portuguese nasals. In: Proceedings of the ICPhS, Saarbrücken, Germany (2007)
19. Parkinson, S.: Portuguese nasal vowels as phonological diphthongs. Lingua 61(2–3), 157–177 (1983)

20. Prasad, A., Ghosh, P.K.: Information theoretic optimal vocal tract region selection from real time magnetic resonance images for broad phonetic class recognition. Comput. Speech Lang. **39**, 108–128 (2016). https://doi.org/10.1016/j.csl.2016.03. 003

21. Ramanarayanan, V., Segbroeck, M.V., Narayanan, S.S.: Directly data-derived articulatory gesture-like representations retain discriminatory information about phone categories. Comput. Speech Lang. **36**, 330–346 (2016). https://doi.org/10. 1016/j.csl.2015.03.004

22. Rao, M., Seth, S., Xu, J., Chen, Y., Tagare, H., Príncipe, J.C.: A test of independence based on a generalized correlation function. Sign. Proces. **91**(1), 15–27 (2011)

23. Saltzman, E.L., Munhall, K.G.: A dynamical approach to gestural patterning in speech production. Ecol. Psychol. **1**(4), 333–382 (1989)

24. Scott, A.D., Wylezinska, M., Birch, M.J., Miquel, M.E.: Speech MRI: morphology and function. Physica Med. **30**(6), 604–618 (2014). https://doi.org/10.1016/j.ejmp. 2014.05.001

25. Sepulveda, A., Castellanos-Domínguez, G., Guido, R.C.: Time-frequency relevant features for critical articulators movement inference. In: Proceedings of the 20th European Signal Processing Conference (EUSIPCO), pp. 2802–2806, August 2012

26. Silva, S., Teixeira, A.: Unsupervised segmentation of the vocal tract from real-time MRI sequences. Comput. Speech Lang. **33**(1), 25–46 (2015). https://doi.org/ 10.1016/j.csl.2014.12.003

27. Silva, S., Teixeira, A.: Quantitative systematic analysis of vocal tract data. Comput. Speech Lang. **36**, 307–329 (2016). https://doi.org/10.1016/j.csl.2015.05.004

28. Silva, S., Teixeira, A., Orvalho, V.: Articulatory-based audiovisual speech synthesis: proof of concept for European Portuguese. In: Proceedings of the IberSPEECH, Lisbon, Portugal, pp. 119–126 (2016)

29. Silva, S., Teixeira, A.J.: Critical articulators identification from RT-MRI of the vocal tract. In: INTERSPEECH, pp. 626–630 (2017)

30. Silva, S., Teixeira, A., Cunha, C., Almeida, N., Joseph, A.A., Frahm, J.: Exploring critical articulator identification from 50Hz RT-MRI data of the vocal tract. In: Proceedings of the INTERSPEECH, pp. 874–878 (2019). https://doi.org/10. 21437/Interspeech.2019-2897

31. Teixeira, A., Vaz, F., Príncipe, J.C.: Nasal vowels after nasal consonants. In: 5th Seminar on Speech Production: Models and Data, Kloster Seon, Alemanha, May 2000

32. Teixeira, A., Vaz, F.: European Portuguese nasal vowels: an EMMA study. In: Proceedings of the INTERSPEECH, Aalborg, Denmark, pp. 1483–1486 (2001)

Comparison of Heterogeneous Feature Sets for Intonation Verification

Mariana Julião[1,2]([✉]) [iD], Alberto Abad[1,2] [iD], and Helena Moniz[1,3,4] [iD]

[1] INESC-ID, Lisbon, Portugal
{mariana.juliao,alberto.abad}@l2f.inesc-id.pt, helena.moniz@inesc-id.pt
[2] Instituto Superior Técnico, Universidade de Lisboa, Lisbon, Portugal
[3] FLUL - Faculdade de Letras da Universidade de Lisboa, Lisbon, Portugal
[4] CLUL - Centro de Linguística da Universidade de Lisboa, Lisbon, Portugal

Abstract. The assessment of intonation, to which intonation verification belongs, has many applications, such as health-impaired people training – from individuals with Parkinson's disease to children with Autism Spectrum Disorders – and second language learning. Most of the approaches that are found in the literature are based on intensive preprocessing of the audio signal and hand-crafted feature extraction methods, and most of those works do not tackle the particularities of the Portuguese language. In this paper, we present our work on intonation assessment, developed from a database of binarily-labelled Portuguese intonation imitation. This has been done using the set of Low Level Descriptors (LLDs) and eGeMAPS, both extracted with the openS-MILE toolkit, and Problem-Agnostic Speech Encoder (PASE) features. We have taken the most informative feature subsets for prosody out of these. Distances between stimulus and imitation – the so-called similarity intonation scores – have been computed applying Dynamic Time Warping (DTW) for different feature subsets, and have afterwards been used as input features of a binary classifier. Performance achieves up to 66.9% of accuracy in the test data set when considering only one feature set, and it increases up to 77.5% for a set of seven features.

Keywords: Intonation assessment · Prosody imitation verification · Multiple feature fusion

1 Introduction

Although often disregarded among other aspects of language, prosody plays a crucial role in human communication, as it provides a wealth of relevant information. It encompasses pitch, rhythm, energy, and voice quality. Intonation corresponds to the variations of pitch, i.e., the melodic contours. Whereas rhythm helps segment the speech stream into smaller units as words and phrases, intonation provides information on the sentence type. For instance, in languages as Portuguese, where yes-no questions are not lexically distinguishable from affirmations, intonation is what allows to decide between these two, or even between

© Springer Nature Switzerland AG 2020
P. Quaresma et al. (Eds.): PROPOR 2020, LNAI 12037, pp. 13–22, 2020.
https://doi.org/10.1007/978-3-030-41505-1_2

an affirmation and an exclamation. It carries information on intent, focus, attitudes and emotions, not to mention all the information it conveys about the speaker.

Prosody is fluidly acquired in typically developing children. Infants have the ability to mimic the melodic aspects of speech long before they are able to articulate words [5,10]. On the other hand, it reveals itself quite hard to master by second language learners [6], as well as children with Autism Spectrum Disorders (ASD). The prosody produced by the latter, according to [15], is reported to include monotonic intonational patterns, misplaced stress patterns, deficits in pitch and intensity control, and differences in voice quality. Furthermore, according to the same authors, observations suggest that these aspects "tend to persist over time, even when other aspects of language improve".

Intonation assessment has been addressed in different ways. These can broadly be classified as assessment (how good the intonation of a segment is), as in [1,4,12,20], and classification of segments (according to their labels, as H or L, for instance) as in [7,11].

This work presents the preliminary experiments in intonation verification in a data set. Firstly recorded as an imitation task, the augmentation of the data set has made it more similar to a verification task, for considering unrelated samples as bad imitations. This is explained in detail in Subsect. 4.1. Unlike what is commonly seen in the literature, instead of using hand-crafted features alongside preprocessing, we have resorted to simple classification algorithms, and to the available general toolkits for feature extraction, with minimal preprocessing.

The relevance of our work is threefold. First, the task of intonation imitation/verification is a fundamental task in prosody assessment, which has a plethora of applications. Then, this problem has not been solved yet, as there is still no reliable way to compare intonation. Finally, to our best knowledge, no similar work has been done for Portuguese. As the number of L2 speakers of Portuguese keeps increasing, a growth in the demand for learning applications is to be expected, and these should not leave prosody assessment aside.

2   Related Work

The seminal work for goodness of imitation by Arias, Yoma, and Vivanco [1] is still a reference these days. The work considers data from second language learners (L2) of English with Spanish as their native language (L1). MFCCs were aligned using a DTW algorithm, which was afterwards used to compare the F0 curves on a frame-by-frame basis. Their data set consisted short sentences, uttered with different intonation patterns by 16 speakers. It achieved an averaged subjective-objective score correlation of 0.88.

Cheng considered recordings of Pearson Test Academic English, rated by at least two human experts [4]. Their main contribution is the use of k-means clustering method to build canonical contour models at the word level for F0 and energy, which provided strong predictors of prosody ratings. For the comparison of sequences, they had extracted word boundary information, and then scaled every word interval to a standard length, after which they applied Euclidean distance, correlation coefficient, and DTW. The authors concluded that, being F0 and energy contours strong predictors of prosody ratings, duration information was the best predictive feature. The linear regression model scores highly correlated with human ratings, $r = 0.80$.

Ma et al. [12] used 48 features based on the normalised F0 measurements, to assess nativeness in a sentence repeat task. Their data set comprised 9k responses from non-native speakers of English, from China and India, and 4k responses from native speakers of US English. The evaluation of the results was done using a weighted F1 score, achieving 0.783 in a text-independent context and 0.741 in a text-dependent one. According to their results, no substantial drop in nativeness detection has been noticed between models trained on polynomial functions on first seven degrees of polynomials and the models trained only on the first three. This means that the "basic descriptive statistics and lower-degree polynomial parameters can capture the primary characteristics".

Also for nativeness assessment, this time focusing on the classification of prosodic contours, the study of Escudero-Mancebo [7] presents a system that computes distances between sequences of prosodic labels. It considers prosodic contours by using a set of metrics based on joint entropy. The data set consisted of fifteen read sentences from the news paragraphs of a bigger corpus, read by a group of Japanese speakers of Spanish. This system performed a pairwise classification, which combined evidence for three complementary types of classifiers (artificial neural networks, decision trees, and support vector machines), which have been combined using a comprehensive fuzzy technique. It allowed for the analysis of the most frequent potential misuses of the Sp_ToBI tones as a cue for possible mistakes that appear in the prosodic productions of non-native speakers.

Automatic intonation classification was done applying multi-distribution DNNs to data from Chinese L2 learners of English [11]. The authors labelled intonation as rising, upper, lower or falling, which are then shrinked into two categories, rising and falling. Ultimately, by considering the last 80 ms of an intonational phrase, they determine the intonation of L2 English speech utterances as either rising or falling, with an accuracy of 93.0%.

3   Imitation Classification Approach

Figure 1 shows the pipeline of the approach followed in this work. First, for both stimulus and imitation speech signal, word segmentation is applied to find start and end of word boundaries (Subsect. 3.1), followed by feature extraction (Subsect. 3.2). Next, the distance between stimulus and imitation is computed using DTW, for each specific feature set (Subsect. 3.3). We refer to the distances obtained with the DTW as *similarity intonation scores*. Then, these intonation scores are fed to a classifier, which classifies them as corresponding to a *good* imitation – stimulus and imitation match – or a *bad* imitation – stimulus and imitation differ (Subsect. 3.4). We try both feeding the classifier one type of intonation score at a time – corresponding to one feature or feature set alone – and

several types of intonation scores (working as different features for the classifier), obtained from different feature sets. We have made two sets of experiences:
in train set and in test set. All the experiments in the train set are done in
cross-validation with leave one speaker out, and will, henceforth, be referred to
as cross-validation.

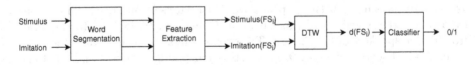

Fig. 1. Intonation comparison approach.

3.1   Word Segmentation

In Portuguese prosodic words, stresses may fall in the last three syllables of
a word, and this happens mostly in the antepenultimate syllable (in our data
set, all words correspond to this case). As Portuguese has a very strong vowel
reduction, prosodic information is by no means evenly spread throughout the
word. On the contrary, most of the information comes in the stressed syllable and
in what comes afterwards. For this reason, we thought of attending specifically
to the words from the beginning of the stressed syllabled until the end. However,
as 3 out of 5 words in our set have the stressed syllable as its first one, this would
not lead to a significant difference. Therefore, we chose to consider the whole
words.

To achieve a proper segmentation of the words, we ran forced alignment with
Kaldi [16] trained with BD-Publico corpus [13]. This provided us the phone
boundaries, with which we have segmented the segments of the recordings to
consider (words). BD-Publico has been constructed to allow for a broad speech
recognition system of continuous speech. Participants from a school of engineering have been recorded reading texts extracted from Público newspaper.

3.2   Feature Sets

In this work, rather than using task-oriented features, we exploit both the large
feature sets obtained with the openSMILE toolkit [8] (LLDs and eGeMAPS)
and the new bottleneck features from PASE [14]. From the openSMILE based
features, we chose the ones which could potentially provide the best prosodic
information: those related to pitch, energy, duration, and voice quality. For all
cases, we normalised each word feature-wise with zero mean and unit variance
before the DTW stage.

LLDs. The set of 130 low-level descriptors corresponds to the ComPaRE 2016
[18] data set. Features were extracted for each utterance with the openSMILE
toolkit [8], for windows of 0.060 s with a step of 0.010 s. From this data set, we
considered separately F0, MFCCs, and energy.

eGeMAPs. The Geneva Minimalistic Acoustic Parameter Set [9] is a set of functionals computed on top of low-level descriptors, designed specifically to provide a common ground for research in various areas of automatic voice analysis, namely paralinguistics. It comprises both the minimalistic set of 62 features (GeMAPS) and the extended set of 88 features (eGeMAPS), the former appending spectral and frequency-related parameters to the minimalist set.

As these are utterance-level features, and as we need to preserve the sequential aspect of the utterances, for the sake of comparison, we have extracted them for sliding windows of 0.200 s and steps of 0.010 s. From the eGeMAPS set, we considered separately the F0, MFCCs, loudness (to which we call "energy", hitherto), and slope.

Bottleneck Features. Recently, a Problem Agnostic Speech Encoder, PASE, has been presented [14]. It can be used to pre-train a network for speech classification tasks or simply as a speech feature extractor. This is a fully-convolutional speech encoder, followed by seven multilayer perceptron workers, which cooperate to solve different self-supervised tasks. After the convolutional blocks, an additional layer projects 512 features to embeddings of dimension 100. It emulates an overlapping sliding window using a set of convolutions, such that the input signal is decimated by a factor of 160. For sampling rates of 16 kHz, as in our case, this is equivalent to a 10 ms stride, which makes these features as usable in our task as the aforementioned ones.

3.3 Dynamic Time Warping

Dynamic Time Warping (DTW) is an algorithm for comparing time sequences [2], allowing for the comparison of time sequences of different length. It starts by building a distance matrix D, $n \times m$, where n and m are the lengths of the sequences to be compared. Each entry $D_{i,j}$, is the distance between entries i and j of the first and the second sequence, respectively, $D_{i,j} = d(x_i, y_j)$, and d is an adequate distance function.

We consider Euclidean and Cosine distances, defined as $|\boldsymbol{x}^2 - \boldsymbol{y}^2|$, and $1 - \frac{\boldsymbol{x} \cdot \boldsymbol{y}}{\|\boldsymbol{x}\|\|\boldsymbol{y}\|}$, respectively. After computing the distance matrix, the algorithm computes a warping path w, such that $d_{DTW}(x,y) = min \sum_{i=1}^{k} D(w_i)$.

The length normalised distance $d_{DTW}(x,y)$ of the two sequences along the warping path corresponds to the similarity intonation scores. In our problem, the sequences correspond to the whole segmented words. Features from the sequences are normalised to zero mean and unit variance before the distances are computed. Intonation scores are also normalised to zero mean and unit variance before classification.

3.4 Classification

For final imitation verification, we used Support Vector Machines (SVM) binary classifiers trained on the similarity intonation scores provided by the DTW stage.

Whereas any other type of classifier might have been used, SVMs were selected for their particular adequacy for tasks with a small training data size, such in our case. Among other machine learning models, SVMs stand out by being powerful discriminators that are able to perform well in a wide variety of tasks, including those where data is scarce, like in our task.

4   Experimental Setup

4.1   Data Set

Our intonation data set has 20 original stimuli recorded by a native female speaker of Standard European Portuguese and reproductions of it by 17 different speakers: 7 female, 10 male, all of them native speakers of Standard European Portuguese and with no known health impairments. The 20 original stimuli correspond to the possible combinations of five words: *banana*, *bolo*, *gelado*, *leite*, and *ovo*; and four intonations: *affirmation*, *question*, *pleasure*, and *displeasure*. Each utterance corresponds, then, to one word uttered with one particular intonation. This data set collection was initially part of a work for prosodic exercises for children with Autism Spectrum Disorders [19].

One non-expert annotator labelled the utterances binarily as *good* or *bad* imitations. After discarding non-suitable recordings, we were left with 335 imitations. The data set was split in train and test data subsets: 13 speakers for train (5 female, 8 male) and 4 speakers for test (2 female, 2 male). As expected from native speakers of the same variant of a language, most of the imitations were labelled as *good*. To increase the number of *bad* imitations in our data set, we have augmented it by adding pairs of stimulus and imitation considering orthogonality between some types of intonation: *Affirmation* orthogonal to *Question*, and *Pleasure* orthogonal to *Displeasure*. In that sense, a good imitation of an affirmation cannot be, at the same time, a good imitation of a question. Therefore, good imitations have been considered bad imitations of their counterpart. With this procedure, the final data sets consist of 494 imitations in the train set (of which 248 are *good* imitations), and 142 imitations in the test set (of which 72 are *good*).

4.2   Cross-Validation Experiments

Discrimination of Similarity Intonation Scores. In this section, we investigate the importance of the similarity intonation scores obtained with each individual feature set, as well as the proper distance metric for each one of them in the DTW stage. We considered the most informative feature sets for our task, according to literature: F0, MFCC, energy, slope – from LLD and eGeMAPS. We have trained SVMs with the intonation scores from each of these feature sets separately (cf. Fig. 1), for both euclidean and cosine distance in the DTW. The results in Table 1 are the average of the accuracies obtained in the SVM with leave-one-speaker-out cross-validation, and the corresponding standard deviations. We have also considered the PASE-BNF features. For each feature set, we highlight the best result between euclidean and cosine. Clearly, the euclidean distance provides better results than the cosine distance for all feature sets except EG_F0. These best results are the ones to be considered hereafter.

Table 1. Cross-validation accuracy (%) and standard deviation for each feature subset.

	LLD			eGeMAPS				PASE-BNF
	F0	MFCC	Energy	F0	MFCC	Energy	Slope	All
euc	**75.5 ± 4.7**	**63.0 ± 6.5**	**64.7 ± 10.2**	67.2 ± 5.0	**61.8 ± 4.4**	**64.1 ± 5.4**	**69.8 ± 6.0**	**59.9 ± 6.8**
cos	68.0 ± 7.2	62.6 ± 8.1	62.6 ± 8.1	**70.8 ± 9.9**	58.8 ± 5.8	61.4 ± 8.0	64.4 ± 4.3	56.6 ± 7.1

Fusion and Selection of Intonation Scores. In this section, we investigate different intonation score combinations at a late fusion stage. That is, we considered the intonation scores computed with the distance metric (euclidean or cosine) which has provided a better performance, and use them to train the imitation classifier. Rather than testing all possible combinations, we run an iterative search approach based on the sequential forward selection (SFS) [17], in which a model is trained with an incremental number of features. Starting with no features, at each iteration the accuracy of the model is tested by adding, one at a time, each of the features that were not selected in a previous iteration. The feature that yields the best accuracy is retained for further processing. The same leave-one-speaker-out cross-validation protocol on the training data partition as previously has been applied.

Feature sets have been chosen with the following order: LLD_F0, EG_slope, LLD_MFCC, PASE-BNF, EG_MFCC, EG_F0, EG_energy, LLD_energy. One can consider that the selection order illustrates the relevance of the features with respect to the task at hand. Therefore, as expected, LLD_F0 is the first feature selected, as it is the one which more directly relates to the task. Afterwards, EG_slope, which is, as well, very much related to the imitation of contours, and LLD_MFCC. Then, the selected set is the PASE-BNF. On the one hand, this is surprising, as it is selected before energy, which is expected to complement the existing information. On the other hand, this is indicative of the properties of this feature set, which does not provide much discriminative power when considered alone, but seems to add robustness when added to the other feature sets. Energy, both LLD and EG come at the end of feature selection. This may be due to the fact that although energy is a parameter of prosody, its correlation with intonation may not be that informative. The blue curve in Fig. 2 shows the mean and deviation accuracy achieved in cross-validation with an increasing number of feature sets selected.

For cross-validation, the best average accuracy was 78.1%, attained for four features selected. Nevertheless, we can see in Fig. 2 that the performance in cross-validation is quite stable across different feature sets, although, as we see from error bars, the variability across speaker folds increases, having a minimum when two feature sets are selected. This can indicate that, although other features can

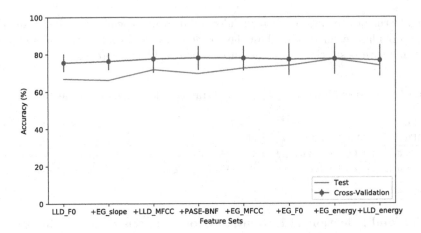

Fig. 2. Accuracy in cross-validation experiments and in the test set for an increasing number of feature sets selected.

Table 2. Accuracy (%) for isolated feature sets in test.

LLD			eGeMAPS				PASE-BNF
F0	MFCC	Energy	F0	MFCC	Energy	Slope	All
66.9	62.0	62.7	49.2	57.7	63.4	60.0	52.8

add relevant information for our task, F0 and EG_slope are the ones achieving the most inter-speaker consistency. Nevertheless, the observations about the relative importance of each feature set and the optimum number of features to select must be taken cautiously due to the considerably high accuracy variance observed.

4.3   Experiments in the Test Set: Results and Discussion

In this subsection, we report the results obtained in the test set when the intonation classifiers are trained using the complete training data set. Table 2 shows results of the intonation imitation classifiers trained using one single intonation score. We notice that, except for the case of EG_F0, there is not a large performance degradation with respect to previous cross-validation experiments. We notice, as well, that in spite of the 8.6% degradation for LLD_F0, this feature set is still the one yielding the best individual results.

When considering the fusion of intonation scores, the order of the selected features follows the order learned in the previous cross-validation experiments. For the best configuration in cross-validation – obtained selecting only four features (78.1%) –, the performance achieved in the test set drops to 69.7%. However, when training the classifiers with seven features, the performance in the test set increases up to 77.5%. This performance difference between the cross-validation and test set results is in line with the degradation already observed from Table 1 to Table 2. The fact that the best result in the test set does not correspond to the set of features which yielded the best result for cross-validation, as pointed out previously, is most likely related with the reduced amount of data and the high variability accuracy observed in cross-validation.

5   Conclusions and Future Work

We investigated the performance of different feature sets for the task of into-nation verification. As a single feature, F0 from the LLD set provided the best performance, with 75.5% of well classified pairs in cross-validation and 66.9% in the test set. The fusion of features led to improved results, as 78.1% for the cross-validation experiments and up to 77.5% in test set. F0 and F0 slopes are the first features chosen for the task, as foreseen. Interestingly, the PASE-BNF come as a relevant part in classification, as they improve the classification in train, but they are also the last features to be added when reaching the max-imum. This is rather encouraging, in the sense that these bottleneck features have been extracted from a network previously extracted for other languages and tasks, and still add robustness to the results.

As future work, we would like to further investigate the possibilities of fusion, namely using tooklits as BOSARIS [3], which would contribute to better tuning each component. We would also like to re-annotate the data set, so that we had a regressive metric for goodness of imitation and could then improve the comparability of our results. The results we have had with the bottleneck features suggest transfer learning should be further addressed in the future tasks with cross-language information.

Acknowledgements. This work was supported by national funds through Fundação para a Ciência e a Tecnologia (FCT), with reference UIDB/50021/2020, through PhD grant SFRH/BD/139473/2018, and project CMUP-ERI/TIC/0033/2014.

References

1. Arias, J.P., Yoma, N.B., Vivanco, H.: Automatic intonation assessment for com-puter aided language learning. Speech Commun. **52**(3), 254–267 (2010)
2. Berndt, D.J., Clifford, J.: Using dynamic time warping to find patterns in time series. In: KDD Workshop, Seattle, WA, vol. 10, pp. 359–370 (1994)
3. Brümmer, N., De Villiers, E.: The BOSARIS toolkit user guide: theory, algorithms and code for binary classifier score processing. Documentation of BOSARIS toolkit, p. 24 (2011)
4. Cheng, J.: Automatic assessment of prosody in high-stakes English tests. In: Twelfth Annual Conference of the International Speech Communication Associ-ation (2011)
5. Christophe, A., Gout, A., Peperkamp, S., Morgan, J.: Discovering words in the continuous speech stream: the role of prosody. J. Phon. **31**(3–4), 585–598 (2003)
6. Chun, D.M.: Discourse Intonation in L2: From Theory and Research to Practice, vol. 1. John Benjamins Publishing, Amsterdam (2002)

7. Escudero-Mancebo, D., González-Ferreras, C., Aguilar, L., Estebas-Vilaplana, E., Cardeñoso-Payo, V.: Exploratory use of automatic prosodic labels for the evaluation of Japanese speakers of L2 Spanish (2016)
8. Eyben, F., Weninger, F., Gross, F., Schuller, B.: Recent developments in openS-MILE, the Munich open-source multimedia feature extractor. In: Proceedings of the 21st ACM International Conference on Multimedia, MM 2013, pp. 835–838. ACM, New York (2013). https://doi.org/10.1145/2502081.2502224, https://doi.acm.org/10.1145/2502081.2502224
9. Eyben, F., et al.: The Geneva Minimalistic Acoustic Parameter Set (GeMAPS) for voice research and affective computing. IEEE Trans. Affect. Comput. **7**(2), 190–202 (2015)
10. Levitt, A.G.: The acquisition of prosody: evidence from French- and English-learning infants. In: de Boysson-Bardies, B., de Schonen, S., Jusczyk, P., McNeilage, P., Morton, J. (eds.) Developmental Neurocognition: Speech and Face Processing in the First Year of Life. NATO ASI Series (Series D: Behavioural and Social Sciences), vol. 69, pp. 385–398. Springer, Dordrecht (1993). https://doi.org/10.1007/978-94-015-8234-6_31
11. Li, K., Wu, X., Meng, H.: Intonation classification for L2 English speech using multi-distribution deep neural networks. Comput. Speech Lang. **43**, 18–33 (2017)
12. Ma, M., Evanini, K., Loukina, A., Wang, X., Zechner, K.: Using F0 contours to assess nativeness in a sentence repeat task. In: Sixteenth Annual Conference of the International Speech Communication Association (2015)
13. Neto, J.P., Martins, C.A., Meinedo, H., Almeida, L.B.: The design of a large vocabulary speech corpus for Portuguese. In: Fifth European Conference on Speech Communication and Technology (1997)
14. Pascual, S., Ravanelli, M., Serrà, J., Bonafonte, A., Bengio, Y.: Learning problem-agnostic speech representations from multiple self-supervised tasks. arXiv preprint arXiv:1904.03416 (2019)
15. Paul, R., Shriberg, L.D., McSweeny, J., Cicchetti, D., Klin, A., Volkmar, F.: Brief report: relations between prosodic performance and communication and socialization ratings in high functioning speakers with autism spectrum disorders. J. Autism Dev. Disord. **35**(6), 861 (2005)
16. Povey, D., et al.: The Kaldi speech recognition toolkit. In: IEEE 2011 Workshop on Automatic Speech Recognition and Understanding. IEEE Signal Processing Society (2011)
17. Pudil, P., Novovičová, J., Kittler, J.: Floating search methods in feature selection. Pattern Recogn. Lett. **15**(11), 1119–1125 (1994)
18. Schuller, B., et al.: The INTERSPEECH 2016 computational paralinguistics challenge: deception, sincerity and native language. In: Proceedings of the 21st ACM International Conference on Multimedia, pp. 2001–2005, September 2016. https://doi.org/10.21437/Interspeech.2016-129
19. da Silva Sousa, M.S.: Prosodic exercises for children with ASD via virtual therapy. Master's thesis, Instituto Superior Técnico, Lisboa, Portugal (2017)
20. Truong, Q.T., Kato, T., Yamamoto, S.: Automatic assessment of L2 English word prosody using weighted distances of F0 and intensity contours. In: Interspeech, pp. 2186–2190 (2018)

The BioVisualSpeech European Portuguese Sibilants Corpus

Margarida Grilo[1] , Isabel Guimarães[1] ,
Mariana Ascensão[1], Alberto Abad[2(✉)] , Ivo Anjos[3] , João Magalhães[3] ,
and Sofia Cavaco[3]

[1] Escola Superior de Saúde do Alcoitão,
Rua Conde Barão, Alcoitão, 2649-506 Alcabideche, Portugal
[2] INESC-ID/Instituto Superior Técnico,
Universidade de Lisboa, Rua Alves Redol 9, 1000-029 Lisboa, Portugal
alberto.abad@inesc-id.pt
[3] NOVA LINCS, Department of Computer Science,
Faculdade de Ciências e Tecnologia, Universidade NOVA de Lisboa,
2829-516 Caparica, Portugal

Abstract. The development of reliable speech therapy computer tools that automatically classify speech productions depends on the quality of the speech data set used to train the classification algorithms. The data set should characterize the population in terms of age, gender and native language, but it should also have other important properties that characterize the population that is going to use the tool. Thus, apart from including samples from correct speech productions, it should also have samples from people with speech disorders. Also, the annotation of the data should include information on whether the phonemes are correctly or wrongly pronounced. Here, we present a corpus of European Portuguese children's speech data that we are using in the development of speech classifiers for speech therapy tools for Portuguese children. The corpus includes data from children with speech disorders and in which the labelling includes information about the speech production errors. This corpus, which has data from 356 children from 5 to 9 years of age, focuses on the European Portuguese sibilant consonants and can be used to train speech recognition models for tools to assist the detection and therapy of sigmatism.

Keywords: Sibilants · European Portuguese corpus · Speech sound disorders

1 Introduction

While most children learn how to speak in their native language and learn how to correctly produce the native language phonemes by the expected ages, for some children, the language acquisition process may be challenging [1]. As reported

---

All authors contributed equally to this work.

© Springer Nature Switzerland AG 2020
P. Quaresma et al. (Eds.): PROPOR 2020, LNAI 12037, pp. 23–33, 2020.
https://doi.org/10.1007/978-3-030-41505-1_3

by Guimarães *et al.* for data on European Portuguese (EP), 8.8% of preschool-aged children suffer from some type of speech sound disorders (SSD) [2]. Many children can surpass their language acquisition difficulties as they grow older and their speech organs develop, but for some children, the speech distortions are not surpassed naturally. These children may need professional help to correct their SSD. Besides, it is important to address these difficulties as early as possible since SSD can affect the child's quality of life and literacy acquisition [3,4].

Sigmatism is a SSD that consists of pronouncing the sibilant consonants incorrectly. The sibilants, which include sounds like [s] in serpent and [z] in zipper, are consonants that are generated by letting the air flow through a very narrow channel towards the teeth [5]. Sigmatism is a very common SSD among children with different native languages [6,7], including EP [8,9].

Speech and language pathologists (SLPs) help children with sigmatism correct the production sibilants with speech exercises that start with the isolated sibilants and then progress to the production of the sounds within syllables and words. While the repetition of the speech exercises is important to practice and master the correct production of the speech sounds, it may lead to the child's weariness and lack of interest on proceeding with the speech exercises. In order to keep children motivated and collaborative during the therapy sessions, SLPs need to adapt the speech and language exercises into fun and appealing activities.

As a contribution to help SLPs motivating children to repeat the tasks that may lead to the correction of their speech disorder, we have been developing serious games for training the production of EP sibilants, which are controlled by the child's voice [10,11]. To make this possible, at its core, the games use speech classifiers that process the child's speech productions. In addition, we have also been developing machine learning approaches to detect the incorrect production of sibilant sounds and help SLPs on assessing if the child has sigmatism [12]. This work is part of the BioVisualSpeech research project, in which we explore multimodal human computer interaction mechanisms for providing bio-feedback in speech and language therapy through the use of serious digital games.

In order to develop the speech classifiers for our serious games for sibilants, we built a children's speech corpus composed of 70 EP single words with sibilant consonants in which the sibilant phoneme occurs either at the initial, middle or final position. The word productions were recorded in three schools, and 365 children from 5 to 9 years of age participated in the data collection task. One of the novelties of this work is that the data annotations include information on the quality of the sound productions according to SLPs criteria. Another novelty is that the set of chosen words focuses on the EP sibilant consonants.

2   Related Work

The availability of speech resources with characteristics similar to the intended application – more specifically, corpora containing manually annotated speech – is of critical importance for the development of robust speech analysis tools.

In particular, modern approaches based on deep neural networks depend on large amounts of training data. To the best of our knowledge, there has not been any previous large scale effort to collect EP speech from children in sibilant production tasks as the one targeted in BioVisualSpeech. Nevertheless, there has been some previous remarkable efforts to collect EP speech recordings of children in a variety of reading tasks. This is the case of the LetsRead database [13] and the CNG database [14]. While none of these corpora contain detailed phonetic annotations in spontaneous naming tasks, these two resources are still extremely valuable for the development of baseline speech and language technological modules tailored for the child population, which can eventually be adapted to specific tasks and/or to atypical children speech characteristics in a later stage.

The **LetsRead** database contains reading aloud recordings of 284 children, whose mother tongue is EP: 147 girls and 137 boys, distributed from 1st to 4th grade. Data of 104 participants, 58 girls and 46 boys, are manually annotated, equally distributed in the 4 grades (26 per grade) and correspond to approximately 5 h and 30 min of speech. The remaining data were automatically aligned with the prompts. The recording sessions were carried out in a classroom with low reverberation and low noise acoustic characteristics. Prompts of 20 sentences and 10 pseudo-words were presented to the children for reading, through a specially developed interface. The sentences used in these recordings were extracted from children fairy tales and grade-specific scholar books. The difficulty degree of the sentences was evaluated accordingly to their phonetic complexity and variety.

The **CNG corpus** contains reading aloud recordings from 510 children, whose maternal language is EP: 285 girls and 225 boys, distributed from ages 3 to 6 (153 participants) and from ages 7 to 10 (357 participants). The recording sessions were carried out at a room with low reverberation and low noise. The prompts were presented to the children for reading, through a specially made interface called "Your Speech". In total, 30 prompts were used for the 3 to 6 age group and 50 prompts for the 7 to 10 age group. The prompts were chosen from a set of four types of prompts: 292 phonetically rich sentences (CETEMPúblico corpus); musical notes; isolated cardinals; and sequential cardinals.

3   Sibilant Consonants and Sigmatism

Different sibilant sounds can be produced by using different parts of the vocal tract. There are two types of EP sibilant consonants: the alveolar sibilants, which are produced with the tongue nearly touching the alveolar region of the mouth, and the palato-alveolar sibilants, which are produced by positioning the tongue towards the palatal region of the mouth (Fig. 1). The vocal folds can either be used or not, resulting in a voiced or a voiceless sibilant, respectively.

The EP sibilant consonants are: [z] as in zebra, [s] as in snake, [ʃ] as the *sh* sound in sheep, and [ʒ] as the *s* sound in Asia. [z], and [s] are both alveolar sibilants, while [ʃ], and [ʒ] are palato-alveolar sibilants. Both [z] and [ʒ] are voiced sibilants, and [s] and [ʃ] are voiceless sibilants.

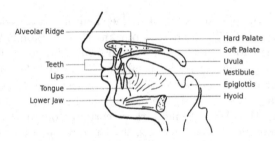

Fig. 1. Main places of articulation in the vocal tract, adapted from [5].

The most usual sibilant mistakes committed by children are distortion errors [2,3]. Distortion errors typically reflect a slight alteration in the production of a sound (e.g., a slight problem with tongue placement). The resulting productions are in the correct phoneme category but lack phonetic precision or accuracy. A common example is the distortion of the [s] consonant into a [θ] sound (as the *th* sound in teeth) when the tongue is wrongly placed between the front teeth or against the upper front teeth, instead of nearly touching the top alveolar ridge.

4   The Sibilants Corpus

The BioVisualSpeech EP sibilants corpus consists of recordings of isolated sibilants (Sect. 4.1) and words that contain sibilant consonants (Sect. 4.2). The corpus development process consisted of three tasks: the screening task, the data collection task (performed within the screening task) and the annotation task, which was divided into two phases. The first phase was conducted during the data collection phase, while the second phase took place afterwards (Fig. 2).

The corpus development process not only served the purpose of building the EP sibilants corpus itself, but was also used as a screening activity to detect any cases of SSD. In fact, while the data described here focuses on the sibilants, the screening task assessed all EP consonant sounds and included several speech and orofacial activities that helped the SLPs to detect not only sigmatism but also other SSD cases. The data collection task consisted of two activities within the screening task that involved sibilant sounds.

The screening task, which took six months, was done in three schools in the district of Lisboa (Portugal). The participating children were all either at pre-school or primary school. We obtained an informed consent from all parents or legal guardians, and the ethics approval was provided by the ethics committee of Escola Superior de Saúde do Alcoitão, Santa Casa da Misericórdia de Lisboa (process number 001/2017).

Several SLP graduate students participated in the screening task, under the supervision of a senior SLP from the BioVisualSpeech team. This means that different children could have interacted with different SLPs during the data collection and screening. During the screening task, the SLPs participating in

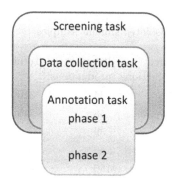
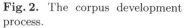

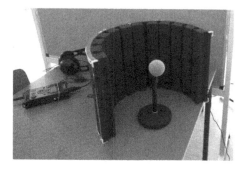

Fig. 2. The corpus development process.

Fig. 3. Equipment used for the recordings: a DAT, a microphone, and acoustic foam.

the study filled in an individual report for each child to inform the parents or legal guardians about the results of the screening.

Our aimed age group was from 5 to 9 year-old children. Whilst data on age-appropriated speech sound production for EP speaking children between 3 and 6;11 years old is available, there have been limited studies including older EP speaking children [2,15]. Nonetheless, evidence for other languages supports the cutoff age between 8 and 9 years old for typical speech sound acquisition to be completed [16].

There were 356 children from this age group participating in the study. Some younger and older children who were in the same classrooms also wanted to participate. We allowed these children to participate for inclusion and non-discriminating reasons. Therefore, while the most significant amount of data of our corpus is from the 356 children (who were in the 5–9 age range), we also have data from some 3, 4, 10 and 11 year old children, and in total we have data from 386 children. The data presented below can include samples from these younger and older children. Also, due to time constraints, not all children participated in all data collection activities, and thus, the data presented for some data collection activities is not from all 386 children.

Children were assessed individually in a quiet room at their school setting by an SLP or an SLP graduated student. One or two other adults (SLP graduate students or researchers from the BioVisualSpeech team) could be present at the room but only the SLP in charge gave the necessary instructions and interacted with the children. Each child had two different screening moments, at different days, to avoid that the children got tired and also to make shorter interruptions of their normal school day.

The equipment used in the data collection task consisted of a dedicated unidirectional condenser microphone, a portable battery powered digital audio tape (DAT) recorder (Sony TCD-D8) and acoustic foam to attenuate background noise (Fig. 3). Due to the children's age group, we did not use head mounted microphones. The recordings were made in a reasonably quiet room at the schools, but in many cases, it was still possible to hear the noise coming from

Table 1. Isolated sibilants – number of children

Age	Girl	Boy	Total
4	0	1	1
5	8	3	11
6	8	8	16
7	19	9	28
8	21	20	41
9	23	19	42
10	3	2	5
11	1	0	1
Total	83	62	145

Table 2. Isolated sibilant samples

Phoneme	Correct productions	Incorrect productions	Total
ʃ	276	34	310
ʒ	257	58	315
s	278	39	317
z	265	49	314
Total	1076	180	1256

the playground and corridors. While the recording conditions were not perfect, having background noise in the data samples is appropriate for our goal since we aim to develop automatic recognition models that are robust enough to be used in SLP's offices or at schools.

The data was recorded continuously, that is, the recorded speech signals include the SLP and the child's speech. Thus, after the data collection task was finished, we had to segment all the recorded speech signals, not only to extract the children relevant speech portions (isolated sibilants or words with sibilants) but also to discard all the speech data from the SLPs.

Below we describe in more detail the data and the protocols used to record the set of isolated sibilants as well the annotation details for this set of sound productions (Sect. 4.1). The set of words with sibilant consonants and its collection is described in Sect. 4.2, while the annotation of these words is discussed in Sect. 4.3.

4.1   Isolated Sibilants

We collected both short and long productions of the isolated sibilants (that is, a version that lasts less than a couple of seconds and another that last a few seconds). The SLP would first ask the child to produce all sibilants sounds in both the short and long versions by illustrating herself how to do it. The order of the sibilants varied, and the order of the version (short or long) also varied.

The goal was to record eight sounds samples for each child (both a short and a long production for each sibilant). A few children were not able to produce some sibilants, so in those cases we are missing those productions, and in other cases the child produced some of the sounds more than once. Table 2 shows the number of correct and incorrect productions of each sibilant. These sound productions were collected from 145 children as not all children did the isolated sibilants activity (Table 1).

Table 3. Words with sibilants

Phoneme	Initial position	Middle position	Final position	Total
ʃ	6	20	13	39
ʒ	5	5		10
s	13	11		24
z	2	6		8

Fig. 4. Stimulus used to suggest the word *mochila*

Table 4. Words with sibilants – number of children

Age	Girl	Boy	Total
5	20	19	39
6	35	35	70
7	51	33	84
8	39	50	89
9	37	37	74
Total	182	174	356

Table 5. Word samples

Phoneme	Incorrect phoneme occur-rences	Total phoneme produc-tions	Words with incorrect sibilants	Total number of words
ʃ	434	11202	422	11455
ʒ	240	2880	240	3333
s	354	6627	322	7024
z	154	2260	154	2616
Total	1182	22969	1138	22830

The data was automatically segmented in a first round and then, in a second round, we manually checked and adjusted the segmentation results. We discarded all the segments containing the SLP's speech. The labelling was performed by the team computer scientists (non-SLP) who were segmenting the data.

The labels contain information about the sound that is expected, and if the sound was correctly produced. The first part of the labels indicates the sibilant that the SLP asked the child to produce, even in cases in which the child produced another sibilant sound correctly. For second part of the label, the production was marked with R for a correct production, and with W for an incorrect production. For instance, if the SLP asked the child to produce a sibilant s_1 and the child produced another sibilant s_2, the sound sample is labeled with $s_1 W$.

4.2   Words with Sibilants

We used a total of 70 words with sibilant consonants. The chosen words start with one of the four sibilant consonants (*e.g.*, *sino*), have the sibilant in a middle position (*e.g.*, *pijama*), or finish with the sibilant [ʃ] (*e.g.*, *livros* or *peixe*).

Ten of these words contain more than one sibilant phoneme (like *cereja*, in which the initial phoneme is [s] and there is a middle phoneme with [ʒ]). The 70 chosen words have 81 sibilant-phoneme occurrences (Table 3). The number of occurrences is not equal for all sibilants because these words were chosen taking into consideration their frequency of appearance in EP, and their semantic predictability [17,18]. Also, [ʃ] is the only sibilant that can occur in word final positions in EP.

In order to have the children produce these words, the stimuli consisted of age-appropriate color images representing the words. We used plain images in a white background and printed in A5 paper (one image per paper sheet) to direct the attention to the aimed word as much as possible. As an example, Fig. 4 shows the image used for one of the words (*mochila*, which is the EP word for backpack and which contains the [ʃ] phoneme in a middle position). In order to have the child pronouncing the word in his/her usual way and not having the child mimicking the SLP pronunciation, the SLP did not say the aimed word. Each picture was shown to the child, who was asked to name it. If the child did not answer, the examiner could give standardized semantic clues.

In total, we collected 22830 samples from these 70 words from the productions of 356 children (Tables 4 and 5). There are 20198 correct word productions and 2632 word samples incorrectly produced. From these incorrectly produced samples, there are 1138 word samples with incorrectly produced sibilants (fourth column of Table 5). In each word with sibilant phoneme x (where x is [ʃ], [ʒ], [s] or [z]), we considered that the sibilant is incorrectly produced when the word contains the sibilant phoneme x, but the child speech production does not contain x, substitutes or has a distortion of x. While this is a good approximation of the real number of word samples with incorrect sibilant productions, it may fail in some cases in which the word production contains the x phoneme but in a different word position/syllable. Also note that the total number of words for all sibilants presented in the table (22830) does not result from adding the numbers in the fifth column since some words can contain more than one sibilant sound.

The second column of Table 5 shows the number of incorrect sibilant productions. The third column of this table shows the total number of occurrences (correct and incorrect) of each sibilant phoneme. Note that one word can have more than one sibilant production, and thus, the total presented in this column (22969) is higher than the total number of word samples (22830).

4.3 Word Samples Annotation

The data was annotated according to SLPs criteria. The first annotation phase was done by the SLP in charge of the recordings and took place during the data collection task. The second annotation phase took place after the data collection task was finished and was done by an SLP and a software engineer.

The annotation during the data collection consisted on marking each target word as either being produced, produced after repetition, or not produced by the recorded child. In the cases where the word was produced, the uttered word was annotated as a correct pronunciation or as an incorrect one. Moreover, each consonant group was labelled as correctly or incorrectly pronounced. Incorrect production was considered (i) for no response or (ii) for detected consonant omission, substitution or distortion. This process was useful for the individual screening reports sent to the children's parents or legal guardians and for speech-language pathology research purposes.

In order to make the recorded data and annotations useful for computerised methods, it was necessary to follow a second annotation stage. In this annotation stage, each recording was manually time aligned to identify the start and end boundaries of each word. Moreover, segments containing speech from the thera-pists or other not interesting events were marked to be later rejected. Moreover, for each of the wrongly uttered words identified in the first stage, the speech assessment methods phonetic alphabet (SAMPA) transcriptions were produced.

The following example illustrates how the word *mochila* was annotated for a wrongly uttered occurrence of this word. The annotation includes the start and end times of the word within the speech sound file, the indication that the word is wrongly uttered (with the symbol * at the end of the word transcription, *mochila**) and the SAMPA transcription *m@sil6* (a correct occurence of the word would be annotated as *muSil6*, which means that this particular example has two pronunciation errors, one for the sibilant [ʃ] and another for the vowel sound [u]):

```
<Turn speaker="spk1" startTime="18.170" endTime="19.129">
    <Sync time="18.170"/>
        mochila*
    <Event desc="m@sil6" type="pronounce" extent="previous"/>
</Turn>
```

5   Conclusion

Here we discuss the several stages for the creation of an EP sibilants corpus. This corpus contains speech data from 356 children from 5 to 9 years of age. While the most significant data is from this age group, the corpus also contains some samples from younger and older children, and thus, in total it has speech data from 386 children from 3 to 11 years of age.

The corpus focuses on the EP portuguese sibilants and can be used to develop automatic classifiers of speech data for tools to assist the detection and therapy of sigmatism. More specifically, the corpus contains samples from the EP isolated sibilants, and words with sibilants either in the initial position, a middle position of the final position.

One of the novelties of the proposed work is that the phoneme and word labeling information indicates if the sound productions are correct or incorrect according to SLPs criteria. Also, the corpus includes samples from children with SSD. Both these features are important to assist the development of automatic speech classifiers that can deal with speech from children with SSD.

Acknowledgements. This work was supported by the Portuguese Foundation for Science and Technology under projects BioVisualSpeech (CMUP-ERI/TIC/0033/2014), NOVA-LINCS (PEest/UID/CEC/04516/2019) and INESC-ID (UIDB/50021/2020). We thank Cátia Pedrosa and Diogo Carrasco for the segmentation and annotation of our corpus, all postgraduate SLP students who collaborated in the data collection task, and the schools and children who participated in the study.

References

1. McLeod, S.: The International Guide to Speech Acquisition. Thomson Delmar Learning, Clifton Park (2007)
2. Guimarães, I., Birrento, C., Figueiredo, C., Flores, C.: Teste de articulação verbal. Oficina Didáctica, Lisboa, Portugal (2014)
3. Preston, J., Edwards, M.L.: Phonological awareness and types of sound errors in preschoolers with speech sound disorders. J. Speech Lang. Hear. Res. **53**(1), 44–60 (2010)
4. Nathan, L., Stackhouse, J., Goulandris, N., Snowling, M.J.: The development of early literacy skills among children with speech difficulties: a test of the critical age hypothesis. J. Speech Lang. Hear. Res. **47**, 377–391 (2004)
5. Guimarães, I.: Ciência e Arte da Voz Humana. Escola Superior de Saúde de Alcoitão (2007)
6. Honová, J., Jindra, P., Pešák, J.: Analysis of articulation of fricative praealveolar sibilant "s" in control population. Biomed. Papers **147**(2), 239–242 (2003)
7. Weinrich, M., Zehner, H.: Phonetiche und Phonologische Störungen bein Kindern. Springer, Heidelberg (2005). https://doi.org/10.1007/3-540-27497-9
8. Figueiredo, A.C.: Análise acústica dos fonemas /s, z/ produzidos por crianças com desempenho articulatório alterado. Master's thesis, Escola Superior de Saúde do Alcoitão, Santa Casa da Misericórdia de Lisboa (2017)
9. Rua, M.: Caraterização do desempenho articulatório e oromotor de crianças com alterações da fala. Master's thesis, Escola Superior de Saúde do Alcoitão, Santa Casa da Misericórdia de Lisboa (2015)
10. Anjos, I., Grilo, M., Ascensão, M., Guimarães, I., Magalhães, J., Cavaco, S.: A serious mobile game with visual feedback for training sibilant consonants. In: Cheok, A.D., Inami, M., Romão, T. (eds.) ACE 2017. LNCS, vol. 10714, pp. 430–450. Springer, Cham (2018). https://doi.org/10.1007/978-3-319-76270-8_30
11. Anjos, I., Marques, N., Grilo, M., Guimarães, I., Magalhães, J., Cavaco, S.: Sibilant consonants classification with deep neural networks. In: Moura Oliveira, P., Novais, P., Reis, L.P. (eds.) EPIA 2019. LNCS (LNAI), vol. 11805, pp. 435–447. Springer, Cham (2019). https://doi.org/10.1007/978-3-030-30244-3_36
12. Anjos, I., Grilo, M., Ascensão, M., Guimarães, I., Magalhães, J., Cavaco, S.: A model for sibilant distortion detection in children. In: Proceedings of the 2018 International Conference on Digital Medicine and Image Processing (DMIP) (2018)
13. Proença, J., Celorico, D., Candeias, S., Lopes, C., Perdigão, F.: The LetsRead corpus of Portuguese children reading aloud for performance evaluation. In: Proceedings of the Tenth International Conference on Language Resources and Evaluation (LREC 2016), Portorož, Slovenia, pp. 781–785. European Language Resources Association (ELRA), May 2016
14. Hämäläinen, A., et al.: The CNG corpus of European Portuguese children's speech. In: Habernal, Ivan, Matoušek, Václav (eds.) TSD 2013. LNCS (LNAI), vol. 8082, pp. 544–551. Springer, Heidelberg (2013). https://doi.org/10.1007/978-3-642-40585-3_68

15. Lousada, M., Mendes, A., Valente, R., Hall, A.: Standardization of a phonetic-phonological test for European-Portuguese children. In: Folia Phoniatrica et Logopaedica: Official Organ of the International Association of Logopedics and Phoniatrics (IALP), vol. 64, pp. 151–156, September 2012
16. Wren, I., McLeod, S., White, P., Miller, L., Roulstone, S.: Speech characteristics of 8-year-old children: findings from a prospective population study. J. Commun. Disord. **46**(1), 53–69 (2013)
17. Charles-Luce, J., Dressler, K.M., Ragonese, E.: Effects of semantic predictability on children's preservation of a phonemic voice contrast. J. Child Lang. **26**, 505–530 (1999)
18. Mestre, I.: Sibilantes e motricidade orofacial em crianças portuguesas dos 5;00 aos 9;11 anos de idade: Estudo preliminar. Master's thesis, Escola Superior de Saúde do Alcoitão, Santa Casa da Misericórdia de Lisboa (2017)

Evaluation of Deep Learning Approaches to Text-to-Speech Systems for European Portuguese

Sebastião Quintas[1,2](✉) and Isabel Trancoso[1,2]

[1] INESC-ID, Lisbon, Portugal
sebastiao.frazao@gmail.com, Isabel.Trancoso@inesc-id.pt
[2] Instituto Superior Técnico, Lisbon, Portugal

Abstract. Deep Learning models are considered state-of-the-art regarding Text-to-Speech, displaying very natural and realistic results. However, it is known that these machine learning methods usually require large amounts of data to operate properly. Due to this, an assessment of the system's ability to generalize to different instances becomes relevant, specially when learning from small data sets to create new voices. This study describes the assessment of a deep learning approach to TTS for European Portuguese. We show that we can use transfer learning techniques to fine-tune a Tacotron-2 model to a specific voice, while preserving speaker identity, without requiring large amounts of data. We also perform a comparison between the developed model and a statistical parametric speech synthesizer enhanced by deep learning, concluding that Tacotron-2 provided an overall better word pronunciation, naturalness and intonation.

Keywords: Deep learning · Transfer learning · European Portuguese · Speaker adaptation · Speech synthesis

1 Introduction

In the past few years, Deep Learning has played an important role in the evolution of Text-to-Speech (TTS) systems. With the development of recent models like Tacotron-2 [1] and WaveNet [2], that are able to produce reliable and very realistic synthesized speech, the resulting quality of Deep Learning methods became comparable to natural speech.

This paper addresses the evaluation of a Tacotron-2 version for European Portuguese (EP) developed in the framework of an MSc Thesis. After briefly outlining the main steps of the development of the baseline version, we shall compare its performance with the one of a previous generation Parametric Speech Synthesizer called Merlin [3] (developed for the same voice bank), which also makes use of Deep Learning (DL). Finally, we will extend the evaluation to two versions of Tacotron-2 obtained by performing speaker adaptation of the developed model to two smaller voice banks.

© Springer Nature Switzerland AG 2020
P. Quaresma et al. (Eds.): PROPOR 2020, LNAI 12037, pp. 34–42, 2020.
https://doi.org/10.1007/978-3-030-41505-1_4

2   Development of the Base Model

In this section we will focus on the development of a Portuguese TTS system that will be the main focus of attention throughout this work. The developed model will also serve as basis for speaker adaptation experiments.

Tacotron-2 [1] is an end-to-end generative text-to-speech model that synthesizes speech directly from characters. Given text and audio pairs, one can train a model completely from scratch with random initialization. It does not require phoneme-level alignment, so it can easily scale to using large amounts of acoustic data accompanied with orthographic transcripts. The working principle of Tacotron-2 is based on a sequence-to-sequence model with attention as a feature generator [4], and an appended WaveNet [2] as a vocoder. Sequence-to-sequence models, also called encoder/decoder models, are deep learning models that aim to map a fixed length input with a fixed length output, where the length of the input and output may differ [5]. Figure 1 displays an overview of the Tacotron-2 architecture, with the encoder on the left side, and the attention-based decoder on the right side, appended by the WaveNet vocoder.

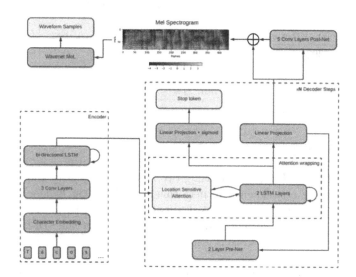

Fig. 1. Tacotron-2 global architecture. Extracted from [7]

WaveNet is a deep neural network used to generate raw audio waveforms by conditioning each audio sample on the previous timesteps. Wavenet's conditional probability distribution is modelled by a stack of dilated convolutional layers. This module replaces the Griffin-Lim vocoder that was proposed in the precursor system, called Tacotron [6].

WaveNet receives as input mel-spectrogram features (80-dimensional vectors, computed every 12.5 ms), which capture both pronunciation of words and various subtleties of human speech, e.g. volume, speed and intonation.

Tacotron-2 is reported to produce state of the art speech synthesis quality [1], achieving a Mean Opinion Score (MOS) of 4.53 ± 0.07 on a 5-point Likert scale (1:bad, 2:poor, 3:fair, 4:good, 5:excellent). This performance is comparable to the MOS achieved by natural recorded speech: 4.58 ± 0.05.

In order to develop this system, we used an open-source implementation of Tacotron-2 by Rayhane Mamah [7].

We trained the system using an in-house Portuguese female Voice Bank called SSF1, whose main characteristics can be found in the first line of Table 1. This database was originally designed for a concatenative based synthesizer in which the main concern was getting a phonetically rich set of sentences, in terms of diphone and triphone coverage. The developed system was trained in two phases, the first one corresponding to Tacotron (mel-spectrogram generator), and the second to WaveNet (waveform generation conditioned on mel-spectrograms).

Table 1. Description of the Voice Banks used throughout this work.

Name	Nr. Utterances	Duration	Gender	Int.	Exc.	Dec.
SSF1	7303	14 h 16 min 28 s	F	11%	0.7%	88.3%
SSF2	728	1 h 3 min 30 s	F	10.3%	0.9%	88.8%
SSM2	728	1 h 0 min 27 s	M	10.3%	0.9%	88.8%

3   Evaluation

We evaluated the resulting system using two metrics [8]: quality and intelligibility. For the quality assessment, we performed an MOS test, where 100 unseen utterances received at least 8 ratings. For natural speech, the score obtained is slightly lower than the one reported in the literature. For the synthetic speech corresponding to SSF1,the score is also lower than the reported one, which may be due to the voice bank size.

For intelligibility assessment, we ran a Semantically Unpredictable Sentence (SUS) test, where 10 unpredictable sentences were transcribed by at least 8 different listeners. Using the obtained transcriptions, we computed the total Word Error Rate (WER) according to:

$$WER(\%) = \frac{Sw + Iw + Dw}{Tw} * 100$$

where Sw stands for substitutions, Iw for insertions, Dw for deleted words and Tw for total number of words. The WER results are shown in the first line of Table 3.

Table 2. Mean Opinion Score test results.

System	MOS
Natural speech	4.42 ± 0.60
SSF1 Basis TTS	3.82 ± 0.69
SSF2 speaker adaptation	3.62 ± 0.68
SSM2 speaker adaptation	3.37 ± 0.84

Table 3. Word Error Rate achieved by the SUS test.

System	WER
SSF1 Basis TTS	1.42%
SSF2 speaker adaptation	0.82%
SSM2 speaker adaptation	7.46%

3.1 Analysis of Grapheme-to-Phoneme Errors

Previous G2P (Grapheme-to-Phoneme) approaches for European Portuguese, including rule-based and neural network approaches [9], have shown that the most common errors concern the transcription of graphemes e and o, to which two different phonological representations can be associated (in stressed syllables), and also the transcription of x whose contextual variation is difficult to predict, since it depends, among other facts, on the time the word entered the lexicon.

In order to assess how Tacontron-2 handles these problematic graphemes, we synthesized a list of 50 words which typically require extra rules or exceptions, and which were not included in SSF1. The system correctly pronounced **78.4%** of these words. Table 4 illustrates some of the difficulties. These results can be seen as promising results, but also point to the need to carefully design a relatively short database of sentences for end-to-end speech synthesis, not just bearing in mind diphone and triphone coverage.

Table 4. Examples of Grapheme-to-Phoneme errors.

Words	Achieved	Target
axila	[6s"il6]	[aks"il6]
trouxe	[tr"oS@]	[tr"os@]
paradoxo	[p6r6d"Oksu]	[p6r6d"oksu]
hexagonal	[eZ6gun"al ˜]	[ez6gun"al˜]
gafanhotos	[g6f6J"OtuS]	[g6f6J"otuS]
bocejos	[bus"EZuS]	[bus"6ZuS]
congénere	[ko˜g"EnEr@]	[ko˜g"En@r@]

Another aspect of G2P that should be evaluated is the disambiguation of homographs. The most common type of errors these word-pairs face concerns again the transcription of graphemes *e* and *o*. Typical rule-based systems handle this disambiguation by a previous part-of-speech module that distinguishes between verbs and nouns. In order to evaluate the way our Tacotron-2 system handles this problem, we synthesized a list of 10 examples that contemplated these word pairs. Table 5 displays the sentences used, where red corresponds to mispronunciations.

Table 5. Homograph test performed. Bold marked words display mispronunciations.

Nr.	Sentence
1	Eu **acordo** no dia do *acordo*
2	Usei a *colher* para *colher* as sementes
3	No *começo* do dia **começo** por dançar
4	Eu **jogo** o *jogo* que ele me deu
5	Estou com **sede** depois de sair da *sede*
6	Eu *olho* para o *olho* da Maria
7	O Rei teve de fazer um *corte* na **corte**
8	Não quero que **sobre** nada *sobre* a mesa
9	Eu *molho* a taç com o *molho*
10	Eu *acerto* no dia de fazer o **acerto**

The results showed that in 3 out of 10 sentences, the developed system produced the correct pronunciation. However, it did not generalize to the same word pairs in different contexts. It is important to state that the words used in this assessment did not have a strong representation in the voice bank, either as a verb or a noun, which again points to a more careful design of the sentence database.

The performance of the G2P system was also evaluated using a set of 70 sentences illustrating different domains: broadcast news, weather forecast, children's books. Tacotron-2 achieved 1.30% mispronunciation rate, at the word level. Some of the errors revealed the inadequate coverage of words with clitics in SSF1.

Although not addressed in this paper, for the sake of space, the pronunciation of acronyms and foreign words also deserves special attention in this context.

4   Comparison with Merlin

Since we had access to synthesized speech obtained by a parametric speech synthesizer enhanced by Deep Learning (Merlin [3]) that was also trained with the SSF1 Voice Bank, we conducted a preference and comparison test.

The preference test devised was performed in a pair comparison way, where after listening to each pair of samples, subjects were asked to choose which one they preferred in terms of naturalness, being able to choose "neutral" if they did not have any clear preference. A total of 10 pairs was subject to evaluation by at least 8 listeners. The results can be found in Table 6, showing a very clear preference towards Tacontron-2. The cases where Merlin was preferred over Tacotron-2 were mainly associated to audible noise and artifacts.

Table 6. Preference test results between the two models.

System	Preference
Tacotron-2	**70.0%**
Merlin	17.5%
Neutral	12.5%

We also compared the performance of both systems regarding G2P, by synthesizing the same set of 70 sentences. Despite the mispronunciation rate being low for both systems, Merlin achieved over twice the rate of Tacotron-2 (2.74% for Merlin, at the word level).

4.1   Interrogative Sentences

It is known that Deep Learning has large data requirements in order to learn specific features. Given the limited representation of interrogative sentences in the SSF1 Voice Bank, we investigated whether the model had learned the specific intonations that characterizes this sentence type or not. We also compared the obtained results with the interrogative sentences achieved by Merlin.

The analysis of the interrogative intonation was made using both yes/no questions, wh-questions, and alternate questions. The results suggest that while Tacotron-2 is able to generalize well to different intonation types [10, 11], Merlin fails to convey any intonation. Figure 2 exemplifies these results with the presence of the same yes/no question synthesized using both Merlin and Tacotron-2. From the pitch contour present in this Figure, one can notice that Merlin fails to output an ascending pitch pattern towards the end of the sentence. Tacotron-2 addresses this issue and is able to produce the characteristic ascending pattern, which is crucial to convey a proper intonation to this interrogative type [10].

The analysis of interrogative intonation produced by our TTS model allowed us to see that the model is generalizing well to different types of interrogative sentences, with simple patterns, but a much more thorough test is needed. We anticipate that the system will face sporadic issues regarding intonation when tested with semantically complex sentences, namely given the very limited training material of this type.

The same type of brief analysis was performed for exclamatory sentences whose coverage is even more reduced in SSF1. Despite the coverage problems,

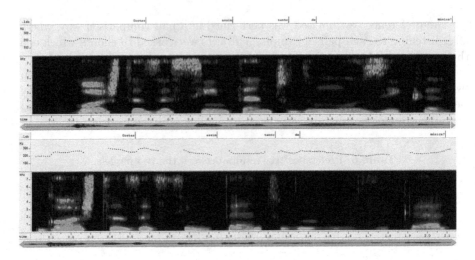

Fig. 2. Spectrogram and pitch contour of the same yes/no question synthesized by Merlin (top) and Tacotron-2 (bottom).

the results for both interrogative and exclamatory sentences for Tacotron-2 can be seen as a promising improvement over Merlin regarding intonation, since Merlin failed to convey any characteristic intonation.

5   Speaker Adaptation Tests

This section concerns the development of two different voices for Tacotron-2, using much smaller voice banks. For this purpose, we used transfer learning in order to fine-tune smaller amounts of data from different speakers to the baseline model previously developed. Fine-tuning can be seen as the process of taking a network model that has already been trained on a given task, and make it perform a second similar task, assuming that the second task shares similar traits.

We used two parallel in-house voice banks to perform speaker adaptation, named SSF2 (female) and SSM2 (male). The characteristics of both voice banks can be found in Table 1. The smaller voice banks had no sentences in common with SSF1.

Similarly to Sect. 2, we also performed the evaluation of our Speaker Adaptation models using a Mean Opinion Score and a Semantically Unpredictable Sentence test.

For the MOS test, we also asked 8 different listeners to rate the naturalness and quality of 100 unseen synthesized sentences. The results obtained can be found in Table 2, compared to the ratings obtained by natural speech and also the previous model.

For the SUS test, we created 10 semantically unpredictable sentences for each model being assessed (SSF2 and SSM2) and each sentence was transcribed at least 8 times. The generated sentences were different for each system assessed with the SUS test. The total Word Error Rate achieved can be found in Table 3. The WER results for SSF2 were lower than those for SSF1, but the difference may not be significant given the limited size of the test set.

The differences in MOS scores between the SSF2 model score and the SSM2 counterpart reflect the much noisier synthetic speech of the SSM2 system, which also affected its overall intelligibility score, specially in plosives.

The speaker adaptation models were able to preserve speaker identity for the two smaller voice banks, but the quality of the female-to-male adaptation was lower than the female-to-female adaptation, as could be expected.

By performing the same analysis on G2P errors, our speaker adaptation models achieved a correctness value of **68%** for the female adaptation and **66%** for the male counterpart. This results were slightly worse than the ones achieved by our base model, which could be expected, and also point to the need for a carefully designed database suggested in Subsect. 3.1.

Concerning the intonation of interrogative sentences, the results were also worse for the two smaller voice banks, showing the need for better representativeness of this type of sentences in smaller voice banks.

6   Conclusions and Future Work

The present work addressed the creation of a Portuguese Text-to-Speech system that can be fine-tuned in order to perform speaker adaptation on smaller voice banks. We showed that we can use transfer learning techniques to fine-tune a Tacotron-2 model to a specific voice, while preserving speaker identity, without requiring large amounts of data. We also performed a comparison between the developed model and a statistical parametric speech synthesizer enhanced by deep learning. From this comparison, we concluded that the end-to-end TTS system provided an overall better word pronunciation, naturalness and intonation than the older model in which Deep Learning was only used to learn the relationship between linguistic and acoustic features.

The performed evaluation was also important to assess how an end-to-end TTS system addresses the pronunciation of graphemes which raise more problems in specific contexts in European Portuguese. To address the lack of representativity of certain words and sentence types in the training set, we suggest specially designed voice banks with a strong presence of different interrogative types and also words of difficult pronunciation (e.g. Table 4), even for the specific task of speaker adaptation.

Acknowledgments. This work was supported by national funds through Fundação para a Ciência e a Tecnologia (FCT) with reference UID/CEC/50021/2019. The authors gratefully acknowledge the contributions of Ana Londral, Sérgio Paulo, Luís Bernardo, and Catarina Gonçalves.

References

1. Shen, J., Pang, R., Weiss, R.J.: Natural TTS Synthesis by Conditioning WaveNet on Mel Spectrogram Predictions. Google Inc., December 2017
2. Oord, A., Dieleman, S., Simonyan, K.: Wavenet: A generative model for raw audio. Google's Deepmind, September 2016
3. Wu, Z., Watts, O., King, S.: Merlin: an open source neural network speech synthesis system. In: 9th ISCA Speech Synthesis Workshop, September 2016
4. Vaswani, A., Shazeer, N., Parmar, N.: Attention is all you need. In: NIPS Proceedings (2017)
5. Sutskever, I., Vinyals, O.: Sequence to sequence learning with neural networks. In: NIPS Proceedings, June 2014
6. Wang, Y., Ryan, R.J., Stanton, D.: Tacotron: Towards End-to-End Speech Synthesis. Google Inc., April 2017
7. Mamah, R.: Open-Source Tacotron-2. https://github.com/Rayhane-mamah/Tacotron-2
8. Synsig: Evaluation. https://www.synsig.org/index.php/Evaluation
9. Isabel, M., Trancoso, M., Viana, C., Silva, F.M.: On the pronunciation of common lexica and proper names in European Portuguese. In: 2nd Onomastica Research Colloquium, December 1994
10. Moniz, H., Batista, F., Trancoso, I., Mata, A.I.: Análise de interrogativas em diferentes domínios. APL, July 2012
11. Truckenbrodt, H.: On rises and falls in interrogatives. Actes d'IDP, June 2009

Evaluation and Extensions of an Automatic Speech Therapy Platform

Anna Pompili[1]([✉])[iD], Alberto Abad[1][iD], Isabel Trancoso[1][iD], José Fonseca[2][iD], and Isabel P. Martins[2][iD]

[1] INESC-ID/IST, Lisbon, Portugal
{anna,alberto.abad,isabel.trancoso}@l2f.inesc-id.pt
[2] Laboratório de Estudos de Linguagem, Faculty of Medicine, University of Lisbon, Lisbon, Portugal

Abstract. Speech and language technology is currently being incorporated into e-health services addressed to the detection, assessment and rehabilitation of different types of speech and language disorders. This is the case of the Portuguese platform VITHEA, which provides remote access to automatic training sessions for aphasia rehabilitation. In VITHEA, patients' answers to semantic confrontation exercises are validated using automatic speech recognition. Text-to-speech synthesis and a virtual agent are exploited to allow a natural multimodal interaction. While the effectiveness of the different technological components has been individually validated, there is a need for the assessment of the overall therapeutic platform. In this work, we report evaluation results of the complete therapeutic platform based on a survey collected from speech and language therapists. The results not only confirmed the significant usefulness of the platform for the treatment of aphasic patients, but also provided very relevant feedback that led to the introduction of additional features and to the development of similar solutions for other diseases.

Keywords: Aphasia · Automatic speech recognition · Keyword spotting · Speech synthesis · Virtual therapy

1 Introduction

Aphasia is a communication disorder caused by a damage to one or more language areas of the brain. It affects various speech and language functionalities, including auditory comprehension, speech production, oral expression, reading and writing. There are several causes of brain injuries affecting communication

This work was funded by Fundação para a Ciência e a Tecnologia (FCT) through the project RIPD/ADA/109646/2009 and partially supported by grant SFRH/BD/97187/2013, by national funds through FCT under project UIDB/50021/2020, and by CMUP-ERI/TIC/0033/2014 Program fund.

P. Quaresma et al. (Eds.): PROPOR 2020, LNAI 12037, pp. 43–52, 2020.
https://doi.org/10.1007/978-3-030-41505-1_5

skills, such as brain tumours, brain infections, severe head injuries, and most commonly, cerebral vascular accidents (CVA). The number of individuals that suffered from a CVA has dramatically increased in the last decades, with approximately 600.000 estimated new cases each year in the EU. Typically, a third of these cases present language disorders [1]. Among the effects of aphasia, the difficulty to recall words is the impairment most commonly presented by aphasic individuals. In fact, it has been reported in some cases as the only residual deficit after rehabilitation [2]. Several studies about aphasia have demonstrated the positive effect of speech-language therapy activities for the improvement of social communication abilities [3]. Moreover, it has been shown that the intensity of therapy positively influences speech and language recovery in aphasic patients [4]. The use of computers for aphasia treatment has been explored since the early eighties [5,6] due to its importance for overcoming resource limitations inherent in the provision of rehabilitation services. Recent commercial products and research laboratory prototypes are currently available for different kinds and degrees of aphasia treatment and in some cases they incorporate speech and language technology (SLT), mainly the use of speech output and virtual agents [7–10]. Up to our knowledge, the only therapeutic tool for word recalling training addressed to Portuguese aphasic patients that makes use of speech recognition technology is the VITHEA platform [11]. The proposed system aims at acting as a "virtual therapist", asking the patient to recall the content represented in a photo or video shown. By means of the use of automatic speech recognition (ASR) technology, the system processes what is said by the patient and decides if it is correct or wrong. The reliability and robustness of the ASR as a word verification tool were evaluated in [12].

In this work, we focus on a user evaluation of the platform, performed with the support of several speech and language therapists experienced in the treatment of aphasic patients. The evaluation was conducted through on-line questionnaires focused on the therapeutic utility, the usability, and the robustness of the platform. Almost 30 speech therapists were involved in the survey, which included a trial phase of the platform with different aphasic patients. This experimental phase also allowed to gather important feedback and comments which have lead to recent extensions of the platform. In the following, in Sect. 2, we first introduce the VITHEA platform with a brief focus on its core components. Then, the evaluation process and its results are described in detail in Sect. 3. Finally in Sect. 4, we present some recent extensions of the platform that have been motivated by the encouraging feedback received through the survey.

2   The VITHEA Platform

The on-line platform described in [11] is the first prototype for aphasia treatment resulting from the collaboration of the Spoken Language Processing Lab of INESC-ID (L^{2}F) and the Language Research Laboratory of the Lisbon Faculty of Medicine (LEL), which has been developed in the context of the activities of the Portuguese national project VITHEA. The VITHEA platform comprises two specific web applications: the patient and the clinician module. The clinician

Fig. 1. Screen-shot of the VITHEA patient application.

module permits speech language therapists to easily create therapy exercises and to manage patient data. The patient module is dedicated to aphasia patients for accessing therapy sessions. The overall flow can be described as follows: when a therapy session starts, the virtual therapist shows to the patient, one at a time, a series of visual or auditory stimuli. The patient is then required to answer verbally to these stimuli by naming the contents of the object or action that is represented. The utterance produced is recorded, encoded and sent via network to the server side. Upon reception, the audio file is processed by an ASR module and the result compared with a set of predetermined textual answers (for the given question) in order to verify the correctness of the patient's input. Finally, feedback is sent back to the patient. The platform is intended not only to serve as an alternative, but most importantly, as a complement to conventional speech-language therapy sessions, permitting intensive and inexpensive therapy sessions to patients, besides providing to the therapists a tool to assess and track the evolution of their patients (Fig. 1).

2.1   Automatic Speech Recognition

The ASR module is the backbone of the system: it is responsible for receiving the patient's speech answer and validating the correctness of the utterance for a given therapeutic exercise. Consequently, it strongly determines the usability of the whole therapeutic platform. The targeted task for automatic word naming recognition consists of deciding whether a claimed word W is uttered in a given speech segment S or not. Keyword spotting is an adequate solution to deal with unexpected speech effects typical in aphasic patients, such as hesitations, doubts, repetitions, descriptions and other speech disturbing factors.

In the current version of the system, acoustic based keyword spotting is applied for word verification. In order to do so, our in-house ASR engine named AUDIMUS [13], that has been previously used for the development of several ASR applications, was modified to incorporate a competing background speech model that is estimated without the need for acoustic model re-training [14].

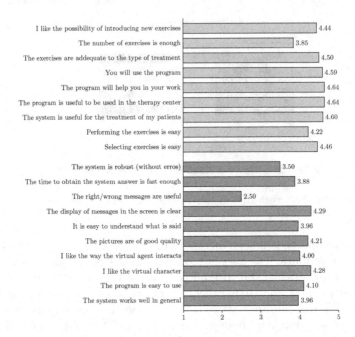

Fig. 2. User evaluation average scores obtained from the collected therapist questionnaires.

2.2   Speech Synthesis and Virtual Character Animation

The VITHEA platform integrates our in-house text-to-speech (TTS) engine named DIXI [15], configured for unit selection synthesis with an open domain cluster voice for European Portuguese. The server uses DIXI to gather SAMPA phonemes [16], their timings and raw audio signal information.

The virtual therapist's representation to the user is achieved through a three-dimensional environment with speech synthesis capabilities. The environment is based on the Unity game engine and contains a 3D model of a cartoon character with visemes and facial emotions. Dynamic text, generated according to the system's flow, is forwarded to the TTS server. Upon the server's reply, the character's lips are synchronized with the synthesized speech.

3   Evaluation of the VITHEA Platform

A subjective evaluation of the overall VITHEA platform has been conducted with the collaboration and involvement of several speech and language therapists from different hospitals and continued care units across the country. All the therapists had previous experience with the platform, in their own language center, with different conditions for each participating subject. Following their experimental phase with the system, the speech therapists were asked to fill a questionnaire about the platform. Besides the answers collected with the questionnaires, therapists were asked to provide additional comments and feedback that were crucial for the later improvement of the therapy platform.

3.1   Evaluation Description

The survey involved 28 therapists, 27 female, 1 male, with an average age of 32 years, and an average professional experience with aphasia patients of 10.5 years.

The questionnaire was meant to assess several aspects of the VITHEA platform, namely its therapeutic utility, robustness, and usability. Therefore, it is divided into questions related with the choice of exercises and materials, with the speech recognition module, and with the human-machine interface. Answers to the questionnaire were given on a numerical scale (derived from the Visual Analogue Scales), where 1 is related to low satisfaction and 5 equals maximum satisfaction for each question. A representative subset of the items contained in the survey is shown in Fig. 2. In this picture, questions have been clustered into two groups: questions related with the therapeutic utility of the platform (shown in light gray), and questions related with robustness and usability (shown in dark gray). The questionnaire also contains open questions that allows collecting information about the convenience of incorporating new exercises and resources, which exercises may not be adequate and should be removed, the usefulness of the evaluation exercises, as well as appropriateness of the use of the program in other related areas (e.g. children with language learning and acquisition problems).

3.2   Evaluation Results

The results of this survey were remarkably good (Fig. 2), achieving an average score of 4.14. The items related with the therapeutic utility have an average score of 4.44, while the ones related to robustness and usability achieved 3.87.

Globally, all the questions concerning the therapeutic utility of the platform provided positive feedback. The exercises presented by the platform are adequate to the type of treatment (4.50), their varieties is reasonably good (3.85), and therapists like the possibility of introducing new exercises and their management features (avg. 4.37). It is worth stressing that the question on whether the system will be helpful in the daily work of the speech therapist received an average score of 4.59, and the question about its use in the therapy center got an even higher score of 4.64.

Many of the questionnaires were submitted before the introduction of several technical improvements that strongly contributed to the increased robustness of the platform. This justifies the average score of 3.50 assigned to the question about system robustness. In fact, it was found an incompatibility between the technology exploited by the first version of the patient module and the operating system installed on some machines of the visited hospitals. The average score to the question related with the time to obtain a response from the system is reasonably good (3.88), specially taking into account that VITHEA is a web application, and each exercise typically involves the transmission of an audio file from the client computer to the server machine. This fact adds a latency strongly dependent on the network congestion.

The worst results (2.50) concerned the question about the feedback messages. In fact, this question may be interpreted in several ways: *is it important to receive feedback? Is the provided feedback adequate? Is the quality of the feedback acceptable?* In the future, the question about the oral feedback should be rephrased, and eventually broken into more than one question. Overall, however, the system usability achieved quite good results: messages on the screen are clear (4.29), patients like the virtual therapist (4.28), and the program is easy to use (4.10). Particularly relevant are the results on the acceptance of the animated character.

4 Recent Improvements Motivated by the Evaluation

The comments received from the speech therapists involved in the evaluation motivated the introduction of considerable extensions to the platform. The most significant one concerns the development of a version customized for mobile devices, described in Sect. 4.1. Additionally, the success of the platform gave rise to new projects targeting different disorders, some of which based on the original platform (Sect. 4.2).

4.1 Adaptation to Mobile Devices

Due to a limitation in the Adobe® API, used to record patients' answers, the patient module of the VITHEA platform was not supported by the most common mobile device's browsers. However, smart-phones and tablets have become mainstream over the last few years, and in some cases, they may be cheaper than a computer, more practical, and even easier to use. Therefore, VITHEA2.0 [17], an enhanced application specifically suited for these devices, has been designed and implemented. With respect to the original web platform, this version pays particular attention to the overall user experience and also introduces new functionalities related with patients' management. In fact, VITHEA2.0 can be used on Android devices by patients, to perform traditional speech therapy exercises, and by clinicians to monitor the progress of their patients.

The application dedicated to patients has been designed with the aim of providing an easy and robust interaction. Patients can customize their experience by managing different options, including the possibility of choosing among three virtual therapists and setting the number of attempts that can be made in an exercise. Particular attention was given to the usability of the interface, which provides a simple and clear design and the possibility of customizing the font size. Visual feedback is also introduced to highlight wrong and right answers. Finally, the application is able to adapt to screens of different sizes and includes

Fig. 3. The interface of the VITHEA2.0 patient application. An example of a visual stimulus (left), and the feedback received when providing a correct answer (right).

an option for verifying the quality of the audio recorded. Figure 3 provides an example of the patient module interface.

Even though the patient application follows the same implementation logic of the web version, the underlying technology is different and raised several integration issues due to the heterogeneity of the standard used. In order to allow different client devices to access the functionalities of the VITHEA back-end, the latter has been restructured into a set of reusable components, adopting the Service Oriented Architecture (SOA) paradigm. The application logic and the ASR engine have been exposed as web services, according to the Representational State Transfer (REST) [18]. The speech recognition process is performed remotely by the in-house speech recognizer AUDIMUS, but the audio is now acquired through the Android microphone, thus overcoming the limitations imposed by Adobe®.

VITHEA2.0 has been designed to be used also by speech therapists and provides additional functionalities with respect to the corresponding web version. In particular, clinicians can now add or remove patients to their profile, send exercises to their patients, and monitor their progress.

4.2 Follow-Up Systems and Projects After VITHEA

The remarkable results achieved with VITHEA motivated the extension of the original platform to the treatment and screening of different diseases. Moreover, VITHEA has been also the basis for the development of novel applications in several follow-up projects.

VITHEA-Kids. VITHEA-Kids [19,20], is an application for Portuguese children suffering from Autism Spectrum Disorder (ASD). ASD is a developmental disability characterized by impairments in social communication that often comprises difficulties in the acquisition of verbal language skills. Symptoms may vary according to the specific diagnosis (i.e., Asperger syndrome, Childhood Disintegrative Disorder etc.), and to the specific characteristics of each child. In general, however, ASD is considered a complex pragmatic language disorder, which significantly influences communication skills. In this sense, the VITHEA-kids allows caregivers to build multiple choice exercises while taking into account the specific needs of each child. In fact, the platform provides an interface that allows to customize various aspects of the interaction. VITHEA-kids has been evaluated with caregivers, who provided positive feedback both in terms of the overall interaction with the application, and for what concerns the ability to easily and quickly complete the tasks assessed.

Cognitive Screening and Stimulation. The VITHEA platform has been also adapted to create a tool for monitoring the evolution of Alzhemeir's Disease (AD) [21]. AD is a neurodegenerative disorder characterized by alterations of memory and of spatial and temporal orientation. The diagnosis is typically based on several screening tests, such as the Mini-Mental State Examination (MMSE), the AD Assessment Scale (ADAS-Cog), and others. Most of these tests include a verbal component provided in response to a visual or spoken stimulus solicited by a therapist. Thus, due to their nature, and the need to continuously monitor the cognitive decline over time, these tests lend themselves naturally to be automated through speech and languages technologies. As far as we know, the adaptation of VITHEA to the monitoring of cognitive decline is the only platform of this type implemented for the Portuguese population.

More recently, a multiplayer game for European Portuguese has been developed with the aim of providing cognitive stimulation to the elderly [22]. The game, based on the format of a quiz, helps elders to exercise their memory while competing with each other, and thus promoting social interaction, which is of major importance for cognitive stimulation. To this end, inspired by the VITHEA platform, the game incorporates a virtual gameshow host and SLT allowing for natural voice interactions. The results of the user satisfaction survey showed the importance of the multiplayer component, reinforcing the potential of this type of system.

Speech Therapy Games for Children. The fundamental ideas of VITHEA have been more recently explored and expanded to develop speech therapy games particularly tailored for the children population. The BioVisualSpeech project [23], and also partially, the TAPAS (Training Network on Automatic Processing of PAthological Speech) H2020-ITN [24], are in fact focused on the development of new tools to assist speech and language pathologists in their daily activities with children presenting speech and language affecting disorders. The former project aims to research natural and multimodal interaction mechanisms for providing bio-feedback in speech therapy through the use of serious (computer) games, with particular focus to therapy of European Portuguese sibilant sounds. The second project focuses on the development of improved ASR modules for children atypical speech to be incorporated into naming based exercises, such as those of VITHEA. In both projects, the incorporation of gamification elements is a key aspect to keep children engaged in the therapy exercises.

5 Conclusion

In this work, we presented the results of the subjective evaluation of an on-line automatic therapy platform called VITHEA. The system is designed to allow Portuguese patients with aphasia to have unlimited access to word recalling therapy sessions. To this end, the tool integrates not only automatic speech recognition technology, but also text-to-speech and virtual character animation. Surveys conducted considered different aspects of the platform, and involved several speech and language therapists, who experimented the program with their own patients in their own medical centre facilities. According to the results of the survey, we can conclude that the VITHEA platform is perceived by therapists as a very useful tool for the treatment of aphasic patients. In addition to these encouraging results, the involvement of health professionals in the evaluation permitted us collecting extremely valuable feedback that contributed to the latter improvement of several aspects of the platform, including the development of a version for mobile devices. Finally, the success and flexibility of the platform allowed its use and extension in other projects targeting different disorders, like AD, ASD, and speech and language affecting diseases in children.

References

1. Pedersen, P., Jorgensen, H., Nakayama, H., Raaschou, H., Olsen, T.: Aphasia in acute stroke: incidence, determinants, and recovery. Ann. Neurol. **38**, 659–666 (1995)
2. Wilshire, C., Coslett, H.: Aphasia and Language. Theory to practice. In: Disorders of Word Retrieval in Aphasia Theories and Potential Applications, pp. 82–107. The Guilford Press (2000)
3. Basso, A.: Prognostic factors in aphasia. Aphasiology **6**(4), 337–348 (1992)
4. Bhogal, S., Teasell, R., Speechley, M.: Intensity of aphasia therapy, impact on recovery. In: Stroke, pp. 987–993 (2003)
5. Colby, K., Christinaz, D., Parkinson, R., Graham, S., Karpf, C.: A word finding computer program with a dynamic lexical-semantic memory for patients with anomia using an intelligent speech prosthesis. Brain Lang. **14**(2), 272–281 (1981)
6. Katz, R., Nagy, V.: A computerized approach for improving word recognition in chronic aphasic patients. In: Brookshire, R. (ed.) Clinical Aphasiology: Conference Proceeding. Minneapolis BRK Publishers (1983)
7. Archibald, L., Orange, J., Jamieson, J.: Implementation of computer-based language therapy in aphasia. Ther. Adv. Neurol. Disord. **2**(5), 299–311 (2009)
8. Adrián, J., González, M., Buiza, J., Sage, K.: Extending the use of spanish computer-assisted anomia rehabilitation program (carp-2) in people with aphasia. J. Commun. Disord. **44**(6), 666–677 (2011)
9. Fink, R., Brecher, A., Sobel, P., Schwartz, M.: Computer-assisted treatment of word retrieval deficits in aphasia. Aphasiology **19**(10–11), 943–954 (2005)
10. Jokel, R., Cupit, J., Rochon, E., Leonard, C.: Relearning lost vocabulary in non-fluent progressive aphasia with MossTalk Words®. Aphasiology **23**(2), 175–191 (2009)

11. Abad, A., et al.: Automatic word naming recognition for an on-line aphasia treatment system. Comput. Speech Lang. **27**(6), 1235–1248 (2013). https://doi.org/10. 1016/j.csl.2012.10.003. http://www.sciencedirect.com/science/articlepii/S0885230 81200085X, special Issue on Speech and Language Processing for Assistive Technology
12. Abad, A., Pompili, A., Costa, Â., Trancoso, I.: Automatic word naming recognition for treatment and assessment of aphasia. In: INTERSPEECH (2012)
13. Meinedo, H., Abad, A., Pellegrini, T., Trancoso, I., Neto, J.: The L^2F broadcast news speech recognition system. In: Proceedings of Fala 2010 (2010)
14. Pinto, J., Lovitt, A., Hermansky, H.: Exploiting phoneme similarities in hybrid HMM-ANN keyword spotting. In: Proceedings of Interspeech, pp. 1610–1613 (2007)
15. Paulo, S., et al.: DIXI - a generic text-to-speech system for European Portuguese. In: Computational Processing of the Portuguese Language, pp. 91–100 (2008)
16. Trancoso, I., Viana, C., Barros, M., Caseiro, D., Paulo, S.: From Portuguese to Mirandese: fast porting of a letter-to-sound module using FSTs. In: Mamede, N.J., Trancoso, I., Baptista, J., das Graças Volpe Nunes, M. (eds.) PROPOR 2003. LNCS (LNAI), vol. 2721, pp. 49–56. Springer, Heidelberg (2003). https://doi.org/ 10.1007/3-540-45011-4_7
17. de Lemos Marques, G.J.: Development of a Mobile Application for Remote Speech Therapy. Master's thesis, Instituto Superior Técnico, Lisbon, Portugal (2019)
18. Fielding, R., Taylor, R.: Principled design of the modern web architecture. ACM Trans. Internet Technol. **2**(2), 115–150 (2002)
19. Mendonça, V., Coheur, L., Sardinha, A.: Vithea-kids: a platform for improving language skills of children with autism spectrum disorder. In: Proceedings of the 17th International ACM SIGACCESS Conference on Computers & Accessibility, pp. 345–346. ACM (2015)
20. Mendonça, V.: Extending VITHEA in order to improve children's linguistic skills. In: Silva, J., Ribeiro, R., Quaresma, P., Adami, A., Branco, A. (eds.) PROPOR 2016. LNCS (LNAI), vol. 9727, pp. 3–11. Springer, Cham (2016). https://doi.org/ 10.1007/978-3-319-41552-9_1
21. Pompili, A., Amorim, C., Abad, A., Trancoso, I.: Speech and language technologies for the automatic monitoring and training of cognitive functions. In: Proceedings of SLPAT 2015: 6th Workshop on Speech and Language Processing for Assistive Technologies, pp. 103–109 (2015)
22. Oliveira, F., Abad, A., Trancoso, I.: A multiplayer voice-enabled game platform. In: PROPOR2020 (submitted)
23. Cavaco, S., et al.: BioVisualSpeech - A platform designed to help speech therapists (2016–2020). https://novasearch.org/biovisualspeech/project.php. Accessed 25 Oct 2019
24. TAPAS - Training Network on Automatic Processing of PAthological Speech (2018–2021). https://www.tapas-etn-eu.org. Accessed 25 Oct 2019

Resources and Evaluation

Resources and Avail5ation

A Dataset for the Evaluation of Lexical Simplification in Portuguese for Children

Nathan S. Hartmann[1,3]($\boxtimes$), Gustavo H. Paetzold[2], and Sandra M. Aluísio[1]

[1] Institute of Mathematics and Computer Science,
University of São Paulo, São Paulo, Brazil
{nathansh,sandra}@icmc.usp.br
[2] Federal Technological University of Paraná, Toledo Campus, Apucarana, Brazil
g.h.paetzold@sheffield.ac.uk
[3] Data Science Team, Itaú-Unibanco, São Paulo, Brazil

Abstract. Most research on Lexical Simplification (LS) addresses non-native speakers of English, since they are numerous and easier to recruit for evaluating resources. Target audiences that are harder to deal with, such as children, are often underrepresented in literature, although simplifying a text for children could facilitate access to knowledge in a classroom setting, for example. This paper presents an improved version of SIMPLEX-PB, a public benchmarking dataset for LS that was subject to multiple rounds of manual annotation in order for it to accurately capture the simplification needs of underprivileged children. It addresses all limitations of the old SIMPLEX-PB: incorrectly generated synonyms for complex words, low coverage of synonyms, and the absence of reliable simplicity rankings for synonyms. The dataset was subjected to an enhancement on the number of synonyms for its target complex words (7,31 synonyms on average), and the simplicity rankings introduced were manually provided by the target audience itself – children between 10 and 14 years of age studying in underprivileged public institutions.

Keywords: Lexical Simplification · Dataset · Benchmark · Children

1 Introduction

Lexical Simplification (LS) has the goal of changing words or expressions for synonyms that can be understood by a larger number of members of a certain target audience. Some examples of such audiences are children, low-literacy readers, people with cognitive disabilities and second language learners [13]. Most automatic systems for LS are structured as a pipeline and perform all or some of the steps illustrated in Fig. 1. The steps are (i) Complex Word Identification (CWI), which selects words or expressions that are considered complex for a reader and/or task; (ii) Substitution Generation (SG) and Selection (SS), which consist of searching for and filtering synonyms for the selected complex words; and (iii) Substitution Ranking (SR), in which the synonyms selected are ranked according to how simple they are [16].

The opinions expressed in this article are those of the authors and do not necessarily reflect the official policy or position of the Itaú-Unibanco.

© Springer Nature Switzerland AG 2020
P. Quaresma et al. (Eds.): PROPOR 2020, LNAI 12037, pp. 55–64, 2020.
https://doi.org/10.1007/978-3-030-41505-1_6

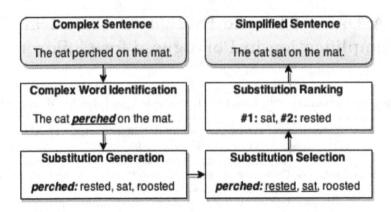

Fig. 1. Lexical simplification pipeline.

Most research on LS addresses the English language [3,11,16,18,19], but there are also studies dealing with many other languages such as Japanese [7], Spanish [1], Italian [17], and Portuguese [5], as well as multilingual and cross-lingual scenarios [8,18,20]. When it comes to target audiences, however, most recent work focuses on non-native speakers of English [13], since they are numerous and easier to recruit for evaluating resources and methods developed. Target audiences that are harder to deal with, from a practical point of view, are often underrepresented in literature, such as children [7,8], although simplifying a text for children of different grades could facilitate access to knowledge in a classroom setting, for example.

Currently, in Brazil, the National Program for Books and Lecturing Material (*Programa Nacional do Livro e do Material Didático (PNLD)*) is an initiative with broad impact on education, as it aims to choose, acquire, and distribute free textbooks to students in public elementary schools. Since 2001, the PNLD has been focusing on selecting and acquiring specific dictionaries for each school year/stage. In this scenario, adapting the level of complexity of a text to the reading ability of a student could substantially influence their improvement and determine whether they reach the level of reading comprehension expected for that school year. The task of LS could greatly help programs such as PNLD to thrive and reduce operational costs through automatization. However, there aren't many publicly available lexical simplification resources for Portuguese. Recently, the SIMPLEX-PB dataset [5] was created and made publicly available as an effort to foment research on LS for Portuguese. However, its first version as pointed out by the authors themselves, the dataset has several limitations preventing its applicability, such as incorrectly generated synonyms for complex words, low coverage of synonyms, and the absence of reliable simplicity rankings for synonyms.

In an effort to address these problems, this paper presents SIMPLEX-PB 2.0, an improved version of SIMPLEX-PB that was subject to multiple rounds of manual annotation in order to solve its limitations. It was also evaluated by children of different school grades attending supplementary classes after school. In Sect. 2, we present a brief literature review on datasets for LS. In Sect. 3 we describe the four steps we used to improve the original SIMPLEX-PB: (i) Synonym expansion via sinonimos.com.br; (ii) Synonym filtering through manual inspection; (iii) Adjudication of instances that had conflicting assessments during manual inspection; and (iv) Interpolation between the original dataset with the new filtered synonyms. In Sect. 4, we introduce our approach to synonym ranking, where we asked children between 10 and 14 years old of different school grades studying in underprivileged institutions and attending supplementary classes after school to order synonyms according to their simplicity. Finally, in Sect. 5 we present our conclusions and our intentions for future work.

2 Related Work

There are several publicly available datasets for training and evaluating LS systems in literature, most of which address the English language. The benchmark compiled by [16] for the SemEval 2012 Text Simplification shared-task was based on the Semeval 2007 Lexical Substitution *gold-standard* (LEXSUB) [11]. The 2007 joint task asked participants to generate substitutes for a target word. The LEXSUB dataset consists of 2,010 sentences, 201 target words each with 10 sentences as contexts which were annotated by 5 native English speakers. It covers mostly polysemous target words, including nouns, verbs, adjectives, and adverbs. For the joint task of 2012, the annotators ranked substitutes for each individual context in ascending order of complexity, thus enabling the joint task in Lexical Simplification. The selected annotators (graduated students) had high proficiency levels in English as second language learners. LSeval [3] was annotated by 55 annotators in which 46 were via Amazon Mechanical Turk platform and 9 were Ph.D. students. This dataset was also based on LEXSUB and in order to transform it to an LS dataset, it was removed from the list of 201 target words the "easy words", remaining 43 words, or 430 sentences. CW Corpus [15] is composed of 731 sentences from the Simple English Wikipedia in which exactly one word had been simplified by Wikipedia editors from the standard English Wikipedia. These simplifications were mined from Simple Wikipedia edit histories and each entry gives an example of a sentence requiring simplification by means of a single lexical edit. This dataset has been used in the Complex Word Identification (CWI) task. In the CWI task of SemEval 2016 [12], 400 non-native English speakers annotated the shared-task dataset, mostly university students or staff. Using the total of 9,200 sentences, 200 of them were split into 20 subsets of 10 sentences, and each subset was annotated by a total of 20 volunteers. The remaining 9,000 sentences were split into 300 subsets of 30 sentences, each of which was annotated by a single volunteer. The CWIG3G2 dataset [19] covers three text genres (professionally written news articles, amateurishly written news articles, and Wikipedia articles) annotated by both native and non-native English speakers. Besides covering single words, they deal with complex phrases (CPs), presenting them for judgment in a paragraph context. CWIG3G2 has balanced annotations from 10 native and 10 non-native speakers. This was the first study on cross-genre and cross-group CWI.

For Japanese, there are two LS datasets available. The SNOW R4 dataset [7], with 2,330 sentences, contains simplifications created and ranked by 5 annotators. These simplifications were rated as appropriate or not based on the following two criteria: if the sentence became unnatural as a result of the substitution and if the meaning of the sentence changed as a result of the substitution. The rank of each target word was decided based on the average of the rank from each annotator, following the previous research [16]. The BCCWJ dataset [8] was built to overcome several deficiencies of SNOW R4 dataset. It is the first controlled and balanced dataset for Japanese lexical simplification with high correlation with human judgment. A crowdsourcing application was used to annotate 1,800 sentences. Five annotators wrote substitutes, five annotators selected a substitution word that did not change the meaning of the sentence and five annotators performed the simplification ranking.

The SIMPLEX-PB dataset contains 1,719 instances following the proportion of content words found in [4] corpus: 56% nouns, 18% adjectives, 18% verbs, and 6% adverbs. From this distribution, the authors also made the subdivision equally distributed to benefit: more frequent words, words with a greater number of synonyms and words with more senses. Altogether, 757 distinct words were a target of simplification. Annotation was performed by three linguists experts for children. Two of them have a MSc and the third one has a Ph.D. The annotator filtered which words were appropriate to replace the original complex word. They also suggested replacements that were not listed. The Ph.D. linguist annotated all sentences and each of the MSc linguists annotated half of them in a double-blind procedure. The Cohen Kappa [2] was 0.74 for the first pair of annotators and 0.72 for the second pair. Table 1 summarizes 7 datasets publicly available for LS in English and Japanese languages. SIMPLEX-PB is presented in the last line.

Table 1. Benchmarks publicly available. In the second column, "Quality of Forms" indicates if there is any problem with the direct substitution of target word(s) by candidate simplifications; in the third column, "Task" shows the two ways the candidates are presented: a long list or only two (simple vs. complex); "Size" indicates sentences (S) or complex phrase annotations (CPs); NNE for Non-native English.

Dataset	Quality of Forms	Task	Size	Language	Target audience
SemEval2012	Inflection problems	List	2,010 S	English	NNE speakers
LSeval	Inflection problems	List	430 S	English	NNE speakers
CW Corpus	Automated creation; Wikipedia based	Binary	731 S	English	Evaluation of CWI systems
SemEval2016	Target words tagged by Freeling	Binary	9,200 S	English	NNE speakers
CWIG3G2	Balanced annotations	Binary	62,991 CPs	English	Native & NNE speakers
SNOW R4	Corrected for meaning preservation & naturalness	List	2,330 S	Japanese	Children & language learners
BCCWJ	Corrected for target audience	List	1,800 S	Japanese	Children & language learners
SIMPLEX-PB	Corrected for inflection errors	List	1,719 S	Portuguese	Children

3   Correcting and Complementing Synonyms

One of the main limitations of the original SIMPLEX-PB dataset was the fact that it had low coverage of synonyms for complex words. In order to enrich SIMPLEX-PB, we extracted synonyms from the online Dictionary of Synonyms for Brazilian Portuguese (https://www.sinonimos.com.br). Much like TeP [10], which was used in the creation of the original SIMPLEX-PB, sinonimos.com.br lists does not contain only the different meanings of registered words, but also a list of synonyms for each sense. In this annotation stage, for each target complex word in SIMPLEX-PB, we queried the senses available at sinonimos.com.br, then manually selected the meaning that best represented the context in which the target complex word was in. This task was conducted by three researchers in total. Two researchers annotated each instance so that we could not only calculate the agreement between them, but also minimize annotation errors. The dataset was split in 12 sections and the annotators were organized in two pairs (the most experienced researcher of the three was part of both pairs). Each pair annotated 6 sections. The overall Kappa annotator agreement score between all annotators was 0.63, which is considered substantial [9].

It is important to note that there is an interesting contrast between our Kappa agreement scores and our raw inter-annotator accordance (the proportion of instances in which both annotators chose the same sense). Inspecting the distributions featured in Fig. 2a, we can notice that the Kappa and accordance distributions differ quite a bit. While accordance has a more uniform distribution around the mean and a lower standard deviation, Kappa features not only a sparser distribution, but also a left skewed distribution representing dataset sections that considerably deviated from the mean at left. Figure 2b reveals the existence of two dataset sections featuring particularly low Kappa agreement scores between the annotators. Because Kappa makes an attempt at filtering "random accordance" between annotators, its penalization for these two sections is much more severe than the accordance distribution suggests.

Out of the 1,719 instances of SIMPLEX-PB, only a set of 114 were not annotated. This happened either because they did not have a registered sense in sinonimos.com.br that fit the context of the target complex word in question or because the context of the complex word had its syntactic/semantic structure compromised, hence preventing a reliable annotation from being made. Annotators agreed on their annotation in 69,2% of the instances (1,192). These instances were automatically enriched with the pertaining synonyms registered in sinonimos.com.br. The remaining 413 instances, for which there was no accordance in annotation, were subjected to an adjudication process. In the adjudication phase, each of the 413 instances were annotated by all three annotators. If all three annotators agreed on the sense of the target complex word, then the instance was kept, otherwise, it was discarded. Because these 413 instances were inherently more challenging to annotate, we figured that it would be best to pass them through this severe filtering process in order to maximize the reliability

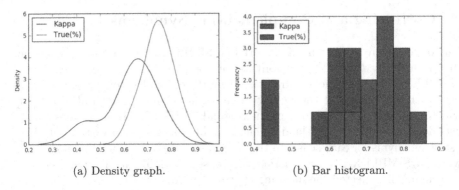

(a) Density graph.   (b) Bar histogram.

Fig. 2. Kappa (in blue) and accordance (in green) distributions for each annotated section of the dataset. (Color figure online)

of our new dataset. The three annotators agreed on 232 instances (56% of the initial 413), meaning that the remaining 181 instances were not updated with new synonyms. After the conclusion of these two annotation steps, a total of 295 instances (17% of the original 1,719) were not updated (for these instances, the original synonyms were kept). Through the new annotation of SIMPLEX-PB synonyms, we had an enrichment potential in 82.8% of the instances. This enrichment increased the mean of the dataset synonyms from 1.43 ± 0.7 to 7.31 ± 5.68, with an average gain of 80% in the number of synonyms presented. This synonym count is close to the 7.36 ± 5.3 average synonyms per complex word found in popular LS datasets for English [14].

4   Ranking Synonyms

Another limitation of the original SIMPLEX-PB dataset was the absence of simplicity rankings for synonyms. Similar LS datasets, such as LexMTurk [6] and BenchLS [14] feature not only synonyms for complex words in context, but also a ranking that orders them with respect to how easy it is for some target audience to understand them. This is a very important piece of annotation because of a variety of reasons, such as (i) it allows for the dataset to capture the needs of a specific target audience, (ii) it allows for supervised lexical simplifiers to be trained more easily, and (iii) it allows for a more thorough, informative evaluation of automatic lexical simplifiers.

Our goal was to make SIMPLEX-PB 2.0 (as we call the new version of the original dataset) a dataset for the training and evaluation of automatic lexical simplifiers for children, so we decided to allow the children themselves to rank the synonyms of SIMPLEX-PB 2.0. The annotation process was conducted with children of different grades attending supplementary classes after school. These classes are part of an educational support program conducted by University of

São Paulo (USP), in São Carlos, Brazil that focuses on helping children from low-income families[1].

First, from the 1,582 instances produced by the adjudication process, we chose 755 that featured at most 5 synonyms. We did this in order to reduce the complexity of the annotation process, since we anticipated that children would have a hard time producing rankings for large sets of synonyms. Some of the instances (25% of them) feature 10 or more synonyms, which would be challenging even for a trained adult to confidently rank. The 755 selected instances feature 412 nouns, 197 verbs, 89 adjectives, 56 adverbs, and 1 preposition. In order to make the annotation process more familiar to the children, we structured it as a series of exams. Each exam had 10 questions (10 instances for annotation). Each question was composed of a sentence with the original target complex word replaced by a series of underscores and a list of words composed by the complex word itself and its synonyms. The children were tasked with ranking the words from simplest to most complex. The original target complex word was also included so we could evaluate whether or not children would prefer for it to be replaced with a synonym. At the very top of all exams we placed a pre-completed instance in order to show the children how they should fill in the test. Figure 3 shows part of one the exams we used.

Fig. 3. Excerpt from an exam used during the synonym ranking phase.

We automatically generated the exams then manually reviewed them in order to correct the inflection of all synonyms. We did this because the synonyms fea-

---

[1] Implemented at USP in 1997, the Pequeno Cidadão Project serves 220 children from low-income families in São Carlos. Every day, accompanied by monitors and staff, they participate in a range of activities such as sports, dance, crafts, lectures and courses. Tutoring is also part of the routine, in addition to medical monitoring. To participate in the project, the child undergoes a socio-economic screening and must be enrolled in a regular school.

tured in SIMPLEX-PB 2.0 are all lemmatized (they are not inflected to the same tense as the target complex word), and hence they could potentially confuse the children. We generated 73 exams with 10 questions each, totalling 730 instances out of the 755 that we initially selected for this step of the annotation process. Our initial goal was to have each exam be taken by either 2 or 3 children so that we could not only calculate the agreement between them, but also produce a dataset that captures the needs of children as a whole more accurately. However, because of some unexpected issues that were out of our control, we could only get answers for 61 exams (83,5% of the original 73), with 27 of them being answered by a single child, 18 of them being answered by 16 children, and 3 of them being answered by 3 children. Some exam questions were left blank. After the exams were concluded, we inspected the agreement between the children. We calculated how frequently children agreed on the simplest synonyms, how frequently they agreed on the two simplest synonyms, and also the Spearman correlation coefficient between their entire rankings. A summary of the results is described in Table 2. When it comes to instances that were answered by two children only, in 43,5% and 27,3% of them there was an agreement on which was the simplest synonym (Top 1 Accordance) and on which were the two simplest synonyms (Top 2 Accordance), respectively. These proportions are quite low when compared to the agreement obtained for instances that were annotated by three children. In 81,5% of these instances there was an agreement between at least two children on the simplest word, and in 58,5% of them at least two children agreed on the two simplest. Furthermore, in 43,9% of them, all three children agreed on the simplest word, and in 14% the children agreed on the two simplest. These results are quite satisfactory, given that our focus was on maximizing agreement on the simplest word. This type of agreement is one of the most desirable traits of a dataset for LS because it increases the reliability of traditional performance measures for automatic lexical simplifiers. Inspecting the instances in the exams we found out some more interesting things. In 68% of instances, the synonym deemed simplest by the children was not the target complex word itself, which strongly suggests that SIMPLEX-PB 2.0 is in fact useful for the training and evaluation of lexical simplifiers. We also noted that the agreement between the children across the instances is inversely proportional to the amount of synonyms they featured (the more synonyms the instance had, the lower the agreement). This is expected, given that children living and studying in underprivileged conditions tend to have a limited vocabulary, which has often caused them to arbitrarily rank the words they have never heard of at the bottom of the synonym ranks. The substantially low Spearman correlation scores the annotations obtained highlight that phenomenon quite well.

The full synonym ranking annotations, including the number of children who annotated each instance, Top 1, Top 2 and Spearman correlation scores can be found within the SIMPLEX-PB 2.0 dataset package[2]. The final version of SIMPLEX-PB 2.0 has synonyms inflected to the same tense as the target complex word in each sentence.

---

[2] Available at https://github.com/nathanshartmann/SIMPLEX-PB-2.0.

Table 2. Accordance between children in synonym ranking.

#Accordances	Top 1	Top 2	Spearman
Instances annotated by 2 children			
Two children	43,5%	27,3%	0,05
Instances annotated by 3 children			
Two children	81,5%	58,5%	0,16
Three children	43,9%	14,0%	

5 Conclusions and Future Work

We presented SIMPLEX-PB 2.0, an expanded and enhanced version of the original SIMPLEX-PB dataset that was subjected to numerous rounds of manual annotation in order for it to accurately capture the simplification needs of underprivileged children. The dataset was subjected to an enhancement on the number of synonyms for its target complex words (7,31 synonyms on average) and the introduction of manual simplicity rankings produced by the target audience itself – children between 10 and 14 years of age studying in underprivileged public institutions in Brazil. In the future, we intend to incorporate rankings produced by more privileged children studying in private schools so that we can further increase the potential applications of SIMPLEX-PB 2.0. Finally, we also aim to conduct a benchmark of many different automatic lexical simplifiers on the dataset.

References

1. Bott, S., Rello, L., Drndarevic, B., Saggion, H.: Can Spanish be simpler? LexSiS: lexical simplification for Spanish. In: Proceedings of COLING 2012, pp. 357–374. The COLING 2012 Organizing Committee, Mumbai, December 2012
2. Cohen, J.: A coefficient of agreement for nominal scales. Educ. Psychol. Measur. **20**, 37–46 (1960)
3. De Belder, J., Moens, M.-F.: A dataset for the evaluation of lexical simplification. In: Gelbukh, A. (ed.) CICLing 2012, Part II. LNCS, vol. 7182, pp. 426–437. Springer, Heidelberg (2012). https://doi.org/10.1007/978-3-642-28601-8_36
4. Hartmann, N., Cucatto, L., Brants, D., Aluísio, S.: Automatic classification of the complexity of nonfiction texts in portuguese for early school Years. In: Silva, J., Ribeiro, R., Quaresma, P., Adami, A., Branco, A. (eds.) PROPOR 2016. LNCS (LNAI), vol. 9727, pp. 12–24. Springer, Cham (2016). https://doi.org/10.1007/978-3-319-41552-9_2
5. Hartmann, N.S., Paetzold, G.H., Aluísio, S.M.: SIMPLEX-PB: a lexical simplification database and benchmark for Portuguese. PROPOR 2018. LNCS (LNAI), vol. 11122, pp. 272–283. Springer, Cham (2018). https://doi.org/10.1007/978-3-319-99722-3_28

6. Horn, C., Manduca, C., Kauchak, D.: Learning a lexical simplifier using Wikipedia. In: Proceedings of the 52nd Annual Meeting of the Association for Computational Linguistics (Volume 2: Short Papers), pp. 458–463. Association for Computational Linguistics, Baltimore, June 2014. https://doi.org/10.3115/v1/P14-2075

7. Kajiwara, T., Yamamoto, K.: Evaluation dataset and system for Japanese lexical simplification. In: ACL (Student Research Workshop), pp. 35–40. The Association for Computer Linguistics (2015)

8. Kodaira, T., Kajiwara, T., Komachi, M.: Controlled and balanced dataset for Japanese lexical simplification. In: Proceedings of the ACL 2016 Student Research Workshop, pp. 1–7. Association for Computational Linguistics (2016)

9. Landis, J.R., Koch, G.G.: The measurement of observer agreement for categorical data. Biometrics **33**(1), 159–174 (1977)

10. Maziero, E., Pardo, T.: Interface de Acesso ao TeP 2.0 - Thesaurus para o português do Brasil. Technical report, University of São Paulo, Brazil (2008)

11. McCarthy, D., Navigli, R.: Semeval-2007 task 10: English lexical substitution task. In: Proceedings of the 4th International Workshop on Semantic Evaluations (SemEval-2007), pp. 48–53. Association for Computational Linguistics (2007)

12. Paetzold, G., Specia, L.: Semeval 2016 task 11: complex word identification. In: Proceedings of the 10th International Workshop on Semantic Evaluation, pp. 560–569. Association for Computational Linguistics (2016)

13. Paetzold, G.H., Specia, L.: A survey on lexical simplication. J. Artif. Intell. Res. **60**, 549–593 (2017)

14. Paetzold, G.H., Specia, L.: Benchmarking lexical simplification systems. In: Proceedings of the 10th International Conference on Language Resources and Evaluation (LREC-2016), pp. 3074–3080 (2016)

15. Shardlow, M.: The CW corpus: a new resource for evaluating the identification of complex words. In: Proceedings of the 2nd Workshop on Predicting and Improving Text Readability for Target Reader Populations, pp. 69–77. Association for Computational Linguistics (2013)

16. Specia, L., Jauhar, S.K., Mihalcea, R.: SemEval-2012 task 1: English lexical simplification. In: *SEM 2012: The First Joint Conference on Lexical and Computational Semantics - Volume 1: Proceedings of the main conference and the shared task, and Volume 2: Proceedings of the Sixth International Workshop on Semantic Evaluation (SemEval 2012), pp. 347–355. Association for Computational Linguistics, Montréal, 7–8 June 2012

17. Tonelli, S., Aprosio, A.P., Mazzon, M.: The impact of phrases on Italian lexical simplification. In: Proceedings of the Fourth Italian Conference on Computational Linguistics (CLiC-it 2017), pp. 316–320. Accademia University Press, Torino (2017)

18. Yimam, S.M., et al..: A report on the complex word identification shared task 2018. In: Proceedings of the 13th BEA. Association for Computational Linguistics (2018)

19. Yimam, S.M., Štajner, S., Riedl, M., Biemann, C.: Cwig3g2 - complex word identification task across three text genres and two user groups. In: Proceedings of the 8° IJCNLP, pp. 401–407. Asian Federation of Natural Language Processing (2017)

20. Yimam, S.M., Štajner, S., Riedl, M., Biemann, C.: Multilingual and cross-lingual complex word identification. In: Proceedings of RANLP, pp. 813–822 (2017)

Situational Irony in Farcical News Headlines

Paula Carvalho[1,2(✉)] (ID), Bruno Martins[2,3] (ID), Hugo Rosa[2] (ID), Silvio Amir[2],
Jorge Baptista[2,4] (ID), and Mário J. Silva[2,3] (ID)

[1] Universidade Europeia, Lisbon, Portugal
pcc@inesc-id.pt
[2] INESC-ID, Lisbon, Portugal
{bruno.g.martins,mjs}@inesc-id.pt, hugohrosa@gmail.com,
silvio.aam@gmail.com, jbaptis@ualg.pt
[3] Instituto Superior Técnico, Universidade de Lisboa, Lisbon, Portugal
[4] Universidade do Algarve, Faro, Portugal

Abstract. Current approaches to the computational modelling of irony mostly address verbal irony and sarcasm, neglecting other productive types of irony, namely situational irony. The function of situational irony is to lay emphasis on (real or fictional) events that evoke peculiar and unexpected images, which usually create a comical effect on the audience. In this paper, we investigate the linguistic and rhetorical devices underlying this phenomenon in a corpus composed of farcical news headlines, aiming at its automatic recognition. Based on a thorough annotation study, we found that in news headlines unexpectedness is mainly achieved by combining terms from different conceptual domains (what we have called out-of-domain contrast). We then explored features for automatically identifying these semantic and pragmatic incongruities and evaluated their discriminating power in a corpus whose irony is expressed by means of out-of-domain contrast. The features explored in our experiments are globally effective in capturing this phenomenon, attaining a six percent improvement in terms of the F-Measure over a baseline that only considers lexical information. Moreover, we observed that the best features typically reported in the literature for identifying incongruity in sarcastic text are not relevant for detecting situational irony in farcical news, thus reinforcing the idea that these phenomena pose different challenges that require distinct modelling approaches.

Keywords: Computational modeling of irony in text · Situational irony · Farcical news headlines · Out-of-domain contrast

1 Introduction

Irony covers distinct rhetorical devices, presenting different linguistic and pragmatic properties that pose particular challenges on its automatic recognition. Among other types, classical rhetoric distinguishes verbal irony from situational irony.

Verbal irony is classically defined as the intentional use of words and phrases to express the opposite of their literal meaning [30] (e.g., 'How brilliant!', instead of 'How stupid!'). This can be achieved by a variety of rhetorical strategies, including sarcasm,

P. Quaresma et al. (Eds.): PROPOR 2020, LNAI 12037, pp. 65–75, 2020.
https://doi.org/10.1007/978-3-030-41505-1_7

hyperbole, rhetorical questions, jocularity, and understatement [9]. On the other hand, situational irony usually involves an incongruity between expectations and reality, that is, a striking contrast between the normal state of affairs and the situation depicted or evoked by speakers [10]. This phenomenon relies, among other features, on unexpectedness, human frailty, and opposition [17] (e.g., 'Army vehicle disappears after being painted with camouflage'). Unexpectedness (i.e., absurdity) is also one of the main properties underlying satire, often present in situational irony [15].

Although situational irony is as complex and productive as verbal irony, it has not received the same attention from the cognitive and computational research communities. In fact, most research in computational modelling of irony focuses on verbal irony and sarcasm [11, 26]; the latter can be viewed as a special case of irony, where the positive literal meaning is perceived as an indirect insult [7]. Moreover, despite the increasing efforts to model some of these concepts, research on computational irony is more concerned with the generic detection of evidences on irony from text and context than with the understanding of the linguistic and rhetorical strategies underlying the ironic intent of messages in a specific type of content.

In this paper, we systematically investigate the expression of situational irony in farcical news headlines, collected from a Portuguese news satire site. Farcical news headlines are presented in a format typical of but rely heavily on irony and deadpan humor to emulate a genuine news source, mimicking credible news sources and stories, and often achieving wide distribution (News Satire, 2015, cited by [21]). In particular, we address two research questions which we deem critical to improve irony understanding and detection, especially in farcical news context:

- What are the most representative linguistic and rhetorical devices underlying situationally ironic events, particularly the ones displayed in news headlines?
- How does the modelling of specific rhetorical devices impact the automatic detection of situational irony?

Our study is based on a corpus of news headlines conveying an ironic intent, collected from *Inimigo Público*[1], a weekly farcical news supplement of a Portuguese mainstream newspaper, *Público*[2]. A set of 2,750 ironic headlines were labeled with information on the rhetorical devices underlying them, following detailed guidelines specifically developed for that purpose. With the resulting corpus, we conducted an inter-annotator agreement study to validate the annotations.

We found that situational irony in farcical headlines frequently uses out-of-domain contrast, i.e. incongruous combinations of entities and concepts belonging to different conceptual domains, as illustrated in the following farcical news headline taken from *Inimigo Público*: 'Gisele Bundchen [a famous top model] and Paulo Portas [a Portuguese political figure] announced their retirement from the runway'. Therefore, we concentrated our efforts in identifying the best features for assessing these contrasts and evaluated their performance with two standard machine learning classifiers.

---

[1] https://inimigo.publico.pt/.

[2] https://www.publico.pt/.

The remainder of the paper is structured as follows: Sect. 2 reviews previous work on the computational modelling of irony. Section 3 describes the corpora created for this study and their annotation process, which enabled the characterization of the most representative rhetorical devices used by each corpus' news source. Section 4 presents our approach to model out-of-domain contrast, underlying situational irony. Section 5 presents the conducted experiments, and Sect. 6 the achieved results. Finally, the main conclusions and future directions are discussed in Sect. 7.

2   Computational Modelling of Irony

Regardless of their specific properties, ironic utterances are claimed to share two intrinsic features: they usually involve an explicit or implicit untruthfulness, and they convey an implicit evaluation [8]. In fact, the perception of ironic utterances by listeners usually requires access to pragmatic information that goes beyond the utterances [25, 26].

Nevertheless, until recently, irony detection models mostly relied on the identification of lexical clues from text, and shallow syntactic parsing. For example, Kreuz and Caucci (2007) explored the importance of several lexical features (e.g., interjections) for identifying sarcastic statements [14]. Similar experiments were conducted by exploring hashtags denoting irony, explicitly inserted in short messages posted by Twitter users [6, 19]. On the other hand, Carvalho et al. (2011) showed that oral and gestural cues, such as emoticons, onomatopoeic expressions for laughter, heavy punctuation marks, quotation marks, and positive interjections, are more efficient in capturing irony than other cues based on more complex linguistic information [5]. However, the presence of some explicit features commonly explored in the literature, like emoticons, is closely related to the content being analyzed. In fact, these symbols are not expected to appear in certain types of content, such as news headlines.

To perform irony detection, Reyes et al. (2013) proposed a model that represents different attributes characterizing verbal irony in text, including unexpectedness and different emotional scenarios [19]. The former aims at capturing both temporal and contextual inconsistencies; the latter tries to capture different subjective dimensions on words. Exploring the idea of incongruity underlying ironic text, they proposed a method to detect sarcasm based on the expression of contrasting (positive vs. negative) sentiments and situations in the same utterance. To capture inter-sentential incongruity, Joshi et al. (2017) also explored the co-occurrence in text of (i) sentiment words, and (ii) sentiment words and phrases, explicitly or implicitly presenting divergent polarity [11]. Nevertheless, incongruity is not exclusively or necessarily expressed in terms of polarity. For example, it can be achieved by combining, in the same linguistic unit (noun phrase, sentence or utterance), entities and events from different semantic or conceptual domains (e.g., 'Cavaco quotes Trump's adviser to assure that Socrates used a microwave to spy on him').

Specifically, regarding the task of determining whether a newswire article is factual or satirical, Burfoot and Baldwin (2009) introduced the notion of validity, which decreases whenever a sentence contains unusual combinations of named entities [4]. Their method identifies the named entities in a given document and queries the web for the conjunction of those entities. Following this idea, Rubin et al. (2015) showed that absurdity, defined as the unexpected introduction of new named entities within satirical news, is a good predictor of satire in fake news, together with part-of-speech information and punctuation marks [21].

The majority of the approaches for irony detection still rely on the linguistic information present in text. However, as observed by Wallace et al. (2014), irony detection usually requires information that cannot be inferred directly from the documents alone [28]. Following this line of reasoning, recent studies, especially those based on Twitter, show that modelling metalinguistic information, such as the author's profile, and the author's historical salient terms, helps to improve irony detection accuracy [2]. Khattri et al. (2015) show that sentiment contrasts towards a given entity in tweets, as posted by an author over time, can provide additional context for sarcasm detection [13]. By exploring comments from reddit, Wallace analyzed contextual features, specifically by combining noun phrases and sentiment extracted from comments with the forum type (e.g. Conservative or Liberal) to which they were posted [27]. Amir et al. (2016) exploited contextual information by leveraging automatically learned user representations [1].

As in verbal irony, the recognition of incongruity or unexpectedness underlying situational irony also requires the access to dynamic information that goes beyond the text. Moreover, we posit that the relevance of the information to be considered strongly depends on the nature of data we intend to analyze.

3   Data Collection and Annotation

We created two different annotated corpora for this study: (i) a corpus used to conduct a preliminary analysis on the linguistic and rhetorical devices underlying situational irony in news headlines (Sect. 3.1); (ii) a gold-standard corpus to support the evaluation of machine learning procedures for irony detection (Sect. 3.2). To assess the reliability of the annotations in the corpus, we conducted an inter-annotator agreement (IAA) study (Sect. 3.3).

3.1   Preliminary Analysis

We started by assembling a corpus from 500 non-factual news headlines, published between January and May 2015 in *Inimigo Público*. The collected headlines were annotated by two linguists, aiming at finding the most prominent linguistic and rhetorical devices used to express situational irony.

This study allowed for the identification of 15 different categories. Some of them fit into the definition of classical rhetorical figures (like antithesis, comparison, hyperbole, metaphor, paradox, parallelism, repetition, and vulgarism), while others rely on a peculiar usage of syntactic and semantic properties (expressive use of adjectives, diminutive suffixes, and "exception" connectors; distributional and idiomatic rupture); and, finally, unusual combinations of nouns and named entities (out-of-domain contrast). Particular linguistic devices or rhetorical strategies not fitting any of the previous categories were classified as *other*. Finally, the cases where no evidence of irony could be detected were signaled as *no evidence*.

Our preliminary analysis allowed making an informed selection of the devices to be considered in the next annotation step, aiming at the creation of a gold-standard corpus to be used in the study and recognition of situational irony. In addition to *other* and *non-evidence*, we selected the following classes: comparison, metaphor, hyperbole, out-of-domain contrast, paradox, and vulgarism. This selection was based both on their relative frequency over the previously annotated corpus, and the agreement rate achieved between annotators. To measure the homogeneity of the annotations, we calculated the inter-annotator agreement, using Krippendorff's Alpha standard metric [16]. For the selected classes of devices, the obtained value was 0.55.

3.2 Gold-Standard Corpus

We assembled a second corpus of 2,500 non-factual headlines, also collected from the satirical newspaper *Inimigo Público*, between April 1, 2009 to October 25, 2015. To later use the corpus as a gold-standard for situational irony detection in news titles, the headlines were annotated with the previously identified rhetorical devices by five students in Communication Sciences, who were previously trained for this task. Table 1 summarizes the type and number of labels assigned by the annotators. On average, annotators identified 1.5 rhetorical devices per headline, and the most representative mechanism used to express situational irony was out-of-domain contrast. This corroborates the results obtained in the preliminary annotation experiments.

Table 1. Distribution of rhetorical devices in the gold-standard corpus.

Device	Example	Occurrences
Comparison	Like Passos Coelho, Jorge Jesus says that Sporting is better in radio broadcasts than in TV broadcasts	84
Metaphor	Al-Qaeda and ISIS are rivals in the race for the Ballon d'Or of Jihadism	810
Hyperbole	Antonio Costa announced that when elected Prime Minister each patient will have 2500 doctors	711
Out-of-Domain	Blatter and Platini suspended from FIFA for 90 days have been invited to the Government of Passos Coelho	1134
Paradox	Charlie Hebdo's cartoonists found the terrorist attack very funny	460
Vulgarism	Athens paid 580 M euros to the IMF but Varoufakis drew a penis on each banknote	151
Other	Cavaco Silva announces his name change to Passaco Silva	321
No-evidence	A Socialist group will propose an extraordinary congress of the Socialist Party after the Presidential election	152

3.3 Inter-annotator Agreement

To evaluate the reliability of the annotated corpus, we conducted an IAA study, based on a data sample composed of 250 news headlines. These include 100 factual headlines (collected from *Público*), and 150 farcical (non-factual) headlines (collected from *Inimigo Público*). The judges involved in the annotation of the gold-standard corpus were asked to both identify the presence of irony in the headlines and select the most relevant rhetoric devices they potentially convey.

Regarding the identification of irony, the agreement achieved by the annotators is substantial, ranging from 0.66 to 0.77 in the ternary classification (i.e. ironic vs. not ironic vs. uncertain), and from 0.76 to 0.80 in the binary classification (ironic vs. not ironic). With respect to the identification of rhetorical devices, the best IAA is achieved for vulgarism (0.75) and out-of-domain contrast (0.60), ranging from substantial to moderate agreement. The lowest agreement observed among the rhetorical devices involves metaphor (0.40) and paradox (0.41).

The apparently low agreement among the annotators was expected given the task complexity and the annotation guidelines, which involved a relatively high number of not always mutually exclusive and complex classes. Since the annotators were asked to select the most prominent linguistic or rhetorical device(s), instead of exhaustively determining the presence or absence of each class individually, having distinct devices assigned by different annotators does not necessarily mean that they disagree or that some of the assignments are incorrect.

Taking into consideration both the agreement results previously reported, and the frequency of each rhetorical device in the corpus, we decided to pursue out-of-domain contrast further, aiming at its automatic modelling and recognition.

4 Modelling Out-of-Domain Contrast

For modelling out-of-domain contrast, we considered shallow linguistic information, like Part-of-Speech (PoS), and additional semantic attributes derived from the application of specific linguistic resources to text (cf. Sect. 5). Regarding PoS information, we specifically calculated the representativeness of content words (namely nouns, adjectives, verbs and adverbs) in news headlines.

Inspired by Burfoot and Baldwin (2009), we also estimated the degree of validity or predictability of a situation, by exploring the relative frequency of co-occurrence of key terms (i.e. named entities) in the web [4]. In our experiments, we extended the notion of key term to common nouns and restricted the search to a specific web resource: a Portuguese news aggregator[3]. It is expected that the named entities and common nouns present in ironic headlines do not co-occur frequently in factual (or literal) news headlines and news stories.

In addition, we tested how the semantic relatedness among concepts may be captured through the computation of the distance between word vectors on the latent semantic space induced by Mikolov et al.'s Skip-gram embeddings [18]. These correspond to dense vector representations that implicitly capture latent aspects of words. The fundamental

---

[3] http://www.programmableweb.com/api/sapo-agenda.

idea behind these language models is that similar words tend to occur in similar contexts [24]. Using these embeddings, we measured the semantic distances (i.e., the cosine distance between the k-dimensional embedding vectors) between pairs of words occurring in the same title. We hypothesize that these distances will exhibit different patterns in the factual and ironic news headlines, given that the expression of irony frequently involves particular linguistic and rhetoric mechanisms, such as intentional repetition of words and phrases, and contrast between words and concepts from different semantic categories.

Finally, following recent studies on incongruity detection [12, 20], we explored sentiment contrasts, based on the sentiment polarity and other affective dimensions, like valence, arousal and dominance, described in sentiment lexicons available for Portuguese. In particular, it is assumed that incongruity may be detected based on the imbalance of positive and negative words in text.

5   Experimental Setup

The above features were first tested in a collection composed of 4,336 farcical headlines collected from *Inimigo Público*, from April 1, 2009 to October 25, 2015. Then, we tested those features in a subset of the gold-standard corpus, composed by 1,134 headlines previously identified by annotators as conveying out-of-domain contrast, and 1,134 others that were not labeled as conveying it.

Both collections were tagged with PoS information, using the NLTK package for Portuguese[4]. Named entity recognition was performed through *Verbetes*, a knowledge base that allows the recognition and disambiguation of public figures and organizations often mentioned in Portuguese news articles[5]. Potential sentiment words and expressions were labeled with information on polarity through the application of *SentiLex*, a sentiment lexicon for Portuguese [22]. Other affective values, such as valence, arousal, and dominance were also assigned to items recognized by the Portuguese version of *ANEW* [23], which was automatically enriched with the affective norms described for approximately 14,000 English lemmas[6] [29].

To calculate the joint and marginal probabilities of the (co)occurrences of named entities and/or common nouns, required for the computation of normalized pointwise mutual information (NPMI) statistics features [3], we first extracted all the simple and compound noun candidates from the corpus using the NLTK PoS tagger. Then, we identified the named entities by querying the Verbetes webservice for each candidate and replaced each match by its canonical form (i.e., the name commonly used to refer each entity in media). Finally, we counted the occurrences and co-occurrences of the (common and proper) nouns extracted from the news headlines over a large repository of Portuguese on-line newspapers, and used that information to compute the aforementioned probabilities. The word embeddings underlying the computation of features based on the semantic distances between word vectors were trained on a large corpus of 533,000 news articles also from the *Público* newspaper.

---

[4] https://www.nltk.org/.

[5] http://labs.sapo.pt/2011/02/verbetes/.

[6] English lemmas were automatically translated into Portuguese using the Google API client for Google Translate.

To ascertain the predictive power of our proposed features, we conducted experiments with two L1-regularized linear classifiers: Logistic Regression (LR) and linear Support Vector Machines (SVM). L1 norm regularization was considered as a means to encourage sparse models that only use the most informative features. As baselines, we considered the same classifiers using only binary bag-of-words (BoW) features.

The evaluation was performed with 10-fold cross-validation, by fitting the models associated to each of the folds on 80%, tuning on 10% and testing on 10% of the data. In each step, the regularization constant was selected with grid search using the training set to fit the model and evaluating on the tuning set. After selecting the optimal regularization constant, and again for each fold, the model was retrained on the union of the train and tune sets and evaluated on the test set.

6 Results and Discussion

Table 2 summarizes the results achieved for the task of detecting out-of-domain contrast. The results are presented in terms of average precision (P), recall (R), and F-measure (F), for both linear classifiers. The table also contrasts the baseline results (BoW) with the ones generated by adding the features described previously (*All Feat*).

The results show that the features used in our experiments globally correspond to good predictors of incongruity resulting from out-of-domain contrast. In fact, both classifiers outperformed the F-Measure of baselines in approximately 6% points.

The same set of features used to detect out-of-domain contrast were then tested to evaluate their impact in discriminating situationally ironic headlines from factual headlines. Table 3 summarizes the results achieved for this task. We observe that simple linear classifiers, based only on bag-of-words features, are quite efficient in distinguishing farcical from factual news titles, achieving an averaged F-measure of 0.85. This supports the insight that the vocabulary chosen by authors is a good predictor for detecting situationally ironic events. However, the integration of the features used to identify out-of-domain contrast significantly improved the results (F = 0.91).

Table 2. Detection of out-of-domain.

Classifier	P	R	F
SVM (BoW)	0.636	0.771	0.680
SVM + All Feat	**0.729**	0.768	**0.747**
LR (BoW)	0.627	**0.787**	0.684
LR + All Feat	0.721	0.782	0.738

Table 3. Detection of situational irony.

Classifier	P	R	F
SVM (BoW)	0.882	0.822	0.851
SVM + All Feat	**0.934**	0.885	**0.909**
LR (BoW)	0.879	0.827	0.852
LR + All Feat	0.929	**0.888**	0.908

Not surprisingly, the results achieved for the specific task of detection of out-of-domain contrast are significantly lower than the ones reported before, given the task specificity. Nevertheless, they reinforce the idea that the features used in our experiments correspond to good predictors of incongruity resulting from out-of-domain contrast.

In fact, both classifiers that used the complete set of features outperformed the F-Measure of baselines in approximately 6% points.

To better understand the impact of each feature subset on the detection of out-of-domain contrast, we carried out an ablation study, measuring the performance of the models obtained when leaving out one feature subset at a time. The obtained results show that the most relevant features underlying out-of-domain contrast rely on the contrast between unrelated common nouns and named entities, both in news articles and head-lines. The exclusion of this feature set from the experiments reduced the best achieved F-Measure by more than 2% points (Table 4).

Table 4. Out-of-domain detection ablation tests.

Feature set	P	R	F
All features (Linear SVM)	0.729	0.768	0.747
All features, except PoS representativeness	0.721	0.751	0.735
All features, except polarity information	0.729	0.773	0.749
All features, except polarity contrast	0.730	0.768	0.748
All features, except affective dimensions and affective contrast	0.661	0.840	0.738
All features, except contrast between N/NE in news headlines	0.727	0.727	**0.727**
All features, except contrast between N/NE in news articles	0.716	0.732	**0.723**
All features, except contrast between NE in news articles	0.729	0.767	0.747
All features, except contrast between NE in news headlines	0.728	0.763	0.745
All features, except semantic volume	0.703	0.749	**0.724**
All features, except semantic distance	0.730	0.768	0.748

To learn the importance of each feature individually, we have also considered the variable weights given by fitting the L1-regularized linear classifiers used in our experiments. We found that, contrarily to nouns, the high use of adjectives in farcical news headlines may signal ironic intent in incongruous utterances. Furthermore, we observed that the indicators typically reported in literature as good predictors of incongruity in text, such as sentiment contrast, do not seem relevant in our data set. In fact, the best feature to identify this rhetorical strategy is the standard deviation measure that contrasts nouns and named entities in news headlines.

Again, to interpret the impact of each feature subset on the detection of situational irony, we carried out an ablation study by measuring the performance of our proposed models, leaving out one of each feature subset at a time. We found that, in this case, the presence of negative words in ironic text is more informative than the positive ones. This differs from verbal irony, which makes a stronger use of positive words [5]. In addition, we observed that ironic headlines make a larger use of verbs, while factual headlines use preferably nouns. Regarding contrasts, the best feature to identify situational irony in news headlines is the standard deviation measure of contrast between nouns/entities, while the minimum value is better at identifying factual news headlines.

7   Main Conclusions and Future Work

We identified the most important rhetorical devices used in a corpus composed of situationally ironic headlines and evaluated how their modelling impacts irony recognition. We conclude that incongruity underlying ironic events often involves out-of-domain contrast, which can be successfully captured by statistically contrasting the co-occurrences of named entities and/or common nouns within a particular headline over the ones historically registered in large repository of semantically related data. Moreover, we found that, unlike verbal irony, sentiment features (like polarity and affective contrasts) are not effective in identifying situational irony, in particular out-of-domain contrast, underlying farcical headlines. As Rubin et al. (2015), we observed that PoS information can be used to detect satire in farcical news [21]. In particular, our results show that the prevalence of adjectives in news headlines may signal ironic intent in incongruous utterances. This research will contribute to a better understanding of the linguistic and rhetorical mechanisms underlying fake news headlines, providing new clues for the automatic recognition of incongruity in situationally ironic news headlines.

Acknowledgments. This work was supported by Fundação para a Ciência e a Tecnologia, through the projects EXPRESS (UTAP-EXPL/EEI-ESS/0031/2014) and DARGMINTS (PCI-01-0155-FEDER-031460), and also through the INESC-ID multiannual funding (UID/CEC/50021/2019).

References

1. Amir, S., Wallace, B., Lyu, H., Carvalho, P., Silva, M: Modelling context with user embeddings for sarcasm detection in social media. In Proceedings of the 20th SIGNLL Conference on Computational Natural Language Learning, pp. 167–177. ACL (2016)
2. Bamman, D., Smith, N.: Contextualized sarcasm detection on Twitter. In: Proceedings of the 9th International Conference on Web and Social Media, pp. 574–577. AAAI Press (2015)
3. Bouma, G.: Normalized (pointwise) mutual information in collocation extraction. In: Proceedings of the International Conference of the German Society for Computational Linguistics and Language Technology, pp. 31–40 (2009)
4. Burfoot, C., Baldwin, T.: Automatic satire detection: are you having a laugh? In: Proceedings of the Joint Conference of the 47th Annual Meeting of the ACL and the 4th International Joint Conference on Natural Language Processing, pp. 161–164. ACL (2009)
5. Carvalho, P., Sarmento, L., Teixeira, J., Silva, M.: Liars and saviors in a sentiment annotated corpus of comments to political debates. In: Proceedings of 49th Annual Meeting of the Association for Computational Linguistics: Human Language Technologies, pp. 564–568. ACL (2011)
6. Davidov, D., Tsur, O., Rappoport, A.: Semi-supervised recognition of sarcastic sentences in Twitter and Amazon. In: Proceedings of the 14th Conference on Computational Natural Language Learning, pp. 107–116. ACL (2010)
7. Dews, S., Kaplan, J., Winner, E.: Why not say it directly? The social functions of irony. Discourse Process. 19(3), 347–367 (1995)
8. Dynel, M.: The irony of irony: irony based on truthfulness. Corpus Pragmat. 1, 3–36 (2017)
9. Gibbs, R.: Irony in talk among friends. Metaphor Symb. 15(1), 2–27 (2000)
10. Gibbs, R.: A new look at literal meaning in understanding what is said and implicated. J. Pragmat. 34(4), 457–486 (2002)

11. Joshi, A., Bhattacharyya, P., Carman, M.: Automatic sarcasm detection: a survey. ACM Comput. Surv. (CSUR) **50**(5), 73 (2017)
12. Joshi, A., Sharma, V., Bhattacharyya, P.: Harnessing context incongruity for sarcasm detection. In: Proceedings of the 53rd Annual Meeting of the Association for Computational Linguistics and the 7th International Joint Conference on Natural Language Processing, pp. 757–762. ACL (2015)
13. Khattri, A., Joshi, A., Bhattacharyya, P., Carman, M.: Your sentiment precedes you: using an author's historical tweets to predict sarcasm. In: Proceedings of the 6th Workshop on Computational Approaches to Subjectivity, Sentiment and Social Media Analysis, pp. 25–30. ACL (2015)
14. Kreuz, R., Caucci, G.: Lexical influences on the perception of sarcasm. In: Proceedings of the Workshop on Computational Approaches to Figurative Language, pp. 1–4. ACL (2007)
15. Kreuz, R., Roberts, R.: On satire and parody: the importance of being ironic. Metaphor Symb. **8**(2), 97–109 (1993)
16. Krippendorff, K.: Reliability in content analysis. Hum. Commun. Res. **30**(3), 411–433 (2004)
17. Lucariello, J.: Situational irony: a concept of events gone awry. J. Exp. Psychol. Gen. **123**(2), 129 (1994)
18. Mikolov, T., Sutskever, I., Chen, K., Corrado, G., Dean, J.: Distributed representations of words and phrases and their compositionality. In: Burges, C.J.C, Bottou, L., Welling, M., Ghahramani, Z., Weinberger, K.Q. (eds.) Advances in Neural Information Processing Systems, vol. 26, pp. 3111–3119. Curran Associates, Inc. (2013)
19. Reyes, A., Rosso, P., Veale, T.: A multidimensional approach for detecting irony in Twitter. Lang. Resour. Eval. **47**(1), 239–268 (2013)
20. Riloff, E., Qadir, A., Surve, P., Silva, L., Gilbert, N., Huang, R.: Sarcasm as contrast between a positive sentiment and negative situation. In: Proceedings of the 2013 Conference on Empirical Methods in Natural Language Processing, pp. 704–714. ACL (2013)
21. Rubin, V., Chen, Y., Conroy, N.: Deception detection for news: three types of fakes. Proc. Assoc. Inf. Sci. Technol. **52**(1), 1–4 (2015)
22. Silva, M.J., Carvalho, P., Sarmento, L.: Building a sentiment lexicon for social judgement mining. In: Caseli, H., Villavicencio, A., Teixeira, A., Perdigão, F. (eds.) PROPOR 2012. LNCS (LNAI), vol. 7243, pp. 218–228. Springer, Heidelberg (2012). https://doi.org/10.1007/978-3-642-28885-2_25
23. Soares, A., Comesana, M., Pinheiro, A., Simões, A., Frade, C.: The adaptation of the affective norms for English words (anew) for European Portuguese. Behav. Res. Methods **44**(1), 256–269 (2012)
24. Sperber, D., Wilson, D.: A synopsis of linguistic theory 1930–1955. In: Studies in Linguistic Analysis, Selected Papers of J. R. Firth 1952–1959, pp. 1–32 (1968)
25. Sperber, D., Wilson, D.: Pragmatics, modularity and mind-reading. Mind Lang. **17**(1–2), 3–23 (2002)
26. Wallace, B.: Computational irony: a survey and new perspectives. Artif. Intell. Rev. **43**(4), 467–483 (2015)
27. Wallace, B.: Sparse, contextually informed models for irony detection: exploiting user communities, entities and sentiment. In: Proceedings of the 53rd Annual Meeting of the Association for Computational Linguistics and the 7th International Joint Conference on Natural Language Processing, pp. 1035–1044. ACL (2015)
28. Wallace, B., Choe, D., Kertz, L., Charniak, E.: Humans require context to infer ironic intent (so computers probably do, too). In: Proceedings of the 52nd Annual Meeting of the Association for Computational Linguistics, pp. 512–516. ACL (2014)
29. Warriner, A., Kuperman, V., Brysbaert, M.: Norms of valence, arousal, and dominance for 13,915 English lemmas. Behav. Res. Methods **45**(4), 1191–1207 (2013)
30. Wilson, D., Sperber, D.: On verbal irony. Lingua **87**, 53–76 (1992)

Inferring the Source of Official Texts: Can SVM Beat ULMFiT?

Pedro Henrique Luz de Araujo[1]([✉]), Teófilo Emidio de Campos[1]([✉]), and Marcelo Magalhães Silva de Sousa[2]

[1] Departamento de Ciência da Computação (CiC), Universidade de Brasília (UnB), Brasilia, Brazil
pedrohluzaraujo@gmail.com, t.decampos@oxfordalumni.org
[2] Tribunal de Contas do Distrito Federal, Zona Cívico-Administrativa, Brasília, DF, Brazil
marcelomsousa@tc.df.gov.br

Abstract. Official Gazettes are a rich source of relevant information to the public. Their careful examination may lead to the detection of frauds and irregularities that may prevent mismanagement of public funds. This paper presents a dataset composed of documents from the Official Gazette of the Federal District, containing both samples with document source annotation and unlabeled ones. We train, evaluate and compare a transfer learning based model that uses ULMFiT with traditional bag-of-words models that use SVM and Naive Bayes as classifiers. We find the SVM to be competitive, its performance being marginally worse than the ULMFiT while having much faster train and inference time and being less computationally expensive. Finally, we conduct ablation analysis to assess the performance impact of the ULMFiT parts.

Keywords: Text classification · Language models · Transfer learning

1 Introduction

Government Gazettes are a great source of information of public interest. These government maintained periodical publications disclose a myriad of matters, such as contracts, public notices, financial statements of public companies, public servant nominations, public tenderings, public procurements and others. Some of the publications deal with public expenditures and may be subject to frauds and other irregularities.

On the other hand, it is not easy to extract information from Official Gazettes. The data is not structured, but available as natural language texts. In addition, the language used is tipically from the public administration domain, which can further complicate information extraction and retrieval.

Natural Language Processing (NLP) and Machine Learning (ML) techniques are great tools for obtaining information from official texts. NLP has been used to automatically extract and classify relevant entities in court documents [3,5].

P. Quaresma et al. (Eds.): PROPOR 2020, LNAI 12037, pp. 76–86, 2020.
https://doi.org/10.1007/978-3-030-41505-1_8

Other works [6, 10, 12, 15] explore the use of automatic summarization to mitigate the amount of information legal professional have to process. Text classification has been utilized for decision prediction [1, 11], area of legal practice attribution [24] and fine-grained legal-issue classification. Some effort has been applied to the processing of Brazilian legal documents [17, 20, 25].

In this paper, we aim to identify the public body of origin of documents fom the Official Gazette of the Federal District. This is a first step in the direction of structuring the information present in Official Gazettes in order to enable more advanced applications such as fraud detection. Even though it is possible to extract the public entity that produced the document by using rules and regular expressions, such approach is not very robust: changes in document and phrase structure and spelling mistakes can greatly reduce its effectiveness. A machine learning approach may be more robust to such data variation.

Due to the small number of samples in our dataset, we explore the use of transfer learning for NLP. We choose ULMFiT [8] as the method due to it being less resource-intensive than other state-of-the-art approaches such as BERT [4] and GPT-2 [19]. Our main contributions are:

1. Making available to the community a dataset with labeled and unlabeled Official Gazette documents.
2. Training, evaluating and comparing a ULMFiT model to traditional bag-of-word models.
3. Performing an ablation analysis to examine the impact of the ULMFiT steps when trained on our data.

2 The Dataset

The data consists of 2,652 texts extracted from the Official Gazette of the Federal District[1]. Handcrafted regex rules were used to extract some information from each sample, such as publication date, section number, public body that issued the document and title. 797 of the documents were manually examined, from which 724 were found to be free of labeling mistakes. These documents were produced by 25 different public entities. We filter the samples with entities who have less than three samples, since this would mean no representation for the public body in either the training, validation or test set. As a result, we end up with 717 labeled examples from 19 public entities.

We then split these samples and the 1,928 unverified or incorrectly labeled texts into two separate datasets. The first for classification of public entity that produced the document and the other for the unsupervised training of a language model.

The classification dataset is formed by 717 pairs of document and its respective public entity of origin. We randomly sample 8/15 of the texts for the training set, 2/15 for the validation set and the remainder for the test set, which results in 384, 96 and 237 documents in each set, respectively. Figure 1 shows the class

---

[1] Available at https://www.dodf.df.gov.br/.

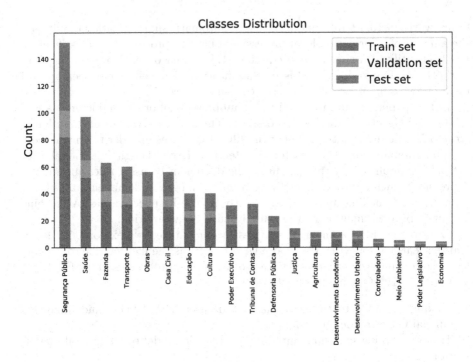

Fig. 1. Class counts for each dataset split.

distribution in each set. The data is imbalanced: *Segurança Pública*, the most frequent class, contains more than 140 samples, while the least frequent classes are represented by less than 5 documents. We handle this by using F_1 score as the metric for evaluation and trying model-specific strategies to handle imbalance, as we discuss in Sect. 4.

Two of the 1,928 texts in the language model dataset were found to be empty and were dropped. From the remaining 1,926, 20% were randomly chosen for the validation set. The texts contain 984,580 tokens in total; after the split, there are 784,260 in the training set and 200,320 in the validation set. In this case we choose to not build a test set since we are not interested in an unbiased evaluation of the language model performance. The data is automatically labeled as an standard language model task where the label of each token is the following token in the sentence.

3   The Models

In this section we describe the transfer learning based approach to text classification used to classify the documents, the bag-of-words method used as a baseline and the preprocessing employed for both approaches.

3.1 Preprocessing

We first lowercase the text and use SentencePiece [14] to tokenize it. We chose SentencePiece because that was the tokenizer used for the pretrained language model (more about that on Sect. 3.3), so using the same tokenization was fundamental to preserve vocabulary. We use the same tokenization for the baseline methods to establish a fair comparison of the approaches.

In addition, we add special tokens to the vocabulary to indicate unknown words, padding, beginning of text, first letter capitalization, all letters capitalization, character repetition and word repetition. Even though the text has been lowercased, these tokens preserve the capitalization information present in the original data. The final vocabulary is composed of 8,552 tokens, including words, subwords, special tokens and punctuation.

3.2 Baseline

For the baseline models, we experiment with two different bag-of-words text representation methods: tf-idf values and token counts. Both methods represent each document as a v-dimensional vector, where v is the vocabulary size. In the first case, the i-th entry of the vector is the tf-idf value of the i-th token in the vocabulary, while in the second case that value is simply the number of times the token appears in the document. Tf-idf values are computed according to the following equations:

$$\text{tf-idf}(t, d) = \text{tf}(t, d) \times \text{idf}(t) \tag{1}$$

$$\text{idf}(t) = \log \frac{1 + n}{1 + \text{count}(t)} + 1, \tag{2}$$

where $\text{tf}(t, d)$ is the frequency of term t in document d, n is the total of documents in the corpus, and $\text{count}(t)$ is the number of documents that contain term t. All document vectors are normalized to have unit Euclidean norm.

We use the obtained bag-of-words to train a shallow classifier. We experiment with both Support Vector Machines (SVM) [7] with linear kernel and Naive Bayes classifiers.

3.3 Transfer Learning

We use Universal Language Model Fine-Tuning (ULMFiT) [8] to leverage information contained in the unlabeled language model dataset. This method of inductive transfer learning was shown to require much fewer labeled examples to match the performance of training from scratch.

ULMFiT amounts to three stages:

Language Model Pre-training. We use a bidirectional Portuguese language model[2] trained on a Wikipedia corpus composed of 166,580 articles, with a total

---

[2] Available at https://github.com/piegu/language-models/tree/master/models.

of 100,255,322 tokens. The tokenization used was the same as ours. The model architecture consists of a 400-dimensional embedding layer, followed by four Quasi-Recurrent Neural Network (QRNN [2]) layers with 1550 hidden parameters each and a final linear classifier on top. QRNN layers alternate parallel convolutional layers and a recurrent pooling function, outperforming LSTMs of same hidden size while being faster at trainining time and inference.

Language Model Fine-Tuning. We fine-tune the forward and backward pre-trained general-domain Portuguese language models on our unlabeled dataset, since the latter comes from the same distribution and the classification task data, while the former does not. As in the ULMFiT paper, we use discriminative fine-tuning [8], where instead of using the same learning rate for all layers of the model, different learning rates are used for different layers. We employ cyclical learning rates [22] with cosine annealing to speed up training.

Classifier Fine-Tuning. To train the document classifier, we add two linear blocks to the language models, each block composed of batch normalization [9], dropout [23] and a fully-connected layer. The first fully-connected layer has 50 units and ReLU [18] activation, while the second one has 19 units and is followed by a softmax activation that produces the probability distribution over the classes. The final prediction is the average of the forward and backwards models. The input to the linear blocks is the concatenation of the hidden state of the last time step h_T with the max-pooled and the average-pooled hidden states of as many time steps as can be fit in GPU memory $H = \{h_1, \cdots, h_T\}$. That is, the input to the linear blocks h_c is:

$$h_c = \text{concat}(h_t, \text{maxpool}(H), \text{averagepool}(H)). \tag{3}$$

4 Experiments

In this section we describe the training procedure and hyperparameters used. All experiments were executed on a Google Cloud Platform n1-highmem-4 virtual machine with a Nvidia Tesla P4 GPU.

4.1 Baseline

To find the best set of hyperparameter values we use random search and evaluate the model on the validation set. Since we experiment with two classifiers (SVM and Naive Bayes) and two text vectorizers (tf-idf values and token counts), we have four model combinations: tf-idf and Naive Bayes, tf-idf and SVM, token counts and Naive Bayes; and token counts and SVM. For each of these 4 scenarios we train 100 models, each iteration with random hyperparameter values.

Vectorizers. For both the tf-idf and token counts vectorizers we tune the same set of hyperparameters: n-gram range (only unigrams, unigrams and bigrams, unigrams to trigrams), maximum document frequency token cutoff (50%, 80% and 100%), minimum number of documents for token cutoff (1, 2 and 3 documents).

Naive Bayes. We tune the smoothing prior α on a exponential scale from 10^{-4} to 1. We also choose between fitting the prior probabilities, which could help with the class imbalance, and just using an uniform prior distribution.

SVM. In the SVM case, we tune two hyperparameters. We sample the regularization parameter C from an exponential scale from 10^{-3} to 10. In addition, we choose between applying weights inversely proportional to class frequencies to compensate class imbalance and giving all classes the same weight.

4.2 Transfer Learning

To tune the best learning rate in both the language model fine-tuning and classifier training scenarios, we use the learning rate range test [21], where we run the model through batches while increasing the learning rate value, choosing the learning rate value that corresponds to the steepest decrease in validation loss. We use Adam [13] as the optimizer.

We fine-tune the top layer of the forward and backwards language models for one one cycle of 2 epochs and then train all layers for one cycle of 10 epochs. We use a batch size of 32 documents, weight decay [16] of 0.1, backpropagation through time of length 70 and dropout probabilities of 0.1, 0.6, 0.5 and 0.2 applied to embeddings inputs, embedding outputs, QRNN hidden-to-hidden weight matrix and QRNN output, respectively, following previous work [8].

In the case of the backward and forward classifiers, in order to prevent catastrophic forgetting by fine-tuning all layers at once, we gradually unfreeze [8] the layers starting from the last layer. Each time we unfreeze a layer we fine-tune for one cycle of 10 epochs. We use a batch size of 8 documents, weight decay of 0.3, backpropagation through time of length 70 and the same dropout probabilities used for the language model fine-tuning scaled by a factor of 0.5.

Similarly to the SVM experiments, in order to handle data imbalance we try applying weights inversely proportional to class frequencies. Nevertheless, this did not contribute to significant changes in classification metrics.

5   Results

Table 1 reports, for each model trained, test set F_1 scores for each class. Due to the small size of the classification dataset, some class-specific scores are noisy because of their rarity, so we also present the average and weighted by class frequency F_1 values and the model accuracy. For the baseline models, we present

Table 1. Classification results (in %) on the test set.

Class	NB	SVM	F-ULMFiT	B-ULMFiT	F+B-ULMFiT	Count
Casa Civil	72.22	74.29	82.35	83.33	**85.71**	18
Controladoria	**80.00**	**80.00**	**80.00**	0.00	66.67	2
Defensoria Pública	**100.00**	**100.00**	**100.00**	**100.00**	**100.00**	8
Poder Executivo	80.00	81.82	78.26	**90.91**	86.96	10
Poder Legislativo	40.00	**100.00**	**100.00**	**100.00**	**100.00**	1
Agricultura	28.57	75.00	**85.71**	75.00	**85.71**	4
Cultura	**91.67**	**91.67**	88.00	**91.67**	**91.67**	13
Desenv. Econômico	**66.67**	**66.67**	28.57	33.33	33.33	4
Desenv. Urbano	75.00	**85.71**	75.00	66.67	**85.71**	4
Economia	**100.00**	**100.00**	**100.00**	**100.00**	**100.00**	1
Educação	70.00	**75.00**	72.00	66.67	**75.00**	13
Fazenda	85.71	88.37	86.36	**90.48**	**90.48**	21
Justiça	**80.00**	75.00	66.67	75.00	66.67	5
Obras	84.85	85.71	87.50	87.50	**90.91**	18
Saúde	91.43	93.94	**95.38**	91.43	94.12	32
Segurança Pública	**97.03**	95.24	95.24	96.15	94.34	50
Transporte	91.89	95.00	87.18	**95.24**	**95.24**	20
Meio Ambiente	80.00	**100.00**	66.67	66.67	66.67	2
Tribunal de Contas	**100.00**	**100.00**	95.65	**100.00**	**100.00**	11
Average F1	79.74	**87.55**	82.66	79.48	84.69	237
Weighted F1	86.86	89.17	87.46	88.14	**89.74**	237
Accuracy	86.92	89.45	87.76	89.03	**90.30**	237

results using the tf-idf text vectorizer, which performed better than the count vectorizer on the validation set. F-ULMFiT, B-ULMFiT and F+B-ULMFiT indicate the forward ULMFiT model, the backward counterpart and their ensemble, respectively.

All models performed better than a classifier that simply chooses the most common class, which would yield average and weighted F_1 scores of 7.35 and 1.83 and an accuracy of 21.10. The SVM and ULMFiT models outperformed the Naive Bayes classifier across almost all categories. All models seem to achieve good results, with weighted F_1 scores and accuracies approaching 90.00%, though we do not have a human performance benchmark for comparison.

Despite the SVM's average F_1 score being higher than the ULMFiT's, the latter has greater weighted F_1 score and accuracy, with a corresponding reduction of 8.06% on test error rate. That being said, the SVM has some advantages. First, it is much faster to train. While the SVM took less than two seconds to train, the ULMFiT model took more than half an hour. In addition, the ULMFiT approach greatly depends on GPU availability, otherwise training would take much more time.

Table 2. Ablation scenarios results (in %) on the test set.

Model	Average F1	Weighted F1	Accuracy
No gradual unfreeezing (f)	82.34 (−0.32)	89.46 (+2.00)	89.87 (+2.11)
No gradual unfreeezing (b)	80.8 (+1.32)	89.07 (+9.03)	89.87 (+0.84)
No gradual unfreeezing (f+b)	82.76 (−1.93)	89.66 (−0.08)	89.87 (−0.43)
Last layer fine-tuning (f)	63.30 (−19.36)	77.39 (−10.07)	78.90 (−8.86)
Last layer fine-tuning (b)	60.48 (−19.00)	77.03 (−11.11)	78.48 (−10.55)
Last layer fine-tuning (f+b)	66.37 (−18.32)	79.60 (−10.14)	81.01 (−9.29)
No LM fine-tuning (f)	28.05 (−54.61)	47.24 (−40.22)	53.59 (−34.17)
No LM fine-tuning (b)	27.32 (−52.16)	39.24 (−48.90)	50.63 (−38.40)
No LM fine-tuning (f+b)	31.48 (−53.21)	46.06 (−43.68)	55.27 (−35.03)
Direct transfer (f)	11.78 (−70.88)	24.33 (−63.13)	32.07 (−55.69)
Direct transfer (b)	8.33 (−71.15)	14.01 (−74.13)	27.85 (−61.18)
Direct transfer (f+b)	11.54 (−73.15)	24.00 (−65.74)	34.60 (−55.70)

Furthermore, SVM training is very straightforward, while the transfer learning scenario requires three different steps with many parts that need tweaking (gradual unfreezing, learning rate schedule, discriminative fine-tuning). Consequently, not only the ULMFiT model has more hyperparameters to be tuned, each parameter search iteration is computationally expensive—the time it takes to train one ULMFiT model is enough to train more than 1,000 SVM models with different configurations of hyper-parameters.

5.1 Ablation Analysis

In this section we analyze the individual impact of ULMFiT's parts on our data. We do so by running experiments on four different scenarios. We use the same hyperparameters as in the complete ULMFiT case and train for the same number of iterations in order to establish a fair comparison. Table 2 presents the results and the difference between the scenario result and the original performance, taking into consideration if it is the forward, backward or ensemble case.

No Gradual Unfreezing. This scenario's training procedure is almost identical to the previously presented, with the exception that gradual unfreezing is not used. In the classifier fine-tuning step though, we instead fine-tune all layers at the same time. This was the least contributing to the performance, with minor reductions to our metrics in the ensemble case.

Last Layer Fine-Tuning. This scenario is similar to the previous one in the sense that we do not perform gradual unfreezing. But while there we fine-tuned all layers, here we treat the network as a feature extractor and fine-tune only the classifier. We see a sharp decrease in performance across all metrics, suggesting that the QRNN network, even though the language model was fine-tuned on domain data, does not perform well as a feature extractor for document classification. That is, to train a good model it is imperative to fine-tune all layers.

No Language Model Fine-Tuning. Here we skip the language model fine-tuning step and instead train the classifier directly from the pre-trained language model, using gradual unfreezing just like in the original model. This results in a great decline in performance, with decreases ranging from about 30 to more than 50 percentual points. Therefore, for our data, training a language model on general domain data is not enough; language model fine-tuning on domain data is essential. This may be due to differences in vocabulary and word distribution between general and official text domains.

Direct Transfer. In this scenario we go one step further than in the previous one: we start from the pre-trained language model and do not fine-tune it. They differ because in the classifier fine-tuning step we do not perform gradual unfreezing, but train all layers at the same time. This results in a even greater performance decrease. The lack of gradual unfreezing here is much more dramatic than in the first scenario. We hypothesize that the language model fine-tuning may mitigate the effects or decrease the possibility of catastrophic forgetting.

Averaging Forward and Backward Predictions. In almost all cases, averaging the forward and backward models predictions results in more accurate results than either of the single models. One possible way of further experimenting is trying other methods of combining the directional outputs.

6   Conclusion

This paper examines the use of ULMFiT, a inductive transfer learning method for natural language applications, to identify the public entity that originated Official Gazette texts. We compare the performance of ULMFiT with simple bag-of-words baselines and perform an ablation analysis to identify the impact of gradual unfreezing, language model fine-tuning and the use of the fine-tuned language model as a text feature extractor.

Despite being a state-of-the-art technique, the use of ULMFiT correspond to a small increase in classification accuracy when compared to the SVM model. Considering the faster training time, simpler training procedure and easier parameter tuning of SVM, this traditional text classification method is still competitive with modern deep learning models.

Finally, our ablation analysis shows that the combination of language model fine-tuning and gradual unfreezing is extremely beneficial. It also suggests that language models, even after fine-tuned on domain data, are not good feature extractors and should be trained also on classification data.

Acknowledgements. This study was financed in part by the Coordenação de Aperfeiçoamento de Pessoal de Nível Superior - Brasil (CAPES) - Finance Code 001. TdC received support from Conselho Nacional de Desenvolvimento Científico e Tecnológico (CNPq), grant PQ 314154/2018-3. We are also grateful for the support from Fundação de Apoio à Pesquisa do Distrito Federal (FAPDF).

References

1. Aletras, N., Tsarapatsanis, D., Preotiuc-Pietro, D., Lampos, V.: Predicting judicial decisions of the European Court of Human Rights: a Natural Language Processing perspective. PeerJ Comput. Sci. **2**, e93 (2016). https://doi.org/10.7717/peerj-cs.93

2. Bradbury, J., Merity, S., Xiong, C., Socher, R.: Quasi-recurrent neural networks. CoRR abs/1611.01576 (2016). http://arxiv.org/abs/1611.01576

3. Cardellino, C., Teruel, M., Alonso Alemany, L., Villata, S.: A low-cost, high-coverage legal named entity recognizer, classifier and linker. In: Proceedings of the 16th International Conference on Artificial Intelligence and Law (ICAIL), London, UK, June 2017, preprint available from https://hal.archives-ouvertes.fr/hal-01541446

4. Devlin, J., Chang, M., Lee, K., Toutanova, K.: BERT: pre-training of deep bidirectional transformers for language understanding. CoRR abs/1810.04805 (2018). http://arxiv.org/abs/1810.04805

5. Dozier, C., Kondadadi, R., Light, M., Vachher, A., Veeramachaneni, S., Wudali, R.: Named entity recognition and resolution in legal text. In: Francesconi, E., Montemagni, S., Peters, W., Tiscornia, D. (eds.) Semantic Processing of Legal Texts. LNCS (LNAI), vol. 6036, pp. 27–43. Springer, Heidelberg (2010). https://doi.org/10.1007/978-3-642-12837-0_2

6. Galgani, F., Compton, P., Hoffmann, A.: Combining different summarization techniques for legal text. In: Proceedings of the Workshop on Innovative Hybrid Approaches to the Processing of Textual Data, HYBRID, pp. 115–123. Association for Computational Linguistics (ACL), Stroudsburg, PA, USA (2012). http://dl.acm.org/citation.cfm?id=2388632.2388647

7. Hearst, M.A.: Support vector machines. IEEE Intell. Syst. **13**(4), 18–28 (1998)

8. Howard, J., Ruder, S.: Fine-tuned language models for text classification. CoRR abs/1801.06146 (2018). http://arxiv.org/abs/1801.06146

9. Ioffe, S., Szegedy, C.: Batch normalization: Accelerating deep network training by reducing internal covariate shift. In: Proceedings of the 32nd International Conference on Machine Learning, vol. 37. pp. 448–456. JMLR.org (2015). http://dl.acm.org/citation.cfm?id=3045118.3045167

10. Kanapala, A., Pal, S., Pamula, R.: Text summarization from legal documents: a survey. Artif. Intell. Rev. (2017). https://doi.org/10.1007/s10462-017-9566-2

11. Katz, D.M., Bommarito, Michael J, I., Blackman, J.: A general approach for predicting the behavior of the Supreme Court of the United States. PLoS ONE (2017). https://doi.org/10.1371/journal.pone.0174698

12. Kim, M.-Y., Xu, Y., Goebel, R.: Summarization of legal texts with high cohesion and automatic compression rate. In: Motomura, Y., Butler, A., Bekki, D. (eds.) JSAI-isAI 2012. LNCS (LNAI), vol. 7856, pp. 190–204. Springer, Heidelberg (2013). https://doi.org/10.1007/978-3-642-39931-2_14

13. Kingma, D.P., Ba, J.: Adam: a method for stochastic optimization. In: International Conference on Learning Representations (ICLR) (2015)

14. Kudo, T., Richardson, J.: SentencePiece: a simple and language independent sub-word tokenizer and detokenizer for neural text processing. In: Proceedings of the 2018 Conference on Empirical Methods in Natural Language Processing: System Demonstrations (EMNLP), pp. 66–71. Association for Computational Linguistics (ACL), Brussels, Belgium, November 2018
15. Kumar, R., Raghuveer, K.: Legal document summarization using latent Dirichlet allocation. Int. J. Comput. Sci. Telecommun. **3**, 114–117 (2012)
16. Loshchilov, I., Hutter, F.: Fixing weight decay regularization in Adam. CoRR abs/1711.05101 (2017). http://arxiv.org/abs/1711.05101
17. Luz de Araujo, P.H., de Campos, T.E., de Oliveira, R.R.R., Stauffer, M., Couto, S., Bermejo, P.: LeNER-Br: a dataset for named entity recognition in Brazilian legal text. In: Villavicencio, A., Moreira, V., Abad, A., Caseli, H., Gamallo, P., Ramisch, C., Gonçalo Oliveira, H., Paetzold, G.H. (eds.) PROPOR 2018. LNCS (LNAI), vol. 11122, pp. 313–323. Springer, Cham (2018). https://doi.org/10.1007/978-3-319-99722-3_32
18. Nair, V., Hinton, G.E.: Rectified linear units improve restricted Boltzmann machines. In: Proceedings of the 27th International Conference on Machine Learning (ICLR), pp. 807–814. Omnipress, USA (2010). https://icml.cc/Conferences/2010/papers/432.pdf
19. Radford, A., Wu, J., Child, R., Luan, D., Amodei, D., Sutskever, I.: Language models are unsupervised multitask learners. OpenAI blog **1**(8) (2019). https://cdn.openai.com/better-language-models/language_models_are_unsupervised_multitask_learners.pdf
20. da Silva, N.C., et al.: Document type classification for Brazil's supreme court using a convolutional neural network. In: 10th International Conference on Forensic Computer Science and Cyber Law (ICoFCS), Sao Paulo, Brazil, 29–30 October 2018. https://doi.org/10.5769/C2018001. Winner of the best paper award
21. Smith, L.N.: No more pesky learning rate guessing games. CoRR abs/1506.01186 (2015). http://arxiv.org/abs/1506.01186
22. Smith, L.N., Topin, N.: Super-convergence: Very fast training of residual networks using large learning rates. CoRR abs/1708.07120 (2017). http://arxiv.org/abs/1708.07120
23. Srivastava, N., Hinton, G., Krizhevsky, A., Sutskever, I., Salakhutdinov, R.: Dropout: a simple way to prevent neural networks from overfitting. J. Mach. Learn. Res. **15**(1), 1929–1958 (2014). http://dl.acm.org/citation.cfm?id=2627435.2670313
24. Şulea, O.M., Zampieri, M., Vela, M., van Genabith, J.: Predicting the law area and decisions of french supreme court cases. In: Proceedings of the International Conference Recent Advances in Natural Language Processing (RANLP), pp. 716–722. INCOMA Ltd. (2017)
25. de Vargas Feijó, D., Moreira, V.P.: RulingBR: a summarization dataset for legal texts. In: Villavicencio, A., Moreira, V., Abad, A., Caseli, H., Gamallo, P., Ramisch, C., Gonçalo Oliveira, H., Paetzold, G.H. (eds.) PROPOR 2018. LNCS (LNAI), vol. 11122, pp. 255–264. Springer, Cham (2018). https://doi.org/10.1007/978-3-319-99722-3_26

Native Language Identification on L2 Portuguese

Iria del Río[(⊠)] [iD]

Centro de Linguística da Universidade de Lisboa, Lisbon, Portugal
igayo@letras.ulisboa.pt

Abstract. This study advances on Native Language Identification (NLI) for L2 Portuguese. We use texts from the NLI-PT dataset corresponding to five native languages: Chinese, English, German, Italian, and Spanish. We include the same L1s as in previous works, and more texts per language. We investigate the impact of different lexical representations, the use of syntactic dependencies and the performance of diverse classification methods. Our best model achieves an accuracy of 0.66 including lexical features, and of 0.61 excluding them. Both results improve previous works on NLI for L2 Portuguese.

Keywords: Native Language Identification · L2 Portuguese · Second language acquisition

1   Introduction

Native Language Identification (NLI) is the task of determining the native language (L1) of an author based on his second language (L2) linguistic productions [1]. The assumption behind NLI is that speakers of the same native language share a series of linguistic patterns in their L2 productions, influenced by their mother tongue. NLI works by identifying those patterns. A major motivation for NLI is studying second language acquisition (SLA). NLI models can enable analysis of inter-L1 linguistic differences, allowing us to study the language learning process and develop L1-specific pedagogical methods and materials.

NLI research is conducted using learner corpora: collections of learner productions in an acquired language, annotated with metadata such as the author's L1 or proficiency. These datasets are the foundation of NLI experiments and their quality and availability has been a key issue since the earliest work in this area.

A notable research trend in recent years has been the extension of NLI to languages other than English [2]. Recent NLI studies on languages other than English include Chinese [3], Norwegian [4], Arabic [5] and European Portuguese [6,7]. The present work extends previous approximations to NLI on European Portuguese. The novel aspects of our work include experimenting with

© Springer Nature Switzerland AG 2020
P. Quaresma et al. (Eds.): PROPOR 2020, LNAI 12037, pp. 87–97, 2020.
https://doi.org/10.1007/978-3-030-41505-1_9

a representation of lexical features that avoids topic bias, measuring the effect of syntactic dependencies on the task or using ensemble classification methods, among others.

The paper is organized as follows: Sect. 2 discusses related work in NLI, Sect. 3 describes the methodology and dataset used in our experiments, and Sect. 4 presents the experimental results. Finally, Sect. 5 presents a brief discussion and concludes this paper with avenues for future research.

2   Related Work

NLI is a recent area of research that connects Natural Language Processing with SLA. The first works in the field appeared in the early 2000s and most significant work has appeared over the last decade [8–12]. The research community has focused on aspects like improving classification [11], studying language transfer effects [13], and applying the linguistic features to other NLP tasks.

NLI is typically modeled as a supervised multi-class classification task. In this experimental design the individual productions of learners[1] are used as training and testing data while the author's L1 information serves as class labels. It has been shown that NLI is challenging even for human experts, with machine learning methods significantly outperforming humans on the same data [15].

There have been two shared tasks focusing on NLI, one in 2013[2] and the other in 2017.[3] In 2013 the dataset used was the TOEFL11 corpus [16], the first dataset designed for NLI. The winning entry was [17], which achieved an accuracy of 0.84. They used an L2-regularized SVM classifier and n-grams of words, Part-of-Speech (POS), and lemmas as features. In addition to normalizing each text to unit length, the authors applied a log-entropy weighting schema to the normalized values, which clearly improved the accuracy of the model.

Growing interest led to another edition of the shared task in 2017, where the task included speech data. The systems that achieved the best performance across the different tracks used ensembles and meta-classifiers. Participants using deep learning-based models and features (e.g. word embeddings) did not outperform traditional classification systems. The use of more sophisticated systems led to substantially higher results than in the previous edition. A detailed report on the findings of the task can be found in [18].

Regarding classification features, NLI employs a wide range of linguistic features, lexical, morphological and syntactic. A more detailed review of NLI methods is omitted here for brevity, but a comprehensive exposition can be found in [19,20]. Some of the most successful features used in previous work include **lexical features** like character n-grams [21], Function word unigrams and bigrams [22], Word and Lemma n-grams; **morphological features** like

---

[1] NLI is usually applied on whole texts, although [14] performs the task also at the sentence level.

[2] https://sites.google.com/site/nlisharedtask2013/home.

[3] https://sites.google.com/site/nlisharedtask/home.

Penn Treebank (PTB) POS n-grams or RASP POS n-grams [22]; and **syntactic features** as Adaptor Grammars (AG) [23], CFG Production Rules [9], Stanford Dependencies with POS transformations [11], and Tree Substitution Grammar (TSG) fragments [10].

Besides classification, another branch of NLI uses models based on these features to generate SLA hypotheses. In [24] the authors make use of L1 and L2 data to identify features exhibiting non-uniform usage in both datasets, using them to create lists of candidate transfer features. [13] proposes a different methodology, using linear SVM weights to extract lists of overused and underused linguistic features per L1 group.

Most English NLI work has been done using two corpora, the *International Corpus of Learner English* [25] and TOEFL11. The first one is a learner corpus of L2 English, fact that implies certain shortcomings for its use in NLI being widely noted [26]. On the other hand, TOEFL11 was specifically designed for NLI, although it only contains argumentative essays, limiting analyses to this genre.

In recent years, NLI research has extended to languages other than English [5,27]. [3] introduced the *Jinan Chinese Learner Corpus* [28] for NLI and their results indicate that feature performance may be similar across corpora and even L1-L2 pairs. Similarly, [4] proposed using the ASK corpus [29] to conduct NLI research using L2 Norwegian data. Recently, the NLI-PT dataset [6] was released for L2 European Portuguese, and [7] constitutes the first attempt to apply NLI techniques to this language. In that work, the authors try to identify five L1s: Chinese, English, German, Italian and Spanish. Since NLI-PT is not topic balanced, they use only non lexical features: functional words, POS and CFG rules, and a linear Support Vector Machine (SVM) classifier. They achieve an accuracy of **0.54** with a mean probability ensemble model. The present paper develops the work presented there, including more data, new linguistic features and classification methods.

3   Data and Method

3.1   Data

Similarly to [7], we used a sub-set of the NLI-PT dataset with texts for five L1 groups: Chinese, English, German, Italian, and Spanish. We chose these five languages because they are the ones with the greatest number of texts in NLI-PT. The dataset has been recently enlarged [30] and thanks to that the number of texts per language we use is much bigger than in [7], where the authors used 215 productions per L1. Table 1 shows the composition of our data.

It is important to note that NLI-PT is not topic balanced in terms of L1 [6]. The reason is that the dataset is the result of merging different learner corpora. Even after regrouping the thematic areas, there are more than 90 different topics in the dataset, with an unbalanced distribution by number of texts or L1.

Texts in NLI-PT have annotations at two levels: POS and syntax. There are two types of POS: a simple POS with only the type of word, and a fine-grained

POS with type of word plus morphological features. Concerning syntactic information, texts are annotated with constituency and dependency representations.

Table 1. Distribution of the five L1s in the NLI-PT dataset in terms of texts, tokens, types, and type/token ratio (TTR).

L1	Texts	Tokens	Types	TTR
Chinese	440	90,424	9,931	0.11
English	409	86,017	10,323	0.12
German	430	92,756	10,713	0.12
Italian	555	129,630	14,779	0.11
Spanish	607	121,452	14,018	0.12
Total	2,441	520,279	59,764	0.12

3.2 Classification Models and Evaluation

We model the task as a standard multi-class classification problem. We test different algorithms and feature vectors created using relative frequency values, in line with previous NLI research [19]. We also experiment with ensemble methods using multiple classifiers.

We perform two types of experiments. First, for testing the impact of linguistic features and algorithms, a single model is trained on each feature type. In these experiments, we use algorithms that have been used previously for NLI and generally for text classification. Multinomial Logistic Regression [31] and Support Vector Machines [32] showed good results in previous NLI work. For SVM we test two versions, one with a linear kernel and another with a rbf kernel (both with the one-vs.-rest (OVR) approach). We experiment also with Ridge Regression [33], and a Multi-Layer Perceptron classifier. For all the algorithms we use the default parameters in the scikit-learn package excepting:

- We set the random state to 7.
- For the RBF kernel SVM model we set gamma to 'scale'.
- With Logistic Regression we use a L2 regularization with a liblinear solver.
- We set the number of epochs to 10 for the Multi-Layer Perceptron.

Once we have identified the best combination of feature plus algorithm, we run experiments using ensemble combinations of classifiers. We test two different strategies: an ensemble method that uses mean probability rule[4] and classifier stacking.

Similar to the majority of previous NLI studies, we report our results as classification accuracy under k-fold cross-validation, with $k = 10$. For generating our folds we use randomized stratified cross-validation which aims to ensure that

---

[4] More details about this approach can be found in [19].

the proportion of classes within each partition is equal [34].[5] We use accuracy as our main metric and we also report per-class precision, recall, and F1 scores. We compare these results against a random baseline.

3.3   Features

Previous research in NLI has shown the importance of using datasets which are balanced in terms of topic and L1. This aspect is particularly relevant for the use of content-based features, which can be topic-related and inflate accuracy [20].

NLI-PT dataset is very heterogeneous and unbalanced in terms of distribution of topics. This is the reason why [7] do not use lexical features, achieving an accuracy of 0.54. In [6], a BOW representation gets an accuracy of 0.7, suggesting the influence of topic bias. It is then clear that the use or not of lexical features has a considerable impact for the NLI-PT dataset. To investigate this impact, we experiment with lexical features and we analyse their behaviour. We consider two types of features: one includes all the words in the text (WLP) and the second one all the words except nouns and adjectives (WLPmod). The rationale behind this decision is that nouns and adjectives carry most of the lexical content in a text and, therefore, it is expected that they are the words more influenced by topic bias. Removing them can therefore help to remove topic bias. To check this assumption, we also perform a chi-squared test to extract the most correlated unigrams and bigrams per L1 for both lexical representations. Finally, instead of a simple bag of words, we chose a richer representation which includes word+lemma+POS for each of the words in a text. In WLPmod, we remove the word and the lemma of all adjectives and nouns and we only keep the POS. For both lexical features we use n-grams of size 1–3.

Besides lexical features, we use a set of morphological and syntactic features that have been proved as useful for NLI. We employ the following topic-independent feature types: fine-grained POS tags, context-free grammar (CFG) production rules and dependency triplets. We extract the features from the annotations in the NLI-PT dataset. POS and CFG were used in [7] with good results. We include also dependencies, not tested before for L2 Portuguese. Grammatical dependencies have been found to be useful for NLI, as they capture a "more abstract representation of syntactic structures" [11,35]. NLI-PT dependencies include POS and lemma. For our experiments, we removed the word form information and we kept only the POS tag. For each of these non lexical features, we experiment with n-grams of different sizes. The maximum size is 4, except for POS, since previous work (and our own results) demonstrates that sequences of order 4 or greater achieve lower accuracy. For feature representation, we normalize the raw counts using TF-IDF weighting.

---

[5] Unfortunately, NLI-PT does not have a specific test set as other NLI datasets like TOEFL11. For this reason, we use 10-fold cv over the whole corpus for all the experiments. This method allows also for a direct comparison with [7].

4   Results

4.1   Individual Feature Types

We first report the CV results obtained using systems trained on different feature types. Results are presented in terms of accuracy in Table 2. These results are compared against a uniform random baseline of 0.20.

Table 2. Classification results under 10 fold cross-validation (accuracy is reported).

Features	LR	MLP	SVMrbf	SVMlin	Ridge
WLP1-3	0.65	**0.66**	0.63	**0.66**	**0.66**
WLPmod1-3	0.56	**0.58**	0.55	**0.58**	**0.58**
POS1	0.42	0.39	0.43	0.42	0.42
POS2	0.55	0.55	0.54	0.55	0.55
POS3	0.56	0.56	0.55	0.56	0.53
POS1-2	0.56	0.56	0.55	0.56	0.56
POS1-3	0.56	**0.58**	0.56	0.57	0.56
DEP1	0.41	0.41	0.41	0.40	0.41
DEP2	0.43	0.43	0.41	0.42	0.41
DEP3	0.41	0.40	0.36	0.39	0.40
DEP4	0.33	0.34	0.31	0.32	0.32
DEP1-2	**0.44**	**0.44**	0.43	0.43	0.43
DEP1-3	0.43	**0.44**	0.42	0.43	0.43
DEP1-4	**0.44**	**0.44**	0.42	0.43	0.42
CFG1	0.42	0.40	0.41	0.41	0.41
CFG2	0.44	0.43	0.44	0.44	0.45
CFG3	0.48	0.47	0.45	0.47	0.47
CFG4	0.45	0.46	0.44	0.46	0.47
CFG1-2	0.45	0.43	0.44	0.44	0.46
CFG1-3	0.48	0.47	0.47	0.47	0.48
CFG1-4	0.49	**0.50**	0.49	**0.50**	0.48

Random baseline **0.20**

As expected, the best result is obtained with the lexical representation that includes nouns and adjectives. The number is close to the 0.7 obtained by [7] with a BOW representation over a different subset of NLI-PT, with the same L1s. When nouns and adjectives are excluded from the representation, and only their POS is kept, the accuracy decreases considerably, and it is in fact the same as for the best POS representation.

These results seem to confirm the intuition that the use of nouns and adjectives inflates the results and probably indicates a topic-classification instead of a L1-classification. In order to investigate this aspect, we performed a test to extract the most correlated unigrams and bigrams per L1 for the two lexical features. For WLP, these n-grams always include proper names connected with the L1 of the text, like *China* or *Macau* for Chinese, *Inglaterra* ('England') for English or *Espanha* ('Spain') and *Madrid* for Spanish. However, in the representation without nouns and adjectives, WLPmod, the most correlated n-grams correspond to verbs or prepositional/verbal phrases which are not topic related. Examples are: *devemos_dever_vmis1p0* ('we should') for Chinese; *è_è_vmip3s0* ('is') (which contains an orthographic mistake) for Italian; *ele_ele_pp3ms00 vai_ir_vmip3s0* ('he goes') for German. Both the low accuracy and the correlated n-grams seem to indicate that excluding nouns and adjectives from a lexical representation reduces topic bias.

For the non lexical features, we can see how accuracy increases as we increase the size of the n-grams. For POS and as previous work has shown, the best representation is 1–3. On the other hand, DEP seems to benefit more of a 1–2 representation. It is interesting to note that the size of the n-grams affects particularly the CFG production rules, which achieve the best results with n-grams of range 1–4, which is not good for POS or DEP.

Concerning the performance of the algorithms, MLP is the algorithm with the best results for the features with the highest accuracy. On average and for the features with the best performance, MLP and SVMlin get the best results, followed by LR and Ridge, and finally by SVMrbf. As a reference, we have ran a test of significance using the results of the models with the best accuracy by type of feature: WLP1-3 with algorithms MLP, SVMlin and Ridge; WLPmod1-3 with the same algorithms; POS1-3 with MLP and SVMlin; DEP1-2 with LR and MLP; CFG1-4 with MLP and SVMlin. Comparing the performance of different algorithms through a test of significance is not a simple task [36], especially if the method used is cross validation, where the samples are not independent. Since the distribution of our data is not normal, and we want to compare more than two samples in some cases, we have chosen the Kruskal-Wallis H-test.[6] The test does not show a significant difference in accuracy for any of the single feature models compared ($p > 0.05$).

4.2   Ensemble Models

Since MLP shows the best results for the most relevant features, we use it as the base classifier for the ensemble experiments. As features, we select the best performing types in the previous experiments: WLPmod, POS1-3, DEP1-2 and CFG1-4. To test the impact of lexical features, we create two types of ensemble models: one including WLPmod (+lex) and another not including this feature (−lex). For classification stacking we use SVMlin as metaclassifier because it has shown good results in a comparative analysis of ensemble methods applied to NLI [20] (Table 3).

---

[6] We are aware that our data violates one of the assumptions of this test, that is, the independence of the samples.

Table 3. Accuracy of ensemble methods.

Ensemble+lex	Stacking+lex	Ensemble−lex	Stacking−lex
0.64	**0.66**	0.61	**0.61**

As expected, ensemble methods help to improve general accuracy, and stacking gets better results than the simple ensemble (using lexical features). The use of lexical features also helps to increase accuracy. We have applied the Kruskal-Wallis H-test to compare the results including and excluding lexical features. For both ensemble and stacking methods, the difference in accuracy is significant ($p \leq 0.05$). We perform a final test to check if the result of our best system was influenced by overfitting. We split the dataset into train (80%) and test (20%) sets, training and testing the system in different portions of data. The accuracy of the Stacking+lex on the test set was **0.7**, +0.04 points over the result obtained using the whole dataset with 10-fold cv.

Table 4. Stacking systems per-class results: precision, recall and the F1-score are reported.

Class	Precision	Recall	F1-Score
CHIN	0.80/0.78	0.86/0.84	**0.83/0.81**
ENG	0.59/0.54	0.54/0.50	0.56/0.52
GER	0.62/0.59	0.59/0.55	0.61/0.57
ITA	0.65/0.59	0.63/0.57	0.64/0.58
SPA	0.64/0.56	0.68/0.59	**0.66/0.57**
Average	0.66/0.61	0.66/0.61	0.66/0.61

In Table 4 we present the results obtained for each L1 in terms of precision, recall, and F1 score as well as the average results on the five classes. Each column shows the results of the two stacking systems, corresponding the first result to stacking+lex and the second to stacking−lex. Looking at individual classes, the results obtained for Chinese are clearly higher than those of other L1s, even when the number of texts is smaller than for Spanish and Italian. The same tendency was observed in [7], and it seems to illustrate the intuition that linguistic distance is directly related to level of performance per class in NLI. This idea is also supported by the confusion matrix in Table 5, which shows, for example, that Spanish and Italian, the two Romance languages, tend to be confused more frequently. On the opposite side, English is the L1 with the lowest accuracy. Again, [7] showed the same pattern. English is the class with less texts in our dataset, but the difference with German (the other Germanic language in the dataset), with +21 texts, does not seem big enough to justify the difference in performance (−0.05 points). If we take a look at the confusion matrix in Table 5 we can see that English texts are confused with all the other L1s in a similar proportion, even with Chinese. One linguistic hypothesis for this behaviour could be that English is a Germanic language (then closer to German) with a high percentage of Latin vocabulary (then close to Spanish and Italian) and with an isolating morphology (then close to Chinese). German, on the contrary, is not so close to the Romance languages in vocabulary, and does have a rich morphological system.

Table 5. Confusion matrix for the Stacking+lex model.

		Predicted class				
		CHI	ENG	GER	ITA	SPA
Actual class	CHI	379	25	13	10	13
	ENG	48	210	53	31	67
	GER	19	53	253	58	47
	ITA	13	25	56	358	103
	SPA	13	50	33	94	417

Table 4 shows also that lexical features have a positive impact for all the L1s, being especially relevant for L1s that are more similar to Portuguese, Spanish and Italian. For Chinese, however, lexical features only increased F1 score in 0.2 points. This fact seems to indicate that, for L1s that are close to the target at all the levels (lexical, morphological and syntactic), the inclusion of lexical information makes a difference to improve accuracy. On the other hand, for L1s that are lexically unrelated and very distant morphosyntactically, the use of morphosyntactic information is enough to get good results.

5   Conclusion and Future Work

This paper presented new experiments on NLI for L2 Portuguese. Our results improve the best result previously obtained in [7], considering both general accuracy and results by class. The presented results are comparable to those of other NLI studies [2], but not as high as those on the largest and most balanced corpora [18]. This is likely a limitation of our data, mainly caused by topic distribution.

We proposed a linguistically motivated method to make use of lexical features while reducing topic bias. This method helped to increase the classification performance for all L1s, especially for those which are more similar to Portuguese. We tested different algorithms and features, defining the most effective combination for our dataset. We also found that n-gram size particularly affects the performance of the CFG production rules. We experimented for the first time with L2 Portuguese with dependencies and an ensemble method that uses stacking classification, obtaining the best results in our experiments.

This study opens several avenues for future research. One of them is investigating the influence of L1 in Portuguese second language acquisition. Such approaches, similar to those applied to English learner data [13], can have direct pedagogical implications. Particularly, we would like to investigate in more detail the impact of the different types of linguistic features in the classification task taking into account the linguistic distance between L1 and L2 Portuguese. We also would like to analyse the possible influence of L3 languages in the task.

Another important step will be the refinement and extension of our dataset, especially in terms of topic distribution by L1.

Acknowledgements. This work was supported by Fundacão para a Ciência e a Tecnologia (postdoctoral research grant SFRH/BPD/109914/2015). We would like to thank the anonymous reviewers for the suggestions and constructive feedback provided.

References

1. Malmasi, S.: Native language identification: explorations and applications. Ph.D. thesis (2016)
2. Malmasi, S., Dras, M.: Multilingual native language identification. Nat. Lang. Eng. **23**(2), 163–215 (2015)
3. Malmasi, S., Dras, M.: Chinese native language identification. In: Proceedings of EACL, Gothenburg, Sweden. Association for Computational Linguistics (2014)
4. Malmasi, S., Dras, M., Temnikova, I.: Norwegian native language identification. In: Proceedings of RANLP, Hissar, Bulgaria, pp. 404–412, September 2015
5. Malmasi, S., Dras, M.: Arabic native language identification. In: Proceedings of the Arabic Natural Language Processing Workshop (2014)
6. del Río, I., Zampieri, M., Malmasi, S.: A Portuguese native language identification dataset. In: Proceedings of BEA (2018)
7. Malmasi, S., del Río, I., Zampieri, M.: Portuguese native language identification. In: Villavicencio, A., et al. (eds.) PROPOR 2018. LNCS (LNAI), vol. 11122, pp. 115–124. Springer, Cham (2018). https://doi.org/10.1007/978-3-319-99722-3_12
8. Wong, S.M.J., Dras, M.: Contrastive analysis and native language identification. In: Proceedings of ALTA, Sydney, Australia, pp. 53–61, December 2009
9. Wong, S.M.J., Dras, M.: Exploiting parse structures for native language identification. In: Proceedings of EMNLP (2011)
10. Swanson, B., Charniak, E.: Native language detection with tree substitution grammars. In: Proceedings of ACL, Jeju Island, Korea, pp. 193–197, July 2012
11. Tetreault, J., Blanchard, D., Cahill, A., Chodorow, M.: Native tongues, lost and found: resources and empirical evaluations in native language identification. In: Proceedings of COLING, Mumbai, India, pp. 2585–2602 (2012)
12. Gebre, B.G., Zampieri, M., Wittenburg, P., Heskes, T.: Improving native language identification with TF-IDF weighting. In: Proceedings of BEA (2013)
13. Malmasi, S., Dras, M.: Language transfer hypotheses with linear SVM weights. In: Proceedings of EMNLP, pp. 1385–1390 (2014)
14. Cimino, A., Dell'Orletta, F., Brunato, D., Venturi, G.: Sentences and documents in native language identification. In: CLiC-it (2018)
15. Malmasi, S., Tetreault, J., Dras, M.: Oracle and human baselines for native language identification. In: Proceedings of BEA (2015)

16. Blanchard, D., Tetreault, J., Higgins, D., Cahill, A., Chodorow, M.: TOEFL11: a corpus of non-native English. Technical report, Educational Testing Service (2013)
17. Jarvis, S., Bestgen, Y., Pepper, S.: Maximizing classification accuracy in native language identification. In: Proceedings of BEA (2013)
18. Malmasi, S., et al.: A report on the 2017 native language identification shared task. In: Proceedings of BEA (2017)
19. Malmasi, S., Dras, M.: Native language identification using stacked generalization. arXiv preprint arXiv:1703.06541 (2017)
20. Malmasi, S., Dras, M.: Native language identification with classifier stacking and ensembles. Comput. Linguist. **44**(3), 403–446 (2018)
21. Tsur, O., Rappoport, A.: Using classifier features for studying the effect of native language on the choice of written second language words. In: Proceedings of the Workshop on Cognitive Aspects of Computational Language Acquisition (2007)
22. Malmasi, S., Wong, S.M.J., Dras, M.: NLI shared task 2013: MQ submission. In: Proceedings of BEA (2013)
23. Wong, S.M.J., Dras, M., Johnson, M.: Exploring adaptor grammars for native language identification. In: Proceedings of EMNLP (2012)
24. Swanson, B., Charniak, E.: Data driven language transfer hypotheses. In: EACL 2014, p. 169 (2014)
25. Granger, S., Dagneaux, E., Meunier, F., Paquot, M.: International Corpus of Learner English (Version 2). Presses Universitaires de Louvain, Louvian-la-Neuve (2009)
26. Brooke, J., Hirst, G.: Measuring interlanguage: native language identification with L1-influence metrics. In: Proceedings of LREC (2012)
27. Malmasi, S., Dras, M.: Finnish native language identification. In: Proceedings of ALTA, Melbourne, Australia, pp. 139–144 (2014)
28. Wang, M., Malmasi, S., Huang, M.: The Jinan Chinese learner corpus. In: Proceedings of BEA (2015)
29. Tenfjord, K., Meurer, P., Hofland, K.: The ASK corpus: a language learner corpus of Norwegian as a second language. In: Proceedings of LREC (2006)
30. del Río, I.: Automatic proficiency classification in L2 Portuguese. Procesamiento del Lenguaje Natural **63**, 67–74 (2019)
31. Genkin, A., Lewis, D.D., Madigan, D.: Large-scale Bayesian logistic regression for text categorization. Technometrics **49**, 291–304 (2007)
32. Joachims, T.: Text categorization with support vector machines: learning with many relevant features. In: Nédellec, C., Rouveirol, C. (eds.) ECML 1998. LNCS, vol. 1398, pp. 137–142. Springer, Heidelberg (1998). https://doi.org/10.1007/BFb0026683
33. Zhang, T., Oles, F.J.: Text categorization based on regularized linear classification methods. Inf. Retrieval **4**(1), 5–31 (2001)
34. Kohavi, R.: A study of cross-validation and bootstrap for accuracy estimation and model selection. In: IJCAI, vol. 14, pp. 1137–1145 (1995)
35. Bykh, S., Meurers, D.: Native language identification using recurring n-grams – investigating abstraction and domain dependence. In: Proceedings of COLING 2012, Mumbai, India, pp. 425–440. The COLING 2012 Organizing Committee, December 2012
36. Dietterich, T.G.: Approximate statistical tests for comparing supervised classification learning algorithms. Neural Comput. **10**(7), 1895–1923 (1998)

Aligning IATE Criminal Terminology to SUMO

Daniela Schmidt[1]([✉])[iD], Avner Dal Bosco[1], Cássia Trojahn[2][iD],
Renata Vieira[1,3][iD], and Paulo Quaresma[3][iD]

[1] Pontifical Catholic University of Rio Grande do Sul, Porto Alegre, Brazil
{daniela.schmidt,avner.bosco}@edu.pucrs.br, renata.vieira@pucrs.br
[2] Toulouse University, Toulouse, France
cassia.trojahn@irit.fr
[3] Évora University, Évora, Portugal
{renatav,pq}@uevora.pt

Abstract. In this paper we apply an ontology matching system in the context of an information extraction project regarding criminal data. Our data comes from social network, in order to make better sense and analysis of the information provided we consider the IATE (InterActive Terminology for Europe) regarding its crime related sub-domain. The alignment of this terminology to an ontology is a further step towards enriching the semantics of the data. We evaluate a recently proposed domain top ontology matcher (based on Wordnet-SUMO previous alignment) to the task of aligning this IATE sub-domain to SUMO, a general purpose top ontology. Another aspect to explore is the use of multi-linguality in the disambiguation problem itself, as in the case of "alvo" (aim as target and not goal) which becomes more clear in the Portuguese than the English version.

Keywords: Ontology matching · IATE terminology · SUMO ontology

1 Introduction

There is an exponential increase of information published in social networks and open access media. This data has been so far exploited in a plethora of NLP applications, from the identification of sexists posts, the identification of fake news to the identification of clues of criminal situations. In our particular domain of interest in this work, it is important to be able to process open access texts, published in the web or in social networks, and to automatically identify criminal concepts and to link them with related concepts in other documents, such as law documents for instance. In order to achieve this goal it is desirable to have a predefined terminology and to be able to relate them to concepts in an existent ontology. This connection would allow formal inference processes and also to relate different but similar cases, helping police researchers to detect potential criminal situations.

P. Quaresma et al. (Eds.): PROPOR 2020, LNAI 12037, pp. 98–108, 2020.
https://doi.org/10.1007/978-3-030-41505-1_10

With that in mind, our adopted terminology for this domain comes from the "InterActive Terminology for Europe"[1] (IATE), which has almost 8 million entries and a classification by subject. We consider in particular the sub-domain Criminal Law. This sub-domain terminology serves thus as an aid to identify concepts in texts. It is important to point out that IATE supports 26 European languages, including Portuguese, Spanish and English, which are the focus of the project that gives context for this work.

Top ontologies describe general concepts (e.g., physical object, event) and relations (e.g., parthood, participation), which are independent of a particular domain. These ontologies, also named *upper* or *foundational*, are usually equipped with a rich axiomatic layer. They have an important role in the construction and integration of domain ontologies, providing a well-founded reference model that can be shared across domains. While the clarity in semantics and a rich formalization of foundational ontologies are important requirements for ontology development [11,15], and improving ontology quality, they may also act as semantic bridges supporting interoperability between domain ontologies [11,14,17].

We use a previously proposed domain-top ontology matcher (based on Word-Net) [25] in order to automatically link the criminal subdomain of IATE to SUMO [19] (Suggested Upper Merged Ontology). We have chosen SUMO for several reasons. It is the only formal ontology that has a complete set of manually-performed correspondences to all 117,000 word senses in WordNet. It is also one of the few ontologies that has a detailed formalization in an expressive logical language. Most ontologies are still simple taxonomies and frame systems, and so assessing the meaning of their terms requires human intuition based on term names and relationships. SUMO includes a computational toolset [21] that allows users to test the logical consistency of its definitions, which provides a guarantee of quality and correctness than just testing type constraints. Lastly, SUMO is large and comprehensive at roughly 20,000 terms and 80,000 hand-written logical axioms, exceeding the size of other open source foundational ontologies by several orders of magnitude.

This is the context of the research project *Agatha – A Platform for Criminal Police Investigation and Intelligence Services*, funded by Portugal 2020, which aims to create an integrated system able to aid police researchers in their work.

The paper is organized as follows, Sect. 2 provides some background on the IATE terminology, top ontologies, in particular SUMO and its alignment with WordNet. In Sect. 3 we discuss related work. In Sect. 4 we described the applied matching approach. The evaluation experiment is presented in Sect. 5. Finally we conclude the paper in Sect. 6.

---

[1] https://iate.europa.eu/.

2   Background

2.1   IATE Criminal Domain

As it was previously referred we used the IATE terminology as the source of relevant concepts. This terminology has almost 8 million entries and it uses the EuroVoc domain for the classification process. EuroVoc is a multilingual thesaurus maintained by the Publications Office of the European Union. It exists in the 24 official languages of the European Union. It contains keywords, organized in 21 domains and 127 sub-domains, which are used to describe the content of documents in EUR-Lex, an official website of European Union law and other public documents of the European Union (EU).

We have selected the criminal subset terminology under the category Law - Criminal Law of IATE, which is composed by 1182 terms (single and compound). Some examples are: "algemas" (handcuffs), "nota falsa" (counterfeit bank note), "falsificação de moeda" (forgery of money).

The relation between such domain concepts and top ontologies gives way for the semantic enrichment of criminal documents. Domain concepts are often specific and represent ideas in a given context, making it difficult to be fully understood. Relating these concepts to broader concepts from top ontologies would allow for semantic treatment of the information being presented.

2.2   Top Ontologies

A top ontology is a high-level and domain independent ontology. The concepts expressed are intended to be basic and universal to ensure generality and expressiveness for a wide range of domains. It is often characterized as representing common sense concepts and is limited to concepts which are meta, generic, abstract and philosophical. Several top ontologies have been proposed in the literature. The reader can refer to [13] for a review of them. Here, we briefly introduce SUMO, which is used in our experiments as a top ontology.

SUMO [19] (Suggested Upper Merged Ontology) provides definitions for general-purpose terms and acts as a foundation for more specific ontologies. It is being used for research and applications in search, linguistics and reasoning. It is an ontology of particulars and universals which has two higher concepts: *physical* and *abstract*. *Physical* represent an entity that has a location in space-time. An *abstract* can be said to exist in the same sense as mathematical objects such as sets and relations, but they cannot exist at a particular place and time without some physical encoding or embodiment.

2.3   WordNet and Its Alignments to Top Ontologies

WordNet [16] is a general-purpose large lexical database of English frequently adopted as an external resource in automatic ontology matching between domain ontologies [24,31,32]. In the following, we discuss its alignments to SUMO ontology.

SUMO to WordNet Alignment. Niles and Pease [20] construct an alignment between SUMO and WordNet 1.6 (a more recent release considers WordNet 3.0). For each identified correspondence, the synset of WordNet is augmented with three information: *(i)* a prefix (&%) that indicates that the term is taken from SUMO; *(ii)* the SUMO concept; and *(iii)* a suffix indicating the kind of relation. The suffix '=' indicates that the correspondence relation is synonymy. '+' indicates that the concept is a hypernym of the associated synset. The instantiation relation is indicated by the suffix '@'. An example of the structure of a correspondence representing a synonymy relation can be seen below, where *"05800611 09 n 02 probe 0 investigation"* corresponds to the synset. The gloss for this synset is defined as *"an inquiry into unfamiliar or questionable activities"*, the prefix *"&%"* indicates that the term is taken from SUMO. *"Investigating"* corresponds to the SUMO concept and the signal *"+"* is the suffix indicating the hyponymy relation.

05800611 09 n 02 probe 0 investigation — an inquiry into unfamiliar or questionable activities &%Investigating+

There are other efforts that provide alignments of WordNet to top ontologies (such as DOLCE, Cyc, and BFO). The reader can refer to [23, 27] for details.

3   Related Work

Matching ontologies from different levels of abstraction, as domain and foundational ontologies, is still an early tackled challenge in the ontology matching field. This is a complex task, even manually, that requires the deep identification of the semantic context of concepts and, in particular, the identification of subsumption relations. The latter is largely neglected by most state-of-the-art matchers. The main problem of matching foundational and domain ontologies using these matching systems is that, despite the variety of approaches, most of them typically rely on string-based techniques as an initial estimate of the likelihood that two elements refer to the same real world phenomenon, hence the found correspondences represent equivalences with concepts that are equally or similarly written. However, in many cases, this correspondence is wrong [26]. In fact, when having different levels of abstraction it might be the case that the matching process is rather capable of identify subsumption correspondences than equivalence, since the foundational ontology has concepts at a higher level. Relatively few matching systems are able to discover other relations than equivalence. The examples are AML, BLOOM, S-Match, TaxoMap and Aroma, many depending on background knowledge as WordNet), with few other propositions in the literature [30, 33].

Approaches dealing with the task of matching top and domain ontologies are mostly based on manual matching [3, 15]. In [3], Geoscience ontologies have been manually aligned to DOLCE (*Descriptive Ontology for Linguistic and Cognitive Engineering*) [5][2] and incompatibilities issues have been discussed.

---

[2] http://www.loa.istc.cnr.it/old/DOLCE.html.

In [15], DOLCE has also been manually aligned to a domain ontology describing services, in order to address its conceptual ambiguity, poor axiomatization, loose design and narrow scope. In [4], several schemata of FactForge (which enables SPARQL querying over the Linked Open Data cloud) have been manually aligned to PROTON (PROTo ONtology) [29][3] in order to provide a unified way to access the data. Manually alignments have also been established between biomedical ontologies and BFO (*Basic Formal Ontology*)[4] [1,7] in [28]. More recently, in [9], the alignment between the T-PAS resource (Typed Predicate-Argument Structures [10]) and DOLCE categories has been manually established, highlighting the distinctions and similarities between the two resources from a cognitive and application-based perspective. One of the few automatic approaches is BLOOMS+ [8], which has been used to automatically align PROTON to LOD datasets using as gold standard the alignments provided in [4]. BLOOMS+ first uses Wikipedia to construct a set of category hierarchy trees for each class in the source and target ontologies. It then determines which classes to align using (1) similarity between classes based on their category hierarchy trees; and (2) contextual similarity between these classes to support (or reject) an alignment. More recently, in [2], automatic classification of foundational distinctions (class vs. instance or physical vs. non-physical objects) of LOD entities is done with two strategies: an (unsupervised) alignment approach and a (supervised) machine learning approach. The alignment approach, in particular, relies on the linking structure of alignments between DBpedia, DOLCE, and lexical linked data, using resources such as BabelNet [18], YAGO [22] and OntoWordNet [6]. For instance, they use the paths of alignments and taxonomical relations in these resources and automated inferences to classifying whether a DBpedia entity is a physical object or not.

4   Matching Approach

The matching approach, detailed in [25], has two main steps. The first step disambiguates the domain concept, selecting the most appropriated WordNet synset; and the second matches the domain concept to the foundational concept via existing correspondences between WordNet and the top ontologies, as detailed below.

4.1   Pre-processing

For the alignment process of the IATE terms a few steps were taken in order to use the matching tool. The task could be summarized as a process of converting the IATE terminology to an OWL ontology. In order to achieve this, we extract a simple list of the english terms from the IATE terminology in rdf format. This list of terms was then processed to remove some special characters and blank

---

[3] http://ontotext.com/proton.
[4] https://github.com/bfo-ontology/BFO/wiki.

spaces. Every entry from the list was taken as a concept in a owl structure. With no further processing, this owl file with terms as concepts was used in the matching tool for the alignment process.

4.2 Synset Disambiguation

In [25], a disambiguation process to select the synset that better expresses the meaning behind the ontology concept is applied. A *context* is constructed from all information available about an ontology entity, including entity naming (ID), annotation properties (usually labels and comments) and information on the neighbours (super and sub-concepts).

This context is used to find the closer synset using Lesk similarity measure. The Lesk measure for word sense disambiguation [12] relies on the calculation of the word overlap between the sense definitions of two or more target words. Given a word w, it identifies the sense of w whose textual definition has the highest overlap with the words in the context of w.

However, in the case of just a list of terms, such as ours, and in the lack of contextual elements, basically the first retrieved synset is applied.

4.3 Identification of Correspondences to SUMO

This step uses existing alignments between SUMO and WordNet 3.0, in order to identify the domain and top concepts correspondences. As SUMO-WordNet alignment is a file containing the synset ID, terms, gloss, and the alignment to top concept and the domain selected synset in searched in this file and, if the synset is found, the domain concept is aligned with the top concept related to the synset.

5 Experiments

As mentioned before we used a subset of criminal terms from the IATE terminology, corresponding to 1182 terms. We extracted the Portuguese, Spanish and English terms, allowing us to process and link sentences written in any of these three languages. The IATE terms were then aligned with SUMO automatically. After the alignment process, we randomly selected 120 terms to evaluate their resulting alignments. For the evaluation procedures, judges had to consider whether the equivalence or subsumption relations found were acceptable for the given domain. Four different judges were involved in the assessment. Each judge was given a random subset of 30 aligned terms to be evaluated, 10 of them were unigrams, 10 bi-grams, 10 n-grams. Judges had access to both english and Portuguese terms, which helped in the evaluation, since an alternative language could help with disambiguation in some cases. After this first step was concluded all evaluations were compiled together so that all judges could discuss the final results. At this phase some discussion was raised. For instance one of the judges first classified the match between the SUMO concept 'Position' to the term 'Smuggler' as correct, given that the definition of Position has the sense of a job, or a position at a company. Although, the others judges considered that a smuggler was not really a job or a company position, so this match was then re-classified as wrong. Another instance was the case of considering 'Aim' and 'PsychologicalAttribute' as a correct match, given that the definition of 'Psychological Attribute' would match with a possible definition of Aim, although it falls in an ambiguous context problem, so it was reclassified as wrong.

These concepts are used to identify potential criminal situations in social media and open access documents and, in the context of the *Agatha* project, A Platform for Criminal Police Investigation and Intelligence Services[5], we are continuously crawling and processing the main social networks (twitter and facebook) and online news and TV.

5.1 Results and Discussion

Table 1. Resulting alignments examples

SUMO Concept	Aligned as	Term	Portuguese translation
Firearm	Equivalent	Firearm	Arma de Fogo
UnilateralGetting	Superclass	Kidnapping	Rapto
IntentionalRelation	Superclass	Bias	Tendenciosidade, Viés
Pistol	Superclass	AirPistol	Pistola de Ar Comprimido
Group	Superclass	CaribbeanFinancial ActionTaskForce	Grupo de Ação Financeira das Caraíbas

Table 1 shows some examples of the resulting alignments. Table 2 shows the evaluation of the alignments found distributed along unigrams (Uni), bigrams (Bi) and larger terms (N). These terms were aligned automatically with a superclass or an equivalent class. The number of alignments considered as correct is 48 out of 87 for superclass relations (55%)–65% for unigrams, 56% for bigrams and 40% for trigrams. This lower accuracy for compound terms was expected since Wordnet is mainly constituted of single words. Regarding equivalence relations the number of correct alignments observed was much lower, 6 out of 33 for equivalence (18%).

Errors occur mainly due to ambiguity, for instance, aim (translated as "alvo" in Portuguese) was automatically classified as mental process (considering the sense of goal, objective), whereas it was the sense of target that was meant, as judges could verify by the Portuguese translation ("alvo").

---

[5] http://agatha-osi.com/en/.

Table 2. Alignments evaluation

Grams	Total	Aligned as		Evaluated			
				Aligned as		Correct	
		Superclass	Equivalent	Superclass	Equivalent	Superclass	Equivalent
Uni	290	197	93	32	8	21	4
Bi	439	391	47	30	10	17	1
N	453	363	90	25	15	10	1
Total	1182	981	230	87	33	48	6

A similar case happened with the compound term "aiming point" (also translated as "alvo" in Portuguese). It was automatically classified as a geometric point (considering the sense of a geometric point in space), whereas the sense was also supposed to mean target.

Another case of error was the term smuggler (translated as 'contrabandista' in Portuguese) which was matched as a position, in the sense of an organizational position.

Yet one more example, the term cellular confinement was automatic classified as a biological attribute, referring to cellular confinement systems, also known as geocells, although it was suppose to refer to a special kind of jail confinement (known as 'solitária' in Portuguese).

6   Concluding Remarks and Future Work

In this paper we propose the use of the IATE terminology and its alignment with SUMO, regarding the criminal domain in order to add semantic knowledge to a social media data set. The first step towards this goal is evaluated in this paper, which is the applicability of recently proposed top domain ontology matchers for linking this terminology to SUMO. The advantages of considering this terminology is its multi-linguality, in that way the alignment may serve to applications in many languages. Thus, the extension of our approach to other European languages is quite straightforward because IATE supports 26 different languages.

Given that we evaluate a direct application of existing resources, without tuning to our specific needs, we consider that we have positive outcomes. For this kind of task we found 65% of precision for superclass alignment of unigrams.

These relations to top ontologies could improve the search and analysis of documents and reports through the use of more abstract concepts. For example, in the IATE terminology, we have terms like 'Kidnapping', 'AirPiracy' and, 'Abduction' that all refer to, or meant to have a similar sense to the idea of something being forcefully taken from somewhere or someone and then possibly hold hostage. After the alignment process all of those terms were matched to the top concept 'UnilateralGetting'. So if we were tasked to find all the reports from some criminal registry that are cases of something being forcefully taken, we could use this broad concept of 'UnilateralGetting' instead of searching for each individual term at IATE. Similarly, we noticed that, at IATE, we have terms like 'AutoloadingShotgun', 'AutomaticShotgun', and 'DoubleBarreledShotgun', they all point to the sense of an object that is used to shoot something. They were all matched to the top concept 'Weapon'. Again we could use this broad concept to optimize services. Consider also a more challenging search, where one needs to find more serious, or violent cases of something being forcefully taken. Now, let the definition of a violent case of a kidnapping be: "a kidnapping that weapons were used". With the setting of the proper axiom we could infer each documents in a criminal registry reports a violent kidnapping based on the existence of the "UnilateralGetting' and 'Weapon' top concepts. Moreover, the use of IATE and top ontologies allow the creation of automatic alerts that, given the identification of specific situations (e.g. 'UnilateralGetting'), inform the police researchers about the potential criminal situation.

For further work we plan to consider ways of adding context to the terms into consideration. Besides, it is also important to focus on multi word expressions. As expected, compound terms were more difficult to deal with and further analysis and adaptation of the employed matching approach is necessary, in particular for n-grams with n greater than 2. We also plan to evaluate the approach on terminology of other domains.

References

1. Arp, R., Smith, B., Spear, A.: Building Ontologies with Basic Formal Ontology. MIT Press, Cambridge (2015)
2. Asprino, L., Basile, V., Ciancarini, P., Presutti, V.: Empirical analysis of foundational distinctions in linked open data. In: Proceedings of the Twenty-Seventh International Joint Conference on Artificial Intelligence, IJCAI 2018, Stockholm, Sweden, 13–19 July 2018, pp. 3962–3969 (2018). https://doi.org/10.24963/ijcai.2018/551
3. Brodaric, B., Probst, F.: DOLCE ROCKS: integrating geoscience ontologies with DOLCE. In: Semantic Scientific Knowledge Integration, pp. 3–8 (2008)
4. Damova, M., Kiryakov, A., Simov, K.I., Petrov, S.: Mapping the central LOD ontologies to PROTON upper-level ontology. In: Workshop on Ontology Matching (2010)
5. Gangemi, A., Guarino, N., Masolo, C., Oltramari, A., Schneider, L.: Sweetening ontologies with DOLCE. In: Gómez-Pérez, A., Benjamins, V.R. (eds.) EKAW 2002. LNCS (LNAI), vol. 2473, pp. 166–181. Springer, Heidelberg (2002). https://doi.org/10.1007/3-540-45810-7_18
6. Gangemi, A., Navigli, R., Velardi, P.: The OntoWordNet project: extension and axiomatization of conceptual relations in WordNet. In: Meersman, R., Tari, Z., Schmidt, D.C. (eds.) OTM 2003. LNCS, vol. 2888, pp. 820–838. Springer, Heidelberg (2003). https://doi.org/10.1007/978-3-540-39964-3_52
7. Grenon, P., Smith, B., Goldberg, L.: Biodynamic ontology: applying BFO in the biomedical domain. In: Studies in Health Technology and Informatics (2004)

8. Jain, P., et al.: Contextual ontology alignment of LOD with an upper ontology: a case study with proton. In: Antoniou, G., et al. (eds.) ESWC 2011. LNCS, vol. 6643, pp. 80–92. Springer, Heidelberg (2011). https://doi.org/10.1007/978-3-642- · 21034-1_6

9. Jezek, E.: Sweetening ontologies cont'd: aligning bottom-up with top-down ontologies. In: Proceedings of the Contextual Representation of Events and Objects in Language Workshop (CREOL), Co-located with the Joint Ontology Workshops, JOWO-2019, Graz, Austria (2019)

10. Jezek, E., Magnini, B., Feltracco, A., Bianchini, A., Popescu, O.: T-PAS; a resource of typed predicate argument structures for linguistic analysis and semantic processing. In: Proceedings of the Ninth International Conference on Language Resources and Evaluation, LREC 2014, Reykjavik, Iceland, 26–31 May 2014, pp. 890–895 (2014)

11. Keet, C.M.: The use of foundational ontologies in ontology development: an empirical assessment. In: Antoniou, G., et al. (eds.) ESWC 2011. LNCS, vol. 6643, pp. 321–335. Springer, Heidelberg (2011). https://doi.org/10.1007/978-3-642-21034-1_22

12. Lesk, M.: Automatic sense disambiguation using machine readable dictionaries: how to tell a pine cone from an ice cream cone. In: Proceedings of the 5th Annual International Conference on Systems Documentation, SIGDOC 1986, pp. 24–26. ACM, New York (1986). https://doi.org/10.1145/318723.318728

13. Mascardi, V., Cordì, V., Rosso, P.: A comparison of upper ontologies. In: Proceedings of the 8th AI * IA/TABOO Joint Workshop on Agents and Industry, pp. 55–64 (2007)

14. Mascardi, V., Locoro, A., Rosso, P.: Automatic ontology matching via upper ontologies: a systematic evaluation. IEEE Trans. Knowl. Data Eng. **22**(5), 609–623 (2010)

15. Mika, P., Oberle, D., Gangemi, A., Sabou, M.: Foundations for service ontologies: aligning OWL-S to DOLCE. In: Proceedings of the 13th International Conference on World Wide Web, pp. 563–572 (2004)

16. Miller, G.A.: WordNet: a lexical database for English. Commun. ACM **38**(11), 39–41 (1995)

17. Nardi, J.C., de Almeida Falbo, R., Almeida, J.P.A.: Foundational ontologies for semantic integration in EAI: a systematic literature review. In: Douligeris, C., Polemi, N., Karantjias, A., Lamersdorf, W. (eds.) I3E 2013. IAICT, vol. 399, pp. 238–249. Springer, Heidelberg (2013). https://doi.org/10.1007/978-3-642-37437-1_20

18. Navigli, R., Ponzetto, S.P.: BabelNet: the automatic construction, evaluation and application of a wide-coverage multilingual semantic network. Artif. Intell. **193**, 217–250 (2012)

19. Niles, I., Pease, A.: Towards a standard upper ontology. In: Proceedings of the International Conference on Formal Ontology in Information Systems, pp. 2–9 (2001)

20. Niles, I., Pease, A.: Linking lexicons and ontologies: mapping wordnet to the suggested upper merged ontology. In: Proceedings of the International Conference on Information and Knowledge Engineering, pp. 412–416 (2003)

21. Pease, A., Benzmüller, C.: Sigma: an integrated development environment for logical theories. AI Commun. **26**, 9–97 (2013)

22. Rebele, T., Suchanek, F.M., Hoffart, J., Biega, J., Kuzey, E., Weikum, G.: YAGO: a multilingual knowledge base from Wikipedia, WordNet, and GeoNames. In: The Semantic Web - ISWC 2016–15th International Semantic Web Conference, Kobe, Japan, 17–21 October 2016, Proceedings, Part II. pp. 177–185 (2016). https://doi.org/10.1007/978-3-319-46547-0_19
23. Reed, S., Lenat, D.: Mapping ontologies into Cyc. In: Proceedings of the Workshop on Ontologies for the Semantic Web, pp. 1–6 (2002)
24. Schadd, F.C., Roos, N.: Coupling of wordnet entries for ontology mapping using virtual documents. In: Proceedings of the 7th Conference on Ontology Matching, pp. 25–36 (2012)
25. Schmidt, D., Basso, R., Trojahn, C., Vieira, R.: Matching domain and top-level ontologies exploring word sense disambiguation and word embedding. In: Emerging Topics in Semantic Technologies (Best Papers from the Workshops at ISWC 2018), pp. 27–38 (2018)
26. Schmidt, D., Trojahn, C., Vieira, R.: Analysing top-level and domain ontology alignments from matching systems. In: Proceedings of the 11th International Workshop on Ontology Matching Co-located with the 15th International Semantic Web Conference (ISWC 2016), Kobe, Japan, 18 October 2016, pp. 13–24 (2016)
27. Seppälä, S.: Mapping WordNet to basic formal ontology using the KYOTO ontology. In: Proceedings of the International Conference on Biomedical Ontology, pp. 1–2 (2015)
28. Silva, V., Campos, M., Silva, J., Cavalcanti, M.: An approach for the alignment of biomedical ontologies based on foundational ontologies. Inf. Data Manag. 2(3), 557–572 (2011)
29. Terziev, I., Kiryakov, A., Manov, D.: Base Upper-level Ontology (BULO) Guidance. Deliverable 1.8.1, SEKT Project (2005)
30. Vennesland, A.: Matcher composition for identification of subsumption relations in ontology matching. In: Proceedings of the Conference on Web Intelligence, pp. 154–161 (2017)
31. Wang, P.: Lily results on SEALS platform for OAEI 2011. In: Proceedings of the 6th International Workshop on Ontology Matching, pp. 156–162 (2011)
32. Yatskevich, M., Giunchiglia, F.: Element level semantic matching using WordNet. In: Meaning Coordination and Negotiation Workshop, pp. 37–48 (2004)
33. Zong, N., Nam, S., Eom, J.H., Ahn, J., Joe, H., Kim, H.G.: Aligning ontologies with subsumption and equivalence relations in linked data. Knowl. Based Syst. 76(1), 30–41 (2015). https://doi.org/10.1016/j.knosys.2014.11.022

The Construction of a Corpus from the Brazilian Historical-Biographical Dictionary

Lucas Ribeiro[1], Jaqueline P. Zulini[2], and Alexandre Rademaker[1,3]($\boxtimes$)

[1] FGV/EMAp, Rio de Janeiro, Brazil
arademaker@gmail.com
[2] FGV/CPDOC, Rio de Janeiro, Brazil
[3] IBM Research, Rio de Janeiro, Brazil

Abstract. We present our ongoing efforts towards the creation of a new Portuguese corpus based on the "Dicionário Histórico-Bibliográfico Brasileiro". The aim to add as many linguistic annotations as possible using widely accepted annotation schemas and distributing all data in standard formats. This first exploratory work revisits what is already done and tests different tools to detect errors and look for the best methods to tackle the problem. Data is available at https://github.com/cpdoc/dhbb-nlp, and it will be continuously improved.

Keywords: Portuguese corpus · Segmentation · Natural language processing

1 Introduction

In this paper we present our ongoing efforts towards the creation of a corpus based on the "Dicionário Histórico-Bibliográfico Brasileiro" (DHBB) [1] that contains almost 12 millions tokens in about three hundred thousand sentences. The DHBB is a reference work, written by historians and social scientists, it contains almost eight thousand entries with information ranging from the life and career trajectories of individuals to the relationships between the characters and events that the country has hosted. This work presents an exploratory approach in order to find the best methods to create a reliable corpus.

In previous articles, some initial efforts to mine the DHBB texts were presented. In [15], the documents were processed by Freeling [13] to annotate named entities and expand the coverage of OpenWordnet-PT [14]. In [9], DHBB was syntactical analysed with two different statistical parsers. Once a preliminary set of relevant entities types and semantic relations was identified, the classification of appositives syntactic annotations regarding the semantic relations was performed in a sample and evaluated. The low agreement on the appositives annotations between the two parsers shown that results are not very reliable. Later on, in [10], DHBB was subject to syntactical analysis by PALAVRAS

© Springer Nature Switzerland AG 2020
P. Quaresma et al. (Eds.): PROPOR 2020, LNAI 12037, pp. 109–117, 2020.
https://doi.org/10.1007/978-3-030-41505-1_11

parser [3] and semantic annotated by AC/DC [5].[1] The problem is that not all PALAVRAS errors were fixed but only proper names segmentation. Besides that, the annotation schema used is not widely adopted.

Our aim is to annotate DHBB (Sect. 2) with as many as possible layers of linguistic information using widely accepted schemas (Sect. 3) shared by the NLP community. This work is also leading us to improve the DHBB itself, since we could detect several problems like encoding issues and typos in the corpus. We start dealing with the problem of text segmentation into sentences (Sect. 4). Due to its format, there are several uncommon abbreviations and quotes, thus turning the segmentation task not trivial. By comparing the segmentation of two different tools, we found the divergent results that suggest possible hard cases. Going further, in Sect. 5, we made a first preliminary experiment on part-of-speech (POS) tagging using the same tool trained on two different corpora. Again, by comparing the outputs, we could make a first confusion matrix and locate where the tools diverge. We also note that comparing the outputs of two different models searching for weakness or inconsistencies in annotation is known strategy, used for instance in [19]. We extend this strategy to segmentation task as well.

2   DHBB

DHBB [1] is an encyclopedia developed and curated by Centro de Pesquisa e Documentação de História Contemporânea do Brasil (CPDOC), from Fundação Getulio Vargas (FGV), and is an important resource for all research, nationally and internationally, interested in Brazilian politics. It was first published in 1984, in four volumes containing 4,500 entries. In the 2001, the resource was increased by one more volume reaching a total of 6,620 entries, and in 2010 its material was made available online,[2] with about 7,500 entries composed of a title, the kind of entry (biographical or thematic), the author of the entry, and the text in a text field. Currently, DHBB has 7,687 entries and data is maintained in text files under version control.[3] The process and rationale of releasing this content from the database and converting it to full text aiming at natural language processing are described by [17]. Each entry became a single text file that received a unique identifier, and new metadata were added, such as the gender of the biographee and the political role she/he had.[4]

As noted before, DHBB was already treated by AC/DC, using PALAVRAS[5] to parse it. However the only mapping for PALAVRAS to other schemas is

---

[1] Data available at https://www.linguateca.pt/acesso/corpus.php?corpus=DHBB. The AC/DC is a online service for corpus browsing and searching but also a data format with attributes added on tokens in the output of the PALAVRAS parser.

[2] https://cpdoc.fgv.br/acervo/dhbb.

[3] https://github.com/cpdoc/dhbb.

[4] In order to preserve the original repository, the present work can be reproduced from https://github.com/cpdoc/dhbb-nlp where all data is available.

[5] The documentation is available at https://visl.sdu.dk/visl/pt/info/.

the one to Universal Dependencies used by [16] but outdated. A corpus with syntactic annotation on a non-widespread schema is less useful. In a language processing pipeline, we usually aspire, for example, that a named entity classifier component can understand the syntactic annotation of the parser, and both results could be easily combined for a further processing step. Particular syntactic annotations force the implementation of mappings not always full content preserving. Furthermore, AC/DC has joint DHBB alongside with other two corpora, the 'Dicionário histórico-biográfico da Primeira República' (DHBPR) and the 'Dicionário da política republicana do Rio de Janeiro'. Our aim is just to deal with the DHBB which is already a big corpus.

Finally, we mention that the texts in DHBB were written with certain independence among their writers, and this directly impacts any computational approach in the corpus. For instance, abbreviations and punctuations were not used consistently. Moreover, some authors may decide to cite another text in the DHBB, whereas others do not, thus leading to a more clean text, without citations or references.

3 Universal Dependencies for Portuguese

As stated in [11], the Universal Dependencies project provides an inventory of dependency relations that are linguistically motivated, computationally useful, and cross-linguistically applicable. It holds two Portuguese corpora since its 2.1 release. The UD Portuguese Bosque corpus (Bosque) [16] is a subset of the Floresta Sinta(c)tica treebank [7] converted to UD annotation style. Bosque currently has 9,365 sentences that were taken from CETENFolha (4,213 sentences in Brazilian PT) and CETEMPublico (5,152 sentences in European PT) corpora. The other Portuguese corpus is the Google Stanford Dependencies (GSD) [12]. This corpus was converted from the Google Universal Dependency Treebank, but we were unable to find information about the origin of the data. Inspecting the sentences manually, we found pieces of evidence of being text collected from newspaper articles, probably between 2010 and 2012.

It is important to emphasize that DHBB and the UD Portuguese corpora have different text styles. DHBB text has an encyclopedia-style; many sentences do not have a subject since, in the same entry, we are usually talking about the same entity. DHBB authors followed a general guideline for making sentences declarative and neutral. The guidelines also suggest the flow of information on each entry (i.e., when describing a politician, the first paragraph contains the city and year of birth and the parents' names, while the second paragraph details the education path, and so on). On the other hand, news from different sources tends to bias convincement and impact on the readers. Vocabulary is much more assorted compared to DHBB, given they are not limited to the history of politicians but cover many domains from sports to science.

4   Text Segmentation

Since manually revising more than three hundred thousand sentences is almost impractical, we adopted a strategy already suggested in the literature. Using two different tools, we segmented DHBB and compared the results, revising the cases where the tools diverge. In that way, we focused on systematic confusions, an approximation for the hard cases that should be manually inspected by humans. The Apache OpenNLP [6] is a machine learning based toolkit for natural language processing. The sentence detector module uses a maximum entropy model to evaluate end-of-sentence characters to determine if they signify the end of a sentence. Sentence Detection can be done before or after tokenization.[6] One important limitation of OpenNLP sentence segmentation module is that it cannot identify sentence boundaries based on the contents of the sentence. A notable example is the first sentence in the articles where the title is mistakenly identified to be the first part of the first sentence.

Freeling [13] is an open-source multilingual processing library providing a wide range of analysis functionalities. Its sentence splitter module receives a list of word objects and returns a list of sentence objects. It uses an options file, where one can tune parameters in order to fit to particularities of the text in question.

In Linguateca processing steps of DHBB,[7] before DHBB was syntactically analyzed with PALAVRAS, the corpus was tokenized and segmented with a Perl library called `Lingua::PT::PLNbase`.[8] As stated on its website, this library was created in 2004, and the main difference of this library compared to Freeling is that it has fewer configuration options, so users have less control over the tokenization and segmentation steps. For instance, Linguateca's tokenizer cannot deal appropriately with characters such as 'º', like *"(...) em seu artigo 14, parágrafos 1º ..."* and has to replace these characters with ASCII symbols, thus making the outputs different from the inputs. We didn't find how to add new abbreviations to the list handled by the library, as we did for Freeling. Table 1 shows the number of sentences of the DHBB parsed with Linguateca, OpenNLP and Freeling.

Table 1. Number of sentences of the DHBB with each parser.

Tool	Number of sentences
Linguateca	312,539
OpenNLP	314,930
Freeling	311,530

---

[6] Here we have used the pre-trained models that adopted segmentation first.

[7] Documented at https://www.linguateca.pt/acesso/anotacao.html.

[8] See https://metacpan.org/pod/Lingua::PT::PLNbase.

We first processed all DHBB files with Freeling and OpenNLP. At first, we found that 3,438 files diverged on segmentation, comprising 44% of the whole DHBB. Looking at the divergent files,[9] we could divide the errors in two groups: (i) problems in the DHBB itself; (ii) confusion of the tools due to uncommon abbreviations, quotations that lasts longer than a sentence, and uncommon quotation symbols.

Comparing the output of the tools was very efficient to find errors on the corpus. We found many occurrences of the unicode non-breaking space character (wrongly in place of normal spaces) in more than 1,700 files. This character confuse both tools in different contexts. During the migration of DHBB data to text files, some sentences have been split into more than one line and some segments were lost, ending up with sentences fragments without a final period. Freeling is able to detect sentences regardless of the presence of line breaks, but OpenNLP is not, it never join separated lines into one sentence. We have fixed many cases and listed some for further review by DHBB editors. Another error is related to many different quotation marks, some not properly balanced. In some cases, we found even hard for humans to identify the quotes given the nesting of quotation marks. Finally, during the migration of DHBB to text files, the titles of the entries are moved from the first line of the text to a metadata field, but many cases remain in the text. We manually cleaned up around 165 files.

Regarding the divergence of the tools, this happens due to uncommon abbreviations, quotations and punctuation symbols. For quotes, Freeling has a fine-tuned control for blocking or not the introduction of sentence split inside a pair of parenthesis-like markers. These markers can be quotes, parenthesis or any other pair of characters. OpenNLP expertise is limited by the data it saw during training. OpenNLP sentence detector was trained with the CoNLL-X shared task [4], the Portuguese part is taken from the Bosque corpus distributed by Linguateca before its conversion to UD (Sect. 3).

Due to DHBB political content, abbreviations of names and initials of political parties are very common on it. We have many occurrences of PP (Partido Progressista), PT (Partido dos Trabalhadores) and names such as 'M. H. Simonsen'. In Freeling, we have some ways to control the segmentation. First, we were able to refine the list of abbreviations that must not be separated of their following dot during tokenization. Since tokenization happens before sentence detection, dots part of abbreviations are not considered candidates for sentence ending characters. When the abbreviation happens in the end of the sentence, a sentence split will only be introduced by Freeling if a sentence ending character is followed by a capitalized word or a sentence start character. That is, a sentence ending with an abbreviation followed by a sentence that starts with a proper name will always confuse Freeling. OpenNLP tends to correctly detect sentences that starts with a quotation mark or a non-standard or multi-character sentences ending marks such as colon, semicolon and ellipsis.

---

[9] We have used the `diff` command line tool inside Emacs editor. This environment provided us a easily way to inspect the differences in the files in an interactive manner.

Finally, we observed that although we could have defined quotation marks as possible sentence start character for Freeling, this option increase the number of errors in our experiments. Regarding OpenNLP training, we found that abbreviation dictionary can also be provided but many details regarding the parameters used by the module are not well-documented.

After we calibrated Freeling parameters, we improved the results and obtained that of the 7,687 files, 2,096 diverged on the number of sentences, comprising 27% of the total. We note that, despite the huge amount of divergent files, when counting the number of divergent sentences, they comprise a total of 2% of the total. Of course, we are aware that we may still have cases of false negative, that is, when the tools agree in a wrong segmentation.

Once we identified the differences between Freeling and OpenNLP, we processed the corpus with `Lingua::PT::PLNbase`. A detailed exploration of the differences was not yet possible due to the following problems. First, the encoding of some files was lost with the mixing of UTF-8 and ISO-8859 code systems. Next, XML tags were included to mark the begin/end of sentences, but the tool did not produce valid XML files (i.e. symbols such as '&' were not converted to '&' and the markup was not a correct tree structure). These errors make difficult the processing of the outputs by an XML parser. Given the results that we had from `Lingua::PT::PLNbase`, we could only count the number of sentences but we could not easy compare the differences of the files.

Finally, we emphasize that this is an initial exploratory approach to decide what methods are the best to tackle the corpus analysis, and also this initial efforts could detect problems in the DHBB itself, providing an improvement of the whole corpus, which will reduce future errors and contribute to make DHBB more reliable.

5   Part-of-Speech Tagging

After tokenization and segmentation, next step will comprise the part-of-speech (POS) tagging. Following the same approach, here we briefly explain our first experiment sharing preliminary results. In order to identify possible errors in POS tagging, we compared the outputs of two different UDPipe [18] models trained on Bosque and GSD corpora when applied to DHBB. As a first approach we made a confusion matrix, shown in Table 2. The rows are GSD tags and the columns are from Bosque. Similar technique was employed in [8].

As a first glance, we found many repeated errors. For example, GSD model tag months as NOUN whereas Bosque model tags them as PROPN. Since many recent revisions of Bosque driven by changes in the UD guidelines [16] were not yet applied to GSD corpus, many differences on the results of the models are expected. Moreover, the difference between the vocabulary and the style between the training data (UD corpora) and DHBB, and the strategy of UDPipe on dealing with out-of-vocabulary words explain a lot of differences too. These will all be subject of future work.

It is worth to explain the choice of UDPipe for this first experiment with POS tagging. UDPipe is easier to run/train using corpora annotated with UD

Table 2. Confusion matrix between GSD and Bosque

	ADJ	ADP	ADV	AUX	CCONJ	DET	INTJ	NOUN	NUM	PART	PRON	PROPN	PUNCT	SCONJ	SYM	VERB	X
ADJ	74193	226	270	14	3	369	0	4845	32	0	90	882	1	0	0	4137	7
ADP	88	409490	683	12	0	1500	0	169	3	0	132	952	0	59	0	190	7
ADV	990	635	41643	96	96	41	0	1609	9	0	113	273	0	15	0	95	0
AUX	109	4	45	36417	3	15	0	112	0	0	18	39	0	0	0	5036	0
CCONJ	9	68	1352	2	50222	12	0	25	0	0	450	107	1	4571	0	26	1
DET	579	3099	92	0	0	293250	0	283	316	0	1134	195	0	0	0	123	0
INTJ	0	0	0	0	0	0	0	0	0	0	0	0	0	0	0	0	0
NOUN	5632	324	921	81	1	160	1	293786	205	0	234	2294	0	14	0	3447	14
NUM	76	182	67	0	0	260	0	346	72184	0	3	474	10	7	0	9	1
PART	13	5	8	0	0	0	0	20	1	0	300	27	0	9	0	6	0
PRON	71	85	48	3	0	558	0	128	1357	0	22890	276	0	970	0	19	5
PROPN	3785	18470	1396	5441	60	1254	9	56300	133	0	647	300078	89	171	39	2476	1
PUNCT	101	4	0	0	1	0	0	611	0	0	6	145	268560	0	36	0	0
SCONJ	0	0	0	0	0	0	0	0	0	0	0	0	0	0	0	0	0
SYM	0	0	0	0	0	0	0	0	0	0	0	0	0	0	52	0	0
VERB	2710	211	656	4771	39	50	0	4695	128	1	54	444	1	11	0	154572	3
X	46	1	2	0	0	11	0	14	0	0	6	12	0	0	1	11	0

tags and following UD guidelines, and it produces UD compatible output. The POS tagger of Freeling does not follow the UD guidelines, and we haven't yet explored the options for training and evaluating the OpenNLP tagger. Moreover, our focus is not on the adaptation of a single tool for processing DHBB, but on the production of consistent data with compatible annotations.

6   Conclusion

As observed by [2], tokenization is a crucial component of language processing, yet there is no widely accepted tokenization method for English texts. In this article, we have shown that the segmentation of texts into sentences is also not a solved problem in general, as many researchers believe. Many language processing tools are trained or fine-tuned to deal with news articles. Still, once they are used to process texts with a different narrative style (such as encyclopedia material) or domain-specific documents, many issues appear unsolved.

The observation that motivates our work is that the current version of DHBB in AC/DC is not complete since (i) the tool used to segment the corpus is not reliable; (ii) the output format of the parsed files is not widely used. Moreover, analyzing the divergence on segmentation led us to detect errors in the corpus itself, thus leading to an improvement of the DHBB.

As we go deeper in the annotation of DHBB, we note that there are several issues that need to be solved in order to properly annotate such important material. We started with segmentation and noticed that relying just on one tool can lead to wrong segmentation, therefore adding different tools is a good technique to identify and correct possible errors, reducing the manual revision effort. We also note that this investigation can lead us to find weakness or inconsistencies on corpora used to train the models for POS tagging and parsing.

After this exploratory analysis, future work will need to be done. For instance, we plan to retrain the OpenNLP sentence detector with fragments of the DHBB manually curated and also add training UDPipe models with manually annotated DHBB texts in order to look for improvements in the POS tagging.

We also note that although the use of machine-learning tools in natural language processing is prevalent, the generality of the pre-trained models is rarely discussed in the literature. The openNLP segmentation model that we used proved to be not well adapted to DHBB style and maybe overfit to the data used for creating it, but training a model with DHBB data would not also make the result a robust model for processing other materials. In that sense, we may be still far from advances in general and reliable language processing techniques.

References

1. de Abreu, A., Lattman-Weltman, F., de Paula, C.J. (eds.): Dicionário Histórico-Biográfico Brasileiro pos-1930. CPDOC/FGV, 3 edn., Rio de Janeiro (2010). http://cpdoc.fgv.br/acervo/dhbb
2. Barrett, N., Weber-Jahnke, J.: Building a biomedical tokenizer using the token lattice design pattern and the adapted Viterbi algorithm. BMC Bioinform. **12**(3), S1 (2011)
3. Bick, E.: The Parsing System Palavras. Automatic Grammatical Analysis of Portuguese in a Constraint Grammar Framework (2000)
4. Buchholz, S., Marsi, E.: CoNLL-X shared task on multilingual dependency parsing. In: Proceedings of the Tenth Conference on Computational Natural Language Learning (CoNLL-X), pp. 149–164. Association for Computational Linguistics, New York City, June 2006. https://www.aclweb.org/anthology/W06-2920
5. Costa, L., Santos, D., Rocha, P.A.: Estudando o português tal como é usado: o serviço ac/dc. In: 7th Brazilian Symposium in Information and Human Language Technology (STIL 2009) (São Carlos Brasil 8–11 de Setembro de 2009) (2009)
6. Apache Software Foundation: Apache OpenNLP. version 1.9.1. (2019). https://opennlp.apache.org
7. Freitas, C., Rocha, P., Bick, E.: Floresta sintá (c) tica: bigger, thicker and easier. In: Teixeira, A., de Lima, V.L.S., de Oliveira, L.C., Quaresma, P. (eds.) International Conference on Computational Processing of the Portuguese Language, pp. 216–219. Springer, Heidelberg (2008). https://doi.org/10.1007/978-3-540-85980-2_23
8. Freitas, C., Trugo, L.F., Chalub, F., Paulino-Passos, G., Rademaker, A.: Tagsets and datasets: some experiments based on Portuguese language. In: Villavicencio, A., et al. (eds.) PROPOR 2018. LNCS (LNAI), vol. 11122, pp. 459–469. Springer, Cham (2018). https://doi.org/10.1007/978-3-319-99722-3_46
9. Higuchi, S., Freitas, C., Cuconato, B., Rademaker, A.: Text mining for history: first steps on building a large dataset. In: Proceedings of 11th Edition of the Language Resources and Evaluation Conference, Miyazaki, Japan, May 2018. http://www.lrec-conf.org/proceedings/lrec2018/summaries/1084.html
10. Higuchi, S., Santos, D., Freitas, C., Rademaker, A.: Distant reading Brazilian politics. In: Navarretta, C., Agirrezabal, M., Maegaard, B. (eds.) Proceedings of the Digital Humanities in the Nordic Countries 4th Conference, vol. 2364, Copenhagen, Denmark, March 2019. http://ceur-ws.org/Vol-2364/
11. Jurafsky, D., Martin, J.H. (eds.): Speech and Language Processing - An Introduction to Natural Language Processing, Computational Linguistics, and Speech Recognition, 3 edn., Stanford (2019). https://web.stanford.edu/jurafsky/slp3/

12. McDonald, R., et al.: Universal dependency annotation for multilingual parsing. In: Proceedings of the 51st Annual Meeting of the Association for Computational Linguistics (Volume 2: Short Papers), pp. 92–97 (2013)
13. Padró, L., Stanilovsky, E.: FreeLing 3.0: towards wider multilinguality. In: LREC2012 (2012)
14. de Paiva, V., Rademaker, A., de Melo, G.: OpenWordNet-PT: an open Brazilian WordNet for reasoning. In: Proceedings of COLING 2012: Demonstration Papers, pp. 353–360. The COLING 2012 Organizing Committee, Mumbai, December 2012. http://www.aclweb.org/anthology/C12-3044, published also as Technical report http://hdl.handle.net/10438/10274
15. Paiva, V.D., Oliveira, D., Higuchi, S., Rademaker, A., Melo, G.D.: Exploratory information extraction from a historical dictionary. In: IEEE 10th International Conference on e-Science (e-Science), vol. 2, pp. 11–18. IEEE, October 2014. https://doi.org/10.1109/eScience.2014.50
16. Rademaker, A., Chalub, F., Real, L., Freitas, C., Bick, E., Valeria De Paiva Universal Dependencies for Portuguese: Universal dependencies for Portuguese. In: Proceedings of the Fourth International Conference on Dependency Linguistics (Depling), Pisa, Italy, pp. 197–206, September 2017
17. Rademaker, A., Oliveira, D.A.B., de Paiva, V., Higuchi, S., e Sá, A.M., Alvim, M.: A linked open data architecture for the historical archives of the Getulio Vargas foundation. Int. J. Digit. Libr. **15**(2–4), 153–167 (2015). https://doi.org/10.1007/s00799-015-0147-1
18. Straka, M., Straková, J.: Tokenizing, POS tagging, lemmatizing and parsing UD 2.0 with UDPipe. In: Proceedings of the CoNLL 2017 Shared Task: Multilingual Parsing from Raw Text to Universal Dependencies, pp. 88–99. Association for Computational Linguistics, Vancouver, August 2017. http://www.aclweb.org/anthology/K/K17/K17-3009.pdf
19. Volokh, A., Neumann, G.: Automatic detection and correction of errors in dependency tree-banks. In: Proceedings of the 49th Annual Meeting of the Association for Computational Linguistics: Human Language Technologies: Short Papers-Volume 2, pp. 346–350. Association for Computational Linguistics (2011)

Natural Language Processing Applications

Making the Most of Synthetic Parallel Texts: Portuguese-Chinese Neural Machine Translation Enhanced with Back-Translation

Rodrigo Santos$^{(\boxtimes)}$, João Silva, and António Branco

NLX—Natural Language and Speech Group, Department of Informatics,
Faculdade de Ciências, University of Lisbon, Campo Grande,
1749-016 Lisbon, Portugal
{rsdsantos,jsilva,antonio.branco}@di.fc.ul.pt

Abstract. The generation of synthetic parallel corpora through the automatic translation of a monolingual text, a process known as back-translation, is a technique used to augment the amount of parallel data available for training Machine Translation systems and is known to improve translation quality and thus mitigate the lack of data for under-resourced language pairs. It is assumed that, when training on synthetic parallel data, the original monolingual data should be used at the target side and its translation at the source side, an assumption to be assessed. The contributions of this paper are twofold. We investigate the viability of using synthetic data to improve Neural Machine Translation for Portuguese-Chinese, an under-resourced pair of languages for which back-translation has yet to demonstrate its suitability. Besides, we seek to fill another gap in the literature by experimenting with synthetic data not only at the source side but also, alternatively, at the target side. While demonstrating that, when appropriately applied, back-translation can enhance Portuguese-Chinese Neural Machine Translation, the results reported in this paper also confirm the current assumption that using the original monolingual data at the source side outperforms using them at the target side.

Keywords: Neural Machine Translation · Synthetic parallel texts · Back-translation · Portuguese · Chinese · Under-resourced translation pair

1 Introduction

Neural Machine Translation (NMT) is known for its good performance and fluent output, but also for requiring large quantities of parallel data to unfold its potential in terms of delivering quality translations. Most of the current research and existing language resources concern the English language, leaving the vast majority of the other language pairs understudied and with relatively little to no data available for NMT engines to be developed. Portuguese-Chinese (PT-ZH) is

© Springer Nature Switzerland AG 2020
P. Quaresma et al. (Eds.): PROPOR 2020, LNAI 12037, pp. 121–130, 2020.
https://doi.org/10.1007/978-3-030-41505-1_12

the language pair being addressed in this study, and it has very little resources available [4], which is somehow disconcerting, especially when one considers the large number of speakers of either language.[1]

Creating synthetic parallel corpora from monolingual data has been used with favorable results as a valid option to overcome the lack of resources in MT for under-resourced language pairs, as monolingual data is much more readily available and in much greater quantity than parallel data [22]. A common technique to achieve this is known as *back-translation*, through which a monolingual text is automatically translated by an existing seed MT system, giving rise to synthetic parallel data, where each sentence s_o from the original monolingual corpus is paired up with its (synthetic) translation s_{mt}. This parallel corpus can then be used to train further MT systems in both directions, either with s_o as source and s_{mt} as target, or with s_o as target and s_{mt} as source.

This paper addresses the viability of improving NMT for PT-ZH, a language pair under-resourced for MT, with synthetic parallel texts. This work studies which translation direction benefits the most from using the synthetic data. That is, it compares (i.i) *synthetic target*: using the generated synthetic data s_{mt} on the target side and the original monolingual data s_o on the source side, with (i.ii) *synthetic source*: doing it the other way around, where the generated synthetic data s_{mt} is used on the source side and the original monolingual data s_o is used on the target side.

This paper also assesses the impact of progressively increasing the amount of synthetic training data through back-translating monolingual texts. Thus, on the one hand, experiments (i.i) and (i.ii) are undertaken for a range of synthetic data sets of increasing sizes, all generated with the same seed MT engine. On the other hand, the results of those experiments are compared with (ii) *bootstrapping*, where a succession of NMT models are trained with a succession of back-translated data of increasing size such that a given model is trained with the synthetic data created with the NMT model trained in the previous stage.

To create the synthetic data, we opted for using Chinese monolingual texts and (machine) translating them into Portuguese given that the quality of the Chinese text is secured by its publishing source and the level of quality of the Portuguese text outcome can be assessed by the authors of this paper, native speakers of Portuguese.

The experiments and their results presented in this paper demonstrate that back-translation can enhance Portuguese-Chinese NMT. They also deliver important lessons, namely lending credence to the assumption that the synthetic source approach, which has been used in the literature, outperforms the synthetic target approach; and that by resorting to a single, initial seed MT engine to generate the synthetic data, both synthetic source and target approaches outperform the bootstrapping approach, which is based on a succession of MT models successively retrained on the synthetic data generated by the models of the previous stages.

---

[1] Data fromethnologue.com ranks Chinese as the language with the most speakers among the approximately 7,000 languages in the world, and Portuguese as the sixth.

The remainder of the paper is organized as follows. Section 2 presents previous work in the literature that is more closely related to the present paper. In Sect. 3, a short overview is provided, of Transformer, the NMT architecture used throughout the experiment reported here. Section 4 describes the experiments that were performed as well as the data sets that were used and Sect. 5 presents the results of the experiments. Finally, Sect. 6 closes the paper, with the discussion of the results and conclusions.

2   Related Work

Back-translation was initially used to create synthetic parallel data in the context of Statistical MT, with encouraging results [22]. Since then it has also been successfully applied to NMT [17] and is now a common practice among the most recent work in the field.[2]

Research on back-translation has addressed several issues, such as (i) exploring methods for picking the sentences that form the synthetic corpus [8]; (ii) testing ways to improve the quality of the obtained corpus by applying to it some filtering [10]; and (iii) assessing the impact on performance of varying the ratio of real to synthetic data in the training set [15].

Other studies have attempted an iterative approach where a system trained on synthetic data is used create an additional batch of synthetic data, which is then added to the training set and used to train a presumably better system that will be used to back-translate even more data, iteratively building towards MT systems and parallel data of higher quality [9,23].

Regarding the language pair in the current study, it is worth noting that there is little research on parallel texts [6,13] and on NMT [16] for PT-ZH reported in the literature and, to the best of our knowledge, there is no published research results on applying back-translation to this language pair.

Also of note is that papers that resort to back-translation use the translated text as source and the original text as target, under the assumption that the model will be able to produce better translations if the original non-synthetic data, which are of presumably good quality, are the target that the system will aim to produce, instead of trying to learn to translate when the target is formed by the output of an MT system since these are presumably noisy synthetic sentences. However, there is not much research either for or against this assumption.

3   NMT Architecture

When using machine translation, it is necessary to process sequences of arbitrary length. To allow NMT to cope with input of variable length, the by now familiar encoder-decoder sequence-to-sequence architecture was proposed [19], where an

---

[2] In the most recent Conference on Machine Translation (WMT'19), nearly two-thirds of the participating systems used back-translation in some way [2].

encoder module, formed by recurrent units, takes the input sentence, one token at each time step, and encodes it into a vector of fixed size. Then, a decoder module, also formed by recurrent units, takes this vector and decodes it, one token at each time step, to produce a target translation.

This architecture achieved good results but still suffered from a major drawback, namely that it forces the encoder to encapsulate the representation of the whole source sentence information into a single vector of fixed size. This bottleneck was overcome by the so-called attention mechanism [1,12], which allows the decoder to access all encoder states, from all time steps, combining them through a weighted sum, thus releasing the encoder from the burden of having to encode the whole sentence in a single vector.

The mechanism of attention has been further exploited by the Transformer model [21], which discards all recurrent units and replaces them with the attention mechanism, resulting in an architecture that has better performance and faster training times. Given this, the Transformer has become the state of the art for NMT and is the architecture used throughout the experiments reported in this paper. In this Section we provide a short overview of Transformer, and refer the interested reader to [21] for more details.

When training, the input to Transformer are the sequences of embeddings of the words in the source and target sentences. However, since the model lacks recurrent units to implicitly track word position in the sentence, this information is explicitly integrated by adding positional embeddings. The input sequences are then fed to the encoder and decoder stacks, which use multi-head self-attention on their inputs, concatenate the output of each head and run the result through a dense layer. On the decoder side, the inputs are masked to block the leakage of future information. For each decoder layer, an additional multi-head attention layer assigns different weights to every encoder state in an averaged sum, similar to the original attention mechanism. Finally, the output of the decoder stack is passed to a softmax that produces a probability distribution over the target vocabulary, and the word with the highest probability is predicted by the model. This is repeated until the target sentence is fully predicted.

4   Experimental Setup

4.1   Seed Corpus and MT System

To obtain a synthetic parallel corpus, one needs a monolingual corpus and a seed MT system with which to back-translate it.

Seed Corpus and MT System. We use the Transformer [21] NMT architecture throughout this work as it is the current state of the art, resorting to the implementation in the Marian framework [11]. The various models trained here follow the setup from the base model described in [21], with 6 encoder and decoder layers, 8 attention heads, and an embedding size of 512. To obtain the seed MT system, Transformer was trained on the UM-PCorpus [6], a PT-ZH parallel corpus with around 1 million sentences from five domains, namely news, technology, law, subtitles, and general.[3] The UM-PCorpus further serves as the *seed corpus* inasmuch as the various back-translated corpora will be added to it.

Test Corpus. Throughout this work, we use the first 1,000 sentences of the corpus News Commentary 11 [20] as the test set (NC11). This corpus is similar to the "newstest" test set used for evaluation in most published research on NMT, and is composed of well curated, high quality translations from the news domain.

Seed System Performance. The seed system scores 13.38 BLEU for the ZH → PT direction and 10.72 BLEU for the PT → ZH direction when evaluated on NC11. These scores are in line with the best results obtained in the literature [16], and will serve as the baseline for the experiments in the present paper.

Monolingual Corpus for Back-Translation. As the monolingual input used to generate the synthetic parallel corpora, we resorted to 6 million Chinese sentences from MultiUN [20], a corpus composed of documents of the United Nations.

Text Pre-processing. Every corpus is pre-processed either with the Moses tokenizer,[4] for Portuguese text, or with the Jieba segmentation tool,[5] for Chinese text. Vocabularies with 32,000 sub-word units [18] are learned separately[6] for both languages of the seed corpus.

4.2 Experiments

Having established a seed corpus and MT system, a test set and a monolingual corpus to back-translate, the following three experiments were undertaken.

Synthetic Source. The approach to training a system on back-translated data commonly found in the literature consists of using the original monolingual corpus on the target side and the synthetic data (obtained by translating the original data) on the source side. This is an option adopted in our experiments as well.

Additionally, given that it is important to monitor the impact of progressively increasing the amount of back-translated data in relation to the seed parallel data, we created three sub-corpora of the synthetic parallel corpus: one with the first 1 million sentences, another with the first 3 million sentences, and yet another with the full 6 million sentences. Each one of these sub-corpora was added in turn to the seed parallel corpus of 1 million sentences and used to train three NMT systems for PT → ZH, which are different from the seed system. Each one of these three systems is trained on a different amount of data and a different

---

[3] The developers of UM-PCorpus also released an additional set of 5,000 sentence pairs (1,000 pairs from each domain) that we used for development purposes.

[4] We use the implementation from https://github.com/alvations/sacremoses.

[5] You may find Jieba at https://github.com/fxsjy/jieba.

[6] We use the implementation from https://github.com/rsennrich/subword-nmt.

ratio of parallel to synthetic data, namely $S^s_{1:1}$, trained on 2 million sentences (1:1 ratio); $S^s_{1:3}$, trained on 4 million sentences (1:3 ratio); and $S^s_{1:6}$, trained on 7 million sentences (1:6 ratio).

Synthetic Target. The case against using synthetic data on the target side comes from the expectation that the new model would aim at producing translations that are noisier, and thus of less quality, than the seed system. However, it is also possible that the eventual negative effect of an increased number of noisy sentences on the target side during training is canceled or even reverted by an increase in the grammatical diversity of those same sentences. And that performance may nevertheless happen to get improved more with synthetic sentences added to the target side, than with them added to the source side.

The back-translated corpus is used to obtain the same three sub-corpora used in the approach described above, with 1 million, 3 million, and 6 million sentences, and each is added in turn to the seed 1 million parallel corpus. The resulting extended corpora are used to train three new MT systems, namely $S^t_{1:1}$ on 2 million sentences (1:1 ratio), $S^t_{1:3}$ on 4 million sentences (1:3 ratio) and $S^t_{1:6}$ on 7 million sentences (1:6 ratio), but now in the ZH → PT direction.

Bootstrapping. The quality of a synthetic corpus is better when the quality of the MT system used to do the back-translation is also better. Since adding synthetic parallel data to the training set should allow creating a better MT system, this suggests that a bootstrapping approach may yield good results. In this approach, an initial portion of synthetic parallel data is used to augment the seed corpus and the resulting, larger data is used to train a second MT system. This system is then used to generate more synthetic parallel data, of presumably better quality than that produced from the seed system in the previous stage. This synthetic data, generated with this second MT system, is used to augment the seed parallel corpus and the result used to train a third MT system. And so on, with similar bootstrapping steps being iterated for larger portions of data.

In this experiment, we take the seed model for the ZH → PT direction and use it to create a synthetic parallel corpus with 1 million sentence pairs, which is added to the seed corpus and used to train a new MT system for ZH → PT.[7] Note that, up to this point, the result is the same as the $S^t_{1:1}$ system trained on 2 million sentence pairs with synthetic data on the target side, described above.

However, in this experiment, this $S^t_{1:1}$ system is used to back-translate 2 million new sentences which are added to the training data, for a total of 4 million sentence pairs, of which 1 million are from the original seed parallel corpus, 1 million from back-translation with the seed system, and 2 million from back-translation with $S^t_{1:1}$. This corpus of 4 million pairs is used to train a new system, $S^t_{1:1:2}$, which is then used to back-translate 3 million new sentences. These new

---

[7] Given the direction ZH → PT provided superior results than the direction PT → ZH in the two non-bootstrapping experiments (as reported in detail in Sect. 5), the direction ZH → PT was the one focused on in the bootstrapping approach.

synthetic parallel sentences are added to the training data, which is used to train yet another model, $S_{1:1:2:3}^{t}$. This last model was trained on a total of 7 million sentences, of which 1 million are from the original seed parallel corpus, 1 million from back-translation with the seed system, 2 million from back-translation with $S_{1:1}^{t}$, and 3 million from back-translation with $S_{1:1:2}^{t}$.

Table 1. BLEU scores (higher values are better)

Approach	Parallel corpus			
	Seed	1:1	1:3	1:6
Synthetic on target side	13.38	14.04	**14.12**	13.39
Bootstrap (target side)	13.38	**14.04**	13.59	11.46
Synthetic on source side	10.72	11.45	**11.84**	11.59

5 Results

This Section describes the evaluation results obtained for the experiments undertaken.

Following common practice in the literature, the evaluation of MT performance resorts to the BLEU metric [14], here implemented by the `multi-bleu.perl` script, part of the Moses[8] toolkit. The performance scores for the different experiments are in Table 1.

Results for Synthetic Source. The bottom line of Table 1 displays the performance scores obtained by incorporating the original monolingual corpus on the target side and the back-translated synthetic data on the source side and training PT → ZH models on this data.

The PT → ZH seed model, which uses no synthetic data, gets 10.72 BLEU points. Every other data point on that table line achieves a score higher than this seed model, with the largest score belonging to the $S_{1:3}^{s}$ model, with 3 million additional synthetic sentence pairs (a ratio of 1:3 of parallel to synthetic data). However, while the trend of increasing BLEU scores, and thus of better translation performance, is visible up to the 3 million sentence data set, translation quality degrades when one adds 6 million synthetic sentences.

The decrease in quality is probably linked to the increase in the ratio of the synthetic parallel data to the original parallel data. Whereas until this data point the addition of noisier data was overcome by the increase of diversity in the training set, with a 1:6 ratio of real to synthetic data the translation quality starts to decrease, with the noise in the synthetic sentences hurting performance.[9]

---

[8] https://www.statmt.org/moses/.

[9] In future work, further experimentation with introduction of noisy sentences could be explored by resorting to text generated by grammars [3,5,7].

Results for Synthetic Target. The first line of Table 1, in turn, shows the scores when the synthetic data is used in the target side for training ZH → PT models. We see improvements in BLEU up to a 1:3 ratio, from the 13.38 points of the seed ZH → PT model to 14.12 points of the $S_{1:3}^t$ model.

Once again, the $S_{1:6}^t$ model, trained on 6 million synthetic sentences, shows a decrease in quality when compared with the previous data point ($S_{1:3}^t$) and is only 0.01 BLEU points above the corresponding seed model, confirming what had been observed in the previous experiment, that a 1:6 ratio of original parallel data to synthetic parallel data starts to hurt translation performance.

Results for Bootstrapping. For the bootstrapping approach, whose scores are displayed in the second line of Table 1, one only sees an improvement in the first iteration, with the $S_{1:1}^t$ model (which is identical to the model in the synthetic target approach). In the subsequent stages, the performance decreases and the last iteration originates the only model ($S_{1:1:2:3}^t$) that is worse than its corresponding seed model, at 1.42 BLEU points below that starting point.

This experimental result seems to indicate that a rapid decrease in quality occurs, which may be a sign that back-translation is performed by increasingly worse models. A model trained on low-quality data will generate a low-quality synthetic parallel corpus, which when used to trained yet another model will only exacerbate the problem, with the initial positive increase (with the $S_{1:1}^t$ model) apparently not having the strength to generate synthetic data that leverages the performance of the systems in the subsequent stages.

6   Discussion and Conclusions

In this paper, we report on research concerning the viability of improving NMT for the language pair PT-ZH by (progressively) increasing the amount of training data through the back-translation of monolingual Chinese texts.

We experimented with different approaches concerning how to resort to synthetic data, with the results obtained having experimentally demonstrated that: (i) back-translation improves NMT performance for PT-ZH, with every approach experimented with surpassing the seed system to some degree; (ii) creating extended parallel texts by having the original monolingual data on the target side and the generated synthetic translations on the source side provide for the best performance improvements, strengthening this previously untested assumption found in the literature; (iii) bootstrapped NMT engines with recurrent back-translation deliver worse performance than progressive engines that rely on back-translation of increasingly larger data sets by a single seed engine; and (iv) progressive back-translation enters a decaying slope after reaching a peak of performance, rather than maintaining a steady increase: this adds to the literature on back-translation, where it is usually assumed that more synthetic data leads to better or similar MT performance.

This last aspect raises an important question.

While most literature points towards a steady increase in performance until reaching a plateau, the current work contradicts them by finding a drop in quality beyond a certain point of added synthetic data. Further studies on back-translation should focus on whether this behavior is found only for under-resourced languages, or even just for this language pair; and if other languages pairs used in other studies have a different tipping point, reached only at even larger quantities of synthetic data.

Acknowledgements. The research reported here was partially supported by POR-TULAN CLARIN—Research Infrastructure for the Science and Technology of Language, funded by Lisboa 2020, Alentejo 2020 and FCT—Fundação para a Ciência e Tecnologia under the grant PINFRA/22117/2016.

References

1. Bahdanau, D., Cho, K., Bengio, Y.: Neural machine translation by jointly learning to align and translate. In: Proceedings of the International Conference on Learning Representations (ICLR) (2015). Available as arXiv preprint arXiv:1409.0473
2. Barrault, L., et al.: Findings of the 2019 conference on machine translation (WMT19). In: Proceedings of the Fourth Conference on Machine Translation (Volume 2: Shared Task Papers, Day 1), pp. 1–61 (2019)
3. Branco, A., Costa, F.: Noun ellipsis without empty categories. In: The Proceedings of the 13th International Conference on Head-Driven Phrase Structure Grammar, pp. 81–101 (2006)
4. Branco, A., et al.: The Portuguese Language in the Digital Age. Springer, Heidelberg (2012). https://doi.org/10.1007/978-3-642-29593-5
5. Branco, A.H., Costa, F.: A computational grammar for deep linguistic processing of portuguese: Lxgram, version a.4.1. Technical report, University of Lisbon (2008)
6. Chao, L.S., Wong, D.F., Ao, C.H., Leal, A.L.: UM-PCorpus: a large Portuguese-Chinese parallel corpus. In: Proceedings of the LREC 2018 Workshop "Belt & Road: Language Resources and Evaluation", pp. 38–43 (2018)
7. Costa, F., Branco, A.: Aspectual type and temporal relation classification. In: Proceedings of the 13th Conference of the European Chapter of the Association for Computational Linguistics, pp. 266–275 (2012)
8. Edunov, S., Ott, M., Auli, M., Grangier, D.: Understanding back-translation at scale. In: Proceedings of the 2018 Conference on Empirical Methods in Natural Language Processing, pp. 489–500 (2018)
9. Hoang, V.C.D., Koehn, P., Haffari, G., Cohn, T.: Iterative back-translation for neural machine translation. In: Proceedings of the 2nd Workshop on Neural Machine Translation and Generation, pp. 18–24 (2018)
10. Imamura, K., Fujita, A., Sumita, E.: Enhancement of encoder and attention using target monolingual corpora in neural machine translation. In: Proceedings of the 2nd Workshop on Neural Machine Translation and Generation, pp. 55–63 (2018)
11. Junczys-Dowmunt, M., et al.: Marian: fast neural machine translation in C++. In: Proceedings of ACL 2018, System Demonstrations, pp. 116–121 (2018)

12. Kuang, S., Li, J., Branco, A., Luo, W., Xiong, D.: Attention focusing for neural machine translation by bridging source and target embeddings. In: Proceedings of the 56th Annual Meeting of the Association for Computational Linguistics (Volume 1: Long Papers), pp. 1767–1776 (2018)
13. Liu, S., Wang, L., Liu, C.H.: Chinese-Portuguese machine translation: a study on building parallel corpora from comparable texts. In: Proceedings of the Eleventh International Conference on Language Resources and Evaluation (LREC 2018), pp. 1485–1492 (2018)
14. Papineni, K., Roukos, S., Ward, T., Zhu, W.J.: BLEU: a method for automatic evaluation of machine translation. In: Proceedings of the 40th Annual Meeting of the Association for Computational Linguistics, pp. 311–318 (2002)
15. Poncelas, A., Shterionov, D., Way, A., de Buy Wenniger, G.M., Passban, P.: Investigating backtranslation in neural machine translation. In: 21st Annual Conference of the European Association for Machine Translation, pp. 249–258 (2018)
16. Santos, R., Silva, J., Branco, A., Xiong, D.: The direct path may not be the best: portuguese-chinese neural machine translation. In: Moura Oliveira, P., Novais, P., Reis, L.P. (eds.) EPIA 2019. LNCS (LNAI), vol. 11805, pp. 757–768. Springer, Cham (2019). https://doi.org/10.1007/978-3-030-30244-3_62
17. Sennrich, R., Haddow, B., Birch, A.: Improving neural machine translation models with monolingual data. In: Proceedings of the 54th Annual Meeting of the Association for Computational Linguistics (Volume 1: Long Papers), pp. 86–96 (2016)
18. Sennrich, R., Haddow, B., Birch, A.: Neural machine translation of rare words with subword units. In: Proceedings of the 54th Annual Meeting of the Association for Computational Linguistics (Volume 1: Long Papers), pp. 1715–1725 (2016)
19. Sutskever, I., Vinyals, O., Le, Q.V.: Sequence to sequence learning with neural networks. In: Neural Information Processing Systems, pp. 3104–3112 (2014)
20. Tiedemann, J.: Parallel data, tools and interfaces in OPUS. In: Proceedings of the Eight International Conference on Language Resources and Evaluation (LREC 2012), pp. 2214–2218 (2012)
21. Vaswani, A., et al.: Attention is all you need. In: Neural Information Processing Systems, pp. 5998–6008 (2017)
22. Wu, H., Wang, H., Zong, C.: Domain adaptation for statistical machine translation with domain dictionary and monolingual corpora. In: Proceedings of the 22nd International Conference on Computational Linguistics-Volume 1, pp. 993–1000 (2008)
23. Zhang, Z., Liu, S., Li, M., Zhou, M., Chen, E.: Joint training for neural machine translation models with monolingual data. In: Thirty-Second AAAI Conference on Artificial Intelligence (2018)

Leveraging on Semantic Textual Similarity for Developing a Portuguese Dialogue System

José Santos[1,2(✉)] (ID), Ana Alves[1,3] (ID), and Hugo Gonçalo Oliveira[1,2] (ID)

[1] CISUC, University of Coimbra, Coimbra, Portugal
santos@student.dei.uc.pt,{ana,hroliv}@dei.uc.pt
[2] DEI, University of Coimbra, Coimbra, Portugal
[3] ISEC, Polytechnic Institute of Coimbra, Coimbra, Portugal

Abstract. We describe an IR-based dialogue system that, in order to match user interactions with FAQs on a list, leverages on a model for computing the semantic similarity between two fragments of Portuguese text. It was mainly used for answering questions about the economic activity in Portugal and, when no FAQ has a higher score than a threshold, it may search for similar interactions in a corpus of movie subtitles and still tries to give a suitable response. Besides describing the underlying model and its integration, we assess it when answering variations of FAQs and report on an experiment to set the aforementioned threshold.

Keywords: Semantic Textual Similarity · Question answering · Dialogue systems · Conversational agents · Machine learning

1 Introduction

Semantic Textual Similarity (STS) aims at computing the proximity of meaning of two fragments of text. Shared tasks on the topic have been organized in the scope of SemEval 2012 [2] to 2017 [7], targeting English, Arabic and Spanish. In 2016, the ASSIN shared task [11] focused on STS for Portuguese, and its collection was made available. It was followed by ASSIN 2 [24], in 2019.

We see a clear application of STS for mapping pairs of sentences that, though possibly having different surface forms, do have a similar meaning (e.g., *What is the procedure for participating?* and *How can I enter?*). In fact, in SemEval 2016 STS task [1], one dataset was on question-question similarity. This capability is extremely useful for dialogue systems that answer natural language questions.

Following this idea, we trained a model for STS in Portuguese and used it as the engine of a dialogue system, dubbed Cobaia. The primary goal of Cobaia is to answer (domain) questions, in a list of Frequently Asked Questions (FAQs). More precisely, it was used for answering questions about the exercise of economic activity in Portugal. Since users will rarely write their questions exactly as they are stored, to simulate user interactions, variations (roughly, paraphrases) of real

© Springer Nature Switzerland AG 2020
P. Quaresma et al. (Eds.): PROPOR 2020, LNAI 12037, pp. 131–142, 2020.
https://doi.org/10.1007/978-3-030-41505-1_13

FAQs on the aforementioned domain were automatically generated with Google Translate API. Others were created manually and can be more "creative". When using the STS model for matching variations with the original FAQs, we computed the proportion of correct matches and confirmed that human-created variations are harder to match. Furthermore, when, for a given interaction, there is no FAQ with similarity higher than a threshold θ, such interaction is labelled as out-of-domain (OOD). Towards a more "humanised" behavior, in this case, Cobaia may retrieve a suitable answer from an OOD corpus of movie subtitles. This often works well for greetings or general chit-chat. We also analyse the impact of setting different values of θ.

In the remainder of the paper, we overview related work on dialogue systems and IR-based natural language interfaces to FAQs. We then describe the STS model, how it was trained, and report on its performance for matching text variations with FAQs. Before concluding, we search for the best threshold and present an example conversation with the resulting system.

2   Related Work

Dialogue systems typically exploit large collections of text, often including conversations. Generative systems model conversations with a neural network that learns to decode sequences of text and translate them to other sequences, used as responses [29]. Such systems are generally scalable and versatile, always generate a response, but have limitations for performing specific tasks. As they make few assumptions on the domain and generally have no access to external sources of knowledge, they can rarely handle factual content. They also tend to be too repetitive and provide inconsistent, trivial or meaningless answers.

Domain-oriented dialogue systems tend to follow other strategies and integrate Information Retrieval (IR) and Question Answering (QA) techniques to find the most relevant response for natural language requests. In traditional IR, a query represents an information need, typically in the form of keywords, to be answered with a list of documents. Relevant documents are generally selected because they mention the keywords, or are about the topics they convey. Automatic QA [30], diversely, finds answers to natural language questions. Answers can be retrieved from a knowledge base [26] or from a collection of documents [17]. This has similarities to IR, but queries have to be further interpreted, possibly reasoned – where Natural Language Understanding (NLU) capabilities may be necessary –, while answers are expected to go beyond a mere list of documents.

Given a user input, IR-based conversational agents search for the most similar request on the corpus and output their response (e.g., [15]). A common approach for finding similar texts computes the cosine between the input vector and indexed texts. This can be combined with alternative ranking functions, learned specifically for that purpose, and achieved, for instance, with a regression model that considers several lexical or semantic features to measure Semantic Textual Similarity (STS, [8]). This is also a common approach of systems participating in STS shared tasks (e.g., [7]), some of which covering pairs of questions and their similarity [1]. A related shared task is Community Question Answering [20,21], where similarity between questions and comments or other questions is computed, for ranking purposes.

STS can also be useful in the development of natural language interfaces for lists of Frequently Asked Questions (FAQs). Due to their nature and structure, the latter should be seen as valuable resources for exploitation. On this context, there has been interest on SMS-based interfaces for FAQs [18], work for QA from FAQs in Croatian [16], and a shared task on this topic, in Italian [6]. For retrieving suitable answers, the similarity between user queries and available FAQs is computed by exploiting word overlap [16], the presence of synonyms [18, 23], or distributional semantic features [12,16].

In opposition to generative systems, IR-based dialogue systems do not handle very well requests for which there is no similar text in the corpus. Though, an alternative IR-based strategy can still be followed, in this case, for finding similar texts in a more general corpus, such as movie subtitles [19].

3   Training a Model for Portuguese STS

Our STS model was developed with a supervised learning approach. Training was performed on the collections of ASSIN and ASSIN 2, comprising a total of ≈20,000 sentence pairs with their similarity score, based on human opinions, ranging between 1 (completely different) and 5 (equivalent).

To compute the STS between sentence pairs, a set of 71 features was initially extracted, which included lexical, syntactic, semantic and distributional. They were obtained with the following Python libraries: NLTK [4], for getting token and character n-grams; NLPPyPort [10] (NLTK with some improvements for Portuguese), for getting Part-of-Speech (PoS) tags, named entities and lemmas; Gensim [25] and scikit-learn [22], for extracting distributional features.

After testing several regression algorithms available in scikit-learn for this purpose, the best results were obtained with a Support Vector Regressor (SVR), with default parameters. It was trained on both train collections of ASSIN and tested individually on each test collection. Performance was assessed with the Pearson correlation (ρ) and Mean Squared Error (MSE) between the values computed and those in the collection.

Having in mind the scalability of the model, we further tried to reduce the dimensionality of the feature set. For this purpose, we explored three types of feature selection methods, also available in scikit-learn: Univariate, Model-based and Iterative Feature Selection. In order to assess which method improved the performance of the model the most, in comparison to each other and to using all features, the model's coefficient of determination R^2 of the prediction was used for each different method. Given the nature of the previous methods, we believe that, to some extent, their application is equivalent to an ablation study.

Therefore, the initial set of 71 features was reduced to 27, which represented the 38% most relevant, according to Univariate Statistics, the method leading to highest performance. The features effectively considered were:

- Jaccard, Overlap and Dice coefficients, each computed between the sets of token 1/2/3-grams and character 2/3/4-grams.
- Averaged token vectors, computed with the following word embeddings: word2vec-cbow, GloVe (300-sized, from NILC [14]), fastText.cc [5], Numberbatch [28] and PT-LKB [13].
- TF-IDF-weighted averaged token vectors, computed with the following word embeddings: word2vec-cbow, GloVe (300-sized, from NILC [14]), fastText.cc [5] and Numberbatch [28].

Table 1 shows the results of the selected model when trained in both training collections ($\approx$12,500 pairs) and tested in each test collection. Since performance was slightly above the official best results in the ASSIN evaluation [11], we were happy with it and moved on to integrate the STS model in our dialogue system (Sect. 4). As more training data should result in better performance, the model was finally trained in both train and test collections, exclusively for integration in the dialogue system.

Table 1. Performance of the STS model in the ASSIN 1 and 2 test collections.

Metric	ASSIN PTPT (2,000 pairs)	ASSIN PTBR (2,000 pairs)	ASSIN 2 (2,448 pairs)
ρ	0.74	0.73	0.73
MSE	0.58	0.36	0.58

4   Integration in a Dialogue System

The developed STS model was used as the engine of Cobaia, an IR-based dialogue system that, primarily, answers questions related to a specific domain. More precisely, given a user interaction, the STS model retrieves the question with highest similarity score, together with its answer. For experimentation purposes, a list of 379 FAQs on the exercise of economic activity in Portugal was used. It contains 120 FAQs from the Guide for the Application of the Legal Regime for Access and Exercise of Trade, Services and Catering Activities (*Guia de Aplicação do Regime Jurídico de Acesso e Exercício de Atividades de Comércio, Serviços e Restauração – RJACSR*), 56 from the Legislation of the Local Accommodation (*Legislação do Alojamento Local*), and 203 from the Business Spot (*Portal Empresa*)[1]. This section describes how paraphrases and other variations of the FAQs were created and used in the evaluation of the STS model in this context, and then reports on the results obtained.

---

[1] FAQs were downloaded from *Balcão do Empreendedor* (BDE) portal, the Portuguese Entrepreneur's Desk, on June 2018.

4.1   Question Variations

To test the STS model in this domain, a more systematic evaluation was carried out. Bearing in mind that users rarely search for the exact question, variations of the original questions were created in two ways: (i) Using the Google Translate API[2] for generating paraphrases of the original questions, as follows: translation of Portuguese to English and back to Portuguese (VG1); the previous result back to English and back to Portuguese (VG2). (ii) Manually, by a group of native Portuguese speaking volunteers, including not only paraphrases of the original questions, but also closely-related/entailed questions, some of which possibly including spelling mistakes (VUC). Such variations were only produced for the RJACSR and Local Accommodation FAQs, but there is more than one variation of this kind for each question, making a total of 451 variations. The 213 questions remaining without a variation are still used as matching candidates.

Table 2 illustrates the resulting dataset, with examples of original questions (P), their variations, and rough English translations. We note that the surface form of the Google Translate (VG) variations is much closer to the original questions than for the human-created (VUC).

4.2   Evaluation Results

The STS model was used for matching question variations with the original questions. The number and proportion of correct matches for each variation group is in Table 3. For comparison purposes, we include results for the original questions (ORI) and two baselines: (i) search on a Whoosh[3] index of our dataset, created with its Portuguese analyzer; (ii) interaction with Chatterbot[4], trained with our dataset and based on the Leventshtein distance. To check whether correct matches are close to the top, for Cobaia, the same table has figures considering their presence in the top-3 and top-5 retrieved candidates.

As expected, due to the nature of each variation group, and apart from the original questions, the best results were for VG1, with 89% correct matches, and increasing when considering the top-3 (96%) and top-5 ranked questions (97%). Results for VG2 are slightly below, due to variation caused by the additional round of translation. Correct matches for VUC variations were ≈63%, and ≈84% in the top-5. We recall that each variation could be mapped to one out of 379 questions. This lower performance was expected, because, as Table 2 shows, VUC variations are more "creative", though also closer to a real-world scenario. In any case, performance is significantly above the tested baselines, which confirms that IR-based dialogue systems may benefit from STS.

---

[2] https://cloud.google.com/translate/docs/.

[3] Whoosh (https://whoosh.readthedocs.io) is a search engine library in Python.

[4] Chatterbot (https://chatterbot.readthedocs.io) is a Python library for generating responses to user input.

Table 2. Examples of the different question variations used to test the system.

Var	Text
P	*Qual a coima aplicável às contraordenações graves?*
	(What is the fine applicable to severe misconducts?)
VG1	*Qual é a multa aplicável à falta grave?*
	(What is the penalty applicable to a severe fault?)
VG2	*Qual é a multa aplicável à falta grave?*
	(What is the penalty applicable to a severe fault?)
VUC	*coima para contraordenação grave*
	(fine for severe misconduct)
P	*Se a exploração do meu apartamento passar para outra pessoa, tenho de fazer um novo registo?*
	(If the exploration of my apartment becomes the responsability of someone else, do I have to do a new registration?)
VG1	*Se a exploração do meu apartamento passar para outra pessoa, preciso fazer um novo registro?*
	(If the exploration of my apartment becomes the responsability of someone else, do I need to do a new registration?)
VG2	*Se a exploração do meu apartamento passar para outra pessoa, preciso me registrar novamente?*
	(If the exploration of my apartment becomes the responsability of someone else, do I need to register it again?)
VUC	*É necessário renovar o registo de um apartamento de que deixei de explorar?*
	(Is it necessary to renew the registration of an apartment that I do not explore anymore?)

Table 3. Performance when tested in all the FAQ variations.

Variations	Questions	Whoosh		Chatterbot		Cobaia					
	#	#	%	#	%	First		Top-3		Top-5	
						#	%	#	%	#	%
ORI	379	378	99.74	373	98.42	370	97.63	379	100	379	100
VG1	379	29	7.65	48	12.66	338	89.18	364	96.04	368	97.10
VG2	379	21	5.54	33	8.71	333	88.09	360	94.98	365	96.31
VUC	451	47	10.42	15	3.33	288	63.86	362	80.27	379	84.04
Total	1,209	97	8.02	102	8.44	959	79.32	1012	83.71	1112	91.98

4.3 Error Analysis

To better understand where the model is failing, we started by looking at incorrect matches for the group with the less amount of variation, VG1. Table 4 has three situations that sum up most issues. Each line has a variation for which an incorrect match was given, the incorrectly given and the correct match.

In the first, the given match (similarity = 4.1) uses the same words as the correct one, except for the last entity. Very similar questions mislead the selection, which suggests that, when similarity is close among the top candidates, more than one candidate could be given. Issues with the second example (similarity = 3.7) were due to the paraphrasing method resulting in too literal translations: *Empresa na Hora* is the name of an initiative, here translated to 'Company on Time', and *levantamento* was translated to 'raise' instead of 'withdraw'. In the last example (similarity = 2.8), the variation became more vague by not saying that registration (*registro*) has to be by transcription (*por transcrição*). Remaining content words were replaced by a synonym (*pedidos↦solicitações*, *efetuar↦fazer*) or by the Brazilian writing (*registo↦registro*). Although character n-gram features should capture the latter, synonymy was not explicitly covered by the reduced STS model, only relatedness.

Table 4. Incorrect matches of variations in VG1.

Variation	Given match	Correct match
Depois de enviar os documentos, ainda preciso enviar os originais ao Registro Comercial?	*Depois de submeter os documentos, ainda preciso de enviar os originais para o RNPC?*	*Depois de submeter os documentos, ainda preciso de enviar os originais para a Conservatória do Registo Comercial?*
Quando é possível aumentar o capital social da "Empresa em Tempo"?	*Quando é possível o levantamento do capital social da Empresa Online?*	*Quando é possível o levantamento do capital social da "Empresa na Hora"?*
Quais solicitações de registro eu posso fazer?	*Para que tipo de sociedades posso fazer registos por depósito?*	*Que pedidos de registo por transcrição posso efetuar?*

5 Out-of-Domain Interactions

A common limitation of IR-based dialogue systems is in handling OOD interactions. Though not always required, to give the system a more human-like behaviour, it would be interesting to have responses for those cases. While there could be a small set of predefined responses, a larger set can be obtained from a corpus of previous conversations, such as movie subtitles. This section reports on the selection of a threshold θ on STS for identifying OOD interactions and then describes a small conversation with Cobaia, the resulting dialogue system.

5.1   Identifying Out-of-Domain Interactions

For labelling an interaction as OOD or not, we simply rely on the STS score of the best candidate FAQ. If it is below a certain θ, we consider it OOD. To set a suitable θ, we inspect its impact in our dataset. Table 5 has the number of correct matches for different values of θ, given that STS scores range between 1 and 5. As only a minority of variations (one for VG1, two for VG2, five for VUC) is correctly matched with questions for which similarity is below 2.5, we set θ to this value. Though we could rely in a more standard method, we aim to avoid, as much as possible, to leave questions for which there is an answer unanswered, due to being considered OOD. For instance, for VUC, $\theta = 3.3$ maximises the difference between true and false positive rates, but this θ considers many questions OOD that, with a lower θ, would be correctly answered. The impact of incorrect answers is further minimised by presenting the matching question together with their answer.

Table 5. Performance of selected STS model when matching FAQ variations with different thresholds on similarity.

Variation	Questions	$\theta = 2$		$\theta = 2.5$		$\theta = 3$		$\theta = 3.5$		$\theta = 4$	
	#	#	%	#	%	#	%	#	%	#	%
ORI	379	370	97.63	370	97.63	370	97.63	370	97.63	370	97.63
VG1	379	338	89.18	337	88.92	327	86.28	286	75.46	183	48.28
VG2	379	333	87.86	331	87.34	321	84.70	276	72.82	170	44.85
VUC	451	286	63.41	281	62.31	240	53.22	167	37.03	68	15.10
Total	1,209	957	79.16	949	78.49	888	73.45	729	60,30	421	34.82

5.2   Answering Out-of-Domain Interactions

Once θ is set, when an interaction is labeled as OOD, Cobaia may look for a suitable answer in the Portuguese part of Subtle [19], a corpus of movie subtitles with 3M interactions. Yet, to minimise the number of out-of-context responses, those with named entities (identified with NLPPyPort's NER module) were removed, leaving us with ≈2.4M. This size still means that computing an STS score with every interaction is not scalable. So, Subtle interactions were indexed in Whoosh and, for each OOD interaction, the 30 most relevant are first retrieved from the index, and STS is computed only for them. The response for the interaction with the highest similarity, also indexed, is finally given.

A conversation session with the resulting system is in Appendix A. User interactions start with **Me:** and system interactions with **Cobaia:**. Conversation starts with the user greeting the Cobaia and Cobaia greeting them back. The user asks for help and Cobaia says 'help' twice. Then, the user makes four questions:

the first, second and fourth are identified by Cobaia as domain questions. To make sure that it is answering the right question, Cobaia's answer starts by *"If your question was..."*, followed by the matched question and its answer as in the list of FAQs. The third question was incorrectly identified as OOD, and no suitable answer was found, nor in Subtle, so Cobaia just says that it did not understand. Finally, the user thanks Cobaia and says *'goodbye'*. Cobaia thanks the user for making it feel lighter (*leve*) and says *'goodbye'* four times.

With the previous and other sessions, we confirmed that it is possible to have a conversation with Cobaia, which is capable of switching between domain and OOD interactions, even though some responses to the latter might be odd.

6   Conclusion

We described how a dialogue system may leverage on STS and presented Cobaia, a Portuguese dialogue system that uses a STS model, trained in the ASSIN collections, for matching user questions (for evaluation purposes, variations of original questions) with FAQs in a list. As expected, performance is higher when questions are made in a similar way to how they are originally written. It further relies on the computed similarity for identifying OOD interactions and, when all FAQs have low similarity, retrieves an interaction from a corpus of subtitles.

Future improvements should focus both on STS and on the dialogue system. For instance, ASSIN contains only declarative sentences, but the model was used for computing question similarity, which is probably not the most suitable scenario. There is work on better understanding the impact of doing this [27] but, to our knowledge, no collection with pairs of Portuguese questions with their STS (e.g., as the one used in SemEval 2016 STS task [1]) is available. It might be interesting to create such a collection in the future. For the moment, an augmented version of the dataset used in this work is freely available, under the name AIA-BDE, from: https://github.com/hgoliv/AIA-BDE.

On additional features to explore, it should be useful to consider domain acronyms, and it might be worth considering the conversation context and integrating contextual word embeddings [9] in the STS model.

Evaluation of Cobaia relied on a set of question variations. While writing them manually is time-consuming, using automatically-created variations can be far from the real scenario, because the user may write the same questions with a significantly different surface form. More sophisticated paraphrase generation methods [3] may be worth exploring for this purpose. Moreover, the error analysis showed that similar FAQs may result in incorrect matches, which can be minimised by providing answers not for one, but for a set of FAQs for which similarity was high. This is already a parameter in the current version of Cobaia.

Finally, although the used FAQs are about economic activity in Portugal, Cobaia may be adapted to other domains, as long as lists of FAQ are available.

Acknolwedgements. This work was funded by FCT's INCoDe 2030 initiative, in the scope of the demonstration project AIA, "Apoio Inteligente a empreendedores (chatbots)".

A   Example Conversation

```
Me:     Olá tudo bem?
Cobaia: Sim, tudo bem.
Me:     Sou o José
Cobaia: É um prazer.
Me:     Ajudas-me?
Cobaia: Ajuda! Ajuda!
Me:     existem empresas que não podem ser configuradas nos contadores empresa no horário
Cobaia: Se a sua pergunta foi: ''Há sociedades que não podem ser constituídas nos balcões
        "Empresa na Hora"?''...
        Sim, é o caso das sociedades cuja constituição careça de autorizações prévias para o
        efeito, das sociedades cujo capital social seja realizado por entradas em espécie,
        das sociedades anónimas europeias, dos agrupamentos complementares de empresas, das
        cooperativas e das ...
Me:     o que são sociedades anónimas
Cobaia: Se a sua pergunta foi: ''O que são Sociedades Anónimas?''...
        Neste tipo de empresa, os sócios limitam a sua responsabilidade ao valor das ações
        por si subscritas. Assim, os credores sociais só se podem fazer pagar pelos bens
        sociais...
Me:     Que medidas de segurança devo aplicar num alojamento local para mais de 10 hóspedes?
Cobaia: Desculpe, não percebi, pode colocar a sua questão de outra forma?
Me:     se tiver um estabelecimento com mais que 9 quartos e não conseguir fazer a alteração
        para empreendimento turístico, tenho de o fechar?
Cobaia: Se a sua pergunta foi: ''O que acontece aos estabelecimentos de alojamento local
        registados ao abrigo da legislação anterior que tenham mais de 9 quartos e não
        consigam por algum motivo fazer a sua alteração para empreendimento turístico? Têm
        de encerrar?''...
        Não, os limites previstos no artigo 11.º do Decreto-Lei n.º 128/2014, de 29 de
        agosto, apenas se aplicam aos estabelecimentos de alojamento local registados após a
        sua entrada em vigor.
Me:     Obrigado pela ajuda!
Cobaia: Obrigado por me porem leve.
Me:     Vou embora
Cobaia: Vou-me embora! Espero que estejas feliz!
Me:     Adeus
Cobaia: Adeus, adeus. Adeus, adeus.
```

References

1. Agirre, E., et al.: SemEval-2016 task 1: semantic textual similarity, monolingual and cross-lingual evaluation. In: Proceedings of 10th International Workshop on Semantic Evaluation (SemEval-2016), pp. 497–511. Association for Computational Linguistics, San Diego, California, June 2016
2. Agirre, E., Diab, M., Cer, D., Gonzalez-Agirre, A.: Semeval-2012 task 6: a pilot on semantic textual similarity. In: Proceedings of 1st Joint Conference on Lexical and Computational Semantics-vol. 1: Proceedings of Main Conference and Shared Task, and, vol. 2: Proceedings of 6th International Workshop on Semantic Evaluation, pp. 385–393. Association for Computational Linguistics (2012)
3. Barreiro, A.: Make it simple with paraphrases: Automated paraphrasing for authoring aids and machine translation. Ph.D. thesis, Universidade do Porto (2009)
4. Bird, S., Klein, E., Loper, E.: Natural Language Processing with Python. O'Reilly Media, Beijing (2009)
5. Bojanowski, P., Grave, E., Joulin, A., Mikolov, T.: Enriching word vectors with subword information. Trans. Assoc. Comput. Linguist. 5, 135–146 (2017)
6. Caputo, A., Degemmis, M., Lops, P., Lovecchio, F., Manzari, V.: Overview of the EVALITA 2016 question answering for frequently asked questions (QA4FAQ) task. In: Proceedings of 3rd Italian Conference on Computational Linguistics (CLiC-it 2016) & 5th Evaluation Campaign of Natural Language Processing and Speech Tools for Italian. Final Workshop (EVALITA 2016). CEUR Workshop Proceedings, vol. 1749. CEUR-WS.org (2016)

7. Cer, D., Diab, M., Agirre, E., Lopez-Gazpio, I., Specia, L.: SemEval-2017 task 1: semantic textual similarity multilingual and crosslingual focused evaluation. In: Proceedings of 11th International Workshop on Semantic Evaluation (SemEval-2017), pp. 1–14. Association for Computational Linguistics (2017)
8. Cui, L., Huang, S., Wei, F., Tan, C., Duan, C., Zhou, M.: Superagent: a customer service chatbot for e-commerce websites. In: Proceedings of 55th Annual Meeting of the Association for Computational Linguistics, ACL 2017, System Demonstrations, pp. 97–102. Association for Computational Linguistics (2017)
9. Devlin, J., Chang, M.W., Lee, K., Toutanova, K.: BERT: pre-training of deep bidirectional transformers for language understanding. In: Proceedings of 2019 Conference of the North American Chapter of the Association for Computational Linguistics: Human Language Technologies, Volume 1 (Long and Short Papers), pp. 4171–4186. Association for Computational Linguistics, Minneapolis, Minnesota, June 2019
10. Ferreira, J., Gonçalo Oliveira, H., Rodrigues, R.: Improving NLTK for processing Portuguese. In: Symposium on Languages, Applications and Technologies (SLATE 2019). OASIcs, vol. 74, pp. 18:1–18:9. Schloss Dagstuhl, June 2019
11. Fonseca, E., Santos, L., Criscuolo, M., Aluísio, S.: Visão geral da avaliação de similaridade semântica e inferência textual. Linguamática **8**(2), 3–13 (2016)
12. Fonseca, E.R., Magnolini, S., Feltracco, A., Qwaider, M.R.H., Magnini, B.: Tweaking word embeddings for FAQ ranking. In: Proceedings of 5th Evaluation Campaign of Natural Language Processing and Speech Tools for Italian, vol. 1749. CEUR-WS (2016)
13. Gonçalo Oliveira, H.: Learning word embeddings from portuguese lexical-semantic knowledge bases. In: Villavicencio, A., Moreira, V., Abad, A., Caseli, H., Gamallo, P., Ramisch, C., Gonçalo Oliveira, H., Paetzold, G.H. (eds.) PROPOR 2018. LNCS (LNAI), vol. 11122, pp. 265–271. Springer, Cham (2018). https://doi.org/10.1007/978-3-319-99722-3_27
14. Hartmann, N.S., Fonseca, E.R., Shulby, C.D., Treviso, M.V., Rodrigues, J.S., Aluísio, S.M.: Portuguese word embeddings: evaluating on word analogies and natural language tasks. In: Proceedings of 11th Brazilian Symposium in Information and Human Language Technology. STIL 2017 (2017)
15. Ji, Z., Lu, Z., Li, H.: An information retrieval approach to short text conversation. ArXiv abs/1408.6988 (2014)
16. Karan, M., Žmak, L., Šnajder, J.: Frequently asked questions retrieval for Croatian based on semantic textual similarity. In: Proceedings of 4th Biennial Intl. Workshop on Balto-Slavic Natural Language Processing, pp. 24–33. Association for Computational Linguistics, Sofia, Bulgaria, August 2013
17. Kolomiyets, O., Moens, M.F.: A survey on question answering technology from an information retrieval perspective. Inf. Sci. **181**(24), 5412–5434 (2011)
18. Kothari, G., Negi, S., Faruquie, T.A., Chakaravarthy, V.T., Subramaniam, L.V.: SMS based interface for FAQ retrieval. In: Proceedings of Joint Conference of the 47th Annual Meeting of the ACL and the 4th International Joint Conference on Natural Language Processing of the AFNLP: Volume 2, pp. 852–860. ACL 2009, Association for Computational Linguistics (2009)
19. Magarreiro, D., Coheur, L., Melour, F.S.: Using subtitles to deal with out-of-domain interactions. In: Proceedings of 18th Workshop on the Semantics and Pragmatics of Dialogue (SemDial), pp. 98–106 (2014)
20. Nakov, P., et al.: SemEval-2017 task 3: community question answering. In: Proceedings of 11th International Workshop on Semantic Evaluation (SemEval-2017), pp. 27–48. Association for Computational Linguistics, August 2017

21. Nakov, P., et al.: SemEval-2016 task 3: community question answering. In: Proceedings of 10th International Workshop on Semantic Evaluation. Association for Computational Linguistics, June 2016
22. Pedregosa, F., et al.: Scikit-learn: machine learning in Python. J. Mach. Learn. Res. **12**, 2825–2830 (2011)
23. Pipitone, A., Tirone, G., Pirrone, R.: ChiLab4It system in the QA4FAQ competition. In: Proceedings of 5th Evaluation Campaign of Natural Language Processing and Speech Tools for Italian, vol. 1749. CEUR-WS (2016). http://ceur-ws.org/Vol-1749/
24. Real, L., Fonseca, E., Oliveira, H.G.: The assin 2 shared task: a quick overview. In: Computational Processing of the Portuguese Language - 13th International Conference, PROPOR 2020, Évora, Portugal, 2–4 March 2020, Proceedings, LNCS. Springer, Heidelberg (2020). https://doi.org/10.1007/978-3-030-41505-1
25. Řehůřek, R., Sojka, P.: Software framework for topic modelling with large Corpora. In: Proceedings of LREC 2010 Workshop on New Challenges for NLP Frameworks, pp. 45–50. ELRA, Valletta, Malta, May 2010
26. Rinaldi, F., Dowdall, J., Hess, M., Mollá, D., Schwitter, R., Kaljurand, K.: Knowledge-based question answering. In: Palade, V., Howlett, R.J., Jain, L. (eds.) KES 2003. LNCS (LNAI), vol. 2773, pp. 785–792. Springer, Heidelberg (2003). https://doi.org/10.1007/978-3-540-45224-9_106
27. Rodrigues, J., Saedi, C., Branco, A., Silva, J.: Semantic equivalence detection: are interrogatives harder than declaratives? In: Proceedings of 11th Language Resources and Evaluation Conference. ELRA, Miyazaki, Japan, May 2018
28. Speer, R., Chin, J., Havasi, C.: Conceptnet 5.5: an open multilingual graph of general knowledge. In: Proceedings of 31st AAAI Conference on Artificial Intelligence, pp. 4444–4451. San Francisco, California, USA (2017)
29. Vinyals, O., Le, Q.V.: A neural conversational model. In: Proceedings of ICML 2015 Deep Learning Workshop. Lille, France (2015)
30. Voorhees, E.M.: The TREC question answering track. Nat. Lang. Eng. **7**(4), 361–378 (2001)

Fake News Detection on Fake.Br Using Hierarchical Attention Networks

Emerson Yoshiaki Okano[1]([✉])(iD), Zebin Liu[2](iD), Donghong Ji[2](iD), and Evandro Eduardo Seron Ruiz[1](iD)

[1] Departamento de Computação e Matemática – FFCLRP,
Universidade de São Paulo, Avenida dos Bandeirantes, 3900 – Monte Alegre,
14040-901 Ribeirão Preto, SP, Brazil
{okano700,evandro}@usp.br
[2] School of Cyber Science and Engineering, Wuhan University, #299, Bayi Road,
Wuchang District, Wuhan 430072, China
dhji@whu.edu.cn, 1579670185@qq.com

Abstract. Automatic fake news detection is a challenging problem in natural language processing, and contributions in this field may induce immense social impacts. This article examines the use of Hierarchical Attention Network (HAN) as a method for automatic fake news detection. We evaluate the proposed models in the Brazilian Portuguese fake news parallel corpus Fake.Br using its original full text, and also in the truncated version. We run the HAN varying the size of word embedding from 100 to 600, and by maintaining and removing the stop words. This method achieved an accuracy of 97% for full texts using the word embedding size of 600 from GloVe. However, when comparing running this method for truncated texts, this method presents similar results (90% accuracy) to the baseline established by the simple machine learning methods presented in the original presentation work of the Fake.Br (89% accuracy). Overall, keeping or removing stop words and varying the size of the word embeddings also shows a negligible advantage.

Keywords: Hierarchical attention networks · Deep learning · Text classification · Fake news

1 Introduction

Lately, the term fake news is of frequent use, a neologism, referring either as misinformation, fabricated news, or false information presented in a way that it may seem factually accurate. Lazer and colleagues define "fake news" as fabricated information that mimics news media content in form but not in organizational process or intent [8]. One of the most notorious cases of fake news in science is related to the 1998 paper by Wakefield [17], published in The Lancet, reporting a link between autism and the measles, mumps, and rubella (MMR) vaccine. As numerous other studies fail to replicate these associations, this is a real sign of falsified data in the original study. Nowadays, Wakefield's dangerous claims are

© Springer Nature Switzerland AG 2020
P. Quaresma et al. (Eds.): PROPOR 2020, LNAI 12037, pp. 143–152, 2020.
https://doi.org/10.1007/978-3-030-41505-1_14

still causing direct harm to children whose parents insist not to vaccinate them due to the alleged lifelong conditions imposed by autism.

Another landmark was in 2016 when the word fake news became very famous due to two decisive political events (the Brexit referendum in the UK and the presidential election in the US). These events coincide with the rise of searches for the term "fake news" in Google[1] in this year. On another hand, this buzzword becomes famous in Brazil in 2018 due to the presidential election.

Presently this fake news nightmare turned to be the high-speed phenomena carrying this fabricated news from cellphones to cellphones, from families to families. The consequences of fake news are everywhere, from the anti-vaccine movement to politics [1].

Recently there has been much effort to fight against fake news. Companies such as Facebook, Google, and Bing have joined forces to create "The Trust Project"[2], that created the Trust indicator which helps people to differentiate real news from fake news.

The content of fake news is rather diverse in terms of topics, styles, and media platforms. To help mitigate the adverse effects caused by fake news, it is of utmost importance to develop methods that automatically detect fake news on social media [14]. Although the language has no direct connection to distinguish real and fake news, legitimate and faked news articles use language differently in ways that can be detected by algorithms. The distinctive ways language is used to detect fake news have been explored by a number of research groups, such as [4, 8,9,11,14] and [16]. In this article, we employ a deep learning based automated detector approach using a three-level Hierarchical Attention Network (HAN) accurate detection of fake news. Regarding the work of Monteiro *et al.* [9] that establishes a baseline classification metric using machine learning techniques, the present work tests the effectiveness of a HAN to detect deception on written texts. We also expect that by applying a HAN model, its attention layers could highlight the most relevant sentences for the classifier.

The remainder of this article is organized as follows. In Sect. 2, we start by overviewing related works on fake news detection. In Sect. 3, we briefly discuss the datasets and explain the network model adopted. The results are presented in Sect. 4, and we conclude in Sect. 5.

2   Related Work

As James Kershner pointed out in his book [7] "So what makes fake news fake? If news refers to an accurate account of a real event, what does fake news mean?" Actually, 'fake news' has become a buzzword. Nowadays, this term does not differentiate misinformation in the media from actually fabricated news, nor a news satire from large-scale hoaxes, rumors. Only recently, on an article by Tandoc Jr. and colleagues [16], the authors clearly identified the dimensions that guided previous definitions of fake news, offering a typology based on such

---

[1] http://bit.ly/2og4zvV.
[2] https://thetrustproject.org.

dimensions that include news satire, news parody, news fabrication, advertising material, propaganda (referring to news stories created by a political entities), and even photo manipulation.

Earlier, Conroy, Rubin, and Chen [4] also propose a typology to asses veracity composed of methods emerging from two major categories, which are: linguistic cue approaches and network analysis approaches. They concluded proposing operational guidelines based on a hybrid approach that combine both previously cited categories. In another article [12], we understand that these same authors inaugurated a more computer methodological focused research on deception detection. They analyzed rhetorical structures, discourse constituent parts, and their coherence relations in deceptive and in real news samples. They further applied a vector space model to cluster the news by discourse feature similarity, achieving 63% accuracy.

Recently Pérez-Rosas and co-authors [11] focused on the automatic detection of fake online news. Their dualistic work consists of two novel datasets, covering seven different news topics, for fake news disclosure; and a set of learning experiments able to detect fake news achieving accuracies of up to 76%. Some of the linguistic features are also presented in the work of Okano and Ruiz [13], where they tested 76 linguistic cues on the Fake.Br [9] parallel corpus and achieved accuracy results of 75% using support vector machines (SVM), random forest, and logistic regression. We address the work of Monteiro and colleagues [9] about the construction of the Fake.Br, the first Brazilian Portuguese parallel fake news corpus, later, on Sect. 3.1.

One of the first attempts to use HAN in social media was aimed to detect rumor in microblogs was reported by [5]. They build a hierarchical bidirectional long short-term memory (BLSTM) model for representation learning. The social contexts were incorporated into the network via attention mechanism in a way that that important semantic information was introduced to the framework for robust rumor detection. They achieved 94% using F1-measure on rumorous Weibo microblogs and 82.5% on tweets.

Hierarchical Attention Networks were first introduced in 2016 by Yang and collaborators [19], a partnership between Carnegie Mellon and Microsoft. As they emphasize, they propose this novel structure that mirrors the hierarchical structure of documents. This model incorporates the knowledge of document structure in the model architecture. It also has two levels of attention mechanisms that, when applied to the word and sentence-level, enable more or less importance to the content when constructing the document representation. They applied this new neural network on six large scale document classification data sets for two classification tasks: sentiment estimation and topic classification, and concluded that the proposed architecture outperforms previous methods by a significant margin.

Following Yang's article, we call attention to the work of Yang, Mukherjee, and Dragut [18] who used an attention mechanism and some linguistic features to recognize satirical cues at the paragraph level. They investigated the difference between paragraph-level features and document-level features and revealed what features are essential at which level. Singhania and collaborators [15] also have tested this three-level hierarchical attention network, which they called 3HAN, but aiming for accurate detection of fake news. By their experiments, they argue that despite other deep learning models, the 3HAN model provides an 'understandable output through the attention weights given to different parts of an article'. In this paper, we innovate by proposing a HAN for document classification written in Brazilian Portuguese as disjoint labels of fake or real news, and also by adopting a categorical cross-entropy as loss function that measures the performance of the classification model in the $[0, 1]$ interval.

3   Dataset and Methods

In this section, we discuss the available dataset and present the algorithms used for fake news detection. We also focus on evaluation metrics for this task.

3.1   Fake.Br Corpus

The Fake.Br Corpus [9] is the first fake news reference corpus for Portuguese. It is composed of aligned pairs of authentic and fake news. This corpus is composed of 7,200 news, where 3,600 are fake news, and 3,600 are their real correspondent news. Table 1 shows the distributions of the news in each category.

Table 1. Sampling distribution per category in Fake.BR. Adapted from Monteiro et al. [9]

Category	Samples (# of)	%
Politics	4180	58.0
TV & Celebrities	1544	21.4
Society & Daily News	1276	17.7
Science & Technology	112	1.5
Economy	44	0.7
Religion	44	0.7

The authors manually collected and analyzed all the fake news from an interval of two years (from 01/2016 to 01/2018) from 4 websites, which are: *Diário do Brasil, A Folha do Brasil, The Journal Brasil* and *Top Five TV*, filtering out the news that presented half-truth. On the other hand, the authors collected the real news using a web crawler from three major Brazilian news agencies: *G1, Folha de São Paulo*, and *Estadão*. After collecting the news, the authors used a lexical similarity measure to choose the most similar real news to the fake news collected. They also performed a manual verification to guarantee that the fake news and real news were subject related.

As the average number of tokens $\bar{t}$ in each corresponding class in Fake.Br is so big, fake news $\bar{t} = 216.1$ tokens and true news $\bar{t} = 1268.5$ tokens, the authors of the Fake.Br also offered a truncated version of the corpus in which both real and fake news, have the same number of characters based on the length (number of tokens) of the shortest of the pair. The HAN was applied to both corpora, the full, and the truncated one.

3.2   Hierarchical Attention Network

We adopt a general HAN architecture for document representation, displayed in Fig. 1, initially proposed by Yang [19]. The overall architecture is represented in two major parts: a word-level attention layer, and a sentence-level attention layer, therefore representing two levels of abstraction. They are both preceded by the corresponding encoders, a word encoder, and a sentence encoder.

Word encoder. Given a sentence with words $w_{it}, t \in [1,T]$ for T maximum number of words per sentence, they are embedded to vectors x_{iT}, see Eq. 1. This model uses a bidirectional GRU network where the words are summarized in two directions, the forward hidden state $\overrightarrow{h}_{it}$ and and backward hidden state $\overleftarrow{h}_{it}$, (Eqs. 2 and 3) therefore summarizing the information of the whole sentence centered around w_{it}, as in Eq. 4.

Word attention layer. The attention mechanism devised in the next phase (seen as α_w in Fig. 1), extracts the most meaningful words to contribute to the sentence meaning. In other words, it gives weights to words considering the importance α_{it} of the word w_{it} to the sentence s_i. In a summary, u_{it} resulted form a one layer MLP, as seen in Eq. 5. Equation 6 represents the importance of the word, which is calculated using the softmax function to get the normalized importance weight α_{it}. Equation 7 refers to the output of the word attention layer, which is the sentence vector s_i, calculated as the weighted sum of the words annotation.

The following equations summarize both processes:

$$x_{it} = W_e w_{it} \qquad (1)$$

$$\overrightarrow{h}_{it} = \overrightarrow{\mathrm{GRU}}(x_{it}), \qquad (2)$$

$$\overleftarrow{h}_{it} = \overleftarrow{\mathrm{GRU}}(x_{it}), \qquad (3)$$

$$h_{it} = [\overrightarrow{h}_{it}, \overleftarrow{h}_{it}] \qquad (4)$$

$$u_{it} = \tanh(W_s h_i + b_s) \qquad (5)$$

$$\alpha_{it} = \frac{\exp(u_{it}^{\top} u_s)}{\sum_t \exp(u_{it}^{\top} u_s)} \qquad (6)$$

$$s_i = \sum_t \alpha_{it} h_{it} \qquad (7)$$

Recalling that $t \in [1,T]$ for all equations above.

Sentence encoder. Similarly to the word encoder layer, we have the sentence encoder, which uses an analogous mechanism. Here we have sentence $s_i, i \in [1, L]$, for L the max number of sentences in a document. Equations 8, 9 and 10 represent the sentence encoder mechanism and, similarly, with word encoder. Here h_i stands for the information of the whole document centered around s_i.

Sentence attention. A similar attention mechanism was implemented to reward the sentences that are more important to the classification. Equations 11, 13 can summarize the sentence attention layer.

$$\vec{h_i} = \overrightarrow{GRU}(s_i), i \in [1, L] \quad (8)$$

$$u_i = \tanh(W_s h_i + b_s) \quad (11)$$

$$\overleftarrow{h_i} = \overleftarrow{GRU}(s_i), i \in [L, 1] \quad (9)$$

$$\alpha_i = \frac{\exp(u_i^\top u_s)}{\sum_i \exp(u_i^\top u_s)} \quad (12)$$

$$h_i = [\vec{h_i}, \overleftarrow{h_i}] \quad (10)$$

$$v = \sum_i \alpha_i h_i \quad (13)$$

Document classification. To classify the document we apply the document vector v through a softmax function as shown in Eq. 14, where W_c is the weight vector and the b_c is the bias vector.

$$p = \text{softmax}(W_c v + b_c) \quad (14)$$

In our work, we used the categorical cross-entropy, Eq. 15, as loss function. There the loss, L, is calculated as the sum of the entropy of all classes M, where y_c is the class label, and p_c is the predicted label.

$$L = -\sum_{c=1}^{M} y_c \log p_c \quad (15)$$

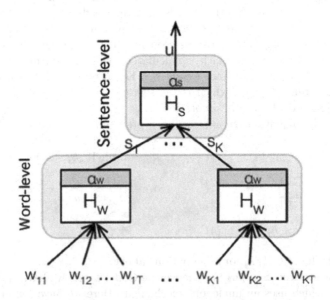

Fig. 1. General architecture of hierarchical attention neural networks for modeling documents. Reprinted from Pappas Popescu-Belis [10]

3.3 Model Configuration

Initially, we performed the preprocessing of the text, converting it to lowercase and removing or not the stop words(NLTK stop words). We then split the documents into sentences using a sentence tokenizer function (NLTK [2]). Each sentence was also split into tokens using the Keras [3] tokenizer.

In the word embedding layer, we used Hartmann et al. [6] pre-trained Global Vectors (GloVe). Actually trained in a large Portuguese multi-genre corpus. In our experiments, we trained models utilizing GloVe with different dimensions ($d = \{100, 300, 600\}$).

For training, we used a batch size of 400, using the Keras Adam optimizer using the default parameters. The models were trained using this configuration during 100 epochs or until the loss did not decrease by at least 10^{-3} for ten successive epochs.

To evaluate the performance of the Hierarchical Attention Network in the task of detection of fake news, we used the same methodology used by Monteiro et al. [9], running the algorithm in two setups: using full texts and using truncated texts. We used the 5-fold cross-validation to evaluate the algorithm calculating the precision, recall, and F-measure metrics for each class, as well as overall accuracy.

4 Results

We performed our experiments using the full texts and the truncated texts. We chose the truncated datasets due to the difference in the number of tokens between the two classes. The average number of tokens in real news is $1,268.5$, and in fake news is 216.1.

In Table 2, we show the results obtained using the full-text dataset, where in the first column we present the setup used where GloVe x are the results obtained using GloVe of x dimensions and SW we removed all stop words. Looking at the results, we can observe that we obtained almost the same result using all the different configurations we proposed: Removing or not the stop words and using different numbers of dimensions of the GloVe model.

Using this model in the full texts, we obtained 97% of accuracy. Considering the significant difference in the number of tokens between the two classes to make this classification task more manageable, we checked the performance of this model in the truncated texts too.

In Table 3, we present the results using the truncated texts. There we can observe that the results obtained using HAN were close, or slightly better, than the results obtained by Monteiro et al. [9], when they mainly used bag of words to obtain an accuracy of 89% in both, fake and real class. One advantage of this model, to be pursued during future studies, is that we can extract an attention map from the attention layers showing the importance of each sentence and each word.

Table 2. Results of the HAN applied on full texts.

	Precision		Recall		F-score		Accuracy
	Fake	True	Fake	True	Fake	True	
GloVe 100	0.9655	0.9695	**0.9694**	0.9653	0.9674	0.9673	0.9674
GloVe 100 SW	0.9696	0.9532	0.9522	0.9700	0.9608	0.9615	0.9611
GloVe 300	0.9666	0.9622	0.9619	0.9667	0.9642	0.9644	0.9643
GloVe 300 SW	0.9672	0.9640	0.9639	0.9672	0.9655	0.9656	0.9656
GloVe 600	**0.9706**	**0.9696**	**0.9694**	**0.9706**	**0.9700**	**0.9700**	**0.9700**
GloVe 600 SW	0.9655	0.9632	0.9631	0.9656	0.9643	0.9643	0.9643

Table 3. Results of the HAN applied on truncated texts.

	Precision		Recall		F-score		Accuracy
	Fake	True	Fake	True	Fake	True	
GloVe 100	0.8966	**0.9038**	**0.9044**	0.8956	0.9004	0.8996	0.9000
GloVe 100 SW	0.8801	0.8884	0.8892	0.8769	0.8840	0.8819	0.8831
GloVe 300	0.9035	0.9018	0.9017	0.9036	0.9026	0.9027	0.9026
GloVe 300 SW	0.8808	0.8983	0.9003	0.8764	0.8899	0.8865	0.8883
GloVe 600	**0.9094**	0.9026	0.9014	**0.9103**	**0.9053**	**0.9064**	**0.9058**
GloVe 600 SW	0.8999	0.8990	0.8989	0.9000	0.8994	0.8995	0.8994

5   Conclusion

We believe the enormous spread of fake news came along with the increasing popularity of social media. In this article, we explored the problem of fake news detection by reviewing the hierarchical attention networks applied to texts written in Brazilian Portuguese. Previously the HAN model has been successfully applied to sentiment analysis [19], where the attention layers were able to select qualitatively informative words and sentences. We expected a similar behavior for this model when applied to distinguish between fake and real news, which did not happen for this corpus. Besides the narrow margin of contrast between fake and real news presented by this deep learning model, this architecture poses a high computing cost to obtain similar results as other comparable lower-cost architectures such as machine learning models [9].

For future work, we want to use the metadata provided in Fake.Br corpus to improve the classification results and also explore the attention map extracted from these texts to verify the importance of each word and sentence to the classification of fake and true news, we also want to use this model in another classification task as well as sentiment analysis in Portuguese texts.

Acknowledgements. This research was supported by Fundação de Amparo à Pesquisa do Estado de São Paulo (FAPESP), process number 2018/03129-8.

References

1. Allcott, H., Gentzkow, M.: Social media and fake news in the 2016 election. J. Econ. Perspect. **31**(2), 211–236 (2017)
2. Bird, S., Klein, E., Loper, E.: Natural Language Processing with Python: Analyzing Text with the Natural Language Toolkit. O'Reilly Media, Inc., Sebastopol (2009)
3. Chollet, F., et al.: Keras (2015). https://keras.io
4. Conroy, N.J., Rubin, V.L., Chen, Y.: Automatic deception detection: methods for finding fake news. Proc. Assoc. Inf. Sci. Technol. **52**(1), 1–4 (2015)
5. Guo, H., Cao, J., Zhang, Y., Guo, J., Li, J.: Rumor detection with hierarchical social attention network. In: Proceedings of the 27th ACM International Conference on Information and Knowledge Management, CIKM 2018, pp. 943–951. ACM, New York (2018). https://doi.org/10.1145/3269206.3271709.https://doi.acm.org/10.1145/3269206.3271709
6. Hartmann, N., Fonseca, E., Shulby, C., Treviso, M., Rodrigues, J., Aluisio, S.: Portuguese word embeddings: evaluating on word analogies and natural language tasks. arXiv preprint arXiv:1708.06025 (2017)
7. Kershner, J.W.: Elements of News Writing. Allyn and Bacon, Boston (2004)
8. Lazer, D.M., et al.: The science of fake news. Science **359**(6380), 1094–1096 (2018)
9. Monteiro, R.A., Santos, R.L.S., Pardo, T.A.S., de Almeida, T.A., Ruiz, E.E.S., Vale, O.A.: Contributions to the study of fake news in Portuguese: new corpus and automatic detection results. In: Villavicencio, A., et al. (eds.) PROPOR 2018. LNCS (LNAI), vol. 11122, pp. 324–334. Springer, Cham (2018). https://doi.org/10.1007/978-3-319-99722-3_33
10. Pappas, N., Popescu-Belis, A.: Multilingual hierarchical attention networks for document classification. arXiv preprint arXiv:1707.00896 (2017)
11. Pérez-Rosas, V., Kleinberg, B., Lefevre, A., Mihalcea, R.: Automatic detection of fake news. In: Proceedings of the 27th International Conference on Computational Linguistics, pp. 3391–3401. Association for Computational Linguistics, Santa Fe, August 2018. https://www.aclweb.org/anthology/C18-1287
12. Rubin, V.L., Conroy, N.J., Chen, Y.: Towards news verification: deception detection methods for news discourse. In: Hawaii International Conference on System Sciences (HICSS48) Symposium on Rapid Screening Technologies, Deception Detection and Credibility Assessment Symposium. Grand Hyatt, Kauai (2015). https://doi.org/10.13140/2.1.4822.8166
13. Ruiz, E.E.S., Okano, E.Y.: Using linguistic cues to detect fake news on the Brazilian Portuguese parallel corpus Fake.BR. In: Proceedings of the 12th Brazilian Symposium in Information and Human Language Technology (2019)
14. Shu, K., Sliva, A., Wang, S., Tang, J., Liu, H.: Fake news detection on social media: a data mining perspective. ACM SIGKDD Explor. Newsl. **19**(1), 22–36 (2017)
15. Singhania, S., Fernandez, N., Rao, S.: 3HAN: a deep neural network for fake news detection. In: Liu, D., Xie, S., Li, Y., Zhao, D., El-Alfy, E.S. (eds.) ICONIP 2017. LNCS, vol. 10635, pp. 572–581. Springer, Cham (2017). https://doi.org/10.1007/978-3-319-70096-0_59
16. Tandoc Jr., E.C., Lim, Z.W., Ling, R.: Defining "fake news": a typology of scholarly definitions. Digit. Journal. **6**(2), 137–153 (2018)
17. Wakefield, A.J.: MMR vaccination and autism. Lancet **354**(9182), 949–950 (1999)

18. Yang, F., Mukherjee, A., Dragut, E.: Satirical news detection and analysis using attention mechanism and linguistic features. arXiv preprint arXiv:1709.01189 (2017)
19. Yang, Z., Yang, D., Dyer, C., He, X., Smola, A., Hovy, E.: Hierarchical attention networks for document classification. In: Proceedings of the 2016 Conference of the North American Chapter of the Association for Computational Linguistics: Human Language Technologies, pp. 1480–1489 (2016)

Screening of Email Box in Portuguese with SVM at Banco do Brasil

Rafael Faria de Azevedo$^{(\boxtimes)}$ (ID), Rafael Rodrigues Pereira de Araujo(ID),
Rodrigo Guimarães Araújo(ID), Régis Moreira Bittencourt(ID),
Rafael Ferreira Alves da Silva(ID), Gabriel de Melo Vaz Nogueira(ID),
Thiago Marques Franca(ID), Jair Otharan Nunes(ID), Klailton Ralff da Silva(ID),
and Emmanuelle Regiane Cunha de Oliveira(ID)

Banco do Brasil S.A., SAUN Quadra 5, Lote B, s/n, Asa Norte,
Brasília, DF 70.040-912, Brazil
{rafael.azevedo,rafael.ferreira,thiago.franca,jotharan,klailtonralff,
emmanuelle.oliveira}@bb.com.br, rafael.f.azevedo.83@gmail.com,
bsb.rafaelaraujo@gmail.com, ratopythonista@gmail.com, reagis@gmail.com,
gabrielmvnogueira@gmail.com
https://www.bb.com.br/

Abstract. This paper describes a tool called ACE, which stands for Assistente Cognitivo de E-mail (Cognitive Email Assistant). It is an application that reads customers emails from a general entrance email box sent to Banco do Brasil. Afterwards, it classifies the emails by their content (message body) and forwards them to other four Specific Email Boxes (SEBs), according to the demand or business of the customer found in the email body. The application was created to automate the screening process of an email box that receives up to 4,000 emails per day. Before ACE existed, the screening process was manually done by up to eight business assistants (employees) of the company. When the application started being used, the number of employees working on the General Email Box (GEB) was reduced to one or two. They are still necessary because ACE does not classify all emails received in the GEB. The machine learning algorithm used in this task is a Support Vector Machine (SVM) with a linear kernel. The efficiency of the system is assured by a curation process coupled with a self-feeding strategy. The F1-Score of the system is 0.9048.

Keywords: Email · Portuguese · Classification · SVM · Banking sector

1 Introduction

Although there is the advancement of social networks, email is still one of the most common ways of communication nowadays, including in the finance industry. Imagine a department that is responsible to attend 5,000 groups of companies where some of them present an annual revenue of up to hundreds of millions of US dollars. This is the reality of one department of Banco do Brasil. The email

P. Quaresma et al. (Eds.): PROPOR 2020, LNAI 12037, pp. 153–163, 2020.
https://doi.org/10.1007/978-3-030-41505-1_15

is the main communication channel when a customer has any issue with your banking products or services. As part of this process, this department has a General Email Box (GEB) that receives emails of any subject from customers (only companies). This email box receives up to 4,000 emails per day in some periods of the month. These quantity does not include spam, it is only customers interactions. To make the screening of all these emails manually, up to eight business assistants (employees) used to be necessary (Fig. 1).

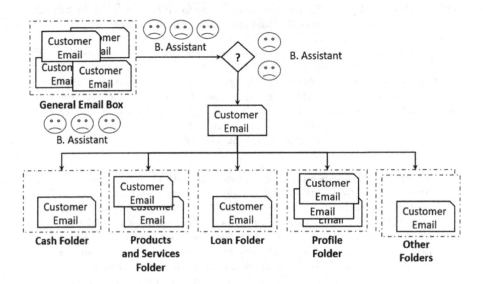

Fig. 1. The manual screening process

As presented in Fig. 1, in the manual screening process, employees have to read or at least have a quick look at each email of the GEB and move it to a folder created to treat emails that corresponds to that content. There are teams dedicated and specialized in each of these folders, as they may have to deal with issues that require a technical and deep knowledge of the subject. Since Banco do Brasil has many products and services, there are many folders in this email box. However, there are four main subjects (folders) that the aforementioned department frequently receives from customers, they are: Cash, Products and Services, Loan and Profile. These four folders were the motivation to create the Assistente Cognitivo de E-mail (ACE), which was a collaboration between the Diretoria de Tecnologia (DITEC) (Board of Technology) and the Diretoria Corporate Bank (DICOR) (Board of Corporate Bank) of Banco do Brasil.

In this paper, a system called ACE that classifies the email body message into four classes is presented. These emails were in Portuguese and belonged to the bank industry. The aim of the application is to save efforts of the business assistants needed to make the screening of emails received in the GEB and, attend customers faster. ACE also provides a way to make the curation of the machine learning model in a semi-automated approach. The solution was built to a specific domain, however, its design can be applied to any email box that daily receives a large quantity of messages and needs a screening (classification) process. The rest of the paper is organized as follows. Section two presents the related works. Section three is about the developed application. Section four presents the discussion and section five presents the conclusions of this work.

2   Related Works

In this section, works related to ACE are presented. The study of email messages as an NLP task comes from the beginning of the internet. At that time, there were works that compared a weighted TF-IDF (Term Frequency–Inverse Document Frequency) and a keyword-spotting rules method called RIPPER to filter (classify) emails [1]. The work of Zhang and Xu presents the enrichment of part of the Enron Corpus [2] with new classes using the Amazon Mechanical Turk[1] [3]. The Eron Corpus has been used in many studies. There are works that classify emails received in contact centers as "needs an immediate response" or "not need an immediate response" [4]. It also makes a classification to discover if the email is "root", "inner" or "leaf", according to its position in the email timeline. Support Vector Machine (SVM) and Naive Bayes were used in the Pine-Info discussion list web archive dataset. The classification of emails in the classes "business" or "personal" is the aim of Alkhereyf and Rambow [5]. They used SVM and Extra-Tree classifiers to build the models. They also extracted social networks features in addition to lexical features from the email content, it includes the use of embeddings (Glove). SmartMail is a prototype system designed to automatically identify tasks in an email. Tasks are usually actions that could be part of a to-do list. They used an SVM with linear kernel, plus different experiments using extracted features and Part-Of-Speech (POS) n-gram features [6]. Zhang and Tetreault proposed to use the email content to generate automatically its subject (title). Their method is a combination of Reinforcement Learning, temporal Convolutional Neural Network (CNN) and bidirectional Long Short-Term Memory (LSTM) [7]. Saini, Saha and Bhattacharyya proposed a Cascaded Self-Organizing Map (SOM) based architecture. SOM is an artificial neural network based model, it uses unsupervised learning to relate the similar input instances to the same region of a map of neurons. This approach can be applied to solve multi-class classification problems where labeled data is limited and classes are highly overlapping to each other, like in email classification. The generation of email vectors needed for classification was done by means of the application Word2vec and TF-IDF explorations [8].

Spam is the most studied subject related to email research. According to Sharaff and Gupta, almost 93% of emails people receive are spam messages [9]. These same researchers proposed a way to reduce the false-positive problem of treating spam email messages. Their method uses metaheuristics-based feature selection methods and employs extra-tree classifier to classify emails into spam.

---

[1]   https://www.mturk.com.

Their method was compared with other two classifiers: Random Forest and Decision Tree. Experiments were made in the UCI library email dataset with 4,601 emails. The metaheuristic methods for features selection were Binary version of Particle Swarm Optimization (BPSO), Particle Swarm Optimization (PSO) and Genetic Algorithm (GA). Youn presented a double level ontology spam filter system called SPONGY (SPam ONtoloGY). They apply a first layer global ontology filter and a second layer user-customized ontology filter. The system also used the C4.5 decision tree algorithm in its hybrid architecture. The global ontology filter presented a 91% spam filtering rate [10]. Gomes and colleagues made a comparison between Naive Bayes and Hidden Markov Model (HMM) to classify spam. The HMM presented the best accuracy [11]. Grbovic et al. presented a method which aims to distinguish whether an email was generated by a human or by a machine (spam). They found a way to group the machine-generated emails into 5 representative classes. The Latent Dirichlet Allocation (LDA) algorithm allowed them to make this discover. The authors had the privilege to work with a corpus with 500 billions emails from Yahoo [12]. Text is not the only input to decide whether an email is or not spam. Harisinghaney and colleagues formulated a method to analyse text and image components of emails trying to classify spam. They compared the algorithms K-Nearest Neighbors (KNN), Naive Bayes and reverse Density Based Spatial Clustering of Applications with Noise (DBSCAN). The method proposed also used the Tesseract Optical Character Recognition (OCR) library [13].

Multi-folder categorization is the second most studied application area related to email [14]. This is the area of the proposed method. Li et al. created a way to classify email messages as sensitive or not for companies. This research is important due to its ability to detect emails with critical data such as intellectual properties and trade secrets issues. Their method is a combination of an incremental Principal Component Analysis (PCA) to reduce the feature dimensionality and a Linear SVM. The method was designed to deal with eight classes. The paper compares the proposed method with an AdaBoost approach and Logistic Regression one [15]. Sethi and colleagues presented a system that allows users to create their own labels, which are used by the system to create folders related to these custom labels. A classifier is trained or re-trained for new classes/labels created by the user. The system was tested with SVM, Naive Bayes and KNN [16].

Regarding to Portuguese, there already are approaches to deal with multi-folder categorization of emails and others approaches. The Email2Vemail project is an example. The motivation of the project was to turn email messages into voice messages in English, Spanish and Portuguese to make the usage of the email as simple as the use of the telephone. A challenging point of the project was the confusion between Portuguese and Spanish, as both languages have resemblances [17]. Another work related to Portuguese is the proposal of a tool to identify moral harassment in emails. The study also proposed a set of words in Portuguese related to bullying in the work environment [18]. Song and Lee [19] proposed a classification of emails in order to move them to the folder related to the email body content. The learning of which folder a message belongs is based on what was learned by the embedding. They tested the learning of the user embeddings from emails based on the sender-recipient network approach with Logistic Regression (LR), Average Perception (AP) and SVM. LR presented the best results. The work of Bhadra et al. [20] proposes a way to classify emails according to its content into custom folders created by the user. The task was tested with two classifiers: Naive Bayes and K-Nearest Neighbors (KNN). A dataset with 1,500 emails was built in their work, with four classes. Naive Bayes presented the best results. In the next section the application is presented.

3   The Application

This section presents the construction of the corpus and other details of ACE like preprocessing, architecture and results.

3.1   Corpus Construction

Natural Language Processing (NLP) with supervised machine learning solutions need a corpus to train and test the model generated by an inductor (classifier), a SVM in this case. In NLP, a dataset is called corpus. The construction of the corpus used by ACE was gradual. To build the corpus, it was necessary to copy three months of emails from production environment to a test environment (development). Packs of 200, 500 and 800 emails were classified by one or more annotators (employees) per day, during a certain period, according to their availability to do the work. Emails were classified into one of the following classes: **cash, products and services, loan** and **profile**. They are the same folders that already existed in the manual process aforementioned.

A senior business assistant was dedicated to construct this corpus. Eventually other two business assistants helped him in this task. This limitation occurred because the project was developed as a pilot one, with no guarantees that it would be useful for the department. Because of this limitation, no evaluation of agreement between annotators was possible (like Cohen Kappa or Fleiss' Kappa). The construction of the corpus was linked with the increase of the F1-Score of the model built by the team. The corpus kept being increased until the responsible of the department understood it was a fair value to deploy the application into production (Fig. 2). When the software was deployed in production, the corpus had almost twelve thousand examples, around three thousand examples per class. The ACE design and results are presented in the next subsections.

3.2   Preprocessing, Architecture and Results

This subsection presents the preprocessing, the architecture and the results of ACE. To improve the prediction of the model, a preprocessing step included the removal of some items: numbers, email signature, greetings, company tags, notices, links, document names, telephone extension, dates, HTML content and

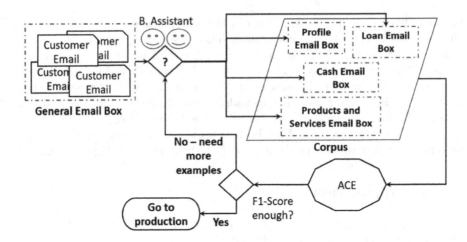

Fig. 2. The initial curation process

special characters. The only feature selection applied was made with the Natural Language Toolkit (NLTK) stopwords[2] list for Portuguese. Afterwards, tokens were turned into features for the classifier via TF-IDF algorithm. Only ASCII characters were kept. ACE works in two different perspectives: its impact in the work of employees that used to deal with the GEB and a machine learning pipeline point of view.

Figure 3 shows the impact of ACE on how the business assistants cope with customers requests. When the GEB receives an email, ACE classifies it. If the score of the classification (threshold) of the email is equal or higher than 0.65, the message is forwarded to the class related to the obtained score (one of four SEBs presented above). If the difference between the highest score and the second highest score is equal or greater than 0.3, the email is also forwarded to the class with the highest score. The sum of the score of all classes is equal to 1.0. The email remains in the GEB if none of the conditions above are satisfied, in this case, it has to be forwarded to the correct SEB manually, by one business assistant. Each SEB has a folder called "curation", as presented in Fig. 3. Business assistants are oriented to move all correctly classified emails to this folder. Once a week, the training process is executed, in order to update ACE. The number of examples in the corpus is incremental, meaning each week the corpus becomes bigger. The process is the same presented in Fig. 4. To retrain the model weekly, an under-sampling strategy is applied. It means that, among the four SEBs, the content of the folder with less emails is withdrawn to train as a whole. The other three folders have the same quantity of emails withdrawn of the folder with less emails. This approach keeps the corpus balanced. For instance, if in the weekly training the curation folder in the SEB called "cash" has 1,300 emails, and SEBs "products and services", "loan" and "profile" have

---

[2] http://www.nltk.org/howto/portuguese_en.html.

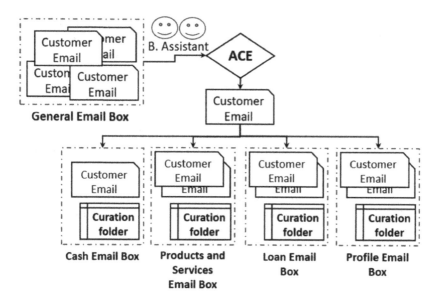

Fig. 3. The automated screening process made by ACE and the maintenance curation phase.

respectively 4,000, 2,700 and 1,900 emails, only 1,300 emails will be taken to training of each SEB. Emails are picked randomly from folders with more emails than the folder with the smallest quantity of emails. ACE freed up to six business assistants to more strategic tasks, improved the life of the ones that still have to manage the emails not classified by the tool and, helped the business assistants to reply the customer faster. It is important to realize that, there was an initial curation to create the corpus capable of creating a satisfactory prediction model and there is a need of keeping the corpus updated, these two phases are represented by Figs. 2 and 3 respectively. Figure 4 presents the ACE machine learning design. Figure 4 represents the machine learning pipeline used by ACE. The SVM inductor[3] is the algorithm that builds the model used in the application. The whole application is implemented in Python 3 with Scikit-learn[4]. The use of SVM was based on many tests performed by the team that built the application. In the test phase, algorithms such as KNN, Naive Bayes, Multilayer Perceptron (MLP) and SVM were evaluated. The best results were reached by SVM. To define the hyper-parameters, the Grid Search algorithm was applied. The Linear Kernel presented the best results in the Grid Search execution. The combination of SVM with Linear Kernel was used in the training and test steps. The different penalty parameter C of the error term used in Grid Search were: 0.025, 0.08, 0.1, 0.5 and 0.8. The stratified 10-fold cross-validation approach prevented the bias problem. ACE has two different results, the metrics of the current

---

[3] https://scikit-learn.org/stable/modules/generated/sklearn.svm.SVC.html.
[4] https://scikit-learn.org/stable/.

model in production and the perception of its efficiency reported by the department team. The SVM model results are: 0.9058 (Precision), 0.9048 (Recall) and 0.9048 (F1-Score). The individual results for classes **products and services, loan, cash** and **profile** are respectively 0.9067, 0.9180, 0.9105 and 0.8840. The efficiency of ACE reported by the department team tells that: in normal days, between 400 and 500 emails remain in the entrance box. In peak days, between 600 and 700 emails remain in the GEB. In normal days, the GEB receives around 2,000 emails. In peak days this number can be near 4,000 emails. The success of ACE is unanimous, according to the department team perception, as the tool brought efficiency to their workflow and diminished their workload. Even with the application deployed in production, it is designed to a continuous update of its corpus, as already explained. So, it is important to say that the results were collected with the corpus version at 30-09-2019. It is intended to expand ACE to other areas of the company which have email boxes that pass through a human screening process.

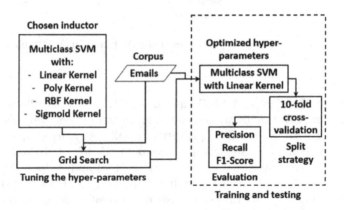

Fig. 4. ACE machine learning architecture

4   Discussion

This section discusses the whole development process of ACE and its results. The email vendor that ACE works with is the IBM Lotus Notes, which is not natively prepared to work with a machine learning application like ACE. To make it possible it was necessary to develop some extra APIs in Lotus Notes, this was possible since Banco do Brasil has a specialist in this tool. When ACE forwards emails from the GEB to the SEB, in fact, it is not the use of the common forward function that exists in any email. It was necessary to create a function that copies the whole object "email" from the GEB to the SEB. It was necessary because the department wanted this functionality, even the customer sending the email to the GEB, it should not appear there and not leave any trace that it has been there before. The ideia was to create the perception that the customer sent the email directly to the SEB. However, when the business assistant who works in the SEB replied the customer, the email had to appear to the customer as "sent by" the email address of the GEB. In other words, the existence of ACE should be transparent to the customer. Related to these challenges, a problem which was solved was that, if the business assistant who works in the SEB added the GEB address in the CC or CCO field, ACE should not start an infinite loop. This was a challenging task, since the whole object "email" had to be copied from the GEB to the SEB, including all fields like CC, CCO etc.

At the beginning of the project, the idea was to use a black box solution in the machine learning part of the application. However, as it was a cloud based solution, the team had to develop the model (using SVM) by themselves, because the email content is sensitive to the company, considering its strategic secrecy and privacy. The GEB reality without ACE only used folders. ACE was developed initially to work with these folders. Nevertheless, when the project was almost accomplished, there was an infrastructure need to change from these folders to SEBs. This change delayed a bit the application of ACE to production, this is just to present how changes happen frequently in companies and the projects have to stick on them. Still following this remark, in about 8 months, all GEBs of the Bank will change its vendor, what will impact ACE again.

The way the corpus is being updated currently is a temporary solution, since the dataset must not grow indefinitely. In the next version of ACE, the team intends to start analysing which examples are significant to increase the prediction quality of the model. A string similarity approach is planned to be used to reach this objective.

ACE has been in production since the end of September/2019. It took more than one year to be finished in its 1.0 version. When the first training and testing actions started, the F1-Score was around 0.05. The continuous increase of the corpus size being curated manually was essential to reach the current F1-Score of 0.9048. The initial threshold (score) required to automatically move an email from the GEB to the SEB was around 0.9. As tests evolved, the business assistants realized that a less value did not affect drastically the quality of the classification. After many experiments, the current threshold (classification score) that controls whether an email stays in the GEB or goes to the SEB is 0.65.

As future work, the business department team wants to add other SEBs in ACE, it is the current study being made by the software development team. A graphical interface that allows the whole management of the application is also being built, the current version is managed via terminal. As other departments want to use the tool, the graphical interface is supposed to have this function either. In its current version, ACE evaluates only the email body, however, tests are programmed to evaluate the attached files that come with many emails, like text files and spreedsheets, since many emails sent by companies present few words in their body, but a lot of information in their attachments.

5   Conclusions

This paper presents a tool called ACE, which in Portuguese stands for Assistente Cognitivo de E-mail (Cognitive Email Assistant), which automatically makes the screening of messages received from customers in a General Email Box (GEB). The challenging project took more than one year and uses a model that is currently with F1-Score of 0.9048. From a business point of view, ACE classifies correctly around 75% of emails received in the GEB. As far as it is known, this is the first paper to report such application that deals with email body classification in Portuguese for the banking sector. As it is an industry application, this paper shows the extra challenges a machine learning software has to face, compared to the ones which are used only in the academic context. As future work, the team intends to use string similarity approaches to improve the quality of the corpus and the model consequently. An embeddings strategy is also planned to be explored in the application, as in other works of the literature [19].

References

1. Cohen, W.W., et al.: Learning rules that classify e-mail. In: AAAI Spring Symposium on Machine Learning in Information Access, pp. 18–25 (1996)
2. Klimt, B., Yang, Y.: The Enron corpus: a new dataset for email classification research. In: Boulicaut, J.-F., Esposito, F., Giannotti, F., Pedreschi, D. (eds.) ECML 2004. LNCS (LNAI), vol. 3201, pp. 217–226. Springer, Heidelberg (2004). https://doi.org/10.1007/978-3-540-30115-8_22
3. Zhang, F., Xu, K.: Annotation and classification of an email importance corpus. In: Proceedings of the 53rd Annual Meeting of the Association for Computational Linguistics and the 7th International Joint Conference on Natural Language Processing (Volume 2: Short Papers), pp. 651–656 (2015)
4. Nenkova, A., Bagga, A.: Email classification for contact centers. In: Proceedings of the 2003 ACM Symposium on Applied Computing, pp. 789–792 (2003)
5. Alkhereyf, S., Rambow, O.: Work hard, play hard: email classification on the Avocado and Enron corpora. In: Proceedings of TextGraphs-11: The Workshop on Graph-Based Methods for Natural Language Processing, pp. 57–65 (2017)
6. Corston-Oliver, S., Ringger, E., Gamon, M., Campbell, R.: Task-focused summarization of email. In: Text Summarization Branches Out, pp. 43–50 (2004)
7. Zhang, R., Tetreault, J.: This email could save your life: introducing the task of email subject line generation. arXiv preprint arXiv:1906.03497 (2019)
8. Saini, N., Saha, S., Bhattacharyya, P.: Cascaded SOM: an improved technique for automatic email classification. In: 2018 International Joint Conference on Neural Networks (IJCNN), pp. 1–8 (2018)
9. Sharaff, A., Gupta, H.: Extra-tree classifier with metaheuristics approach for email classification. In: Bhatia, S.K., Tiwari, S., Mishra, K.K., Trivedi, M.C. (eds.) Advances in Computer Communication and Computational Sciences. AISC, vol. 924, pp. 189–197. Springer, Singapore (2019). https://doi.org/10.1007/978-981-13-6861-5_17
10. Youn, S.: SPONGY (SPam ONtoloGY): email classification using two-level dynamic ontology. Sci. World J. **2014** (2014). 11 pages

11. Gomes, S.R., et al.: A comparative approach to email classification using Naive Bayes classifier and hidden Markov model. In: 2017 4th International Conference on Advances in Electrical Engineering (ICAEE), pp. 482–487 (2017)

12. Grbovic, M., Halawi, G., Karnin, Z., Maarek, Y.: How many folders do you really need?: classifying email into a handful of categories. In: Proceedings of the 23rd ACM International Conference on Conference on Information and Knowledge Management, pp. 869–878 (2014)

13. Harisinghaney, A., Dixit, A., Gupta, S., Arora, A.: Text and image based spam email classification using KNN, Naive Bayes and Reverse DBSCAN algorithm. In: 2014 International Conference on Reliability Optimization and Information Technology (ICROIT), pp. 153–155 (2014)

14. Mujtaba, G., Shuib, L., Raj, R.G., Majeed, N., Al-Garadi, M.A.: Email classification research trends: review and open issues. IEEE Access **5**, 9044–9064 (2017)

15. Li, M., Park, Y., Ma, R., Huang, H.Y.: Business email classification using incremental subspace learning. In: Proceedings of the 21st International Conference on Pattern Recognition (ICPR2012), pp. 625–628 (2012)

16. Sethi, H., Sirohi, A., Thakur, M.K.: Intelligent mail box. In: Satapathy, S.C., Mandal, J.K., Udgata, S.K., Bhateja, V. (eds.) Information Systems Design and Intelligent Applications. AISC, vol. 435, pp. 441–450. Springer, New Delhi (2016). https://doi.org/10.1007/978-81-322-2757-1_44

17. Pereira, H., Teixeira, P., Oliveira, L.C.: Email2Vmail — an email reader. In: Mamede, N.J., Trancoso, I., Baptista, J., das Graças Volpe Nunes, M. (eds.) PROPOR 2003. LNCS (LNAI), vol. 2721, pp. 189–192. Springer, Heidelberg (2003). https://doi.org/10.1007/3-540-45011-4_29

18. Nunes, A.V., Freitas, C.O., Paraiso, E.C.: Detecção de Assédio Moral em e-mails in I Student Workshop on Information and Human Language Technology, São Carlos. I Student Workshop on Information and Human Language Technology-7th Brazilian Symposium in Information and Human Language Technology. POA: SBC 1, pp. 01–05 (2009)

19. Song, Y., Lee, C.-J.: Learning user embeddings from emails. In: Proceedings of the 15th Conference of the European Chapter of the Association for Computational Linguistics: Volume 2, Short Papers, vol. 2, pp. 733–738 (2017)

20. Bhadra, A., Hitawala, S., Modi, R., Salunkhe, S.: Email classification using supervised learning algorithms. In: Saeed, K., Chaki, N., Pati, B., Bakshi, S., Mohapatra, D.P. (eds.) Progress in Advanced Computing and Intelligent Engineering. AISC, vol. 564, pp. 81–90. Springer, Singapore (2018). https://doi.org/10.1007/978-981-10-6875-1_9

Back to the Feature, in Entailment Detection and Similarity Measurement for Portuguese

Pedro Fialho[1,3][✉] [ID], Luísa Coheur[1,2] [ID], and Paulo Quaresma[1,3] [ID]

[1] INESC-ID Lisboa, Lisbon, Portugal
pedro.fialho@l2f.inesc-id.pt
[2] Instituto Superior Tecnico, Universidade de Lisboa, Lisbon, Portugal
[3] Universidade de Évora, Évora, Portugal

Abstract. This paper describes a system to identify entailment and quantify semantic similarity among pairs of Portuguese sentences. The system relies on a corpus to build a supervised model, and employs the same features regardless of the task. Our experiments cover two types of features, contextualized embeddings and lexical features, which we evaluate separately and in combination. The model is derived from a voting strategy on an ensemble of distinct regressors, on similarity measurement, or calibrated classifiers, on entailment detection. Applying such system to other languages mainly depends on the availability of corpora, since all features are either multilingual or language independent. We obtain competitive results on a recent Portuguese corpus, where our best result is obtained by joining embeddings with lexical features.

Keywords: Entailment · Semantic similarity · Feature engineering

1 Introduction

The ability to identify if two sentences share equivalent semantics is of use to systems that organize data, as in clustering of news and user comments, or that accept natural language inputs to be matched against a knowledge base, as in question answering and dialogue management. In this work we focus on the equivalence between two sentences.

Text semantics are generically represented in embeddings, as obtained from distributional methods that model the semantics of words from their proximity to neighbor words in large collections of text such as Wikipedia [12]. Hence, embeddings are available for many languages, including Portuguese. Sentence embeddings can be derived by compositional methods on word embeddings [19]. The cosine of two embeddings is a popular form of computing the similarity of their corresponding sentences.

Semantic similarity for sentences may also originate from hand-designed lexical features that cover different forms of similarity between a pair of sentences.

© Springer Nature Switzerland AG 2020
P. Quaresma et al. (Eds.): PROPOR 2020, LNAI 12037, pp. 164–173, 2020.
https://doi.org/10.1007/978-3-030-41505-1_16

Each such metric outputs the semantic similarity of an input pair of sentences, according to a particular rationale that may require resources not available in all languages. However, most such metrics are language independent, or depend on resources available in many languages.

Lexical features are typically supported by plausible motivations on linguistic equivalence, which allow human interpretation. Embeddings are sourced from linear algebra, hence lack an interpretation for each feature.

We employ Portuguese embeddings and hand-designed lexical features to two related but conceptually distinct semantic equivalence tasks: entailment detection and similarity measurement. Namely, a target sentence entails a source sentence if its semantics can be derived from the source sentence, and two sentences are similar, or a paraphrase, if expressing the same meaning irrespective of their order. Hence, entailment is a unidirectional relation between two sentences, similarity is bidirectional, and both imply measuring semantic equivalence. Despite the differences, we use the same type of features to address both tasks.

Particularly, we built a system to identify if a sentence entails, contradicts or is neutral to another sentence, and to measure the semantic overlap among the two sentences with a continuous score between 0 and 5. Our system applies machine learning supervised on the SICK-BR corpus [16], which provides Portuguese sentence pairs annotated with the mentioned outcomes.

We represent each pair of sentences by multilingual embeddings, for all languages in Wikipedia, and lexical features that are either multilingual or language independent, hence our system can be applied to other languages than Portuguese, according to corpora availability.

In the following we present related work on Sect. 2, our approach on Sect. 3, and its experimental setup in Sect. 4. The results are reported and discussed in Sect. 5, including example analysis. Finally, we conclude and plan future work in Sect. 6.

2 Related Work

A benchmark for systems aimed at Recognizing Textual Entailment (RTE) was initially developed in the PASCAL challenge series [2]. RTE is defined as a classification task that may include target labels such as entailment, contradiction and neutral (no semantic relation).

To compare the performance of systems measuring semantic similarity, various shared tasks on Semantic Textual Similarity (STS) were defined in Semeval [1], including cross-lingual and multilingual tracks [4], which however did not cover Portuguese. STS is a regression task, where the aim is to find a continuous value between 0 and 5 for the similarity among two sentences.

To the best of our knowledge, the first corpus to include entailment labels and similarity values for Portuguese sentences was ASSIN [7], provided in a shared task of the same name. For English, the same type of annotations are found in SICK [11], a corpus of image and video captions annotated by crowd-sourcing.

Recently, a translation of SICK sentences to Portuguese was made available in the SICK-BR corpus [16], which we employ in our experiments.

Systems that participated in the ASSIN shared task employed various approaches for entailment detection and similarity measurement in Portuguese, which include features from similarity metrics on various text representations [6], word embeddings built with word2vec [12] from the Portuguese Wikipedia [3,9], and features based on syntactic properties and lexical semantics [13], also applied in compositional methods to derive sentence similarity from word similarities [8]. Metrics on multiple text representations was the approach with best performance on one of the tracks, and is our choice for experiments with lexical features.

Recently, the BERT model [5] was made available, and achieved state of the art results on various Natural Language Processing (NLP) tasks for English, as those in the GLUE benchmark [18], which is aimed at finding a single natural language representation for multiple NLP tasks.

While word2vec produces a static embedding for a word, BERT generates a dynamic embedding according to the context in which a word is employed, and may even generate the embedding of a sentence pair, if the aim is to verify entailment on the pair [5]. Training a BERT model is expensive on time and resources, but models based on Wikipedia were made available, also on various languages covered by Wikipedia, including Portuguese [15].

3   Modelling Equivalence for Portuguese Sentences

Currently available resources to assess the similarity between Portuguese sentences include embeddings and similarity metrics. We use both, separately and in combination, to compile vectors of distinct features, and produce a model for each type of feature vector by supervised learning on a Portuguese corpus.

Given a corpus where each example is composed by a pair of sentences and its target outcome is a label and/or continuous value related to the equivalence between the two sentences, we obtain its model from two distinct types of feature vector: (a) the embedding of each sentence pair according to BERT, and (b) a vector of scores from similarity metrics on distinct equivalence aspects.

In this work we employ such system to a Portuguese corpus annotated with entailment labels and similarity values. Therefore, we produce a classification and a regression model for each type of feature vector, such that the same type of features is employed for both tasks.

3.1   BERT Embeddings

Embeddings are well known for the ability to produce competitive results on various NLP tasks without task adaptation, and for their ease of availability on various languages since input text does not requires annotation.

We obtain Portuguese embeddings from BERT [5], a deep learning architecture based on bidirectional transformers, a recent concept in neural networks [17].

Namely, we employ the multilingual and cased version of the BERT Base model, which produces embedding vectors with 768 dimensions, and applies to raw text that was not transformed by lower casing or accent removal. Such embeddings are sourced from pre-trained models provided with the original BERT release.

Embeddings are a popular resource to score the similarity between two sentences, whether directly from their cosine similarity, or by forming a feature vector, such as from the concatenation of two embeddings, and building a regression model based on supervised learning. The latter may also be targeted to detect entailment relations, by using a classification model.

BERT produces the embedding of a sentence pair, for an input formatted as a sentence followed by token "|||" and followed by the other sentence[1]. We format sentence pairs in such manner before input to BERT, and the resultant embedding is the feature vector for the pair, which we employ in building a model by supervised learning.

3.2 Lexical Features

The output of a similarity metric is a score for the similarity between two sentences. Various of such metrics exist, where some are applicable to inputs composed by heterogeneous symbols, such as the Jaccard coefficient. We employ a previously released system that generates 96 features for a pair of sentences, based on applying such metrics to various representations of text. Namely, lexical features are obtained from the INESC-ID@ASSIN [6] system, since it achieved state of the art results on the European Portuguese track of the ASSIN challenge [7]. These include similarity metrics aimed at text, such as BLEU, but also metrics on symbols, such as Jaccard. Each of such metrics is applied to the original sentences, but also to alternative representations of such text, such as obtained from phonetic encoding. A comprehensive descriptive of such metrics and representations is available in [6].

3.3 Non Deep Learning Methods

We leverage data modelling techniques prior to current deep learning architectures.

Both for classification and regression, we employ a voting strategy on a set of different models, to leverage different learning strategies at once. For regression, voting consists in averaging predictions from a set of models, while for classification different strategies of computing the output class may apply, whether based on the classes predicted by each classifier or by averaging prediction confidences.

For classification, each classifier was calibrated so that the confidence of predicting an example as belonging to a certain class is approximately the percentage of examples of that class.

---

[1] https://github.com/google-research/bert.

4   Experimental Setup

In the following we describe our choice of corpus, machine learning algorithms and their parameters, and evaluation metrics for the global system performance.

4.1   The SICK-BR Corpus

As previously mentioned, our system is evaluated on the SICK-BR corpus [16], a Brazilian Portuguese translation of the SICK [11] corpus on entailment and semantic similarity. The original SICK was the target corpus for a shared task on Semeval 2014 [10].

As in the original SICK corpus, SICK-BR is composed of 4906 test examples, 495 trial/development examples and 4439 train examples. We train our machine learning algorithms on both train and trial, and for the current experiments we did not search for optimal parameters, which would rely on the trial partition.

Each example is annotated with a continuous value between 0 and 5, for how similar the two sentences are, and a text label for the relationship between the two sentences, with the 3 possible values of *neutral, contradiction* and *entailment*, and a distribution of 5595 examples of neutral, 2821 of entailment and 1424 of contradiction. More information is available in each example, such as the original English sentence, but it is out of the scope of our evaluation, and hence redirected to the original corpus description at [11].

The development of SICK-BR only targeted sentence translation, hence it is also a parallel corpus to SICK, since original annotations did not change. On such basis, we situate our results within those of the Semeval task [10], to find if our current approach on Portuguese is competitive to the 2014 best approaches on English. More recent Semeval tasks exist for RTE and STS, covering modern approaches in NLP technology, but the 2014 edition is the only targeted exclusively at the SICK corpus.

4.2   Machine Learning Choices

All machine learning was performed in *scikit-learn* [14].

Classifiers were chosen after ablation analysis of various combinations, without tuning parameters and choosing those that achieved the best results in less processing time to build the model. The resulting set is composed of a Support Vector Machine with linear kernel (LIBLINEAR implementation), a Multi Layer Perceptron and a Random Forest of 100 Decision Trees.

In voting we consider that all models have the same weight, and for classification we employ a strategy named "soft voting" in *scikit-learn*, in which the output class is chosen by averaging the prediction probabilities that each classifier reports for a certain class, and choosing the highest class average using argmax.

All classifiers are calibrated with the Platt method of fitting a logistic regression on prediction probabilities, named "sigmoid" in *scikit-learn*.

Soft voting and calibration do not apply to regression.

4.3   Evaluation Metrics

The performance of our system on entailment detection is measured with Accuracy, Precision, Recall and F-measure (F1, as we consider precision and recall to have the same weight/importance). For similarity measurement, and as in the Semeval edition that employs the English SICK corpus, we report Pearson, Spearman and Mean Squared Error (MSE).

A lower MSE is better, while for the remaining metrics a higher value is better. All metrics for entailment detection produce values in the 0 to 1 range, hence we report such results in percentages.

As the entailment task on SICK-BR configures a multi class classification setup, and the Precision, Recall and F1 metrics are based on the assumption that a positive label exists (as in binary classification), such metrics are calculated by an average among binary classifications, one for each class such that the positive label represents belonging to the class. We chose to average by an unweighted mean (named *macro* in *scikit-learn*) that considers all classes as equally important, despite their unbalanced distribution in SICK-BR.

5   Results and Discussion

We evaluated the performance of lexical features and embeddings, both isolated and combined, and present the results of each such configuration in Table 1 for classification of entailment labels and on Table 2 for regression of similarity values.

Table 1. Results on entailment detection.

Feature type	Accuracy	F1	Precision	Recall
ASSIN features	76.39%	73.72%	77.52%	71.16%
BERT-base, multilingual	80.64%	79.41%	82.63%	77.06%
ASSIN + BERT	80.96%	79.78%	83.01%	77.39%

Table 2. Results on similarity measurement.

Feature type	Pearson	Spearman	MSE
ASSIN features	0.741	0.68	0.461
BERT-base, multilingual	0.774	0.687	0.426
ASSIN + BERT	0.776	0.684	0.428

BERT is a modern model with proven success in various NLP tasks [18], hence it reaches better results than using only lexical features. However, we notice performance increases when combining BERT embeddings with lexical features, which although small are consistent on all metrics except for MSE, where the best result is obtained by using only BERT embeddings.

As we did not find other systems employing SICK-BR, we situate our results within those of the Semeval edition that employed SICK.

Semeval results for entailment detection on the SICK corpus reached a maximum accuracy of 84.6% (83.6% for the second best result) and a minimum of 48.7% (67.2% for second worst result). For similarity measurement we only consider results with MSE below 1, which correspond to the most competitive systems. The best result reaches 0.828 Pearson, 0.769 Spearman and 0.325 MSE, and the worst result is 0.628 Pearson, 0.597 Spearman and 0.662 MSE [10]. For both tasks, our results on SICK-BR situate between the middle result and the best result on SICK, hence we assume our approach as competitive.

Of 4906 test examples, 274 were not correctly classified when using BERT features, where most are entailment or neutral examples. Particularly, using BERT features results in classification of such entailment and contradiction examples as neutral, which is less harmful as error in a NLP pipeline than, for instance, classifying a contradiction as entailment. In Fig. 1 we present two of such examples, with low and high word overlap respectively. The example with high word overlap is the most likely to be classified as entailment, but BERT does not provide an interpretation of its features for us to inspect.

A mulher faminta está comendo
A mulher está comendo

Está nevando em dois cachorros que brincam
Dois cachorros estão brincando na neve

Fig. 1. Entailment examples that were correctly classified by lexical features, and wrongly classified as neutral by BERT.

BERT is also the only feature type that enables the correct classification of 482 examples, also mostly entailment or neutral examples. Among such cases we found 36 contradiction examples that were classified as entailment when using lexical features, and in most one of the sentences is the negation of the other, as shown in Fig. 2 where the top example explicitly employs the word "not", while in the other the negation is only identifiable by semantic analysis, as it translates approximately to "a dog is in the water/a dog is out of the water".

Lexical features are mostly aimed at measuring similarity from common words, such that the few words that negate the whole sentence do not impact the features that focus on common words regardless of their polarity, which are most of the lexical features. Although a few features derive from a metric that identifies negation from a fixed and small list of words, such as "not" or "nobody", no feature in our system is designed to interpret negations out of the scope of such short list.

A pessoa está entrando na água
A pessoa não está indo para dentro da água

Um cachorro com pelo dourado está na água
Um cachorro com pelo dourado está fora da água

Fig. 2. Contradiction examples that were wrongly classified as entailment by lexical features, but were correctly classified with BERT.

6   Conclusion

We employed two distinct forms of features for entailment detection and similarity measurement in Portuguese. Our method is supervised in the SICK-BR corpus, which is a Portuguese translation of the SICK corpus, originally for English. As annotations were left intact, SICK-BR is a parallel corpus to SICK, and we compare our results in the Portuguese SICK-BR to those reported for the English SICK in a shared task designed for the 2014 Semeval workshop [10].

Although the resources to compute similarity features on Portuguese are still more limited and scarce than those available for English in 2014, we were able to achieve competitive performance. As a modern model, BERT reaches better results than lexical features. However, our best result was obtained by joining lexical features to BERT embeddings, hence proving that such features increase system performance if appended to BERT embeddings.

Future work includes exploring other sources of features already available for Portuguese, such as from syntactic analysis, search of optimal parameters for machine learning algorithms, and further analysis of language usage in examples that fail with embeddings but not with lexical features. Future work also includes fine tunning BERT, by employing its architecture to model SICK-BR tasks.

Acknowledgements. This work was supported by national funds through Fundação para a Ciência e Tecnologia (FCT) with reference UID/CEC/50021/2019 and by FCT's INCoDe 2030 initiative, in the scope of the demonstration project AIA, "Apoio Inteligente a empreendedores (chatbots)", which also supports the scholarship of Pedro Fialho.

References

1. Agirre, E., Diab, M., Cer, D., Gonzalez-Agirre, A.: Semeval-2012 task 6: a pilot on semantic textual similarity. In: Proceedings of the First Joint Conference on Lexical and Computational Semantics - Volume 1: Proceedings of the Main Conference and the Shared Task, and Volume 2: Proceedings of the Sixth International Workshop on Semantic Evaluation, SemEval 2012, pp. 385–393. Association for Computational Linguistics, Stroudsburg (2012). http://dl.acm.org/citation.cfm?id=2387636.2387697

2. Bar-Haim, R., Dagan, I., Szpektor, I.: Benchmarking applied semantic inference: the PASCAL recognising textual entailment challenges. In: Dershowitz, N., Nissan, E. (eds.) Language, Culture, Computation. Computing - Theory and Technology. LNCS, vol. 8001, pp. 409–424. Springer, Heidelberg (2014). https://doi.org/10.1007/978-3-642-45321-2_19

3. Barbosa, L., Cavalin, P., Guimarães, V., Kormaksson, M.: Blue man group no assin: usando representações distribuídas para similaridade semântica e inferência textual. Linguamática 8(2), 15–22 (2016). https://www.linguamatica.com/index.php/linguamatica/article/view/v8n2-2

4. Cer, D., Diab, M., Agirre, E., Lopez-Gazpio, I., Specia, L.: SemEval-2017 task 1: semantic textual similarity multilingual and crosslingual focused evaluation. In: Proceedings of the 11th International Workshop on Semantic Evaluation, SemEval-2017, Vancouver, Canada, pp. 1–14. Association for Computational Linguistics, August 2017. https://doi.org/10.18653/v1/S17-2001. https://www.aclweb.org/anthology/S17-2001

5. Devlin, J., Chang, M.W., Lee, K., Toutanova, K.: BERT: pre-training of deep bidirectional transformers for language understanding. In: Proceedings of the 2019 Conference of the North American Chapter of the Association for Computational Linguistics: Human Language Technologies, Volume 1 (Long and Short Papers), Minneapolis, Minnesota, pp. 4171–4186. Association for Computational Linguistics, June 2019. https://doi.org/10.18653/v1/N19-1423

6. Fialho, P., Marques, R., Martins, B., Coheur, L., Quaresma, P.: Inesc-id@assin: Medição de similaridade semântica e reconhecimento de inferência textual. Linguamática 8(2), 33–42 (2016). https://www.linguamatica.com/index.php/linguamatica/article/view/v8n2-4

7. Fonseca, E., Borges dos Santos, L., Criscuolo, M., Aluísio, S.: Visão geral da avaliação de similaridade semântica e inferência textual. Linguamática 8(2), 3–13 (2016). https://www.linguamatica.com/index.php/linguamatica/article/view/v8n2-1

8. Freire, J., Pinheiro, V., Feitosa, D.: FlexSTS: um framework para similaridade semântica textual. Linguamática 8(2), 23–31 (2016). https://www.linguamatica.com/index.php/linguamatica/article/view/v8n2-3

9. Hartmann, N.: Solo queue at assin: Combinando abordagens tradicionais e emergentes. Linguamática 8(2), 59–64 (2016). https://www.linguamatica.com/index.php/linguamatica/article/view/v8n2-6

10. Marelli, M., Bentivogli, L., Baroni, M., Bernardi, R., Menini, S., Zamparelli, R.: SemEval-2014 task 1: evaluation of compositional distributional semantic models on full sentences through semantic relatedness and textual entailment. In: Proceedings of the 8th International Workshop on Semantic Evaluation, SemEval 2014, Dublin, Ireland, pp. 1–8. Association for Computational Linguistics, August 2014. https://doi.org/10.3115/v1/S14-2001. https://www.aclweb.org/anthology/S14-2001

11. Marelli, M., Menini, S., Baroni, M., Bentivogli, L., Bernardi, R., Zamparelli, R.: A SICK cure for the evaluation of compositional distributional semantic models. In: Proceedings of the Ninth International Conference on Language Resources and Evaluation, LREC-2014, Reykjavik, Iceland, pp. 216–223. European Languages Resources Association (ELRA), May 2014

12. Mikolov, T., Sutskever, I., Chen, K., Corrado, G.S., Dean, J.: Distributed representations of words and phrases and their compositionality. In: Burges, C.J.C., Bottou, L., Welling, M., Ghahramani, Z., Weinberger, K.Q. (eds.) Advances in Neural Information Processing Systems 26, pp. 3111–3119. Curran Associates, Inc. (2013). http://papers.nips.cc/paper/5021-distributed-representations-of-words-and-phrases-and-their-compositionality.pdf
13. Oliveira Alves, A., Rodrigues, R., Gonçalo Oliveira, H.: ASAPP: Alinhamento semântico automático de palavras aplicado ao português. Linguamática **8**(2), 43–58 (2016). https://linguamatica.com/index.php/linguamatica/article/view/v8n2-5
14. Pedregosa, F., et al.: Scikit-learn: machine learning in Python. J. Mach. Learn. Res. **12**, 2825–2830 (2011)
15. Pires, T., Schlinger, E., Garrette, D.: How multilingual is multilingual BERT? In: Proceedings of the 57th Annual Meeting of the Association for Computational Linguistics, Florence, Italy, pp. 4996–5001. Association for Computational Linguistics, July 2019. https://doi.org/10.18653/v1/P19-1493
16. Real, L., et al.: SICK-BR: a Portuguese corpus for inference. In: Villavicencio, A., et al. (eds.) PROPOR 2018. LNCS (LNAI), vol. 11122, pp. 303–312. Springer, Cham (2018). https://doi.org/10.1007/978-3-319-99722-3_31
17. Vaswani, A., et al.: Attention is all you need. In: Guyon, I., et al. (eds.) Advances in Neural Information Processing Systems 30, pp. 5998–6008. Curran Associates, Inc. (2017). http://papers.nips.cc/paper/7181-attention-is-all-you-need.pdf
18. Wang, A., Singh, A., Michael, J., Hill, F., Levy, O., Bowman, S.: GLUE: a multi-task benchmark and analysis platform for natural language understanding. In: Proceedings of the 2018 EMNLP Workshop BlackboxNLP: Analyzing and Interpreting Neural Networks for NLP, Brussels, Belgium, pp. 353–355. Association for Computational Linguistics, November 2018. https://doi.org/10.18653/v1/W18-5446. https://www.aclweb.org/anthology/W18-5446
19. Wu, L., et al.: Word mover's embedding: from Word2Vec to document embedding. In: Proceedings of the 2018 Conference on Empirical Methods in Natural Language Processing, Brussels, Belgium, pp. 4524–4534. Association for Computational Linguistics, October–November 2018. https://doi.org/10.18653/v1/D18-1482. https://www.aclweb.org/anthology/D18-1482

Emoji Prediction for Portuguese

Luis Duarte$^{(\boxtimes)}$, Luís Macedo, and Hugo Gonçalo Oliveira

CISUC, University of Coimbra, Coimbra, Portugal
lduarte@student.dei.uc.pt, {hroliv,macedo}@dei.uc.pt

Abstract. Besides alternative text-based forms, emojis became highly common in social media. Given their importance in daily communication, we tackled the problem of emoji prediction in Portuguese social media text. We created a dataset with occurrences of frequent emojis, used as labels, and then compared the performance of traditional machine learning algorithms with neural networks when predicting them. Either considering five or ten of the most popular emojis, an LSTM neural network clearly outperformed Naive Bayes in the latter task, with F1-scores of 60% and 52%, respectively, against 33% and 23%.

Keywords: Emojis · Portuguese · Automatic prediction · Machine learning · Social media

1 Introduction

Text is the most popular method of communication in social networks like Facebook and Twitter [4]. Yet, in order to include the most information possible in the least possible content, it was not long until alternative forms of communication started to be used, namely for aspects that are hard to describe in only a few words. Such forms go beyond abbreviations (e.g., *lol, imo, btw, afaik*), and include hashtags (e.g., #propor2020), emoticons (e.g., :), : (, :P) and their consequent evolution to emojis (e.g., 😍, 😭, 🙄), which became very popular in latter years [13]. Emojis are small icons that, originally, represented the status of a human face. Recently, they started to cover also concepts in domains like food, objects, or flags, and there is work on the generation of new emojis for representing currently uncovered concepts [5].

Finding methods for predicting emoji usage may be useful for private messaging [9], chat [20], and, in general, social media applications that take advantage of the text recommendation feature. It is thus no surprise that scientific work on the usage and prediction of emojis is increasing. One of such works, and the main inspiration for this study, is the task of emoji prediction [2], which sees the emoji as the label for a short text, in this case, in English or Spanish, and proposes its automatic prediction. However, different languages represent different realities, and socio-cultural differences should play an important role when it comes to communication in social media. In fact, when directly adapting what is done for other languages, often English, some information might be lost during

© Springer Nature Switzerland AG 2020
P. Quaresma et al. (Eds.): PROPOR 2020, LNAI 12037, pp. 174–183, 2020.
https://doi.org/10.1007/978-3-030-41505-1_17

the translation process (see [17]). Therefore, we decided to recreate the task of emoji prediction, but for Portuguese.

We follow a supervised approach in the development of a set of classifiers for the automatic prediction of popular emojis, given a short text (i.e., a tweet) written in Portuguese. Such models include traditional machine learning algorithms, like Naive Bayes, as well as Recurrent Neural Networks with a Long Short Term Memory (LSTM) layer, which helped us conclude that, similarly to other tasks for which there is enough data, these networks have a clearly better performance on this task (e.g., $F1 = 52\%$ against $F1 = 23\%$) and are less affected by data unbalance. On the other hand, Naive Bayes and other traditional models have the advantage of being interpretable (i.e., the most relevant features considered for each emoji can be analysed) and help us better understand the problem. Yet, due to their low performance, this is not always much useful.

In the remainder of the paper, we overview related work on emojis and their prediction (Sect. 2); we describe the methodology followed (Sect. 3), including insights on the data and the validation of different prediction models; and we present the main results obtained for emoji prediction, using the best models (Sect. 4). We conclude with a short discussion (Sect. 5).

2   Related Work

Emojis have been used in social media for a few years and can be seen as the evolution of emoticons [13], towards better expressiveness. Currently, they are so popular that, besides being available in most social media platforms, mainstream media has started to use them in advertisement, marketing campaigns and slogans. Emojis started to be a topic of interest in Natural Language Processing (NLP), in the scope of Sentiment Analysis (SA) and Emotion Recognition (ER). For instance, Shiha and Ayvaz [15] observed that emojis were used in Twitter for adding expressiveness to positive and negative events, thus helping to classify sentiment. Towards better methods for SA and ER, several resources were developed, such as lexicons that assign polarities [12] or emotion values [14] to emojis. There is work on the relation between certain emojis and expressed emotions [19], also including recent work [6] in Portuguese. Among other results, in the latter, emotion-related emojis are predicted, using traditional machine learning approaches, but performance is low (F1≈ 23%), apparently because a large number of semantically-close emojis (62) was considered.

Although visually the same, differences on emoji usage across languages/ regions has been studied [3,21], with the main conclusion that the interpretation of some emojis is language-dependent. Barbieri et al. [2] organised a shared task on emoji prediction for short texts in English and Spanish, which lead to interesting conclusions. Emoji prediction is hard and emoji usage is indeed different in the two target languages. For instance, emojis like 🔥 and 💦 are used in different contexts, while others like (💜, 😍) have more consistent usage.

In previous work [1], the task of emoji prediction was investigated for English and best results were achieved with a Bidirectional LSTM neural network [8,

10], where the inputs of the LSTMs are character embeddings learned from the data to which pretrained word embeddings are concatenated. In opposition to word embeddings, character embeddings capture orthographically similar words, which is better for handling inflections of the same word. A related task is emoji recommendation in dialogue systems [20] or private messages [9], where methods like LSTM neural networks and Random Forest have been applied.

3   Methodology

We see emoji prediction as a multiclass classification problem, where a classifier has to predict a suitable emoji for a short text. Our approach to this problem is based on supervised machine learning. We learn a set of classifiers from training data and then assess them in testing data. This section presents the datasets used, including some decisions taken, and describes the classification models explored for emoji prediction.

3.1   Data

Considering all possible emojis would make our goal impractical, as it did in previous work [6]. We thus followed Barbieri et al. [1] and made an initial selection of 18 emojis, based on their popularity and visual differences[1], displayed in Fig. 1. We cover part of the emojis in Barbieri et al. [1], with minor differences, as we tried to include emojis related to different emotions (e.g., 😈, 💔, 😫) and flags of the Portuguese-speaking countries with the bigger communities in Twitter (🏳, 🏴).

Fig. 1. List of all the emojis considered for this work

Our dataset consisted of tweets written in Portuguese and retrieved in real-time from Twitter, between 16th September and 9th October 2019, with the help of Tweepy[2] for accessing the Twitter Streaming API. Also, as in previous work [1], we only considered tweets with an emoji at the end of the text, because the relation between text and emoji is more clear this way.

Extracted tweets helped us concluding that the frequency of different emojis was significantly different. Therefore, we ended up removing texts using the least

---

[1] Real-time usage of emojis in Twitter is available in http://emojitracker.com.
[2] Available in http://www.tweepy.org.

frequent emojis in the original selection. The eight discarded emojis are those on the right-hand side of Fig. 1 and make up only about 1% of the dataset.

The resulting dataset comprises 215,367 tweets using one of the ten different emojis in the left-hand side of Fig. 1. After removing emojis from each tweet and using them as the target label, this dataset was used for training and validation of our models. For testing purposes, another dataset was created with the same method, this time with 49,523 tweets retrieved between 9th and 15th October, using the same ten emojis. Table 1 describes the train and test datasets, with the proportion of texts using each emoji and two examples of each.

Table 1. Emoji distribution in train and test dataset

Emoji	Train	Test	Example
	50,994	12,395	Gente, e essa música, sou apaixonada nela
	(23.7%)	(25.1%)	Linda demais essa garota
	47,665	9,876	Domingo falamos então seus perdedores
	(22.1%)	(19.9%)	Posso até ser feio mais eu sou Maneirão
	31,474	6,453	Essa sim é a garota mais linda do mundo
	(14.6%)	(13.0%)	simplesmente a melhor série de comédia de todos os tempos brigada
	28,996	6,555	Queria um celular novo, o meu está todo lixado
	(13.5%)	(13.2%)	Vou pro dentista
	18,675	3,954	Se inscreva no canal do meu amigo
	(8.7%)	(8.0%)	Não perdi o celular na aula, grande dia
	14,332	2,946	Maldita a hora que torci o pé
	(6.7%)	(5.9%)	kkkkkkkkkkkkkkk que ódio
	10,039	2,545	Que dor na minha garganta
	(4.7%)	(5.1%)	1000 reais p concertar minha moto
	5,656	1,531	"pra uma menina ela joga bem" o machismo nessa frase é absurdo
	(2.6%)	(3.1%)	Q ressaca
	4514	1869	mano esse calor tá sendo uma amostra grátis do inferno
	(2.1%)	(3.8%)	Demaaaais! Super ansiosos pra sexta!!!!
	3,022	1,399	Não sei o que fazer ... Mas pronto é seguir em frente
	(1.4%)	(2.8%)	Eu confio plenamente em vocês para partirem essa m**** toda!!! Vamos

In both datasets, emoji distribution is consistent with their popularity. Even though we discarded less frequent emojis, data distribution per class is still clearly unbalanced, which may cause problems when training the classifiers, e.g., it might lead to overfitting to the predominant classes. Towards better generalisation, all username and URL mentions were replaced by @USERNAME and @URL, respectively, while the '#' symbol was removed from hashtags. This is common in tweet classification approaches (e.g., [16]).

3.2 Classifiers

The first set of classifiers is based on traditional machine learning, as in previous work for Portuguese [6], includes Naives Bayes (NB) and Support Vector Machines (SVM), in addition to Random Forest, all with implementation in the scikit-learn library[3]. They are all based on the representation of each tweet by its TF.IDF-weighted vector, using scikit-learn's *TfidfVectorizer*, after removing stopwords[4]. An extensive search (grid-search) with different numbers of features (100 to 5,000) and different n-gram intervals ($n = 1$ to $n = 1, 2, 3, 4, 5$) in the train dataset suggested that we used the 3,000 features with highest frequency in the dataset and that those features covered not only tokens, but also bigrams ($n = 2$) and trigrams ($n = 3$).

The second set of classifiers is based on neural networks, one with simple LSTM layers and one with Bidirectional LSTM layers (as in previous work for English [1]). They were based on the Keras implementation[5], but the Keras Tokenizer had the same parameters as those for the traditional classifiers.

After some experiments on the train dataset, towards the optimisation of specific neural network parameters, the best results were obtained for the following: an embedding layer followed by an LSTM, with dropout set to 20% and 100 units, and a dense layer with 5 or 10 units, depending on the number of emojis to predict. The addition of more layers decreased the performance of the network. Exploiting pretrained embeddings or learning character-based embeddings, as in previous work for English [1], was left for future work, mainly because we were working with less training data.

When using the selected parameters, the performance of the selected classifiers in a 10-fold cross-validation on the train dataset is reported in Table 2. Similarly to Duarte et al. [6], the best traditional method was NB, which outperformed the other two in precision, recall and F1-score. Yet, it was outperformed by both neural network architectures, with the best performance achieved by the simple LSTM, also on the three metrics.

Table 2. Macro average results of 10-fold cross-validation in the train dataset.

Model	Precision	Recall	F1
Naive Bayes	49% ± 3%	42% ± 2%	47% ± 3%
SVM	46% ± 2%	39% ± 2%	42% ± 1%
Random Forest	47% ± 2%	41% ± 3%	44% ± 3%
LSTM	**53% ± 4%**	**48% ± 2%**	**51% ± 2%**
Bi-LSTM	50% ± 1%	46% ± 2%	48% ± 2%

Based on this validation, we decided to use the NB and LSTM-based classifiers in the evaluation scenarios described in the following section.

---

[3] See   https://scikit-learn.org/stable/tutorial/text_analytics/working_with_tex_data.html for using scikit-learn with textual data.

[4] We used NLTK's Portuguese stopword list, https://www.nltk.org.

[5] https://keras.io.

4   Results

This section reports on the performance of the best classifiers (Sect. 3.2), in the test dataset (Sect. 3.1). Results are presented for two scenarios: first, when considering a smaller set with the five most frequent emojis (five classes); then for a larger set with the ten considered emojis (ten classes).

4.1   Scenario 1: Prediction of Five Emojis

Models for this scenario were trained only in data using the five most popular emojis. This consists of $\approx 80\%$ of all train dataset and should pose an easier challenge, both because there are less classes to predict and unbalance is lower. Table 3 shows the results for the best two models in the validation phase: NB and LSTM neural network. Even though differences were not so pronounced during the validation, here, the LSTM neural network clearly outperforms the NB model in all metrics for all five emojis, e.g. with macro-$F1 = 60\%$ against macro-$F1 = 33\%$, respectively. We notice that NB is highly affected by data unbalance, with very low performance for the emoji with less training instances ($F1 = 8\%$ for 👍, in $\approx 9\%$ of the dataset), and higher for the most frequent emojis (e.g., $F1 = 49\%$ for 😂, in $\approx 24\%$). This does not happen with the LSTM network, where, for instance, the second best $F1$ is for the least frequent emoji ($F1 = 63\%$ for 👍). We may thus conclude that, similarly to other NLP tasks (e.g., [11,18]), in this multiclass scenario, involving social media text, and for which much data is available, the LSTM-based classifier is better-suited than NB.

Table 3. Results obtained for the five most popular emojis

	Naive Bayes			LSTM		
	Precision	Recall	F1	Precision	Recall	F1
😂	42%	59%	49%	56%	78%	65%
😭	35%	31%	26%	64%	49%	55%
❤	32%	24%	27%	61%	44%	55%
😍	28%	21%	29%	61%	56%	58%
👍	13%	5%	8%	76%	53%	63%
Total Macro	32%	35%	33%	62%	60%	60%
Total Micro	30%	28%	28%	64%	56%	59%

The main advantage of NB is that, in opposition to the LSTM, it is not black-box, so we can look at the features considered and their relevance, which might help on better understanding the problem. Table 4 reveals the most relevant features considered by NB for each emoji. Given how challenging this problem was to the NB classifier, many features do surprisingly make sense. For instance, the words *amo* (love) and *linda* (pretty) are associated with 😍 and ❤, which suggests potential confusion when predicting these emojis. This also happens for the word *tranquilo* (ok), associated with 😎 and 👍. Furthermore, some slang words with negative connotation, like *seca* (drag) or *porra* (damn), are associated with 😵, some positive, like *perfeita* (perfect), are associated with 👍, and the word *rir* (laugh) is associated with 😂.

Table 4. Most relevant features by emoji for Naive Bayes in the 5-emoji scenario.

Emoji	Relevant features
😍	amo, maravilhosa, perfeitos, desejo, linda
😌	sentimento, tranquilo, obg, rir, subscrevam
♥	linda, parabéns, amo, anjo, voltou
😵	quero, seca, porra, inventar, querendo
👍	perfeita, amanhã, tranquilo, dormir, cuidando

4.2 Scenario 2: Prediction of Ten Emojis

In this scenario, models are trained in the full train dataset and tested in the full test dataset, i.e., we used the same instances as in the previous experiment, plus the remaining ≈20%, where five additional emojis are used. This adds extra difficulty in two ways: classifiers must predict twice the number of classes as before, and there are not as many instances of the additional emojis as for the previous. Table 5 shows the results in this scenario, again using the best models in the validation phase (Sect. 3.2).

Table 5. Results obtained for all the considered emojis

	Naive Bayes			LSTM		
	Precision	Recall	F1	Precision	Recall	F1
😍	30%	37%	33%	52%	59%	55%
😌	26%	42%	33%	47%	68%	56%
♥	31%	23%	26%	54%	46%	50%
😵	16%	14%	15%	49%	45%	47%
👍	9%	3%	5%	69%	52%	59%
😵	4%	3%	3%	61%	45%	52%
💜	15%	6%	9%	54%	25%	34%
😷	45%	32%	33%	77%	49%	60%
🔥	1%	0%	0%	65%	37%	48%
👍	17%	12%	14%	83%	48%	61%
Total Macro	**23%**	**25%**	**23%**	**54%**	**53%**	**52%**
Total Micro	**19%**	**17%**	**18%**	**61%**	**47%**	**52%**

As expected, performance decreases for both models and, again, the LSTM clearly outperforms NB. Data balancing still played a role in the latter model, with $F1 = 0$ for the second least frequent emoji (🔥), though this trend is less clear. For instance, even when compared to less frequent emojis, performance was still very low for 👍, which might also indicate that this emoji is used in more varied contexts, and thus harder to predict. Second worst performance was for the sixth more frequent emoji ( ).

Not only performance was better for the LSTM network, but its drop of performance, when compared to the five-emoji scenario, was also smoother than for NB. All emojis are predicted with $F1$ between 47% ( ) and 61% ( ), except for , with $F1 = 34\%$, but still much higher than with NB ($F1 = 9\%$). Again, this suggests that this emoji is used in more varied contexts, which is confirmed by the two examples in Table 1, but needs further inspection for stronger conclusions. It is the kind of situation where it would be useful to interpret the results of the LSTM network.

When tackling the prediction of emojis, Barbieri et al. [1] also performed experiments considering five, ten and twenty emojis, with best results obtained by a Bi-LSTM network. Although results are not comparable, because we focused on a different language, different emojis, and used less data, overall, our $F1$-scores are slightly lower in the five-emoji ($F1 = 63\%$) and slightly higher in the ten-emoji scenario ($F1 = 47\%$). They only present results by emoji in the twenty-emoji scenario but, looking at emojis considered in both works, it is interesting to see that the best-performing emojis are not the same. For instance, Barbieri et al. [1] reports low $F1$ for ($F1 = 27\%$) and ($F1 = 13\%$), while, for these emojis we did not get significantly worse $F1$. In fact, for the former, F1 was above average. Such differences might be related to the aforementioned cultural differences among languages and their impact on emoji utilisation. Target emojis might also play a role here, i.e., Barbieri et al. may have considered emojis more semantically-similar to those with a lower performance, making the specific task of predicting them harder. Looking at the SemEval-2018 task [2], best results for both English and Spanish are also different. In this case, the best $F1$ among all teams, for both languages, was for ($F1 = 88\%$ for English, $F1 = 70\%$ for Spanish), in both cases with a great margin over the others. This was not the case in our experiment.

5   Final Notes

Classifiers for emoji prediction may rely on the huge amounts of text using emojis that are currently produced in social media. Inspired by previous work for English and Spanish [1,2], and having in mind cultural differences between languages, we tackled the task of emoji prediction for Portuguese. We explored both traditional machine learning and deep learning models and confirmed that best results are obtained with the latter, namely a neural network with a LSTM layer. The main drawback of such a model is its black-box nature, in opposition to NB, for which we can inspect the most relevant features considered and thus understand the problem better. Results also suggest that NB is more affected by data unbalance, highly present in our datasets because data were extracted in real-time and not all emojis have the same popularity. To confirm this, we further trained new models in balanced versions of the train dataset but, instead of improvements, performance was lower for an under-sampled and for an over-sampled version. Due to lack of space, these results were not reported.

Since optimisation plays a great role in neural networks, it is something to work on in the future. We further aim to explore the usage of character and word embeddings learned from social media, thus including dense-vector representations of emojis (see, e.g., [7]) that could be used in the first layer of the neural network.

Given the current impact of emojis in communication and the availability of data, for which few or no annotation effort is required (i.e., emojis are our labels), it would be interesting to organise a shared task on emoji prediction, possibly following SemEval-2018's [2], but targeting Portuguese. This would be a nice way of involving all interested researchers, of comparing the large number of possible approaches and optimisations for this task and, of course, advancing the state-of-the-art.

Acknowledgements. This work was developed in the scope of the SOCIALITE Project (PTDC/EEISCR/2072/2014), co-financed by COMPETE 2020, Portugal 2020 – Operational Program for Competitiveness and Internationalization (POCI), European Union's ERDF (European Regional Development Fund), and the Portuguese Foundation for Science and Technology (FCT).

References

1. Barbieri, F., Ballesteros, M., Saggion, H.: Are emojis predictable? In: Proceedings of the 15th Conference of the European Chapter of the Association for Computational Linguistics: Volume 2, Short Papers, Valencia, Spain, pp. 105–111. ACL, April 2017
2. Barbieri, F., et al.: SemEval 2018 task 2: multilingual emoji prediction. In: Proceedings of the 12th International Workshop on Semantic Evaluation, pp. 24–33 (2018)
3. Barbieri, F., Kruszewski, G., Ronzano, F., Saggion, H.: How cosmopolitan are emojis?: exploring emojis usage and meaning over different languages with distributional semantics. In: Proceedings of the 24th ACM International Conference on Multimedia, pp. 531–535. ACM (2016)
4. Chen, X., Vorvoreanu, M., Madhavan, K.: Mining social media data for understanding students' learning experiences. IEEE Trans. Learn. Technol. **7**(3), 246–259 (2014)
5. Cunha, J.M., Martins, P., Machado, P.: Emojinating: representing concepts using emoji. In: Proceedings of the ICCBR 2018 Workshop on Knowledge-Based Systems in Computational Design and Media (KBS-CDM), Stockholm, Sweden (2018)
6. Duarte, L., Macedo, L., Gonçalo Oliveira, H.: Exploring emojis for emotion recognition in portuguese text. In: Moura Oliveira, P., Novais, P., Reis, L.P. (eds.) EPIA 2019. LNCS (LNAI), vol. 11805, pp. 719–730. Springer, Cham (2019). https://doi.org/10.1007/978-3-030-30244-3_59
7. Eisner, B., Rocktäschel, T., Augenstein, I., Bošnjak, M., Riedel, S.: emoji2vec: learning emoji representations from their description. In: Proceedings of The Fourth International Workshop on Natural Language Processing for Social Media, Austin, TX, USA, pp. 48–54. ACL Press, November 2016

8. Graves, A., Fernández, S., Schmidhuber, J.: Bidirectional LSTM networks for improved phoneme classification and recognition. In: Duch, W., Kacprzyk, J., Oja, E., Zadrożny, S. (eds.) ICANN 2005. LNCS, vol. 3697, pp. 799–804. Springer, Heidelberg (2005). https://doi.org/10.1007/11550907_126
9. Guibon, G., Ochs, M., Bellot, P.: Emoji recommendation in private instant messages. In: Proceedings of the 33rd Annual ACM Symposium on Applied Computing, pp. 1821–1823. ACM (2018)
10. Hochreiter, S., Schmidhuber, J.: Long short-term memory. Neural Comput. **9**(8), 1735–1780 (1997)
11. Huang, Z., Xu, W., Yu, K.: Bidirectional LSTM-CRF models for sequence tagging. CoRR abs/1508.01991 (2015)
12. Novak, P.K., Smailović, J., Sluban, B., Mozetič, I.: Sentiment of emojis. PLoS ONE **10**(12), e0144296 (2015)
13. Pavalanathan, U., Eisenstein, J.: Emoticons vs. emojis on Twitter: a causal inference approach. arXiv preprint arXiv:1510.08480 (2015)
14. Rodrigues, D., Prada, M., Gaspar, R., Garrido, M.V., Lopes, D.: Lisbon emoji and emoticon database (LEED): norms for emoji and emoticons in seven evaluative dimensions. Behav. Res. Methods **50**(1), 392–405 (2018)
15. Shiha, M., Ayvaz, S.: The effects of emoji in sentiment analysis. Int. J. Comput. Electr. Eng. (IJCEE.) **9**(1), 360–369 (2017)
16. Suttles, J., Ide, N.: Distant supervision for emotion classification with discrete binary values. In: Gelbukh, A. (ed.) CICLing 2013. LNCS, vol. 7817, pp. 121–136. Springer, Heidelberg (2013). https://doi.org/10.1007/978-3-642-37256-8_11
17. Van Nes, F., Abma, T., Jonsson, H., Deeg, D.: Language differences in qualitative research: is meaning lost in translation? Eur. J. Ageing **7**(4), 313–316 (2010)
18. Wang, Y., Huang, M., Zhu, X., Zhao, L.: Attention-based LSTM for aspect-level sentiment classification. In: Proceedings of the 2016 Conference on Empirical Methods in Natural Language Processing, Austin, Texas, pp. 606–615. Association for Computational Linguistics, November 2016
19. Wood, I.D., Ruder, S.: Emoji as emotion tags for tweets. In: Proceedings of the Emotion and Sentiment Analysis Workshop LREC2016, Portorož, Slovenia, pp. 76–79 (2016)
20. Xie, R., Liu, Z., Yan, R., Sun, M.: Neural emoji recommendation in dialogue systems. CoRR abs/1612.04609 (2016). http://arxiv.org/abs/1612.04609
21. Zhao, P., Jia, J., An, Y., Liang, J., Xie, L., Luo, J.: Analyzing and predicting emoji usages in social media. In: Companion Proceedings of the the Web Conference 2018, pp. 327–334. International World Wide Web Conferences Steering Committee (2018)

Vitality Analysis of the Linguistic Atlas of Brazil on Twitter

Arley Prates M. Nunes[1,2], Luis Emanuel N. de Jesus[1,2],
Daniela Barreiro Claro[1,2(✉)] ⓘ, Jacyra Mota[1,3] ⓘ, Silvana Ribeiro[1,3] ⓘ,
Marcela Paim[1,3], and Josane Oliveira[1,3]

[1] Federal University of Bahia, Ondina Campus, Salvador, Bahia, Brazil
{dclaro,alib}@ufba.br
[2] FORMAS Research Group, Computer Science Department, LaSiD Laboratory,
Institute of Mathematics and Statistical, Salvador, Bahia, Brazil
formasresearchgroup@gmail.com
http://www.formas.ufba.br
[3] Institute of Letters, ALiB Project, Conselho Nacional de Desenvolvimento
Científico e Tecnológico (CNPQ), Salvador, Bahia, Brazil

Abstract. The diversity of the linguistic reality of Brazil is analyzed through the Linguistic Atlas of Brazil (ALiB). ALiB's first publication covered 25 capitals of Brazil into the volume 1 and 2 of the Atlas. Taking into account the semantic-lexical map from ALiB, this paper analyzes the vitality of the ALiB terms through Twitter. Two methods are proposed: one lexical that deals with the lexical variations of ALiB terms on Twitter, and the other reflects the disambiguation of Twitter terms with similar meaning to those of the project. The results highlight that some terms are no longer used or not employed in a social network. On the other hand, some terms cataloged by ALiB continue to be used by Brazilians even in social media.

Keywords: Linguistic map · Sociolinguistics · Vitality · Twitter

1 Introduction

Natural language is the most common way to communicate, either by speech or writing. According to [7], sociolinguistics observe patterns of linguistic behavior within a speech community. Linguists and dialectologists came together to elaborate on a Linguistic Atlas of Brazil, in which the main objective is to describe the linguistic reality of Brazil [9].

The ALiB Project (Linguistic Atlas of Brazil) was conceived since 1950 and supported by the Brazilian government through decree no. 30,643, of March 20, 1952, which determined its creation, but prevented by numerous difficulties [9]. Only from 1996 onwards, the ALiB Project resumed, and the research started through linguistic surveys.

In 2014, the ALiB Project published its first two volumes, which corresponds to the analysis of sociolinguistic variation in 25 capitals of Brazil [2]. According

ⓒ Springer Nature Switzerland AG 2020
P. Quaresma et al. (Eds.): PROPOR 2020, LNAI 12037, pp. 184–194, 2020.
https://doi.org/10.1007/978-3-030-41505-1_18

to [3], 1100 informants were contacted, and the phonetic-phonological (including prosody questions), morphosyntactic, and semantic-lexical questionnaires were applied.

The collection of these data began more than two decades ago. Since then, each term has been studied into diverse linguistic departments. At the same time, the spread of social networks has influenced Brazilian daily lives. Thus, a new challenge has risen on ALiB Project: the need to evaluate the linguistic vitality of ALiB terms in social media. Twitter was chosen due to its domain independence, its text documents, and the locality of the people who use it.

From ALiB, only the semantic-lexical questionnaire was used, which provides the lexical variants of Brazilian informants located throughout the Brazilian territory. This questionnaire has 202 questions and a variety of answers from informants. From ALiB [2], 35 distinct lexical terms were observed, and this set was used throughout Twitter searches. Some of these terms are not probable to occur on Twitter. However, in this first moment, we do not make a distinction of these terms to observe the ALiB comportment against social media.

This work analyzes the linguistic vitality of the ALiB terms through two approaches using a Twitter *corpus* obtained from February to March 2019. The first approach was a lexical analysis that verified the occurrence of the ALiB term presented on Twitter. The second approach was a semantic analysis that identifies the meaning of ALiB terms found in tweets through a lexical disambiguation method to prove their vitality. Results obtained highlighted that some terms are no longer used or are not employed on social media. On the other hand, some terms cataloged by ALiB continue to be employed by Brazilians even on social netwroks such as Twitter.

This paper is organized into sections as follows. Section 2 presents the materials, Sect. 3 describes our approach, and Sect. 4 explains the experiments performed and each result. Section 5 presents related works, and Sect. 6 discusses some findings and threats. Finally, Sect. 7 concludes and presents some future work.

2 Materials

Our approach has manipulated mainly three materials: a Corpus from Twitter, a dictionary to verify the presence of ambiguity, and a thesaurus to provide disambiguation of the terms. Materials are detailed in the following sections.

2.1 Twitter Corpus

Our corpus was obtained through Twitter via the API (Application Programming Interface) that gets the data, which is daily shared on the Twitter digital platform [8]. It was collected through the tweets and replies, from February to March 2019, totaling 2,692,460 tweets, published in Brazilian Portuguese language. These tweets are stored into JSON format. Each JSON line represents a tweet and its respective attributes. This corpus was organized into 270 JSON files with 1000 tweets per file containing approximately 16 MB (MegaBytes), which resulted in a corpus with over 17 GB (GigaBytes).

2.2 Lexicon Analysis

The lexical analysis was based on the semantic-lexical questionnaire obtained from ALiB Project. Lexical variants were provided by Brazilian informants located throughout the national territory. These data were published in the first volume of the Linguistic Atlas of Brazil [2], presenting only data from the capitals of Brazil. From the application of this questionnaire to the informants, the surveys that have information regarding the locality are gathered and thus it is possible to generate the maps from ALiB. For instance, MAP L23 - "amarelinha" corresponds to informants' answers to the question "a game where children scratch a figure on the floor, made up of numbered squares, throw a pebble and jump with one leg". Among the answers, the following variations stand out: "academia", "avião", "maré", "macaco", "macaca", "macacão", "amarelinha", "caracol" and "sapata".

Table 1 presents the 7 maps and their respective lexical variations.

Table 1. Linguistic maps - ALiB Project

MAPS	VARIATIONS
AMARELINHA	ACADEMIA, AVIÃO, MARÉ, MACACO, MACACA, MACACÃO, AMARELINHA, CARACOL, SAPATA
SUTIÃ	SUTIÃ, CORPETE, CALIFOM, PORTA-SEIO, GOLEIRO
PROSTITUTA	PUTA, PRIMA, PROSTITUTA, RAPARIGA, GAROTA DE PROGRAMA, MERETRIZ, QUENGA, BISCATE, RAMPEIRA, RAMEIRA
BRINQUEDO DE EMPINAR COM VARETA	QUADRADO, CORUJA, PIPA, PAPAGAIO, PEIXINHO, RAIA, PANDORGA, RABIOLA, CANGULA, CURICA, PEPETA
BRINQUEDO DE EMPINAR SEM VARETA	AVIÃO, PIPA, PAPAGAIO, RATINHO, RAIA, PERIQUITO, BOLACHINHA, PANDORGA, CURICA, CAIXOTINHO, CAIXOTINHA, CAPOCHETA, JERECO
BALA/CONFEITO/BOMBOM	BALA, BOMBOM, QUEIMADO, CARAMELO, CONFEITO
SINALEIRO/SEMÁFORO/SINAL	SINAL, FAROL, SEMÁFORO, SINALEIRO, SINALEIRA, LUMINOSO

2.3 Semantic Analysis

The semantic analysis aimed to identify the same meaning from the terms of ALiB Project found on Twitter. Such terms may be in the same context as the ALiB linguistic maps. A knowledge-based approach using the Lesk [6] method of lexical disambiguation of meaning using OpenWordNet-PT was employed.

Lesk [6] algorithm aims to disambiguate specific words in short sentences. Authors in [1] proposed to use WordNet instead of traditional dictionaries. WordNet [5] is a lexical database and was originally created for the English language.

Words are organized into synsets, that is, sets of synonymous forms that represent a concept. These synsets are interconnected through semantic relationships such as hyponymy/hyperonymy, meronymy/holonymy, and antonymy, forming a taxonomy of concepts [5].

WordNet for Portuguese began around the year 2000. Since then, specific tesaurus emerged, such as WordNet-BR and OpenWordNet-PT. OpenWordNet-PT was motivated by the need for an accessible and affordable WordNet that allowed knowledge sharing with the scientific community [11].

OpenWordnet-PT [12], abbreviated as OpenWN-PT, maps the synsets from English to the Portuguese correspondent. Information from Wikipedia articles in Portuguese is used to aggregate relevant information in OpenWN-PT [12]. Currently OpenWN-PT, according to [11], has 43,925 synsets, among which 32,696 correspond to nouns, 4,675 verbs, 5,575 to adjectives and 979 adverbs. We used the OpenWordnet-PT in our Semantic Analysis to disambiguate some of the ALiB terms. We deeply explain our approach in the following sections.

3   Our Methods

The process of vitality investigation was divided into two analyzes, as shown in Fig. 1: lexical and semantic analysis. Our Twitter corpus, now on called TwitterALiB, was used on both methods.

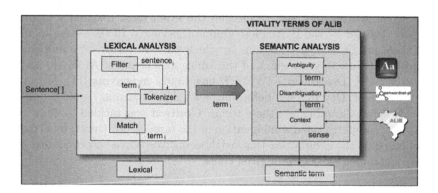

Fig. 1. Vitality analysis of ALiB terms.

3.1   Lexicon Method

Our lexical method aims to identify the occurrence of ALiB terms on TwitterALiB *corpus*. Our analysis was structured into four steps:

1. FILTER: A filter is performed in the corpus to retrieve only users from the Brazilian capitals;
2. TOKENIZER: it is divided into two steps:

(a) terms with single words, for instance: "macaxeira";
(b) terms with multi-words, for instance: "chuva de gelo";
3. MATCH: It consists in comparing the tweet term according to the type of token: single word or multi word.

Then, each ALiB term, which is ambiguous, was manipulated by our Semantic method.

3.2 Semantic Method

Our semantic analysis consists in verifying if the terms found in the tweets have the same meaning used in the ALiB Project. For instance: Given a target word (ALiB term) in a context (tweet), a sense disambiguation algorithm is applied to choose the best meaning of a target word present in a context. Our semantic method is depicted in Fig. 1:

1. AMBIGUITY: Identify ambiguous ALiB terms through an online dictionary[1] from the Portuguese language;
2. DISAMBIGUATION: Query definitions of ambiguous terms in OpenWN-PT; Include new definitions into the OpenWN-PT for terms identified as ambiguous.
3. CONTEXT: Performs disambiguation through Lesk algorithm adapted to Portuguese;

The terms used in this work totalized 215 terms distributed in 23 semantic-lexical maps. **Ambiguity** was verified on the seven most frequently linguistic maps over Twitter by the Portuguese Online Dictionary. In the seven linguistic maps, there are 68 lexical variations in which only 24 terms were ambiguous. **Disambiguation** analyzed which of the ambiguous terms of ALiB are present at OpenWN-PT. Despite OpenWN-PT has 43,925 synonyms [11], few ALiB terms are present. Due to a few definitions with ALiB meaning, some definitions were included to disambiguate these terms. **Context** was tackled by Lesk algorithm which computes the disambiguation of the target word (term) in a context (tweet) based on the assumption that neighboring words in a target context tend to share a common subject in a given context.

4   Experiments and Results

Experiments were performed to identify the vitality of ALiB terms in the Twitter context, analyzing the occurrence of terms by the most extensive distribution throughout Brazil. This is one of the methodologies adopted by ALiB Project and similarly used to guide the analysis of vitality in this work [2].

Two experiments were performed to verify the vitality of ALiB terms on Twitter. The first experiment checks the occurrence of terms in tweets, and the second experiment disambiguates the terms from tweets, verifying that they have the same meaning as the ALiB Project.

---

[1] https://www.dicio.com.br.

4.1   Lexicon Experiments

Our lexical experiment carried the terms from ALiB. Seven linguistic maps were chosen: MAP L15-prostituta, MAP L20-brinquedo de empinar c/vareta (toy to stack with rod), MAP L21-brinquedo de empinar s/vareta (toy to stack without rod), MAP L23-amarelinha, MAP L24-bala, MAP L25-sutiã and MAP L27-semáforo. Among these terms, "bala", "queimado", "sinal", "semáforo", "farol" are ambiguous as definitions on the Online Dictionary of Portuguese Language. Thus, it is necessary to analyze their meaning to identify if they correspond with the sense of the ALiB.

4.2   Semantic Experiments

Semantic experiments focused on tweets in which terms are ambiguous. Table 2 lists each linguistic map from ALiB and the occurrence on Twitter.

Table 2. Terms from ALiB with similar sense on Twitter

Sutiã		Prostituta 1		Bala	
ALiB	Twitter	ALiB	Twitter	ALiB	Twitter
Sutiã	Sutiã	Prostituta	Puta	Bala	Bala
Corpete	Corpete	Mulher...	Prostituta	Bombom	Bombom
Califon		Puta	Garota de Programa	Caramelo	Caramelo
Porta-seio		Rapariga	Meretriz	Confeito	
Goleiro		Meretriz	Rapariga	Queimado	
		Rameira	Biscate		
		Outras			

It is observable that for the first linguistic map (L25 - Sutiã), only "sutiã" and "corpete" was found in Twitter. For the linguistic map (L15 - Prostituta), almost all terms also occur in Twitter.

Additionally, a manual examination was performed to validate the results from the semantic method. This manual examination aimed to disambiguate the terms which were not disambiguated by Lesk algorithm. Each term was verified manually over the tweet, remarking the meaning for each tweet. The notes were: the direction of ALiB, sense not found, and other senses. This type of annotation occurred in sentences that possess ambiguity or possess little information to indicate the meaning.

5   Results

A survey of each linguistic map occurrences was carried out, with the quantity of 509 of MAP L15 - Prostituta 1, 226 of MAP L25 - Sutiã and 87 of MAP L24 - bala.

MAP L15 - Prostituta 1 provided a wide lexical variation within the highest number of occurrences on Twitter, something that consolidates the information mapped by the ALiB research project. Indeed, this term is so vast that it resulted in the publication of two maps on ALiB Atlas.

Regarding the term "prostituta" found on Twitter, 30 of them had the same sense of ALiB in 7 capitals concentrated in the northeast and the south of Brazil. As regards the distribution of terms, Twitter differs from ALiB map because it has the term "puta" with the most extensive distribution followed by the term "prostituta". Considering the vitality, the term "prostituta", "mulher..." and "puta" maintain their presence. Despite the fact that the term "puta" was the most widely distributed in the state of São Paulo, Rio de Janeiro, and Vitória in ALiB maps, it lost in Twitter and where almost permuted by the term "prostituta". Such a phenomenon occurred with opposite characteristics in Recife, Belo Horizonte, Curitiba, and Porto Alegre where the term "puta" was consolidated.

Evaluating the occurrence of "garota de programa" and "biscate", which are linked to others in ALiB is validated with terms of low occurrence in the country. However, "rameira/rampeira", "rapariga" and "meretriz" have their vitality compromised in relation to data collected by this work since there was no occurrence.

Fig. 2. ALiB and Twitter distribution (MAP L15 - prostituta 1)

MAP L25 - sutiã obtained 13 occurrences on Twitter with the same sense used in the ALiB Project. At almost all capitals, the distribution was given by the term "sutiã", confirming the same information collected by ALiB within the MAP L25 - sutiã [2].

With the analysis based on the distribution of terms, the capitals Manaus, Recife, Curitiba, Sao Paulo and Rio de Janeiro provided the assessment of the vitality of terms based on research from ALiB and Twitter. Among these capitals, Curitiba and Rio de Janeiro obtained the same results, having the term "sutiã" in 100% of occurrences. In the capitals Manaus, Sao Paulo and Rio de Janeiro the results brought divergence. In Manuas and Recife, the term "corpete" and, in São Paulo, the term "califom" did not appear in the tweets.

An interesting aspect in the construction of this map is the verification of the terms in the Federal District, state that was not covered by the ALiB project due to the time of foundation of the state and the aspects that interfered with the linguistic variation of the region. In this case, on twitter, there was an occurrence of "sutiã" and "corpete".

Fig. 3. ALiB and Twitter distribution (MAP L25 - sutiã)

Regarding MAP L24 - bala (Fig. 4), 87 occurrences of this term were extracted from twitter. Among these, 17 occurrences were in the same sense of the ALiB term, with its distribution in 6 states, distributed in the northeast, south, and center-west regions.

In the northeast region, São Luís obtained the hegemony of the term "bombom" from the tweets in disagreement with the term "bala", presented in MAP L24 - bala from ALiB. In Recife, the terms "caramelo", "confeito" and "bombom" did not appear in the sense of ALiB terms. Only the term "bala" occurred in the sense of ALiB.

In the south, Rio de Janeiro and São Paulo presented two terms. In São Paulo, it was verified the aggregation of the terms "bombom" and "caramelo", as similar in Rio de Janeiro where the terms "bombom" and "caramelo" also appeared. On the other hand, in Minas Gerais, there was no variation on the results from ALiB neither on Twitter, consolidating the term "bala" as preponderant in this capital.

Similar to MAP L15 - prostituta 1, MAP L24 - bala also obtained results on Twitter for the Federal District. The terms "confeito" and "queimado" are not active on Twitter due to the non-occurrence; however, the terms "bala", "bombom" and "caramelo" remain vital in the Portuguese language in social networks.

Fig. 4. ALiB and Twitter distribution (MAP L24 - bala)

6   Related Works

The main work related to this is the ALiB project [2]. Other works have focused on vitality, such as [13] and [10] and lexical disambiguation. Authors in [13] conducts an analysis of the vitality of the Italian language in a small community of Araguaia, Marechal Floriano, Espírito Santo to analyze the factors that lead to the maintenance or loss of a minority language. Similarly, authors in [13] also uses as a theoretical basis the document Language Vitality and Endangerment from UNESCO 2003 [4]. However, it differs mainly by two issues. The population is very small, Italian immigrants living in a small region of Brazil and the approach of vitality analysis was made by applying questionnaires with themes related to the history and social of Italian people.

In the work [10], authors studied methods of meaningless lexical disambiguation in a Brazilian Portuguese corpus. However, wordnet-PR (Princeton) is used as a sense repository as a multilingual approach, in which automatic

Portuguese-English translators are used. In addition, Nóbrega evaluated the use of wordnet-BR[2] however, at the date of publication, this wordnet was still under development.

Thus, the present work aims differently to analyze the vitality of lexical variants of Brazilian Portuguese based on ALiB terms.

7   Discussions and Challenges

From our lexical and semantic perspectives, some important issues must be discussed. OpenWordnet-PT is one of the WordNets for Brazilian Portuguese based on wordnet-PR, which is continually being improved. Therefore the word sense from ALiB is particular in some cases, not even being present in a dictionary. Thus, it is important to discuss how we can improve it and where it must be included. The use of the Lesk algorithm requires a lot of definitions (gloss) in wordnet. This can be a limiting factor to disambiguate some of the ALiB terms.

We analyzed seven ALiB maps with ambiguous and unambiguous terms, but only two of them contain ambiguous terms in tweets. MAP L15 - prostituta 1 had one ambiguous term: prima (cousin). MAP L24 - bala had two ambiguous terms: bala (candy) and queimado (candy).

In the work [4], authors propose six factors that describe the vitality of a language or its danger of disappearance. The vitality of lexical variations from Brazil requires further study. Within Twitter, it is not possible to state that Brazilian Internet users no longer use the ALiB terms. We can state that the term was not found on social media. Moreover, the location from Twitter needs a substantial analysis due to its inaccurate information characteristics.

Another challenge was concerned with the period in which Twitter data was collected. During this period, many subjects and content posted on Twitter were related to facts happening at the publication time. Thus, this can interfere with domain variability.

8   Conclusion

This work investigated the vitality of ALiB term against Twitter. We evaluated the answers from the semantic-lexical questionnaire in the ALiB project to the appearance of Twitter data. We observed that some ALiB terms are still present in daily Brazilian Portuguese, even in social networks. Other terms completely disappeared in social media. As future work, we would like to improve our corpus with a year collection from twitter to better cover a variety of domains. We also would like to cover other types of social media to spread the chance to find similar ALiB sense terms.

Acknowledgements. Authors would like to thank FAPESB, CNPQ and Capes for their financial support.

---

[2] http://www.nilc.icmc.usp.br/wordnetbr/index.html.

References

1. Banerjee, S., Pedersen, T.: An adapted lesk algorithm for word sense disambiguation using WordNet. In: Gelbukh, A. (ed.) CICLing 2002. LNCS, vol. 2276, pp. 136–145. Springer, Heidelberg (2002). https://doi.org/10.1007/3-540-45715-1_11
2. Cardoso, S., et al.: Atlas Linguístico do Brasil. EDUEL (2015). https://books.google.com.br/books?id=rMyCDwAAQBAJ
3. Cardoso, S.A.M.: Projeto atlas linguístico do brasil - projeto alib: Descrição e estágio atual. Revista da ABRALIN **18**(1) (2009)
4. Drude, S., et al.: Language vitality and endangerment (2003). https://unesdoc.unesco.org/ark:/48223/pf0000183699. Accessed 20 Apr 2019
5. Fellbaum, C., Miller, G.: WordNet: An Electronic Lexical Database, Language, Speech, and Communication. MIT Press, Cambridge (1998). https://books.google.at/books?id=Rehu8OOzMIMC
6. Lesk, M.: Automatic sense disambiguation using machine readable dictionaries: how to tell a pine cone from an ice cream cone. In: Proceedings of the 5th Annual International Conference on Systems Documentation, pp. 24–26. Citeseer (1986)
7. Lucchesi, D., Araújo, S.: A Teoria da Variação Línguística (2011). http://www.vertentes.ufba.br/a-teoria-da-variacao-linguistica. Accessed 18 Apr 2019
8. Makice, K.: Twitter API: Up and Running Learn How to Build Applications With the Twitter API, 1st edn. O'Reilly Media Inc., Sebastopol (2009)
9. Mota, J.A., Paim, M.M.T., Ribeiro, S.S.C. (eds.): Documentos 5 - Projeto Atlas Linguístico do Brasil Avaliação e Perspectivas. Quarteto (2015). https://alib.ufba.br/sites/alib.ufba.br/files/documentos_5.pdf
10. Nóbrega, F.A.A.: Desambiguação lexical de sentidos para o português por meio de uma abordagem multilíngue mono e multidocumento. Ph.D. thesis, Universidade de São Paulo (2013)
11. Oliveira, H.G., de Paiva, V., Freitas, C., Rademaker, A., Real, L., Simões, A.: As wordnets do português. In: Oslo Studies in Language, vol. 7, no. 1, pp. 397–424 (2015)
12. de Paiva, V., Rademaker, A., de Melo, G.: OpenWordNet-PT: an open Brazilian wordnet for reasoning. In: Proceedings of COLING 2012: Demonstration Papers, pp. 353–360. The COLING 2012 Organizing Committee, Mumbai, India, December 2012. http://www.aclweb.org/anthology/C12-3044
13. Peres, E.P.: Análise da vitalidade do vêneto em uma comunidade de imigrantes no espírito santo. Revista (Con) Textos Linguísticos **5**(5), 94–110 (2011)

Fact-Checking for Portuguese: Knowledge Graph and Google Search-Based Methods

Roney Lira de Sales Santos$^{(\boxtimes)}$ and Thiago Alexandre Salgueiro Pardo

Interinstitutional Center for Computational Linguistics (NILC),
Institute of Mathematical and Computer Sciences, University of São Paulo,
São Carlos, SP, Brazil
roneysantos@usp.br, taspardo@icmc.usp.br

Abstract. The propagation of fake news may influence a large number of people on a wide range of subjects. Once the spread of fake news reached a critical point, relevant initiatives to fight them have emerged. In this paper, we adapt from English a knowledge graph-based method for fact-checking and propose a new one based on Google search, following content-based strategies for tackling deception in Portuguese, differently from what has been previously done in linguistic-based approaches. Our results are promising and indicate new ways to deal with the deceptive content detection issue.

Keywords: Fake news · Fact-checking · Knowledge graph · Google search

1 Introduction

Deception is a general term that includes kinds of content such as fake news, rumors, hoaxes, irony and sarcasm. [3] claims that deception may be intentionally produced and transmitted in order to create a false impression or conclusion. Currently, fake news are the most famous type of deception, as it has gained substantial attention in recent years, evolving to a passionately criticized Internet phenomenon [12].

Fake news detection is defined as the prediction of the chances of a particular news article (news report, editorial, expose, etc.) being intentionally deceptive, using varied approaches [20]. Such approaches may be defined by the type of detection they use, being divided in linguistic-based and content-based approaches, according to the taxonomy proposed by [27]. Linguistic-based approaches attempts to identify clues from the language writing style and characteristics, such as part of speech tags, semantics, spelling errors, and content diversity, among others, to construct detection models [14,16,21]. Content-based approaches focuses on what is being transmitted, that is, on identifying the meaning of the content passed to the user. Fact-checking models try to tackle this issue.

© Springer Nature Switzerland AG 2020
P. Quaresma et al. (Eds.): PROPOR 2020, LNAI 12037, pp. 195–205, 2020.
https://doi.org/10.1007/978-3-030-41505-1_19

Formally, fact-checking is the task of evaluating whether the statements made, in both written and spoken language, are true, which is usually done by trained professionals [24]. These professionals should evaluate past speeches, debates, legislation, images and known facts to perform the task of fact-checking and, combined with their reasoning, reach a verdict. According to [11], depending on the complexity of the statement, this whole process may take from less than an hour to a few days. For this reason, this process has been the subject of requests from the journalism community for the development of computational tools to automate parts of this task [2,7].

In this context, with the desire to help filling the existent gap in fake news detection and minimizing the problem of spread of fake news in the web, in this paper we report our efforts to build an automatic fact-checking approach for the Portuguese language. Following some of the ideas of [6], we perform experiments of veracity detection by exploring a knowledge graph extracted from Wikipedia infoboxes in Portuguese. We also propose a baseline approach based on Google searches, trying to reproduce the usual human behavior to check information. It is important to highlight that approaches for fake news detection in Portuguese already exist. They are linguistic-based and achieve good overall results (see, e.g., [14]). However, to the best of our knowledge, we report in this paper the first content-based approaches for Portuguese.

The remainder of this paper is organized as follows. Section 2 briefly introduces the main related work in the area. Section 3 presents the fact-checking approaches that we investigate, while experiments and results are reported in Sect. 4. Some final remarks are made in Sect. 5.

2   Related Work

Automatic fact-checking is a relatively recent task. We briefly report below some of the main attempts to tackle it.

In [25], the authors define fact-checking in a computational way, using the specific context of the statement and considering it as a binary classification task, but there are cases where the statements are not completely fake or true, thereby placing it in intermediate classes as "mostly truth" or "half-truth". This type of classification brought other approaches that include such classes [15,19].

The work of [24] is quite complete in relation to the directions that should be taken into account in the fact-checking task. The authors consider that a frequent entry for fact-checking approaches is a triple (subject, predicate, object), once this type of input facilitates fact-checking in structured datasets (and also semi-structured ones). More specific cases may be found when the triples require more complex representations (for example, a statement that contains several participants – subjects – should be represented in multiple triples [8]) or when it is necessary to disambiguate the entities and their properties [13].

Given the type of input that the fact-checking system receives, it is necessary to find a way to manipulate the information to have the expected result. Knowledge graphs are widely used in the literature [23,26] and provide a rich set of structured information related to world knowledge stored in a machine-readable format that supports the task of checking facts [24]. In [6], the authors use the topology of a knowledge graph to find the shortest path among nodes that represent the entities in given statements and consider that this proximity may indicate true or fake content. This is one of the approaches that we test in this paper, as we explain later.

Although papers use the classification of the statement on a scale between false and true, other works highlight alternative ways of checking content, such as verifying whether the statement is common sense [10], a rumor [28], a clickbait [4,17], if the title of the text is related to its body (of news) [5], reliability of news articles, classifying them as reliable, hoax, satire or advertisement [18] and other types of content checking such as non-factual, unimportant or check-worthy sentences [11].

3   Fact-Checking Approaches

We start by exploring the proposal of [6], which represents statements extracted from Wikipedia's infoboxes through triples (subject, predicate, object). The set of such triples are combined to produce a knowledge graph, which reflects all the factual relationships between the entities mentioned in the statements. Additionally, we present an approach that retrieves Google's search results and evaluate if the information available in the results (the snippets) shows some cue that discriminates if the news are fake. The subsections below detail each of the approaches.

3.1   Wikipedia's Knowledge Graph (WKG)

[6] claims that, in a knowledge graph, distinct paths between the subject and object typically provide different factual support for the statement that those nodes represent, even if the paths contain the same number of intermediate nodes. Generic entities often provide weaker support because these nodes link to many entities and yield little specific information, such as *cidade* ("city") or *futebol* ("soccer"). On the other hand, the entities inside the path may be very specific and provide stronger support.

The Wikipedia's infobox database for Portuguese language was found in DBPedia Project[1]. There are a lot of databases that represent the infoboxes in several languages. Detailed information about this and some descriptional data are shown in Sect. 4.

The authors affirm that the resulting knowledge graph represents most of the factual relationships among the entities mentioned in Wikipedia's infobox statements. Then, given a new statement, the authors expect it to be true if there is a direct edge or a short path connecting the subject to its object within the knowledge graph. However, if the statement is false, they should have neither

---

[1] Available at https://wiki.dbpedia.org/develop/datasets/downloads-2016-10.

edges nor short paths that connect subjects and objects. In addition, the short paths, called *semantic proximity* by the authors, are calculated as a measure of the truth value $\tau(e) \in [0, 1]$ of a new statement $e = (s, p, o)$, which has its value obtained by the path evaluation function $maxW(P_{s,o})$, following the equation below:

$$W(P_{s,o}) = W(v_1, ..., v_n) = \left[1 + \sum_{i=2}^{n-1} \log k(v_i) \right]^{-1} \tag{1}$$

where $v_1, ..., v_n$ is the set of nodes that are between the subject s (v_1) and the object o (v_n), and $k(v_i)$ is the v_i's entity degree, i.e., the number of statements within the knowledge graph that the entity participates in.

The calculation of the truth value $\tau(e)$ maximizes semantic proximity, which is equivalent to finding the shortest path between the subject and the object [22]. Therefore, given a new statement that already contains an edge e connecting the entities related by the predicate p, the value of $\tau(e)$ is equal to 1, the maximum value that may be assigned to the statement. Otherwise, if the nodes representing the subject and the object are connected via other nodes, the value of $\tau(e)$ decreases proportionally to the increase in the number of nodes between the subject and the object.

Our objective in the replication of this proposal is (i) to verify the availability of the necessary information for Portuguese, building a knowledge graph from Wikipedia, and, with it, (ii) to implement the analysis proposal and evaluate the results.

3.2   Proposal with Google's Search Results (GSR)

The baseline approach proposed in this work is based on the results of Google search, trying to reproduce the usual behavior that people have in quickly searching for news to check their veracity. Specifically, we want to measure if, when a person uses the Google search with the title or some other parts of the news, the visualized search results are clear in indicating if the news are true or not.

When a news text is submitted to our proposed process, its title is extracted, which usually contains the most relevant news information. Then Google search is performed with the words of the title, returning two important results for us: the snippets and links to the resulting texts.

The snippets are the texts that summarize or show the beginning of the news of the links resulting from the search in Google. Usually, in a Google search result, the snippets are just below the link information.

All the resulting texts in the first search page are then analyzed. In this way, we adopted the proposal of [9], which claims that, to find potentially relevant sources, it is more common to look only at the first few results or 'hits' on the first page in the browser. For this, each one of the results is submitted to a verification step: if one of the terms that characterize falsity occurs, that news is classified as fake. Otherwise, the news is considered true. The following words (including their variations for gender and number in Portuguese) were considered as indications of fake content: *fake, falso* ("false"), *mentira* ("lie"), *calúnia* ("calumny"), *inverídico* ("untrue"), *enganoso* ("deceptive"), *farsa* ("scam"), *ilusório* ("illusory"), *ilegítimo* ("illegitimate"), *boato* and *rumor* ("rumor").

4   Experiments and Results

We report in this section our experiment setup and the achieved results. For the WKG method, we also explain how to build the knowledge graph for Portuguese and compare the results of our method to the English results obtained by [6].

4.1   The WKG Method

Initially, the construction of the knowledge graph for Portuguese was based on data collected by the DBPedia project [1]. For comparison purposes with the results of [6], the graph for Portuguese was constructed from three datasets of triples that are in the DBPedia project: (i) the *"Instance Types"* dataset, which contains triples in the form (subject, *"is-a"*, class), where "class" is a category of the DBPedia ontology; (ii) the *"Infobox Properties"* dataset, which contains the triples that were extracted from the infoboxes; and (iii) the *DBPedia Ontology*, which was used to reconstruct the full ontological hierarchy of the graph, as well as in [6].

Overall, the three datasets contain 7,853,605 lines, in which the largest one represents the information of the infoboxes, with 7,273,995 lines, followed by the dataset of types and ontology, with 578,847 and 746 lines, respectively. It is noteworthy that the lines that had the predicate "subClassOf" were the basis for reconstructing the ontology. For example, *park* is a subclass of *place*, creating an edge between these two nodes in the graph. It is important to mention that all the information was in English, being necessary to translate the words before including them in the graph.

In the end, the graph is formed by 1,778,677 entity nodes linked by 3,646,144 undirected edges, being much smaller than the graph of [6], which contains 3 million entity nodes and approximately 23 million edges. As in [6], triples which contained numbers, useless information - as image, url, and align symbols - and unique characters (size 1) have been discarded, since they never appear as subjects in other triples.

We performed an experiment with the WKG method to validate simple factual statements in Portuguese, using Eq. 1. Here we submit several simple statements about history and geography. For the purpose of comparison with [6], we used the same model of statements, which were in the form "p_i was married to s_j" and "c_i is the capital of e_j", where p_i is a Brazilian president, s_j is the spouse of a Brazilian president, c_i is a city and e_j is a Brazilian state or a country.

All the data were obtained from Wikipedia[2]. Simple statements were formed by combining each of the N subject entities with each of the N object entities.

---

[2] The data is available at http://tiny.cc/fum86y.

For example, we have "Brasília is the capital of Brazil", but we also have "Brasília is the capital of Portugal". Performing this procedure, we got: (i) Brazilian presidential couples with $N = 24$ and 576 statements; (ii) Brazilian state capitals, with $N = 27$ and 729 statements; and (iii) world capitals, with $N = 180$ and 32,400 statements. For avoiding bias and having a fair experiment, if a triple indicating a true statement was already present in the knowledge graph, we removed it from the graph before computing the truth value, as well as [6] did.

The truth value was calculated for the statements in each area and organized in three matrices, which we refer by *matrices of statements*. Figure 1 contains the results for the two best results (states and countries), with the graph in English by [6] represented at the left and the graph in Portuguese represented at the right side. In each matrix, the subjects are represented in rows and objects are represented in columns. In the diagonals, the true statements were represented and the higher truth values were mapped to colors of increasing intensity.

It is possible to see that in the statements related to capitals, the resulting matrices with truth values are similar, with the diagonal representing the true statements being very clear, both for English and Portuguese. The experiment related to the Brazilian presidents had a poor result due to the few connections that come from the nodes representing the spouses to the presidents (degree avg $= 5$), in which they always pass by nodes that have high degree (connected node max degree avg $= 10,064$), making the truth value to considerably decrease.

Finally, to show the accuracy of the fact checker method for Portuguese, we estimate the probability that $\tau(e) > \tau(e')$, in which e is a true statement and e' is a false statement (as well as we made to build the truth value matrices). We compare our results to the results of [6]. Table 1 shows the results.

Table 1. Accuracy of the fact checker

Area	English [6]	Portuguese
Presidential couples	0.98	0.46
State capitals	0.61	0.90
World capitals	0.95	0.87
Avg.	0.84	0.74

Overall, the results are encouraging. Considering that the graph for Portuguese is significantly smaller than for English, the accuracy is surprisingly good.

4.2   The GSR Method

In the GSR proposal, we use the journalistic news of the FAKE.BR CORPUS [14] as test set. This corpus has 7,200 news, being 3,600 fake and 3,600 true samples. Here, we used only the title of each news for performing the search. Then, we perform the Google searches with three types of queries related to the news title:

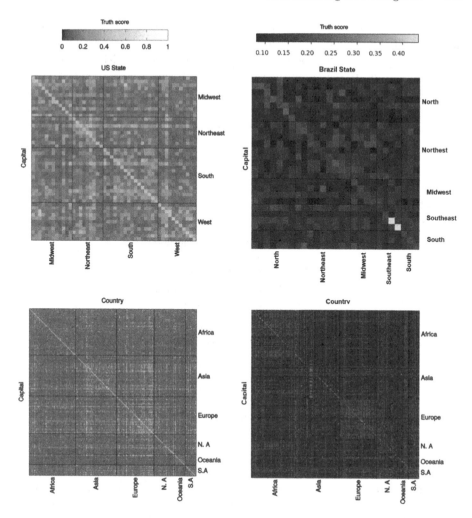

Fig. 1. Resulting matrices of simple factual statements for capitals: English at the left and Portuguese at the right side

the entire title (E1); the title without stopwords (E2); and the entire title with quotes in order to search for the exact word ordering (E3).

As we explained in the Sect. 3.2, we defined whether a news item was fake if there were any words in the snippets or link texts that might indicate fake content, and true if there was not. The file with the fake-related terms used for this evaluation is available online[3]. We evaluate the success of this fake detection strategy with the most common metrics, such as Precision (P), Recall (R), F1 Score (F1) for each class, and Accuracy (A) for both classes.

---

[3] Available at http://tiny.cc/zxm86y.

By applying GSR method to the true and fake news of FAKE.BR CORPUS, the results of the evaluation metrics for all experiments are shown in Table 2. The E2 takes into account the most important words in the title, which might lead to more accurate search on the subject, and for this, we adopted the NLTK stopwords for Portuguese. In the execution of this experiment, we noticed that some news were released in manual fact-checking sites, but the snippets and the text in the links had no word that discriminated that the news was fake, classifying them as true. We then did another test (E2-alt) by checking the occurrence of these fact-chekcing sites in the links, such as *Boatos.org*[4], *E-Farsas*[5], *Aos Fatos*[6] and *Agência Lupa*[7]. We keep the Google search query without stopwords. Finnaly, in the E3 we could evaluate the search when each snippet has the full title.

Table 2. Results for GSR method

Experiment		P	R	F1	A
E1	Fake	0.71	0.12	0.20	0.53
	True	0.52	0.95	0.67	
E2	Fake	0.71	0.13	0.23	0.54
	True	0.52	0.94	0.67	
E2-alt	Fake	0.76	0.24	0.36	**0.68**
	True	0.60	0.98	0.74	
E3	Fake	1.00	0.01	0.01	0.51
	True	1.00	1.00	1.00	

We realized that our best Google-based method is the one that uses the news title without stopwords and that considers the site information in the links (E2-alt). This is somehow expected as we previously knew which sites were important for this purpose (what causes the method to be partially supervised, therefore). After this, the second best method was the one with the news title without stopwords (E2). More than this, we may also see that the recall for the fake news are very low in all the methods, and all of them are better at dealing with true news. This can be explained by the fact that the words that indicate fake news appear in a few snippets, classifying most news as true.

The results may indicate that we should also explore the content of the retrieved documents (and not only the snippets and links) to improve the fake news detection with this kind of method. Interestingly, this is exactly what we would expect humans to do in a manual fact-checking task.

---

[4] https://www.boatos.org/.
[5] http://www.e-farsas.com/.
[6] https://aosfatos.org/.
[7] https://piaui.folha.uol.com.br/lupa/.

Finally, it is important to stress that we could not directly compare the knowledge graph method to the Google one, as we used different test data and evaluation strategies. Future work must make such comparison feasible, as we comment in what follows.

5   Final Remarks

In this paper, we have presented two methods for fact-checking for Portuguese, following the content-based strategy. One of them, adapted from English, uses knowledge graphs built from Wikipedia data to check the veracity of statements. The other one, based on Google search, was used to check whether news were true or not. The achieved results were surprisingly good, but show that there is still room for improvements.

On the knowledge graph side, we expect to run the method over graphs built from journalistic texts, adapting the method to perform fake news detection (and making it possible to compare it with other methods). This brings some challenges, as determining the right way to check veracity in the graph and extracting the relevant triples from a large corpus of news (using, for instance, Open Information Extraction systems), besides proposing a new truth value $\tau(e)$ in order to use the predicate information in a more direct way. On the Google search side, more informed strategies might be used, incorporating to the process more information from the retrieved documents.

To the interested reader, more information about this work may be found at OPINANDO project webpage (https://sites.google.com/icmc.usp.br/opinando/).

Acknowledgments. The authors are grateful to CAPES and USP Research Office (PRP 668) for supporting this work.

References

1. Auer, S., Bizer, C., Kobilarov, G., Lehmann, J., Cyganiak, R., Ives, Z.: Dbpedia: a nucleus for a web of open data. In: Proceedings of The Semantic Web: 6th International Semantic Web Conference, pp. 722–735 (2007)
2. Babakar, M., Moy, W.: The state of automated factchecking. Technical report, Full Fact (2016)
3. Burgoon, J.K., Buller, D.B., Guerrero, L.K., Afifi, W.A., Feldman, C.M.: Interpersonal deception: Xii. information management dimensions underlying deceptive and truthful messages. Commun. Monogr. **63**(1), 50–69 (1996)
4. Chakraborty, A., Paranjape, B., Kakarla, S., Ganguly, N.: Stop clickbait: detecting and preventing clickbaits in online news media. In: Proceedings of the IEEE/ACM International Conference on Advances in Social Networks Analysis and Mining, pp. 9–16 (2016)
5. Chesney, S., Liakata, M., Poesio, M., Purver, M.: Incongruent headlines: yet another way to mislead your readers. In: Proceedings of the Empirical Methods in Natural Language Processing Workshop: Natural Language Processing Meets Journalism, pp. 56–61 (2017)

6. Ciampaglia, G.L., Shiralkar, P., Rocha, L.M., Bollen, J., Menczer, F., Flammini, A.: Computational fact checking from knowledge networks. PloS One **10**(6), 1–13 (2015)
7. Cohen, S., Li, C., Yang, J., Yu, C.: Computational journalism: a call to arms to database researchers. In: Proceedings of the 5th Biennial Conference on Innovative Data Systems Research, pp. 148–151 (2011)
8. Doddington, G., Mitchell, A., Przybocki, M., Ramshaw, L., Strassel, S., Weischedel, R.: The automatic content extraction (ACE) program - tasks, data, and evaluation. In: Proceedings of the Fourth International Conference on Language Resources and Evaluation, pp. 837–840 (2004)
9. Eysenbach, G., Köhler, C.: How do consumers search for and appraise health information on the world wide web? qualitative study using focus groups, usability tests, and in-depth interviews. BMJ **324**(7337), 573–577 (2002)
10. Habernal, I., Wachsmuth, H., Gurevych, I., Stein, B.: The argument reasoning comprehension task: identification and reconstruction of implicit warrants. In: Proceedings of the 2018 Conference of the North American Chapter of the Association for Computational Linguistics: Human Language Technologies, vol. 1 (Long Papers), pp. 1930–1940 (2018)
11. Hassan, N., et al.: The quest to automate fact-checking. In: Proceedings of the Computation + Journalism Symposium, pp. 1–5 (2015)
12. Klein, D., Wueller, J.: Fake news: a legal perspective. J. Internet Law **20**(10), 6–13 (2017)
13. McNamee, P., Dang, H.: Overview of the tac 2009 knowledge base population track. In: Proceedings of the Text Analysis Conference, pp. 111–113 (2009)
14. Monteiro, R.A., Santos, R.L.S., Pardo, T.A.S., de Almeida, T.A., Ruiz, E.E.S., Vale, O.A.: Contributions to the study of fake news in portuguese: new corpus and automatic detection results. In: Proceedings of the Computational Processing of the Portuguese Language Conference, pp. 324–334 (2018)
15. Nakashole, N., Mitchell, T.M.: Language-aware truth assessment of fact candidates. In: Proceedings of the 52nd Annual Meeting of the Association for Computational Linguistics (vol. 1: Long Papers). vol. 1, pp. 1009–1019 (2014)
16. Pérez-Rosas, V., Mihalcea, R.: Experiments in open domain deception detection. In: Proceedings of the Conference on Empirical Methods in Natural Language Processing, pp. 1120–1125 (2015)
17. Potthast, M., Kiesel, J., Reinartz, K., Bevendorff, J., Stein, B.: A stylometric inquiry into hyperpartisan and fake news. In: Proceedings of the 56th Annual Meeting of the Association for Computational Linguistics (vol. 1: Long Papers), pp. 231–240 (2018)
18. Rashkin, H., Choi, E., Jang, J.Y., Volkova, S., Choi, Y.: Truth of varying shades: analyzing language in fake news and political fact-checking. In: Proceedings of the 2017 Conference on Empirical Methods in Natural Language Processing, pp. 2931–2937 (2017)
19. Rogerson, K.S.: Fact checking the fact checkers: verification web sites, partisanship and sourcing. In: Proceedings of the American Political Science Association Annual Meeting (2013)
20. Rubin, V.L., Conroy, N.J., Chen, Y.: Towards news verification: deception detection methods for news discourse. In: Proceedings of the Hawaii International Conference on System Sciences, pp. 5–8 (2015)

21. Rubin, V.L., Conroy, N.J., Chen, Y., Cornwell, S.: Fake news or truth? using satirical cues to detect potentially misleading news. In: Proceedings of 15th Annual Conference of the North American Chapter of the Association for Computational Linguistics: Human Language Technologies, pp. 7–17 (2016)

22. Simas, T., Rocha, L.M.: Distance closures on complex networks. Netw. Sci. **3**(2), 227–268 (2015)

23. Thorne, J., Chen, M., Myrianthous, G., Pu, J., Wang, X., Vlachos, A.: Fake news stance detection using stacked ensemble of classifiers. In: Proceedings of the Empirical Methods in Natural Language Processing Workshop: Natural Language Processing meets Journalism, pp. 80–83 (2017)

24. Thorne, J., Vlachos, A.: Automated fact checking: task formulations, methods and future directions. In: Proceedings of the 27th International Conference on Computational Linguistics, pp. 3346–3359 (2018)

25. Vlachos, A., Riedel, S.: Fact checking: task definition and dataset construction. In: Proceedings of the ACL Workshop on Language Technologies and Computational Social Science, pp. 18–22 (2014)

26. Vlachos, A., Riedel, S.: Identification and verification of simple claims about statistical properties. In: Proceedings of the Conference on Empirical Methods in Natural Language Processing, pp. 2596–2601 (2015)

27. Zhou, L.: An empirical investigation of deception behavior in instant messaging. IEEE Trans. Prof. Commun. **48**(2), 147–160 (2005)

28. Zubiaga, A., Aker, A., Bontcheva, K., Liakata, M., Procter, R.: Detection and resolution of rumours in social media: a survey. ACM Comput. Surv. **51**, 32:1–32:36 (2018)

Extraction and Use of Structured and Unstructured Features for the Recommendation of Urban Resources

Brenda Salenave Santana[(✉)] and Leandro Krug Wives

PPGC – Instituto de Informática, Universidade Federal do Rio Grande do Sul,
Caixa Postal 15.064 – 91.501-970, Porto Alegre, RS, Brazil
{bssantana,wives}@inf.ufrgs.br

Abstract. Urban Computing is concerned about the exploration and understanding of urban systems using data generated by itself. The objective of this paper is to describe an approach to analyze information expressed in social networks to help the recommendation of urban resources. This process considers different structured and unstructured features like resource's location, reviews polarity, and user profile reliability. Therefore, we use text and Web mining techniques to extract those features and then apply traditional recommendation algorithms considering different combinations to identify if they provide better results. Results were compared, and we found that for neighborhood algorithms, the proposed approach presented better results when compared to traditional methods.

Keywords: Recommendation indicators · Data analytics · Urban resources

1 Introduction

In the context of urban centers, the analysis of urban elements involves the application of a range of strategies to understand infrastructural, physical and socio-economic systems, and the use and management of states such as transportation, environment, health, housing, and economy [10]. Thus, Urban Computing is an emerging area focused on the exploration and understanding of urban systems, leveraging new data sources.

The recommendation of the resources available in ubiquitous environments requires the evaluation of different samples of information [12], not limited to structured data, thus reinforcing the relevance of data mining techniques. For instance, recommendation approaches should analyze urban resources not only for the information itself but also for its origin (i.e., trustworthiness), polarity (i.e., how positive or negative it is) and the date of its creation (i.e., if it can be considered still relevant given the time elapsed since its inception).

© Springer Nature Switzerland AG 2020
P. Quaresma et al. (Eds.): PROPOR 2020, LNAI 12037, pp. 206–214, 2020.
https://doi.org/10.1007/978-3-030-41505-1_20

In this context, this work is concerned with stimulating the smart use of urban resources[1] present in ubiquitous environments, facilitating the integration of citizens through the use of more accurate recommendation methods. For this, the objective of this work is to explore the use of different combined recommendation indicators generated from unstructured data, improving their recommendation process. Those can then be presented in a way adapted to each user, varying according to their level of knowledge, needs, and context.

The rest of the study is organized as follows. Section 2 presents related work. Section 3 describes our approach to create urban resources indicators from the extraction and application of local-based social network (LBSN) features for the recommendation process. Section 4 presents the dataset used and maps the extraction and use of the recommendation indicators. Section 5 presents experiments and results, and discuss improvements and the possible limitations provided with the use of our approach. Finally, the study is concluded in Sect. 6, with some closing remarks and future work.

2   Related Work

It is possible to find in the literature different approaches that seek to improve results obtained through the recommendation of points of interest in urban environments [2,3,7]. Thus, different works propose the use of information modeled under a unified structure that takes into consideration features to improve the performance of POI indications in LBSNs. This type of research has shown that it is possible to identify the perception of urban areas in a scalable way, supporting essential mechanisms to help people better understand the semantics existing in different regions of the city.

In this work, unlike proposals described in related work, we chose to use multiple textual and temporal information from LBSNs as a way to generate analysis features for the aggregated data under a unified recommendation structure. So, differently from previous work, in the understanding that different attributes may have different degrees of relevance for the user, this work evaluates the impact of the combination of multiple features. Moreover, in this way, to apply the generated estimate to recommendation algorithms, to achieve better accuracy rates in the recommendation of urban resources.

3   Proposed Approach

Platforms aimed at providing information and reviews of tourism-related content, such as LBSNs, offer filtering mechanisms, including ratings and reviews. However, they often do not consider the user context and interests during searches, nor even make recommendations by combining such factors.

---

[1] In this paper, Urban resources or Points of Interest (POI) are understood as the elements that make up a city, which may include different categories, such as leisure, transport, security, community spaces, and local businesses.

Alternatively, in some situations, it is possible to consider incremental aspects in the evaluation, but recommendation explanations are not presented to the users. Thus, the present work is based on the assumption that aggregating information extracted from textual elements (reviews) with structured data (properties of resources, personal information, interest, and context of users) would help in this process.

The proposed approach is divided into four main steps: Data Collection, Data Analysis, Recommendation of Urban Resources, and Evaluation. With such a process, the objective is to evaluate the use of auxiliary indicators in the recommendation process, as well as the analysis of aspects related to data arranged in different forms and structures.

3.1 Data Collection

A crawler was developed to collect information available in a LBSN, and it captures the name, location, and type of the establishment, as well as its indicators like the number and the average of evaluations, opinions, number of favorable or unfavorable votes to the comments, and also the number of evaluations previously performed by the current user. As LBSN source for our studies, Foursquare was adopted, since it presents one of the most popular location-based social networks [2].

We also extracted data from an open data portal (*DataViva*), which is a free platform for visualizing social and economic data of Brazilian cities, giving greater completeness to the model. As a data source for Brazilian cities in general, the DataViva platform was used to collect official information from municipalities (e.g., description, geographic location, as well as social and economic aspects), aiming to complement the system, making it more robust and informative.

3.2 Data Analysis

A descriptive analysis was carried out to categorize, characterize, consolidate data, and convert it into useful information. To analyze different aspects of information (e.g., polarity, reliability, and influence of the publication date) that cover different types of data aspects, Eqs. 1, 2, 3 and 4 are then proposed, which permeate different approaches of the objectified analyzes.

In order to prioritize more up-to-date information, Eq. 1 is used to apply an exponential decay. Where *diff* represents the difference between the current day and the day the comment was made. Thus, recent reviews tend to exert more influence.

$$e^{(-diff/50)} \tag{1}$$

To analyze the expressed polarities in the reviews text, two Portuguese sentiment lexicons were used, OpLexicon 3.0 [9] and SentiLex [8] to complement expressions not contemplated by the first one. Equation 2 refers to the polarity analysis performed on the reviews. Based on the lexicons, the sum of polarities of the same comment is extracted. Those dictionaries classify positive words with a positive value (1), negative with a negative value (-1), and neutral as zero (0), respectively.

$$\sum lex\_polarity\_score \tag{2}$$

When analyzing a comment, it is of interest to know more than the information explicitly expressed in the text; thus, when evaluating the reliability of information, Eq. 3 ponders the number of positive ($votes\_up$) and negative ($votes\_down$) votes for all n comments and also the number of evaluations (n_tips) already performed on the site by the user who generated the comment i which is analyzed.

$$\log_2 votes\_up_i - \log_2 votes\_down_i + \ln(n\_tips_i + 1) \tag{3}$$

In order to put the data on a scale equivalent to that used in LBSN, a standardization of the results was performed with Eqs. 1, 2 and 3 over a predetermined interval. We used min-max normalization, i.e., a method that resizes the range of resources to a closed interval. In this case, the restricted range from one to ten was used for converting the data to a mode equivalent to that used by the social network based on the analyzed location.

To combine the previously presented features Eq. 4 considers them for each comment analyzed by also considering parameterizable variables of weight. These variables (α, β, and γ) represent the degree of relevance of each estimate previously calculated.

$$\sum_{i=1}^{n} polarity_i * \alpha + trust_i * \beta + decay\_date_i * \gamma \tag{4}$$

After the application of the Eq. 4, the results obtained are then again normalized at a closed interval between one and ten.

3.3   Recommendation of Urban Resources

This step applies the knowledge extracted from the analyses performed, evaluating them as possible indicators to be used in the process of recommending available resources. Therefore, standard recommendation algorithms are used, seeking to analyze the effects of the use of such indicators in this process.

This stage is realized through the use of Surprise[2], which is a Python library to construct and analyze recommender systems where several algorithms are integrated, focusing on the prediction of regressions. It is important to state that those algorithms have different parameters, and we have evaluated different variations of them to obtain better results for the application (details are in the next sections).

---

[2] http://surpriselib.com/.

3.4 Evaluation

The cross-validation [5] technique was used to evaluate the generalization capacity of the models. Such a technique is employed in problems where the goal is the prediction, so we try to estimate how accurate this model is to a new set of data. As designated in [6] , $k = 5$ and $k = 10$ was used in k-fold cross-validation for predicting error estimation, since low bias was presented with the use of such values. Using this technique, we evaluated the Mean Absolute Error (MAE) and Root Mean Squared Error (RMSE) metrics. These are used to measure the accuracy of continuous variables, according to [11], and are also widely used for evaluation in recommendation systems.

Then, a non-parametric hypothesis test (Wilcoxon [4]) is used to compare the two related measurements (rates) to evaluate whether their position measurements are the same in the case where the samples are dependent. This test is often used in samples of model evaluation metrics to ascertain whether the skill difference between machine learning models is significant.

4   Extraction and Use of Indicators

For the application of such proposed techniques analysis, we decided to analyze data from the Brazilian city of Gramado [1], since this is considered by sites as TripAdvisor as one of the main touristic winter destinations in the country. We collected all data available until December 20, 2018.

In the end, we had collected relevant data from both sources, which after different filtering and pre-processing stages resulted in the following set: establishments name, latitude, longitude, average rating, total of rates, reviews text, date and down/up votes, user ID and total user tips from Foursquare; and city name, general profile, total population, and life expectancy. To better organize the representation of the obtained data, a knowledge representation model based on an ontology specifically build by us was elaborated in the domain of smart cities, where it was possible to gather such information.

With the focus on the extraction of features from the Web, we employed the approaches described in Sect. 3.1. Thus, we sought to explore information considered relevant for surveying the intrinsic characteristics present in the dataset analyzed.

Using Eq. 4, we combine different features (polarities and reliability) into Eq. 1 by applying to each comment a decay factor on the date in which it was carried out, prioritizing the most recent evaluations, and helping us to understand distinct aspects of the data.

Figure 1 presents an example of a recommendation that can be generated from the use of such features and indicators. In this paper, we highlight the general characteristics found in the data analysis of a given establishment. It also shows the suitability of users who carried out the evaluations and their respective polarities, which resulted in the estimated rating generated.

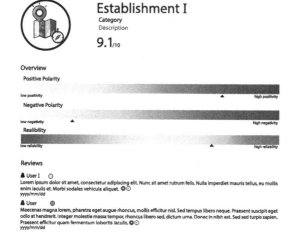

Fig. 1. Application Example of the features (reliability, polarity, and temporality) into an urban resources recommender system

5 Results and Discussion

To validate the use of the proposed indicators in the process of the recommendation of urban resources, we applied the proposed metric, previously generated using different features in traditional recommendation algorithms. The execution of the algorithms was also done using the pattern evaluation (user explicit rating) of the establishments in the analyzed environment.

Using *Surprise* library, *K*-NN and SVD based algorithms were applied with their respective variations. A sequence of tests was performed varying the parameters of each one for each metric evaluated to achieve better results in the recommendation process with these algorithms. A library feature, called *GridSearchCV*, was then used to answer which combination of parameters produces the best results. The execution of each algorithm and its variations were then performed using the parameter combination generated by the tool.

Table 1 presents the respective weights and standard deviations achieved during the different implementations of the algorithms using each of the metrics compared (the standard metric used by the studied LBSN and metric proposed with the use of indicators). Thus the results represent the respective means and standard deviations using 10 *folds* for cross-validation of the algorithms.

When comparing the results achieved for each algorithm using the MAE and RMSE metrics over 30 executions, it was possible to notice that the use of standard metric performed better in 100% of the cases, when using algorithms based on matrix factorization (SDV and SVD++). Already for the algorithms that are directly derived from a basic approach of closer neighbors, the use of the proposed metric was better in all cases of comparison. As we can see in Table 2. In this table, we present the percentage of times each approach was better when compared to another.

Table 1. Averages and standard deviations obtained through the application of the MAE and RMSE metrics during the generated executions.

	MAE				RMSE			
	Stardard metric		Proposed metric		Stardard metric		Proposed metric	
Algoritmo	Mean	Standard deviation	Mean	Standard deviation	Mean	Standard deviation	Mean	Standard deviation
SVD	0.224628	0.010352	0.259426	0.008512	0.349781	0.034429	0.465482	0.027394
SVD++	0.169321	0.010577	0.21516	0.008744	0.408688	0.055431	0.412578	0.032038
KNN (user)	1.495882	0.033332	1.220767	0.028342	1.938904	0.05991	1.567626	0.047501
KNN (item)	1.040791	0.03367	0.866297	0.041528	1.583225	0.071083	1.292741	0.052349
KNN Baseline (user)	1.259964	0.030242	0.103477	0.003226	1.670258	0.053814	0.191285	0.039884
KNN Baseline (item)	1.335254	0.032025	0.103352	0.003473	1.72822	0.056223	0.191461	0.039523

Table 2. Comparison of the use of the metrics evaluated for each evaluation rate tested.

	MAE		RMSE	
Algorithm	Stardard metric	Proposed metric	Stardard metric	Proposed metric
SVD	100.00%	0.00%	100.00%	0.00%
SVD++	100.00%	0.00%	100.00%	0.00%
KNN (user)	3.33%	96.67%	0.00%	100.00%
KNN (item)	3.33%	96.67%	0.00%	100.00%
KNN Baseline (user)	3.33%	96.67%	0.00%	100.00%
KNN Baseline (item)	3.33%	96.67%	0.00%	100.00%

Thirty executions were executed for statistical validation purposes, using cross-validation with 10 folds to perform a more consistent validation on the results obtained. Thus, from the extraction of the absolute mean error measures achieved using each rating approach, the Wilcoxon test was applied since it can be used in samples of model evaluation metrics by checking whether the difference of prediction among machine learning models is significant.

The null hypothesis used in the test consists of the assumption that both samples were taken from a population with the same distribution and, therefore, the same population parameters. Thus, it is assumed that after the calculation of the significance test in the sample set and the null hypothesis is rejected, there is evidence to suggest that the samples were drawn from different populations and, in turn, the difference between the estimates may be significant.

When performing the Wilcoxon test on the data samples employing an alpha value of 0.05, that is, 95% confidence, for all algorithms tested, the null hypothesis was rejected. These results represent non-uniformity in the distribution of the samples, so it is possible to state that there are significant differences between the results obtained with both of the rating approaches used.

With these experiments, better results were obtained with the use of the proposed metric applying the use of features extracted from the analysis in Foursquare data, through the use of algorithms based in the neighborhood. However, in cases where the use of the commonly used rating metrics proved to be better (algorithms based on matrix factorization), the error rate measured with the use of indicators remains low, as can be seen in Table 1. This result accentuates the applicability of the use of such indicators in the urban recommendation process.

6   Final Remarks

This work proposed an analysis of features extracted from location-based social networks on applying them as indicators in the process of the recommendation of urban resources. To this end, we have proposed ways of extracting and quantifying indicators such as the polarity of the evaluation comments of each establishment, the reliability of the information provided by users based on the number of contributions previously provided and also the relevance of reviews based on the time factor (i.e., date of publication). To evaluate the metric, our experiments were performed with standard algorithms of recommendation systems, trying to compare this new estimative of rating with the use of traditional LBSNs rating, using the usual metrics of evaluations.

When evaluating the mean error obtained during the application of the recommendation algorithms based on matrix factorization, it is estimated that in 100% of the cases, the use of the standard evaluation used presents a smaller error than the use of the proposed estimate. However, it should be noted that in these cases, the error is maintained with a low average and standard deviation. Already with the application of neighborhood-based algorithms, in all experiments, the use of the suggested estimate keeps with better results when compared to the traditional evaluation. However, in these cases, for both approaches, the error is higher than one.

The results achieved with the use of both metrics were compared using Wilcoxon tests with 95% confidence. These portrayed the non-uniformity in the distribution of the samples, evidencing significant differences between the results obtained with the approaches used. Thus, it is concluded that the applicability of the proposed estimate is feasible since, for the most commonly used approaches in analogous research aimed at the recommendation of urban elements, neighborhood-based algorithms are mainly applied. Also, the use in algorithms performed by processing with factorization cannot be declinable since they have demonstrated good accuracy and are still capable of improvement.

References

1. de Geografia e Estatística IBGE, I.B.: Gramado RS - Panorama. Instituto Brasileiro de Geografia e Estatística - IBGE, Rio de Janeiro (2019). https://cidades.ibge.gov.br/brasil/rs/gramado/panorama

2. Gao, H., Tang, J., Hu, X., Liu, H.: Content-aware point of interest recommendation on location-based social networks. In: AAAI, pp. 1721–1727 (2015)
3. García, K., Velasco, S., Mendoza, S., Decouchant, D.: A matchmaking algorithm for resource discovery in multi-user settings. In: Proceedings of the 2014 IEEE/WIC/ACM International Joint Conferences on Web Intelligence (WI) and Intelligent Agent Technologies (IAT) - Volume 03, pp. 352–359. WI-IAT 2014, IEEE Computer Society, Washington, DC, USA (2014). https://doi.org/10.1109/WI-IAT.2014.188
4. Gehan, E.A.: A generalized wilcoxon test for comparing arbitrarily singly-censored samples. Biometrika **52**(1–2), 203–224 (1965)
5. Kohavi, R., et al.: A study of cross-validation and bootstrap for accuracy estimation and model selection. In: IJCAI. vol. 14, pp. 1137–1145. Montreal, Canada (1995)
6. Rodriguez, J.D., Perez, A., Lozano, J.A.: Sensitivity analysis of k-fold cross validation in prediction error estimation. IEEE Trans. Pattern Anal. Mach. Intell. **32**(3), 569–575 (2010). https://doi.org/10.1109/TPAMI.2009.187
7. Santos, F.A., Silva, T.H., Ferreira Loureiro, A.A., Villas, L.A.: Uncovering the perception of urban outdoor areas expressed in social media. In: 2018 IEEE/WIC/ACM International Conference on Web Intelligence (WI), pp. 120–127, December 2018. https://doi.org/10.1109/WI.2018.00-99
8. Silva, M.J., Carvalho, P., Costa, C., Sarmento, L.: Automatic expansion of a social judgment lexicon for sentiment analysis. Technical report, TR 10–08, University of Lisbon, Faculty of Sciences, LASIGE, December 2010. http://hdl.handle.net/10455/6694, doi: 10455/6694
9. Souza, M., Vieira, R.: Sentiment analysis on Twitter data for portuguese language. In: Caseli, H., Villavicencio, A., Teixeira, A., Perdigão, F. (eds.) PROPOR 2012. LNCS (LNAI), vol. 7243, pp. 241–247. Springer, Heidelberg (2012). https://doi.org/10.1007/978-3-642-28885-2_28
10. Thakuriah, P.V., Tilahun, N.Y., Zellner, M.: Big data and urban informatics: innovations and challenges to urban planning and knowledge discovery. In: Thakuriah, P.V., Tilahun, N., Zellner, M. (eds.) Seeing Cities Through Big Data. SG, pp. 11–45. Springer, Cham (2017). https://doi.org/10.1007/978-3-319-40902-3_2
11. Yang, X., Guo, Y., Liu, Y., Steck, H.: A survey of collaborative filtering based social recommender systems. Comput. Commun. **41**, 1–10 (2014)
12. Ying, J.J.C., Lu, E.H.C., Kuo, W.N., Tseng, V.S.: Urban point-of-interest recommendation by mining user check-in behaviors. In: Proceedings of the ACM SIGKDD International Workshop on Urban Computing, pp. 63–70. UrbComp 2012, ACM, New York, NY, USA (2012). https://doi.org/10.1145/2346496.2346507, http://doi.acm.org/10.1145/2346496.2346507

Semantics

A Portuguese Dataset for Evaluation of Semantic Question Answering

Denis Andrei de Araujo[1] , Sandro José Rigo[1(✉)] , Paulo Quaresma[2] ,
and João Henrique Muniz[1]

[1] Applied Computing Graduate Program, University of Vale do Rio dos Sinos (UNISINOS),
São Leopoldo, Brazil
denis.andrei.araujo@gmail.com, rigo@unisinos.br,
joaohenriquemuniz@gmail.com
[2] Department of Informatics, University of Évora, Évora, Portugal
pq@uevora.pt

Abstract. Research on question answering tools over open linked data is increasing, and that brings the necessity of resources to allow for the evaluation and comparison of such systems. Question Answering over Linked Data (QALD) is a traditional benchmark event that occurs annually since 2011. However, although the multilingual task is available since its third edition, there is a necessity to foster the actual Portuguese Language resources present in this event benchmark. In this paper, we describe the development of the Portuguese language as a QALD corpus complement. The corpus is based on an existing QALD multilingual corpus and comprises 258 sentences used for the event challenge in 2017. We constructed a second corpus to allow direct comparison with the DBPedia Portuguese content. The main topics to highlight are the adopted methodology, which results in corpus related to frequent Brazilian Portuguese use of the language, and the work on adapting the answers to the DBPedia PT knowledge base, providing a corpus to evaluate Portuguese QA systems accurately.

Keywords: Question Answering · Open linked data · Annotated corpus

1 Introduction

Question Answering (QA) is a research area explored since the sixties [5, 8, 12, 18], recently fostering the development of Semantic QA systems (SQA), aiming to rely on linked databases to find requested answers [3]. A significant amount of work has been published in this area, stimulated by the growth of the open linked databases [2, 10, 14, 17, 19].

The development of datasets and specific frameworks for the evaluation of new algorithms and to promote the SQA systems benchmark is necessary to foster the research in this area. There is a growing number of such datasets and also of events held exclusively to evaluate and compare different approaches [14, 15]. Most of them are specifically designed for the English language [4, 6, 11, 15]. To the best of our knowledge, we did find little evidence of corpus SQA systems assessment for the Portuguese language [11].

© Springer Nature Switzerland AG 2020
P. Quaresma et al. (Eds.): PROPOR 2020, LNAI 12037, pp. 217–227, 2020.
https://doi.org/10.1007/978-3-030-41505-1_21

The QALD is a traditional benchmark event that occurs annually since 2011 [16]. The QALD has included a multilingual task since its third edition. Nevertheless, there is a necessity to foster the availability of Portuguese Language resources in this event benchmark. In this article, we describe the creation of a corpus in Portuguese developed from the dataset available in the QALD 7 multilingual challenge. On the importance of having resources to assess SQA systems also in the Portuguese language, we feel motivated to develop and make available a resource that could be used both to evaluate and to compare SQA systems that focuses on the Portuguese language. The paper describes two main contributions, which are the creation of a Portuguese Dataset to support the Semantic Question Answering benchmark, and the adaptation of this dataset to use the data available in DBPedia Portuguese version (DBPedia PT)[1].

2 Adopted Methodology

The development of a benchmark dataset requires clear definitions of the evaluation scope, avoiding the influence of preconceived ideas and prejudices [1]. Besides, it is also necessary to take into account that the benchmark datasets should present a realistic degree of difficulty, which stimulates the participants' competition, but at the same time does not produce such artificial data that they do not find a similar context in real-world situations. We verified these fundamental properties in the report describing the procedures adopted for configuring the QALD benchmark dataset for the multilingual task [7]. The Portuguese benchmark dataset for SQA systems was created using the QALD dataset. The first part of each entry in the QALD benchmark dataset comprises the language reference, the natural language sentence, and the relevant keywords for that sentence. When using the dataset to perform benchmarks, it is expected the applications to perform the sentence analysis and after this, define which are the essential keywords. The next step of our methodology translates the questions and selects the keywords for each sentence. The final step involves the adaptation of the answers contained in the dataset.

We selected the training and test datasets used in the seventh edition of QALD (QALD-7) for this work. These datasets are available in a publicly accessible repository in JSON format. The questions are represented in the question section of the file by a set of fields: the question original language ("language" field), the question itself ("string" field), and the corresponding keywords ("keyword" field). The QALD-7 training file contains 258 questions in up to nine different languages: German, English, Spanish, Farsi, French, Hindi, Italian, Dutch, and Romanian. Except for the Persian language with 98 questions and the Romanian with 168 questions, we translated all 258 training questions into the seven other languages. In the test file, we have 43 questions translated into the same languages as the training file.

2.1 Translation of Question Sentences

We decided that the translation would consider Portuguese spoken in Brazil since the research group involved in this work have only native speakers from this country. The

---
[1] http://pt.dbpedia.org/.

translation of the questions was carried out by two members of the research group: a linguist with a specialization in English and a computing researcher with a specialization in Natural Language Processing. The questions translation was carried out independently by the two researchers, and we combined the results into a single listing. We adopted this procedure to avoid a biased translation. The two lists of translations were compiled into a single listing by agreement between the two researchers. There were divergences between the two translations and the choice of words to formulate the question, which is quite natural given the different training of both researchers and the flexibility of the Natural Language. Such divergences were solved considering the usual way of formulating the question in Portuguese spoken in Brazil, and also using the translations already available in the dataset for the other languages. The main divergences between the translations carried out by the two researchers occurred in the references to geopolitical entities and cinematographic works. We have in Fig. 1 examples to illustrate these divergences. In sentence 1 of Fig. 1, we can verify that the name of the country (United States) has been replaced by the word form usually adopted to refer to the citizens of that country (American).

Proposed translations:
1 Quem foi a esposa do presidente dos EUA Lincoln?
  (Who was the wife of U.S. president Lincoln?)
2 Quem é o prefeito da capital da Polinésia Francesa?
  (Who is the mayor of the capital of French Polynesia?)
3 Quais são os cinco condados de Nova Iorque?
  (What are the five boroughs of New York?)
4 Quem é o prefeito de Rotterdam?
  (Who is the mayor of Rotterdam?)
Final Translations:
1 Quem foi a esposa do presidente americano Lincoln?
  (Who was the wife of the American president Lincoln?)
2 Quem é o prefeito da capital da Polinésia Francesa?
  (Who is the mayor of the capital of French Polynesia?)
3 Quais são os cinco condados de New York?
  (What are the five boroughs of New York?)
4 Quem é o prefeito de Rotterdam?
  (Who is the mayor of Rotterdam?)

Fig. 1. Examples of divergences between the proposed translation and the one adopted

We changed the proposed translation due to the decision to follow the pattern adopted in the other Romance languages [13] present in the dataset: Spanish, French, Italian, and Romanian. The basis for this decision is the fact that the Portuguese language is part of this set of languages that evolved from Latin, having for this reason similarities concerning the style and semantics of writing [9]. We established as a procedure for the translation to follow the pattern adopted by most Romance languages or, in case of divergence, to observe the procedure most commonly adopted in Portuguese spoken in Brazil. Analyzing the translations for the other Romance languages presented in Fig. 1, we verified that the inclusion of the name of the country to the detriment of the gentile occurred only in the Italian version, reason why we modified the initially proposed translation, aiming to follow the pattern adopted by most other Romance languages. Although the other divergences presented in Fig. 1 also originate from the application of the same rule (follow the pattern adopted by most Romance languages), we could observe different results in the final text. French Polynesia (sentence 2), for example, was translated to Portuguese, whereas for New York (sentence 3) remained in its English version. The city of Rotterdam was proposed in English (sentence 4) and was maintained in the final text by the application of the rule of consonance with the other Romance languages.

2.2 Selection of Keywords

For the step of selecting keywords, we used the same pattern of selection adopted by the other Romance languages present in the dataset. In the rare cases where there was disagreement in the selection of keywords, we performed an analysis involving all available translations, including the English and German languages. Figure 2 shows an example in which further analysis was needed. We observed three different procedures for the selection of keywords in Romance languages: (1) Restrict themselves to the use of words that are contained in the sentence ignoring the interrogative pronoun (Spanish); (2) insertion of words not found in the original sentence (Italian and French); and (3) use of words contained in the question including the interrogative pronoun (Romanian).

```
"question": [
{ "language": "en",
    "string": "When did Operation Overlord commence?",
    "keywords": "when, Operation Overlord, commence" },
{ "language": "pt_BR",
    "string": "Quando começou a Operação Overlord?",
    "keywords": "começou, Operação Overlord"},
{ "language": "es",
    "string": "¿Cuándo comenzó la operación Overlord?",
    "keywords": "comienzo, operación Overlord "},
{ "language": "it",
    "string": "Quando è iniziata l'operatione Overlord?",
    "keywords": "data di inizio, operatione Overlord"},
{ "language": "fr",
    "string": "Quand a commencé l'opération Overlord?",
    "keywords": "date de commencement, opération Overlord"},
{ "language": "ro",
    "string": "Când a început operaţiunea Overlord?",
    "keywords": "când, început, operaţiunea Overlord"} ], ...
```

Fig. 2. Example of mismatch in keyword selection.

For cases like this, we used again on the procedures adopted in the Romance languages closest to Portuguese, following this order of influence: Spanish, Italian, French, and Romanian. Thus, for the case of divergence presented in Fig. 2, we defined that the keywords for the Portuguese question "When did Operation Overlord begin?" would be "started" and "Operation Overlord". This was influenced by the selection of words adopted in the Spanish, observing the conjugated verb in the first person singular of the Perfect Past. After the selection of the keywords, we contacted the people responsible for the QALD challenge and made available the work developed. The organizers of the event received well our initiative, and after receiving guidance on the procedures for making the material we produce available, we had the gratifying reward of having our contribution integrated into the official QALD repository[2].

2.3 Adaptation of QALD-7 Queries and Responses to DBPedia PT

To improve the dataset QALD-7 quality, we decided to adapt the answers to the DBPedia PT knowledge base. To adapt the training dataset and testing the QALD multilingual task, we analyzed each one of the 258 QALD-7 questions to identify the changes that would be required in the dataset, considering DBPedia PT as the knowledge base to be used for the location of the answers. The analysis procedure started by identifying the necessary changes to the SPARQL query for each question.

Each DBPedia version (EN and PT) autonomously chooses the details of its vocabulary. However, it is not only the queries that needed to be changed for the adaptation to DBPedia PT. The answers also demanded changes, as they can be different elements, such as a URI or a literal. In the course of the work of adapting the dataset to DBPedia PT, we observed that the differences between DBPedia EN and DBPedia PT are present in such extension that all SPARQL queries needed to be changed.

2.4 Necessary Adaptations

After the migration of the 258 questions from QALD-7 datasets to DBPedia PT, we developed strategies to make the necessary data adaptations. After the conclusion of this work, we began the cataloging and investigation of these strategies. We identified five different processes that allowed us to carry out dataset adaptation to DBPedia PT, which we here called the SPARQL query construction, simple response, wrong answer, unanswered question.

2.4.1 SPARQL Query Construction

We begin the construction of the equivalent SPARQL query for DBPedia PT by analyzing the original query of QALD, seeking to identify first the references to proper names, that is, to identify the elements of the query that refer to the proper nouns present in the question. For example, for the question of Fig. 3, we identified which elements of the query to DBPedia EN (item 2 of Fig. 3) refers to the noun Paris. In the query, Paris is referred by the element <http://dbpedia.org/resource/Paris>. We named this procedure as search for the equivalent reference.

---

[2] https://github.com/ag-sc/QALD/tree/master/7/data.

> **1. Question**:
> Who is the mayor of Paris?
> **2. SPARQL query for DBPedia EN**:
> SELECT DISTINCT ?uri
> WHERE { <http://dbpedia.org/resource/Paris>
>   <http://dbpedia.org/ontology/mayor> ?uri }
> **3. SPARQL query for DBPedia PT**:
> SELECT DISTINCT ?uri
> WHERE { <http://pt.dbpedia.org/resource/Paris>
>   <http://pt.dbpedia.org/property/prefeito> ?uri }

Fig. 3. SPARQL query and response in DBPedia EN and PT for a question

If we do not find an equivalent reference, this means that the QALD-7 question has no response in DBPedia PT. We then have a standard procedure for the unanswered question cases, which we describe in detail in Sect. 2.4.4. If the equivalent reference is found, then we must identify the equivalent relation, that is, to identify which predicate used in DBPedia PT is the equivalent to the predicate of DBPedia EN. This is a more complicated process to accomplish because predicates do not follow a single pattern, as in the case of references. In the case of the question presented in Fig. 3, we can see that the predicate used in DBPedia EN is <http://dbpedia.org/ontology/mayor> (item 2 of Fig. 3) is not directly related to the predicate used in the query to the DBPedia PT <http://pt.dbpedia.org/property/prefeito> (item 3 of Fig. 3). They have different URI bases (http://dbpedia.org and http://pt.dbpedia.org) and also different domains (ontology and property).

In our approach, we adopted as initial procedure the verification of the existence of a predicate in DBPedia PT that contains in its URI a Portuguese translation of the term used in English. Therefore, for the example showed in Fig. 3, we look for a predicate in the DBPedia PT that contains a translation to the mayor. We do that by listing all triples of DBPedia PT which subject is <http://pt.dbpedia.org/resource/Paris> and the Portuguese translation to the mayor term as the predicate. The result of this query returns that the equivalent predicate in the DBPedia PT is the <http://pt.dbpedia.org/property/ prefeito>. If the procedure of searching for the equivalent predicate by the translation fails, we perform a new query in DBPedia PT, this time with the equivalent reference and the predicate originally used in the DBPedia EN. For example, if the query did not return any response, we would execute a new query the DBPedia PT, using <http:// pt.dbpedia.org/resource/Paris> as subject and the original DBPedia EN as a predicate (<http://dbpedia.org/ontology/mayor>).

We always use the first search for the equivalent predicate by translation. We adopted this procedure because we understand that it is the most appropriate approach for the production of a dataset for the validation of SQA systems for Portuguese since we prefer to use the predicate expressed in Portuguese other than the predicates expressed in other languages. However, the procedures described above do not always result in locating an equivalent predicate. If both procedures fail, we make a more general attempt to locate the equivalent predicate: analyze all triples in the DBPedia PT that contain the equivalent reference, filtering the triples until the desired equivalent predicate is found. If the equivalent predicate is not found, it means that the QALD-7 question can not be answered based on the information represented in DBPedia PT, resulting in a question not answerable, which will be detailed in a separate section later on. If the process of constructing the new SPARQL query is successful, that is, all the equivalent references and predicates have been found, we can proceed to the final step: analyze the answers found and make the changes in the JSON file.

2.4.2 Simple Answers

If, after the process of constructing the new SPARQL query, we run it on the DBPedia PT and get a return that can be considered as the correct answer to the question, we have a simple case of inserting the response into the JSON. We classify as simple answers, even the responses that are not compatible with the original response as long as the information returned is the correct answer.

The procedure for simple answers is to only update the JSON of the original response, replacing the contents of the item sparql and item value. There may be instances where DBPedia PT has a correct response whose type is different from the original type. We consider that this type of situation is also a simple answer because the only difference concerning the example presented above is that it is necessary to update the type field, which in our view still characterizes it as a simple case to be solved.

2.4.3 Wrong Answers

We can receive incorrect or incomplete answers when using the data from DBPedia. This happened during the work of adapting QALD-7 responses to DBPedia PT. The origin of the errors, both DBPedia EN and DBPedia PT, according to the survey we did concerning QALD-7 questions, originated both directly from wrong data and from the lack of Wikipedia articles that allowed us to respond correctly. Given this situation, we conclude that the best approach we could take to produce a dataset to benchmark SQA systems would be to consider the feedback obtained from the knowledge base query, disregarding the accuracy of the returned response. Thus, in this context, we consider the answers returned by the SPARQL queries would be the correct answers, regardless of whether or not they are consistent with the real-world facts. We believe that this is the most coherent procedure with the objectives of the artifact that we intend to make available because the SQA system can only return an answer to what is represented in the knowledge base. If the information in the knowledge base is wrong or incomplete, but is the answer returned by the query to the question, we consider that the SQA system has achieved its goal.

2.4.4 Non-existent Response

The original purpose of QALD-7 is evaluating the performance of SQA systems based on DBPedia EN knowledge. As the questions were formulated considering this content, some of them are related to information that is not represented in DBPedia PT, being impossible to obtain the answer. Questions like "How tall is Amazon Eve?" can not be answered based on DBPedia PT because there is no information about Amazon Eve in this knowledge base since there is no Wikipedia article about this person.

The number of QALD-7 questions with non-existent answers in DBPedia PT is quite expressive: 41.86% of the questions in the test dataset and 45.58% in the training questionnaire, resulting in an overall score of 44.96% of unanswered questions. We observed that there were also unanswered questions in the original dataset of QALD-7. If we execute the query of the example shown in Fig. 4 using the SELECT command, we should get an empty answer, since no triple matches the research being done.

```
1. Question:
  Is James Bond married?
2. JSON file with SPARQL query and answer from DBPedia EN:
"query": {
  "sparql": "
    PREFIX dbo: <http://dbpedia.org/ontology/>
    PREFIX res: <http://dbpedia.org/resource/>
    ASK WHERE { res:James_Bond dbo:spouse ?uri. }"},
"answers": [{
    "head": {},
    "results": {},
    "boolean": false }]
```

Fig. 4. QALD-7 unanswered question example.

We realized that all questions with no answer were of the boolean type. All non boolean QALD-7 questions were formulated so that the answer was found in DBPedia EN. The research group involved in the project concluded that it would be interesting to evaluate the ability of the SQA systems to conclude that the question could not be answered with the information stored in the knowledge base. Hence, it was decided that questions with non-response would be held in the Portuguese dataset being constructed.

All non-existent answer questions are easily identifiable in the JSON structure since they were represented by the insertion of empty query and answer items (item 2 of Fig. 4). This is the only case in which we do not follow the representation patterns established in the original QALD-7 dataset since representing non-Boolean questions with non-existent answers has become a specific case of the Portuguese dataset.

2.4.5 General Statistics on Adapting Responses

We obtained a corpus containing 258 questions in Portuguese, with corresponding key-words and answers, which can be used to evaluate the performance of SQA systems in relation to a knowledge base that uses vocabulary in Portuguese to represent the infor-mation. Regarding the search for answers in DBPedia PT, 32,17% of the questions had compatible answers between DBPedia EN and DBPedia PT. As already mentioned, we had about half of the questions with no response (44.96%). In addition to non-existent answers, we also had 22.87% of divergent answers among the knowledge bases, that is, different answers to the same question (Table 1).

Table 1. Problems in the process of adapting QALD-7 responses to DBPedia PT.

Answers	Boolean quest.	Non bool. questions	Total	%
Compatible	17	66	83	32,17
Divergent, error in DBPedia EN	3	7	10	3,88
Divergent, error in DBPedia PT	17	13	30	11,63
Incomplete in DBPedia PT	–	14	14	5,43
Extra data in DBPedia PT	–	5	5	1,94
Not existent in DBPedia PT	–	116	116	44,96
Total	37	221	258	

Regarding the divergent answers, we had cases where the DBPedia EN response was wrong (3.88%), and the DBPedia PT response was wrong (11.63%). Completing the cases of divergent answers, specifically for the questions that had a response list, there were cases where there were either missing elements in the list of DBPedia PT (5.43%) and sometimes there were responses that were more than expected (1.94%).

3 Corpus Application Possibilities

The translation of the QALD-7 questions was approved and integrated into the official QALD repository. From the integration of our translations into qald-7-train-multilingual.json, SQA systems for processing queries in Portuguese can use this dataset to check the performance of your systems in relation to DBPedia in English. In this regard, the application should processes this file, loading the questions by submitting them to the SQA system, and finally comparing the responses returned by the system with the ones in the JSON file. If the objective is to evaluate the performance of the SQA system against the Portuguese version of DBPedia, then one should download the files qald-7-test-multilingual-PT.json or qald-7-train-multilingual-PT.json that we make available in a repository (URL removed for consistency with TACL submission anonymization requirement) and perform the same process described above, with the difference that should be used the DBPedia version 2016-10 in Portuguese as knowledge base. The system to be used in both cases is the same. This flexibility was one of the objectives of having followed the QALD standard in adapting the paired dataset to DBPedia PT. The Portuguese SQA systems can evaluate their performance against to DBPedia PT and/or EN.

Regarding the use of the dataset with SQA systems on DBPedia PT, we suggest analyzing the possibility of performing the evaluation experiment in two separate moments, with and without the nonexistent answers. As we discussed earlier, it is interesting to note the ability of the SQA system to recognize that the question can not be answered based on information from the knowledge base. However, this is a specific feature of the SQA system whose performance can be assessed separately. Because non-response questions follow a unique pattern of representation in the JSON file (empty answers field), it is quite simple to evaluate the performance of SQA systems concerning this task.

4 Conclusions

We presented in this article the procedures adopted for the production of two evaluation artifacts for SQA systems that aim to process questions in Portuguese. We have described in detail the processes adopted and the decisions we take against situations faced, illustrating them with specific examples. We seek to present all decisions and respective justifications to make both the context and the adopted options transparent and reproducible. Our purpose in reporting and illustrating these issues is to motivate researchers in the production of computational resources to evaluate systems dedicated to Portuguese language processing.

We understand that there are exciting opportunities left by the work we presented, such as changing questions with non-existent answers, in such a way that the structure and purpose of the question remain but that it is possible to respond based on DBPedia PT data. Another possibility would be to use the procedures as a basis for the translation of the current QALD base of questions, starting from a base of procedures already standardized, adapting them, or increasing them to deal with the possible new situations of the current corpus. This approach would undoubtedly represent a valuable work for those developing SQA systems in Portuguese mainly, but also for those who are searching for multilingual solutions.

Acknowledgements. This research was supported by CWI Software, Brazilian Higher Education Personnel Improvement Coordination (CAPES), Unisinos University and Évora University.

References

1. Asakura, T., Kim, J.-D., Yamamoto, Y., Tateisi, Y., Takagi, T.: A quantitative evaluation of natural language question interpretation for question answering systems. In: Ichise, R., Lecue, F., Kawamura, T., Zhao, D., Muggleton, S., Kozaki, K. (eds.) JIST 2018. LNCS, vol. 11341, pp. 215–231. Springer, Cham (2018). https://doi.org/10.1007/978-3-030-04284-4_15
2. Atzori, M., Mazzeo, G.M., Zaniolo, C.: QA3: a natural language approach to question answering over RDF data cubes. Semant. Web **10**, 587–604 (2019)
3. Bauer, F., Martin, K.: Linked Open Data: The Essentials. Edition mono/monochrom, Vienna (2011)
4. Berant, J., Chou, A., Frostig, R., Liang, P.: Semantic parsing on freebase from question-answer pairs. In: Proceedings of the 2013 Conference on Empirical Methods in Natural Language Processing, pp. 1533–1544 (2013)
5. Fischer, B.S.: A Deductive Question Answering System. Harvard University (1964)
6. Antoine, B., Usunier, N., Chopra, S., Weston, J.: Large-scale simple question answering with memory networks (2015)
7. Cimiano, P., Lopez, V., Unger, C., Cabrio, E., Ngonga Ngomo, A.-C., Walter, S.: Multilingual question answering over linked data (QALD-3): lab overview. In: Forner, P., Müller, H., Paredes, R., Rosso, P., Stein, B. (eds.) CLEF 2013. LNCS, vol. 8138, pp. 321–332. Springer, Heidelberg (2013). https://doi.org/10.1007/978-3-642-40802-1_30

8. Cordell, G.: Theorem proving by resolution as a basis for question-answering systems. Mach. Intell. **4**, 183–205 (1969)
9. Anderson, H.R.: External History of the Romance Languages, vol. 2. Elsevier Publishing Company, Amsterdam (1974)
10. Xin, H., Dang, D., Yao, Y., Ye, L.: Natural language aggregate query over RDF data. Inf. Sci. **454**, 363–381 (2018)
11. Maksym, K., Rodrigues, M., Teixeira, A.: DBPedia based factual questions answering system. IADIS Int. J. WWW/Internet **15**(1), 80–95 (2017)
12. Lehnert, W.G.: The Process of Question Answering: A Computer Simulation of Cognition, vol. 978. Lawrence Erlbaum, Hillsdale (1978)
13. Posner, R.: The Romance Languages. Cambridge University Press, Cambridge (1996)
14. Tasar, C.O., Komesli, M., Unalir, M.O.: Systematic mapping study on question answering frameworks over linked data. IET Software **12**, 461–472 (2018)
15. Unger, C., et al.: Question answering over linked data (QALD-4). In: Working Notes for CLEF 2014 Conference (2014)
16. Usbeck, R., Ngomo, A.-C.N., Haarmann, B., Krithara, A., Röder, M., Napolitano, G.: 7th open challenge on question answering over linked data (QALD-7). In: Dragoni, M., Solanki, M., Blomqvist, E. (eds.) SemWebEval 2017. CCIS, vol. 769, pp. 59–69. Springer, Cham (2017). https://doi.org/10.1007/978-3-319-69146-6_6
17. Wang, M., Liu, J., Wei, B., Yao, S., Zeng, H., Shi, L.: Answering why-not questions on SPARQL queries. Knowl. Inf. Syst. **58**(1), 169–208 (2019)
18. Woods, W.: The lunar sciences natural language information system. BBN report (1972)
19. Zafar, H., Napolitano, G., Lehmann, J.: Formal query generation for question answering over knowledge bases. In: Gangemi, A., et al. (eds.) ESWC 2018. LNCS, vol. 10843, pp. 714–728. Springer, Cham (2018). https://doi.org/10.1007/978-3-319-93417-4_46

Exploring the Potentiality of Semantic Features for Paraphrase Detection

Rafael Torres Anchiêta$^{(\boxtimes)}$ and Thiago Alexandre Salgueiro Pardo

Interinstitutional Center for Computational Linguistics (NILC),
Institute of Mathematical and Computer Sciences (ICMC),
University of São Paulo (USP), São Carlos, SP, Brazil
`rta@usp.br, taspardo@icmc.usp.br`

Abstract. Paraphrase is defined as the repetition of something written or spoken using different words. In this paper, we adopt a feature engineering strategy to perform paraphrase detection at the sentence level. In particular, we explore the potentiality of semantic features, as the similarity between two semantic graphs, a distance function between sentences and the cosine similarity between embedded sentences, using them within several machine learning-based classifiers. We evaluate our approach on the ASSIN benchmark corpus and achieve 80.5% of F-score, outperforming some other detection methods for Portuguese.

Keywords: Paraphrase detection · Semantics · Machine learning

1 Introduction

According to Bhagat and Hovy [5], paraphrases are sentences or phrases that convey the same meaning using different wording, i.e., they represent alternative surface forms in the same language expressing the same semantic content of the original forms [19]. For example, sentences 1 and 2 are paraphrases of each other.

1. It is a strange term, but we have got used to it.
2. This term is strange, however, we are accustomed to it.

Automatically detecting paraphrases may be useful for several Natural Language Processing (NLP) tasks, for instance, summarization [15], question answering [20], plagiarism detection [22], semantic parsing [31] and machine translation [29], among others.

Despite the importance of detecting paraphrases, few studies have focused on this task for the Portuguese language. Moreover, the reported achieved results are still far from the ones for the English language. For Portuguese, the achieved results are under 40% of F-score, whereas, for English, the results are over 85%. One possible reason for the few studies in Portuguese is that authors have focused on the related task of textual entailment recognition, which is the task of deciding whether the meaning of one text may be inferred from another one [12].

© Springer Nature Switzerland AG 2020
P. Quaresma et al. (Eds.): PROPOR 2020, LNAI 12037, pp. 228–238, 2020.
https://doi.org/10.1007/978-3-030-41505-1_22

In this paper, we perform feature engineering to develop a new method to identify whether two sentences are paraphrases of each other. In particular, we explore 4 semantic features: Word Mover Distance (WMD) [16], Smooth Inverse Frequency (SIF) [3], the cosine between two embedded sentences (COS), and the similarity between sentences encoded as Abstract Meaning Representation (AMR) graphs [4]. We train some classifiers, as Support Vector Machine (SVM), Naïve Bayes (NB), Decision Trees (DT), Neural Networks (NN) and Logistic Regression (LR), and evaluate them on the ASSIN benchmark corpus [11], reaching the best F-score of 80.5% with the SVM classifier, outperforming some other methods for Portuguese.

The remaining of this paper is organized as follows. Section 2 describes the main related work. In Sect. 3, we present the used corpus. Section 4 details our paraphrase identification method and the adopted features. In Sect. 5, we report our experiments and the achieved results. Finally, Sect. 6 concludes the paper, indicating future research.

2 Related Work

For the Portuguese language, there are few approaches that strictly tackle the paraphrase detection task. At this point, it is important to let clear that there is a subtle difference between paraphrase detection and similarity/entailment identification, as claimed in [30]. For the latter task, other works do exist. Following [30], we specifically focus on the former approaches.

Cordeiro et al. [10] developed a metric named *Sumo-Metric* for semantic relatedness between two sentences based on the overlapping of lexical units. Although the authors evaluated their metric on a corpus for the English language, the metric is language-independent.

Rocha and Cardoso [28] modeled the task as a supervised machine learning problem. However, they handled the issue as a multi-class task, classifying sentence pairs into entailment, none, or paraphrase. Thus, they employed a set of features of the lexical, syntactic, and semantic levels to represent the sentences in numerical values, and fed these features into some machine learning algorithms. They evaluated their method on the training set of the ASSIN corpus, using both European and Portuguese partitions. The method obtained 0.52 of F-score using a SVM classifier.

Souza and Sanches [30] also dealt with the problem with supervised machine learning. However, their objective was to explore sentence embeddings for this task. They used a pre-trained FastText model [7] and the following features: the average of the vectors, the value of Smooth Inverse Frequency (SIF), and weighted aggregation based on Inverse Document Frequency (IDF). With these features, their method reached 0.33 of F-score using a SVM classifier on balanced data of the ASSIN corpus for European and Portuguese partitions.

Consoli et al. [9] analyzed the capabilities of the coreference resolution tool CORP [13] for identification of paraphrases. The authors used CORP to identify noun phrases that may help to detect paraphrases between sentence pairs. They evaluated their method on 116 sentence pairs from the ASSIN corpus, achieving 0.53 of F-score.

For the English language, recent works have focused on deep learning models [17,18,32] because of the availability of large corpora. These works achieve F-scores over 85%.

3   The Corpus

To evaluate our model, we used the ASSIN corpus [11]. It contains 10,000 sentence pairs, 5,000 written in Brazilian Portuguese and 5,000 in European Portuguese. Each language has 2,500, 500, and 2,000 pairs for training, development, and testing, respectively, as shown in Table 1.

Table 1. Organization of the ASSIN corpus

Language	Training	Development	Testing
Brazilian Portuguese	2,500	500	2,000
European Portuguese	2,500	500	2,000

The data in the corpus is organized into three categories: entailment, none, and paraphrase. Table 2 presents the distribution of these categories in the corpus. As we can see, the corpus is unbalanced concerning the paraphrase label, since the proportion of entailment and none labels is much higher than paraphrases. For example, the none label has 73.16% of examples in the corpus and the entailment label has 20.80%. Together, they sum 93.96% of the examples in the corpus.

Table 2. Distribution of labels in the ASSIN corpus

Label	Brazilian Port.			European Port.			Total #	Proportion %
	Train.	Dev.	Test.	Train.	Dev.	Test.		
Entailment	437	92	341	613	116	481	2,080	20.80
None	1,947	384	1,553	1,708	338	1,386	7,316	73.16
Paraphrase	116	24	106	179	46	133	604	6.04

In this paper, we used both European and Brazilian Portuguese languages for paraphrase detection. In Table 3, we show examples of paraphrase pairs in the corpus.

Table 3. Examples of paraphrase pairs for Portuguese

Language Variety	Sentences
Brazilian	(1) *De acordo com o site TMZ, a cantora Britney Spears comprou uma nova casa*
	(2) *Segundo informações divulgadas pelo site TMZ, Britney Spears está de casa nova* (In English, "According to the TMZ website, singer Britney Spears bought a new home.")
European	(3) *Hitler não queria exterminar os judeus na época, ele queria expulsar os judeus*
	(4) *Naquela altura, Hitler não queria exterminar os judeus mas sim expulsá-los* (In English, "Hitler did not want to exterminate the Jews, but to expel them.")

4   Paraphrase Identification Method

Although the ASSIN corpus has three labels, we joined the entailment and none labels into one unique label named "non-paraphrase", which is our negative class. Table 4 shows the new configuration of the ASSIN corpus.

Table 4. New distribution of labels in the ASSIN corpus

Label	Brazilian Port.			European Port.			Total #	Proportion %
	Train.	Dev.	Test.	Train.	Dev.	Test.		
Non-paraphrase	2,384	476	1,894	2,321	454	1,867	9,396	93.96
Paraphrase	116	24	106	179	46	133	604	6.04

We did this modification to formulate the task as a binary classification problem, since we aim to identify whether a sentence pair shows a paraphrase or not. Thus, we formulate the problem in the following way. Let S be a set of sentence pairs. We provide input data in the form of $(x_1^{(i)}, x_2^{(i)}, b^{(i)})$ for $i \in [n]$, where n is the number of training sentences, $x_1^{(i)}$ and $x_2^{(i)}$ are the input sentences, and $b^{(i)} \in \{0, 1\}$ indicates a binary classification that informs whether $x_1^{(i)}$ and $x_2^{(i)}$ are paraphrases of each other. In summary, the aim is to learn a classifier c that, given unseen sentence pairs, classifies whether they are paraphrases, as in Eq. 1.

$$c : S \times S \to 0, 1 \tag{1}$$

To classify these sentence pairs, we extract some semantic features. We focused on semantic features because detecting paraphrases involves understanding the meaning of the sentences. Some of the adopted features need to be modeled as word embeddings, which are vectors of real-valued numbers that represent particular words. As the ASSIN corpus is small to train embedding models, we used pre-trained word embeddings [14] and evaluated different models such as Word2Vec [23], FastText [7], and Glove [25] with dimensions of 50, 100, and 300. For Wor2Vec and FastText, we analyzed two training methods: Skip-Gram and CBOW. We describe the extracted features in what follows.

Word Mover Distance (WMD). It is a feature that assesses the distance between two documents even when they have no words in common [16]. It measures the dissimilarity between two text documents as the minimum amount of distance that embedded words of one document need to "travel" to reach the embedded words of another document. It is important to notice that WMD is a distance function, i.e., the lower the distance value is, the more similar the documents are. For getting the WMD distance, we first tokenized and removed stopwords of the sentences, using the Natural Language Toolkit (NLTK) [6]; next, we got the embeddings for the words of the sentences; finally, to get the WMD distance, we used the method from Gensim library [27] that receives a sentence pair encoded as word embeddings as input and returns the WMD value.

Cosine of Word Embeddings (COS). For calculating the cosine similarity between sentences, we got the embeddings for the words, computed the average of the word embeddings for each sentence, and calculated the cosine similarity between these vectors, applying Eq. 2, where $\vec{u} \cdot \vec{x}$ is the dot product of the two vectors.

$$\cos \theta = \frac{\vec{u} \cdot \vec{x}}{\|\vec{u}\| \|\vec{x}\|} \tag{2}$$

Smooth Inverse Frequency (SIF). Computing the average of the word embeddings, as in the cosine similarity, tends to give too much weight to words that may be irrelevant [3]. SIF tries to solve this problem, giving more weight to words that contribute to the semantics of the sentence. For this purpose, Eq. 3 is used, where a is a hyper-parameter set to 0.001 by default and $p(w)$ is the estimated word frequency in the corpus.

$$SIF(w) = \frac{a}{(a + p(w))} \tag{3}$$

Abstract Meaning Representation (AMR). It is a semantic representation language designed to capture the meaning of a sentence [4]. This language represents sentences as directed acyclic graphs, where the nodes are concepts and edges represent the relation among them, explicitly showing semantic features, as semantic roles, word sense disambiguation, negation, and others. Therefore, sentences with the same meaning should result in similar graphs. For instance, the sentences "James did not see the girl who wanted him." and "James did not see the girl who he was wanted by." may be encoded as the AMR graph

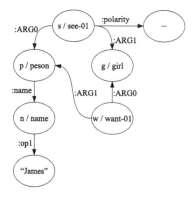

Fig. 1. An example of AMR graph. The `see-01` node is the root of the graph, the `person` node indicates a named entity, and the `polarity` relation illustrates a negation. One may also see PropBank-like semantic roles. For more details, we suggest consulting the original AMR paper [4].

shown in Fig. 1. To take this information into account, we parsed the sentence pairs into AMR graphs using a rule-based AMR parser [1] and computed the similarity between the graphs using the SEMA metric [2].

Following the feature extraction step, we used some classifiers to evaluate our approach. We used Support Vector Machine (SVM), Naïve Bayes (NB), Decision Trees (DT), Neural Networks (NN), and Logistic Regression (LR) in the Scikit-Learn library [24]. In what follows, we detail our experiments and the obtained results.

5   Experiments and Results

After extracting the features, we used the ASSIN corpus with two labels, as shown in Table 4, to evaluate our approach. As we can see, the corpus is very unbalanced concerning the paraphrase label. This causes difficulties to the learning, since a classifier will learn much more about non-paraphrase information. To mitigate this issue, we applied the SMOTE (Synthetic Minority Over-sampling Technique) technique [8] to balance the data. It creates synthetic data for the minority class in order to obtain a balanced corpus.

After evaluating different pre-trained word embeddings with the extracted features to feed the classifiers, the best setting was reached with the SVM classifier with linear kernel and the Word2Vec model of 300 dimensions using the Skip-Gram as training method. Table 5 shows the obtained results with that setting in both unbalanced and balanced version of the corpus.

To compare with our approach, we developed a baseline method based on the word overlap between the sentence pairs. First, we tokenized the sentence pairs; next, we computed the number of tokens in the intersection between the sentence pairs; we, then, applied the SMOTE technique to balance the data; and,

Table 5. Results of the SVM classifier for paraphrase detection

	Class	Precision	Recall	F-score
Unbalanced	Paraphrase	0.20	0.81	0.32
	Non-paraphrase	0.98	0.80	0.88
Balanced	Paraphrase	0.80	0.82	0.81
	Non-paraphrase	0.81	0.80	0.80

at last, we trained the SVM classifier. In addition to the baseline method, we also compared our approach with the method of Souza and Sanches [30], since they used the same corpus and oversampling technique. In Table 6, we present a comparison among the approaches.

Table 6. Comparison among approaches for paraphrase identification

Method	F-score
Souza and Sanches [30]	0.333
Baseline	0.730
Our approach	**0.805**

One may see that our approach outperforms the related work, achieving results close to those for the English language. Moreover, using the same pre-trained word embeddings and classifier above, we investigated the importance of each feature in the classification, as depicted in Fig. 2.

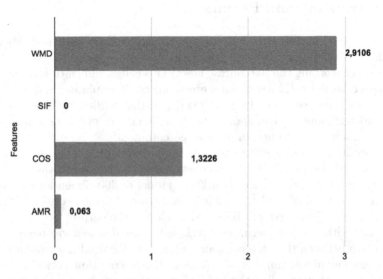

Fig. 2. Importance of each feature

Overall, the features WMD, COS, and AMR are more relevant for classification, while SIF did not contribute to it. We believe that the SIF feature fails because the corpus is small and this metric uses information about the estimated frequency of words.

We performed an ablation study aiming to investigate how each feature may improve the classification. Table 7 presents the results for the study using the SVM classifier. We can see that the WMD + COS and WMD + COS + AMR features achieved the best F-score values (0.805). However, the AMR feature had little contribution to classification, since the WMD + COS reached higher value.

Table 7. Ablation study with the features for the SVM classifier

Features	F-score
WMD	0.800
COS	0.740
AMR	0.580
WMD + COS	**0.805**
WMD + AMR	0.803
WMD + COS + AMR	**0.805**

Another conclusion is that the COS feature alone produced better results than the AMR feature alone. This is relevant because such measures follow different semantic paradigms: COS is based on the word embeddings, which "implicitly" represent semantics, while AMR "explicitly" indicates the semantic constituents of the text passage of interest. The achieved result may reflect that embedding learning is currently more robust than AMR learning/parsing, but may also indicate that our feature computation did not take full advantage of AMR potentiality. This issue remains for future exploration.

We performed a detailed error analysis and could realize that automatically distinguishing paraphrase from entailment cases is not a trivial task, as a paraphrase may be viewed as a mutual (or bidirectional) entailment. Textual entailment is the relationship between a text T and a hypothesis H, where $T \rightarrow H$ (T entails H), while a paraphrase may be viewed as $T \rightarrow H$ and $H \rightarrow T$. Because of this, SVM misclassified the sentence "*Segundo Lagarde, esse fenômeno deverá levar o FMI a revisar para baixo a previsão de crescimento.*" and "*Esse fenômeno deve levar o FMI a revisar para baixo as projeções de crescimento.*" as paraphrases, whereas it also missclassified the sentences "*Nunca antes um pontífice havia ido ao plenário das Casa Legislativas dos Estados Unidos.*" and "*Ele será o primeiro papa no plenário da Casa Legislativa dos Estados Unidos.*" as non-paraphrases.

Treating such subtleties in classification and investigating which types of paraphrases were not identified remain for future work.

6   Final Remarks

In this paper, we explored the potentiality of semantic features in a machine learning solution to detect paraphrases for the Portuguese Language. We evaluated our approach on the ASSIN benchmark corpus, achieving 80.5% of F-score, outperforming some reported results on the literature for Portuguese.

Future work includes exploring other semantic features and classification strategies, looking for more data to run deep learning methods. A new feature that may be promising to the task comes from discourse structuring studies, in particular, from the works on parsing texts according to the Cross-document Structure Theory [26], which is a discourse model that predicts some paraphrase-like relations among text passages. Discourse parsers for Portuguese already exist (see, e.g., [21]) and might be used.

To the interested reader, the source code and trained models that we tested are available online (http://github.com/rafaelanchieta/paraphrase-detection). Additional information about this work may be found at the OPINANDO project webpage (https://sites.google.com/icmc.usp.br/opinando/).

Acknowledgements. The authors are grateful to *Instituto Federal do Piauí* (IFPI) and USP Research Office (PRP 668) for supporting this work.

References

1. Anchiêta, R.T., Pardo, T.A.S.: A rule-based AMR parser for portuguese. In: Simari, G.R., Fermé, E., Gutiérrez Segura, F., Rodríguez Melquiades, J.A. (eds.) IBERAMIA 2018. LNCS (LNAI), vol. 11238, pp. 341–353. Springer, Cham (2018). https://doi.org/10.1007/978-3-030-03928-8_28
2. Anchiêta, R.T., Cabezudo, M.A.S., Pardo, T.A.S.: SEMA: an extended semantic evaluation metric for amr. In: (To appear) Proceedings of the 20th International Conference on Computational Linguistics and Intelligent Text Processing (2019)
3. Arora, S., Liang, Y., Ma, T.: A simple but tough-to-beat baseline for sentence embeddings. In: Proceeding of the 5th International Conference on Learning Representations (2017)
4. Banarescu, L., et al.: Abstract meaning representation for sembanking. In: Proceedings of the 7th Linguistic Annotation Workshop and Interoperability with Discourse, pp. 178–186 (2013)
5. Bhagat, R., Hovy, E.: What is a paraphrase? Comput. Linguist. **39**(3), 463–472 (2013)
6. Bird, S., Klein, E., Loper, E.: Natural language processing with Python: analyzing text with the natural language toolkit. O'Reilly Media, Inc., Sebastopol (2009)
7. Bojanowski, P., Grave, E., Joulin, A., Mikolov, T.: Enriching word vectors with subword information. Trans. Assoc. Comput. Linguist. **5**, 135–146 (2017)
8. Chawla, N.V., Bowyer, K.W., Hall, L.O., Kegelmeyer, W.P.: Smote: synthetic minority over-sampling technique. J. Artif. Intell. Res. **16**, 321–357 (2002)
9. Consoli, B.S., Neto, J.F.S., de Abreu, S.C., Vieira, R.: Análise da capacidade de identificação de paráfrase em ferramentas de resolução de correferência. Linguamática **10**(2), 45–51 (2018)

10. Cordeiro, J., Dias, G., Brazdil, P.: A metric for paraphrase detection. In: International Multi-Conference on Computing in the Global Information Technology, pp. 1–7. IEEE (2007)
11. Fonseca, E., Santos, L., Criscuolo, M., Aluísio, S.: Assin: Avaliação de similaridade semântica e inferência textual. In: Proceedings of the 12th International Conference on the Computational Processing of Portuguese, pp. 13–15 (2016)
12. Fonseca, E.R., dos Santos, L.B., Criscuolo, M., Aluísio, S.M.: Visão geral da avaliação de similaridade semântica e inferência textual. Linguamática **8**(2), 3–13 (2016)
13. Fonseca, E., Sesti, V., Antonitsch, A., Vanin, A., Vieira, R.: Corp: Uma abordagem baseada em regras e conhecimento semântico para a resoluçao de correferências. Linguamática **9**(1), 3–18 (2017)
14. Hartmann, N., Fonseca, E., Shulby, C., Treviso, M., Silva, J., Aluísio, S.: Portuguese word embeddings: evaluating on word analogies and natural language tasks. In: Proceedings of the 11th Brazilian Symposium in Information and Human Language Technology, pp. 122–131 (2017)
15. Jing, H., McKeown, K.R.: Cut and paste based text summarization. In: Proceedings of the 1st North American chapter of the Association for Computational Linguistics conference, pp. 178–185. Association for Computational Linguistics (2000)
16. Kusner, M., Sun, Y., Kolkin, N., Weinberger, K.: From word embeddings to document distances. In: Proceedings of the 32nd International Conference on Machine Learning, pp. 957–966 (2015)
17. Lan, W., Xu, W.: Neural network models for paraphrase identification, semantic textual similarity, natural language inference, and question answering. In: Proceedings of the 27th International Conference on Computational Linguistics, pp. 3890–3902 (2018)
18. Liu, X., He, P., Chen, W., Gao, J.: Multi-task deep neural networks for natural language understanding. In: Proceedings of the 57th Annual Meeting of the Association for Computational Linguistics, pp. 4487–4496. Association for Computational Linguistics (2019)
19. Madnani, N., Dorr, B.J.: Generating phrasal and sentential paraphrases: a survey of data-driven methods. Comput. Linguist. **36**(3), 341–387 (2010)
20. Marsi, E., Krahmer, E.: Explorations in sentence fusion. In: Proceedings of the 10th European Workshop on Natural Language Generation (ENLG-05) (2005)
21. Maziero, E.G., del Rosário Castro Jorge, M.L., Pardo, T.A.S.: Revisiting cross-document structure theory for multi-document discourse parsing. Inf. Process. Manag. **50**(2), 297–314 (2014)
22. McClendon, J.L., Mack, N.A., Hodges, L.F.: The use of paraphrase identification in the retrieval of appropriate responses for script based conversational agents. In: Proceedings of the 27th International Flairs Conference, pp. 196–201 (2014)
23. Mikolov, T., Chen, K., Corrado, G., Dean, J.: Efficient estimation of word representations in vector space. In: Proceedings of International Conference on Learning Representations Workshop (2013)
24. Pedregosa, F., et al.: Scikit-learn: machine learning in Python. J. Mach. Learn. Res. **12**, 2825–2830 (2011)
25. Pennington, J., Socher, R., Manning, C.: Glove: global vectors for word representation. In: Proceedings of the 2014 conference on empirical methods in natural language processing (EMNLP), pp. 1532–1543 (2014)

26. Radev, D.: A common theory of information fusion from multiple text sources step one: cross-document structure. In: Proceedings of the 1st SIGdial Workshop on Discourse and Dialogue, pp. 74–83. Association for Computational Linguistics, Hong Kong, China, October 2000

27. Řehůřek, R., Sojka, P.: Software Framework for Topic Modelling with Large Corpora. In: Proceedings of the LREC 2010 Workshop on New Challenges for NLP Frameworks, pp. 45–50 (2010)

28. Rocha, G., Lopes Cardoso, H.: Recognizing textual entailment and paraphrases in Portuguese. In: Oliveira, E., Gama, J., Vale, Z., Lopes Cardoso, H. (eds.) EPIA 2017. LNCS (LNAI), vol. 10423, pp. 868–879. Springer, Cham (2017). https://doi.org/10.1007/978-3-319-65340-2_70

29. Sekizawa, Y., Kajiwara, T., Komachi, M.: Improving Japanese-to-English neural machine translation by paraphrasing the target language. In: Proceedings of the 4th Workshop on Asian Translation (WAT2017), pp. 64–69 (2017)

30. Souza, M., Sanches, L.M.P.: Detecção de paráfrases na língua portuguesa usando sentence embeddings. Linguamática **10**(2), 31–44 (2018)

31. Su, Y., Yan, X.: Cross-domain semantic parsing via paraphrasing. In: Proceedings of the 2017 Conference on Empirical Methods in Natural Language Processing, pp. 1235–1246 (2017)

32. Tomar, G.S., Duque, T., Täckström, O., Uszkoreit, J., Das, D.: Neural paraphrase identification of questions with noisy pretraining. In: Proceedings of the First Workshop on Subword and Character Level Models in NLP, pp. 142–147 (2017)

Portuguese Language Models and Word Embeddings: Evaluating on Semantic Similarity Tasks

Ruan Chaves Rodrigues[1(✉)], Jéssica Rodrigues[2],
Pedro Vitor Quinta de Castro[1], Nádia Felix Felipe da Silva[1],
and Anderson Soares[1]

[1] Institute of Informatics, Federal University of Goiás, Goiânia, Brazil
ruanchaves93@gmail.com, {pedrovitorquinta,nadia,anderson}@inf.ufg.br
[2] Department of Computer Science, Federal University of São Carlos,
São Carlos, Brazil
jsc.rodrigues@gmail.com

Abstract. Deep neural language models which achieved state-of-the-art results on downstream natural language processing tasks have recently been trained for the Portuguese language. However, studies that systematically evaluate such models are still necessary for several applications. In this paper, we propose to evaluate the performance of deep neural language models on the semantic similarity tasks provided by the ASSIN dataset against classical word embeddings, both for Brazilian Portuguese and for European Portuguese. Our experiments indicate that the ELMo language model was able to achieve better accuracy than any other pretrained model which has been made publicly available for the Portuguese language, and that performing vocabulary reduction on the dataset before training not only improved the standalone performance of ELMo, but also improved its performance while combined with classical word embeddings. We also demonstrate that FastText skip-gram embeddings can have a significantly better performance on semantic similarity tasks than it was indicated by previous studies in this field.

Keywords: Deep neural language models · Semantic textual similarity · Portuguese language

1 Introduction

The application of deep learning methods to Natural Language Processing (NLP) is possible due to the representation of words as vectors in a low-dimensional continuous space. These traditional word embeddings are static: each word has a single vector, regardless of its context [20,21]. This generates several problems, especially that all the senses of a polysemic word have to share the same

---

The source code for the experiments described in this paper has been published on GitHub at https://github.com/ruanchaves/elmo.

P. Quaresma et al. (Eds.): PROPOR 2020, LNAI 12037, pp. 239–248, 2020.
https://doi.org/10.1007/978-3-030-41505-1_23

representation. Recent developments in the field produced deep neural language models such as ELMo [23] and BERT [10], which have successfully created contextualized word representations, word vectors that are sensitive to the context in which they appear. Using contextualized representations rather than static embeddings has resulted in significant improvements in a variety of NLP tasks, such as question answering and coreference resolution.

In this paper, we present experiments carried out to evaluate different word representation models for Portuguese, including both Brazilian and European variants, for semantic similarity tasks. To our knowledge, this is the first paper to evaluate deep neural language models on semantic similarity tasks in the Portuguese language.

Our experiments indicate that, if fine-tuning is not applied to any language model, then the ELMo language model is able to achieve better accuracy than any other pretrained model which has been made publicly available for the Portuguese language. We have found that performing vocabulary reduction on the corpus before training not only improved the standalone performance of ELMo, but also improved its performance while combined with classical word embeddings. We also demonstrate that FastText skip-gram embeddings [2] can have a significantly better performance on semantic similarity tasks than it was indicated by previous studies in this field.

In Sect. 2 we describe some of the approaches for generating deep neural language models proposed in the literature. The approaches investigated in this paper are described in Sect. 3. The experiments carried out for evaluating deep neural language models for Portuguese are described in Sect. 4. Section 5 finishes this paper with its conclusions and proposals for future work.

2   Related Work

Hartmann et al. [12] trained 31 word embedding models using FastText, GloVe, Wang2Vec and Word2Vec. The authors evaluated them intrinsically on syntactic and semantic analogies and extrinsically on POS tagging and sentence semantic similarity tasks. The authors contribute with a variety of pre-trained word embeddings, intrinsic and extrinsic task comparisons, and preprocessing and evaluation codes. We used this work as a baseline for deep neural language models.

Quinta de Castro et al. [6] evaluated the four different types of word embeddings pre-trained by [12] and performed an extrinsic evaluation of them in the Named Entity Recognition (NER) task. The authors used only 100-dimensional word embeddings, applying them to the same BiLSTM-CRF deep learning architecture from [15], and improved the previous state-of-the-art on the HAREM [26] benchmark for Portuguese language using Wang2Vec [16] embeddings.

An ELMo [23] model trained for Portuguese has been previously evaluated by Quinta de Castro [7] on NER tasks for the IberLEF evaluation [11].

Quinta de Castro [7] also made their model publicly available through the AllenNLP library[1]. The authors experimented different scenarios of NER with Portuguese corpora, using a BiLSTM-CRF network from the AllenNLP library. The results achieved state-of-the-art performance using the optimal values for them.

Santos et al. [27] assessed how different combinations of static word embeddings and contextualized embeddings impact NER for the Portuguese language. The authors show a comparative study of 16 different combinations of static and contextualized embeddings and evaluate NER performance using the HAREM benchmark. The best NER system outperforms the state-of-the-art in Portuguese NER by 5.99 in absolute percentage points.

Quinta de Castro [5] evaluated different combinations of word representations, such as character level embeddings, static word embeddings from [12] and ELMo embeddings [23] on the NER task. The author performed a comparative study on two different domains for the Portuguese language (general and legal), performing the pre-training of the ELMo embeddings for each domain, and comparing them to a fine-tuned version of the model on different NER corpora, for each domain. The author reached a new state-of-the-art for the HAREM benchmark using the fine-tuned ELMo embeddings, combined with 100-dimensional Wang2Vec embeddings.

To our knowledge, this is the first paper to evaluate deep neural language models on semantic similarity tasks in the Portuguese language. The semantic similarity task provided by the ASSIN dataset is equivalent to the Semantic Textual Similarity Benchmark (STS-B), and works that evaluated deep neural language models on the STS-B task, such as [22], can be taken as a reference for what to expect of its performance in other linguistic contexts.

3   Word Representations

In this paper, two ways of word representation were evaluated in semantic similarity tasks for Portuguese: contextualized and static word representations. They were tested both individually and also pairwise concatenated with each other, and each approach is explained in the next sections.

3.1   Static Word Representations

Word representations are numerical vectors which can represent words or concepts in a low-dimensional continuous space, reducing the inherent sparsity of traditional vector-space representations [25]. These vectors, also known as embeddings, are able to capture useful syntactic and semantic information, such as regularities in natural language. They are based on the distributional hypothesis, which establishes that the meaning of a word is given by its context of occurrence [3]. A numerical vector representing a word can be visualized in a continuous vector space, accepting algebraic operations such as the cosine distance.

---

[1] https://allennlp.org/elmo.

The ability of static word embeddings to capture knowledge has been exploited in several tasks, such as Machine Translation [20], Word Sense Disambiguation [9] and Language Understanding [18].

Although very useful in many applications, the static word embeddings, like those generated by Word2Vec [19], GloVe [21], Wang2Vec [16] and FastText [2] have an important limitation: each word is associated with only one vector representation, ignoring the fact that polysemous words can assume multiple meanings. This limitation is called *Meaning Conflation Deficiency*, which is a mixture of possible meanings in a single word [4]. For instance, in the phrase *"My mouse was broken, so I bought a new one yesterday."* the word *"mouse"* should be associated with its meaning of being a *computer device*, rather than the *animal called mouse*. Figure 1 is an illustration of this Meaning Conflation Deficiency in a 2D semantic space.

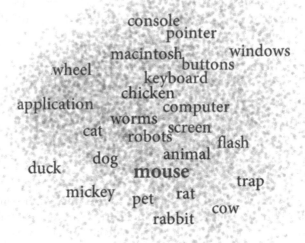

Fig. 1. Example of meaning conflation deficiency of ambiguous word "mouse". The words in blue refer to the sense of animal and the words in green to the sense of device. (Color figure online)

Because they create a single representation for each word, a notable problem with static word embeddings is that all senses of a polysemous word must share a single vector.

3.2   Contextualized Word Representations

The limitations of static word embeddings have led to the creation of context-sensitive word representations. ELMo [23], BERT [10], and GPT-2 [24] are examples of deep neural language models that are fine-tuned to create models for a wide variety of downstream NLP tasks. As GPT-2 is not yet available for the Portuguese language, we performed our experiments solely on ELMo and a multilingual version of BERT. The internal representations of words for these language models are called contextualized word representations because they are a function of the entire input sentence, and in this study, sentence embeddings were built through the summation of these representations. The success of this approach suggests that these representations capture highly transferable and task-agnostic properties of natural languages [17].

ELMo. [23] is a two-layer bidirectional LSTM language model, built over a context independent character CNN layer and originally trained on the Billion Word Benchmark dataset [8], consisting primarily of newswire text. In order to obtain a representation for each word, we performed a linear concatenation of all three ELMo layers, without learning any task-specific weights. During our experiments, we considered two ELMo language models that were exclusively trained for the Portuguese language. The first model has been made publicly available through the AllenNLP library. The second model was trained by ourselves in an attempt to improve on the accuracy of this public model: although it took the same dataset used by the first model as its starting point, words that occurred less than three times were removed from the dataset before training the model. Such additional vocabulary reduction step was accompanied by suitable adjustments on the softmax layer and the network architecture.

BERT. [10] is a deep Transformer [28] encoder trained jointly as a masked language model and on next-sentence prediction, originally trained on the concatenation of the Toronto Books Corpus [29] and the English Wikipedia. As with GPT, we do not fine-tune the encoder weights. We utilized the publicly released BERT-multilingual model, which was simultaneously trained on the Wikipedia dumps for 104 different languages. In order to achieve better accuracy on the semantic similarity task, we considered only the final layer of the model for generating its sentence embeddings.

4   Experiments and Results

In this section we show the experiments carried out to evaluate the two approaches under investigation: word embeddings (Word2Vec, FastText) and deep neural language models (ELMo, BERT) on semantic similarity tasks.

4.1   Evaluation

Based on [12], this experiment is a task of semantic similarity between sentences where the use of neural language models is evaluated. Word embeddings were chosen as baselines.

Dataset. ASSIN (Avaliação de Similaridade Semântica e Inferência Textual) was a workshop co-located with PROPOR-2016 which encompassed two shared-tasks regarding: (i) semantic similarity and (ii) entailment. We chose the first one to evaluate our contextualized vectors extrinsically in a semantic task. In ASSIN, the participants of the semantic similarity shared-task were asked to assign similarity values between 1 and 5 to pairs of sentences (gold score). The workshop made available the training and test sets for Brazilian (PT-BR) and European (PT-EU) Portuguese.

Algorithm. The objective of this task is to predict, through a linear regression, the similarity score between two sentences. The model is trained in the training set, which contains sentence pairs with the gold score. The prediction occurs in the test set, which contains sentence pairs without the gold score. As we have this same test set with the gold score, it is possible to calculate Pearson's Correlation (ρ) and Mean Squared Error (MSE) between them. These results show how much the automatic prediction has approached the human prediction.

The results were obtained after training a linear regressor with the cosine similarity between the summations of the word representations of each sentences' words, in a procedure almost equivalent to what has been performed by [12]. However, we applied the following changes to his original approach: for word embeddings, we avoided most occurrences of out of vocabulary words by applying to the test set the same tokenization and normalization steps which were performed on the training set before the word embeddings were trained. These steps were described by [12] and we performed them through their standard implementation.

This approach significantly reduced the amount of out-of-vocabulary words for word embeddings, and the remaining ones were simply ignored, instead of being replaced by a single UNKNOWN token. In the case of language models, such as ELMo and BERT, no preprocessing was applied, and whenever evaluating the combination of a language model and a word embedding, we simply performed the concatenation of the sentence embeddings produced from each source.

Evaluation Metrics. The Pearson correlation coefficient measures the linear relationship between two datasets: one annotated by the participants and another which is output by the system. Like other correlation coefficients, this one varies between -1 and $+1$ with 0 meaning no correlation. Correlations of -1 or $+1$ mean an exact linear relationship. The Mean Squared Error (MSE) of an estimator measures the average of the squares of the errors, that is, the average squared difference between the estimated value and what was expected.

Discussion of Results. Table 1 shows the performance of our models for the Brazilian Portuguese and European Portuguese test sets, through the Pearson's Correlation (ρ) and mean squared error (MSE).

All semantic similarity tests for word embeddings listed by [12] were repeated during our experiments. Although most word embeddings retained exactly the same relative accuracy, FastText skip-gram embeddings have exhibited a noticeable increase in performance; in fact, the FastText skip-gram embedding at 1000 dimensions achieved the best standalone accuracy among all word embeddings considered for the ASSIN semantic similarity task. This happened because the approach deployed by [12] produced a higher amount of out-of-vocabulary (OOV) words, and the FastText embeddings were abnormally sensitive to their adopted strategy of replacing all OOV words by a single UNKNOWN token. [14] provides a survey of OOV word replacement techniques that can avoid this handicap. We therefore conclude that the performance oscillations in FastText word embeddings reported by [12] should first be regarded as a result of their approach to word preprocessing and OOV word replacement after the training stage, rather than as a by-product of intrinsic properties of the word embeddings themselves.

Furthermore, three language models were evaluated, both in isolation and in combination with each one of the word embeddings made publicly available by [12]: BERT, and ELMo with and without vocabulary reduction. While the concatenation of ELMo without vocabulary reduction with any word embeddings resulted in a worse result than using ELMo by itself, the reduced version of ELMo significantly improved its accuracy after being concatenated with Word2Vec embeddings. Such an improvement has not been achieved by any other word embedding. The best combination of Word2Vec and reduced ELMo is reported in Table 1: results belong to the concatenation of the reduced version of ELMo with a Word2Vec embedding that has 1000 dimensions and follows the Continuous Bag of Words (CBOW) model.

It is also important to notice that, while ELMo retained a relatively stable performance across the Brazilian and European versions of the dataset, BERT-

Table 1. Best results for extrinsic evaluation on the semantic similarity task. Arrows indicate whether lower ($\downarrow$) or higher ($\uparrow$) is better. A hyphen (-) indicates the absence of either a word embedding or a language model. All word embeddings present in the table below have 1000 dimensions.

Word embedding	Language model	PT-BR		PT-EU	
		ρ ($\uparrow$)	MSE ($\downarrow$)	ρ ($\uparrow$)	MSE ($\downarrow$)
Word2Vec (CBOW)	ELMo, reduced	**0.632**	**0.457**	**0.654**	**0.709**
-	ELMo, reduced	0.618	0.472	0.627	0.735
-	ELMo	0.611	0.479	0.620	0.745
-	BERT-multilingual	0.604	0.483	0.564	0.813
FastText (skip-gram)	-	0.590	0.496	0.571	0.796

multilingual loses a measurable portion of its accuracy while performing semantic similarity tasks in European Portuguese. In all likelihood, such a steep decline happens due to the imbalanced proportion between Brazilian and European Portuguese articles in Wikipedia, on which BERT-multilingual was trained.

5   Conclusion and Future Work

Our experiments have shown that the ELMo model that has been made publicly available through the AllenNLP library is already able to consistently perform better on semantic similarity tasks than multilingual versions of BERT that have not been subject to fine-tuning, or classical word embeddings, even when both the Brazilian and European dialects of the Portuguese language are taken into account. Although results for word embeddings superior to those achieved by ELMo have already been reported in the literature, they combine multiple word embeddings [13] or combine a word embedding with several linguistic features [1].

Furthermore, we have also seen that vocabulary reduction not only improved its standalone performance, but made it suitable to be concatenated with Word2Vec embeddings on semantic similarity tasks, which seems to suggest that vocabulary reduction made ELMo favorable to ensemble approaches for improving on its accuracy.

In the future, we should also evaluate if similar results would happen on other downstream tasks, such as sentiment analysis, part-of-speech tagging and named entity recognition. And given the current lack of pretrained deep language models in the Portuguese language, we may also consider introducing in our next experiments not only existing multilingual models, but also more deep language models trained by ourselves, optimized to work exclusively with the Portuguese language.

References

1. Alves, A., Gonçalo Oliveira, H., Rodrigues, R., Encarnaçao, R.: ASAPP 2.0: advancing the state-of-the-art of semantic textual similarity for Portuguese. In: 7th Symposium on Languages, Applications and Technologies (SLATE 2018). Schloss Dagstuhl-Leibniz-Zentrum fuer Informatik (2018)
2. Bojanowski, P., Grave, E., Joulin, A., Mikolov, T.: Enriching word vectors with subword information. Trans. Assoc. Comput. Linguist. **5**, 135–146 (2017)
3. Bruni, E., Tran, N.K., Baroni, M.: Multimodal distributional semantics. J. Artif. Intell. Res. **49**, 1–47 (2014)
4. Camacho-Collados, J., Pilehvar, M.T.: From word to sense embeddings: a survey on vector representations of meaning. J. Artif. Intell. Res. **63**, 743–788 (2018)
5. de Castro, P.V.Q.: Aprendizagem Profunda para Reconhecimento de Entidades Nomeadas em Domínio Jurídico. Master's thesis, Universidade Federal de Goiás (2019)

6. Quinta de Castro, P.V., Félix Felipe da Silva, N., da Silva Soares, A.: Portuguese named entity recognition using LSTM-CRF. In: Villavicencio, A., et al. (eds.) PROPOR 2018. LNCS (LNAI), vol. 11122, pp. 83–92. Springer, Cham (2018). https://doi.org/10.1007/978-3-319-99722-3_9
7. de Castro, P.V.Q., da Silva, N.F.F., da Silva Soares, A.: Contextual representations and semi-supervised named entity recognition for Portuguese language (2019)
8. Chelba, C., et al.: One billion word benchmark for measuring progress in statistical language modeling. arXiv preprint arXiv:1312.3005 (2013)
9. Chen, X., Liu, Z., Sun, M.: A unified model for word sense representation and disambiguation. In: Proceedings of the 2014 Conference on Empirical Methods in Natural Language Processing (EMNLP), Doha, Qatar, pp. 1025–1035. Association for Computational Linguistics, October 2014. https://doi.org/10.3115/v1/D14-1110, https://www.aclweb.org/anthology/D14-1110
10. Devlin, J., Chang, M.W., Lee, K., Toutanova, K.: BERT: pre-training of deep bidirectional transformers for language understanding (2018)
11. Glauber, R.: IberLEF 2019 Portuguese named entity recognition and relation extraction tasks (2019)
12. Hartmann, N., Fonseca, E., Shulby, C., Treviso, M., Rodrigues, J., Aluisio, S.: Portuguese word embeddings: evaluating on word analogies and natural language tasks. arXiv preprint arXiv:1708.06025 (2017)
13. Hartmann, N.S.: Solo queue at assin: Combinando abordagens tradicionais e emergentes. Linguamática **8**(2), 59–64 (2016)
14. Hu, Z., Chen, T., Chang, K.W., Sun, Y.: Few-shot representation learning for out-of-vocabulary words (2019)
15. Lample, G., Ballesteros, M., Subramanian, S., Kawakami, K., Dyer, C.: Neural architectures for named entity recognition. arXiv preprint arXiv:1603.01360 (2016)
16. Ling, W., Dyer, C., Black, A.W., Trancoso, I.: Two/too simple adaptations of Word2Vec for syntax problems. In: Proceedings of the 2015 Conference of the North American Chapter of the Association for Computational Linguistics: Human Language Technologies, pp. 1299–1304 (2015)
17. Liu, Y., et al.: RoBERTa: a robustly optimized BERT pretraining approach. arXiv preprint arXiv:1907.11692 (2019)
18. Mesnil, G., He, X., Deng, L., Bengio, Y.: Investigation of recurrent-neural-network architectures and learning methods for spoken language understanding. In: Interspeech, pp. 3771–3775 (2013)
19. Mikolov, T., Chen, K., Corrado, G., Dean, J.: Efficient estimation of word representations in vector space. arXiv preprint arXiv:1301.3781 (2013)
20. Mikolov, T., Le, Q.V., Sutskever, I.: Exploiting similarities among languages for machine translation (2013)
21. Pennington, J., Socher, R., Manning, C.: GloVe: global vectors for word representation. In: Proceedings of the 2014 Conference on Empirical Methods in Natural Language Processing (EMNLP), pp. 1532–1543 (2014)
22. Peters, M., Ruder, S., Smith, N.A.: To tune or not to tune? adapting pretrained representations to diverse tasks. arXiv preprint arXiv:1903.05987 (2019)
23. Peters, M.E., et al.: Deep contextualized word representations (2018)
24. Radford, A., Narasimhan, K., Salimans, T., Sutskever, I.: Improving language understanding by generative pre-training (2018). https://s3-us-west-2.amazonaws.com/openai-assets/research-covers/language-unsupervised/language_understanding_paper.pdf
25. Salton, G., Wong, A., Yang, C.S.: A vector space model for automatic indexing. ACM Commun. **18**(11), 613–620 (1975). https://doi.org/10.1145/361219.361220

26. Santos, D., Cardoso, N.: Reconhecimento de entidades mencionadas em português. Linguateca **7**(7), 1 (2007). Portugal
27. Santos, J., Consoli, B., dos Santos, C., Terra, J., Collonini, S., Vieira, R.: Assessing the impact of contextual embeddings for Portuguese named entity recognition. In: 2019 8th Brazilian Conference on Intelligent Systems (BRACIS), pp. 437–442. IEEE (2019)
28. Vaswani, A., et al.: Attention is all you need. In: Advances in Neural Information Processing Systems, pp. 5998–6008 (2017)
29. Zhu, Y., et al.: Aligning books and movies: towards story-like visual explanations by watching movies and reading books. In: Proceedings of the IEEE International Conference on Computer Vision, pp. 19–27 (2015)

Relation Extraction for Competitive Intelligence

Sandra Collovini[1]([⊠]) [iD], Patricia Nunes Gonçalves[2], Guilherme Cavalheiro[1],
Joaquim Santos[1] [iD], and Renata Vieira[1,3] [iD]

[1] Pontifícia Universidade Católica do Rio Grande do Sul (PUCRS),
Porto Alegre, Brazil
`{sandra.abreu,guilherme.bonfada,joaquim.santos}@acad.pucrs.br,`
`renata.vieira@pucrs.br`
[2] Cooperativa de Crédito Sicredi, Av. Assis Brasil, Porto Alegre, RS 3940, Brazil
`patricia_ngoncalves@sicredi.com.br`
[3] Universidade de Évora, Evora, Portugal
`renatav@uevora.pt`

Abstract. Competitive intelligence (CI) has become one of the major
subjects for strategic process in an organization in the recent years. CI
gives support to the strategic business area and works as a sensor, showing managers how to position their organization as competitive in the
market. In this paper, we show how Relation Extraction supports CI to
collect and organize external information from unstructured data collected from newspaper, blogs, magazines and informational portals.

Keywords: Relation Extraction · Natural Language Processing ·
Competitive Intelligence

1 Introduction

The task of Relation Extraction from texts is one of the main challenges in
the area of Information Extraction, considering the required linguistic knowledge and the sophistication of the language processing techniques employed.
The objective of this task is to show how identifying and classifying semantic
relations that occur between entities recognized in a given text contribute to
competitive intelligence. The access to an increasing world of information and
the deployment of cutting edge information technologies empowers the modern
corporation to understand itself and its markets. In the last decades this kind of
work has been done without the support of specific computational tools, nowadays current NLP and AI technology are reaching the required maturity to help
organizing such unstructured information.

Competitive Intelligence (CI) is a structured survey model for unstructured
facts and data analysis to support the company's decision making in its strategic
planning [27]. The possible applications of CI are manifold, such as constantly
updating of the company's strategy; building scenarios for business evolution;

© Springer Nature Switzerland AG 2020
P. Quaresma et al. (Eds.): PROPOR 2020, LNAI 12037, pp. 249–258, 2020.
https://doi.org/10.1007/978-3-030-41505-1_24

anticipate changes in the competitive environment; discover new competitors in advance; assist in choosing partnerships, mergers and acquisitions; reduce business risk; detect threats and opportunities; learn about new technology products, processes, political, legal or regulatory changes. In order to study the market, we need to develop scenarios and analyze a great quantity of data, which requires great human effort. To structure and organize the data, we turn to Relation Extraction as a resource for support in information extraction [25].

The aim of this work is to generate a knowledge basis that shows the relation between Fintechs with the objective of monitoring the financial market for Competitive Intelligence. For this purpose, we apply relation extraction to news collected from diverse information sources, such as newspapers and magazines.

This paper is organized as follows. In Sect. 2, we review some related work. Relation extraction framework is presented in Sect. 3. In Sect. 4, we describe the experiments and we discuss the corresponding results. We conclude in Sect. 5.

2   Related Work

In general, knowledge available in texts is expressed by relations between entities (designated by noun phrases). Open Information Extraction (OIE) systems aim at extracting a large set of triples (arg1, rel, arg2) from a corpus without requiring human supervision. In these triples "arg1" and "arg2" are strings meant to denote entities and "rel" is a string meant to denote a relation between "arg1" and "arg2". In [17], the authors present a review of the literature in Open IE through a systematic mapping study.

A great variety OIE systems has been developed in recent years, some of these systems are for Portuguese language [2]. Gamallo and Garcia [16] proposed a multilingual dependency-based Open IE system (DepOE), which was used to extract triples from the Wikipedia considering four target languages: Portuguese, Spanish, Galician and English. Gamallo et al. [14] proposed a multilingual rule-based Open IE system (ArgOE). It is configured for English, Spanish, French, Galician and Portuguese. Gamallo and Garcia [15] proposed a suite of tools, called Linguakit for extraction, analysis, annotation or linguistic correction. LinguaKit allows you to perform various tasks, such as lemmatization, POS-tagging or syntactic parsing, also including sentiment analysis applications, relation extraction, summarization, among others. This tool covers Portuguese, Spanish, English, and Galician. Claro et al. [8] investigate the area of Multilingual Open Information Extraction, exploring Portuguese and English languages.

Regarding systems for Portuguese, three of them [4,5,7] took part in the ReRelEM track of Second HAREM [6]. Cardoso [5] developed the REMBRANDT system to recognize all categories of named entities and relations between them ("identity", "inclusion", "placement" and "other"). Brucksen et al. [4] presented the SeRELeP system aimed at recognizing three relations: "identity", "inclusion" and "placement". Chaves [7] developed SEI-Geo, that dealt only with the Place category and its relations. Santos et al. [21] presented the News2Relations system for extracting relations from titles of news written in Portuguese, dealing with relations of the type (subject, verb, object). Santos and Pinheiros [24] presented the RePort system, a method of Open IE for Portuguese based on the ReVerb system [13] for English. Collovini et al. [10] proposed the extraction and structuring of open relations between named entities from Portuguese texts. Collovini and Vieira presented a system for Portuguese Open Relation Extraction (RelP) [1], which extracts any relation descriptor that describes an explicit relation between named entities (Organization, Person and Place categories) for the organization domain.

More recently, a shared task regarding Named Entity Recognition (NER) and Relation Extraction (RE) for Portuguese was proposed in IberLEF (Iberian Languages Evaluation Forum) 2019[1] [12].

In this work we combine together previous NER and RE Portuguese systems presented in the literature into a unified framework, for the purpose of finding relations among organizations, according with the specific need of a company. The framework is described in the next section.

3   RelP++: A Relation Extraction Framework

Figure 1 shows the overview of RelP++, our Framework to Relation Extraction developed in this work. Our approach is divided into the following modules:

1. NLP Pre-processing is responsible for sentence segmentation and tokenization. Our first module is responsible for breaking and to separating all the words, punctuation and markings that are within the sentence. To develop this module we use NLTK Toolkit[2] for Python.
2. Named Entity Recognition (NER) module processes the tokens provided by the previous module, extracts, and classifies named entities into Person, Organization and Location. The classification is made by a predictive model previously trained by Santos et al. [23].
3. NE's Matcher is an entity matcher algorithm, which means that this part of the process is focused on creating a link between all entities previously identified by NER. This module receives as input a file (CoNLL format [20]) tagged with named entity types, which will pass through a pipeline of analysis, and combine these entities, generating pairs of named entities into the sentences.
4. The feature module is responsible for generating feature vectors for each pair of the named entities and also for the words in between.
5. The CRF model module is responsible for applying the model generated from these features vectors.

Named Entity Recognition: Named Entity Recognition (NER) is a classic Natural Language Processing (NLP) task and consists in identifying and classifying certain mentions in a given text [22]. For example, "A Giro.Tech <B-ORG> garante ao FIDC <B-ORG> um risco muito menor de fraudes." ('Giro.Tech

---

[1]   https://iberlef.sepln.org/.
[2]   https://www.nltk.org.

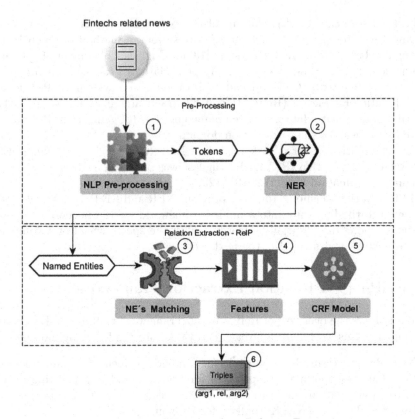

Fig. 1. Overview of Framework to Relation Extraction

<B-ORG> gives FIDC *<B-ORG>* a much lower risk of fraud.'). Where *<B-ORG>* means that the previous token has been classified as an entity of the Organization category.

For the NER module in this framework we used a prediction model previously trained by Santos et al. [23], currently state-of-the-art work for the Portuguese language. To generate the predictive model, the authors used the BiLSTM-CRF Neural Network together with highly representative Language Models (LM). In this sense, BiLSTM-CRF receives a Stacking Embeddings, which are LM compositions, and represents the inputs based on this stacking. Two LMs were used: Word Embeddings (WE) and Flair Embeddings. For WE, we used Word2Vec-Skip-Gram trained with 1 billion tokens by Hartman et al. [18]. For Flair Embeddings we used FlairBBP, trained with 4.9 billion tokens. According to Akibik et al. [3], Flair Embeddings is a type of Contextulized Embeddings, which assume textual inputs as strings and automatically extract features from that level through an LSTM network, just as at the word level they also capture information.

Relation Extraction

In this framework, we used the RelP system [1], built for open relation extraction for Portuguese texts. RelP extracts any relation descriptors expressing an explicit relation occurring between pairs of named entities (Organization, Person or Place) in organization domain. For example, "Mellissa Penteado, CEO do Bancoin" ('Mellissa Penteado, the CEO of Bancoin), we have the triple (Mellissa_Penteado, CEO of, Bancoin). The method used to classify the relation descriptor is the probabilistic model Conditional Random Fields (CRF) [19], considering the representation scheme IO and features defined in previous works [9,11].

In this work, we used a new version of the RelP system that only uses open source resources. The RelP classification step was reimplemented, which involves the encoding in features vectors and the corresponding class that represents data input for the classifier. The features have been rewritten using information from Cogroo[3] [26]. The sets of features are: Part-Of-Speech (e. g. POS tag); lexical (e. g. canonic form), syntactic (e. g. syntactic tag); patterns (e. g. noun followed by a preposition); among others. Feature vectors were generated for the pair of the named entities and also for the words between them, resulting in a vector with 51 elements for each word. The CRF model is generated from these features vectors; for every feature, it is attributed a certain weight, resulting in a weight matrix. From this matrix, the model is capable of classifying the relation descriptors in new sentences, not tagged yet.

4   Evaluation on a Real Scenario

We applied our framework on a real scenario proposed by Sicredi, with the objective of extracting relation descriptors that express relations between Organizations, Places and Person from news about Startups and Fintechs. The application process was divided as follows:

Training: A CRF model was trained for posterior application in news of interest. Thus, the RelP system was applied to the RE corpus [1,12] and to a few more sentences about the financial market annotated from news, totaling 510 positive examples and 367 negative examples. We applied a 10-fold cross-validation in this data in order to generate the trained model.

Test: To apply the trained model, 200 news about Fintechs were collected by the Sicredi Competitive Intelligence in the period of August 2018 to September 2019. These news were collected from online newspapers, magazines and information portals. They served as input for the process illustrated in Fig. 1. In module 1, prepossessing steps, such as segmentation and tokenization, were applied to the sentences contained in the news. Following, in module 2 – NER –, the named entities of categories Organization, Person and Place contained in these sentences were identified. Next, in module 3, the sentences that did not contain any pair of named entities of interest were discarded, remaining 142 sentences as candidates for relation extraction.

---

[3] http://ccsl.ime.usp.br/cogroo/.

Besides that, we consider only one named entity pair each time. Thus, if there were more than one pair of named entities, these sentences were duplicated for each different pair of named entities. After this process, there was a total of 403 candidates of relation instances, which are the input for module 4. We added to each sentence-entity pair input the annotation of the relation descriptors. This manual annotation was performed by two annotators, and resulted in 124 positive instances and 279 negative instances (where there is no relation regarding the current pair).

In the next module, the feature vectors for the 403 test sentences were generated. Finally, the trained CRF module was applied to these instances, resulting in the relation triples.

4.1   Results and Discussion

RelP was thus applied to the 403 input instances. It resulted in 68 identified relations (IR) from which 47 were correct (CR). Table 1 presents the results of Precision $(P = CR/IR)$, Recall $(R = CR/TR)$ and F-measure $(F = (2 * P * R)/(P + R))$ of the system.

Table 1. Evaluation

Reference	Identified	Correct	Precision	Recall	F-measure
124	68	47	69%	37%	48%

The 68 extracted instances were distributed as: 37 cases regarding Organizations, 18 cases of Organization and Person, and 13 cases of Organization and Place. In general, correct triples (positive instances) express relevant relations for the intended focus, for example: relations of affiliation between Person and Organization; relations of partnerships and financial support between Organizations; relations of placement between Organizations and Places, among others. Table 2 illustrates positive instances of relations.

Table 2. Positive examples

Sentences	Triples
1. A **Kroton** anunciou uma parceria com o **Cubo_Itaú** que (...)	(Kroton, anunciou uma parceria com, Cubo_Itaú)
2. A GIRA acaba de receber um aporte do fundo **Venture_Brasil_ Central**, gerido pela **Cedro_Capital**	(Venture_Brasil_Central, gerido por, Cedro_Capital)
3. **Fernando_Montanari**, diretor de Negócios da **Neon_Pagamentos** (...)	(Fernando_Montanari, diretor de Negócios de, Neon_Pagamentos)

From these results, we observed that, out of 21 incorrectly classified triples, 7 cases refer to wrong entity delimitation, for instance, only "CEO" in example 4 in Table 3 was classified as Person, where the more useful information would be "Rodrigo Ventura". In example 7, only "SC" was classified whereas "Startup SC" (Organization) would be more helpful. There are 4 cases of incorrect triples due to the complexity of the sentence, as in examples 5 and 6 in Table 3, in the first one the relation occur between entities "Ribbit_Capital" and "Guiabolso", and in the second one there is no relation between the selected entity pair.

Table 3. Incorrect examples

Sentences	Triples
4. Por meio deste programa, temos acesso aos recursos para executarmos o projeto, ressalta Rodrigo_Ventura, **CEO** e co-fundador da **88i**	(CEO, co-fundador, 88i)
5. A rodada foi liderada pela Kaszek_Ventures, investidora do **Nubank**, e Ribbit_Capital,que investiu no **Guiabolso**	(Nubank, investiu em, Guiabolso)
6. A Firgun trabalha em parceria com organizações Não-governamentais (ONG) que atuam na periferia,como a Afrobusiness e a **Barca**, que atendeu Maria_Pimentel, da Parça_Progresso_Confecções, do **Jardim_Ângela**, zona sul de São_Paulo	(Barca, de, Jardim_Ângela)
7. O programa de capacitação Startup **SC**,iniciativa do **Sebrae_de_Santa_Catarina**, (...)	(SC, iniciativa de, Sebrae_de_Santa_Catarina)

4.2   Data Visualization

Considering our main target application, which is for the Competitive Intelligence at Sicredi, we organize the triples retrieved by our Framework of Relation Extraction into a Tool of Data Visualization named ArDoq[4].

It is a corporate tool already in use by Sicredi for data visualization. Figure 2 presents two ways of data visualization: (A) shows a graph visualization that allows navigation between entities; (B) shows the same relations in other format, representing the entities as boxes and their respective relations. The Data Visualization tool was made available by the Competitive Intelligence team of analysts to support decision making for the enterprise's strategies.

---

[4]   https://www.ardoq.com.

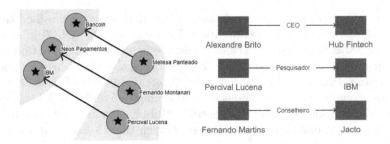

Fig. 2. (A) Visualization using Graph - (B) Visualization using box

5   Conclusion

In this work we discuss the application of NER and RE tool to a news data set collected in the context of Sicredi Bank's Competitive Intelligence, where 200 news about Fintechs were selected to build a knowledge base. By applying our RE framework we were able to track events and facts in the financial market. It is not possible to present comparative results at this stage, since our application considers only relations among named entities, whereas other tools for RE consider noun phrases in general for the generation of the relation triples.

As positive outcomes of this work we can cite: the development of a pipeline of Relation Extraction using Open Source tools, which enables replication of the experiments for other texts, the framework code is available[5]; a new RE CRF model trained more annotated data; the end-to-end development of a knowledge base related to Fintechs that was made available to Competitive Intelligence analysts for decision support.

The academy-enterprise collaboration, as seen in this work, is important not only to the application of tools developed by research groups, but also to evolve systems on the Portuguese language research field. Further research will focus in augmenting the training set for Relation Extraction by adding more complex examples, which would improve the system's ability to capture even more complex relations. Also, there is ongoing work on mapping tests execution to substitute the CRF model for Neural Networks models in order to explore new processing capacity.

References

1. Collovini de Abreu, S., Vieira, R.: RelP: Portuguese open relation extraction. Knowl. Organ. **44**(3), 163–177 (2017)
2. Abreu, S.C., Bonamigo, T.L., Vieira, R.: A review on relation extraction with an eye on Portuguese. J. Braz. Comput. Soc. **19**, 553–571 (2013)
3. Akbik, A., Blythe, D., Vollgraf, R.: Contextual string embeddings for sequence labeling. In: Proceedings of the 27th International Conference on Computational Linguistics, COLING 2018, Santa Fe, New Mexico, USA, pp. 1638–1649 (2018)

---

[5] GitHub: https://github.com/relpplus/versions/RelpPlus_1_0_0.

4. Brucksen, M., Souza, J.G.C., Vieira, R., Rigo, S.: Sistema serelep para o reconhecimento de relações entre entidades mencionadas. In: Mota, C., Santos, D. (eds.) Segundo HAREM, chap. 14, pp. 247–260. Linguateca (2008)
5. Cardoso, N.: Rembrandt - reconhecimento de entidades mencionadas baseado em relações e análise detalhada do texto. In: Mota, C., Santos, D. (eds.) Segundo HAREM, chap. 11, pp. 195–211. Linguateca (2008)
6. Carvalho, P., Oliveira, H.G., Mota, C., Santos, D., Freitas, C.: Segundo harem: Modelo geral, novidades e avaliação. In: Mota, C., Santos, D. (eds.) Desafios na avaliação conjunta do reconhecimento de entidades mencionadas: O Segundo HAREM. Linguateca (2008)
7. Chaves, M.S.: Geo-ontologias e padrões para reconhecimento de locais e de suas relações em textos: o sei-geo no segundo harem. In: Mota, C., Santos, D. (eds.) Segundo HAREM, chap. 13, pp. 231–245. Linguateca (2008)
8. Claro, D.B., Souza, M., Castellã Xavier, C., Oliveira, L.: Multilingual open information extraction: challenges and opportunities. Information 10(7), 228 (2019)
9. Collovini, S., de Bairros P. Filho, M., Vieira, R.: Analysing the role of representation choices in Portuguese relation extraction. In: Mothe, J., Savoy, J., Kamps, J., Pinel-Sauvagnat, K., Jones, G.J.F., SanJuan, E., Cappellato, L., Ferro, N. (eds.) CLEF 2015. LNCS, vol. 9283, pp. 105–116. Springer, Cham (2015). https://doi.org/10.1007/978-3-319-24027-5_9
10. Collovini, S., Machado, G., Vieira, R.: Extracting and structuring open relations from Portuguese text. In: Silva, J., Ribeiro, R., Quaresma, P., Adami, A., Branco, A. (eds.) PROPOR 2016. LNCS (LNAI), vol. 9727, pp. 153–164. Springer, Cham (2016). https://doi.org/10.1007/978-3-319-41552-9_16
11. Collovini, S., Pugens, L., Vanin, A.A., Vieira, R.: Extraction of relation descriptors for Portuguese using conditional random fields. In: Bazzan, A.L.C., Pichara, K. (eds.) IBERAMIA 2014. LNCS (LNAI), vol. 8864, pp. 108–119. Springer, Cham (2014). https://doi.org/10.1007/978-3-319-12027-0_9
12. Collovini, S., et al.: IberLEF 2019 Portuguese named entity recognition and relation extraction tasks. In: Proceedings of the Iberian Languages Evaluation Forum co-located with 35th Conference of the Spanish Society for Natural Language Processing, IberLEF@SEPLN 2019, Bilbao, Spain, September 24th, 2019. CEUR Workshop Proceedings, vol. 2421, pp. 390–410. CEUR-WS.org (2019)
13. Fader, A., Soderland, S., Etzioni, O.: Identifying relations for open information extraction. In: EMNLP, pp. 1535–1545 (2011)
14. Gamallo, P., Garcia, M.: Multilingual open information extraction. In: Pereira, F., Machado, P., Costa, E., Cardoso, A. (eds.) EPIA 2015. LNCS (LNAI), vol. 9273, pp. 711–722. Springer, Cham (2015). https://doi.org/10.1007/978-3-319-23485-4_72
15. Gamallo, P., Garcia, M.: Linguakit: uma ferramenta multilingue para a análise linguística e a extração de informação. Linguamática 9(1), 19–28 (2017)
16. Gamallo, P., Garcia, M., Fernández-Lanza, S.: Dependency-based open information extraction. In: Proceedings of the Joint Workshop on Unsupervised and Semi-Supervised Learning in NLP, Avignon, France, pp. 10–18. Association for Computational Linguistics (2012)
17. Glauber, R., Claro, D.B.: A systematic mapping study on open information extraction. Expert Syst. Appl. 112, 372–387 (2018)
18. Hartmann, N., Fonseca, E.R., Shulby, C., Treviso, M.V., Rodrigues, J.S., Aluísio, S.M.: Portuguese word embeddings: evaluating on word analogies and natural language tasks. In: STIL (2017)

19. Lafferty, J.D., McCallum, A., Pereira, F.C.N.: Conditional random fields: probabilistic models for segmenting and labeling sequence data. In: Proceedings of the Eighteenth International Conference on Machine Learning, ICML 2001, San Francisco, CA, USA, pp. 282–289. Morgan Kaufmann Publishers Inc. (2001)
20. Sang, T.K., Erik, F.: Introduction to the CoNLL-2002 shared task: language-independent named entity recognition. In: Proceedings of CoNLL 2002, pp. 155–158 (2002)
21. Santos, A.P., Ramos, C., Marques, N.C.: Extração de Relações em Títulos de Notícias Desportivas. In: INFORUM 2012, Simpósio de Informática, Lisbon, Portugal (2012)
22. dos Santos, C.N., Guimarães, V.: Boosting named entity recognition with neural character embeddings. In: Proceedings of the Fifth Named Entity Workshop, NEWS@ACL 2015, Beijing, China, pp. 25–33 (2015)
23. Santos, J., Consoli, B., dos Santos, C., Terra, J., Collonini, S., Vieira, R.: Assessing the impact of contextual embeddings for Portuguese named entity recognition. In: 8th Brazilian Conference on Intelligent Systems, BRACIS 2019, Bahia, Brazil, 15–18 October 2019, pp. 437–442 (2019)
24. Santos, V., Pinheiro, V.: Report: Um sistema de extração de informações aberta para língua portuguesa. In: Proceedings of the X Brazilian Symposium in Information and Human Language Technology (STIL). SBC, Natal, RN, Brazil (2015)
25. Sauter, V.L.: Competitive intelligence systems. In: Handbook on Decision Support Systems 2. International Handbooks Information System, pp. 195–210. Springer, Heidelberg (2008). https://doi.org/10.1007/978-3-540-48716-6_10
26. Silva, W.D.C.d.M.: Aprimorando o corretor gramatical cogroo. Master's thesis, Universidade de São Paulo, São Paulo (2013)
27. Weiss, A.: A brief guide to competitive intelligence: how to gather and use information on competitors. Bus. Inf. Rev. **19**, 39–47 (2002)

Natural Language Processing Tasks

Evaluating Methods of Different Paradigms for Subjectivity Classification in Portuguese

Luana Balador Belisário, Luiz Gabriel Ferreira,
and Thiago Alexandre Salgueiro Pardo[✉]

Interinstitutional Center for Computational Linguistics (NILC),
Institute of Mathematical and Computer Sciences (ICMC),
University of São Paulo (USP), São Carlos, SP, Brazil
{luana.belisario,luizgferreira}@usp.br, taspardo@icmc.usp.br

Abstract. This paper presents the study and comparison of methods of different paradigms to perform subjectivity classification of sentences in Portuguese. This task is part of the sentiment analysis area and consists of automatically identifying the presence or not of opinative information in texts of interest. We have investigated methods based on sentiment lexicons, graphs, machine learning and word embeddings, using datasets of different domains. We achieve good results, outperforming the previous approaches for Portuguese.

Keywords: Sentiment analysis · Subjectivity classification

1 Introduction

Texts published on social media have been a valuable source of information for companies and users, as the analysis of this data helps improving/selecting products and services of interest. Due to the huge amount of data, techniques for automatically analyzing user opinions are necessary. The research field that investigates these techniques is called Sentiment Analysis, also known as Opinion Mining.

The subjectivity analysis is one of the first steps in opinion mining. In this task, the documents of interest, which may be complete texts, sentences or even shorter text passages, are classified as subjective or objective [6]: when classified as objective, they express facts (for example, "I bought a Philco netbook in Nov/2010"); otherwise, when said subjective, they express opinions or sentiments ("This book is very good, it is incredibly deep!"). Differently from the objective sentence, it is possible to notice in the subjective example that the author of the review liked the book, as s/he used expressions like "very good" and "incredibly". These words that evidently denote opinion and polarity are called sentiment words. Table 1 shows some other labeled sentences that occurred in the Computer-BR corpus used in [11]. One may see that the subjective sentences can be further divided into "positive" and "negative" polarities. The objective sentences, despite having adjectives that could indicate opinions, like *boas* ("good", in English) and *baum* (misspelled form of *bom* - "good"), do not express opinions about the products. Besides the orthographic errors, it is worth noting that the examples include

P. Quaresma et al. (Eds.): PROPOR 2020, LNAI 12037, pp. 261–269, 2020.
https://doi.org/10.1007/978-3-030-41505-1_25

Table 1. Examples of labeled sentences in the Computer-BR corpus [11].

Sentence	Polarity
Alguem me indica marcas boas de notebook?	Objective
Esse Not é baum? Alguem sabe?	Objective
Sem notebook de novo... Parece brincadeira de mau gosto	Subjective/Negative
Logo um precioso notebook Dell lindíssimo chega aqui em casa tô mt feliz	Subjective/Positive

abbreviations and vocabulary typical of the language use in the web that must be taken into consideration when developing methods for sentiment analysis.

The relevance of the subjectivity classification may be evidenced by its application in other tasks. For instance, in polarity classification, filtering out objective sentences is interesting (see, e.g., [1]); in opinion summarization, subjective sentences are much more important (see, e.g., [7]). Despite the relevance of the task, to the best of our knowledge, there is only one previous work specifically dedicated to subjectivity classification for the Portuguese language - the work of Moraes et al. [11]. Therefore, in this paper, we focus our efforts in this task.

We start by reproducing the experiments of Moraes et al. and extending the evaluation of their methods to two other corpora, aiming to evaluate their robustness for other domains. In this approach, we evaluate methods for subjectivity classification based on sentiment lexicons and Machine Learning (ML) techniques. We then explore other methods for the task: one that uses word embeddings in a ML-based approach and another one based on graphs. We show that the methods have varied performances for the different domains, but that some methods are more stable than others. We also show that one of the new methods outperforms the previous results for Portuguese. We end the paper by performing a detailed error analysis and discussing factors that influence the results.

In the next section, we briefly present the relevant related work. In Sect. 3, we introduce the corpora used in this study. Section 4 details the investigated methods, while the results are reported in Sect. 5. Some final remarks are made in Sect. 6.

2 Related Work

Moraes et al. [11] are the only known authors to specifically investigate the theme of subjectivity classification for Portuguese. They created a corpus of tweets on the area of technology. This corpus - called Computer-BR - was manually labeled and preprocessed to increase the efficiency of the applied methods. Inspired by the approaches for English, the tested methods were based on the use of sentiment lexicons and ML approaches. The best result with lexicon-based methods was 64% in f-measure, while ML-based methods reached 75%.

In a related task - polarity classification - Vilarinho and Ruiz [13] propose a classification method based on word graphs (named SentiElection) to predict if sentences show positive or negative polarities. They use a training set to create "positive" and "negative" graphs and then each test sentence is added to both graphs, being classified according to the graph that produces better centrality measurements. The best achieved classification result was 82% in f-measure in an airline dataset.

In this paper, we have tested these and other methods for the subjectivity classification task. We detail the methods in Sect. 4, but, before, we introduce the corpora that we use and the related data preprocessing that we perform.

3 The Corpora

We have used three corpora to evaluate the explored methods. All of them are composed of material collected from the web. Two of them present sentences related to technology products, while the other presents sentences related to book reviews.

The Computer-BR corpus of Moraes et al. [11] has 2,317 sentences with user messages about the technology area, commenting about notebooks. It is worth noting that this corpus is not balanced, with approximately 72.4% of the sentences belonging to the objective class. We also used a corpus of electronic product reviews with 230 sentences that we took from the well-known Buscapé corpus [5] and subsequently manually labeled them. As Computer-BR, this corpus presents unbalance, with about 70% of sentences labeled as subjective. In addition to the technology domain, we used a corpus composed of book review sentences, taken from the ReLi corpus [4], Amazon website and the Skoob social network, with 270 sentences equally divided between subjective and objective sentences, which were also manually labeled.

The evaluation of the methods with these three corpora is relevant, as it is widely known in the area that sentiment analysis tools are very sensitive to the domain, producing different results. More than this, we have three different balancing situations: one corpus with more objective sentences, one with more subjective sentences and one with the ideal situation of balanced classes. Such evaluation scenarios may allow a more interesting assessment of the robustness of the classification methods.

Finally, as the three corpora are composed of sentences taken from the web and are domain-specific, it is possible to find a large number of abbreviations, spelling errors and specialized jargon, which affect the performance of automatic classification methods. To soften this problem, some preprocessing steps were applied to the corpora. First, the sentences were normalized with the help of the *Enelvo* textual normalization system [2], which, to the best of our knowledge, is the best system for Portuguese for this task. After that, stopwords (as they appear in the *Natural Language Toolkit* - NLTK), punctuation marks, numbers and other special characters were removed.

4 The Methods

4.1 Lexicon-Based Method

The first method we tested was the traditional lexicon-based one, following the best configuration proposed by Moraes et al. [11]. It uses a heuristic that relies on a sentiment lexicon with pre-classified words. The words are associated with a value 1 if they are positive, -1 if negative and 0 if neutral. The subjectivity of a sentence is computed by simply summing the polarities of the words that compose it. If the result assumes a value different from 0, the sentence is considered "subjective"; if the value is zero, the sentence is considered "objective". Due to the simplicity of the method, there is no treatment of negation, irony and adverbs, whose functions would be to intensify, neutralize or even change the orientation of the sentiment words. More than this, one may realize that this method is quite naive as it would classify a sentence with equal number of positive and negative words as "objective", as the positive values would cancel the negative ones, resulting in a 0 value.

Also following Moraes et al., we have used Sentilex-PT [3] and WordnetAffectBR [12] sentiment lexicons to test the method.

4.2 Graph-Based Method

We also tested the best configuration of the graph-based classification method of Vilarinho and Ruiz [13], which evaluates each sentence of interest in relation to reference objective and subjective graphs, adopting the class that produces the best centrality measurement in the graphs.

The objective and subjective graphs are built from a training corpus in a way that the nodes are the words and the links represent the sequence they appear. For example, considering a *word frame* (window) of size 3, the phrase "I love pizza" would produce (i) nodes labeled as "I", "love" and "pizza" and (ii) directed edges from "I" to "love", from "I" to "pizza" and from "love" to "pizza". Following this strategy, we built the objective graph from the objective sentences and the subjective graph from the subjective sentences in the training set. To classify a new sentence (in the test set), the method incorporates the sentence in each of the graphs and computes three global centrality measures - Eigenvector Centrality, Katz Index, and PageRank. For each measure, the graph with the highest value scores 1 point. In the end of this process, the sentence is classified according to the graph that scored best.

For each corpus we used, to compose our (objective and subjective) training sets, we considered an amount of sentences computed as 70% of the sentences in the set with the least number of instances. This way, both objective and subjective graphs are built with the same number of sentences, avoiding any bias that different number of sentences might bring. The remaining sentences in the corpora are used for testing.

4.3 Machine Learning-Based Methods

Three ML-based methods were evaluated. Two are replications of the proposals of Moraes et al. [11] and the other is a different proposal using word embeddings.

Following Moraes et al., two classification techniques (Naive-Bayes and SVM) were tested, using the traditional bag of words representation, which considers the words in a sentence as distinct features. To perform feature selection, we quantify the relevance of the words in each class to select those that will form the bag of words. Two metrics were used for this: the first is simply the frequency of the word in the class; the second metric is the *Comprehensive Measurement Feature Selection* (CMFS) proposed in [14], which aims to calculate the relevance of the words in each class considering their occurrences in other classes.

We used the *scikit-learn* package to run the methods. For Naive-Bayes, the "ComplementNB" implementation was used with the standard library hyper-parameters and the 99 most relevant words (excluding those that were in both objective and subjective sets - which is the "exclusion" configuration proposed by Moraes et al.). For SVM, the "SVC" implementation was used and gamma was changed from standard to "auto", with penalty parameter C set to 30, with 60 words from each class (also using the "exclusion" configuration). These configurations in both methods were the ones that produced the best results for each case.

In our ML variant method, we used word embeddings, i.e., the vector representation of words learned from their contexts of occurrence. As described in [10], with the vector representation, it is possible to obtain values of semantic similarity between terms. Thus, we used the word embeddings to assist in two fronts of the task: (i) to give representativeness to subjective terms that were not present in the classification models (as consequence of not being present in the training data or, otherwise, simply being filtered out by the feature selection techniques of Moraes et al.) and (ii) to obtain a way to represent the whole sentence for classification, without the limitations of the bag of words representation.

The word embeddings were trained with the use of the well-known *gensim* library, with approximately 86 thousand sentences taken from the Buscapé corpus [5]. We used a dimension of 600, a window size of 4 words and only words that had more than 4 occurrences. The used model was the Continuous Bag of Words (CBOW), trained with 100 epochs. Such configuration was the one that produced the best results for this approach. To represent the whole sentence, we explored methods that combine the vectors of the words of a sentence and generate a final vector that can represent its semantics. The best result was produced by the usual strategy of simply adding the word vectors.

The vector of each sentence was used to train a multi-layered neural network with input layer of size 600, one hidden layer (20 neurons for the Computer-BR corpus and 100 for the other two corpora), and an output layer with 2 neurons. The network receives the sentence vector and returns the class ("objective" or "subjective"). The tested activation functions were Rectified Linear Unit (ReLU) and Softmax for hidden and output layers, respectively. We used 30 epochs for the Computer-BR and 20 for the other two corpora. The neural network was implemented using the *keras* library.

5   Results and Discussion

To evaluate the effectiveness of the presented methods, tests were performed on the 3 described corpora. The ML and graph-based methods were evaluated with 3-fold cross-validation (in order to get close to the 70/30 training-testing corpus division used for the graph-based method). For the lexicon-based method, as a training set was not necessary, the test was performed on the full corpora (but taking the average of the results for the corresponding three folds, in order to have a fair comparison of results).

The achieved average results for the three corpora are shown in Tables 2, 3 and 4, in which the best overall accuracy values are in bold. Values for the classical precision,

266   L.B. Belisário et al.

recall and f-measure for the "subjective" and "objective" classes are displayed, as well as the overall accuracy for each method.

The best accuracy results were achieved by the ML-based methods, and we may consistently see that our neural network (trained with word embeddings) was better than SVM, which, in turn, was better than Naive-Bayes (NB). Such results indicate that word embeddings may in fact help in the task. In general, we can also affirm that the graph-based method was slightly better than the lexical-based ones, as there were only two cases where it produced worse results.

One may notice that the domain does affect the results, as many previous works in the area claim. The greatest variations happen for the lexicon-based methods, which produce accuracy results from 0.239 (for electronic products) to 0.738 (for Computer-BR). The graph and ML-based methods, although presenting some variation, look more stable across the domains. In two of the corpora (Computer-BR and book reviews), the WordnetAffectBr lexicon produced better results.

Regarding the ML-based methods, it is possible to see that the classes with more data are benefited, as expected. For the Computer-BR corpus, with more objective instances, the f-measure for the objective class was higher than for the subjective class; for the electronic products, with more subjective instances, the opposite happened; for the balanced corpus of book reviews, the results were close for both classes.

A detailed error analysis showed several interesting issues that remain to be solved in future work. For the ML-based methods of Moraes et al. [11], many mistakes happen due to the lack of information about some words. This fact occurs more often for electronic products and Computer-BR, where the language is more informal, with low frequency

Table 2. Results for Computer-BR corpus.

Measures	Lexicon-based methods		Graph-based method	ML-based methods		
	Sentilex-PT	WordnetAffectBR		NB	SVM	Neural network
Precision (Objective)	0.763	0.749	0.826	0.875	0.801	0.859
Recall (Objective)	0.776	0.959	0.751	0.764	0.926	0.874
F-measure (Objective)	0.769	0.841	0.780	0.816	0.859	0.866
Precision (Subjective)	0.390	0.616	0.475	0.536	0.678	0.653
Recall (Subjective)	0.370	0.156	0.561	0.714	0.399	0.625
F-measure (Subjective)	0.379	0.248	0.494	0.612	0.498	0.637
Overall accuracy	0.664	0.738	0.699	0.750	0.780	**0.805**

Table 3. Results for corpus of book reviews.

Measures	Lexicon-based methods		Graph-based method	ML-based methods		
	Sentilex-PT	WordnetAffectBR		NB	SVM	Neural network
Precision (Objective)	0.490	0.518	0.545	0.759	0.782	0.806
Recall (Objective)	0.600	0.931	0.723	0.736	0.830	0.863
F-measure (Objective)	0.539	0.665	0.652	0.747	0.805	0.831
Precision (Subjective)	0.524	0.730	0.674	0.763	0.831	0.865
Recall (Subjective)	0.413	0.181	0.536	0.782	0.783	0.804
F-measure (Subjective)	0.461	0.288	0.596	0.772	0.806	0.832
Overall accuracy	0.504	0.545	0.627	0.761	0.806	**0.832**

Table 4. Results for corpus of electronic product reviews.

Measures	Lexicon-based methods		Graph-based method	ML-based methods		
	Sentilex-PT	WordnetAffectBR		NB	SVM	Neural Network
Precision (Objective)	0.320	0.187	0.270	0.450	0.395	0.772
Recall (Objective)	0.771	0.908	0.656	0.420	0.166	0.492
F-measure (Objective)	0.451	0.310	0.381	0.410	0.230	0.599
Precision (Subjective)	0.925	0.795	0.887	0.870	0.833	0.893
Recall (Subjective)	0.621	0.084	0.595	0.850	0.942	0.968
F-measure (Subjective)	0.741	0.151	0.710	0.858	0.884	0.929
Overall accuracy	0.649	0.239	0.607	0.777	0.798	**0.880**

terms and several terms that have similar meanings. As an example, we have the following sentences in Computer-BR: *Notebook da Positivo é péssimo, credo! Melhor notebook é Dell*. The words *péssimo, credo* and *melhor* clearly characterize the polarity of the sentences. However, such words rarely appear in the corpora and end up not being selected (by the feature selection process of Moraes et al.), leaving irrelevant terms that have no polarity (as *Notebook, Dell* and *Positivo*) as features in the classification.

Regarding the lexicon-based method, because it is simply based on searching and counting sentiment words, it is not possible to effectively deal with possible polarity deviations, such as sarcasm and irony, adverbs of negation and intensity, and disambiguation of words. For example, the method has problems to classify the sentence *O processador desse notebook é pouco eficiente*, where the *pouco* adverb changes the polarity of the *eficiente* word. Going deeper, by analyzing a sample of 400 misclassified sentences of Computer-BR (which was chosen for this analysis because it is the corpus in common with the work of Moraes et al.) by the best lexicon-based method of Moraes et al., we could see that: 53% of the classification errors were due to the non-treatment of polarity deviations; 25% of them had implicit opinions (embedded in objective sentences); 17% of them were subjective sentences that were misclassified as objective sentences because the sum of polarities was zero; 5% of them had sentiment words that were not in the lexicons.

In what follows, we present some final remarks.

6   Final Remarks

This paper presented the investigation of methods of different paradigms for performing subjective classification for Portuguese language. We tested the lexicon and machine learning-based proposals of Moraes et al. [11], the graph-based method of Vilarinho and Ruiz [13] and a variant method using word embeddings, showing that we outperform the previous approaches for Portuguese. Our error analysis shows that, despite the good results, much remains to be done.

In the future, we intend to investigate more-informed methods that are capable of dealing with the phenomena that affect sentence classification, as negation, intensity and irony/sarcasm. Of particular interest is the study of the discourse structure of the objective and subjective content. In our empirical analysis, we could notice some discourse-related patterns that might help producing more interesting features for classification. Discourse parsers available for Portuguese (e.g., the ones of [8] and [9]) might be useful in this study.

To the interested reader, more information about this work may be found at the OPINANDO project webpage (https://sites.google.com/icmc.usp.br/opinando/).

Acknowledgments. The authors are grateful to FAPESP (2018/11479-9) and USP Research Office (PRP 668) for supporting this work.

References

1. Avanço, L.V., Nunes, M.G.V.: Lexicon-based sentiment analysis for reviews of products in Brazilian Portuguese. In: The Proceedings of the 3rd Brazilian Conference on Intelligent Systems (BRACIS), pp. 277–281 (2014)
2. Bertaglia, T.F.P., Nunes, M.G.V.: Exploring word embeddings for unsupervised textual user-generated content normalization. In: The Proceedings of the 2nd Workshop on Noisy User-generated Text (WNUT), pp. 112–120 (2016)
3. Carvalho, P., Silva, M.J.: SentiLex-PT: Principais Características e Potencialidades. Oslo Stud. Lang. **7**(1), 425–438 (2015)
4. Freitas, C., Motta, E., Milidiú, R., Cesar, J.: Vampiro que brilha… rá! Desafios na anotação de opinião em um corpus de resenhas de livros. In: The Proceedings of the XI Encontro de Linguística de Corpus (ELC), pp. 1–12 (2012)
5. Hartmann, N.S., et al.: A large opinion corpus in Portuguese - tackling out-of-vocabulary words. In: The Proceedings of the Ninth International Conference on Language Resources and Evaluation (LREC), pp. 3865–3871 (2014)
6. Liu, B.: Sentiment analysis and opinion mining. Synth. Lect. Hum. Lang. Technol. **5**, 168 (2012)
7. López Condori, R.E., Pardo, T.A.S.: Opinion summarization methods: comparing and extending extractive and abstractive approaches. Expert Syst. Appl. (ESWA) **78**, 124–134 (2017)
8. Maziero, E.G., Hirst, G., Pardo, T.A.S.: Adaptation of discourse parsing models for Portuguese language. In: The Proceedings of the 4th Brazilian Conference on Intelligent Systems - BRACIS, pp. 140–145 (2015)
9. Maziero, E.G., Hirst, G., Pardo, T.A.S.: Semi-supervised never-ending learning in rhetorical relation identification. In: The Proceedings of the Recent Advances in Natural Language Processing - RANLP, pp. 436–442 (2015)
10. Mikolov, T., Corrado, G., Chen, K., Dean, J.: Efficient estimation of word representations in vector space, pp. 1–12. arXiv:1301.3781 (2013)
11. Moraes, S.M.W., Santos, A.L.L., Redecker, M., Machado, R.M., Meneguzzi, F.R.: Comparing approaches to subjectivity classification: a study on Portuguese Tweets. In: Silva, J., Ribeiro, R., Quaresma, P., Adami, A., Branco, A. (eds.) PROPOR 2016. LNCS (LNAI), vol. 9727, pp. 86–94. Springer, Cham (2016). https://doi.org/10.1007/978-3-319-41552-9_8
12. Pasqualotti, P.R., Vieira, R.: WordnetAffectBR: uma base lexical de palavras de emoções para a língua portuguesa. Revista Novas Tecnologias na Educação **6**(2), 1–10 (2008)
13. Vilarinho, G.N., Ruiz, E.E.S.: Global centrality measures in word graphs for Twitter sentiment analysis. In: The Proceedings of the 7th Brazilian Conference on Intelligent Systems (BRACIS), pp. 55–60 (2018)
14. Yang, J., Liu, Y., Zhu, X., Liu, Z., Zhang, X.: A new feature selection based on comprehensive measurement both in inter-category and intra-category for text categorization. Inf. Process. Manage. **48**(4), 741–754 (2012)

Sentence Compression for Portuguese

Fernando A. A. Nóbrega[1][✉], Alipio M. Jorge[2], Pavel Brazdil[3],
and Thiago A. S. Pardo[1]

[1] Interinstitutional Center for Computational Linguistics (NILC), Institute
of Mathematical and Computer Sciences, University of São Paulo, São Paulo, Brazil
fernandoasevedo@gmail.com,taspardo@icmc.usp.br
[2] LIAAD - INESC TEC/FCUP, University of Porto, Porto, Portugal
amjorge@fc.up.pt
[3] LIAAD - INESC TEC/FEP, University of Porto, Porto, Portugal
pbrazdil@fep.up.pt

Abstract. The task of Sentence Compression aims at producing a
shorter version of a given sentence. This task may assist many other
applications, as Automatic Summarization and Text Simplification. In
this paper, we investigate methods for Sentence Compression for Portuguese. We focus on machine learning-based algorithms and propose
new strategies. We also create reference corpora/datasets for the area,
allowing to train and to test the methods of interest. Our results show
that some of our methods outperform previous initiatives for Portuguese
and produce competitive results with a state of the art method in the
area.

Keywords: Sentence Compression · Linguistic features · Datasets

1 Introduction

The Sentence Compression (SC) task aims at producing a shorter paraphrase (a
reduced or compressed version) for a given input sentence [13]. It may be useful
for many Natural Language Processing (NLP) applications. For instance, in the
Summarization research field, it is usual to select relevant sentences from the
source texts and to compress them for including in the summary [3,5,10,13–
15,21].

Most of the methods for SC follow a deletion approach [3,5,7,13,17,23,24,
26], in which a sentence is reduced by removing some of its elements. In this
scenario, the SC task may be handled as a sequence of deletion actions over
an input sentence s, in which an action i decides if the element $e_i \in s$, which
is usually a token or a syntactic constituent, should or should not be removed
from s. Such decisions rely on shallow and syntactic information. For instance, as
shallow features, some systems look at the position of the token in the sentence,
if it occurs inside parentheses or close to some negation word. As syntactic
information, it is possible to analyze the part of speech (POS) tag of the token

© Springer Nature Switzerland AG 2020
P. Quaresma et al. (Eds.): PROPOR 2020, LNAI 12037, pp. 270–280, 2020.
https://doi.org/10.1007/978-3-030-41505-1_26

or the structure of the syntactic tree (as the distance of a token to the root in the respective tree).

Naturally, the decision of whether removing a word or not is directly influenced by the previous decisions. Therefore, one of the most important clues that have been employed in SC methods is an indication of previous decisions [10,12,20]. From the point of view of machine learning, this kind of information is easily available in the training dataset. However, when a trained model is used to compress new sentences, this information/feature depends on previous classification outputs. This way, a wrong decision for an element t_i in the input sentence may produce future cascade errors. Aiming at the reduction of errors in the compressed sentences, some authors [13,23,24] have used manual constraints and/or language models as indicative features. However, some more recent works propose SC systems based on machine learning techniques only [10].

Additionally to the above challenges, the language to which the SC system is applied may have some influence in the results, as the deletion decisions directly depend on the language structure/grammar. In this paper, we focus our study on the Portuguese language. To the best of our knowledge, there are only two SC systems that were built and evaluated for Portuguese [12,20].

In this paper, we extend the model that was introduced by Nóbrega and Pardo [20] with new features based on syntactic trees in order to produce better compressed sentences. We evaluate different sentence processing orderings, which affect the deletion decisions that are taken, and also propose a variant method that requires simpler preprocessing for the input sentences, avoiding the errors that more sophisticated NLP tools may produce. Finally, to train and test the SC methods, we create reference corpora/datasets, by adapting an existent corpus to the task and automatically producing another one. Our results show that some of our SC methods outperform the existent approaches for Portuguese and produce competitive results with a state of the art method in the area.

The paper is organized as follows. We briefly introduce the main related work in Sect. 2. The datasets that we use are presented in Sect. 3. Our methods and the investigated features are presented in Sect. 4. In Sect. 5, we present and discuss the achieved results. Some final remarks are presented in Sect. 6.

2   Related Work

Several different approaches may be found for the SC task, including noisy-channel modeling [13,24], Integer Linear Programming [3,8,16,23], and decision trees [12,13], deep learning [10,26] and other varied machine learning methods [20]. Here, we detail three of them: the ones for Portuguese [12,20], which is the language of interest in this paper, and the proposal of [10], which we adapt to Portuguese, as it is one of the most relevant approaches in the area and is among the state of the art methods in the task (as evidenced by [26]).

In [12], SC is modeled as a traditional classification task. The authors handle it as a sequence of decisions over an input sentence, in which the method decides whether each token will be removed. For this purpose, they investigate syntactic and semantic features (as POS and named entity categories) produced by the PALAVRAS parser [6] and other features based on the documents that the input sentences come from (as frequency of tokens and position of the sentences). Such approach produces promising results (the authors report a F-measure value of 0.80), but the evaluation is very limited, as the dataset used is too small.

Nóbrega and Pardo [20] try different machine learning techniques (Decision Tree, Logistic Regression, Multilayer Perceptron, Naïve Bayes, and Support Vector Machine). Differently from other approaches in the area, the authors explore three different application situations for feature extraction (considering the Sentence, Document, and Summary scopes), which restrict the kind of information that is available. For instance, in Automatic Summarization, a SC system may have access to the data from the input Sentence s, from the Document where s come from, and also from the output Summary being produced. Their experiments show that there is no much difference among these distinct situations. Overall, the best approach achieves an F-measure value of 0.88, outperforming the results of [12] on the same dataset.

Filippova et al. [10] present a SC method based on Long Short-Term Memory (LSTM) neural networks, in which each token in an input sentence is represented by an embedding vector with 256 dimensions that was obtained by a skip-gram model [18]. The authors try different features, as the embedding of the words and their parents in the corresponding syntactic trees, if the parents have been removed and the previous predicted label. In the best network configuration, the authors achieve good results in their experiments (0.82 of F-measure).

3 The Datasets

We have used two datasets, in which there are sentence pairs with long (original) sentences and their respective reduced versions. We consider that a sentence s_r is a possible reduction of another sentence s_l when we may produce s_r after deleting none or more tokens from s_l. This way, it is possible to have some pairs with identical sentences (s_r is equal to s_l) in our datasets. We have included these cases in order to have examples with sentences that must not be compressed (as, in machine learning, negative examples are as important as positive ones). These restrictions have also been used in [20].

Our first dataset was built based on the Priberam Compressive Summarization Corpus (PCSC) [2], in which there are 874 sentence pairs. A subset of them was also used by [20]. The second one is a collection of 7,056 pairs that were automatically collected based on the methodology proposed in [11].

The PCSC corpus has 801 news documents that are organized (by subject) into 80 collections. In each collection, there are two multi-document summaries that were manually produced by humans using compression of sentences. Given this characteristic of PCSC corpus, Nóbrega and Pardo [20] automatically found the respective long (original) version for each sentence of each summary in PCSC (in a document-summary alignment process). For ambiguous cases, the shorter sentences were maintained in the dataset in order to have training examples that allow the maximal number of token deletions. Furthermore, in order to maintain the data unbiased, the eventual duplicated pairs were removed. After this process, we have ended with 874 valid candidate pairs. We will refer to this collection as the PCSC-Pairs corpus.

The amount of data in the PCSC-Pairs dataset is still tiny if compared to SC experiments for the English language (Filippova et al. [10], for example, used a dataset with 12,000 sentence pairs). This way, we have used the methodology that was proposed by [11] in order to collect a larger dataset. Initially, we have used a set of 1,008,356 news documents that were collected from the G1[1] news portal, which is a very famous and renowned news agency in Brazil. After that, following [11], we analyzed each pair of title and respective first sentence of each document in order to pick as candidate pairs those in which the first one is a reduction of the second one. We ended with 7,024 pairs. We refer to this dataset as the G1-Pairs corpus.

4   Our Methods

Following the previous work for Portuguese [12,20], we also handle the deletion-based SC as a machine learning classification task: given a sentence s with a sequence of tokens (including punctuation marks) $\{t^1, t^2, ..., t^n\}$, we want to build a classifier that answers *"yes"* or *"no"* to the following question for each token $t \in s$: "should we remove this token t from s?". Thus, each token t in a given sentence s in our datasets is considered an instance.

We initially run experiments with Logistic Regression, which reached the best results in [20]. However, differently from [20], we only use features that may be extracted from the input sentences, not considering the other application situations, as the authors concluded that all of them produced similar results. We have also included other features that were not considered by the authors in their original proposal.

Our first SC model uses information from dependency syntactic trees produced by PALAVRAS parser [6]. To extract the features, we use two different approaches for sentence reading: from left to right (or sequentially, from token 1 to n in the sentence), and based on the corresponding syntactic trees, in which we first read the root of the trees and then we follow the dependencies. These processes show us distinct ways to make deletion decisions over the tokens in a given sentence and it also allows us to use different values for features that require previous decisions (labels) over other tokens. The Table 1 shows an example of this processes. As we may see, the second approach give us a more syntactic reading, starting from the main verb in the sentence to the others words and, finally, punctuation marks. Here, it is important to note that, for example, features based on previous decisions (tokens that were removed or not) are null for the token "será" (main verb) in the second approach. On the other hand, this scenery does not occurs in the sequential process.

---

[1] http://www.g1.com.br.

Table 1. Example of the sequential and tree based reading/decision processes.

Sequential:	O confronto de hoje será contra Cuba, às 22h
Tree based:	será confronto O de hoje contra Cuba, às 22h

We employ features based on the structure of syntactic trees and we add them in the best model of Nóbrega and Pardo [20] in order to produce better compressed sentences. The features of [20] are organized into a few main sets, as follows:

- **Shallow Features**: inside-parentheses (if a token t occurs inside parentheses); token-position (if t occurs in the beginning of the sentence, being one of the 20% first tokens, in the end, being among the last 20% tokens, or in the middle of s); is-stopword (if t is a stopword); token-window (the two previous and two next tokens in the sentence); token-itself (the token t itself).
- **Syntactic and Semantic Features**: token-POS (the POS tag for t); POS-window (the POS tag of the two previous and two next words in the sentence); token-syntactic-function (available syntactic functions of t in the dependency tree); token-semantic (semantic information of t, as named entity and semantic class labels also produced by the parser).
- **Context Features**: two boolean values that indicate whether the two previous tokens of t were removed or not from the input sentence.

We also make use of the information that dependency trees provide about the hierarchy of the tokens. With this information, we may conclude, for instance, that, if a token f is removed from the sentence and f is the father of the token t (it means that t is connected to f and t occurs below f in the tree), we probably should also remove t. Based on the previous idea, we propose the following new feature sets:

- **Tree Structure Features**: token-is-root (if t is the root of the tree); token-is-on-left (if t occurs on the left of its father in the sentence); token-father (the token of the father itself).
- **Context Tree Feature**: father-removed (a boolean value that indicates if the father of the token was removed or not from the input sentence).

In a similar way to [20], we have used stemmed tokens for the features that use the tokens themselves. In addition to this step, we have changed the values of numbers (with or without decimal symbols) to the tag <NUM> for these features. This way, we may reduce the dimension of the model and we may use more representative values, as we consider that the actual identity of numbers occurring before or after a given token is not relevant to the SC task.

From a technical point of view, the PALAVRAS parser [6] may be not useful in some contexts. For instance, this parser has its own sentence delimitation process, which sometimes splits a given sentence into two or more sentences; and it is not a free software. Furthermore, even though automatic tools in general produce fewer errors in dependency trees than in constituency trees, we still must handle the possible mistakes made by them. Thus, we proposed a second SC model – a simplified one. This model uses a POS tagger [1], which performs a simpler sentence processing than that made by a full syntactic parser, in order to extract the features. This way, we use almost all the features that were applied in our previous model, but not those derived from syntactic trees. We end up with the following features:

- **Simplified Features**: inside-parentheses; token-position; is-stopword; token-window; token-itself; token-POS (the POS tag for t); POS-window (the POS tags of the two previous and two next tokens).

To deal with the cascade errors, we also run DAGGER[2] [22]. DAGGER is an iterative schema that calibrates classifiers, aiming to handle structured prediction problems, in which a decision i has high dependency on the previous decisions and will also be required for the next decisions, as it happens in the SC task. Basically, given a classifier c, DAGGER creates new training instances based on the outputs of c in the dataset in order to build new and more robust classifiers. This way, the features that require previous decisions of c will receive new values based on the actual output of c during this process. Furthermore, the mistakes made by c will be available during training and assist the production of better classifiers. In other words, DAGGER produces new classifiers based on actual previous outputs in order to reduce the amount of cascade errors.

Still aiming to improve the quality of the output sentences by reducing the amount of mistakes that occur because of cascade errors, we have followed [19] and also trained Conditional Random Fields (CRF) models (instead of Logistic Regression). The main goal for using CRF is to train our models based on structured sequences of instances. In this case, we train our models with sentences instead of tokens of sentences individually. As the CRF already uses information on the previous labels, we have removed the context features. Furthermore, we have only used the sequential reading process of the input sentences.

5   Experimental Setup and Results

We have performed our experiments under two different setups. In the first one, we have used the 10-fold cross-validation strategy with our two datasets individually and also with a mix of them. In the second one, to test the robustness of the models, we have used just the biggest dataset (G1-Pairs) for training and the PCSC-Pairs for testing.

We have scored the methods based on their respective answers for each individual instance (token in an input sentence) and we also compared the reduced sentences that they have produced with their respective reference/gold standard versions. In the first case, we have used the traditional metrics of Precision, Recall and F-Measure (F-1) of the machine learning area; in the second one, we

---

[2] We have also performed experiments with an alternative method, the SEARN algorithm [9], but this did not produce better results.

counted the number of wrong decisions for each sentence, computing a proportion of wrong classifications (the minimal and maximal errors indicate that an
output sentence and its respective gold standard are totally equal or completely
different, respectively). We evaluated the methods in the actual application scenario, in which the features that require previous outputs were filled based on
the current classification outputs.

We compared our results with the best system that was proposed by Nóbrega
and Pardo [20] and also with the LSTM-based approach that was described by
Filippova et al. [10]. As this last approach requires more data in order to show
better results, we have not used this system in the cross-validation evaluation,
but only in the second evaluation setup: we have trained it with the G1-Pairs
dataset and evaluated on the PCSC-Pairs.

Table 2 shows the average evaluation results for each method in the cross-
validation setup. We use the labels +SEQ and +TREE in order to identify the
cases in that we adopt the sequential and tree-based reading processes, respectively. We indicate the use of DAGGER and CRF with the labels +DAGGER
and +CRF, respectively. Due to space limitation, we only show the results for
the case that we mixed the PCSC-Pairs and G1-Pairs corpora. The obtained
results for the other cases were quite similar.

Table 2. Achieved results for 10-fold cross-validation

Method	Precision	Recall	F-1	Avg Error
Nóbrega and Pardo [20]	0.88	0.88	0.88	0.12
Our Model + Seq	0.89	0.89	0.89	0.10
Our Model + Seq + CRF	**0.90**	**0.89**	**0.90**	**0.10**
Our Model + Seq + DAGGER	0.76	0.79	0.78	0.21
Our Model + Tree	0.89	0.89	0.89	0.11
Our Model + Tree + DAGGER	0.81	0.82	0.81	0.15
Our Simplified Model	0.88	0.88	0.88	0.11
Our Simplified Model + CRF	**0.92**	**0.90**	**0.91**	**0.12**
Our Simplified Model + DAGGER	0.69	0.69	0.69	0.32

We may see that some of our models outperform the approach of Nóbrega and
Pardo [20] in all the configurations and for all the metrics, by tiny differences.
Furthermore, the best model based on the sequential reading has higher evaluation score than the one based on tree reading. It shows us that following the
standard left to right sentence processing may be worthy. We have also observed
that the DAGGER algorithm did not improve the scores of the proposed methods. However, one may notice that the CRF algorithm has usually produced
better performances.

Our best simplified model shows better performance than the more complete
method, but slightly penalizes the average error. This scenario indicates that the

context of a given isolated token t (the two previous or two next tokens of t, their respective POS tags and if the two previous tokens in relation to t were or not removed) is good enough to decide if t must be removed or not from an input sentence, but the absence of more sophisticated features may cause readability problems. Similar results were also reached in the experiments performed by Filippova et al. [10].

Table 3 shows the results for our another experiment setup (i.e., training our methods in the G1-Pairs corpus and evaluated them in the PCSC-Pairs corpus). As we have more training data, it was possible to include the approach of Filippova et al. [10].

Table 3. Achieved results when training on G1-Pairs and testing on PCSC-Pairs

Method	Precision	Recall	F-1	Avg Error
Nóbrega and Pardo [20]	0.63	0.53	0.47	0.49
Filippova et al. [10]	0.84	0.84	0.84	0.16
Our Model + Seq	**0.86**	**0.85**	**0.85**	**0.15**
Our Model + Seq + CRF	0.85	0.84	0.84	0.16
Our Model + Seq + DAGGER	0.85	0.84	0.84	0.16
Our Model + Tree	0.66	0.48	0.33	0.56
Our Model + Tree + DAGGER	0.65	0.48	0.32	0.56
Our Simplified Model	0.62	0.57	0.55	0.43
Our Simplified Model + CRF	**0.86**	**0.85**	**0.85**	**0.15**
Our Simplified Model + DAGGER	0.63	0.57	0.54	0.44

We may see that the evaluation scores are less expressive than in the 10-fold cross-validation evaluation. This probably occurs because of the different nature of the datasets, which makes the task harder. Confirming the previous results, the simplified model using CRF is among the best methods. The complete model with sequential reading produced similar results, but using more sophisticated features. We may also see that the Average Error that was produced by the two models is visibly better than the error of most of the other methods. Overall, it is clear that our best models outperformed the work of Nóbrega and Pardo [20], advancing the state of the art for Portuguese.

The tree-based approaches do not show good results, with a higher average error. It suggests that there are relevant differences in the syntactic trees from the training and test datasets. Furthermore, a wrong decision for a given token in this method may produce significant cascade errors.

Finally, it is interesting to notice that our best methods present slightly better scores than the method proposed by Filippova et al. [10]. They are competitive in performance, but our approaches are much simpler and require less training data than the one of Filippova et al.

As illustration, we show below some original sentences with (good and bad) compressions produced by our models:

- *Duas escolas ficaram destruídas e estão a ser retirados os alunos.* ("Two schools were destroyed and the students are being rescued.") −> *Estão a ser retirados os alunos.* ("The students are being rescued.")
- *Os Estados Unidos vão começar a armar os rebeldes sírios, marcando assim um crescendo do envolvimento norte-americano no conflito.* ("The United States will start to sell arms to the rebels in Syria, which increases north-american involvement in the war.") −> *Estados Unidos vão começar a armar rebeldes crescendo.* ("The United States will start to sell arms to the rebels increases.")
- *O plano estabelece um empréstimo no valor total de 78 mil milhões de euros até Junho de 2013.* ("The project defines a loan of EUR 78 thousand million until June 2013.") −> *Plano estabelece 78 mil milhões.* ("Project defines 78 thousand million.")

6   Final Remarks

We have explored machine learning-based models for the sentence compression task for Portuguese. We have extended a method that was proposed in [20], have proposed a simpler version of it, and, to train and test the methods, have assembled two datasets. Our results showed that we outperformed the existent approaches for Portuguese and produced competitive results with a state of the art approach in the area.

Some issues about the methods that we investigated remain as future work. As one may notice, we have not specified any compression rate, as it was directly learned from the datasets. Therefore, it may be interesting to study strategies that produce reduced sentences of different sizes for the same input. Our methods might also make use of context information to do more than to select words to remove: a desirable behavior would be to select words to remove that are not *relevant* to the message that the text wants to convey. This might avoid removing, e.g., the important fact about the "school destruction" in one of the examples in the previous section.

Finally, future work also includes the investigation of abstractive methods for sentence compression, as the ones proposed in [4,25]. Although the production of such sentences is harder than in the deletion-based approach, such strategy may produce more human-like sentences.

To the interested reader, more information about this work (including the datasets and the source code for the SC methods) may be found at the SUCINTO project webpage (www.icmc.usp.br/~taspardo/sucinto).

Acknowledgments. The authors are grateful to CAPES, FAPESP (2015/17841-3) and USP Research Office (PRP 668) for supporting this work. This work is also financed by National Funds through the Portuguese funding agency, FCT − *Fundação para a Ciência e a Tecnologia*, I.P., within project UID/EEA/50014/2019.

References

1. Aires, R.V.X.: Implementação, adaptação, combinação e avaliação de etiquetadores para o português do brasil. Master's thesis, Instituto de Ciências Matemáticas e de Computação (2000)
2. Almeida, M.B., Almeida, M.S.C., Figueira, A.F.T.M.H., Mendes, P., Pinto, C.: A new multi-document summarization corpus for European Portuguese. In: Language Resources and Evaluation Conference, Reykjavik, Iceland, pp. 1–7 (2014)
3. Almeida, M.B., Martins, A.F.T.: Fast and robust compressive summarization with dual decomposition and multi-task learning. In: Proceedings of the Annual Meeting of the Association for Computational Linguistics, Sofia, Bulgaria, pp. 196–206. Association for Computational Linguistics (2013)
4. Baziotis, C., Androutsopoulos, I., Konstas, I., Potamianos, A.: SEQ^3: differentiable sequence-to-sequence-to-sequence autoencoder for unsupervised abstractive sentence compression. In: Proceedings of the 2019 Conference of the North American Chapter of the Association for Computational Linguistics: Human Language Technologies, Minneapolis, Minnesota, vol. 1 (Long and Short Papers), pp. 673–681. Association for Computational Linguistics, June 2019
5. Berg-Kirkpatrick, T., Gillick, D., Klein, D.: Jointly learning to extract and compress. In: Proceedings of the International Conference on Computational Linguistics, Portland, Oregon, pp. 481–490. Association for Computational Linguistics (2011)
6. Bick, E.: The Parsing System Palavras, Automatic Grammatical Analysis of Portuguese in a Constraint Grammar Framework. Aarhus University Press, Aarhus (2000)
7. Cohn, T., Lapata, M.: Sentence compression beyond word deletion. In: Proceedings of the International Conference on Computational Linguistics, pp. 137–144 (2008)
8. Cordeiro, J., Dias, G., Brazdil, P.: Rule induction for sentence reduction. In: Correia, L., Reis, L.P., Cascalho, J. (eds.) EPIA 2013. LNCS (LNAI), vol. 8154, pp. 528–539. Springer, Heidelberg (2013). https://doi.org/10.1007/978-3-642-40669-0_45
9. Daumé III, H., Langford, J., Marcu, D.: Search-based structured prediction. Mach. Learn. J. **75**, 297–325 (2006)
10. Filippova, K., Alfonseca, E., Colmenares, C., Kaiser, L., Vinyals, O.: Sentence compression by deletion with LSTMs. In: Proceedings of the 2015 Conference on Empirical Methods in Natural Language Processing, Lisbon, Portugal, pp. 360–368. Association for Computational Linguistics (2015)
11. Filippova, K., Altun, Y.: Overcoming the lack of parallel data in sentence compression. In: Proceedings of the 2013 Conference on Empirical Methods in Natural Language Processing, Seattle, Washington, USA, pp. 1481–1491. Association for Computational Linguistics (2013)
12. Kawamoto, D., Pardo, T.A.S.: Learning sentence reduction rules for Brazilian Portuguese. In: Proceedings of the 7th International Workshop on Natural Language Processing and Cognitive Science, Funchal, Madeira, Portugal, pp. 90–99 (2010)
13. Knight, K., Marcu, D.: Statistics-based summarization - step one: sentence compression. In: Proceedings of the Seventeenth National Conference on Artificial Intelligence and Twelfth Conference on Innovative Applications of Artificial Intelligence, pp. 703–711 (2000)

14. Li, C., Liu, F., Weng, F., Liu, Y.: Document summarization via guided sentence compression. In: Proceedings of the Conference on Empirical Methods in Natural Language Processing, Seattle, Washington, USA, pp. 490–500. Association for Computational Linguistics (2013)
15. Madnani, N., Zajic, D., Dorr, B., Ayan, N.F., Lin, J.: Multiple alternative sentence compressions for automatic text summarization. In: Proceedings of the Document Understanding Conference (2007)
16. Martins, A.F.T., Smith, N.A.: Summarization with a joint model for sentence extraction and compression. In: Proceedings of the NAACL HLT Workshop on Integer Linear Programming for Natural Language Processing, pp. 1–9 (2009)
17. McDonald, R.: Discriminative sentence compression with soft syntactic evidence. In: Proceedings of the 11st Conference of the European Chapter of the Association for Computational Linguistics, pp. 297–304 (2006)
18. Mikolov, T., Sutskever, I., Chen, K., Corrado, G., Dean, J.: Distributed representations of words and phrases and their compositionality. In: Proceedings of the Advances in Neural Information Processing Systems, pp. 3111–3119 (2013)
19. Nguyen, M.L., Shimazu, A., Horiguch, S., Ho, B.T., Fukushi, M.: Probabilistic sentence reduction using support vector machines. In: Proceedings of the 20th international conference on Computational Linguistics, Geneva, Switzerland, pp. 137–144. Association for Computational Linguistics (2004)
20. Nóbrega, F.A.A., Pardo, T.A.S.: Investigating Machine learning approaches for sentence compression in different application contexts for Portuguese. In: Silva, J., Ribeiro, R., Quaresma, P., Adami, A., Branco, A. (eds.) PROPOR 2016. LNCS (LNAI), vol. 9727, pp. 245–250. Springer, Cham (2016). https://doi.org/10.1007/978-3-319-41552-9_25
21. Qian, X., Liu, Y.: Fast joint compression and summarization via graph cuts. In: Proceedings of the Conference on Empirical Methods in Natural Language Processing, pp. 1492–1502. Association for Computational Linguistics (2013)
22. Ross, S., Gordon, G.J., Bagnell, J.A.: A reduction of imitation learning and structured prediction to no-regret online learning. In: Proceedings of the 14th International Conference on Artificial Intelligence and Statistics, Fort Lauderdale, FL, USA, pp. 627–635 (2011)
23. Thadani, K., McKeown, K.: Sentence compression with joint structural inference. In: Proceedings of the Seventeenth Conference on Computational Natural Language Learning, pp. 65–74 (2013)
24. Turner, J., Charniak, E.: Supervised and unsupervised learning for sentence compression. In: Proceedings of the 43rd Annual Meeting on Association for Computational, pp. 290–297 (2005)
25. Yu, N., Zhang, J., Huang, M., Zhu, X.: An operation network for abstractive sentence compression. In: Proceedings of the 27th International Conference on Computational Linguistics, Santa Fe, New Mexico, USA, pp. 1065–1076. Association for Computational Linguistics (2018)
26. Zhao, Y., Luo, Z., Aizawa, A.: A language model based evaluator for sentence compression. In: Proceedings of the 56th Annual Meeting of the Association for Computational Linguistics (Volume 2: Short Papers), Melbourne, Australia, pp. 170–175. Association for Computational Linguistics (2018)

An Investigation of Pre-trained Embeddings in Dependency Parsing

Juliana C. Carvalho de Araújo[1(✉)], Cláudia Freitas[1],
Marco Aurélio C. Pacheco[1], and Leonardo A. Forero-Mendoza[2]

[1] PUC-Rio, Rio de Janeiro, Brazil
jaraujo.ele@gmail.com, claudiafreitas@puc-rio.br, marco@ele.puc-rio.br
[2] UERJ, Rio de Janeiro, Brazil
leofome@gmail.com

Abstract. In recent years, research in Natural Language Processing has witnessed an explosion in the application of neural networks and word embeddings. The goal of this paper is to explore how different word embedding models affect the performance of a dependency parser based on neural networks, and demonstrate that it is possible to reduce the cost of parsing using pre-trained embeddings. In order to do that, a jPTDP model was proposed. The results indicate the efficiency of the jPTDP as a dependency parser and the advantages of using embeddings with pre-trained words. The best results were obtained through the use of GloVe.

Keywords: Dependency parser · Portuguese treebank · Word embeddings

1 Introduction

Systems that perform information extraction (IE) usually take into account different types of linguistic annotation, such as part of speech (POS) and syntactic dependencies [1,2]. In recent years, Natural Language Processing (NLP) has witnessed an explosion in the application of neural networks and word embeddings, especially when it comes to dependency parsing (DP) tasks [3–6]. For example, using a system which includes embeddings based on syntactic dependencies, [7] obtained the best results in the semantic relation extraction task of SemEval 2018 [8].

In general, words are regarded as the basic unit of input for NLP algorithms. Consequently, it is crucial that they are provided with meaningful representations. Word embedding is a set of language modeling and feature learning techniques in NLP where words or phrases from the vocabulary are mapped from a space with many dimensions per word to a continuous vector space with a much lower dimension.

Word embedding algorithms generate dense, or highly informative, representations of words in texts based on their distribution in context. As a result,

© Springer Nature Switzerland AG 2020
P. Quaresma et al. (Eds.): PROPOR 2020, LNAI 12037, pp. 281–290, 2020.
https://doi.org/10.1007/978-3-030-41505-1_27

the representations are better fit to specify the input layer for artificial neural networks. From a linguistic point of view, the approach is clearly in line with (old) ideas that privilege the context that the words are inserted in order to define their meaning. Some examples are Saussure's idea of linguistic value [9], Firth [10], the slogan "you shall know a word by the company it keeps", and Wittgenstein's advice: "don't ask for the meaning, ask for the use".

A significant advantage of using distributed semantics in the form of word embeddings as a resource for the dependency parsing is that the semantics are able to substitute manual feature engineering. The most advanced word embedding models can be a competitive advantage in large corpora [11]. In the dependency parsing, most of the neural parsers use pre-trained word embeddings [12]. As to Portuguese language, initiatives such as Universal Dependencies (UD) project [13] made available systems able to perform multilingual processing with satisfying results, which can also benefit the Portuguese language.

In addition, for Portuguese, there are already available pre-trained embeddings sets: ([14], [15], and [16], that trained embeddings for the Oil & Gas domain). In [14], different word embedding models trained on a Portuguese corpus are evaluated on a POS tagging task. In this paper, we evaluate pre-trained word embeddings as fine tuning on a DP task.

One of the goals of our work is to understand the impact of using different pre-trained word embeddings in the task of dependency parsing for processing the Portuguese language. The second one is to demonstrate that it is possible to reduce the cost of parsing using pre-trained embeddings. Therefore we chose the neural parser Joint Pos Tagging Dependency Parser (jPTDP) [6] for our experiments. This choice is not random: it is an open source parser that is easy to use and allows training data from scratch. jPTDP achieved excellent results as a dependency parser in the CoNLL-2018 [12] shared task test sets "Big", "PUD" and "Small" for Portuguese [6].

We use pre-trained embeddings as GloVe (provided by [14]) and FastText (CBOW) (provided by [14] and [15]) with the 300, 600, and 1000 dimensionality settings, and compared it to the from scratch embedding layer training for the same dimensions. We know, on the one hand, that the larger the dimensionality, the better the performance. On the other hand, the recent work of [17] warns us about the high financial and environmental costs of recent neural network models for NLP, and this is one of the reasons for looking for a less costly scenario.

2   Dependency Parsing Strategies

The structural aspects of the text refer to the arrangement of words in a sentence and the way the contexts amongst them are interrelated. This organisation is often represented by grammatical relationships between words, also known as dependencies. Dependency is the notion that syntactic units are connected to each other by directed links that describe their relationships.

Dependency parsers assign syntactic structures to sentences in the form of trees. There are generally two kinds of dependency parsing algorithms, namely

Transition-based Dependency Parsing [18] and Graph-based Dependency Parsing [6,19]. In Graph-based parsing, a model is trained to score all possible dependency arcs between words, and decoding algorithms are subsequently applied to find the most likely dependency graph. This strategy scores a large number of dependency graphs which is time consuming. A Transition-based parser only builds one tree, scores transitions between states, and gradually builds up dependency graphs on the side.

Typically, a disambiguation task in dependency parsing is to derive a single dependency tree τ for a given sentence s. The parsing problem is to find the mapping of an input of s using tokens $w_1, ..., w_n$, for a dependency tree τ that represents its grammatical structure and defines its relationships. Some parsers solve this problem by obtaining a single analysis for each sentence. Others, instead, lessen ambiguity by using POS tags to allow lexical-morphological aspects and syntax to interact [6].

3   Word Embeddings

Word embeddings have great practical importance since they can be used as pre-computed high-density features to Machine Learning models, significantly reducing the amount of training data required in a variety of NLP tasks [20]. The core concept of word embeddings is that every word used in a language can be represented by a vector of real numbers. Word embeddings are N-dimensional vectors that try to capture word-meaning and context in numerical values.

Most word embeddings are created based on the notion that words that occur in the same contexts tend to have similar meanings. There are a variety of methods to generate this mapping such as neural networks [21] [15] and dimensionality reduction on the word co-occurrence matrix [22] [23].

Global Vectors (GloVe) [23] is an unsupervised learning algorithm for obtaining vector representations for words. Its training is performed on aggregated global word-word co-occurrence statistics from a corpus. Both GloVe and Word2vec [21] learn the representations based on the contexts of the words in a sentence. However, Word2vec leverage local contexts whereas GloVe utilizes the global contexts in the form of global co-occurrence statistics. FastText [24] is another word embedding method that is an extension of Word2vec [21]. Instead of learning vectors for words directly, FastText represents each word as a bag of n-gram character. Each character n-gram is mapped to dense vectors and the sum of these dense vectors represents the word.

By leveraging the sub word information, FastText offers better representations for rare words because even if the words are rare, their character n-grams appear across the words in the corpus. In addition, Mikolov et al. [21] have shown that training Word2vec using Continuous Bag of Words (CBOW) and Skip-gram could improve performance in various text classification tasks. Both have their own advantages and disadvantages. According to Mikolov [21], Skip Gram works well with small amounts of data and represents rare words.

4 Method

4.1 Corpus

The parser was trained in UD-Portuguese-Bosque corpus, as made available in releases 2.2 and 2.4 (current release) of the UD project. Created in 2002 under the scope of Floresta Sintá(c)tica [25], [26], a Linguateca's project, Bosque is one of the most used annotated Portuguese corpora – it contains 9,368 sentences and 227,653 tokens extracted from Brazilian and Portuguese newspapers. The Bosque-UD version is the result of a conversion process from the output of PALAVRAS parser and linguistic revision, as described in [27]. As part of the UD release, the corpus is released in train, dev and test partitions. We used the release 2.2 since it is part of the data used in two shared tasks for Universal Dependencies parsing, CoNLL 2017 and CoNLL 2018. Since its release according to UD framework, the corpus has been continuously revised, and this is why we wanted to test version 2.4 as well.

4.2 Baseline: UDPipe

DPipe is a trainable pipeline for tokenizing, tagging, lemmatizing and parsing Universal Treebanks [28]. UDPipe is language independent and can only be trained with files in the CoNLL-U format. It is available as a binary for Linux/Windows/OS X, as a library for C++, Python, Perl, Java, C#, and as a web service.

4.3 Parser: jPTDP

jPTDP v2 (Joint POS Tagging Dependency Parser) [6] is a joint model which uses BiLSTMs to learn feature representations shared amongst POS tagging and dependency parsing. jPTDP can be seen as an extension of the graph-based dependency parser [4], replacing POS tag embeddings with LSTM-based character-level word embeddings. The model uses a bidirectional LSTM, followed by an MLP layer and a softmax layer to predict part of the POS tags (trained with gold standard). Figure 1 illustrates the jPTDP [6] architecture.

Dependency trees are formalised as directed graphs. The arc factor analysis approach learns arc scores in graphs. The decoding algorithm will find the maximum spanning tree of these arc scores, i. e., the analysis tree with the highest score on the graph:

$$score(s) = \underset{\hat{y} \in \mathcal{Y}(s)}{\mathrm{argmax}} \sum_{(h,m) \in \hat{y}} score_{arc}(h, m) \tag{1}$$

Where Y(s) is the set of all possible dependency trees for the input sentence s, and $score_{arc}(h, m)$ measures the arc score between the main word and the modifying word in s. The arc is scored using MLP with a single node output layer (MLP_{arc}) in BiLSTM resource vectors:

$$score_{arc}(h, m) = MLP_{arc}(v_h \circ v_m) \tag{2}$$

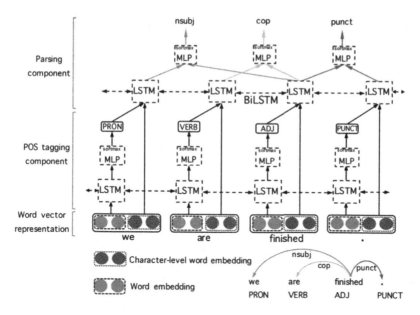

Fig. 1. Proposed architecture. Source [6]

v_h and v_m are biLSTM-based shared resource vectors, representing the words h and mths in s, respectively. Then the model calculates the loss based on the hinge loss. Dependency types are predicted similarly. Another MLP is used in the biLSTM resource vector to predict the type relationship of head modifier arc.

The parser illustrated in Fig. 1 was trained with Bosque Portuguese-UD with and without pre-trained word vectors. In the pre-trained case we used pre-trained Portuguese word vectors provided by [29] and [14].

Given that the focus of these experiments is to evaluate the behavior of the parser with different word embedding combinations, we set the jPTDP hyper-parameters as:

- Epochs: 5
- LSTM Dimension: 256
- Number of LSTM Layers: 2
- Number of Hidden Neurons (MLP): 100
- Character Embedding Dimension: 150
- POS Embedding Dimension: 100

5   Results

Although there was a relatively small number of epochs, the result was satisfactory compared to the results of Conll 2018 [12]. The parser with the aforementioned hyperparameters and pre-trained GloVe embedding with 600 dimension would have reached 10th, 9th and 5th place considering the LAS, UAS and UPOS metrics respectively. It is worth noting that the system with the best performance with LAS, for example, was trained with 100 epochs.

The parser outperformed UDPipe Web results (Table 1 in all metrics for all tested configurations (see Tables 1 and 2).

Table 1. Results UDPipe web

Release	UPOS	LAS	UAS	CLAS	BLEX	MLAS
2.2	95.88	82.28	85.41	75.54	72.21	67.52
2.4	95.71	82.74	86.63	75.62	72.58	67.51

Given the reduced number of epochs used, it seems that pre-trained word embeddings lead the parser to be less costly without sacrificing accuracy. It can be interpreted that the model could identify more semantic signals from the pre-trained embeddings than it did from the training data through the embedding layer.

Table 2. Experiment results (F1)

Embedding	Release	Size	UPOS	LAS	UAS	CLAS	BLEX	MLAS
Trained	2.2	300	96.20	84.70	88.10	79.01	79.09	73.70
		600	96.48	84.83	88.12	79.16	79.16	73.95
		1000	96.28	85.01	88.02	79.55	79.55	74.16
	2.4	300	95.94	85.01	88.82	79.07	79.07	74.73
		600	96.53	84.63	88.39	78.26	78.26	73.84
		1000	96.36	84.57	88.52	77.99	77.99	73.50
GloVe [14]	2.2	300	96.42	85.37	88.55	80.19	80.19	74.81
		600	96.40	**86.20**	**89.09**	**80.85**	**80.85**	**75.46**
		1000	**96.53**	85.27	88.31	79.91	79.91	74.55
	2.4	300	**96.79**	85.62	**89.55**	79.28	79.28	74.93
		600	96.67	85.57	89.53	79.70	79.70	75.13
		1000	96.59	**85.71**	89.35	**79.81**	**79.81**	**75.33**
FastText [14]	2.2	300	96.47	84.73	87.88	79.28	79.28	73.76
		600	96.35	84.05	87.29	79.00	79.00	73.32
		1000	96.35	84.48	87.95	79.02	79.02	73.32
	2.4	300	96.69	84.96	88.87	78.82	78.82	74.05
		600	96.54	84.80	88.72	78.41	78.41	73.85
		1000	96.37	84.03	88.29	77.63	77.63	72.48
FastText [29]	2.2	300	96.42	85.79	88.86	80.64	80.64	75.05
	2.4		96.69	85.48	89.16	79.10	79.10	75.06

As a critical hyperparameter, the choice of dimensionality of word vectors has huge influence on the performance of a word embedding [30]. An embedding with a small dimension is typically not expressive enough to capture all possible word relations, whereas one with a very large dimension suffers from over-fitting. Besides, the number of parameters for a word embedding directly affects training time and computational costs. Therefore, large dimensions tend to increase model complexity, slow down training speed, and add inferential latency, all of which are constraints that can potentially limit model applicability and deployment [31]. In fact, through the experiments, it was possible to notice that the use of pre-trained embeddings influence on the results and performance. For Portuguese, [14] reports that GloVe produced the worst results for both POS tagging and sentence similarity. However, we noticed that the same method gave better results with both UPOS and DP, which is interesting, since neither dependency parsing nor POS are considered semantic tasks. Nonetheless, since the parser combines benefits from character, the FastText performance was suboptimal.

A curious fact is the drop in results for version 2.4, since 2.4 means a version better than the previous ones. However, as can be found in [32], the linguistic revision process dealt mainly with errors derived from the automatic conversion underlying the first release, as detailed in [27]. Still according to [32], the 2.4 version eliminated wrong patterns (and, then, false consistency), and this might explain the decrease in the model performance.

6   Concluding Remarks

In this paper, we conducted an experiment with pre-trained embeddings and dependency parsing. The main motivation was to test how much a simple – that is, less expensive – scenario could yield good results. The approach taken has shown that the jPTDP model benefits from the use of pre-trained word vectors. In particular, GloVe obtained a satisfactory result in the dependency parsing task for Portuguese, even though few epochs were used. In short, the use of pre-trained embeddings act as a fine tuning in neural parser weights initialization, providing greater convergence over a smaller number of epochs. In future works, we intend to investigate the use of newer embedding methods such as ELMO [33] and BERT [34] which, in addition to capturing polysemy, capture more accurate resource representations that may lead to better model performances. As a second contribution, we also provide some metrics regarding v.2.4 of the Bosque-UD corpus.

Acknowledgements. The authors would like to thank CNPq, CAPES and ANP for funding and supporting research.

References

1. Hobbs, J.R., Riloff, E.: Information extraction. In: Indurkhya, N., Damerau, F. (eds.) Handbook of Natural Language Processing, pp. 511–532. CRC Press, Boca Raton (2010)

2. Niklaus, C., Cetto, M., Freitas, A., Handschuh, S.: A survey on open information extraction. In: Proceedings of the 27th International Conference on Computational Linguistics, Association for Computational Linguistics, Santa Fe, New Mexico, USA, pp. 3866–3878 (2018)
3. Smith, A., de Lhoneux, M., Stymne, S., Nivre, J.: An investigation of the interactions between pre-trained word embeddings, character models and POS tags in dependency parsing. In: Proceedings of the 2018 Conference on Empirical Methods in Natural Language Processing, Association for Computational Linguistics, Brussels, Belgium (2018). https://doi.org/10.18653/v1/D18-1291
4. Kiperwasser, E., Goldberg, Y.: Simple and accurate dependency parsing using bidirectional LSTM feature representations. Trans. Assoc. Comput. Linguist. **4**, 313–327 (2016)
5. Dozat, T., Manning, C.D.: Deep biaffine attention for neural dependency parsing. In: 5th International Conference on Learning Representations, ICLR 2017, Toulon, France, 24–26 April 2017, Conference Track Proceedings (2017)
6. Nguyen, D.Q., Verspoor, K.M.: An improved neural network model for joint POS tagging and dependency parsing. In: CoNLL Shared Task (2018)
7. Nooralahzadeh, F., Øvrelid, L., Lønning, J.T.: SIRIUS-LTG-UiO at SemEval-2018 task 7: convolutional neural networks with shortest dependency paths for semantic relation extraction and classification in scientific papers. In: Proceedings of The 12th International Workshop on Semantic Evaluation, SemEval@NAACL-HLT 2018, New Orleans, Louisiana, USA, 5–6 June 2018, pp. 805–810 (2018)
8. Gábor, K., Buscaldi, D., Schumann, A.-K., QasemiZadeh, B., Zargayouna, H., Charnois, T.: SemEval-2018 task 7: semantic relation extraction and classification in scientific papers. In: Proceedings of the 12th International Workshop on Semantic Evaluation, Association for Computational Linguistics, New Orleans, Louisiana, pp. 679–688 (2018). https://doi.org/10.18653/v1/S18-1111
9. de Saussure, F.: Course in General Linguistics. Columbia University Press, New York (2011)
10. Firth, J.R.: A synopsis of linguistic theory 1930–1955. In: Firth, J.R. (ed.) Studies in Linguistic Analysis, pp. 1–32. Blackwell, Oxford (1957)
11. Dhingra, B., Liu, H., Salakhutdinov, R., Cohen, W.W.: A comparative study of word embeddings for reading comprehension, CoRR abs/1703.00993. arXiv:1703.00993
12. Zeman, D., et al.: CoNLL 2018 shared task: multilingual parsing from raw text to universal dependencies. In: Proceedings of the CoNLL 2018 Shared Task: Multilingual Parsing from Raw Text to Universal Dependencies, Association for Computational Linguistics, Brussels, Belgium, pp. 1–21 (2018). https://doi.org/10.18653/v1/K18-2001
13. de Marneffe, M.-C., et al.: Universal Stanford dependencies: a cross-linguistic typology. In: Proceedings of the Ninth International Conference on Language Resources and Evaluation (LREC 2014), European Language Resources Association (ELRA), Reykjavik, Iceland, pp. 4585–4592 (2014)
14. Hartmann, N., Fonseca, E., Shulby, C., Treviso, M., Silva, J., Aluísio, S.: Portuguese word embeddings: evaluating on word analogies and natural language tasks. In: Proceedings of the 11th Brazilian Symposium in Information and Human Language Technology, Sociedade Brasileira de Computação, Uberlândia, Brazil, pp. 122–131 (2017)
15. Bojanowski, P., Grave, E., Joulin, A., Mikolov, T.: Enriching word vectors with subword information. Trans. Assoc. Comput. Linguist. **5**, 135–146 (2017)

16. da Silva Magalhães Gomes, D., Evsukoff, A.G., Cordeiro, F.C.: Word, embeddings em português para o domínio específico deÓleo e gás. In: Rio Oil & Gas, : Instituto Brasileiro de Petróleo, Gás e Biocombustíveis (IBP), p. 2018. Instituto Brasileiro de Petróleo, Gás e Biocombustíveis (IBP), Rio de Janeiro, Brazil (2018)
17. Strubell, E., Ganesh, A., McCallum, A.: Energy and policy considerations for deep learning in NLP. In: Proceedings of the 57th Annual Meeting of the Association for Computational Linguistics, Association for Computational Linguistics, Florence, Italy, pp. 3645–3650 (2019). https://doi.org/10.18653/v1/P19-1355
18. Gómez-Rodríguez, C., Shi, T., Lee, L.: Global transition-based non-projective dependency parsing. In: Proceedings of the 56th Annual Meeting of the Association for Computational Linguistics (Volume 1: Long Papers), Association for Computational Linguistics, Melbourne, Australia, pp. 2664–2675 (2018). https://doi.org/10.18653/v1/P18-1248
19. Dozat, T., Qi, P., Manning, C.: Stanford's graph-based neural dependency parser at the CoNLL 2017 shared task, pp. 20–30 (2017). https://doi.org/10.18653/v1/K17-3002
20. Kurita, S., Søgaard, A.: Multi-task semantic dependency parsing with policy gradient for learning easy-first strategies. In: ACL (2019)
21. Mikolov, T., Corrado, G., Chen, K., Dean, J.: Efficient estimation of word representations in vector space 1–12 (2013)
22. Deerwester, S., Dumais, S.T., Furnas, G.W., Landauer, T.K., Harshman, R.: Indexing by latent semantic analysis. J. Am. Soc. Inf. Sci. 41(6), 391–407 (1990)
23. Pennington, J., Socher, R., Manning, C.: Glove: global vectors for word representation. In: Proceedings of the 2014 Conference on Empirical Methods in Natural Language Processing (EMNLP), Association for Computational Linguistics, Doha, Qatar (2014). https://doi.org/10.3115/v1/D14-1162
24. Grave, E., Bojanowski, P., Gupta, P., Joulin, A., Mikolov, T.: Learning word vectors for 157 languages. In: Proceedings of the International Conference on Language Resources and Evaluation (LREC 2018) (2018)
25. Afonso, S., Bick, E., Haber, R., Santos, D.: Floresta sint'a(c)tica: a treebank for Portuguese. In: Rodrigues, M.G., Araujo, C.P.S. (eds.) Proceedings of the Third International Conference on Language Resources and Evaluation (LREC 2002), ELRA, Paris, pp. 1698–1703 (2002). http://www.linguateca.pt/documentos/AfonsoetalLREC2002.pdf
26. Freitas, C., Rocha, P., Bick, E.: Floresta sintá(c)tica: bigger, thicker and easier. In: Teixeira, A., de Lima, V.L.S., de Oliveira, L.C., Quaresma, P. (eds.) PROPOR 2008. LNCS (LNAI), vol. 5190, pp. 216–219. Springer, Heidelberg (2008). https://doi.org/10.1007/978-3-540-85980-2_23
27. Rademaker, A., Chalub, F., Real, L., Freitas, C., Bick, E., de Paiva, V.: Universal dependencies for Portuguese. In: Proceedings of the Fourth International Conference on Dependency Linguistics (Depling), Pisa, Italy, pp. 197–206 (2017)
28. Straka, M., Strakova, J.: Tokenizing, POS tagging, lemmatizing and parsing UD 2.0 with UDPipe, pp. 88–99 (2017). https://doi.org/10.18653/v1/K17-3009
29. Mikolov, T., Grave, E., Bojanowski, P., Puhrsch, C., Joulin, A.: Advances in pretraining distributed word representations. In: Proceedings of the International Conference on Language Resources and Evaluation (LREC 2018) (2018)
30. Yin, Z., Shen, Y.: On the dimensionality of word embedding. In: Bengio, S., Wallach, H., Larochelle, H., Grauman, K., Cesa-Bianchi, N., Garnett, R. (eds.) Advances in Neural Information Processing Systems 31, pp. 887–898. Curran Associates Inc. (2018)

31. Wu, Y., et al.: Google's neural machine translation system: Bridging the gap between human and machine translation, CoRR abs/1609.08144 (2016)
32. de Souza, E., Freitas, C.: UD Portuguese Bosque from 2.3 to 2.4 - the linguistic revision. Technical report, PUC-Rio (2019)
33. Peters, M., et al.: Deep contextualized word representations. In: Proceedings of the 2018 Conference of the North American Chapter of the Association for Computational Linguistics: Human Language Technologies, Volume 1 (Long Papers), Association for Computational Linguistics, New Orleans, Louisiana, pp. 2227–2237 (2018). https://doi.org/10.18653/v1/N18-1202
34. Devlin, J., Chang, M.-W., Lee, K., Toutanova, K.: BERT: pre-training of deep bidirectional transformers for language understanding. In: NAACL-HLT (2019)

Segmentation of Words Written in the Latin Alphabet: A Systematic Review

Marcelo A. Inuzuka$^{(\boxtimes)}$ ⓘ, Acquila S. Rocha$^{(\boxtimes)}$ ⓘ,
and Hugo A. D. Nascimento$^{(\boxtimes)}$ ⓘ

Instituto de Informática – Universidade Federal de Goiás (UFG),
Caixa Postal 131, Goiânia, GO 74.001-970, Brazil
{marceloakira,acquilarocha,hadn}@inf.ufg.br

Abstract. In this systematic literature review (SLR) we summarize studies that address the word segmentation problem (WSP) for Latin-based languages. We adopted the protocol of Kitchenham et al. for the review. The search in academic repositories found 771 works, from which 89 were selected. After a quality assessment step, 69 papers were chosen for data extraction. The results point to a divergence in terminology of this problem, two of which are more relevant, having specific techniques, corpus and application context: compound splitting and identifier splitting. We analyze the state of the art of each context, pointing out differences and similarities in approaches. We hope that these results can serve as a guide for future investigations and advancement of WSP.

Keywords: Natural language processing · Word segmentation · Identifier splitting · Compound splitting · Systematic literature review

1 Introduction

Word segmentation (WS) is a task of the natural language processing (NLP) area that consists of dividing a string into constituent parts for serving a given purpose. This task is similar to word tokenization, but differs as we will see more below. Depending on the linguistic context or the application domain, this task varies in taxonomy. In the present article, we perform a systematic literature review (SLR) of WS applied on texts written in the Latin alphabet.

The motivation of this work originated in experiences of the processing of legal texts in Portuguese. Due to errors in converting PDF file format to plain text, long spurious strings have emerged such as 'decisãoanteriorjáservecomomandadodeprisãopreventivaeofício' that should be corrected to 'decisão anterior já serve como mandado de prisão preventiva' (previous decision already serves as a warrant for custody). Looking for solutions to the problem, we found the *nltk.tokenize* library, which in turn has a sub-module *nltk.tokenize.stanford_segmenter*[1], but only supports Chinese and Arabic languages. In a prior exploratory research, we found some word segmentation tools

---

[1] Available at https://www.nltk.org/_modules/nltk/tokenize/stanford_segmenter.html.

© Springer Nature Switzerland AG 2020
P. Quaresma et al. (Eds.): PROPOR 2020, LNAI 12037, pp. 291–302, 2020.
https://doi.org/10.1007/978-3-030-41505-1_28

in English with technical analysis, but without scientific benchmarks[2]. These initial experiences motivated us to conduct a systematic literature review.

Word segmentation (WS) and word tokenization (WT) can be confused each other, as both produce sub-strings as a result. The difference is at the input strings and whether or not word delimiters (WDs) are supported, such as spaces or punctuation. In languages such as Portuguese or English, it is normal for the WT input string to be made up of several words separated by WDs and if not, WS can be used to get the tokens separated. In languages like Chinese, there are no WDs, so WS is most commonly employed. This way, WS can be used as a WT subtask if there is any string that needs to be segmented. Following, we focus on a formal description of the *word segmentation problem* (WSP) what can be defined as an optimization problem. A general formulation for it can be: given a string s, consisting of non-delimiting characters of words, find a split of s into a list of words $W = <w_1, w_2, \ldots, w_n>$, with $w_1 \cdot w_2 \ldots \cdot w_n = s$ and $|w_i| \geq 1$, so that an objective function $f(W)$ is optimized and a set of constraints are satisfied. There is a considerable amount of different WSP definitions in the literature, each one with a particular aim and set of constraints. A common and simple specialization of the general formulation is to ignore f (or make it constant) and to ensure that every w_i belongs to a given dictionary. Another specialization of the problem is to find a segmentation W with minimum number of splits. This can be formalized as: $Minimize\ F(W) = |W|$ constrained to have every w_i belonging to a dictionary. It is also possible to deal with imprecision or errors in s. In that case, $f(W)$ could measure how the terms in W deviate from their most similar words in a dictionary. A usual constraint for that case would be to enforce that every word in W is at most k characters different from its closest valid word in the dictionary. Different WSP formulations, in general, demand distinct algorithmic approaches for proving a good solution.

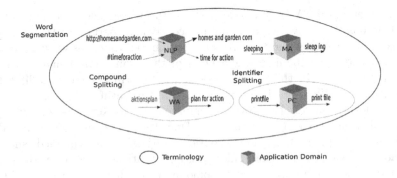

Fig. 1. Word Segmentation application domains

Word segmentation tasks also vary in method and in taxonomy according to the application domain, as seen in Fig. 1. **Word Alignment (WA)** is a task

---

[2] Example of tool: http://www.grantjenks.com/docs/wordsegment/.

in machine translation used for translating texts from a language to another. Languages that have a high amount of compounds, like German, make this task more difficult, because compounds has to be splitted to find corresponding words to the target language. For example: translate the German compound 'aktionsplan' to the English words 'plan for action'. In these contexts, the WS task is called *compound splitting*. **Program comprehension (PC)**. In software engineering, WS is used to analyze source code by dividing identifiers such as variable names that can usually be divided into acronyms or understandable parts. For example: 'printfile' to 'print file'. In this context, WS is called *identifier splitting*. **Social analytics (SA)**. In order to gain a better understanding of the Web, WS can be used to analyse hashtags and domain names (URLs). For example: 'homesandgardens' to 'homes and gardens'. In this context, WS is also employed and can called *hashtag splitting* or *domain name splitting*, respectively. **Morphological analysis (MA)**. A word can be analyzed in morphemes in order to understand its formation. For example: sleep-ing, dis-member-ed, etc. WS is also used in this context [3]. **Natural language processing (NLP)**. This is the most general case, in which the input text has been affected by noise [2] such as typos, OCR errors, char-code conversion errors, speech-to-text conversion error, etc.

The methodological framework applied for the development of this work follows the recommendations of Kitchenham [4], which establish a sequence of steps for producing consistent, auditable, and reproducible systematic reviews. The methodology suggested by the authors involves three stages: creating a review protocol, conducting the review, and presenting the results. The following sections reflect this methodology.

2   Review Protocol

We now present the planning stage of the SLR methodology. This section is divided into 4 subsections. Section 2.1 establishes the review questions; Sect. 2.2 presents the keywords and the search strategies; Sect. 2.3 defines the inclusion and the exclusion criteria; and Sect. 2.4 defines a quality evaluation.

2.1   Research Questions

The main objective of the SLR was to answer the following question: "What is the state of the art in WS methods?". Some more specific questions that unfolded the previous one were formulated: (RQ.1): What are the differences in WS methods in specific contexts? (RQ.2) Which technique performed best in specific contexts? (RQ.3) What is the state of the art in WS in the Portuguese language context?

2.2   Search Strategy

Conducting searches takes into account three primary factors: study sources, search keys, and scope delimitation. Nine study sources[3] were chosen considering previous SLRs and informal conversations with literature review experts: ACM Digital Library (AC), arXiv (AX), Google Search (GO), Google Scholar (GS), IEEE Xplore (IX), Scopus (SC), SpringerLink (SL), Science Direct (SD) and Web of Science (WS). In order to formulate search criteria, we separated the search into three types of aspects: search elements (SE - Table 1), search restrictions (SR - Table 2) and search filters (SF - Table 3). A search string (SS) consists of a combination of SE, and finally of using SR and SF to limit the results, as showed in Table 4.

Table 1. Search elements

Reference	SE - Search elements
SE1	*'compound splitting' OR 'identifier splitting'*
SE2	*'word segmentation'*
SE3	*'natural language processing' OR 'NLP'*
SE4	*'segmentação' OR 'separação' OR 'segmentação lexical' OR 'processamento de palavras compostas' OR 'análise léxica'*
SE5	*'segmentação de palavras'*
SE6	*'processamento de linguagem natural' OR 'PLN'*
SE7	*'palavras compostas' OR 'palavras coladas' OR 'palavras grudadas'*

Table 2. Search restrictions

R1=philosophical, R2=education, R3=chemistry, R4=gear, R5=mechanical, R6=biomedical, R7=engineering, R8=optical, R9=pharmacologic, R10=pharmaceutic, R11=surgery, R12=organic, R13=alloy, R14=biochemical, R15=physics, R16=molecular, R17=disorders, R18=medical, R19=urology, R20=energy, R21=cardiology, R22=clinical, R23=simulation, R24=radio, R25=chemical, R26=philosophy, R27=cultural, R28=psychology, R29=chinese, R30=urdu, R31=thai, R32=vietnamese, R33=myanmar, R34=khmer, R35=arabic, R36=jobs, R37=tibetan, R38=ad, R39='call for papers', R40=japanese, R41=ocr, R42=biologic, R43=handwritten, R44=burmese, R45=infant, R46=lao, R47=geoscience, R48=javanese, R49='question answering'

It is necessary to apply search restrictions in order to limit the amount of search results to a viable number of works to read. For example, in the Table 2, we

---

[3] Study sources details is documented at JSON file: https://git.io/Je0DZ.

use search restrictions to eliminate results outside the desired domain (education, philosophical, etc.) and language (chinese, thai, etc.).

Table 3. SF - Search filters

Reference	Elements
F1	Published from 2014 to 2019
F2	Search content in English
F3	Search content in Portuguese
F4	Science computation area
F5	From first 200 best ranked results
F6	Ad-hoc assessment

For each search engine, one or two searches were performed. This was necessary due to the large amount of results in some specific searches and limitations of the search string length. To facilitate the documentation of the searches, a database in JSON format has been edited[4], as well as a bash script has been created[5]. These components allow to generate the desired search strings. For example, for repeating the search IX2 - second search in the IEEE XPlore Digital Library, we can execute the command 'gen-search-string' as described in Fig. 2.

```
$ ./gen-search-string.sh SE2 SE3 R18 R29 R30 R31 R32 R34 R35 R37 R43

( "word segmentation") AND ( "natural language processing" OR "NLP") -medical
-chinese -urdu -thai -vietnamese -khmer -arabic -tibetan -handwritten
```

Fig. 2. Generating a search string with a bash script

Note that only SE and SR items were combined, since the SF value for the example above is 'None'. In searches that have filters it is necessary to apply them in the web interface of the digital library. For example, the GS2 search has filters F1 and F2. So, it is necessary to select the options 'publish from 2014 and 2019' and 'search content in English' (see the Table 3). With this approach, it was possible to experiment and apply different search strings in an efficient way.

2.3 Inclusion/Exclusion Criteria

Inclusion and exclusion criteria were defined for guiding the selection of relevant studies. For a study to be selected, we considered that all inclusion criteria should be met, as well as not meeting any exclusion criteria.

---

[4] Details of search strings are also available at: https://git.io/Je0DZ.

[5] A bash script file was created to generate search strings: https://git.io/Je0DC.

Table 4. SS - Search strings

Search	Elements	Restrictions	Filters	N. of results
GS1	$SE1 \wedge SE3$	{R2, R3, R5, R6, R7, R29}	F1	114
GS2	$SE2 \wedge SE3$	{R29, R30, R31, R32, R33, R34, R35, R36, R37, R18, R40, R43, R45, R41}	$F1 \wedge F2$	57
GS3	$SE4 \wedge SE6 \wedge SE7$	None	F3	135
GS4	$SE5 \wedge SE6$	None	F3	30
SD1	SE1	{R7, R8, R9, R10, R11, R3, R12, R13, R14, R15, R16, R17, R18, R19, R20, R21}	None	24
SD2	$SE2 \wedge SE3$	{R29, R30, R31, R32, R33, R34, R35, R37, R18, R40, R28, R41, R42}	None	11
IX1	$SE1$	None	None	11
IX2	$SE2 \wedge SE3$	{R29, R30, R32, R31, R34, R35, R37, R18, R43}	None	72
AC1	$SE1$	None	None	43
AC2	$SE2 \wedge SE3$	{R29, R30, R31, R32, R34, R35, R18, R43, R44, R33, R45, R40}	None	26
SC1	$SE1$	None	F4	59
SC2	$SE2 \wedge SE3$	{R29, R30, R31, R32, R46, R35, R18, R43, R33, R37, R44, R40, R47, R48, R49}	F4	69
WS1	$SE1$	None	None	30
WS2	$SE2 \wedge SE3$	{R29, R18, R43, R40, R32, R35, R37, R30, R31, R33}	None	26
SL1	$SE1$	{R22, R23, R24, R25, R7, R3, R26, R18, R27, R15, R28}	None	39
SL2	$SE2 \wedge SE3$	{R29, R18, R43, R40, R32, R46, R35, R37, R30, R31, R33, R41, R7, R45, R2, R49}	None	17
AX1	$SE2$	{R29, R35, R40, R45, R32, R34, R37, R43}	F6	56
GO1	$SE2 \wedge SE3$	{R29, R30, R31, R32, R33, R34, R35, R36, R37, R38, R18, R39}	$F5 \wedge F6$	10

In this sense, we chose the following inclusion criteria: (IC1) having full text available; (IC2) having an abstract; (IC3) being written in English or in Portuguese; (IC4) being a scientific study or a grey literature. As scientific studies, we considered papers, technical reports, surveys, master dissertations and doctoral thesis. As grey literature [4], we included technical reports, preprints, work in progress, software repositories with source codes, and documentations in web portals. For the later, we accepted web portals with relevant publication volume and with good evaluation from their users, or simply by an *ad-hoc* assessment. The exclusion criteria were: (EC1) not addressing WS; (EC2) addressing specific African language studies; (EC3) addressing specific Asian language studies.

2.4 Quality Assessment (QA)

The following quality assessment questions were devised: (QA1) Are the research context described in the study? (QA2) Is the research methodology clearly explained in the study? (QA3) Is data and performance analysis evidently explained in the study?

For each question, three possible answers were established - Yes, Partially, and No. These answers were assigned to a score of 1, 0.5 and 0.0, respectively. Thus, each study could reach a maximum of 3.0 points and a minimum of 0.0 points. All studies below 2.0 points were disqualified (excluded).

3 Conducting the Review

By using the search strings, we found and downloaded the resulting references in the BibTeX format[6]. All digital libraries exported to this format except Springer-Link (SL), which references were available only in CSV and had to be converted to BibTex using the csv2bib tool[7]. The SLR was managed using Parsifal[8] that, in addition to importing the BibTex items, also supported reference duplicate detection, selection, classification and data extraction.

In the selection stage, 771 studies were obtained as candidates. By reading the title and the abstract (when available) of each study, 604 papers were rejected, 89 were detected as duplicates, and 78 were approved. In the classification stage, from the 78 selected papers, 9 were eliminated with a score equal to or below 2.0 points and 69 were classified for data extraction. The data extraction step used a form created according to the Table 5. At this stage, it was necessary to download the full text of all classified studies for a complete reading. The Zotero software[9] was employed for managing and sharing these texts.

The data extracted from the studies at the last step is shown in Table 6, with references available in a BibTeX file[10].

4 SLR Results

In this section, we answer the research questions, based on the extracted data.

---

[6] Bibtex is used in LaTeX documents to describe references: http://www.bibtex.org/.
[7] csv2bib converts CSV to bibtex. See https://github.com/jacksonpradolima/csv2bib.
[8] Parsifal is a web software for managing SLR. https://parsif.al/.
[9] Zotero helps to collect and organize research references. https://www.zotero.org/.
[10] The complete references in Table 6 can be downloaded at https://git.io/Je0D8.

Table 5. Data extraction form

Description	Type	Values
Q1. What type of corpus is used?	Select one	G=Generic, PC=Parallel Corpus, SD=Specific Domain, O=Other
Q2. What is utilization domain?	Select one	GU=General Use, MT= Machine Translation, OU=Other Use, SE=Software Engineering, SN=Social Network Analysis
Q3. What languages did the study address?	Select many	C=Chinese[a], E=English, F=French, G=German, O=Other, P=Portuguese, S=Spanish, U=Universal, V=Various
Q4. What terminology is used?	Select one	CS=Compound Splitting, IS=Identifier Splitting, WS=Word Segmentation
Q5. What type of corpus is tested?	Select one	G=General, H=Hashtag, I=Identifiers, C=Compounds, U=URL
Q6. Did the work involve deep learning technique? Which one?	Select many	LSTM=Bi/Long Short-Term Memory, RNN=Bi/Recurrent Neural Network, CNN=Convolutional Neural Network, GRU=Gated Recurrent Units, N=No, O=Other, SNLM=Segmental Neural Network Model, T2T=Tensor2Tensor MTM
Q7. Did the work use word embedding? Which ones?	Select one	CE=Char Embedding, N=No, O=Other, WE=Word Embeddings
Q8. Did the work use different techniques from deep learning? Which one?	Select many	CRF=Conditional Random Field, DP=Dynamic Programing, WD=Word Dictionary, EA=Expand Abreviations, LA=Lexical Analysis, MA=Morphological Analysis, MS=Morpheme Segmentation, NA/NI=Not Applicable/Not Informed, O=Other, N=NGRAM, PT=Pos Tagging, ST=Statistic Techniques, SW=Stop Words List, TE=Text Entailment, VA=Viterbi Algorithm

[a] Chinese is not the primary language evolved in this works

4.1 RQ.1: What Are the Differences in WS Methods in Specific Contexts?

According to the data survey, when considering the use of the term 'compound splitting' as a specific context of the WS task for segmenting compound words, we obtained 21 studies: 7, 9, 13, 14, 16, 18, 19, 21, 22, 26, 27, 28, 30, 35, 37, 47, 49, 51, 52, 53, 56, 58, 69 – see Table 6. This represents 34.7% of the total amount of papers. There is no occurrence of usage of deep learning techniques in these studies. The most used methods are based on statistical techniques (ST), morphological analysis (MA) and lexical analysis, appearing in 7, 5 and 4 studies, respectively. In the context of this problem, the German language (G) was the one with the highest number of occurrences, as well as in the machine translation application (MT).

In the context of identifier splitting, 14 studies were found (20% from the total): 2, 4, 5, 8, 11, 24, 29, 38, 39, 50, 54, 57 and 59. The techniques of word dictionary (WD) and expand abbreviations (EA) appeared in 4 and 2 studies respectively. Deep learning (DL) was used in two works (29 and 54), and the most used language was English, in all occurrences.

Table 6. Data Extracted from the studies

N	Reference	Q1	Q2	Q3	Q4	Q5	Q6	Q7	Q8
1	(Smith et al. 2018)	G	G	U, V	WS	G	LSTM, RNN	CE	CRF
2	(Binkley et al. 2013)	SD	ES	E	IS	I	N	N	NA/NI
3	(Aken et al. 2011)	O	G	E	WS	G	RNN	N	ST
4	(Hill et al. 2014)	SD	ES	E	IS	I	N	N	NA/NI
5	(Guerrouj et al. 2014)	SD	ES	E	IS	I	N	N	NA/NI
6	(Wang et al. 2015)	G	G	E	WS	G	N	N	ST
7	(Shishkova et al. 2016)	SD	T	G, E	CS	C	N	N	O
8	(Guerrouj et al. 2010)	SD	ES	E	IS	I	N	N	
9	(Lee et al. 2007)	G	G	E, V	CS	G	N	N	ST, NG
10	(Wang et al. 2015)	G	G	E	WS	U	N	N	ST
11	(Dit et al. 2011)	SD	ES	E	IS	I	N	N	O
12	(Doval et al. 2018)	G	G	V	WS	G	RNN	N	NG
13	(Kraaij et al. 1998)	O	G	O	CS	C	N	N	NA/NI
14	(Ordelman et al. 2003)	SD	G	E, O	CS	C	N	N	NA/NI
15	(Shao et al. 2017)	SD	G	V	WS	G	RNN, GRU	N	VA, NG, MS
16	(Khaitan et al. 2009)	G	O	E	CS	U	N	N	ST, NG, SW
17	(Liang et al. 2014)	SD	G	V	WS	G	N	N	NA/NI
18	(Henrich et al. 2011)	SD	O	G, E	CS	C	N	N	MA
19	(Rigouts Terryn et al. 2016)	SD	T	O	CS	C	N	N	O, PT
20	(Baziotis et al. 2019)	SD	G	E	WS	H	RNN	N	NA/NI
21	(Koehn et al. 2003)	PC	T	G, E	CS	C	N	N	ST, LA
22	(Jagfeld et al. 2017)	PC	G	G	CS	C	N	N	TE, LA
23	(Garbe et al. 2019)	O	G	E	WS	G	N	N	DP, O
24	(Carvalho et al. 2015)	SD	ES	E	IS	I	N	N	NA/NI
25	(Hewlett et al. 2011)	G	G	U	WS	G	N	N	NA/NI
26	(Sugisaki et al. 2018)	SD	G	G	CS	C	N	N	MA, LA
27	(Escartín et al. 2014)	PC	T	G, S	CS	G	N	N	PT
28	(Alfonseca et al. 2008)	PC	T	G, E	CS	C	N	N	ST
29	(Li et al. 2018)	SD	ES	E	IS	I	CNN, LSTM	N	CRF
30	(Fritzinger al. 2010)	O	T	G	CS	C	N	N	MA, ST
31	(Johnson et al. 2009)	G	G	O	WS	G	N	N	ST
32	(Chen et al. 2016)	G	G	V	WS	G	N	N	NA/NI
33	(Paul et al. 2011)	PC	G	C, E, V	WS	G	N	N	O
34	(Paul et al. 2009)	PC	T	C, E, V	WS	G	N	N	O
35	(Macherey et al. 2011)	PC	T	G, E, V	CS	C	N	N	MA, DP, O
36	(Kawakami et al. 2018)	G	G	C, E	WS	G	LSTM, SNLM	N	LA, O
37	(Ma et al. 2016)	SD	T	G, U	CS	C	N	N	NA/NI
38	(Corazza et al. 2012)	SD	ES	E	IS	I	N	N	DW, EA, O
39	(Enslen et al. 2009)	SD	ES	E	IS	I	N	N	EA, DW
40	(Macháček et al. 2018)	G	T	G, V	WS	G	T2T	O	MA
41	(Moreau et al. 2019)	G	G	U	WS	G	RNN	N	NA/NI
42	(Sennrich et al. 2015)	G	T	V	WS	G	N	N	NA/NI
43	(Yang et al. 2017)	G	G	C	WS	G	LSTM	N	NA/NI
44	(Jenks et al. 2019)	G	G	E	WS	G	N	N	
45	(Reuter et al. 2016)	G	R	E, P	WS	H	N	N	PT, NG, O
46	(Srinivasan et al. 2012)	O	R	E	WS	U	N	N	ST
47	(Cöster et al. 2004)	SD	O	O	CS	C	N	N	O
48	(Wu et al. 2012)	SD	G	E	WS	G	N	N	O

(continued)

Table 6. (*continued*)

N	Reference	Q1	Q2	Q3	Q4	Q5	Q6	Q7	Q8
49	(Weller-Di et al. 2017)	SD	T	G	CS	C	N	N	NA/NI
50	(Hucka et al. 2018)	G	ES	E	IS	I	N	N	NA/NI
51	(Daiber et al. 2015)	O	T	O	CS	C	N	WE	NA/NI
52	(Shapiro et al. 2016)	G	G	O	CS	G	N	N	NG
53	(Clouet et al. 2014)	G	G	E, V	CS	G	N	N	ST
54	(Markovtsev et al. 2018)	SD	G	V	IS	I	LSTM, CNN	N	O
55	(Popović et al. 2006)	G	G	V	WS	G	N	N	PD, NG
56	(Norvig et al. 2019)	SD	T	G, E	CS	G	N	N	ST
57	(Guerrouj et al. 2013)	SD	ES	E	IS	I	N	N	DW, O
58	(Ziering et al. 2016)	G	O	G, V	CS	C	N	N	MA, PT, O
59	(Guerrouj et al. 2012)	SD	ES	E	IS	I	N	N	DW, O
60	(Shao et al. 2018)	G	G	C, F, E, P, V	WS	G	RNN	CE	NA/NI
61	(Kazakov et al. 2001)	O	G	F	WS	G	NA	NA	MA, O
62	(Roshani et al. 2014)	G	G	U	WS	G	N	N	VA
63	(Tambouratzis et al. 2009)	O	G	V	WS	G	N	N	MA
64	(Sun et al. 2013)	G	G	U	WS	G	N	N	O
65	(Gabay et al. 2008)	G	G	O	WS	G	N	N	PT
66	(Wang et al. 2011)	G	G	E	WS	U	N	N	ST
67	(Hewlett et al. 2011)	G	G	U	WS	G	N	N	O
68	(Stahlberg et al. 2012)	PC	G	S, E, V	WS	G	N	N	O
69	(Owczarzak et al. 2014)	G	G	V	CS	G	N	N	LA

In the more general context, which uses the term 'word segmentation', the largest number of studies were found, 34 (49.3%) in total. In this context, DL techniques were more frequent, about 11 studies (32% of the total). When DL is employed, RNN and LSTM techniques prevail, with 7 and 3 occurrences. Otherwise, statistics, POS tagging (PT) and N-Grams (N) techniques are the most frequent ones, with 12, 5 and 5 occurrences respectively.

Figure 3(a) shows the number of the selected scientific production from 1998 to 2019 in each specific word segmentation context (WS, CS, IS). On average, since 1998, there was an increase of the number of studies in the three segmentation contexts. CS and WS received more publications at the period 2016–2019.

4.2   RQ.2: Which Technique Performed Best in Specific Contexts?

To obtain the state of the art of the WS techniques reliably, it is necessary to apply benchmarking on standardized corpus. Common corpus were found for the IS context, but there was no standardization when considering CS and WS.

In Fig. 3(b) we analyzed the occurrence of DL techniques from 1998 to 2019. We note that, since 2010, it has been an increase in DL and a decrease in the use of other approaches, denoting a certain interest of the scientific community in that technique. Thus, we can say that the use of DL is a trend in recent years.

In the IS context, study 29 (see Table 6) presents a state of the art new technique based on deep learning, called CNN-BiLSTM-CRF, that outperformed other techniques such as LINSEN, LIDS and DTW.

In the context of CS, there is no standardized corpus either. In general, metrics are based on the performance of CS usage applied in machine translation, where BLEU was the most used. However, Escartín [1] suggested a way to mediate CS performance using precision, recall and F-measure metrics.

In the context of WS, there is no standardized corpus. However, in studies 12 and 41, there is an attempt to establish comparative metrics, with precision of .906 and .813 respectively. The most commonly cited technique - in studies 44, 20 and 23 - was based on dynamic programming. Study 65 proposes techniques for generating a standardized corpus using Wikipedia. The corpus 'Google Web Trillion Word Corpus' in English was cited in study 44. There are other studies that present situations with specific corpus: hashtag splitting (45, 32 and 46) and domain splitting (33, 46 and 10).

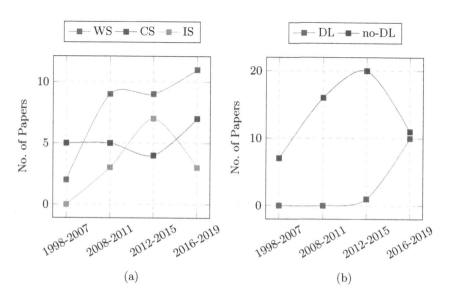

Fig. 3. At the left side (a) shows the use of WS, CS and IS from 1998 to 2019 and at the right side (b) shows the use of DL techniques from 1998 to 2019

4.3   RQ.3: What Is the State of the Art in WS in the Portuguese Language Context (PL)?

The authors in [5], developed a way of extract English compounds from the WordNet[11]. The same approach could be used at Portuguese scenario, but we could not find any corpus annotations of compound words in the most recent WordNets[12]. In order to know how many compound words exist in PL, we extracted 1804 words from a website[13]. Most of these words consisted of open

---

[11] https://wordnet.princeton.edu.
[12] http://www.clul.ulisboa.pt/en/ and http://wordnet.pt/.
[13] http://www.linguabrasil.com.br/palavras-compostas.php.

compounds (929), when a delimiter character separates the two parts of the word. According to the formal definition (Sect. 1), a problem consisting of a word with delimiter character does not characterize a WSP. In addition, compared with English and German, the number of closed compounds (without a delimiter character) in PL is much lower.

In this SLR, only 9 studies (1, 25, 37, 41, 45, 60, 62, 64 and 67) are considered universal, and only 2 (45 and 60) of them make direct reference to PL. Paper 45 refers to a specific application in hashtags and paper 60 is considered universal. In the studies, no software with direct support to the Portuguese language was found. All of them would need integration with specific training corpus in PL. Therefore, objective data for performance benchmarking are lacking. Considering this information, we can state that, compared to other languages, specific studies of WS for PL are lacking.

5 Discussion and Conclusions

In this SLR, we formally defined the problem of segmenting words written in the Latin Alphabet, present in many application domains and with different denominations. Several contexts were found and enumerated. The most relevant contexts are: word segmentation (WS), identifier splitting (IS) and compound splitting (CS) in natural language processing, software engineering and machine translation domains, respectively. We conducted a survey of techniques employed in each context, as well as a historical analysis of the use of deep learning techniques in recent years. Through data extraction and analysis, we conclude that, for each context, some specific techniques are more often then others. The most mature context in establishing a state of the art with standardized corpus is the IS. In the other contexts (CS and WS), there is no standard corpus.

References

1. Escartín, C.P.: Chasing the perfect splitter: a comparison of different compound splitting tools. In: LREC, pp. 3340–3347, May 2014
2. Garbe, W.: Fast Word Segmentation of Noisy Text (2018). https://towardsdatascience.com/fast-word-segmentation-for-noisy-text-2c2c41f9e8da
3. Kazakov, D., Manandhar, S.: Unsupervised learning of word segmentation rules with genetic algorithms and inductive logic programming. Mach. Learn. **43**(1–2), 121–162 (2001). https://doi.org/10/fng8qb, https://www.scopus.com/inward/record.uri?eid=2-s2.0-0035312598&doi=10.1023%2fA%3a1007629103294&partnerID=40&md5=eaae5dc95f7c91cc97525afdf2bb2c17, 144
4. Kitchenham, B., Charters, S.: Guidelines for performing systematic literature reviews in software engineering. EBSE Technical report 2, January 2007
5. Pedersen, T., Banerjee, S., Patwardhan, S.: compounds.pl - extract compound words (collocations) from WordNet - metacpan.org. https://metacpan.org/pod/distribution/WordNet-Similarity/utils/compounds.pl

A Deep Learning Model of Common Sense Knowledge for Augmenting Natural Language Processing Tasks in Portuguese Language

Cecília Silvestre Carvalho[1]([✉]), Vládia C. Pinheiro[1], and Lívio Freire[2]

[1] Universidade de Fortaleza, Fortaleza, Brazil
ceciliacarvalhoo@gmail.com, vladiacelia@gmail.com
[2] Universidade Federal do Ceará (UFC), Fortaleza, Brazil
livio.amf@gmail.com

Abstract. Despite the richness and vastness of the common-sense knowledge bases, we argue that common-sense knowledge has to be integrated into the target applications (Text Classification, Dialogue systems, Information Extraction systems, etc.) more effectively. In order to consider this common-sense knowledge in target applications, we propose a deep learning model of common-sense knowledge in Portuguese language, which can be easily coupled in Natural Language Understanding (NLU) systems in order to leverage their performance. More specifically, the model is composed by a neural network LSTM (Long Short Term Memory) that receives a text from the target application, for example, an user message in a dialog, a response to a user tweet, a news text; and selects and learns what is the best set of common-sense relations to return to the target application, which should be considered in the target learning model or system. We implemented the common-sense learning module in two target applications - a Stance Classification system and an End-to-End Dialogue system. In both cases, incorporating the deep learning model improved the results.

Keywords: Common sense knowledge · Deep learning · LSTM

1 Introduction

World knowledge is required to leverage several Natural Language Understanding (NLU) systems. [11] argue that people respond to each other's utterances in a meaningful way not only by paying attention to the latest utterance of the conversational partner itself but also by recalling relevant information about the concepts covered in the dialogue and integrating it into their responses. In this sense, they propose end-to-end dialogue systems by augmenting them with common-sense knowledge, integrated in the form of external memory. [9] define a method that aims at increasing the accuracy of the traditional systems of keyphrase

© Springer Nature Switzerland AG 2020
P. Quaresma et al. (Eds.): PROPOR 2020, LNAI 12037, pp. 303–312, 2020.
https://doi.org/10.1007/978-3-030-41505-1_29

extraction, expanding the training set with not-in-text terms, obtained from an inference process using world knowledge models. As final result, the method overcomes the limitation of identifying keyphrases that do not appear in the text and/or in the corpus.

In the context of Artificial Intelligence (AI), world knowledge is commonly referenced by common-sense knowledge that is the set of background information that an individual is intended to know or assume and the ability to use it when appropriate [1,2,6]. Several common-sense knowledge bases have been constructed during the past decade, such as ConceptNet [10] and SenticNet [3]. In Portuguese, we highlighted the base InferenceNet [8] that contains the inferential content of concepts, defined and agreed upon in a community or area of knowledge. For instance, when we read the news "João murdered his wife by shooting her to death after an argument on Solon Pinheiro Street", we are able to refute an assertion that the type of weapon used in the crime was a "cold weapon" because we, users of natural language, know the conditions in which the concepts "to shoot" and "to murder" can be used. Another motivating example is illustrated in Fig. 1, where the piece of knowledge "Computer is used to watch movies" is required to generate the best answer to the dialog.

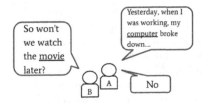

- Computer is used to work ("Computador é usado para trabalhar", in Portuguese)

- Computer is used to watch movies ("Computador é usado para assistir filmes", in Portuguese)

Fig. 1. Dialogue examples and common-sense representation.

Despite the richness and vastness of the common-sense knowledge bases, we argue that common-sense knowledge has to be integrated into the target applications (Text Classification, Dialogue systems, Information Extraction systems, etc.) more effectively. The amount of common sense relations (triples (arg1;semantic relation;arg2)) is huge, and they are spread out in networks, making it difficult to choose which pieces of knowledge are, in fact, relevant. In this work, our goal is learning which set of common-sense relations best fits the target application by developing an external memory module, based on Deep Learning techniques, rather than forcing the system to encode it (the common-sense relations) in model parameters as in traditional methods.

In order to consider this common-sense knowledge in target applications, we propose a deep learning model of common-sense knowledge in Portuguese language, which can be easily coupled in NLU systems in order to leverage their performance. More specifically, the model is composed by a neural network LSTM (Long Short Term Memory) that receives a text from the target application, for example, an user message in a dialog, a response to a user tweet, a news text; and selects and learns what is the best set of common sense relations to return to the target application, which should be considered in the target learning model or system. We implemented the common sense learning module in two target applications - a Stance Classification system and an End-to-End Dialogue system. In both cases, incorporating the deep learning model improved the results.

2   Background Knowledge

2.1   World Knowledge in NLU Systems

In [11] was developed a general-theme Chatbot that uses common-sense knowledge as external information. They used a Tri-LSTM encoder with a new LSTM layer to process the common-sense knowledge. The dataset used was from Twitter and composed of 1.4M dialogue pairs. They used the ConceptNet [10] as common sense database. In the experimental evaluation, $N = 10$ responses were passed to the system, where one answer was positive and the other negative. The result achieved for Recall@1 was 77.5%. In [9] the authors proposed to improve the performance of the keyphrase extraction task by expanding training data using not-in-text terms obtained through an inference process using common-sense knowledge bases. The authors argue that even words that are not present in the text can be related to the text and possibly chosen as keyphrases. The achieved results show performance improvement for the task of keyphrases extraction by 5% on average.

2.2   Common Sense Knowledge Bases

Some existing Common Sense Knowledge bases are ConceptNet [10] and InferenceNet [8]. These bases provide world knowledge to Artificial Intelligence applications. InferenceNet [8] is a knowledge base that provides semantic-inferentialism knowledge for the Portuguese language, with 186.047 concepts related through 842,392 relationships in the format type rel(c1, c2). The ConceptNet [10] is a Knowledge graph that represents relations between words/phrases with assertions, for example, "a dog has a tail" and can be represented as (dog, HasA, tail). The ConceptNet contains 21 million edges and over 8 million nodes. There are 83 languages that contain at least 10,000 nodes. The vocabulary size for the Portuguese is 473,709.

3   A Deep Learning Model of Common Sense Knowledge

In this paper, we propose a deep learning model that assists the use of common-sense knowledge in NLU tasks – DeepCS Model. Common sense knowledge bases are vast and rich, and deciding which knowledge to consider in the application is a challenge. Thus, the proposed model retrieves the set of common-sense knowledge from knowledge bases (CSKB) such as ConceptNet, InferenceNet, and SenticNet and learns the best combination of relations that can contribute to the target app. Figure 2 presents the general architecture of the DeepCS. A target application sends the application's text(s) from the training dataset - INPUT A (a question or a tweet) for the pre-processing CS module and INPUT B (the response or a tweet reply) for DeepCS Module - and receives a word vector with the best common-sense sentence. Figure 2 presents a general RNN architecture that uses common-sense knowledge as extra information. In this architecture, INPUT_A represents the target text, and INPUT_B represents the text to be sorted. Both Inputs are from the dataset available for training. INPUT_C represents X common sense sentences related to INPUT_A. As shown in Fig. 2, they were applied to pre-trained Word Embeddings, such as GloVe Embeddings [7]. That is, each word found in the entries was replaced by a numeric vector that represented it. INPUT_A and B are processed by a neural network architecture generating the representations. Then input is multiplied by a matrix W learned by the neural network and with the result is applied a hadamard product with INPUT_B, as shown in Eq. 1. The result had1 will be used in the future with the knowledge of common sense returned from DeepCS.

$$f(input_a, input_b) = (input_a * W) \circ input_b \tag{1}$$

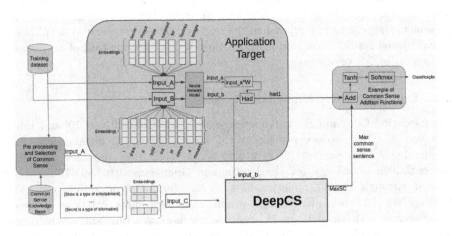

Fig. 2. General architecture of the Deep Learning Model of common-sense Knowledge.

Pre-processing and Selection of the Common Sense knowledge

As shown in Fig. 3, this module receives de INPUT_A and performs tokenization, stop words and numbers removal, word lemmatization, and vocabulary creation V. Then, for each word in the vocabulary V, N common-sense knowledge can be returned from the CSKB. This knowledge composes an H-list of common sense sentences that can be used in the current task. The next step is to relate each example of INPUT_A to a set of sentences listed in H. Thus, X common-sense knowledge can be chosen for each INPUT_A if there is a word in common. For example, "[[The police]] can [[catch a thief]]" could be related to the example of INPUT_A "French police publishes photos of suspect in yesterday's Montrouge shooting. Maybe the same people in Kosher market http://t.co/j5nQIl4Ytu", because in both sentences, the common-sense relation and the INPUT_A, there is the word "police". Finally, these selected common-sense knowledge also goes through a preprocessing step that performs tokenization, stopwords and numbers removal, word lemmatization, and new words are added to vocabulary V.

Fig. 3. Pipeline of the preprocessing and common sense extraction step.

Processing and Learning of Common Sense Knowledge by the Neural Network Model DeepCS

The stage in which common sense knowledge is processed is called DeepCS, a neural network designed to learn which knowledge best assists in the classification task. This network receives as INPUT_C, a number of X common sense knowledge related to INPUT_A, and also receives INPUT_B. DeepCS will return a representation of common sense knowledge called MaxSC with highest relation to INPUT_B. With the result MaxSC given by the DeepCS network it is possible to perform processes that result in the application target, for example, in Fig. 2, the result of the multiplication had1 was added to the knowledge representation MaxSC, then further processes were performed until a classification was returned.

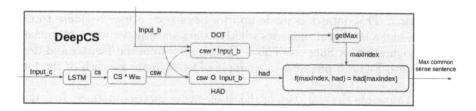

Fig. 4. The DeepCS architecture.

In Fig. 4, the architecture of the DeepCS neural network model is presented in detail. The model receives common-sense sentences that are processed by an LSTM, resulting in the output cs. Then, cs is multiplied by a matrix W, where the values are learned by the network, generating the output csw. In addition to common-sense Knowledge relations, the module also receives the INPUT_B that corresponds to the text to be sorted. The csw and INPUT_B are multiplied, as shown in Eq. 2.

$$f(Input_b, csw) = csw * Input_b \qquad (2)$$

From the result of multiplication 2 is extracted the highest value index, called $maxIndex$. Next, a Hadamard product [5] with csw and INPUT_B information is presented, as shown in Eq. 3, generating the had result.

$$f(csw, Input_b) = csw \circ Input_b \qquad (3)$$

Finally, the greatest common sense relationship is returned by value in the $maxIndex$ position, as shown in Eq. 4. This result is returned by the DeepCS model as $MaxSC$.

$$f(maxIndex, had) = had[maxIndex] \qquad (4)$$

The DeepCS module is decoupled of the target application and can be reused in several natural language processing tasks, improving the representation and the common-sense learning.

4   Experimental Evaluation

4.1   Target Application A - Stance Classification

With the ease of acquiring information over the Internet, it is becoming increasingly important to identify which news is true in order to avoid the spread of rumors. The Stance Classification task is a subtask in the Rumors verification task and consists of classifying a user response in relation to a target post (a tweet) as a comment, a denial, a question or a support. It is believed that analyzing the stance of a text in response to a target would help in the detection of a rumor. We use the dataset provided by SemEval-2019 for Stance Classification task 7. This dataset is made up of a news text, a user response to the news text, and a label that indicates whether the user response was a Comment, Negation, Question, or Support. This data was taken from the Twitter and Reddit platforms. Figure 5 presents an example of tweet/reply for each of the four classes.

Table 1 presents the statistics of the Stance Classification dataset. It is possible to notice that there is an imbalance between the classes, where comment represents more than 50% of the dataset for both training and testing. Common sense knowledge used in this experiment was downloaded from ConceptNet [10]. With the vocabulary created from the entries, each word should return at most ConceptNet's three common-sense relationships [10]. This returned 7980 common-sense relationships. For each tweet target given as INPUT_A, five common-sense relations was listed in H. For comparison, two scenarios were tested for the Stance Classification problem. The first scenario describes a neural network model using LSTM that receives only Input A and Input B

Comment

Tweet: Police reports released this morning indicate Mike Brown was a suspect in a "strong-armed" robbery in #Ferguson

Reply: It's a little scary to know they shoot and kill people suspected of crimes in Ferguson. @DIANAZOGA @AntonioFrench

Query

Tweet: UPDATE: 13 people being held hostage in #Sydney shop, Opera House evacuated after suspicious package found: reports http://t.co/n4D3yGjso9

Reply: @FoxNews why are you not airing the situation in Sydney ?

Deny

Tweet: MORE: Police believe three gunmen were involved in shootings in Ottawa this morning and are looking for two shooters. http://t.co/IHV4galEtC

Reply: @CBSNews That's not what they just said at the Press Conference!

Support

Tweet: UPDATE: #CharlieHebdo's editor-in-chief was killed in attack - Magazine's lawyer http://t.co/kLKwMSlo7g

Reply:@SputnikInt May he rest in peace.

Fig. 5. Examples of the stance classification dataset.

as input. This scenario does not use common sense knowledge in its processing. In the first scenario the entries are replaced with 100-dimensional GloVe [7] pre-trained Word Embeddings and processed by an LSTM. The hyperparameters values for the LSTM layer are 128 units, activation Tanh, recurrent dropout = 0.2, dropout = 0.2 and return sequences set to false. So, there is a multiplication between INPUT_A and a matrix W learned by the network. Finally, the inputs are multiplied and passed to a softmax function that returns the model result. For training was used batch size of size 3 and the optimizer used was ADAM. In second scenario, the Deep Learning Common Sense Knowledge (DeepCS) module is applied by adding a new input for common sense knowledge. For each input, five common sense sentences were passed to the module. Common sense knowledge relations are also replaced by pre-trained GloVe 100-word Word Embeddings and like other inputs processed by a 128-unit LSTM layer. This model was trained during 20 size 3 batch size epochs.

Table 1. Statistics of the Stance Classification Dataset.

	Comment	Deny	Query	Support	Total
Train	3519	378	395	925	5217
Test	1181	82	120	102	1485

Table 2. Experiments Results with the use of DeepCS module in Stance Classification application target.

	Recall	Accuracy	F1 score	Comment	Deny	Query	Support
Scenario 1	0.6228	0.6228	0.3581	0.7660	0.1388	0.3406	0.1867
Scenario 2	0.6484	0.6484	0.3740	0.7883	0.1678	0.3870	0.1526

A Table 2 presents the results obtained in scenarios 1 and 2. Analyzing the values, it is possible to notice that scenario 2 (that use the DeepCS module) obtained better results compared to scenario 1, with an increase of 0.02 in the F1-Score metric. All classes presented the best results in scenario 2, except class Support. We argue that this class is very similar to the class Comment.

4.2 Target Application A – Chatbot in the Portuguese Language

Previous experiments, presented in [4], showed improved performance in the task of classifying the best answer in a Chatbot in the Portuguese Language, when applied DeepCS module in this target application. This application consists of a neural network that, given a question, aims to choose the best answer from a set of possible answers. This kind of Chatbot is known as retrieval based. It was used as dialogues corpus of a Chatbot in operation of the Clinic SIM, clinic that operates in the Brazilian Northeast. The corpus was organized with user input, system response, dialog classification, and common sense knowledge statements related to user input. In order to train the network, it is necessary a coherent data set, where system response makes sense with user input, and incoherent, where system response makes no sense with user input. For the training set, 12544 examples were used, divided equally between coherent and incoherent. For the 3136 test set examples, half coherent and half inconsistent, were used. Table 3 presents the results for scenarios 1 and 2 of the dialog system. Scenario 1 corresponds to tests made without the use of common sense knowledge. In Scenario 2, common sense knowledge was added to the neural network model. The results show improvement in all the metrics used in these tests being more noticeable for the Recall metric.

Table 3. Experiments Results with the use of DeepCS module in Chatbot application target.

Coherent		
	Scenario 1	Scenario 2
Recall	0.5389	0.6734
Precision	0.5682	0.5708
F1 measure	0.5644	0.5802

5   Conclusion

This paper proposes a neural network model called DeepCS for the use of common sense knowledge in various tasks in Natural Language Processing, called application targets. Despite the richness and vastness of the common-sense knowledge bases, we argue that common-sense knowledge has to be integrated into the target applications (Text Classification, Dialogue systems, Information Extraction systems, etc.) more effectively. The DeepCS module of common-sense knowledge in Portuguese language, which can be easily coupled in NLU systems in order to leverage their performance. More specifically, the model is composed by a neural network LSTM (Long Short Term Memory) that receives a text from the target application, for example, an user message in a dialog, a response to a user tweet, a news text; and selects and learns what is the best set of common sense relations to return to the target application, which should be considered in the target learning model or system Specifically for this research, the model was used for the Stance Classification task, a rumor detection subtask. Stance classification aims to classify a user reply to a social news post as comment, question, denial or support. Two scenarios were created for comparison. The first scenario did not use the DeepCS model, receiving only the tweet news post and the reply message. Already in the second scenario, it receives as input new source post, reply message and common sense knowledge. The use of the DeepCS model as a source of extra information showed a slight performance improvement in the metric F1-score. The DeepCS model was used in a second application target – a Chatbot in the Portuguese Language. The result in Scenario 2 was better 2%. As future work, it would be interesting to analyze the performance of the DeepCS model in other tasks, for example, tasks that use a single input. Another important point for evolution is to test different parameters and architectures for the neural network model. Regarding common-sense knowledge, using different common sense bases, such as InferenceNet [8], and varying the parameters in the preprocessing of knowledge, are analyzes that can influence the performance of the DeepCS module.

References

1. Cambria, E., Hussain, A.: Sentic Computing: A Common-Sense-Based Framework for Concept-Level Sentiment Analysis. SC, vol. 1. Springer, Cham (2015). https://doi.org/10.1007/978-3-319-23654-4
2. Cambria, E., Hussain, A., Havasi, C., Eckl, C.: Common sense computing: from the society of mind to digital intuition and beyond. In: Fierrez, J., Ortega-Garcia, J., Esposito, A., Drygajlo, A., Faundez-Zanuy, M. (eds.) BioID 2009. LNCS, vol. 5707, pp. 252–259. Springer, Heidelberg (2009). https://doi.org/10.1007/978-3-642-04391-8_33
3. Cambria, E., Poria, S., Hazarika, D., Kwok, K.: Senticnet 5: discovering conceptual primitives for sentiment analysis by means of context embeddings. In: Thirty-Second AAAI Conference on Artificial Intelligence (2018)

4. Carvalho, C., Pinheiro, V., Freire, L.: Um modelo para sistema de diálogo fim-a-fim usando conhecimento de senso comum. In: XII Symposium in Information and Human Language Technology and Collocates Events (2019)
5. Horn, R.A.: The hadamard product. In: Proceedings of Symposia in Applied Mathematics, vol. 40, pp. 87–169 (1990)
6. Minsky, M.: The Society of Mind. Simon & Schuster, New York (1985, 1986)
7. Pennington, J., Socher, R., Manning, C.: Glove: global vectors for word representation. In: Proceedings of the 2014 Conference on Empirical Methods in Natural Language Processing (EMNLP), pp. 1532–1543 (2014)
8. Pinheiro, V., Pequeno, T., Furtado, V., Franco, W.: InferenceNet.Br: expression of inferentialist semantic content of the portuguese language. In: Pardo, T.A.S., Branco, A., Klautau, A., Vieira, R., de Lima, V.L.S. (eds.) PROPOR 2010. LNCS (LNAI), vol. 6001, pp. 90–99. Springer, Heidelberg (2010). https://doi.org/10.1007/978-3-642-12320-7_12
9. Silveira, R., Furtado, V., Pinheiro, V.: Learning keyphrases from corpora and knowledge models. Nat. Lang. Eng. 1–26 (2019)
10. Speer, R., Chin, J., Havasi, C.: Conceptnet 5.5: an open multilingual graph of general knowledge. In: Thirty-First AAAI Conference on Artificial Intelligence (2017)
11. Young, T., Cambria, E., Chaturvedi, I., Zhou, H., Biswas, S., Huang, M.: Augmenting end-to-end dialogue systems with commonsense knowledge. In: Thirty-Second AAAI Conference on Artificial Intelligence (2018)

Linguistic Analysis Model for Monitoring User Reaction on Satirical News for Brazilian Portuguese

Gabriela Wick-Pedro[1](✉) , Roney L. S. Santos[2], Oto A. Vale[1] ,
Thiago A. S. Pardo[2] , Kalina Bontcheva[3] , and Carolina Scarton[3]

[1] Federal University of São Carlos, São Carlos, Brazil
gwpedro@estudante.ufscar.br, otovale@ufscar.br
[2] University of São Paulo, São Carlos, Brazil
roneysantos@usp.br, taspardo@icmc.usp.br
[3] The University of Sheffield, Sheffield, UK
{k.bontcheva,c.scarton}@sheffield.ac.uk

Abstract. The presence of misleading content on the web and messaging applications has proven to be a major contemporary problem. This context has generated some initiatives in Linguistics and Computation to investigate not only the informative content but also the media in which this mis/disinformation circulates. This paper describes one initiative, in particular, with satire. We present a linguistic analysis based on Brazilian Portuguese satirical news, seeking to understand how a user receives and shares this type of information and which are the main linguistic characteristics of these comments. We note that, while many users understand satirical content, many use the virtual/social environment to express a general comment about the news subject or even to make a toxic comment about a public person. Through this work, we intend to collaborate with the detection of misleading content and understand the behaviour of the user of social media, avoiding the improper sharing of this kind of news.

Keywords: Satire News · User generated content · Deception

1 Introduction

Recently, the media has undergone some changes. The reader began to consume news not only in print but also in virtual form. Social media has facilitated the dissemination of news from a variety of sources and can be shared from one person to another without editorial oversight [1]. This new mode of information dissemination allows a wider reach of different types of users, which facilitates the reproduction of mistaken or misleading news.

We prefer not to adopt the term "fake news" because we believe that some of the content circulating on networks is not fake but written out of context or misinterpreted. Under these conditions, according to Wardle [7], the information

© Springer Nature Switzerland AG 2020
P. Quaresma et al. (Eds.): PROPOR 2020, LNAI 12037, pp. 313–320, 2020.
https://doi.org/10.1007/978-3-030-41505-1_30

may have varied interpretations and will depend on who creates and shares it, as well as the judgment given by the reader to the content.

Considering the users' interpretation, we note the need to study the impact of satirical news on social media. Satirical news are usually composed of complex linguistic mechanisms such as irony and humour. Moreover, these news may intentionally create a false belief in readers' minds [3], since satirical content is highly context-dependent. If a reader does not understand the joke in the text or is inattentive, a misinterpretation can occur, where (s)he understands it as true news and not a joke. These falsehoods are intentionally used and ask to be unveiled. However, as each reader has different world knowledge, some relationships between true and false information may be not realised and misinformation can be disseminated.

Studies related to information distortion [4,6,9] consider the concept of satirical news within the deceptive content typology. According to Rubin et al. [4], there are three traditional types of misleading content: (i) fabricated news: usually produced by what is called the brown press or tabloids; (ii) rumours: news that are disguised to deceive the public and may be carelessly spread by traditional news agencies; and (iii) satirical news: similar to real news, but are created for humour. In this work, satire is understood as a subtle and fun way to critique something of society, appearing in different media such as cartoons, television shows and news [5].

Wardle and Derakhshan [8] state that "we need to examine how wrong information is being consumed, interpreted and acted on." Thus, we hypothesised that there are linguistic marks that may characterise possible comments in which the user did not understand the satire of the news. Therefore, this paper aims to perform an analysis for Brazilian Portuguese about how satirical news are understood and shared by social media users. The analysis was based on data automatically extracted from the Twitter[1] page of Sensacionalista[2], a Brazilian satiric news website that plays with various topics of Brazilian daily news.

To the best of our knowledge, this is the first work to focus on monitoring user-generated content for understanding, reacting, and disseminating satirical news. Through this study, besides identifying possible satirical news that were mistakenly shared as true, it might be possible to identify bot use in tweets, toxic content and hate speech.

2   Data

The choice of Twitter as a data source is because it allows the extraction of tweets in real-time through APIs. This work is based on a collection of tweets collected using the GATE Cloud Twitter Collector[3], a tool that allows the quick and easy extraction of tweets from a specific page, geographic location or by searching for certain keywords.

[1] https://twitter.com.
[2] https://www.sensacionalista.com.br.
[3] https://cloud.gate.ac.uk.

About 36,000 tweets related to the Sensacionalista's Twitter[4] page were collected between August and September 2019. Much of the news is mainly about Brazilian political content. Searching and analysing subjectivity in a text is a long task and requires attention of the researchers. As a result, we chose to focus on only a portion of the data, totaling approximately 18,000 tweets. These tweets were classified into four types:

- **Comments and replies:** as well as sharing, the user makes a comment and/or gives an opinion about the news;
- **Retweets:** the user just shares the news;
- **Links:** users use images or videos to add comments; and,
- **Sensacionalista** posts.

The most representative tweets are Retweets (with 90.85% of user posts), followed by Comments and Replies (with 8.44%), which will be analysed in this paper.

3   Method and Analysis

In this section, we present our method for analysis and description of the extracted data. First, in order to understand users' behavior in relation to satirical news, we have carefully read the comments, separating them into categories related to user intent. We understand as intent what the user intends to express in his/her comment, i.e., questioning the subject of the news or making a positive or negative comment about an event or a person. We also sought to observe whether or not the user understood the satire present in the news. Then, after the analysis, we studied some linguistic characteristics present in the comments.

3.1   Categories

When we analyse the tweets selected as *Comments and Replies*, we see that users maintain a pattern when expressing themselves on satire in the published news. Some use the social network to question a real issue present in satirical news. Others prefer to make a positive or negative comment about a subject or present person that appears in the news. Besides, some users may understand satire and other inattentive users may overlook the humor in the text. Thus, these extracted comments were divided into five categories:

Category 1 (C1): The user will generally give his or her opinion on the content of the news or on matters related to the posted news.

(1) *O curioso é que o pão francês na verdade não é francês.*
     (It is interesting that the French bread is not really French.)

---

[4] https://twitter.com/sensacionalista

Category 2 (C2): Comments in which satire is understood by the user.

(2) *Kkkkkkk essa foi muito engraçada.*
    (Kkkkkkkk that was very funny.)

Category 3 (C3): Toxic comments about news content.

(3) *Verme não produz tanta fumaça.*
    (Worm does not produce so much smoke.)

Category 4 (C4): Positive comments on news content.

(4) *Sérgio Moro é sensacional, incomodou geral.*
    (Sérgio Moro is sensational, bothered overall)

Category 5 (C5): Doubtful comments. In this category a comment can be understood as ironic, but there is also doubt about the user's understanding of satire.

(5) *Isso aí. Vamos arrumar o Brasil. Um desafio!!!*
    (That's right. Let's fix Brazil. A challenge!!!)

Table 1 presents some characteristics of the defined categories: number of tokens, number of tweets in each category and their frequency, respectively. It is worth pointing out that, from the 1,548 comments originally classified as Comments and Replies, 138 tweets that contained only a quote from another user or sequences of letters that carried no meaning were discarded from the analysis.

Table 1. Classification of the collected tweets.

Categories	Qtd. Tweets	Tokens	Frequency (%)
Category 1	683	17.540	48.43%
Category 2	432	4.052	30.63%
Category 3	202	6.329	14.32%
Category 4	10	686	0.12%
Category 5	83	1.931	5.88%

3.2 Linguistic Features

After categorising the comments, we analysed the tweets, considering some linguistic aspects of each category, such as use of hashtags, emoticons, laughter, adjectives and punctuation. To search for these characteristics, Unitex[5] was used, a computational linguistic program that allows the manipulation of large corpora in several languages.

---

[5] https://unitexgramlab.org.

4   Results and Discussion

This section presents the results obtained through a linguistic analysis of the categories found in tweets. Thus, we first divide the amount of language characteristics of a category by the amount of tokens for that category, as shown in Fig. 1. Next, we divide the amount of language characteristics of each category by the total quantity (of all categories) tokens, as shown in Fig. 2.

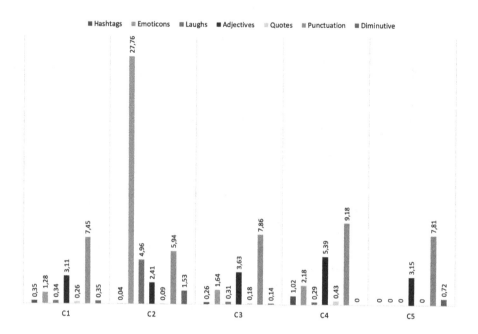

Fig. 1. Frequency of linguistics features in the categories.

C1 is the category with the highest linguistic markup in relation of the total amount of tokens in the analysed data. In other words, hashtags, adjectives, quotes and punctuation characteristics are more frequent in C1. As predicted, emoticons and laughter are more common in C1. Moreover, considering the frequency of linguistic characteristics and the number of tokens in their category, it is observed that the use of adjectives and punctuation in C4 is significant.

Another important point for the analysis of users' reactions to satirical news is the use of adjectives, as, regardless of category, they are necessary for directing opinion (i.e., positive or negative). Thus, greater attention was given to this class. Table 2 shows the total use of adjectives in the analysed data. Despite a higher frequency for negative adjectives, there is a certain balance between positive and neutral adjectives.

The classification of these adjectives took place semi-automatically. Firstly, we used the LIWC dictionary for Portuguese [2] to classify the adjectives that are

318   G. Wick-Pedro et al.

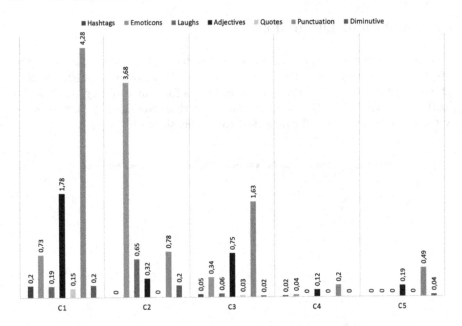

Fig. 2. Frequency total of linguistic features in the categories.

Table 2. Main characteristics of the defined categories.

Adjectives	Qtd. tokens	Frequency%
Positives	102	26.91%
Negative	165	43.53%
Neutral	112	29.55%

in its dictionary. For each adjective, we searched if one of the LIWC classifications had the index '126' or '127', which means 'positive' or 'negative' emotions. Then, the polarity was assigned to the adjective as long as one of the indexes appeared in the dictionary. If the adjective was not in LIWC dictionary in its argument form (for instance, *cômico* – comic), we made a change in the algorithm by getting the stem form of the adjective, for example, *cômic**, which was the form present in LIWC dictionary. After that, if the adjective was still not found, then it was manually classified. The Algorithm 1 shows the pseudocode of this procedure.

Table 3 presents the use of positive, negative and neutral adjectives. As expected, positive adjectives are more frequent in C4 and negative adjectives in C3. It is also observed that there is polarity stability between the adjectives in C5.

Algorithm 1. Adjective polarity assignment by LIWC

Require: LIWC
1: **procedure** ADJECTIVE_POLARITY(*adjective*)
2:     **if** *adjective* or *adjective_stem* is present in LIWC **then**
3:         **if** list of numbers associated to the adjective category includes '126' **then**
4:             *adjective_polarity* ← 'positive'
5:         **else if** the list includes '127' **then**
6:             *adjective_polarity* ← 'negative'
7:         **end if**
8:     **end if**
9:     **if** *adjective* is not present in LIWC **then**
10:         *adjective_stem* ← GET_STEM(*adjective*)
11:         back to 2
12:     **end if**
13:     **if** *adjective_stem* is not present in LIWC **then**
14:         **return** error: manually analyze and label the adjective
15:     **end if**
16: **end procedure**

Table 3. Adjective polarity arrangement in the analysed categories.

Categories	Positive	Negative	Neutral
Category 1	25.84%	37.28%	36.86%
Category 2	55.00%	27.50%	17.50%
Category 3	23.75%	56.25%	20.00%
Category 4	73.91%	21.73%	04.34%
Category 5	27.77%	38.88%	33.33%

5 Conclusions

We present a linguistic analysis based on data extracted from the Sensacional-ista's Twitter page, seeking to observe their reactions to the satire present in the news. It is possible to state that most users use satirical news to be able to comment not only on the news but on the whole context in which the news is inserted. We also observed that there is a great interaction of users who understand the satirical and humor effect present in the news.

Understanding user intent is a complex job to accomplish. We observed how the analysis of tweets is an exhausting and time-consuming task to perform in a manual way, as it requires extreme attention from the reader for the interpretation of explicit and implicit information in the language structure. If we think about the computational spectrum, there is a variability of the issues addressed by the Sensacionalista due to changes in actual events, which can make it difficult, for example, to train machine learning algorithms in recognizing the intent and discussed subject.

We also observed that in C5 there are no linguistics characteristics that stand out from the others. Thus, as it is the category of possible comments where satire has not been understood and users may mistakenly share as true news, we can say that the linguistic characteristic of this category is that it is not as linguistically marked as C2, C3 and C4 and not as frequent as C1.

As future work, we intend to increase the analysis for data that have not yet been categorised and classified and seek to identify other linguistic characteristics present in the analysed comments. We do not focus on possible ironic comments because it is a more elaborate language mechanism that needs attention for its comprehension. However, this is a task to be accomplished in the future.

Finally, we hope to contribute to mapping users on social media, especially their reactions to fake content circulating on networks. Also, it was possible to identify that many of the adjectives analysed were not in the LIWC dictionary for Portuguese. Therefore, the identification and manual classification of the polarity of the adjectives used in this research can be inserted in the dictionary in the future.

To the interested reader, more information about this work may be found at OPINANDO project webpage (https://sites.google.com/icmc.usp.br/opinando/).

Acknowledgments. The authors are grateful to CAPES and USP Research Office (PRP 668).

References

1. Allcott, H., Gentzkow, M.: Social media and fake news in the 2016 election. J. Econ. Perspect. **31**(2), 211–236 (2017)
2. Balage Filho, P.P., Pardo, T.A.S., Aluísio, S.M.: An evaluation of the brazilian portuguese LIWC dictionary for sentiment analysis. In: Proceedings of the 9th Brazilian Symposium in Information and Human Language Technology, Fortaleza, Ceara, Brazil, pp. 215–219 (2013)
3. Rubin, V., Conroy, N., Chen, Y., Cornwell, S.: Fake news or truth? using satirical cues to detect potentially misleading news. In: Proceedings of the Second Workshop on Computational Approaches to Deception Detection, pp. 7–17. Association for Computational Linguistics, San Diego (2016)
4. Rubin, V.L., Chen, Y., Conroy, N.J.: Deception detection for news: three types of fakes. In: Proceedings of the 78th ASIS&T Annual Meeting: Information Science with Impact: Research in and for the Community, pp. 1–4. American Society for Information Science, Silver Springs (2015)
5. Singh, R.K.: Humour, irony and satire in literature. Int. J. Engl. Lit. **3**(4), 63–72 (2012)
6. Tandoc Jr., E.C., Lim, Z.W., Ling, R.: Defining "fake news": a typology of scholarly definitions. Digital Journalism **6**(2), 137–153 (2018)
7. Wardle, C.: Fake news. It's complicated. First Draft News 16 (2017)
8. Wardle, C., Derakhshan, H.: Information disorder: toward an interdisciplinary framework for research and policy making. Council of Europe report **27** (2017)
9. Zaryan, S.: Truth and trust: how audiences are making sense of Fake News. Master's degree, Lund University (2017)

Multilinguality

Word Embeddings at Post-Editing

Marcio Lima Inácio[1]([⊠]) [iD] and Helena de Medeiros Caseli[1,2] [iD]

[1] NILC - Interinstitutional Center for Computational Linguistics
Instituto de Ciências Matemáticas e de Computação,
Universidade de São Paulo, São Carlos, SP 13566-590, Brazil
marciolimainacio@usp.br
[2] LALIC - Laboratório de Linguística e Inteligência Computacional
Departamento de Computação, Universidade Federal de São Carlos,
São Carlos, SP 13565-905, Brazil
helenacaseli@ufscar.br

Abstract. After more than 60 years of research in Machine Translation, it has not been possible yet to develop a perfect fully automatic translation system for unlimited purposes. Thus, it is still necessary post-editing to correct possible mistranslations output by the Machine Translation system. Several approaches have been proposed in order to also automate the post-editing task. This work addresses one of the main steps of an automatic post-editing tool: the automatic proposition of word replacements for a Machine Translation output. To do so, we propose a novel method based on bilingual word embeddings. In the experiments present in this paper we show the effectiveness of this approach in two of the most frequent lexical errors: 'not translated word' and 'incorrectly translated word'.

Keywords: Automatic post-editing · APE · Bilingual word embeddings · Machine translation

1 Introduction

Machine Translation (MT) is an important and extensively researched area in the field of Natural Language Processing (NLP), in which the goal is to automatically produce an equivalent sentence (in some target language) from an input sentence (in some source language). Many approaches have been developed to perform this task, such as rule-based MT [1], statistical MT [14] and, most recently, neural MT [3].

Although lots of effort have been applied into developing better MT systems, it is not yet possible to generate a perfect fully automatic translation for unrestricted domains. Regarding the Brazilian Portuguese, one of the languages investigated in this work, this statement has been confirmed by previous works, such as [7] and [17], for rule-based (RBMT) and statistical MT (SMT), respectively.

Caseli [7] presented that the best MT systems for Brazilian Portuguese at that point translated incorrectly more than 50% of the input sentences. Subsequently, in a detailed study regarding MT's error analysis [17], the same was

P. Quaresma et al. (Eds.): PROPOR 2020, LNAI 12037, pp. 323–334, 2020.
https://doi.org/10.1007/978-3-030-41505-1_31

found for a Phrase-based Machine Translation System (PBSMT), for which 67% of the translated sentences in Brazilian Portuguese had one or more translation errors.

Concerning the most recent MT approach, the Neural Machine Translation (NMT), Popović [23] compared the output between a PBSMT system and a NMT system, for English, German and Serbian. The author affirms that, although the NMT output seemed more fluent in the target language, it still contains errors. It has also been described that the output of the NMT system degrades as the length of the input sentence grows. Moreover, Popović [23] also states that NMT models have difficulty in translating prepositions and ambiguous words.

As the first error analysis of a NMT system for Brazilian Portuguese, we followed the error typology and annotation guidelines developed by Martins and Caseli [17] and analysed 400 sentences automatically translated by a NMT system from English to Brazilian Portuguese.[1] The results of this MT error annotation process are presented in Table 1.

As it is possible to observe, the Lexical category is the most frequent one (72.71% in test-a and 66.37% in test-b), particularly the 'absent word' (29.79% in test-a and 31.21% in test-b), 'incorrectly translated word' (18.27% in test-a and 20.61% in test-b) and 'not translated word' (12.89% in test-a and 9.70% in test-b) subcategories.

Many methods have been proposed to correct automatically the output of MT systems in a process named Automatic Post Editing (APE) [4,15,17]. Our work performs this task by employing bilingual word embeddings to correct two of the most frequent lexical errors: 'not translated word' (*notTrWord*) and 'incorrectly translated word' (*incTrWord*) errors.

The rest of the paper is organised as follows: Sect. 2 presents an overview of APE methods. Section 3 focuses on the definition of Bilingual Word Embeddings followed by their usage on our approach for APE in Sect. 4. Finally our results and conclusions are presented in Sects. 5 and 6, respectively.

2   Related Work

There are different approaches to solve the APE problem. In the rule-based one, rules are used by the APE system to transform the incorrect MT output into a post-edited sentence in the target language. These rules can be handwritten by human specialists [16] or automatically learned from the source sentence, the target (reference) sentence and the output of the MT system [18].

One example of rule-based APE is [9], which focuses on extracting rules automatically, through TBL (Transformation-Based Learning), to correct exclusively lexical errors produced by a RBMT system. The author worked with texts

---

[1] The baseline NMT system was trained using the OpenNMT [13] tool and the FAPESP corpus [2]. The test corpus is composed of 300 sentences from FAPESP's test-a and 100 sentences from FAPESP's test-b, which were manually annotated using the BLAST [26].

Table 1. Manual NMT's error analysis – amount (#) and percentage (%) of MT errors by category in the output of the baseline NMT model when translating from English to Brazilian Portuguese

Error category	Error subcategory	test-a		test-b	
		#	%	#	%
Syntactic errors	Number agreement	52	6.51	19	5.76
	Gender agreement	56	7.01	16	4.85
	Verbal inflection	0	0.00	23	6.97
	PoS	3	0.38	4	1.21
	TOTAL	**111**	**13.90**	**62**	**18.79**
Lexical errors	Extra word	94	11.76	16	4.85
	Absent word	238	29.79	103	31.21
	Not translated word	103	12.89	32	9.70
	Incorrectly translated word	146	18.27	68	20.61
	TOTAL	**581**	**72.71**	**219**	**66.37**
N-gram	Absent n-gram	22	2.75	5	1.52
	Not translated n-gram	3	0.38	1	0.30
	Incorrectly translated n-gram	64	8.01	35	10.61
	TOTAL	**89**	**11.14**	**41**	**12.43**
Reordering	Order	17	2.13	8	2.42
	TOTAL	**17**	**2.13**	**8**	**2.42**
TOTAL		**798**	**100**	**330**	**100**

translated from English to Danish and obtained an improvement of 4% in BLEU score [22] (from 59.5 to 63.5).

Specifically for the Portuguese language, Martins [18] also uses TBL to extract post-editing rules in order to correct the output of a SMT system. These rules were employed in the correction of all types of errors presented in Table 1, except 'Not Translated Word' and 'Incorrectly Translated Word'. It is important to notice that these are exactly the errors that are being addressed in this paper.

Another approach applied for APE is based on SMT techniques [15,25]. In this case, the most common strategy is to take the output of the MT system (as the source) and the reference sentence (as the target), and train a SMT system to perform a monolingual translation from the incorrect version of a sentence (the MT's output) to its correct version (the reference sentence).

As an example, Lagarda et al. [15] applied statistical APE of RBMT outputs (from English to Spanish) in two corpora: Parliament (consisting of parliament speeches) and Protocol (consisting of medical protocols). The authors obtained an improvement of 19.3% (from 29.1 BLEU score to 48.4) for the Parliament corpus and 4.1% improvement for the Protocol corpus (from 29.5 to 33.6 BLEU score).

Similar to the statistical method, neural models have also been recently applied to APE [12,21], emulating a monolingual translation process in which the input (source) sentence is the automatically translated and the output (target) sentence is its correct version.

More recently, a novel dual-attention model has been investigated by Junczys-Dowmunt and Grundkiewicz [12] for neural post-editing of texts translated from English into German. This neural model has two encoders that enable the decoder to take into account both the output of the MT system and the original sentence in the source language. This approach has improved the BLEU score in 2.5% (from 66.9 to 69.4).

3   Bilingual Word Embeddings

Word embeddings are being extensively applied in NLP applications. They are numerical vectors used to represent words (sentences, characters, etc.) which relies on the linguistic distributional hypothesis [10], which states that the meaning of a word is given by the record of co-occurrences patterns of that word in a corpus. Therefore the semantic similarities of two or more words can be measured in terms of geometric distances – usually the cosine distance – between the vectors that represent each one. For instance, the English words *car* and *automobile* can co-occur with words like *street*, *petrol* and *driver*, consequently the vectors of both words tend to be near each other, indicating that these words carry some semantic similarity.

There are also works which explore the implementation of multilingual embeddings, which can represent the meaning and the relationship between words in one or more languages [5,8].

In this work we investigate the applicability of bilingual word embeddings in automatic post-editing of automatically translated sentences. The correlation between word embeddings and the meaning of words can be explored in APE systems, due to the fact that the same meaning must be retained between the source and the target sentences. To illustrate the power of these bilingual word embeddings, Table 2 shows the five words most similar (close) to the English word *science* in the bilingual space trained for the experiments reported in this paper.[2]

4   Proposed Approach

The APE approach proposed in this paper is presented in Fig. 1. Following the model of [18], the post-editing process consists of three main steps: (1) error identification, (2) generation of suggestions for correction and (3) correction. In this way, given an automatically translated sentence, the system is able to

---

[2] The bilingual space used in our experiments was trained by MUSE [8] from the Wikipedia corpus and made available by the authors under https://github.com/facebookresearch/MUSE.

Table 2. Five most similar words, in English and in Portuguese, to the English word *science*

English		Portuguese	
sciences	0.7091	*ciência*	0.7876
biology	0.6729	*ciências*	0.6624
humanities	0.6610	*nanociência*	0.6507
physics	0.6509	*astrobiologia*	0.6500
nanoscience	0.6488	*biologia*	0.6100

generate a post-edited sentence. In this paper, we focus only on step 2 (suggestion generation).[3] For now, the step 3 (correction) is implemented as just the replacement of the incorrect word by the suggested one without any adjustment in gender, number or other morphological feature.

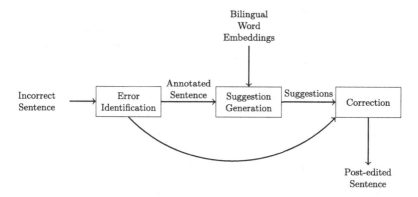

Fig. 1. Fluxogram of the APE system operation

The APE tool implemented following this architecture, the WE@PE tool, is available at https://github.com/LALIC-UFSCar/WE-PE-tool.

4.1   Suggestion Generation at WE@PE

The second step of our APE tool produces suggestions for each error identified by the first step. This module is **the main contribution** of this work.

In the experiments presented in this paper, the bilingual word embeddings were generated using the MUSE tool [8], which creates a bilingual vector space from pre-trained monolingual embeddings. As our monolingual embedding model, in this work we used the same method of [8]: FastText [6]. This

---

[3] We have also implemented step 1 but due to space limitations it will not be presented in this paper. Further information about this step can be found at [11].

method is an extension of the widely used skip-gram model [19] but which also takes into account the morphological information during vector generation.

MUSE creates a bilingual vector space from these pre-trained monolingual embeddings through operations of translation, rotation and uniform scaling. To do so, MUSE trains two neural network models: the discriminator and the mapping. The discriminator model is responsible for the identification of the language of an input vector. On the other hand, the mapping model is in charge of updating the multilingual vector space taking into account both monolingual vector spaces, by applying linear transformations, such that the distribution from both languages approximate to each other.

As a result, given an input source word, some geometric measurement (*e.g.* the cosine similarity measure) can be used to find the most similar source and target words in the generated bilingual space as already illustrated in Table 2.

So, in the approach proposed here for the APE's second step, the automatically annotated sentences (output of the first step) and the bilingual word embeddings are given as input. Then, the APE's suggestion generation module delivers the TOP-5 best suggestions for correction. More specifically, for each English word annotated with *notTrWord* or *incTrWord*, the APE finds the five closest Portuguese embeddings using the cosine similarity measure. The distributional hypothesis guarantees that these Portuguese embeddings have similar or related meanings to the original English word.

5   Experiments and Results

The evaluation was carried out regarding two categories of lexical errors – not translated word (*notTrWord*) and incorrectly translated word (*incTrWord*) – manually identified in 300 sentences from FAPESP's test-a and 100 sentences from FAPESP's test-b (as already mentioned in Sect. 1).

For the purpose of comparison, a baseline has been implemented using a bilingual dictionary generated automatically using the GIZA++ alignment tool [20] on the FAPESP Corpus.[4] This baseline selects the TOP-5 words, regarding the frequency of alignments, in the target language (Portuguese) aligned to the source word (in English). If the source word has been aligned to less than five different words, all the alignments are selected.

In the following sections we describe the results obtained with the intrinsic and the extrinsic evaluations.

5.1   Intrinsic Evaluation

For evaluating the suggestions generated automatically by our approach (WE) and the baseline one (Dict.), we developed an annotation interface[5]. In this interface, each error occurrence is represented as a triple of source (*src*), reference

---

[4] Available at http://www.lalic.dc.ufscar.br/portal/.

[5] Available at: https://github.com/lalic-ufscar/we-pe-tool.

Table 3. Number of error occurrences for *incTrWord* error

Evaluation	Number of occurrences					
Total number of occurrences	test-a		test-b		TOTAL	
	146		68		214	
	WE	Dict.	WE	Dict.	WE	Dict.
Ignored	56	62	23	25	79	87
No suggestion	28	15	5	3	33	18
Effectively evaluated	62	69	40	40	102	109
At least one correct suggestion	37	48	22	27	59	75
At least one partially correct suggestion and no correct one	9	10	7	8	16	18
All suggestions incorrect	16	11	11	5	27	16

(*ref*) and automatically translated (*sys*) sentences, with all aligned words related to that specific error highlighted. Five suggestions for correction are shown in the bottom of this interface (labeled as APE) and for each one the human judge was asked to mark as: correct, partially correct or incorrect.

Correct suggestions are those which fit perfectly on the translated sentence, with no need for further adjustments. Incorrect suggestions, in turn, are the ones for each their lemma do not correspond to any possible translation for the original source word.

Suggestions could also be classified as partially correct when: (i) they have a lemma which is suitable to the meaning of the sentence, still needing some adjustments to be considered correct, or (ii) they resemble the original meaning of the source, even if they do not have the same meaning (e.g., one possible suggestion for the word 'windpipe', which best translation is '*traquéia*', in Portuguese, was '*pescoço*' which is best translated to 'neck', in English).

The detailed results are presented separately for each lexical error category in Tables 3 (*inc-TrWord*) and 4 (*not-TrWord*). There was 214 instances of *inc-TrWord* and 135 of *not-TrWord* considering both test-a and test-b. From these instances, some have been ignored since we consider that they could not be evaluated without taking into account their context (e.g. prepositions and articles). We also ignored cases in which the error has been caused by part of speech mistakes, for instance the word *may*, which can be both the verb ('*poder*', in Portuguese) and the month ('*maio*', in Portuguese).

For other instances, the evaluated approach (WE or Dict.) did not give any suggestion. The absence of suggestions has two main causes: (i) the lack of alignment between the incorrect or not translated word to some word in the source sentence, and (ii) words (*e.g.* proper nouns and abbreviations) which may not be in the vector space (or the dictionary) as they are rare (or did not occur) on the training corpus used to generate the embeddings (or dictionary).

So, for the *incTrWord*, 102 and 109 instances were effectively evaluated regarding WE and Dict., respectively. For the *notTrWord*, 97 and 76 instances

Table 4. Number of error occurrences for *notTrWord* error

Evaluation	Number of occurrences					
Total number of occurrences	test-a		test-b		TOTAL	
	103		32		135	
	WE	Dict.	WE	Dict.	WE	Dict.
Ignored	12	10	0	0	12	10
No suggestion	17	36	7	13	24	49
Effectively evaluated	74	57	25	19	97	76
At least one correct suggestion	43	39	9	8	52	47
At least one partially correct suggestion and no correct one	18	12	11	10	29	22
All suggestions incorrect	13	6	5	1	18	7

were effectively evaluated for WE and Dict., in this order. To allow the comparison of results obtained by our proposed approach (WE) and the baseline one (Dict.) we calculated the precision and recall values as:

$$precision = \frac{\#(partially)correct\_instances}{\#evaluated\_instances} \qquad (1)$$

$$recall = \frac{\#(partially)correct\_instances}{\#existing\_instances} \qquad (2)$$

Table 5 brings the lower and upper bounds for precision and recall for the evaluated approaches (WE and Dict.). The lower bounds were calculated considering only the instances with at least one correct suggestion while the upper bounds also take into consideration the partially correct suggestions.

Table 5. Precision and recall values

	incTrWord		notTrWord	
	WE	Dict	WE	Dict
Precision	57.84–73.53%	68.81–85.32%	53.61–83.50%	61.84–90.79%
Recall	27.57–35.05%	35.05–43.46%	38.52–60.00%	34.81–51.11%

As can be notice from the values in Table 5, the Dict. had a better precision and a better recall in most of the cases, except the recall for the not translated words. This fact show that the Dict. is more precise but WE can bring correct or partially correct suggestions for cases were the Dict. did not found any. This indicates that it can be beneficial to combine both methods to improve results.

5.2   Extrinsic Evaluation

We also evaluated the best (TOP-1) suggestions in the APE scenario. To do so, we calculated the BLEU scores[6] for the original translations (without APE) and for the translations post-edited with the replacement of the incorrect or not translated word by the best suggestion generated by our approach (APE with WE) and by the statistical dictionary (APE with Dict.). If there are no suggestions, the original (wrong) word is kept.

The results obtained by post-editing the sentences can be seen in Table 6.

Table 6. BLEU values for original and post-edited sentences

Model	$incTrWord$		$notTrWord$	
	test-a	test-b	test-a	test-b
Without APE	46.85	35.02	45.51	29.49
APE with WE	47.05	35.09	45.94	29.55
APE with Dict	47.35	35.35	46.27	29.74

These values may substantiate an observation during the previous evaluation that there are cases in which the best (correct) suggestion is not the top 1st. There are also the cases regarding partially correct suggestions, which would need further adjustments (such as number and gender agreement), that are not considered as correct by the BLEU score.

6   Conclusions and Future Work

In this paper we have presented the first experiments using word embeddings to generate possible suggestions for an APE system. The results reported here show that the proposed approach is a promising one since it is able to generate correct suggestions in cases were the statistical dictionary was not.

Ideas for future work include the investigation of sense-specific word embeddings [24] in spite of traditional ones to solve the ambiguity problem (*e.g.* the English word *may* that can be a verb and a month). For the last correction step, we suggest taking the lemma of the best ranked correction suggestion and apply to it the necessary adjustments (verbal inflection, number/gender agreement, etc.) before using it to replace the incorrect word. The implementation of this final step would shift the partially correct instances to the correct class resulting in a positive impact in BLEU scores.

We also acknowledge the restriction of this work, specially for dealing with cases in which the source is aligned to more than one word. Currently, we take

---

[6] The BLEU scores were calculated using the Moses toolkit (https://github.com/moses-smt/mosesdecoder/blob/master/scripts/generic/mteval-v14.pl) taking into account only those sentences annotated with this specific error.

into account only the first word aligned. The method is also strongly dependent to alignments between the incorrect word in the translated sentence and the words in the source sentence.

Better methods for ranking the suggestions can also be investigated, since in some cases the most valuable correction was not in the first position of the TOP-5 list ordered by similarity (cosine distance in the current version).

It is also a research path the extension of the methods developed in this work for other error categories. We suppose that bilingual word embeddings can also be employed, with some rework, to handle 'absent word', 'not translated N-gram' and 'incorrectly translated N-gram' errors.

Acknowledgements. This work has been developed with the support from São Paulo Research Foundation (FAPESP), grants #2016/21317-0 (Undergraduate research grant) and #2016/13002-0 (MMeaning Project).

References

1. Armentano-Oller, C., et al.: Open-source Portuguese–Spanish machine translation. In: Vieira, R., Quaresma, P., Nunes, M.G.V., Mamede, N.J., Oliveira, C., Dias, M.C. (eds.) PROPOR 2006. LNCS (LNAI), vol. 3960, pp. 50–59. Springer, Heidelberg (2006). https://doi.org/10.1007/11751984_6
2. Aziz, W., Specia, L.: Fully automatic compilation of a Portuguese-English parallel corpus for statistical machine translation. In: STIL 2011, Cuiabá, MT, Outubro 2011
3. Bahdanau, D., Cho, K., Bengio, Y.: Neural machine translation by jointly learning to align and translate. In: Bengio, Y., LeCun, Y. (eds.) 3rd International Conference on Learning Representations, ICLR 2015, San Diego, CA, USA, 7–9 May 2015, Conference Track Proceedings (2015). http://arxiv.org/abs/1409.0473
4. Béchara, H., Rubino, R., He, Y., Ma, Y., Genabith, J.: An evaluation of statistical post-editing systems applied to RBMT and SMT systems. In: Proceedings of COLING 2012, pp. 215–230. The COLING 2012 Organizing Committee (2012). http://aclweb.org/anthology/C12-1014
5. Bérard, A., Servan, C., Pietquin, O., Besacier, L.: MultiVec: a multilingual and multilevel representation learning toolkit for NLP. In: The 10th Edition of the Language Resources and Evaluation Conference (LREC 2016), May 2016
6. Bojanowski, P., Grave, E., Joulin, A., Mikolov, T.: Enriching word vectors with subword information. Trans. Assoc. Comput. Linguist. **5**, 135–146 (2017). https://doi.org/10.1162/tacl_a_00051. https://www.aclweb.org/anthology/Q17-1010
7. Caseli, H.M.: Indução de léxicos bilíngües e regras para a tradução automática. Ph.D. thesis, ICMC-USP, May 2007
8. Conneau, A., Lample, G., Ranzato, M., Denoyer, L., Jégou, H.: Word translation without parallel data. In: Proceedings of the Sixth International Conference on Learning Representations, May 2018
9. Elming, J.: Transformation-based correction of rule-based MT. In: Proceedings of EAMT, pp. 219–226 (2006)
10. Harris, Z.S.: Distributional structure. Word **10**(2–3), 146–162 (1954)

11. Inácio, M.L.: Pós-edição automática e semanticamente motivada de traduções em português do Brasil. Monografia de Trabalho de Conclusão de Curso de Graduação em Ciência da Computação, UFSCar (Universidade Federal de São Carlos), São Carlos, Brasil (2018). 93 p. http://www.lalic.dc.ufscar.br
12. Junczys-Dowmunt, M., Grundkiewicz, R.: An exploration of neural sequence-to-sequence architectures for automatic post-editing. In: Proceedings of the Eighth International Joint Conference on Natural Language Processing (Volume 1: Long Papers), pp. 120–129. Asian Federation of Natural Language Processing (2017). http://aclweb.org/anthology/I17-1013
13. Klein, G., Kim, Y., Deng, Y., Senellart, J., Rush, A.: OpenNMT: open-source toolkit for neural machine translation. In: Proceedings of ACL 2017, System Demonstrations, pp. 67–72. Association for Computational Linguistics (2017). http://aclweb.org/anthology/P17-4012
14. Koehn, P., et al.: Moses: open source toolkit for statistical machine translation. In: Proceedings of the 45th Annual Meeting of the ACL on Interactive Poster and Demonstration Sessions, ACL 2007, pp. 177–180. Association for Computational Linguistics, Stroudsburg (2007). http://dl.acm.org/citation.cfm?id=1557769.1557821
15. Lagarda, A.L., Alabau, V., Casacuberta, F., Silva, R., Díaz-de Liaño, E.: Statistical post-editing of a rule-based machine translation system. In: Proceedings of Human Language Technologies: The 2009 Annual Conference of the North American Chapter of the Association for Computational Linguistics, Companion Volume: Short Papers, pp. 217–220. Association for Computational Linguistics (2009). http://aclweb.org/anthology/N09-2055
16. Mareček, D., Rosa, R., Galuščáková, P., Bojar, O.: Two-step translation with grammatical post-processing. In: Proceedings of the Sixth Workshop on Statistical Machine Translation, pp. 426–432. Association for Computational Linguistics (2011)
17. Martins, D.B.J., Caseli, H.M.: Automatic machine translation error identification. Mach. Transl. 29(1), 1–24 (2015). https://doi.org/10.1007/s10590-014-9163-y
18. Martins, D.B.J.: Pós-edição automática de textos traduzidos automaticamente de inglês para português do Brasil. Master's thesis, PPG-CC-UFSCar, February 2014. https://repositorio.ufscar.br/bitstream/handle/ufscar/563/5932.pdf
19. Mikolov, T., Sutskever, I., Chen, K., Corrado, G., Dean, J.: Distributed representations of words and phrases and their compositionality. CoRR abs/1310.4546 (2013). http://arxiv.org/abs/1310.4546
20. Och, F.J., Ney, H.: The alignment template approach to statistical machine translation. Comput. Linguist. 30(4), 417–449 (2004). https://doi.org/10.1162/0891201042544884
21. Pal, S., Naskar, S.K., Vela, M., van Genabith, J.: A neural network based approach to automatic post-editing. In: Proceedings of the 54th Annual Meeting of the Association for Computational Linguistics (Volume 2: Short Papers), vol. 2, pp. 281–286 (2016)
22. Papineni, K., Roukos, S., Ward, T., Zhu, W.J.: BLEU: a method for automatic evaluation of machine translation. In: Proceedings of the 40th Annual Meeting on Association for Computational Linguistics, pp. 311–318. Association for Computational Linguistics (2002)
23. Popović, M.: Language-related issues for NMT and PBMT for English–German and English–Serbian. Mach. Transl. (2018). https://doi.org/10.1007/s10590-018-9219-5

24. Silva, J.R., Caseli, H.M.: Generating sense embeddings for syntactic and semantic analogy for Portuguese. In: Proceedings of the XII Symposium in Information and Human Language Technology and Collocates Events, Salvador, BA, 15–18 October 2019, pp. 104–113 (2019). http://comissoes.sbc.org.br/ce-pln/stil2019/proceedings-stil-2019-Final.pdf, (Best Paper)
25. Simard, M., Goutte, C., Isabelle, P.: Statistical phrase-based post-editing. In: Human Language Technologies 2007: The Conference of the North American Chapter of the Association for Computational Linguistics; Proceedings of the Main Conference, pp. 508–515. Association for Computational Linguistics (2007). http://aclweb.org/anthology/N07-1064
26. Stymne, S.: Blast: a tool for error analysis of machine translation output. In: Proceedings of the 49th Annual Meeting of the Association for Computational Linguistics: Human Language Technologies: Systems Demonstrations, pp. 56–61. Association for Computational Linguistics (2011)

Argument Identification in a Language Without Labeled Data

João Rodrigues$^{(\boxtimes)}$ and António Branco

NLX—Natural Language and Speech Group, Department of Informatics Faculdade de Ciências, University of Lisbon, 1749-016 Campo Grande, Lisboa, Portugal
{joao.rodrigues, antonio.branco}@di.fc.ul.pt

Abstract. This paper addresses the issue of how to obtain processing tools for argument identification for the vast majority of the languages that, differently from English, have little to no relevant labeled data.

This issue is addressed by taking an under-resourced language as a case study, namely Portuguese, and by experimenting with three techniques to cope with the scarceness of data: to obtain labelled data by machine translating data sets from another language labelled with respect to argument identification; to transfer to the argument identifier the language knowledge captured in distributional semantic models obtained during the resolution of other tasks for which more data exist; to expand data for argument identification with text augmenting techniques.

The results obtained demonstrate that it is possible to develop argument identification tools for under-resourced languages with a level of performance that is competitive to the ones for languages with relevant language resources.

Keywords: Argument identification · Argument mining · Machine translation · Learning transfer · Data augmentation · Under-resourced languages · Portuguese

1 Introduction

Automatic argument mining may support a number of high-level applications, including argument search, decision making, automated reasoning, or user review analysis, among several others. As a consequence, there has been an increasing interest on the research about argument mining, which is visible in the range of shared tasks that have been addressed in the last editions of the SemEval workshop [10].

The language processing task of argument mining faces a number of challenges, among which a most notorious one is the lack of a widespread consensus about the most appropriate analysis of arguments. Arguments have different components, e.g. premises and claims, may be related under different possible relations, e.g. attack, support, etc., and have different levels of quality, e.g. persuasiveness, convincing, etc. Many different analysis for arguments have been

© Springer Nature Switzerland AG 2020
P. Quaresma et al. (Eds.): PROPOR 2020, LNAI 12037, pp. 335–345, 2020.
https://doi.org/10.1007/978-3-030-41505-1_32

proposed in the literature, with different types of components and relations [31], and with different argumentation schemes and models, i.e. patterns of propositions that form an argument—for which the Walton [33] schemes and Toulmin [32] models are two well known proposals.

There has been nevertheless a reasonable consensus in the literature that the overall task of argument mining can be usefully broken down into a chain of subsidiary sub-tasks that include, for instance, argument identification, component identification, relation extraction and argument quality assessment [31].

As the mainstream techniques to handling argument mining are mostly based on machine learning, another notorious challenge for argument mining concerns the scarcity of data, and in particular of data sets conveniently annotated with the information about the components, quality, etc., of arguments. Language resources with good quality for argument mining are expensive to develop— requiring the manual labor of annotating massive amounts of data —, and while a few currently exist for English, very little is available yet for the vast majority of the other approximately 7,000 languages in the world.

In this paper, we focus on the initial sub-task of automatic argument mining, namely on argument identification, which consists of taking as input a segment of text and returning whether it is an argument or not. We report on the results of applying a number of approaches that may help to address the scarceness of data for argument mining in a language that is less-resourced than English. As a case study of an under-resourced language in this respect, we consider Portuguese [2–4], for which very little data is available yet for argument mining [23].

Concerning the task of argument identification, we pursue here a twofold goal. On the one hand, by resorting to machine translation [16, 24, 27], we report on performing argument identification with state of the art techniques over a data set in Portuguese that results from translating a mainstream data set in English annotated with argument identification.

On the other hand, taking that translated data set as a basis, we report on a number of subsequent experiments with approaches that seek to further mitigate the data scarceness in argument identification. We will report on transfer learning from distributional semantic models, also known as word embeddings, obtained from data sets of Portuguese that are much larger than the data set obtained for argument identification via translation.

We will report also on further experiments to mitigate data scarcity by resorting to a range of data augmenting techniques, from the simpler one of randomly inserting QWERTY characters, to the more complex one of generating segments with the help of Transformer-based models (BERT [7] and GPT-2 [22]).

Experiments and results presented in this paper demonstrate that, having Portuguese as case study, the approaches we propose provide substantive enhancements for argument mining in languages that are under-resourced in terms of data sets relevant for argument identification, allowing to develop argument identifiers whose performance is competitive to the ones for languages with relevant language resources, like English.

2   Related Work

Like the study in [23], our work also addresses an argument mining task in Portuguese and apply techniques to mitigate the lack of annotated resources, including by applying triangulation supported by machine translation [6]. However, while we address the sub-task of argument identification, [23] addressed the sub-task of argumentative relation identification. These authors used a cross-lingual setting between a source data set in English and a target data set in Portuguese, and explored two techniques, a projection and a direct-transfer technique. In the projection technique, the (English) source data set was automatically translated and a machine learning algorithm was trained on the (Portuguese) target data set. In the direct-transfer technique, a machine learning algorithm was trained on the source data and fine-tuned to the target data.

Several publications have reported on experiments that resorted to distributional semantic models aiming at enhancing several language processing tasks, [19,25,26] including argument mining for English. These kind of models have been used as features to predict argument structure [18,21] and argument convincingness [29], or used in the embedding layer of neural networks to identify attack or support argumentative relations [5,15]. The enhancement of machine learning algorithms with different distributional semantic models has been evaluated also on an argument component identification task [9] by comparing two neural network architectures (Convolutional and Long-Short Term Memory) that were tested with three distributional representations, the word2vec [20], the dependency-based embeddings [17] and factuality/certainty-indicating embeddings. To the best of our knowledge, the present paper is the first to report on the argument identification task for Portuguese enhanced with transfer learning from distributional semantic models and with the use of transformer-based language models as generators of augmented data.

3   Experiments

To address our research goals, three main experiments are undertaken.[1] The first one relies on an intermediate translation step. An English annotated data set, created specifically for the argument identification task, is automatically translated into Portuguese. Over these two data sets, a state-of-the-art machine learning algorithm, namely BiLSTM, is applied to the argument identification task. Having the performance scores for the two data sets will permit us to have an insight into how much the noise introduced by the machine translation procedure affects the argument identification task in the target language. In other words, this will permit us to have an insight into how useful is this approach to address argument identification in a language that is under-resourced for this task.

---

[1] The source code to reproduce these experiments are available at https://github.com/nlx-group/argument-identification.

The second experiment explores transfer learning from distributional semantic models for Portuguese to enhance the machine learning model in the argument identification task obtained in the first experiment.

Finally, the third experiment consists of applying a range of different data augmentation techniques, including the generation of data improved by the fine-tuning of a transformer-based language model.

3.1 First Experiment: Machine Translation

The corpus used in the three experiments for Portuguese is obtained from a mainstream data set in English, the UKP Sentential Argument Mining Corpus [30], which is translated into Portuguese by resorting to Google Translate. Examples from this data set are presented in Table 1.

The English data set was created by including texts on eight controversial topics in each one of these domains: news, editorials, blogs, debate forums, and encyclopedia articles. By taking into account the respective topic, each sentence in the corpus was manually annotated as being an argument or a non-argument. This corpus has approximately 25k sentences of which 10k are labeled as arguments and 15k as non-arguments. The definition for argument followed by the annotators was *a span of text expressing evidence or reasoning that can be used to either support or oppose a given topic.*

Table 1. Sample from the data set: the first two sentences are from the UKP corpus; the last two are their Portuguese Google translations.

Sentence	Label
We need a safe, genuinely sustainable, global and green solution to our energy needs, not a dangerous diversion like nuclear power	*argument*
There are many notable authors of books and articles that render scientific findings available in lay language to a wider public	*non-arg*
Precisamos de uma solução segura, genuinamente sustentável, global e verde para nossas necessidades de energia, não de uma diversão perigosa como a energia nuclear	*argument*
Existem muitos autores notáveis de livros e artigos que disponibilizam descobertas científicas em linguagem leiga para um público mais amplo	*non-arg*

For the Portuguese data set, we adopted the same split proportion as in the original (English) data set, that is, 70% of the total instances for training, 10% for development and 20% for testing.

As the machine learning approach to address the argument identification task, we implemented in Tensorflow [1] a Bidirectional Long Short-Term Memory

(BiLSTM) neural network [12,28]. This network used a trainable embedding layer for the input, instantiated with random embeddings using the FastText [14] 1M words as the vocabulary, that was followed by a single BiLSTM layer with 48 units, and was used to tune a model with a hyper-parameters grid search.[2]

When experimented with the English data set, this set up obtained a performance for argument identification in line with the state of the art, namely an F-measure of 0.7220, which compares very competitively with the F-measure of 0.6580 obtained from the state-of-the-art models reported in [30].

A reason to explain this difference is the following. Although both models use the same data set and split proportions for training, development and testing, in [30] the aim was to evaluate cross-topic argumentation mining, cross-testing each of the 8 topics by training in 7 of them and evaluating on the eighth topic. In our work, in turn, we did not aim at a cross-topic approach. We randomize the data set before splitting it, and by training with data also on the same topic a higher F-measure was obtained.

We applied the same machine learning algorithm for the Portuguese data set. The same procedures were repeated, using the same hyper-parameters and a randomized embedding layer with the Portuguese version of FastText 1M words. We obtained an F-measure of 0.7228, which indicates a competitive performance when compared to the English counter-part (0.7220) developed under the same settings but with data sets specifically annotated for this language. We evaluated the same model on 60 manually reviewed sentences from the test set and obtained a delta of 0.0320 in comparison with the machine translated output. This leads us to believe that the resulting data set for Portuguese is suitable for the argument identification task in Portuguese, and thus that (machine) translation may be a good enough option for under-resourced languages in what concerns obtaining labeled data for the development of argument identifiers.

3.2   Second Experiment: Learning Transfer

Aiming at enhancing the performance of the argument identification tool, we sought to transfer knowledge to the respective machine learning classifier from different word embeddings of Portuguese.

We choose to experiment with semantic spaces of different natures, namely from: (a) FastText [14], a distributional semantic space that takes morphological information into account; (b) multilingual word vectors [8], which are jointly learned embeddings from parallel data; and (c) GloVe and word2vec models created with the models from STIL2017 [11]. All the distributional semantic models had the same vector size of 300 units.

---

[2] The best hyper-parameters were: 10 epochs, batch size of 64, sequence length of 30, learning rate of 0.01, dropout of 0.8, 48 LSTM units and a softmax cross-entropy with an Adam optimization. We manually experimented with the grid search values, and used an early stop technique using the best F-measure obtained from the development data set. An 0.7576 F-score was obtained on this data set from the average of 10 runs. Each trial took approximately 10 min in a GeForce RTX 2080 GPU.

Table 2. Second Experiment - Performance of the argument identifier enhanced with learning transfer techniques, measured with Accuracy, F-measure, Precision and Recall.

Model	Accuracy	F-measure	Precision	Recall
Baseline	0.6734	0.7228	0.6872	0.7627
Word embeddings				
Fasttext	**0.7056**	0.7433	0.7252	0.7640
CMU	0.6984	0.7338	0.7239	0.7449
GloVe	0.7038	0.7399	0.7263	0.7553
CBow	0.6984	0.7370	0.7200	0.7579
Contextual word embeddings				
BERT	**0.7588**	0.7580	0.8619	0.6764

We created a different model with each one of these three semantic spaces encoded in the word embedding layer of the neural network. In all three models, this layer was non-trainable, that is the weights for the embeddings were fixed during all the learning phases. Thus, all of the learning parameters resided solely on the parameters found in the BiLSTM layer, obtained from the baseline hyperparameter grid search.

Given the latest transformer-based architectures, such as BERT [7], have been the state of the art in several natural language processing downstream tasks, we also experimented with the transfer of knowledge from a BERT fine-tuned for Portuguese. BERT is a bidirectional encoder that learns from the left and right context for each word in a sentence and is trained on two tasks: a mask language task and a sentence prediction task. While in the previous distributional semantic models, the neural network has an embedding layer encoding the respective semantic space, BERT is itself a neural network with the semantic space encoded through several neural network layers.

We fine-tuned a pre-trained multi-language BERT model resorting to adapters.[3] An adapter [13] re-purposes a neural network model by adding a new neural network layer, typically a top-layer, and while the original neural layers are kept frozen, the new layer is fine-tuned. This approach reduces the number of parameters necessary for retraining a model thus achieving a faster convergence. Here the training and development sets were used for the fine-tuning.

The results obtained are displayed in Table 2. The baseline is the argument identifier obtained in the first experiment, with an accuracy of 0.6734. All the other models surpassed this baseline. The fine-tuned BERT model outperformed

---

[3] We used the *multi_cased_L-12_H-768_A-12* model. The best hyper-parameters found were a maximum sequence length of 128, a learning rate of 2e-4, 8 training epochs, and a batch size of 32. We manually experimented with the grid search values of the maximum sequence length, learning rate and the number of training epochs. Each trial took approximately 25 min using a GeForce RTX 2080 GPU.

all the other models, with an accuracy of 0.7588, more than 8 points higher than the baseline score.[4]

3.3   Third Experiment: Data Augmentation

Seeking to further enhance the performance of the argument identifier, we experimented with data augmentation techniques. To obtain a series of comparable results, we adopted the base BiLSTM classifier (with the hyper-parameters initially tuned) for all experiments, except when BERT was used, which has its own neural architecture and parameters. To keep with the series of experiments, we resorted to the model with word embeddings that led to the best improvement of the BiLSTM performance in the second set of experiments. We resorted to the Fasttext as the base setup for the third set of experiments, and to its accuracy as the baseline performance.

The performance of several models was investigated, that were obtained in several data augmentation exercises. In each of these exercises, the generated data was added individually to the original training data set. We used the same hyper-parameters as in the previous experiments. The labels (argument or non-argument) of the synthetic sentences are made identical to the labels of the respective base sentences.

First, we resorted to data augmentation techniques that involve the handling of characters: (a) for each randomly picked character c in text, concatenate to it a *QWERTY* character, which corresponds to a key of the *QWERTY* layout keyboard that is a neighbor of the key corresponding to character c; (b) for each randomly picked position in text, concatenate a *randomly* picked character; and (c) *delete* characters at random in text.

Second, we used techniques that involve the handling of words. For each word w randomly picked in text: (a) *insert* another word after it; and (b) *replace* it by another word. The new word, to be inserted, is a most semantically similar word to w, where semantic similarity is determined by the smallest cosine of the angles between vectors of words in a distributional semantic space. Three semantic spaces were experimented with, namely Fasttext, GloVe and BERT.

Finally, we resorted to synthetic data where sentences are generated with the help of a language model, namely the GPT-2 model [22]. Each sentence in the original training data is used as the context for GPT-2 to generate three other (synthetic) sentences. GPT-2 is a large transformer-based language model trained on the word prediction task from a 40 GB of web data corpus. It outperforms several other language models on a number of language tasks, thus being a good option to generate text.

Given that the original models of GPT-2 were trained with English corpora, we trained three *355M parameter* models for Portuguese, with three Portuguese corpora from different domains: Wikipedia;[5] CetemPúblico, with articles from

---

[4] It is worth recalling that on pair with the baseline, BERT is the only other model taking advantage of a fine-tuning and hyper-parameter grid-search.

[5] Portuguese Wikipedia data dump of 01/09/2015.

Table 3. Third Experiment - Performance of the argument identifier enhanced with data augmentation techniques, measured with Accuracy, F-measure, Precision and Recall.

Augmentation	Accuracy	F-measure	Precision	Recall
Baseline	0.7056	0.7433	0.7252	0.7640
Character handling				
Insert QWERTY	0.7019	0.7175	0.7619	0.6788
Insert random	**0.7087**	0.7315	0.7541	0.7116
Delete random	0.7025	0.7201	0.7588	0.6858
Word handling				
Insert Fasttext	**0.7169**	0.7491	0.7419	0.7570
Insert GloVe	0.7150	0.7500	0.7366	0.7665
Insert BERT	0.7146	0.7494	0.7361	0.7649
Replace Fasttext	0.7078	0.7328	0.7498	0.7185
Replace GloVe	0.7145	0.7436	0.7473	0.7427
Replace BERT	0.7112	0.7285	0.7678	0.6947
Sentence handling				
Generate Wikipedia	**0.7174**	0.7479	0.7453	0.7513
Generate CetemPúblico	0.7071	0.7390	0.7390	0.7423
Generate Europarl	0.7079	0.7300	0.7567	0.7091

the Público newspaper; and Europarl, with transcriptions of debates from the European Parliament. We used the gpt-2-simple module.[6] Accordingly, the initial data set with 25 k sentences (translated into Portuguese) doubled in size to 50 k sentences with each character or word handling technique for data augmentation experimented with, and quadrupled to 100 k sentences with each sentence handling technique.

The results are presented in Table 3. Every technique experimented with led to improved performance of the argument identifier, except in the cases of the *QWERTY* and *Delete* exercises, yet only with a slight decay with respect to the baseline with an accuracy score of 0.7056. The best solution is obtained with GPT-2 trained with Wikipedia, scoring 0.7174 accuracy.

The gain of over 1 accuracy point seems to indicate that the advantage obtained by having more data only modestly offsets the noise introduced by labeling the generated sentences, as an argument or a non-argument, with the same label of their context sentences.

---

[6] gpt-2-simple was obtained from https://github.com/minimaxir/gpt-2-simple. We used a generation length of 60 units, the top 3 tokens and one sample per sentence. The training of each model and respective data generation took approximately 3 days using a GeForce RTX 2080 GPU.

4   Conclusions

In this paper, we address the issue of how to obtain argument identification tools for the vast majority of the approximately 7,000 languages of the world that, differently from English, have little to no labeled data that permits the training of solutions for this language processing task. We sought to tackle this issue by taking a language that is under-resourced for this task as a case study, namely Portuguese, and by experimenting with three types of techniques to cope with the scarceness of curated data: to obtain (seed) data by machine translating data from other languages labelled with respect to argument identification (i.e. from English); to transfer to the (seed) argument identifier the language knowledge captured in distributional semantic models (word embeddings) obtained with other language processing tasks for which more data exist; to augment the seed data (initially obtained by translation) with techniques that transform it into new versions of them by handling characters, words or sentences.

The results obtained demonstrate that it is possible to obtain argument identification tools for under-resourced languages with a level of performance (0.7228 F-score) that is competitive with the performance of the tools for the languages with relevant resources (0.7220 F-score for English under the same experimental settings), by translating the later and then training a (BiLSTM based) argument identifier on the output, in the target under-resourced language.

They demonstrate also that some performance gains can be obtained, though somewhat modest (over 1 accuracy point), with data augmenting techniques, with sentence handling techniques contributing better than word handling ones, which in turn contribute better than character handling ones.

The results of the experiments undertaken demonstrate also that it is possible to improve the performance of the seed identifier by transferring the language learning captured in distributional semantic models obtained during the training for other language processing tasks that may resort only to unlabelled data. As expected, contextual word embeddings support larger improvements (over 12 accuracy points) than non-contextual word embeddings (over 3 accuracy points) over the 0.6734 accuracy baseline. Concomitantly, these experiments happen also to set the state of the art in 0.7588 accuracy for argument identification in Portuguese.

Acknowledgments. The research reported here was partially supported by PORTU-LAN CLARIN—Research Infrastructure for the Science and Technology of Language, funded by Lisboa 2020, Alentejo 2020 and FCT—Fundação para a Ciência e Tecnologia under the grant PINFRA/22117/2016.

References

1. Abadi, M., et al.: Tensorflow: large-scale machine learning on heterogeneous systems (2015). https://www.tensorflow.org/, software available from tensorflow.org
2. Branco, A.: A língua portuguesa face ao choque tecnológico digital. Revista do Instituto Internacional da Língua Portuguesa **2**, 28–36 (2013)

3. Branco, A.: We are depleting our research subject as we are investigating it: in language technology, more replication and diversity are needed. In: Proceedings of the Eleventh International Conference on Language Resources and Evaluation (LREC 2018) (2018)
4. Branco, A., et al.: The Portuguese Language in the Digital Age. Springer, Heidelberg (2012). https://doi.org/10.1007/978-3-642-29593-5
5. Cocarascu, O., Toni, F.: Identifying attack and support argumentative relations using deep learning. In: Proceedings of the 2017 Conference on Empirical Methods in Natural Language Processing, pp. 1374–1379 (2017)
6. Costa, F., Branco, A.: TimeBankPT: a timeML annotated corpus of Portuguese. In: Proceedings of the International Conference on Language Resources and Evaluation, pp. 3727–3734 (2012)
7. Devlin, J., Chang, M.W., Lee, K., Toutanova, K.: BERT: pre-training of deep bidirectional transformers for language understanding. In: Proceedings of the 2019 Conference of the North American Chapter of the Association for Computational Linguistics: Human Language Technologies, Volume 1 (Long and Short Papers), pp. 4171–4186 (2019)
8. Ferreira, D.C., Martins, A.F., Almeida, M.S.: Jointly learning to embed and predict with multiple languages. In: Proceedings of the 54th Annual Meeting of the Association for Computational Linguistics (Volume 1: Long Papers), pp. 2019–2028 (2016)
9. Guggilla, C., Miller, T., Gurevych, I.: CNN-and LSTM-based claim classification in online user comments. In: Proceedings of COLING 2016, the 26th International Conference on Computational Linguistics: Technical Papers, pp. 2740–2751 (2016)
10. Habernal, I., Wachsmuth, H., Gurevych, I., Stein, B.: SemEval-2018 task 12: the argument reasoning comprehension task. In: Proceedings of the 12th International Workshop on Semantic Evaluation, pp. 763–772 (2018)
11. Hartmann, N., Fonseca, E., Shulby, C., Treviso, M., Silva, J., Aluísio, S.: Portuguese word embeddings: evaluating on word analogies and natural language tasks. In: Proceedings of the 11th Brazilian Symposium in Information and Human Language Technology, pp. 122–131 (2017)
12. Hochreiter, S., Schmidhuber, J.: Long short-term memory. Neural Comput. **9**(8), 1735–1780 (1997)
13. Houlsby, N., et al.: Parameter-efficient transfer learning for NLP. In: International Conference on Machine Learning, pp. 2790–2799 (2019)
14. Joulin, A., Grave, E., Bojanowski, P., Mikolov, T.: Bag of tricks for efficient text classification. In: Proceedings of the 15th Conference of the European Chapter of the Association for Computational Linguistics: Volume 2, Short Papers, pp. 427–431 (2017)
15. Koreeda, Y., Yanase, T., Yanai, K., Sato, M., Niwa, Y.: Neural attention model for classification of sentences that support promoting/suppressing relationship. In: Proceedings of the Third Workshop on Argument Mining (ArgMining2016), pp. 76–81 (2016)
16. Kuang, S., Li, J., Branco, A., Luo, W., Xiong, D.: Attention focusing for neural machine translation by bridging source and target embeddings. In: Proceedings of the 56th Annual Meeting of the Association for Computational Linguistics (Volume 1: Long Papers), pp. 1767–1776 (2018)
17. Levy, O., Goldberg, Y.: Dependency-based word embeddings. In: Proceedings of the 52nd Annual Meeting of the Association for Computational Linguistics, vol. 2, pp. 302–308 (2014)

18. Li, L., Mao, L., Chen, M.: Word embedding and topic modeling enhanced multiple features for content linking and argument/sentiment labeling in online forums. In: Proceedings of the MultiLing 2017 Workshop on Summarization and Summary Evaluation Across Source Types and Genres, pp. 32–36 (2017)

19. Maraev, V., Saedi, C., Rodrigues, J., Branco, A., Silva, J.: Character-level convolutional neural network for paraphrase detection and other experiments. In: Filchenkov, A., Pivovarova, L., Žižka, J. (eds.) AINL 2017. CCIS, vol. 789, pp. 293–304. Springer, Cham (2018). https://doi.org/10.1007/978-3-319-71746-3_23

20. Mikolov, T., Sutskever, I., Chen, K., Corrado, G.S., Dean, J.: Distributed representations of words and phrases and their compositionality. In: Advances in Neural Information Processing Systems, pp. 3111–3119 (2013)

21. Pathak, A., Goyal, P., Bhowmick, P.: A two-phase approach towards identifying argument structure in natural language. In: Proceedings of the 3rd Workshop on Natural Language Processing Techniques for Educational Applications, pp. 11–19 (2016)

22. Radford, A., Wu, J., Child, R., Luan, D., Amodei, D., Sutskever, I.: Language models are unsupervised multitask learners. OpenAI Blog **1**(8), 9 (2019)

23. Rocha, G., Stab, C., Cardoso, H.L., Gurevych, I.: Cross-lingual argumentative relation identification: from English to Portuguese. In: Proceedings of the 5th Workshop on Argument Mining, pp. 144–154 (2018)

24. Rodrigues, J.A., Rendeiro, N., Querido, A., Štajner, S., Branco, A.: Bootstrapping a hybrid MT system to a new language pair. In: Proceedings of the Tenth International Conference on Language Resources and Evaluation (LREC 2016), pp. 2762–2765 (2016)

25. Rodrigues, J.A., Saedi, C., Maraev, V., Silva, J., Branco, A.: Ways of asking and replying in duplicate question detection. In: Proceedings of the 6th Joint Conference on Lexical and Computational Semantics (* SEM 2017), pp. 262–270 (2017)

26. Saedi, C., Rodrigues, J., Silva, J., Maraev, V., et al.: Learning profiles in duplicate question detection. In: IEEE 18th International Conference on Information Reuse and Integration (IEEE IRI 2017), pp. 544–550. IEEE (2017)

27. Santos, R., Silva, J., Branco, A., Xiong, D.: The direct path may not be the best: Portuguese-Chinese neural machine translation. In: Moura Oliveira, P., Novais, P., Reis, L.P. (eds.) EPIA 2019. LNCS (LNAI), vol. 11805, pp. 757–768. Springer, Cham (2019). https://doi.org/10.1007/978-3-030-30244-3_62

28. Schuster, M., Paliwal, K.K.: Bidirectional recurrent neural networks. IEEE Trans. Signal Process. **45**(11), 2673–2681 (1997)

29. Simpson, E., Gurevych, I.: Finding convincing arguments using scalable Bayesian preference learning. Trans. Assoc. Comput. Linguist. **6**, 357–371 (2018)

30. Stab, C., Miller, T., Schiller, B., Rai, P., Gurevych, I.: Cross-topic argument mining from heterogeneous sources using attention-based neural networks. In: Proceedings of the 2018 Conference on Empirical Methods in Natural Language Processing, pp. 3664–3674 (2018)

31. Stede, M., Schneider, J.: Argumentation mining. Synth. Lect. Hum. Lang. Technol. **11**(2), 1–191 (2018)

32. Toulmin, S.E.: The Uses of Argument. Cambridge University Press, Cambridge (2003)

33. Walton, D.: Argumentation theory: a very short introduction. In: Simari, G., Rahwan, I. (eds.) Argumentation in Artificial Intelligence, pp. 1–22. Springer, Boston (2009). https://doi.org/10.1007/978-0-387-98197-0_1

Natural Language Inference for Portuguese Using BERT and Multilingual Information

Marco Antonio Sobrevilla Cabezudo[(✉)] [iD], Marcio Inácio[iD],
Ana Carolina Rodrigues[iD], Edresson Casanova[iD],
and Rogério Figueredo de Sousa[iD]

NILC - Interinstitutional Center for Computational Linguistics
Instituto de Ciências Matemáticas e de Computação,
Universidade de São Paulo, São Carlos 13566-590, Brazil
{msobrevillac,marciolimainacio,ana2.rodrigues,edresson,rogerfig}@usp.br

Abstract. Recognizing Textual Entailment, also known as inference recognition, aims to identify when the meaning of a piece of text contains the meaning of another fragment of text. In this work, we investigate multiples approaches for recognizing inference in the ASSIN dataset, an entailment recognition corpus for Portuguese. We also investigate the consequences of adding external data to improve training in two different forms: multilingual data and automatically translated corpus. Our results outperform, using the multilingual pre-trained BERT model, the current state-of-the-art for the ASSIN corpus. Finally, we show that using external data did not improve the performance of the model or the improvements are not significant.

Keywords: Natural Language Inference · BERT · Multilingual training · Cross-lingual training

1 Introduction

The task of recognizing textual entailment, also known as inference recognition, consists of identifying when the meaning of a piece of text contains the meaning of another fragment of text. For Natural Language Processing (NLP) purposes, textual entailment is defined as "a directional relationship between pairs of text expressions, denoted by T (the entailing "Text") and H (the entailed "Hypothesis"), in which T entails H if humans reading T would typically infer that H is most likely true" [7]. Recognizing meaning connections between distinct linguistics expression is part of regular communication and, as an automated task, it may help to improve several other applications in Natural Language Processing, such as Question Answering, Semantic Search and Information Extraction.

Initially driven by the PASCAL Challenges [6], a variety of datasets to be used in entailment task was released in the last decade, including Multi-Genre

© Springer Nature Switzerland AG 2020
P. Quaresma et al. (Eds.): PROPOR 2020, LNAI 12037, pp. 346–356, 2020.
https://doi.org/10.1007/978-3-030-41505-1_33

Natural Language Inference (MultiNLI) corpus [17][1], the Cross-Lingual Natural Language Inference (XNLI) corpus [5][2] and the Stanford Natural Language Inference (SNLI) corpus[3].

For the Portuguese language (PT), the ASSIN corpus [11], was made available as part of a shared task in 2016. ASSIN contains pairs of informative (journalistic) sentences compiled with both Brazilian and European variants of Portuguese manually annotated for three classes: entailment, paraphrase and none, differently from previous English datasets, which contain labels for entailment, contradiction and none.

Multiple approaches have been tested to improve textual inference recognition, from grammar-based to the exploitation of WordNet relations [3]. In the last decade, textual inference has been tested in the light of supervised learning algorithms. Moreover, with the advent of Deep Learning [12], new techniques are being explored in NLP, resulting in great improvements over classic approaches.

In particular, pre-trained language representations have been proven effective for this task [8]. A broadly known one is the Bidirectional Encoder Representations from Transformers (BERT)[4]. BERT has been used effectively in multiple tasks like Paraphrase detection, Semantic Text Similarity, among others [8]. Also, BERT was the first fine-tuned representation model that achieved state-of-the-art performance for a large number of sentence and token-level tasks, even outperforming task-specific architectures. Besides its recently promising results, as far as we know, BERT has not been tested in the original ASSIN corpus.

In this work, we analyze multiples approaches of using BERT for inference recognition task in Portuguese. As target data, we use the ASSIN corpus. We also investigate the consequences of adding external data to improve training in two different forms: multilingual data and an automatic translated corpus, as Cross-Lingual Data Augmentation has been proven to increase performance for some NLP tasks [16].

Our work can be summarized in three different approaches: firstly, we evaluate the inference performance after fine-tuning BERT on sentence-pairs exclusively from ASSIN. Secondly, we balance the original corpus adding translated English sentence-pairs from an external source and fine-tune BERT on this new dataset. Thirdly, we explore multilingual training by incorporating more English sentence-pairs from external source during BERT fine-tuning. Finally, based on the results on test data, we manually analyze a sample of the best translated data along with their gold annotation.

Our results outperform [10], which has been reported as the current state-of-the-art (SOTA) for inference on the ASSIN corpus. It also shows the weakness of adding extra data from an external source to improve training.

This paper is organized as follows. Firstly, we discuss previous related work in Sect. 2. Afterwards, we summarize the ASSIN dataset in Sect. 3, followed by

---

[1] Available at https://www.nyu.edu/projects/bowman/multinli/.
[2] Avialable at https://www.nyu.edu/projects/bowman/xnli/.
[3] Available at https://nlp.stanford.edu/projects/snli/.
[4] Available at https://github.com/google-research/bert.

our experiments in Sect. 5 and the results in Sect. 6. Finally, some conclusions are presented in Sect. 7.

2 Related Work

There are numerous works on textual inference for multiple languages. However, due to differences in corpora for different languages, we report mainly works that used the ASSIN corpus, ensuring a fair comparison with our work.

INESC-ID@ASSIN [9] is a method based on lexical features, such as string edit distance, BLEU score, lexical overlapping, ROUGE score, among others, totalling 96 features. These features have been used for training a Support Vector Machine (SVM) model, which, in the best experiment, obtained a F1 score of 0.71 for Brazilian Portuguese (PT-BR) and 0.66 for European Portuguese (PT-PT).

In [15], the usage of named entities as a feature was explored, along with word similarity, count of semantically related tokens, and whether both sentences have the same verb tense and voice. The authors reported only the result for PT-PT obtaining a F1 score of 0.73.

Word embeddings similarity has also been explored in [2]. For classification they explored the use of SVM and Siamese Networks [4]. The best reported experiment achieved a F1 score of 0.52 for PT-BR and 0.61 for PT-PT.

In [1] the authors presented two approaches. The first one, called Reciclagem, was based only on heuristics over semantic networks. The second one, named ASAPP, explores the use of lexical, syntactic, and semantic features extracted from texts. The best experiment got an F1 of approximately 0.5 for PT-BR and 0.59 for PT-PT.

The current SOTA for the ASSIN corpus, considering all dataset samples, has been achieved by the Infernal system [10]. The authors explored features that include syntactic knowledge, embedding-based similarity along with other well-established features that deal with word alignments, totalling 28 features. When considering the entire dataset, i.e. both PT-BR and PT-PT, the Infernal system reached a F1 score of 0.72, currently the best result reported for this dataset.

3 ASSIN Dataset

The ASSIN dataset[5] consists of 10,000 pairs of sentences tagged with similarity grading and inference classification [11]. Inference tags can be three: *None* (N), when both sentences are not related in any way, *Entailment* (E), when the second sentence is a direct inference of the first one, and *Paraphrase* (P), when both sentences convey exactly the same meaning.

The corpus contains pairs of sentences in both Brazilian and European Portuguese, each language variant with splits for training (with 2,500 pairs), development (with 500 instances) and test (2,000). It is important to notice that the splits provided in the corpus are unbalanced, as can be seen in Table 1.

---

[5] Available at http://nilc.icmc.usp.br/assin/.

Table 1. Class frequencies in the splits for the ASSIN corpus

	E			N			P		
	Train	Dev	Test	Train	Dev	Test	Train	Dev	Test
Brazilian Portuguese	437	97	341	1,947	384	1553	116	24	106
European Portuguese	613	116	481	1,708	338	1386	179	46	133
Total	1,050	208	822	3,655	722	2939	295	70	239

Taking into account the statistics presented in Table 1, it is crucial to deal with unbalanced data, specially in the training set in which the *none* class is more frequent (73.1%) when compared with the other two classes (21% and 5,9% for *entailment* and *paraphrase* respectively). This process is reported in the following sections.

4   BERT

BERT is a method for pre-training language representations that allows fine-tuning strategies. In other words, BERT can be pre-trained in a large collection of texts and the training results can be used to different NLP tasks, such as sentiment analysis and inference recognition [8]. BERT is trained using a masked language model (MLM), in which parts of the input are randomly hidden to be predicted based only on their context. Also, the authors also use a next sentence prediction task that jointly pre-trains text-pair representations.

In order to use the pre-trained model for a classification task, an additional output layer can be added and the model trained with labeled data from the specific task, resulting in the updating of the parameters. This process is known as fine-tuning.

Fine-tuning approaches require a pre-trained model and labeled task oriented data. As far as we know, there is no pre-trained BERT model specifically for Portuguese. However, there is a multilingual pre-trained BERT that includes Portuguese[6]. The multilingual model was released by the Google Research group and incorporate 104 languages, such as Spanish and English.

5   Experiments

As previously mentioned, we analyze how BERT performs on Natural Language Inference (NLI) for Portuguese. Specifically, three different settings are analyzed in order to evaluate the contribution of data augmentation into BERT. Additionally, we perform a similar experiment with the SOTA [10]. All these experiments are performed on the ASSIN corpus.

---

[6] The model is available at https://storage.googleapis.com/bert_models/2018_11_23/ multi_cased_L-12_H-768_A-12.zip.

5.1   Fine Tuning BERT on the ASSIN Corpus

Firstly, we use BERT as a pre-trained model and use it to fine-tune on the NLI task. Specifically, we use the multilingual pre-trained BERT model[7], concatenate the premise and the hypothesis with [SEP], prepend the sequence with [CLS], and feed the input to BERT. Then, the representation for [CLS] is fed into a softmax layer for NLI task.

Thus, we use this model to train the NLI task. The hyperparameters to be considered in the training are 7 epochs, a learning rate of 0.00002, a batch size of 22 and a maximum sequence length of 128 tokens.

5.2   Balancing the ASSIN Corpus

As previously described, the ASSIN corpus is highly unbalanced, being Paraphrase and Entailment the minority classes. This may affect the model performance during training, therefore we decided to balance the dataset first.

Due to the fact that there is no other PT corpora available focused on the same task, English (EN) corpora are chosen to balance the number of class instances. Specifically, we use sentence pairs from the XNLI dataset for entailment, which contains 7,500 sentence pairs equally distributed among three classes: entailment, contradiction and none. We also use sentence pairs from the Microsoft Research Paraphrase Corpus (MRPC), which is a dataset focused on paraphrase detection containing 4,075 instances, among which 2,753 are paraphrases and 1323 are not. This way, we build a translated corpus. To achieve this goal, we use the Machine Translation model provided by Google Translate API[8][9]. In total, 4,600 sentence-pairs are selected (2,300 for entailment and 2,300 for paraphrase) and incorporated to the original ASSIN dataset for training.

In order to measure the contribution of the translation quality, i.e., whether the use of higher-quality translations produces a better performance in comparison with lower ones, three sets are built: one composed by translations randomly selected (Random-PT), one composed by the highest-quality translations (Best-PT), and one composed by the lowest-quality translations (Worst-PT).

Because there are no PT references to measure the quality of the translations automatically, back-translation is performed. Thus, PT sentences (translations) are translated back to EN sentences and, then, quality scores are measured comparing EN references with EN sentences (back-translations). The quality scores of the sentences are calculated using the harmonic mean between ROUGE [13] and BLEU [14] scores (called F score). Table 2 shows the statistics about the quality of the sentence-pairs selected.

---

[7] We use the multilingual cased BERT-Base, which comprises 104 languages, 12-layer, 768-hidden, 12-heads, and 110M parameters.

[8] Google Translate API is used due to its good results obtained in Machine Translation. Available at https://cloud.google.com/translate/.

[9] It is worth noting that Google Translate API does not allow us to distinguish between European and Brazilian Portuguese. However, it is known that the model is more biased towards Brazilian Portuguese.

Table 2. Translation quality values (F score) in each set of sentence pairs selected from the translated corpus for data augmentation

	Entailment		Paraphrase	
	Mean	Std	Mean	Std
General	0.58	0.25	0.69	0.16
Best-PT	0.84	0.08	0.74	0.10
Random-PT	0.59	0.25	0.69	0.16
Worst-PT	0.29	0.17	0.65	0.14

Finally, BERT and the SOTA are trained on each balanced dataset using the same parameters as previously described in Subsect. 5.1. It is important to notice that there may be some overlap between each quality set, specially for paraphrase, as the MRPC corpus is smaller.

5.3 Multilingual Data Augmentation on the ASSIN Corpus

Due to the high cost of translating, the possibility to deal with inadequate translations and the possibility to use multilingual representations from Multilingual BERT, the final experiment consists of expanding the dataset using English instances instead of Portuguese ones (translations). Thus, the following settings are proposed:

(1) Adding the English version of the same 4,600 random sentence-pairs described in the previous experiment (2,300 for entailment and 2,300 for paraphrase)
(2) Adding 5,753 English sentence-pairs, 3,000 for entailment and 2,753 for paraphrase (all paraphrase instances of the MRPC corpus)

Note that all sentence-pairs added belong either to the XNLI dataset or the MRPC dataset. The XNLI dataset is a sub-corpus of the Multi-Genre NLI Corpus [17], which is a corpus for Natural Language Inference that covers a wide range of genres of spoken and written text. This way, XNLI dataset may contain instances from domains different from the ASSIN dataset and this may adversely affect the model's performance. Therefore, other subset of sentence-pairs is selected. Specifically, sentence-pairs from government domain[10] in the Multi-Genre NLI corpus are selected.

Additionally, we incorporate more sentence-pairs from entailment and neutral classes (belonging to different domains of the Multi-Genre NLI corpus) into the ASSIN dataset to compare the importance of the domain and the amount of data. In general, the following settings are proposed:

(3) Adding 5,753 sentence-pairs, 3,000 for entailment (government domain) and 2,753 for paraphrase

---

[10] This domain could be more related to the news texts domain of the ASSIN dataset.

(4) Adding 12,753 sentence pairs, 5,000 for neutral (government domain), 5,000 for entailment (government domain) and 2,753 for paraphrase
(5) Adding 12,753 sentence pairs, 5,000 for neutral (different domains), 5,000 for entailment (different domains) and 2,753 for paraphrase
(6) Adding 22,753 sentence pairs, 10,000 for neutral (different domains), 10,000 for entailment (different domains) and 2,753 for paraphrase

6   Results and Discussion

The results of all experiments for both Brazilian (PT-BR) and European Portuguese (PT-PT) can be seen in Tables 3 and 5. Table 3 shows the results of fine-tuning BERT on ASSIN, the current SOTA, and the results of both methods when the best translations (B-PT), the worst translations (W-PT), or translations selected randomly (R-PT) are incorporated into the ASSIN dataset.

In general, fine-tuning BERT on ASSIN presents the best results, outperforming the results of the current SOTA [10] in both variants of Portuguese (accuracy of 90.03% and F1 score of 0.81 in all test set).

Table 3. Results obtained by both BERT and SOTA models using the ASSIN dataset with and without incorporating translated sentence pairs

	PT-BR		PT-PT		All	
	Acc.	F1	Acc.	F1	Acc.	F1
BERT	**90.00%**	**0.78**	**90.05%**	**0.83**	**90.03%**	**0.81**
SOTA [10]	87.30%	0.71	85.75%	0.72	86.52%	0.72
BERT + B-PT	87.55%	0.73	87.00%	0.75	87.28%	0.74
BERT + R-PT	87.15%	0.72	87.70%	0.77	87.42%	0.75
BERT + W-PT	87.45%	0.72	87.00%	0.74	87.22%	0.73
SOTA + B-PT	82.30%	0.63	82.75%	0.69	82.53%	0.66
SOTA + R-PT	81.80%	0.62	82.25%	0.68	82.03%	0.66
SOTA + W-PT	81.20%	0.61	82.10%	0.69	81.65%	0.65

Concerning the contribution of adding translated data, Table 3 shows that the use of translations produces the worst results in both methods (BERT and SOTA). Also, although it is possible to verify that higher-quality translation produces better results (in comparison to the others), these results indicates no considerable difference in performance between them.

In order to identify possible causes of these results, a sample with 250 pairs of sentences of the best translation set was carefully and manually analyzed. An example of translated sentences are show in Table 4. Sentences were evaluated concerning two characteristics:

1. **Translation error:** sentences that had one or more words wrongly translated, including collocations issues, were considered negative for translation error.

2. **Naturalness:** sentences that did not have words wrongly translated and the meaning could be understood, but also did not sound natural in Portuguese, were considered negative for naturalness.

Sentences that were considered not negative for both, translation error and naturalness, were considered good translations. The evaluation showed that 18% of analysed pairs had at least one word translation error and 8% had sentences considered negative for naturalness.

Table 4. Examples of translated sentences

Original in English / Translated sentence (Portuguese)	Translation problem
In central Chungchong province, a landslide caused a Seoul-bound Saemaeul Express train to derail, injuring 28 people, local television said *Na província central de Chungchong, um deslizamento de terra fez com que um trem Saemaeul Express, com destino a Seul, atrapalhasse, ferindo 28 pessoas, informou a televisão local*	Translation error *atrapalhasse* instead of *descarrilhasse*
Beginners who can stay afloat can learn to breathe through the tube and peer through the mask in minutes *Iniciantes que podem se manter à tona podem aprender a respirar através do tubo e espiar através da máscara em minutos*	naturalness
I mow my own lawn and water myself *Eu corto meu próprio gramado e me rego*	Translation error *me rego* instead of *eu mesmo*

Table 5 shows the results of augmenting data using English sentence-pairs from the XNLI dataset (entailment), Multi-Genre NLI corpus (entailment and neutral), and MRPC (paraphrase) according with the settings described in Subsect. 5.3. In general, the results show that the English data lead to improvements, however, this improvement is not significant.

In comparison to the use of translations, the same random English sentence-pairs (setting 1) do not harm the performance as much as the translated version (although the performance is still harmed). Thus, it is possible to affirm that translations, even the highest-quality ones, lose information about the entailment or paraphrase relations. Also, the small drop in the performance is due to the fact that sentence-pairs from XNLI dataset belong to several domains (not only news texts as ASSIN).

Another possible cause that harms the performance is related to the annotation divergences between multiple corpora. The analysis of sentences pairs also

Table 5. Results obtained by the BERT model with data augmentation thorough the incorporation of sentence pairs in English

	PT-BR		PT-PT		All	
	Acc.	F1	Acc.	F1	Acc.	F1
Base	90.00%	**0.78**	90.05%	**0.83**	90.03%	**0.81**
SOTA [10]	87.30%	0.71	85.75%	0.72	86.52%	0.72
(1) Base + Random/2.3K (E) + 2.3K (P)	89.85%	**0.78**	90.00%	**0.83**	89.92%	**0.81**
(2) Base + Random/3K (E) + All (P)	89.75%	0.77	90.50%	**0.83**	90.12%	**0.81**
(3) Base + Government/3K (E) + All (P)	89.90%	0.77	90.20%	**0.83**	90.05%	**0.81**
(4) Base + Government/5K (N) + 5K (E) + All (P)	89.95%	**0.78**	90.25%	**0.83**	90.10%	**0.81**
(5) Base + Random/(5K) N + 5K (E) + All (P)	**90.15%**	**0.78**	90.25%	**0.83**	**90.20%**	**0.81**
(6) Base + Random/(10K) N + 10K (E) + All (P)	89.80%	**0.78**	**90.55%**	**0.83**	90.18%	**0.81**

revealed divergences in labels choices. A considerable part of MRPC pairs, in which the classes are either *paraphrases* or *none*, should have an entailment relation considering all three classes from the ASSIN dataset (*entailment, paraphrases* and *none*). An analogue annotation distinction was noted in sentence pairs from XNLI, which has no paraphrase label class. Paraphrases pairs have been marked as entailment, opposing to the paraphrase-entailment distinction in ASSIN.

Regarding the sentence-pairs extracted from domains similar to the ASSIN (3 and 4 in Table 5), it may be seen that there is not a significant contribution (3). However, major improvements are obtained when neutral sentence-pairs are incorporated. This may be confirmed by the setting 5, where, although sentence-pairs from different domains are incorporated, the performance suffers a higher improvement. This could suggest that English neutral sentence-pairs may help to differentiate the classes. Finally, the limitation of the domains may be outperformed incorporating more sentence-pairs (6), even if they belong to different domains.

7   Conclusions and Future Works

This paper analyzes how well different approaches of classification using BERT perform in inference recognition on the ASSIN dataset. We also examine the consequences of adding external data to improve training in two different forms: automatically translated and multilingual corpus. Fine-tuning BERT on the ASSIN corpus presented the best results, largely outperforming the current best results in both variants of Portuguese. The addition of automatically translated sentences shows the worst results among all tested models, suggesting that translation errors have a high impact on the performance for this task. The results of multilingual training with addition of data in English did not show great improvement compared to training on the original ASSIN dataset. Based on the analyses of a sample from the English data, we hypothesise that the low improvement is a consequence of differences in each corpus composition: we found annotation divergences and content (textual genre domain) differences.

A future deeper analysis of the translation errors and annotation distinctions among multiple corpora may lead to further conclusions about our hypothesis.

Acknowledgments. The authors are grateful to CAPES for supporting this work, and would like to thank NVIDIA for donating the GPU.

References

1. Alves, A.O., Rodrigues, R., Oliveira, H.G.: Asapp: alinhamento semântico automático de palavras aplicado ao português. Linguamática **8**(2), 43–58 (2016)
2. Barbosa, L., Cavalin, P., Guimaraes, V., Kormaksson, M.: Blue man group no assin: Usando representações distribuídas para similaridade semântica e inferência textual. Linguamática **8**(2), 15–22 (2016)
3. Burchardt, A., Pennacchiotti, M., Thater, S., Pinkal, M.: Assessing the impact of frame semantics on textual entailment. Nat. Lang. Eng. **15**(4), 527–550 (2009)
4. Chopra, S., Hadsell, R., LeCun, Y., et al.: Learning a similarity metric discriminatively, with application to face verification. In: CVPR, vol. 1, pp. 539–546 (2005)
5. Conneau, A., et al.: XNLI: evaluating cross-lingual sentence representations. In: Proceedings of the 2018 Conference on Empirical Methods in Natural Language Processing. pp. 2475–2485. Association for Computational Linguistics, Brussels, Belgium, October – November 2018. https://doi.org/10.18653/v1/D18-1269, https://www.aclweb.org/anthology/D18-1269
6. Dagan, I., Glickman, O., Magnini, B.: The PASCAL recognising textual entailment challenge. In: Quiñonero-Candela, J., Dagan, I., Magnini, B., d'Alché-Buc, F. (eds.) MLCW 2005. LNCS (LNAI), vol. 3944, pp. 177–190. Springer, Heidelberg (2006). https://doi.org/10.1007/11736790_9
7. Dagan, I., Roth, D., Sammons, M., Zanzotto, F.M.: Recognizing textual entailment: models and applications. Synth. Lect. Hum. Lang. Technol. **6**(4), 1–220 (2013)
8. Devlin, J., Chang, M.W., Lee, K., Toutanova, K.: BERT: Pre-training of deep bidirectional transformers for language understanding. In: Proceedings of the 2019 Conference of the North American Chapter of the Association for Computational Linguistics: Human Language Technologies, Volume 1 (Long and Short Papers), pp. 4171–4186. Association for Computational Linguistics, Minneapolis, Minnesota, June 2019. https://doi.org/10.18653/v1/N19-1423, https://www.aclweb.org/anthology/N19-1423
9. Fialho, P., Marques, R., Martins, B., Coheur, L., Quaresma, P.: INESC-ID at ASSIN:: measuring semantic similarity and recognizing textual entailment. Linguamática **8**(2), 33–42 (2016)
10. Fonseca, E., Aluísio, S.M.: Syntactic knowledge for natural language inference in Portuguese. In: Villavicencio, A., et al. (eds.) PROPOR 2018. LNCS (LNAI), vol. 11122, pp. 242–252. Springer, Cham (2018). https://doi.org/10.1007/978-3-319-99722-3_25
11. Fonseca, E.R., dos Santos, L.B., Criscuolo, M., Aluísio, S.M.: Visao geral da avaliaçao de similaridade semântica e inferência textual. Linguamática **8**(2), 3–13 (2016)

12. Goodfellow, I., Bengio, Y., Courville, A., Bengio, Y.: Deep Learning, vol. 1. MIT Press Cambridge, Cambridge (2016)
13. Lin, C.Y.: Rouge: A package for automatic evaluation of summaries. In: Proceedings of the Workshop on Text Summarization Branches Out (WAS 2004), pp. 25–26 (2004). https://doi.org/10.1.1.111.9426
14. Papineni, K., Roukos, S., Ward, T., Zhu, W.J.: Bleu: a method for automatic evaluation of machine translation. In: Proceedings of the 40th Annual Meeting on Association for Computational Linguistics, ACL 2002, pp. 311–318. Association for Computational Linguistics, Stroudsburg, PA, USA (2002). https://doi.org/10.3115/1073083.1073135
15. Rocha, G., Lopes Cardoso, H.: Recognizing textual entailment: challenges in the portuguese language. Information **9**(4), 76 (2018)
16. Singh, J., McCann, B., Keskar, N.S., Xiong, C., Socher, R.: Xlda: cross-lingual data augmentation for natural language inference and question answering. arXiv preprint arXiv:1905.11471 (2019)
17. Williams, A., Nangia, N., Bowman, S.: A broad-coverage challenge corpus for sentence understanding through inference. In: Proceedings of the 2018 Conference of the North American Chapter of the Association for Computational Linguistics: Human Language Technologies, Volume 1 (Long Papers), pp. 1112–1122. Association for Computational Linguistics (2018)

Exploiting Siamese Neural Networks on Short Text Similarity Tasks for Multiple Domains and Languages

João Vitor Andrioli de Souza(✉) [ID], Lucas Emanuel Silva E Oliveira[ID],
Yohan Bonescki Gumiel[ID], Deborah Ribeiro Carvalho[ID],
and Claudia Maria Cabral Moro[ID]

Graduate Program on Health Technology (PPGTS), Pontifical Catholic University of Paraná (PUCPR), Curitiba, Brazil
`joao.vitor.andrioli@gmail.com, {lucas.oliveira,yohan.gumiel,`
`ribeiro.carvalho,c.moro}@pucpr.br`

Abstract. Semantic textual similarity algorithms are essential to several natural language processing tasks as clustering documents and text summarization. Many shared tasks regarding this subject were performed during the last few years, but generally, focused on a unique domain and/or language. Siamese Neural Network (SNN) is well known for its ability to compute similarity requiring less training data. We proposed a SNN architecture incorporated with language-independent features, aiming to perform short text similarity calculation in multiple languages and domains. We explored three different corpora from shared tasks: ASSIN 1 and ASSIN 2 with Portuguese journalistic texts and N2C2 (English clinical texts). We adapted the SNN proposed by Mueller and Thyagarajan (2016), in two ways: (i) the activation functions were changed to the ReLU, instead of the sigmoid function, and; (ii) we incorporated the architecture to accept three new lexical features and an embedding layer to infer the values of the pre-trained word embeddings. The evaluation was performed by the Pearson correlation (PC) and the Mean Squared Error (MSE) between the models' predicted values and corpora's gold standard. Our approach achieved better results than the baseline in both languages and domains.

Keywords: Semantic Textual Similarity · Siamese neural networks · Shared tasks

1 Introduction

The Semantic Textual Similarity (STS) algorithms aim to measure how close a text is to another, regarding its semantic meaning. The STS is crucial for many important Natural Language Processing (NLP) applications, such as Question Answering, Text Summarization, Information Retrieval, and Plagiarism Detection [1].

© Springer Nature Switzerland AG 2020
P. Quaresma et al. (Eds.): PROPOR 2020, LNAI 12037, pp. 357–367, 2020.
https://doi.org/10.1007/978-3-030-41505-1_34

The STS methods gained a boost of interest since the SemEval shared-tasks[1] included a task where participants need to calculate similarity scores between a collection of text pairs and benchmark their results against human-made scores.

Several approaches were proposed as a STS solution, including the use of lexical similarity baselines (e.g., Jaccard Similarity, N-Grams, Cosine Similarity), methods based on large corpora information (e.g., Latent Semantic Analysis - LSA), WordNet-based inference, pre-trained word representations (i.e., distributed and contextual embeddings), and Machine Learning (ML) classifiers (e.g., SVM, Neural Networks) inputted with some of the previous approaches as features.

Considering these two events: *2019 n2c2 Shared-Task - Track 1: n2c2/OHNLP Track on Clinical Semantic Textual Similarity*[2] and the *ASSIN 2 - II Semantic Similarity and Textual Inference Evaluation*[3], both are shared-tasks related to STS, the first one focuses on the clinical domain with a database of English texts, while the second has Portuguese texts extracted from journalistic domain. Is it possible that one single architecture executes STS in both tasks?

Keeping in mind the aspiration to build a single methodology that uses the same architecture and features and can be applied for both tasks, we looked for an STS approach that is language and domain-independent. Neural Networks very often outperform traditional ML models without the need for linguistic features, facilitating its use in any language.

A Neural Network architecture called Siamese Neural Network (SNN) is well known for its ability to compute the similarity between two instances of any kind. The SNNs are composed of two or more equal subnetworks, sharing the same configuration with the same weights and parameters, which are updated in parallel during the learning phase [2]. Besides that, it is possible to configure the network according to the task, including the use of many neural network types like CNNs and LSTMs.

Furthermore, unlike other neural network architectures, the SNNs require less training data and are less susceptible to overfitting than other architectures, proving to be an ideal solution to STS, especially if we consider the limited amount of data provided in shared tasks, as stated by [3].

Moreover, the SNNs have been successful in various tasks like quality estimation for language generation [4], signature image verification [4], human face verification [5], textual entailment and text similarity [6].

Considering the current scenario, we propose a SNN architecture incorporated with language-independent features and pre-trained Word Embeddings (WE), aiming to perform short text similarity calculation in multiple languages and domains. Our hypothesis is that it is possible to realize language and domain-independent STS by exploiting SNNs with additional lexical features and pre-trained WE.

---

[1] http://ixa2.si.ehu.es/stswiki/index.php/Main_Page.

[2] https://n2c2.dbmi.hms.harvard.edu/track1.

[3] https://sites.google.com/view/assin2.

2 Related Work

In this section, we review the short text similarity shared tasks and point out popular STS approaches. Moreover, we overview the SNN architecture, which recently has been used to solve STS tasks.

2.1 Short Text Similarity Shared Tasks

The STS algorithms are essential to several NLP tasks that go from clustering similar documents in a text classification application to finding and removing similar sentences in an extractive summarization method. In addition, the advent of the STS shared tasks led to a boost of related work, including the proposal of new methods, development of shared STS datasets and standardization of similarity scores.

The **International Workshops on Semantic Evaluation (SemEval)** already proposed six shared-tasks on STS [1, 7–11] since the first one in 2012. Initially, they focused on the English language only, but then in 2014, they started to include Spanish as well. The field evolution and proposal of new methods is evident when we look through SemEval STS tasks.

Wrapping-up, the methods evolved from knowledge-based (i.e., WordNet) and classical ML algorithms to Neural Networks, WE and complex ensembles. In addition, the shared tasks defined the 1 to 5 numerical value as a standard score for STS [8] and led to new standard STS databases like the SICK corpus [12].

The SemEval initiatives encouraged the **ASSIN (Semantic Similarity and Textual Inference Evaluation) shared tasks**, which worked with short text similarity, but for the Portuguese language. The first edition [13] was in 2016 and counted with 6 teams. It is worth to highlight that the participants explored similar approaches than the SemEval 2015. The winning team used WE and TF-IDF [14]. The ASSIN second edition (ASSIN 2) results were not officially published by the time we submitted this article, but organizers disclosed that nine teams participated in the task.

The Department of Biomedical Informatics (DBMI) of the Harvard Medical School organized the **2019 n2c2 Shared-Task - Track 1: n2c2/OHNLP Track on Clinical Semantic Textual Similarity**. This task diverges from SemEval because it utilizes clinical texts extracted directly from the patient's Electronic Health Records (English), which can affect general domain NLP methods performance. Thirty-three teams submitted results, with almost 100 system runs (each team could send three runs); however, as the ASSIN 2, the official results are not yet published.

2.2 Siamese Neural Networks

Siamese Neural Network is an architecture that contains two or more identical subnetworks that have the ability to parallelly process entities and share the parameters between the layers. Figure 1 outlines a SNN architecture.

The first mention to SNN occurred in [4], where they compared signature images to verify the authenticity of them compared with the original. The SNN was used to calculate the Similarity between both images, and consequently certify its veracity. Another project that explored SNN to perform image classification was [5], which developed a human face verification system that used two Convolutional Networks arranged as a SNN. The system outputs if a pair of faces are from the same person.

Recently a few initiatives started to explore SNNs aiming to execute text similarity calculations [2, 3, 6, 15, 16]. They choose SNN because they needed an architecture built exclusively for similarity computation. Moreover, the SNN showed its efficacy to overcome training data limitations, especially when attached with large pre-trained WE, behavior that was discussed in [2, 6].

Barrow and Peskov [16] developed the first work describing a single model for multiple language processing. Although they simply used Google Translate to translate the text to English, and then inputted the translated text to the model. The Machine Translation impacted negatively the results for other languages.

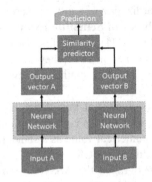

Fig. 1. The Siamese Neural Network architecture. Shaded boxes represent shared parameters that are updated simultaneously.

Considering that just a few studies explored SNNs, recently [3] evaluated seven SNN variants on the SICK [12] and SemEval 2017 datasets [11], each one using different neural networks types and parameters (e.g., LSTMs, Bi-LSTMs, GRUs, Attention mechanisms). They outperformed the baseline approach [2].

3   Methods

3.1   Datasets

We explored three different datasets in our experiments, i.e., ASSIN 1, ASSIN 2 and N2C2, all of them containing a collection of sentence pairs with their respective similarity/relatedness scores, which were manually annotated. Table 1 shows the dataset sizes, while Tables 2 and 3 exemplifies some sentence pairs and scores.

The ASSIN 1 and ASSIN 2 datasets are written in Portuguese language, composed of 10,000 and 9,448 sentence pairs respectively. The scores range from 1 to 5, where 1 stands for no similarity and 5 for maximum similarity.

The N2C2 dataset consists of 2,054 English sentence pairs originated from clinical domain texts, containing highly domain-specific clinical terminologies, ontologies, heterogeneous sentence structures, among many other clinical text issues. The scores range from 0 to 5, where 0 signifies completely dissimilar and 5 completely equivalent sentences.

Table 1. The number of text pairs in each corpus.

Corpus	N2C2	ASSIN 1 (BR)	ASSIN 1 (PT)	ASSIN 2
Training	1,642	2,500	2,500	7,000
Test	412	2,500	2,500	2,448
Total	2,054	5,000	5,000	9,448

Table 2. Text pairs from ASSIN 1 and ASSIN 2 with their respective descriptions and similarity score.

ASSIN 1 & ASSIN 2		
1	Description	The two sentences are totally unrelated
	S1	*Não tem água sendo bebida por um gato*
	S2	*Um caminhão está descendo rapidamente um morro*
	Score	**1.0**
2	Description	The two sentences are not equivalent but have similar actions or objects
	S1	*A senhora não está cortando a carne*
	S2	*A senhora está rachando um ovo para a batedeira*
	Score	**1.9**
3	Description	The two sentences are not equivalent, but share some details
	S1	*Um cachorro preto escuro e um cachorro castanho claro estão brincando no quintal*
	S2	*A luz no quintal está pregando truques no escuro no cachorro castanho e preto*
	Score	**3.1**
4	Description	The two sentences are mostly equivalent
	S1	*O menino pequeno com cabelo castanho está pulando de uma cadeira marrom para o chão*
	S2	*Um jovem menino está pulando de uma cadeira*
	Score	**4.2**
5	Description	The two sentences are completely equivalent
	S1	*Um homem de terno está de pé em frente a um microfone e cantando*
	S2	*O homem de terno está de pé de frente para um microfone e cantando*
	Score	**5.0**

3.2 Model Architecture and Features

The SNN history of good results in other similarity related studies [4, 5] and observations about their low susceptibility to overfitting and fewer data requirements [3] led us to believe that this is the right architecture for the multi-language and multi-domain STS task. Furthermore, there is an insufficient number of studies applying SNN for STS, and a lot of ground to be explored by further studies.

We replicated from scratch the SNN architecture proposed in [2]. Also, we adapted this architecture in two ways: (i) the activation sigmoid function was changed to a ReLU function because instead of values between 0 and 1 produced by the sigmoid function, we needed values ranging between 0 or 1 to 5; (ii) we incorporated three new lexical features, as shown in Fig. 2. Three dense layers with 100 units were added after the lexical similarities (Dense 2, 3 and 4) and a final dense layer with 50 units to infer from the values of the WE and the three lexical features layers. The hyperparameters used are listed below:

- Embedding Layer Dimension size: 100
- Number LSTM cells: 300
- Number Dense 1, 2, 3 & 4 units: 100
- Number Dense 5 units: 50
- Drop Rate LSTM: 0.17
- Drop Rate Denses: 0.25
- Activation Function: ReLU
- Epochs: 100

Table 3. Text pairs from N2C2 with their respective descriptions and similarity score.

N2C2		
1	Description	The two sentences are totally unrelated
	S1	*Patient has not been the victim of other types of abuse*
	S2	*Information collected has not been verified by the patient*
	Score	**0.0**
2	Description	The two sentences are not equivalent but have similar actions or objects
	S1	*Zantac 150 mg tablet 1 tablet by mouth one time daily as needed*
	S2	*Melatonin 3 mg tablet 2 tablets by mouth every bedtime as needed*
	Score	**1.0**
3	Description	The two sentences are not equivalent, but share some details
	S1	*Strattera 40 mg capsule 1 capsule by mouth one time daily*
	S2	*Arimidex 1 mg tablet 1 tablet by mouth one time daily*
	Score	**2.5**
4	Description	The two sentences are mostly equivalent
	S1	*Thank you for contacting the XXX Anticoagulation Clinic*
	S2	*"Thank you for choosing the Name, M.D.. care team for your health care needs!"*
	Score	**4.0**
5	Description	The two sentences are completely equivalent
	S1	*I have reviewed her note in the electronic medical record*
	S2	*Collateral history was reviewed from the electronic medical record*
	Score	**5.0**

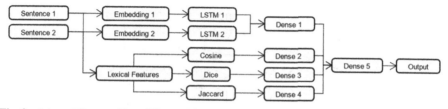

Fig. 2. Adapted Siamese Neural Network incorporated with lexical similarity features, embedding layers and adjusted dense layers.

Due to our corpora language and domain particularities, we focused on language and domain-independent features. For instance, syntactic (e.g., POS-Tagger, dependency parser) and semantic features (e.g., Named Entity Recognition) are often dependent on tools created to work in specific languages and domains, although they can improve the final version, this work includes only the features that can be easily accessed within any language (e.g., lexical features).

Lexical features were computed with similarity metrics such as Cosine similarity, Dice coefficient and Jaccard index (see Eqs. 1, 2 and 3) to represent the number of common tokens of both sentences, the inputs are the sets of words in the sentences. The use of all the three metrics instead of just one was due to preliminary experiments, which have shown an improvement of 5% over the separated metrics.

$$Cosine(A, B) = \frac{A \cap B}{\sqrt{A}\sqrt{B}} \tag{1}$$

$$Jaccard(A, B) = \frac{A \cap B}{A \cup B} \tag{2}$$

$$Dice(A, B) = \frac{2 * A \cap B}{A + B} \tag{3}$$

Two previous STS work for Portuguese [14, 17] utilized the available collection of pre-trained WE for the Portuguese language [18], insomuch we used the 300-sized vector of word2vec CBOW model from this collection. For the English language, we used the 300-sized GoogleNews vector[4].

We also trained our own set of WE directly from each English and Portuguese raw datasets texts, using the train and test set as input to a CBOW word2vec from the gensim library with a 100-sized vector, window of size 5 and minimum count of size 1 and compared both the trained and pre-trained embeddings.

3.3 Experimental Setup

To better understand the importance of the lexical features, our SNN with lexical features model was compared to a SNN model without the lexical features, both with the word2vec and the pre-trained WE. A simple baseline was also compared with the SNN, which is the lexical word overlap of the sentences that represent the proportion of words in common in a pair, given as input to linear regression. The experimental setup is outlined in Fig. 3.

---

[4] https://code.google.com/archive/p/word2vec/.

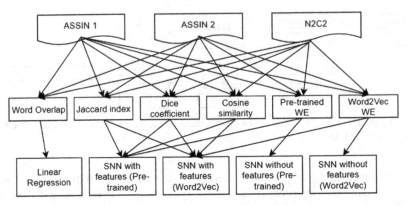

Fig. 3. Overview of the complete experimental setup, with the five compared approaches.

Due to the randomness and variations of single runs, each result shown is the mean of 3 separated runs. The results are evaluated by the Pearson correlation (PC) and the Mean Squared Error (MSE) between the predicted values of the models and the given gold standard of the datasets. The Pearson correlation measures how linearly the values are related and the Mean Squared Error (MSE) estimates the average squared difference between the values, giving the error of the prediction.

4 Results

The results of our experiments are shown in Table 4 comparing the Baseline and the SNN with and without the lexical features. We calculated the Pearson Correlation and the MSE for each model and dataset.

Table 4. Comparison for the Baseline and the SNN with and without the lexical features, with the word2vec WE trained with the corpus and the pre-trained WE (best results for each database are in bold).

		Baseline		SNN (word2vec)				SNN (Pre-trained)			
		ρ	mse	ρ		mse		ρ		mse	
Corpus				No feat	feat	No feat	feat	No feat	feat	No feat	feat
N2C2		0.53	1.84	0.60	0.59	**1.45**	1.72	0.58	**0.64**	1.75	1.58
ASSIN 1	BR	**0.63**	**0.46**	0.52	0.46	0.67	0.68	0.50	0.52	0.60	0.57
	PT	**0.64**	**0.75**	0.53	0.55	0.94	0.83	0.54	0.57	0.81	**0.75**
	BR + PT	**0.63**	**0.60**	0.51	0.51	0.75	0.75	0.52	0.55	0.70	0.65
ASSIN 2		0.57	0.75	0.58	0.68	0.91	**0.61**	0.64	**0.69**	0.78	0.74
ASSIN 1 & 2		0.62	0.73	0.57	0.62	0.85	0.77	0.61	**0.64**	0.75	**0.71**

* *no feat* denotes the SNN using only the WE.
* *feat* denotes the SNN using the WE and the Lexical Features.

In comparison with the baseline, the SNN approach was more significant for the ASSIN 2 with an improvement of 0.12 in Pearson and 0.14 in MSE. The N2C2 corpus achieved 0.11 higher Pearson and 0.39 lower MSE, and for the ASSIN 1, the baseline demonstrated to achieve better results than the SNN. The Pre-Trained WE achieved better results than the word2vec trained on the dataset for almost all datasets.

5 Discussion

We achieved better results than the baseline for N2C2 and ASSIN 2 corpora. However, our approach had worst results than the baseline for the ASSIN 1 corpus, corroborating with [15] that achieved poor results using SNN in this corpus. Some additional error analysis is needed to know why this architecture does not perform well in ASSIN 1 corpus, our hypothesis is that the training data do not represent the test data so well, maybe this explains why the ASSIN 1 top team used a totally unsupervised approach [14]. Additionally, our approach got worst results than [18] that used a diversity of language-dependent features and achieved 0.76 of Pearson and 0.45 of MSE for the ASSIN 1 PT & BR dataset, which is somehow expected, as it was an approach built specifically for Portuguese, as opposed to our attempt to build something for any language.

One possible reason for the N2C2 lower performance compared to ASSIN 2 could be the clinical nature of the N2C2 data, maybe a lot of the clinical terminologies present in this dataset are not present in the Google News pre-trained WE model. It would be interesting to use some clinical WE model and compare the results. Not only that, the word2vec with the full vocabulary has achieved the worst results, this may be due to the high vocabulary sparsity and the lack of data for training a well representative WE.

One important aspect to mention is that our results with a large pre-trained WE achieved better results than our own small one in most runs. This aspect confirms previous work [19] in which larger pre-trained WE achieved better results for a classification task than a small-sized specific model.

Our proposal to use a single methodology with equal architecture and features to perform STS in (i) Portuguese and English languages; (ii) journalistic and clinical domains. A limitation here is the need for a large pre-trained WE model specific for each language. As future work, we intend to assess a multi-lingual WE model like BERT[5] to turn our method completely language-independent. It is worth noting that besides providing a vocabulary for multiple languages, the BERT model could also take advantage of its contextual aspects to improve the similarity scores.

Very recent work already explored additional SNN configurations [3], and the results are very promising. By the time we ended our experiments this work was not yet published. We want to benchmark their models on our datasets and try to incorporate the lexical features that we used in our work and explore new ones as well.

---

[5] https://github.com/google-research/bert/blob/master/multilingual.md.

6 Conclusion

We conclude that a single Siamese Neural Network architecture incorporated with simple lexical features can perform a Short Text Similarity task in multiple languages and domains, even if we consider the dependency of a large pre-trained word vector. Since the process to generate a pre-trained model is completely unsupervised and can be easily replicated for other languages. Moreover, it is possible to explore multi-lingual contextual embeddings like BERT.

References

1. Agirre, E., Cer, D., Diab, M., Gonzalez-Agirre, A.: SemEval-2012 task 6: a pilot on semantic textual similarity. In: *SEM 2012 - 1st Joint Conference on Lexical and Computational Semantics, pp. 385–393. Association for Computational Linguistics, Montréal, Canada (2012)
2. Mueller, J., Thyagarajan, A.: Siamese recurrent architectures for learning sentence similarity. In: AAAI 2016, pp. 2786–2792. AAAI Press, Phoenix, Arizona (2016)
3. Ranasinghe, T., Orasan, C., Mitkov, R.: Semantic textual similarity with siamese neural networks. In: RANLP 2019, Varna, Bulgaria (2019)
4. Bromley, J., Guyon, I., LeCun, Y., Säckinger, E., Shah, R.: Signature verification using a "Siamese" time delay neural network. In: NIPS 1993 Proceedings of the 6th International Conference on Neural Information Processing Systems, pp. 737–744. Morgan Kaufmann Publishers Inc., Denver, Colorado (1993)
5. Chopra, S., Hadsell, R., LeCun, Y.: Learning a similarity metric discriminatively, with application to face verification. In: 2005 IEEE Computer Society Conference on Computer Vision and Pattern Recognition (CVPR 2005), pp. 539–546. IEEE, San Diego, CA, USA (2005)
6. Neculoiu, P., Versteegh, M., Rotaru, M.: Learning text similarity with siamese recurrent networks. In: Proceedings of the 1st Workshop on Representation Learning for NLP, pp. 148–157. Association for Computational Linguistics, Stroudsburg, PA, USA (2016)
7. Agirre, E., Cer, D., Diab, M., Gonzalez-Agirre, A., Guo, W.: *SEM 2013 shared task: semantic textual similarity. In: *SEM 2013 - 2nd Joint Conference on Lexical and Computational Semantics, pp. 32–43. Association for Computational Linguistics, Atlanta, Georgia, USA (2013)
8. Agirre, E., et al.: SemEval-2014 task 10: multilingual semantic textual similarity. In: Proceedings of the 8th International Workshop on Semantic Evaluation (SemEval 2014), pp. 81–91. Association for Computational Linguistics, Dublin, Ireland (2014)
9. Agirre, E., et al.: SemEval-2015 task 2: semantic textual similarity, English, Spanish and pilot on interpretability. In: Proceedings of the 9th International Workshop on Semantic Evaluation (SemEval 2015), pp. 252–263. Association for Computational Linguistics, Denver, Colorado (2015)
10. Agirre, E., et al.: SemEval-2016 task 1: semantic textual similarity, monolingual and cross-lingual evaluation. In: Proceedings of the 10th International Workshop on Semantic Evaluation (SemEval-2016), pp. 497–511. Association for Computational Linguistics, San Diego, California (2016)
11. Cer, D., Diab, M., Agirre, E., Lopez-Gazpio, I., Specia, L.: SemEval-2017 task 1: semantic textual similarity multilingual and crosslingual focused evaluation. In: Proceedings of the 11th International Workshop on Semantic Evaluation (SemEval-2017), pp. 1–14. Association for Computational Linguistics, Vancouver, Canada (2017)

12. Bentivogli, L., Bernardi, R., Marelli, M., Menini, S., Baroni, M., Zamparelli, R.: SICK through the SemEval glasses. Lang. Resour. Eval. **50**, 95–124 (2016). https://doi.org/10.1007/s10579-015-9332-5

13. Fonseca, E.R., dos Santos, L.B., Criscuolo, M.: Visão Geral da Avaliação de Similaridade Semântica e Inferência Textual. In: Linguamática, pp. 3–13 (2016)

14. Hartmann, N.S.: Solo queue at ASSIN: Combinando abordagens tradicionais e emergentes. Linguamatica. **8**, 59–64 (2016)

15. Barbosa, L., Cavalin, P., Guimarães, V., Kormaksson, M.: Blue man group at ASSIN: using distributed representations for semantic similarity and entailment recognition. Linguamática. **8**, 15–22 (2016)

16. Barrow, J., Peskov, D.: UMDeep at SemEval-2017 Task 1: end-to-end shared weight LSTM model for semantic textual similarity. In: Proceedings of the 11th International Workshop on Semantic Evaluation (SemEval-2017), pp. 180–184. Association for Computational Linguistics, Stroudsburg, PA, USA (2017)

17. Alves, A., Oliveira, H.G., Rodrigues, R., Encarnação, R.: ASAPP 2.0: advancing the state-of-the-art of semantic textual similarity for Portuguese. OpenAccess Ser. Informatics. **62**, 1–12 (2018). https://doi.org/10.4230/OASIcs.SLATE.2018.12

18. Hartmann, N.S., Fonseca, E., Shulby, C.D., Treviso, M.V, Rodrigues, J.S., Aluísio, S.M.: Portuguese word embeddings: evaluating on word analogies and natural language tasks. In: Proceedings of the 11th Brazilian Symposium in Information and Human Language Technology, pp. 122–131. Sociedade Brasileira de Computação, Uberlândia, MG, Brazil (2017)

19. e Oliveira, L.E.S., et al.: Learning Portuguese clinical word embeddings: a multi-specialty and multi-institutional corpus of clinical narratives supporting a downstream biomedical task. Stud. Health Technol. Inform. **264**, 123–127 (2019). https://doi.org/10.3233/SHTI190196

CrossOIE: Cross-Lingual Classifier for Open Information Extraction

Bruno Souza Cabral, Rafael Glauber, Marlo Souza,
and Daniela Barreiro Claro[✉] [iD]

FORMAS Research Group, Computer Science Department, LaSiD Laboratory,
Institute of Mathematics and Statistics, Federal University of Bahia,
Salvador, Bahia, Brazil
formasresearchgroup@gmail.com
http://www.formas.ufba.br

Abstract. Open information extraction (Open IE) is the task of extracting open-domain assertions from natural language sentences. Considering the low availability of datasets and tools for this task in languages other than English, recently it has been proposed that multilingual resources can be used to improve Open IE methods for different languages. In this work, we present the CrossOIE, a multilingual publicly available relation tuple validity classifier that scores Open IE systems' extractions based on their estimated quality and can be used to improve Open IE systems and assist in the creation of Open IE benchmarks for different languages. Experiments show that our model trained using a small corpus in English, Spanish, and Portuguese can trade recall performance for up to 27% improvement in precision. This result was also archived in a zero-shot scenario, demonstrating a successful knowledge transfer across the languages.

Keywords: Open information extraction · Cross-lingual · Multilingual

1 Introduction

Open information extraction (Open IE) is the task of extracting knowledge from large collections of textual documents [3]. Different from other approaches, an important characteristic of Open IE is its domain-independence; that is, it does not require the specification of known semantic relations to be extracted.

As noted by Glauber and Claro [14], major advances in the last year in the area o Open IE have mainly focused on the English language. Although the relevance of the English language may seem natural for Open IE due to its origins within Web as a corpus paradigm, it has been recognized by the scientific community that the focus on English and its particularities may induce significant bias in the area [4]. In this context, Claro et al. [6] propose the use of multilingual resources and methods to construct more robust and linguistically supported methods and applications.

© Springer Nature Switzerland AG 2020
P. Quaresma et al. (Eds.): PROPOR 2020, LNAI 12037, pp. 368–378, 2020.
https://doi.org/10.1007/978-3-030-41505-1_35

Recent work on unsupervised representation learning provides evidence that the robust cross-lingual representations [5,17,22,28] can offer a possible solution for the development of natural language processing systems. Moreover, such systems can be applied for different languages by learning models for a target language using annotated data from other languages.

In this work, we introduce the CrossOIE, which uses multilingual language models to help assess the quality of Open IE system extractions. Our method can develop better Open IE systems and benchmarks for different languages, given the difficulties of manually constructing such datasets [16,18]. CrossOIE enables the classification of generated extractions of any previous developed Open IE tool, independently of the language or type of implementation. The main contributions of this paper are: first, a freely available calibrated cross-lingual framework that learns the classification task directly, bypassing other hand-crafted patterns and alleviating error propagation; second, we conduct experiments on datasets in three languages (English, Portuguese and Spanish), comparing two cross-lingual embeddings (BERT and XLM). Besides, we evaluate the model for zero-shot learning, i.e., we evaluate whether the model could usefully classify Portuguese extractions trained only on English extractions.

The remainder of this paper is structured as follows. Section 2 presents our related work, and Sect. 3 describes our approach, our CrossOIE. This Section formalizes and presents the CrossOIEs architecture. Section 4 shows our experiments, our setup up and results. We discuss some important issues. We conclude in Sect. 5 and present some envisioning work.

2 Related Work

Recently, new machine learning-based approaches for Open IE [8,26,27,31] have been proposed, leading to a new generation of Open IE systems. While these systems represent the state-of-the-art in the area, their focus on the English language and need of annotated data make it hard to generalize their results to other languages. For the Portuguese language, early methods use linguistically-inspired patterns for extraction, such as ArgOE [13], or adaptation of methods for the English language, such as SGC_2017 [25] and RePort [21]. Recently, new pattern-based methods have risen as the new state-of-the-art for the language [7] such as InferPORToie [24], PragmaticOIE [23], and DptOIE [15]. As far as we know, new data-based methods have not been proposed yet for Portuguese due to the lack of resources for this task [20].

Regarding multilingual methods, both ArgOE [13] and PolyglotIE [2] are based on the construction of linguistic resources, such as grammars and semantic role labeling parsers, for each language supported by the system. As such, these methods are poorly scalable to other low-resource languages. Faruqi and Kumar [12], on the other hand, apply an English-specific Open IE system coupled with a machine translation model to project extractions to other languages. We believe the lack of robust translation models for several languages and the inherent errors in translation technology, e.g., dealing with domain-specific knowledge, limit the scope of the approach.

Recently, Claro et al. [6] conducted a systematic mapping study of multilingual Open IE methods. The authors report that there are significant research gaps in the area, such as lack of benchmarks and evaluation methodologies for intrinsic evaluation methods. They also point out that few multilingual methods explore multi- or cross-lingual information to improve their extractions. Our work attacks this latter gap and can be used to construct multilingual benchmarks of Open IE. Different from other methods, the only linguistic resource required by our classifier are multilingual language models, which can be trained in an unsupervised manner. We also point out that the resulting classifier can be used to construct Open IE datasets or it can be coupled with naïve methods, such as general lexical-based patterns, to build more accurate Open IE systems for multiple languages.

3   CrossOIE

3.1   Problem Definition

Let $X = \langle x_1, x_2, \cdots, x_n \rangle$ be a sentence composed of tokens x_i, an Open IE extractor is a function that maps X into a set $Y = \langle y_1, y_2, \cdots, y_j \rangle$ being a set of tuples $y\_i = \langle rel_i, arg1_i, arg2_i, \cdots, argn_i \rangle$, which describe the information expressed in sentence X. In this work, we assume that the tuples are always in the format of $y = (arg_1, rel, arg_2)$, where $arg1$ and $arg2$ are noun phrases, not necessarily formed from tokens present in X, and rel is a descriptor of a relation holding between arg_1 and arg_2.

Given a sentence X as above, we are interested in deciding for each extraction $y_i \in Y$ whether y_i is a valid extraction from X and the confidence score for such classification. An Open IE extraction assessment classifier can be expressed as a decision function that for each sentence X and extractions Y, returns a pair $(Z, P) \in \{0,1\}^{|Y|} \times [0,1]^{|Y|}$, where $Z = \langle z_1, z_2, \cdots, z_n \rangle$ is a binary vector s.t. $z_i = 1$ denotes that y_i is a valid extraction, and $P = \langle p_1, p_2, \cdots, p_n \rangle$ is a probability vector, s.t. p_i denotes that extraction y_i has an associated probability p_i of being classified as z_i, given the input sentence X.

3.2   Cross-Lingual Contextual Embedding

For training our classifier, we use multilingual word embeddings models to construct vector representations of sentences' inputs and extractions. In these models, tokens are mapped into a high dimensional vector space, whose geometry preserves some syntactic and semantic traces of the words [11].

Multilingual word embedding are models that represent words of multiples languages into a shared semantic representation space. As such, this models are able to represent semantic similarities between words in different languages. For example, the representation of *cow* in English would appear close to *vaca* in Portuguese, because they refer to the same animal. In our experiments we have chosen to work with Multilingual BERT (M-BERT) [10] and XLM [17] multilingual representation models, since both are contextual embeddings, i.e. the meaning of the word is represented taking its context into consideration, that are readily available for use and have been trained for Portuguese language, among the varieties of the languages represented in the models.

3.3   Model Architecture

Our general architecture and classifier are illustrated in Fig. 1. The proposed framework takes a sentence X and a list of extractions Y, each one following the same structure $y_i = \langle arg_1, rel, arg_2 \rangle$. The first step is to split the sentence in tokens (or words for simplicity). Then we feed the sentence X and the list of extractions Y to the multilingual word embedding models to compute the representation of each token in the sentence. These representations are combined into a single representation for the sentence and relation using the average vector representation computed as:

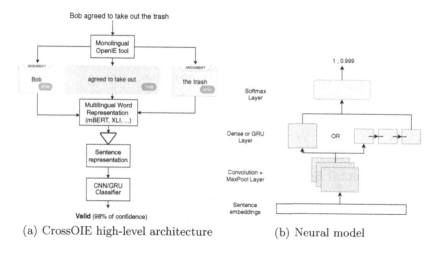

(a) CrossOIE high-level architecture   (b) Neural model

Fig. 1. Architecture overview

$$AverageEmbeddings = \frac{1}{n} \sum_{i=1}^{n} Emb\_x_i \tag{1}$$

For the extractions $y_i = \langle arg1, rel, arg2 \rangle \in Y$, each component of the triple is separately represented and these representations are finally aggregated by the Eq. 2, and passed a single feature vector to the classifier.

$$
\begin{aligned}
SentenceEmbeddings = {}&AverageEmbeddings(Emb\_arg_1) \\
&\oplus AverageEmbeddings(Emb\_rel) \\
&\oplus AverageEmbeddings(Emb\_arg_2)
\end{aligned} \tag{2}
$$

We evaluated two different architectures, CNN and GRU. Both are neural network models with a multilayer structure, namely convolutional layers, followed by a Softmax layer to obtain the scores of different labels. The score is then calibrated using an Isotonic regression [29].

4 Experiments

4.1 Dataset

Our dataset is composed of relations extracted by Open IE systems, namely ClausIE, OLLIE, ReVerb, WOE, and TextRunner, from texts in Portuguese, English, and Spanish, and manually labeled as valid or invalid. A valid extraction corresponds to a coherent triple with the sentence. These linguistic resources were obtained through the studies of [9,13]. The statistics of the dataset are summarized in Table 1.

Table 1. Dataset statistics

	# Sentences	# Extractions
Portuguese	103	209
English	500	7093
Spanish	159	367

4.2 Experimental Setup

We implemented our neural Open IE classifier architecture using the Flair Framework [1], with a modified version of Kashgari[1]. Multilingual BERT model (cased, 104 languages) [10] and XLM (MLM, 17 languages) [17] are employed to map words into contextualized representations.

Our model is trained on 80 epochs, with mini-batches of 4. The CNN classifier starts with a convolution layer of 128 units with a kernel size of 3, followed by a Max pool layer and Dense Layer with 64 units. Finally, it uses a Softmax activation layer. The GRU classifier has a similar network but uses a GRU layer with 100 units in place of the Dense Layer. The activation function in all Dense and Convolution layers is a Rectified Linear Unit (ReLU). An Adadelta [30] optimizer with a Learning rate of 1.0 and rho=0.95 was employed to train our model.

For each single-language test, we split the dataset for train and test using a 5-fold cross-validation strategy. However, for the zero-shot test, we train the classifier with all datasets, excluding the language to be tested (e.g., the zero-shot test for Portuguese is trained using the full English and Spanish datasets and

---

[1] https://github.com/BrikerMan/Kashgari.

evaluated on the full Portuguese dataset). The split is done on a sentence level, to this end the splits have an equal number of sentences, but a different number of extractions. We report our results on the weighted average by the number of extracted facts for each test folds using the standard Precision (P), Recall (R), F1-measure and finally, the Matthews correlation coefficient (MCC) [19] is used in machine learning as a measure of the quality of the classifier. To compute Precision-Recall curves, we select the n extractions with the highest confidence score and compute the classifier's precision. The code for our experiments is available at https://github.com/FORMAS/CrossOIE.

4.3   Evaluation and Results

In the experiments, we compare the results of employing M-BERT embeddings against XLM embeddings, using two classifier models, CNN and GRU. We also analyze two scenarios, zero-shot learning for Spanish and Portuguese, and the results for a specific language, trained with the cross-validation protocol. The single language results are depicted in Fig. 2. The zero-shot results are demonstrated in Fig. 3. A summary with the best-performing models can be seen in Table 2. We provide the original distribution of the data in each datasets (Original), as well as, best achieved Precision (Best Precision) and F1 (Best F1) performances. The highest scores are highlighted in bold.

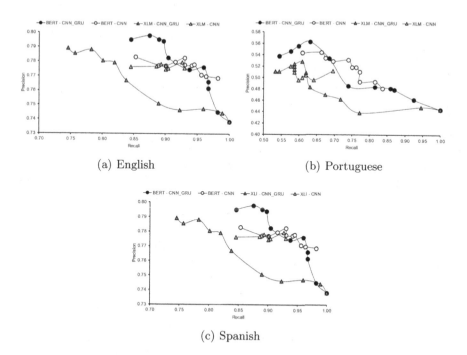

Fig. 2. Language-specific performance

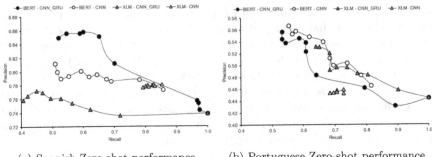

(a) Spanish Zero-shot performance   (b) Portuguese Zero-shot performance

Fig. 3. Zero-shot performance

4.4   Discussion

Overall M-BERT seems to achieve a better and more robust performance than XLM for the task of validity prediction. Regarding the evaluation of single languages, by all metrics other than recall, our classifier achieved better performance. In English, the BERT CNN-GRU (confidence of 0.6) generated the highest Precision score of 0.566, a 24% improvement with a slightly F1 improvement of 1.5%. Moreover, BERT CNN (confidence of 0.999) got the highest F1 score of 0.6528 (+4.5%) and a precision increase to 0.52 (+14.6%). Likewise, the Portuguese got the highest precision of 0.563, a 27.9% improvement with BERT-CNN_GRU (confidence of 0.8), and an F1 of 0.59 (−2.8%). The BERT-CNN classifier (confidence of 0.9) got the best F1 score of 0.6181 (+1.8%). Finally the Spanish results demonstrate that the BERT- CNN (confidence of 0.9) got the highest precision of 0.794 (+7.5%) with an F1 of 0.842 (−0.8%), and the BERT-CNN (confidence of 0.9999) archived the best F1 among the Spanish classifiers, with a score of 0.862 (+1.5%) and a precision of 0.768 (+4.0%). Those classifiers got a Matthews Correlation Coefficient greater than 0.2. Although this is a modest result, this work use only the word representation as features for the classifier, and the extracted triples are from the state-of-art Open IE tool. This shows that the classifiers have converged to a solution and are consistently better than a random oracle considering the class imbalance.

The zero-shot classification is a task where the classifier is evaluated on a language not seen during the training. For Portuguese, the zero-shot classifier with the best Precision, a BERT_CNN (confidence of 0.8), got a score of 0.558 (+25%) with a F1 0.567 (−1%). The classifier with the best F1 was also a BERT_CNN (confidence of 0.995) with a score of 0.6154 and a Precision of 0.504(+13%). For the Spanish zero-shot classifier, the results were the following: The best precision classifier, a BERT-CNN_GRU(confidence of 0.8), got a precision score of 0.858 with a 16% improvement, and a F1 of 0.7072 (−16.7%). The classifier with the best F1, the BERT-CNN_GRU(confidence of 0.8), got a F1 of 0.812 (−4.3%) and a precision boost of 4.7% to 0.773. The result in zero-shot is expected to be lower than when trained with a specific language. Nevertheless, this is a good indicator

Table 2. Metrics scores for languages classifiers

	Precision	Recall	F1	Accuracy	MCC
Zero-shot Portuguese					
Original	0.4444	**1.0000**	0.6154	0.4444	0.0
Best Precision (C:0.8 - BERT-CNN)	**0.5579**	0.5761	0.5668	**0.6087**	**0.21**
Best F1 (C:0.995 - BERT-CNN)	0.5037	0.7391	**0.6154**	0.5604	0.163
Zero-shot Spanish					
Original	0.7384	**1.0000**	0.849	0.7384	0.0
Best Precision (C:0.8 - BERT-CNN_GRU)	**0.8579**	0.6015	0.7072	0.6322	**0.281**
Best F1 (C:0.98 - BERT-CNN_GRU)	0.7572	**0.9668**	**0.849**	**0.7466**	0.173
Portuguese					
Original	0.4402	**1.0000**	0.6113	0.4402	0.0
Best Precision (C:0.8 - BERT-CNN_GRU)	**0.5631**	0.6304	0.5949	**0.6184**	**0.237**
Best F1 (C:0.9 - BERT-CNN)	0.5313	0.7391	**0.6182**	0.5942	0.209
Spanish					
Original	0.7384	**1.0000**	0.8495	0.7384	0.0
Best Precision (C:0.9 - BERT-CNN_GRU)	**0.7941**	0.8466	0.8422	0.7520	**0.283**
Best F1 (C:0.9999 - BERT-CNN)	0.7688	0.9815	**0.8622**	**0.7684**	0.280
English					
Original	0.4543	**1.0000**	0.6247	0.4543	0.0
Best Precision (C:0.6 - BERT-CNN_GRU)	**0.5667**	0.7200	0.6342	**0.6222**	**0.262**
Best F1 (C:0.999 - BERT-CNN)	0.5206	0.8749	**0.6528**	0.5767	0.237

of a successful transfer learning between languages. Our results demonstrate that the classifiers did learn something, as the minimal MCC score was 0.16.

While in the single language experiments, the results of the classifier are more robust, in the sense that the decline in Precision is much more nuanced for almost all representations in the three languages, in the zero-shot experiments, however, this decline is much more pronounced. These results indicate that there may be a discrepancy between the datasets for each language regarding the relations extracted. This discrepancy may arise from the fact that the datasets were created using (i) different Open IE systems for each language (ii) annotated by different teams at different times, and (iii) using texts of different linguistic styles - for English, encyclopedic, journalistic and user-generated (Web pages), for Spanish and Portuguese, encyclopedic texts- and domains - multiple domains for English and Spanish and domain-specific for Portuguese. It may also be the case that linguistic parameters of each language, such syntactic structure and stylistic choices of each language community, may play an important role on structuring information through language and, as such, on how this information is extracted.

It is also worth noticing that the English dataset is considerably larger than both datasets for Spanish and Portuguese, thus in the zero-shot learning, it may dominate the training process and overfits the classifier to the English dataset-specific characteristics. As such, experiments with a higher number of languages to provide the classifier with a more diverse set of examples is recommended.

5   Conclusion and Future Work

In this work, we presented the CrossOIE, a cross-language binary classifier utilizing only cross-language embeddings as training features. The evaluation results demonstrated that a single model could improve the output of multiple state-of-art systems across three languages: Portuguese, English, and Spanish. This shed light that cross-lingual embeddings could be a useful resource to enable better cross-lingual Open IE systems.

In the future, we plan to evaluate the use of richer features such as part-of-speech tags, morphology tags, lemmas, and dependency trees. Another point of improvement would test the solution in larger datasets, and utilize some techniques to improve the classifier such as Fine-tuning the classifier on the Open IE tuples.

Acknowledgements. Authors would like to thank FAPESB, CNPQ and Capes for their financial support.

References

1. Akbik, A., Bergmann, T., Blythe, D., Rasul, K., Schweter, S., Vollgraf, R.: FLAIR: an easy-to-use framework for state-of-the-art NLP. In: Proceedings of the 2019 Conference of the North American Chapter of the Association for Computational Linguistics (Demonstrations), pp. 54–59 (2019)
2. Akbik, A., Chiticariu, L., Danilevsky, M., Kbrom, Y., Li, Y., Zhu, H.: Multilingual information extraction with polyglotie. In: COLING (Demos), pp. 268–272 (2016)
3. Batista, D.S., Forte, D., Silva, R., Martins, B., Silva, M.: Extracçao de relaçoes semânticas de textos em português explorando a dbpédia e a wikipédia. Linguamatica 5(1), 41–57 (2013)
4. Bender, E.M.: Linguistically naïve != language independent: why NLP needs linguistic typology. In: Proceedings of the EACL 2009 Workshop on the Interaction between Linguistics and Computational Linguistics: Virtuous, Vicious or Vacuous? pp. 26–32. Association for Computational Linguistics, Athens, March 2009. https://www.aclweb.org/anthology/W09-0106
5. Chen, X., Awadallah, A.H., Hassan, H., Wang, W., Cardie, C.: Zero-resource multilingual model transfer: Learning what to share. arXiv preprint arXiv:1810.03552 (2018)
6. Claro, D., Souza, M., Castellã Xavier, C., Oliveira, L.: Multilingual open information extraction: challenges and opportunities. Information 10(7), 228 (2019)
7. Collovini, S., et al.: IberLEF 2019 Portuguese named entity recognition and relation extraction tasks. In: Proceedings of the Iberian Languages Evaluation Forum (IberLEF 2019), vol. 2421, pp. 390–410. CEUR-WS.org (2019)
8. Cui, L., Wei, F., Zhou, M.: Neural open information extraction. arXiv preprint arXiv:1805.04270 (2018)

9. Del Corro, L., Gemulla, R.: Clausie: clause-based open information extraction. In: Proceedings of the 22nd International Conference on World Wide Web, pp. 355–366. ACM (2013)
10. Devlin, J., Chang, M.W., Lee, K., Toutanova, K.: Bert: Pre-training of deep bidirectional transformers for language understanding. arXiv preprint arXiv:1810.04805 (2018)
11. Ettinger, A.: What BERT is not: Lessons from a new suite of psycholinguistic diagnostics for language models. arXiv preprint arXiv:1907.13528 (2019)
12. Faruqui, M., Kumar, S.: Multilingual open relation extraction using cross-lingual projection. arXiv preprint arXiv:1503.06450 (2015)
13. Gamallo, P., Garcia, M.: Multilingual open information extraction. In: Pereira, F., Machado, P., Costa, E., Cardoso, A. (eds.) EPIA 2015. LNCS (LNAI), vol. 9273, pp. 711–722. Springer, Cham (2015). https://doi.org/10.1007/978-3-319-23485-4_72
14. Glauber, R., Claro, D.B.: A systematic mapping study on open information extraction. Expert Syst. Appl. **112**, 372–387 (2018)
15. Glauber, R., Claro, D.B., de Oliveira, L.S.: Dependency parser on open information extraction for Portuguese texts - DptOIE and DependentIE on IberLEF. In: Proceedings of the Iberian Languages Evaluation Forum (IberLEF 2019), vol. 2421, pp. 442–448. CEUR-WS.org (2019)
16. Glauber, R., de Oliveira, L.S., Sena, C.F.L., Claro, D.B., Souza, M.: Challenges of an annotation task for open information extraction in Portuguese. In: Villavicencio, A., et al. (eds.) PROPOR 2018. LNCS (LNAI), vol. 11122, pp. 66–76. Springer, Cham (2018). https://doi.org/10.1007/978-3-319-99722-3_7
17. Lample, G., Conneau, A.: Cross-lingual language model pretraining. arXiv preprint arXiv:1901.07291 (2019)
18. Léchelle, W., Gotti, F., Langlais, P.: Wire57: A fine-grained benchmark for open information extraction. arXiv preprint arXiv:1809.08962 (2018)
19. Matthews, B.W.: Comparison of the predicted and observed secondary structure of t4 phage lysozyme. Biochimica et Biophysica Acta (BBA)-Protein Structure **405**(2), 442–451 (1975)
20. Sanches, L.M.P., Cardel, V.S., Machado, L.S., Souza, Marlo, Salvador, L.N.: Disambiguating open IE: identifying semantic similarity in relation extraction by word embeddings. In: Villavicencio, A., et al. (eds.) PROPOR 2018. LNCS (LNAI), vol. 11122, pp. 93–103. Springer, Cham (2018). https://doi.org/10.1007/978-3-319-99722-3_10
21. Pereira, V., Pinheiro, V.: Report-um sistema de extração de informações aberta para língua portuguesa. In: Proceedings of Symposium in Information and Human Language Technology, pp. 191–200. Sociedade Brasileira de Computação (2015)
22. Pires, T., Schlinger, E., Garrette, D.: How multilingual is multilingual bert? arXiv preprint arXiv:1906.01502 (2019)
23. Sena, C.F.L., Claro, D.B.: Pragmatic information extraction in Brazilian Portuguese documents. In: Villavicencio, A., et al. (eds.) PROPOR 2018. LNCS (LNAI), vol. 11122, pp. 46–56. Springer, Cham (2018). https://doi.org/10.1007/978-3-319-99722-3_5
24. Sena, C.F.L., Claro, D.B.: Inferportoie: a Portuguese open information extraction system with inferences. Nat. Lang. Eng. **25**(2), 287–306 (2019). https://doi.org/10.1017/S135132491800044X
25. Sena, C.F.L., Glauber, R., Claro, D.B.: Inference approach to enhance a Portuguese open information extraction. In: Proceedings of the 19th International Conference on Enterprise Information Systems - Volume 1: ICEIS, pp. 442–451, INSTICC, ScitePress, Porto (2017). https://doi.org/10.5220/0006338204420451

26. Stanovsky, G., Michael, J., Zettlemoyer, L., Dagan, I.: Supervised open information extraction. In: Proceedings of the 2018 Conference of the North American Chapter of the Association for Computational Linguistics: Human Language Technologies, Volume 1 (Long Papers), pp. 885–895 (2018)

27. Sun, M., Li, X., Wang, X., Fan, M., Feng, Y., Li, P.: Logician: a unified end-to-end neural approach for open-domain information extraction. In: Proceedings of the Eleventh ACM International Conference on Web Search and Data Mining, pp. 556–564. ACM (2018)

28. Wu, S., Dredze, M.: Beto, bentz, becas: The surprising cross-lingual effectiveness of BERT. CoRR abs/1904.09077 (2019). http://arxiv.org/abs/1904.09077

29. Zadrozny, B., Elkan, C.: Transforming classifier scores into accurate multiclass probability estimates. In: Proceedings of the Eighth ACM SIGKDD International Conference on Knowledge Discovery and Data Mining, pp. 694–699. ACM (2002)

30. Zeiler, M.D.: Adadelta: an adaptive learning rate method. arXiv preprint arXiv:1212.5701 (2012)

31. Zhang, S., Duh, K., Van Durme, B.: MT/IE: cross-lingual open information extraction with neural sequence-to-sequence models. In: Proceedings of the 15th Conference of the European Chapter of the Association for Computational Linguistics: Volume 2, Short Papers, pp. 64–70 (2017)

One Book, Two Language Varieties

Anabela Barreiro[1]([⊠]), Ida Rebelo-Arnold[2], Fernando Batista[1,3],
Isabel Garcez[4], and Tanara Zingano Kuhn[5]

[1] INESC-ID, Lisbon, Portugal
anabela.barreiro@inesc-id.pt
[2] Universidad de Valladolid, Valladolid, Spain
[3] Instituto Universitário de Lisboa (ISCTE-IUL), Lisbon, Portugal
[4] Universidade de Lisboa, Lisbon, Portugal
[5] CELGA-ILTEC, Universidade de Coimbra, Coimbra, Portugal

Abstract. This paper presents a comparative study of alignment pairs,
either contrasting expressions or stylistic variants of the same expression
in the European (EP) and the Brazilian (BP) varieties of Portuguese. The
alignments were collected semi-automatically using the CLUE-Aligner
tool, which allows to record all pairs of paraphrastic units resulting from
the alignment task in a database. The corpus used was a children's literature book *Os Livros Que Devoraram o Meu Pai* (The Books that
Devoured My Father) by the Portuguese author Afonso Cruz and the
Brazilian adaptation of this book. The main goal of the work presented
here is to gather equivalent phrasal expressions and different syntactic constructions, which convey the same meaning in EP and BP, and
contribute to the optimisation of editorial processes compulsory in the
adaptation of texts, but which are suitable for any type of editorial process. This study provides a scientific basis for future work in the area
of editing, proofreading and converting text to and from any variety of
Portuguese from a computational point of view, namely to be used in
a paraphrasing system with a variety adaptation functionality, even in
the case of a literary text. We contemplate "challenging" cases, from a
literary point of view, looking for alternatives that do not tamper with
the imagery richness of the original version.

Keywords: European and Brazilian Portuguese · Stylistic choices ·
Variety distinction · Variety adaptation tool · Paraphrasing · Text
adaptation · Editing and proofreading · Editorial process

1 Introduction

This paper focuses on comparing alignments, i.e., pairs of paraphrastic units used
in the Portuguese (original version) and Brazilian (adapted version) editions
of the children's literature book *Os Livros Que Devoraram o Meu Pai* (*The*

This work was supported by national funds through Fundação para a Ciência e a
Tecnologia (FCT) with reference UID/CEC/50021/2019.

© Springer Nature Switzerland AG 2020
P. Quaresma et al. (Eds.): PROPOR 2020, LNAI 12037, pp. 379–389, 2020.
https://doi.org/10.1007/978-3-030-41505-1_36

Books that Devoured My Father) by the Portuguese author Afonso Cruz. The comparative analysis intends to verify what kind of alterations were made in the adaptation process. The methodology used in this research work consists of: (i) at an early stage, building sentence-level alignments of the entire book, contemplating, on the one side, EP, and, on the other side, BP; (ii) feed the CLUE-Aligner tool with the parallel corpus; (iii) perform multi-layer lexical unit, multiword, or expression-level alignments (not only with lexical, but also with syntactic and stylistic implications); (iv) analyse and categorise each alignment from a constrastive linguistics point-of-view, i.e., from an approach that seeks to describe the differences and similarities between the pair of language varieties; (v) establish a typology of contrasts between EP and BP; and finally, (vi) discuss the implications of linguistic changes in the constitution of the new text, in semantic terms, also occasionally analyzed from the literary and/or cultural perspectives, i.e., does the conversion respect the intention of the author's original idea? Does it change the nature of the meaning intended by the author? Etc.

From a linguistic point of view, the specific objective of our work is to identify, analyze, categorise and discuss a selection of simple lexical units, multiwords, phrases, and expressions, which are alternating in the two varieties, i.e., which present differences between the author's choices in the EP variety (original version) and the corresponding solutions adopted in the conversion to BP. The chosen methodology focuses on the functional grammar-based contrastive linguistic analysis [11], implemented with the aid of computational treatment tools based on the eSPERTo project and using semiautomatic alignments generated by the CLUE-Aligner [5].[1]

From a literary point of view, and based on the same linguistic selection, we will analyze the validity of the editorial choices in the BP edition on two fronts: (1) the rationale of the author's choices in the EP edition according to their polysemy, intentional "strangeness", rhythmic richness, and network of meaning relations in the context in which they arise and with the work as a whole; (2) evaluation of the qualitative equivalence in the reception of both editions regarding the same parameters stated in (1), considering that, both the EP and the BP editions can be worked in classroom context by a target audience of the same age group. Based on the results achieved in this work, we also intend to: (a) encourage the gathering of linguistic resources for the purposes of mediation of literature in Portuguese, mother tongue and/or foreign language; (b) question the importance of literary mediation, whether personalized by the editor, the reviewer or the teacher, with regard to literary reception; (c) present a range of editorial and reading mediation alternatives that will preserve the text of the

---

[1] The corpora of the study are the EP and the BP editions of the aforementioned book, building on previous research work, where we have already discussed in detail certain linguistic phenomena, such as the position of clitic pronouns in EP and BP [12] or the contrast between languages (in this case, language varieties) that tend to use more contractions than others, such as contractions of prepositions with determiners in the case of EP [3].

original edition and thus (d) increase and enrich the level of linguistic, literary and cultural knowledge among readers of both the EP and the BP varieties of Portuguese.

The editorial process has significant implications in the quality of a literary text, as well as in the quality of reception. Therefore, a careful proofreading is indispensable in any editorial task. We highlight the literary implications in the examples.

The present study is part of a broader project that proposes lines of comparative analysis of Brazilian editions of literary works by Portuguese authors and Portuguese editions of literary works by Brazilian authors. We argue that the development of the comparative study of these editions plays an important role in a more fruitful transatlantic relationship regarding literary creation in Portuguese and the promotion of cultural and linguistic diversity, especially empowering language users to access the full richness of a language spoken on both sides of the Atlantic Ocean. In the near future, it will be pertinent to foster the development of tools to assist editors, reviewers and teachers, as well as students and readers from the Portuguese-speaking countries in several continents, either from the point of view of mediation and literary reception or from the point of view of awareness of the linguistic contrasts between the language varieties in the Portuguese-speaking communities spread around the world.

2   Related Work

In recent years, editorial revision processes have benefited not only from linguistic reflections and orientations, but also from natural language processing tools, which can serve to develop corpora analyses, generation and summarisation of texts, translation, paraphrasing, among others. In an attempt to complement tools that aid in writing systems available in the market (mostly spelling and superficial grammar correction), [2] created a paraphrase generation system called eSPERTo, an acronym for *Sistema de Parafraseamento para Edição e Revisão de Texto* (System of Paraphrasing in Editing and Revision of Text [9], which aims to assist in various tasks, such as summarizing and answering questions [10], language teaching, support for machine translation ([2]; controlled technical writing, editing and proofreading, stylistic adaptation ([12], and text conversion between language varieties [4], among others. In the last case study, the use of the tool allowed us to analyze the paraphrastic units of a complete literary work in the EP and BP varieties of Portuguese, following some previously performed experimental works of adaptation between them (cf. [4,12])). In this context, we outline a more global, dynamic and respectful course for the divergences and convergences that make Portuguese one of the richest languages on our planet, taking a further step towards its internationalization [14].

3   Parallel Corpus

Our corpus consists of the full text of two editions of Afonso Cruz's book, namely, the original in EP and its version in BP. The reasons that led to the choice of this parallel corpus are related to: (1) it is a literary work targeting children and a young public, and for this reason it can be argued that the adaptation of the text requires a more incisive treatment, since the understanding of the text, in the adapted version, should be equivalent to that of the original text's target audience; (2) it is included in the lists of the Portuguese National Reading Plan, recommended for autonomous reading of the 3rd cycle (12–14 years); (3) it integrates the lists of the National Library School Program in 2013 in Brazil, as recommended reading in the final years of elementary school; (4) the text of the Brazilian edition presents significant differences in relation to that of the Portuguese edition.

4   Methodology

The parallel corpus contains 1,260 pairs of sentences.[2] Phrases are displayed in grid-like CLUE-Aligner, where the EP phrase appears vertically forming multiple columns and the BP phrase appears horizontally forming multiple rows. The intersection of words in columns and rows forms a matrix where each word corresponds to a cell. The alignment task involves mapping boundaries, according to linguistic analysis criteria. Figure 1 presents the mapping of the alignment of the paraphrastic units of the sentences in example (1).

(1) EP - *Por vezes a voz dela fica um pouco* **amarrotada.**
     BP - *Por vezes, a voz dela fica um pouco* **enrouquecida.**
     EN - *Sometimes, her voice gets a bit wrinkled/hoarse.*

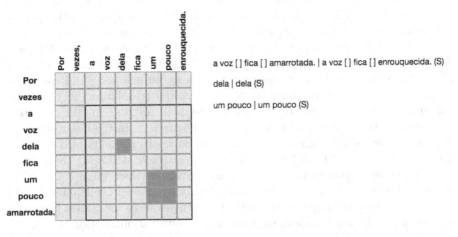

Fig. 1. EP versus BP paraphrastic units. (Color figure online)

---

[2] The most frequent linguistic contrasts of this parallel corpus have been listed and discussed in [13], whose focus was on word sequences analyses.

Figure 1 illustrates the alignment of the EP–BP structures *a voz [] fica []*
amarrotada—a voz [] fica [] enrouquecida, where the only difference is in the
adjectival forms: *amarrotada* (wrinkled) in EP, and *enrouquecida* (hoarse) in
BP. The way to represent the basic structure is to extract the insertions (*dela*
(her) and *um pouco* (a bit), whose alignment mapping is represented in green),
which get automatically aligned by design of the CLUE-Aligner tool.

5 Types of Linguistic Phenomena in EP–BP Alignments

The alignment task resulted in a wide variety of contrastive phenomena, some
purely lexical (e.g., *apanhei o comboio—peguei o trem* (I caught the train)), other
purely syntactic (e.g., *a trabalhar—trabalhando* (walking)) while others, both
lexical and syntactic (e.g., *correu mal—deu tudo errado* (it went (all) wrong)).
The most common contrastive phenomena found in the EP–BP paraphrastic
alignments were lexical, either **Variety Distinction**, or **Lexical Choice**.

Variety Distinction (VAR) represents contrastive alignments where one of
the elements in the pair is either only used or common in one of the varieties
of Portuguese, either EP or BP (e.g., *apelido—sobrenome*). **Lexical Choice**
(LEX-choice) represents the writer's/editor's choice as a variety user, even if both
expressions would be virtually accepted by readers in either one of the speakers communities. Lexical Choice covers a large amount of paraphrastic units in
the corpus, and sometimes it is hard to explain why the editor has changed the
expression used in the source text. Some of those unnecessary changes could
derive into a misinterpretation of what is variety distinction and what variety
distinction implies, i.e., when looking at the EP–BP alignments from the perspective of a student of Portuguese as a foreign language, one might interpret
the changes in BP as "necessary" changes due to the low acceptability of the
original expression in EP (variety distinction). However, it is a matter of choices
by the Portuguese author and the Brazilian editor as users of each variety of
Portuguese, not a variety distinction. This will be the subject of further research
on variety adaptation in the field of editing and proofreading.

The most well-know variants are of lexical and spelling nature (e.g.,
crónicas—crônicas (stories); *relva—grama* (grass); *casa de banho—banheiro*
(bathroom); *rapariga—garota* (girl, young lady), *carteirista—ladrão de carteira*
(pickpocket), etc.). These variants have been widely described, including in early
EP-BP contrastive works developed by computational linguists [16], [6], and can
be easily found in a contrastive dictionary. Also vastly studied within the Framework of the Lexicon-Grammar have been the contrasts between support verb
constructions and morpho-syntactic related single verbs (e.g., ***entrou dentro
dum livro—adentrou** um livro* (went inside a book)). Therefore, we will focus,
from now on, on contrasts that involve different types of lexical choices and
syntactic transformations. It should be noted that the following presentation of
the analysed linguistic phenomena does not reflect corpus-frequency order, but
rather a set of interesting alignments; some of them happen to be also highly
frequent.

Verb Tenses—One of the most consistent pervasive phenomena is the use of different verb tenses between EP and BP, especially the use of the Past Perfect Compound versus the use of the Past Tense, as demonstrated in example (2). Although we consider that there is no justification for this amendment, because it is always preferable to respect the original text, and we are not in the presence of an error, this substitution of verb tenses consists of a stylistic choice, which does not really represent any change in meaning.

(2) *EP - o meu pai **tinha previsto** uma coisa <u>destas</u>.*
    *BP - <u>ele</u> **previu** uma coisa <u>dessas</u>.*
    EN - my father/he (had) predicted such a thing.

VINF (CLITIC) vs PRO-RELque (CLITIC) VSUBJ—Example (3) illustrates a productive phenomenon that consists of a stylistic choice, used in any one of the Portuguese varieties. The syntactic structure of the paraphrasing pair contains two clauses, a main clause and a dependent one. The verb of the main clause can select an infinitive construction (*para me sentar*) (to sit down) or a relative clause (*que me sentasse*) (that I sit down). However, literature is also made of details and, in this case, the verb *dizer* (say) is more assertive than the verb *pedir* (ask), so our editorial choice would be to keep the verb of the EP version. However, on the other hand, in BP, the expression with the verb *dizer* has a connotation of "order", and that might be the reason why the Brazilian editor chose the verb *pedir*.

(3) *EP - Ela disse<u>-me</u> **para me sentar***
    *BP - Ela pediu **que** <u>eu</u> **me sentasse***
    EN - She said/asked me to sit down

PREP-a VINF vs VGER-ndo—One of the most frequent phenomenon contrasting EP and BP is the typically known variety contrast between the use of the verbal construction constituted by the preposition *a* with the infinitive form of the verb in EP and the use of the gerundive form of the verb [PREP(a) VINF vs VGER-ndo] (e.g., *a olhar*—*olhando* (looking) or as in example (4), *a caminhar*—*caminhando* (walking)).

(4) *EP - senti-me **a caminhar** pela grande Avenida Nevski*
    *BP - senti-me **caminhando** pela grande avenida Nevski*
    EN - I felt walking through the large Nevski Avenue

CONTR-PREPDET vs PREP DET—In general, the use of contractions is more prolific in EP than in BP. As illustrated in (5), contractions (e.g., *dum*) occur mostly between a preposition (e.g., *de*) and a determiner, an article (*um*). By replacing the verb *preguiçava* (lazed) in EP by *descansava* (relaxed) in BP, the reader looses an incisive and more visual effect, especially occurring with the subject: *o nariz* (the nose).

(5) *EP - O nariz <u>preguiçava</u> em cima **dum** bigode preto*
    *BP - O nariz <u>descansava</u> em cima **de um** bigode preto*
    EN - The nose lazed/relaxed on the top of a black moustache

2nd vs 3rd PERS-SG—Example (6) shows the use of the second versus the third person singular form of the verb (e.g., *Atreve-te—Atreva-se* (Dare ('yourself')). The absence of a subject pronoun or noun both in EP and BP is due to the use of the Imperative verb tense.

(6)　EP - **Atreve-te**
　　BP - **Atreva-se**
　　EN - *Dare ('yourself')*

PRO-DROP V PREP vs PRO V—EP tends to be a stronger pro-drop variety than BP. Example (pro-drop) contrasts the absence of the subject pronoun in EP with the realisation of the pronoun *vocês* (you) in BP.

(7)　EP - *É a verdade objetiva como <u>haverão de</u> perceber*
　　BP - *É a verdade objetiva, como* **vocês** <u>*vão*</u> *perceber*
　　EN - *It is the objective truth, as you will understand*

DET vs NO-DET B4 PRO-POSS—Example (8) illustrates the use of a determiner versus the use of no-determiner, in the context of an antecedent of a possessive pronoun (e.g., *os seus gestos—seus gestos* (his gestures)). In general, EP tends to use the determiner, while BP tends to avoid it. The change from *cuidados* (elegant) to *cuidadosos* (careful) is unnecessary (the meanings of these words is equivalent in both varieties of Portuguese) and amends the original meaning, because *cuidados* is not an unquestionable synonym of *cuidadosos*.

(8)　EP - *fico sempre fascinado a olhar para* **os seus** *gestos* <u>*cuidados*</u>
　　BP - *sempre fico fascinado observando* **seus** *gestos* <u>*cuidadosos*</u>
　　EN - *I always get fascinated when I look at his elegant/careful gestures*

Word Order—A common conversion strategy between the EP and the BP versions is the word order, which implies words from different parts of speech. Example (9) illustrates the change in the word order of the quantifier *todos* (all). However, examples in the corpus exemplify changes in the word order of adjectives (e.g., *mundo* **enfadonho**—**enfadonho** *mundo* (boring world)), adverbs (e.g., **aqui** *me trouxe*—*me trouxe* **aqui** (brought me here)), or subjects, either pronouns (e.g., *Que poderia* **eu**—*Que* **eu** *poderia* (What could I) or nouns *Como se chama* **o senhor**?—*Como* **o senhor** *se chama*?) (What's your name?)). These editorial choices has different literary implications, which we will not explain in the present work.

(9)　EP - *com aqueles livros* **todos** *sentados nas prateleiras*
　　BP - *com* **todos** *aqueles livros sentados nas prateleiras*
　　EN - *with all those books (all) sitting in the shelves*

Word Reduction and Word Augmentation—The corpus presents many cases of word reduction and word augmentation in a phrase or expression from EP into BP. In example (10), the author of the original text seeks proximity

386 A. Barreiro et al.

with his young readers through the use of the interrogative cleft structure *é que* (where *is it that* he is?), which is typically used in the spoken language modality. Several authors have pointed out that the interrogative cleft structure is easily found in children's language (cf. [1,8], among others), and the target of this book are young readers, so we would maintain the original form in EP.

(10) *EP - Onde é que ele está?*
   BP - Onde ele está?
   EN - Where is (it that) he (is)?

In example (11), the Portuguese author seeks to build a fun word game by following the participial adjective *encolhida* (shrunk) by the title of a book *A Servidão Humana* (The Human Servitude). This diversion effect is lost in the BP version with the introduction of the noun *volume* (volume) before the book's title. We interpret this option of the BP editor as an attempt to make clear to the young reader what the sentence is about.

(11) *EP - encolhida entre o A Servidão Humana de Sommerset Maugham e um livro de Herberto Helder*
   BP - encolhida entre o volume de A Servidão Humana, de Sommerset Maugham, e um livro de Herberto Helder
   EN - crouched between the (volume of) Human Servitude by Sommerset Maugham and a book by Herberto Helder

SG vs PL N or NPs—Several instances of the contrast between the use of singular versus the use of the plural form of a noun phrase happen in the corpus, as in example 12 (e.g., *no cabelo—nos cabelos* (in the hair), where the author of the original text chooses the singular form often used in the spoken modality to more easily approach his target audience. On the other hand, the reviewer chooses the plural form, used in a higher register. The use of plural and singular in nominal agreement and its relation to higher or lower registers and spoken modality have been discussed in the literature (cf. [7,15], among others).

(12) *EP - O meu melhor amigo não tinha óleo no cabelo*
   BP - Meu melhor amigo não tinha óleo nos cabelos
   EN - My best friend didn't have oil in the hair

6 Quantitative Results

The quantitative results in Table 1 show that there are 4 major types of linguistic phenomena in the EP–BP alignments: (i) the use of different syntactic structures (SYNT) (37.4%); (2) the use of different lexical choices (LEX-choice) (30,6%); (iii) different lexicon (including words, and multiword units) based on variety distinctions (VAR) (15,1%); and (iv) the combination of the use of different lexical choices plus different syntactic structures (LEX-choice+SYNT) (10.8%).

A considerable percentage of alignments were identical (SAME), either due to the design of CLUE-Aligner, which automatically aligns insertions in non-contiguous multiwords, whether these insertions are different or identical in EP and BP (it often happens that they are identical and they add up to type SAME). There are a few counts of the combination of the use of variety contrasts in distinct syntactic structures (VAR+SYNT), and of alignments where there is a clear evidence of semantic deviation (SEM DEV) from the original text in the edited text, for reasons which only the editor knows (or does not know, i.e., natural human errors, lack of knowledge of the exact meaning of the word, multiword, or expression in the original or the lack of understanding of the author's intended meaning).

Table 1. Distribution of linguistic phenomena in EP–BP Alignments by most common **types**

Type	Count	Percent	Alignment example	Translation
SYNT	325	37.4%	*dir-lhe-ei—lhe direi*	(I) will tell him/her
LEX-choice	266	30.6%	*esquecidos—absortos*	forgotten—absorbed
VAR	131	15.1%	*apanhei o comboio*	(I) caught the train
			—peguei o trem	—(I) caught the train
LEX-choice+SYNT	94	10.8%	*vê-se*	it can be seen
			—está aparente	— it is clear/obvious
SAME	38	4.4%	*depois—depois*	then
VAR+SYNT	8	0.9%	*que vê ali na relva*	that he sees in the grass
				—there in the grass
SEM DEV	7	0.8%	*mais nada*	nothing else/more
			—tudo	—everything
Total	869	100%		

For the sake of space, we will not present here the distribution of linguistic phenomena in the EP–BP alignments by the most common **subtypes**. However, we present, in Table 2, the most frequent EP–BP alignments within the subtype LEX-choice (5 or more occurrences). From these, with more than 10%, there are noun, verb, adjective and preposition differences, and verb tense differences. The table is self-explanatory.

Table 2. Most frequent EP–BP Alignments in the **LEX-choice** type

LEX-choice	Count	Percent	Alignment example	Translation
N-diff	38	19.9%	*cheiro—odor*	smell—odour
V-diff	36	18.8%	*tremi—estremeci*	(I) shook—shuddered
ADJ-diff	27	14.1%	*massuda—corpulenta*	chunky—corpulent
V-tense	26	13.6%	*havia saído—saíra*	had left—left
PREP-diff	24	12.6%	*atrás de—após*	afterwards—after
EXPR	17	8.9%	*em suores—transpirado*	in sweat—perspired
PRO-DEM-diff	9	4.7%	*estas—essas*	these—those
ADV-diff	8	4.2%	*depressa—rapidamente*	fast—quickly
V-diff+V-tense	6	3.1%	*aconteceu—acontecera*	it happened
Total		100%		

7 Conclusions

We compared the EP and BP editions of the children's literature book *Os Livros que Devoraram o Meu Pai* (The Books that Devoured my Father), by Portuguese author Afonso Cruz, and analyzed the equivalence between the pairs of paraphrastic units found in this literary text. The alignment was done semi-manually by Portuguese and Brazilian linguists. We classified the pairs of paraphrastic units according to their syntactic-semantic, stylistic or varietal nature. The results are of wide interest, but it is impossible to describe them all in this paper. Therefore, we selected just narrower pervasive linguistic phenomena, namely the conversion of/contrast between verb tenses, nominal agreement, word order and collocation of elements in the phrase, such as determiners and pronouns, in the original EP text and in its Brazilian version, and discuss it from the linguistic point of view, with the perspective of literary text adaptation in mind. We put together a set of paraphrastic pairs that can enrich paraphrasing tools including text conversion between the EP and the BP varieties. The problems diagnosed are very similar to those that occur in translations, where editors often require a conventional type of translation writing, even when authors write in an unusual and unconventional way, thus losing the linguistic richness of the original work. As such, many literary options, which were intentionally chosen to arouse strangeness or used for playful reasons, are eventually lost or made explicit in such a way that they are emptied of their initial "richness". In the same way, some expressive resources in the EP original edition, and, therefore, naturally closer to the author's choices, are lost in the BP edition.

References

1. Cavalcante de Araújo, R.: Sobre as interrogativas clivadas (básicas) QU e polares. Fórum Linguístico **16**(1), 3530–3544 (2019)
2. Barreiro, A.: Make it Simple with Paraphrases: Automated Paraphrasing for Authoring Aids and Machine Translation. Ph.D. thesis, Universidade do Porto, Porto, Portugal (2009)
3. Barreiro, A., Batista, F.: Contractions: to align or not to align, that is the question. In: Proceedings of the COLING-Workshop on Linguistic Resources for NLP (2018)
4. Barreiro, A., Mota, C.: Paraphrastic variance between European and Brazilian Portuguese. In: Zampieri, M., Nakov, P., Ljubešić, N., Tiedemann, J., Malmasi, S., Ali, A. (eds.) Proceedings of the Fifth Workshop on NLP for Similar Languages, Varieties and Dialects (VarDial), COLING 2018, Association for Computational Linguistics (2018)
5. Barreiro, A., Raposo, F., Luís, T.: CLUE-aligner: an alignment tool to annotate Pairs of paraphrastic and translation units. In: Proceedings of the 10th Edition of the Language Resources and Evaluation Conference, LREC 2016, pp. 7–13. European Language Resources Association (2016)
6. Barreiro, A., Wittmann, L., Pereira, M.: Lexical differences between European and Brazilian Portuguese. INESC J. Res. Dev. **5**(2), 75–101 (1996)
7. Castilho, A.: Nova Gramática do Português Brasileiro. Contexto (2010)
8. Kato, M.A., Ribeiro, I.: Cleft sentences from Old Portuguese to Modern Portuguese, pp. 123–154. John Benjamins (2009)
9. Mota, C., Barreiro, A., Raposo, F., Ribeiro, R., Curto, S., Coheur, L.: eSPERTo's paraphrastic knowledge applied to question-answering and summarization. In: Barone, L., Monteleone, M., Silberztein, M. (eds.) NooJ 2016. CCIS, vol. 667, pp. 208–220. Springer, Cham (2016). https://doi.org/10.1007/978-3-319-55002-2_18
10. Mota, C., Carvalho, P., Raposo, F., Barreiro, A.: Generating paraphrases of human intransitive adjective constructions with Port4NooJ. In: Okrut, T., Hetsevich, Y., Silberztein, M., Stanislavenka, H. (eds.) NooJ 2015. CCIS, vol. 607, pp. 107–122. Springer, Cham (2016). https://doi.org/10.1007/978-3-319-42471-2_10
11. Neves, M.H.M.: A gramática funcional. Texto e linguagem, Martins Fontes (1997). https://books.google.pt/books?id=auYbAQAAIAAJ
12. Rebelo-Arnold, I., Barreiro, A.: EP-BP paraphrastic alignments of verbal constructions involving the clitic pronoun lhe. In: International Conference on Computational Processing of Portuguese, PROPOR 2018. Springer (2018)
13. Rebelo-Arnold, I., Barreiro, A., Kuhn, T.Z., Garcez, I., Batista, F.: III Simpósio Internacional História, Cultura e Relações de Poder: Revoluções no Mundo Lusófono, chap. Análise Comparativa das Edições Portuguesa e Brasileira da Obra Os Livros Que Devoraram o meu Pai, de Afonso Cruz. Editora LiberArs (2019). http://www.lusosofia.net/
14. Santos, D.: O Português como Língua num Mundo Global: problemas e potencialidades, chap. Português internacional: alguns argumentos, pp. 49–66. Centro de Estudos Lusíadas da Universidade do Minho (2016)
15. Scherre, M.M.P.: Reanálise da concordância nominal em português. Ph.D. thesis, Universidade Federal do Rio de Janeiro, Rio de Janeiro, Brasil (1988)
16. Wittmann, L., Pêgo, T., Santos, D.: Português Brasileiro e Português de Portugal: algumas observações. In: Atas do XI Encontro Nacional da APL, pp. 465–487. Associação Portuguesa de Linguística, Lisboa, Portugal (1995)

Short Papers

Speech Breathing and Expressivity: An Experimental Study in Reading and Singing Styles

Plínio A. Barbosa[1]([✉]) [iD], Sandra Madureira[2], Mario A. S. Fontes[2], and Paulo Menegon[2]

[1] UNICAMP, Campinas, Brazil
pabarbosa.unicampbr@gmail.com
[2] PUCSP, São Paulo, Brazil

Abstract. This paper introduces an experimental study on the role of breathing patterns and acoustic characteristics on the appraisal of emotional content in two speech styles. The corpus is a song lyrics, read and sung by six professional lyrical singers, three men and three women. Three breathing parameters (breath cycle duration, inhalation duration and inhalation amplitude), twelve acoustic parameters, related to fundamental frequency, intensity, spectral tilt and Long Term Analysis, and one semantic descriptor (emotional impact) were analyzed. Results showed stylistic, gender and individual differences. Reading mainly differentiated from singing in relation to the three breathing measures and six acoustic measures. The durations of the breath cycles and the inhalations were higher in singing than in reading and in men than in women. The amplitude of the inhalation was an important factor in separating reading and singing in terms of emotional impact.

Keywords: Breathing · Read speech · Singing

1 Introduction

The investigation of the expression of emotion in speech has focused mainly on vocal and face characteristics [1]. As pointed out by [2] in their investigation of the acoustic characteristics and perception of emotion expressivity in singing, the acoustic characteristics of speech expressivity have been extensively investigated in recent phonetic literature and are highly relevant to the study of sung performances.

Given the importance of the sound symbolism codes, which refer to the acoustic [3], respiratory, phonatory and articulatory characteristics [4, 5] in determining speech style expressivity [6], it is our goal in this study to investigate the role of breathing patterns associated with the acoustic characteristics derived from production characteristics of reading and singing styles on the appraisal of the emotional expressive content. Besides differences between styles (longer breath cycles and deeper inhalation in singing) and genders (longer inhalations for men and faster onset of speech after breath cycle for females) as found in [7, 8], we hypothesize that individual differences in breathing patterns are greater in the singing style than in the reading style since strategies of

© Springer Nature Switzerland AG 2020
P. Quaresma et al. (Eds.): PROPOR 2020, LNAI 12037, pp. 393–398, 2020.
https://doi.org/10.1007/978-3-030-41505-1_37

breath control used by professional singers might vary more [9], that abdomen breathing patterns are longer and deeper than thoracic ones in singing than in reading and that different expressive configuration features may interfere on the judgment of emotional impact.

2 Methodology

2.1 Corpus

The corpus is a well-known Brazilian song lyrics. It is called "Melodia Sentimental" (Sentimental Melody). It is a twenty-verse poem, part of the musical piece "A Floresta do Amazonas" (The Amazon Forest) composed by the Brazilian maestro Heitor Villa-Lobos. It was written in the fifties, last century, by the poetess Dora Vasconcelos to the film "Green Mansions" directed by Mel Ferrer.

2.2 Subjects

Two kinds of subjects participated in the experiment. They were the production task subjects and the perception task subjects. The production task subjects were professional lyric singers, three women, aged 25 to 40 years old, and three men, aged from 35 to 55 years old. Two of the female singers were sopranos and one was a mezzo-soprano. The three male singers were bass baritones. The perception task subjects (judges) were 30 Music undergraduate students, aged from 20 to 30 years old.

2.3 The Production and Perception Tasks Performed by the Subjects

The production task consisted in reading the song lyrics and singing it. All participants, the professional lyric singers, were aware of the song lyrics and had sung it before the recording for the present research work.

The perception task consisted in listening to the recordings and assessing the subjects' performances in reading and singing. A form with the semantic descriptor "emotional impact" (EmoIM) and a 5-point rating scale was given to the participants, the judges, to assess reading and singing performances. The recordings were presented randomly in two sessions. In the first session, the readings of the lyrics were evaluated and, in the second, the singing.

The judges had to choose the level which better corresponded to what they evaluated in terms of speaker's/singer's expressivity. The semantic differential scale comprised from left to right the following items: very low emotional impact, low emotional impact, neutral (moderate), high emotional impact and very high emotional impact. After listening to the instructions, which were given in Brazilian Portuguese, the judges were presented with the audios of the reading/singing. The order of the recordings was randomized between the judges. The 5-level scale was linearly transformed to a scale between -1 and 1 (0 corresponding to the neutral choice) to ensure comparable magnitudes with the z-scored acoustic parameters [10].

2.4 Data Recording

The technique used to record the breathing patterns was the Respiratory Inductance Plethysmography (RIP). As a recording device was used the RespTrack, equipment designed and built at Stockholm University by Johan Stark. The data were collected with the subjects at stand position. The RespTrack measures changes in the cross-sectional area of the rib cage and the abdomen by means of two belts: one placed on the armpits and the other on the navel. The RespTrack traces 3 kinds of graphs relative to breathing patterns: one corresponding to the abdomen, one to the thorax and one that sums both abdominal and thoracic breathing movements.

The acoustic data was recorded by a Shure Headset SM7B microphone in the Phonetics Lab at PUCSP (LIAAC-Pontifical Catholic University of São Paulo). The distance from the headset microphone to the labial commissure was controlled.

2.5 Analytical Procedures

The RespTrack derives values for the thorax, abdomen and the sum (thorax + abdomen) from the signals acquired from the belts. These values were submitted to a 5-point moving average smoothing technique to eliminate prosodic irrelevant ripples and tracings were derived from these. Breathing measures were then extracted manually: the breath group duration from two consecutive inhalation onsets (DurBG); the duration of the inhalation phase (DurIN) and the amplitude of the inhalation (AMP-IN).

The acoustic measures were automatically extracted by the ExpressionEvaluator script developed by [10] for Praat [11]. This script extracts 12 acoustic measures related to fundamental frequency, intensity, spectral tilt and Long Term Average Spectrum (LTAS). They are: fundamental frequency: f0 median (mdnf0), inter-quartile semi-amplitude (sampquartisf0), skewness, and 0.995 quantile (quant99, 5f0); fundamental frequency derivative: df0 mean (medderivf0), standard deviation (desvpaddf0), and skewness (assimdf0div10); intensity measures: intensity skewness (assimint); spectral tilt: spectral tilt mean (medinclinespec), standard deviation desvadinclinespec), and skewness (assiminclinespec); Long-Term Average Spectrum (LTAS): frequency standard deviation (desvapadltas).

In order to correlate the breathing, acoustic and perceptual data, the Principal Component Analysis (PCA) and the Multiple Factor Analysis (MFA) have been applied with FactorMInerR [12] in the R environment. PCA is a multivariate analysis method which involves three steps: finding a common structure among variables; describing the specificity of each group of variables by means of correlation analysis; and comparing the resulting values by means of the individual analyses of the variables MFA, when applied to quantitative data only is an extension of PCA.

Sixteen variables, listed just above, were analyzed and correlated: three breathing measures, twelve acoustic measures and one perceptual measure. These variables were into three groups: Gc1(Acoustic Variables); Gc2(Breathing Variables) and Gc3 (Perceptual Variables). All measures were normalized by z-score. In order to verify the correlation among the groups of variables the Lg coefficient was used. The Lg coefficient measures the degree of correlation between groups of variables. The higher the Lg coefficient, the higher the link between the groups.

3 Results

In separating the reading/singing styles, the most influential variables in dimension 1 were: quant99, 5f0 (0.91; p = 0); DurBG (0.90; p = 0.0001); EmoIM (0.88, p = 0.0001); mednf0 (0.83; p = 0.0009); sampquartisf0 (0.81; p = 0.0013); medderivf0 (0.74; p = 0.0055); DurIN (0.67; p = 0.0165); assimdf0div10 (−0.59; p = 0.0421) and AmpIN (−0.85; p = 0.0004. In dimension 2, the most influential variable was assiminclinespec (0.81; p = 0.0015). The acoustic measures (Gc1) showed the highest Lg coefficient (97.8%). Table 1 presents the values characterizing each group.

Table 1. Lg coefficient values per group of variables: acoustic (Gc1), breathing (Gc2) and Semantic (Gc3).

	Gc1	Gc2	Gc3	MFA
Gc1	1.2445	0.6743	0.4093	**0.9771**
Gc2	0.6743	1.0424	0.5097	0.9344
Gc3	0.4093	0.5097	1	0.8054
MFA	**0.9771**	0.9344	0.8054	1.1404

The most influential variable in determining the emotional impact was the AMP-IN. Singing was judged as having higher impact and was characterized by lower values of AMP-IN (inverse function considering the ratio in relation to the maximum of amplitude). A male subject got the highest emotional impact values in both styles. Figure 1 shows the projection of the variables in two dimensions (Dim1 & Dim2). The dimensions in Multivariate Analysis correspond to various arrangements in which data from various sources are categorized. These various arrangements can be visualized in a graphic display in which the variables are represented by arrows plotted in two dimensions. The

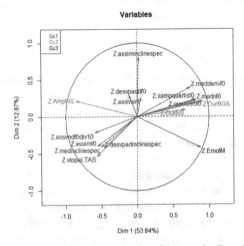

Fig. 1. Variable distribution in the 3 groups analyzed (Acoustic; Breathing and Semantic).

longer the arrows the more relevant the variable in the dimension. Figure 1 is such a kind of graphic, since it displays the variable projections.

In Fig. 1, the most projected variable in the vertical axis (Dimension 2) is an acoustic measure: the assimininclinespec which concerns spectrum tilt. In the horizontal axis (Dimension 1) the most projected variables are: the EmoIM (Emotional Impact), the Amplitude of Inhalations (AmpINS), the Duration of the Breath Groups (DurBGS), the f0 median (mednf0) and f0 derivative median (medderivf0). The remaining variables are less projected than those, that is, they are not as relevant to explain the data.

In Table 2, the means and their standard derivations of AmpIN for Sex (Female and Male), Style (Reading and Singing) and Breathing Type (Abdomen/Torax) are given. Standard derivations are given between parentheses. In singing, values are higher than in reading for both females and males. Larger differences of AmpIN between abdomen and thorax measures in singing are found in men (27% higher than in women).

Table 2. Breathing measures and their standard deviations (in parentheses) in relation to sex and style variables. F stands for female, M for male, R for Reading, S for Singing, A for Abdomen, T for Torax, DurIn for Duration of Inhalation, DurBG for Duration of Breath Group and AmpIN for Amplitude of Inhalation.

Sex	Style	BT	DurIN	DurBG	AmpIN	Sex	Style	BT	DurIN	DurBG	AmpIN
F	R	A	0.84 (0.28)	3.41 (0.77)	0.77 (0.13)	M	R	A	0.78 (0.35)	2.59 (1.26)	0.81 (0.02)
F	R	T	0.81 (0.32)	3.21 (0.73)	0.78 (0.10)	M	R	T	0.78 (0.42)	2.83 (1.06)	0.74 (0.11)
F	S	A	1.19 (0.16)	7.36 (0.95)	0.57 (0.12)	M	S	A	1.09 (0.26)	6.44 (0.95)	0.66 (0.11)
F	S	T	1.20 (0.32)	7.29 (1.01)	0.41 (0.23)	M	S	T	1.06 (0.16)	6.64 (1.20)	0.35 (0.14)

4 Discussion

The higher LG coefficients of acoustic measures signaled their better explanatory power of the data under analysis. Breathing and acoustic differences between sexes were found to be smaller than the ones between styles. Our hypotheses that the Singing and Reading styles were differentiated in terms of breathing patterns were also confirmed.

From the acoustic point of view the Reading and Singing styles were mainly distinguished by fundamental frequency related measures, whose perceptual correlate is pitch, and by spectral tilt which is an important factor in signaling differences concerning voice quality settings. Breathing patterns reflected longer breath groups and higher amplitude of inhalation in Singing. As Singing was considered as displaying more emotional impact than Reading, pitch and voice quality perception cued both by varying breathing and acoustic characteristics are thought to play an expressive role and confirm the hypothesis that different expressive configuration features might interfere on the judgment of emotional impact.

5 Conclusion

Our hypotheses were confirmed and results have showed that the amplitude of the inhalation is a very important factor to be considered in determining the emotional impact in singing expressivity, and that together with breathing inhalation, cycle durations and f0 features, it is important in separating the two styles.

References

1. Scherer, K.: Vocal communication of emotion: a review of research paradigms. Speech Commun. **40**, 227–256 (2003)
2. Sundberg, J., Salomão, G., Scherer, K.: Analyzing emotion expression in singing via flow glottograms, long-term-average spectra, and expert listener evaluation. J. Voice (2019). https://doi.org/10.1016/j.jvoice.2019.08.007
3. Ohala, J.J.: Sound symbolism. In: Proceedings of the 4th Seoul International Conference on Linguistics (SICOL), pp. 98–103. Linguistics Society of America (1997)
4. Gussenhoven, C.: Intonation and interpretation: phonetics and phonology. In: Proceedings of the 1st International Conference on Speech Prosody, pp. 47–57 (2002)
5. Gussenhoven, C.: Foundations of intonational meaning: anatomical and physiological factors. Top. Cogn. Sci. **8**, 425–434 (2016)
6. Madureira, S.: Intonation and variation: the multiplicity of forms and senses. Dialectologia (Special Issue) **VI**, 54–74 (2016)
7. Barbosa, P., Madureira, S.: The interplay between speech and breathing across three Brazilian portuguese speaking styles. In: Proceedings of the 9th International Conference on Speech Prosody 2018, pp. 369–373 (2018)
8. Madureira, S., Barbosa, P.A., Fontes, M.A., Menegon, P.S.: Comparação entre características respiratórias e fonético-acústicas em fala e canto: um estudo de caso. In: Moutinho, L.C., Coimbra, R.L., Rei, E.F., Sousa, J. Bautista, A.G. (orgs.) Estudos em variação linguística nas línguas românicas, vol. 1, 1 edn., pp. 357–374. Universidade de Aveiro, Aveiro (2019)
9. Sundberg, J.: Breathing behavior during singing. STL-QPSR **33**(1), 49–64 (2003)
10. Barbosa, P.A.: Detecting changes in speech expressiveness in participants of a radio program. In: Proceedings of Interspeech, pp. 2155–2158 (2009)
11. Boersma. P., Weenink, D.: Praat: doing phonetics by computer (2016). http://www.praat.org/
12. Husson, F., Josse, J., Lê, S., Mazet, J.: FactoMineR: multivariate exploratory data analysis and data mining with R (version 1.25) [R package] (2013)

Exploring Portuguese Word Embeddings for Discovering Lexical-Semantic Relations

Tiago Sousa[1], Ana Alves[1,2] (iD), and Hugo Gonçalo Oliveira[2,3(✉)] (iD)

[1] ISEC, Polytechnic Institute of Coimbra, Coimbra, Portugal
a21220135@alunos.isec.pt
[2] CISUC, University of Coimbra, Coimbra, Portugal
[3] DEI, University of Coimbra, Coimbra, Portugal
{ana,hroliv}@dei.uc.pt

Abstract. Word2vec-like word embeddings are known for keeping linguistic regularities and thus good for solving analogies. Following this, we explore such embeddings for Portuguese in the discovery of lexical-semantic relations, which can be used for augmenting lexical-semantic knowledge bases. In this exploratory approach, we tested different methods for discovering relations of different types and confirm that word embeddings can be used, at least, for suggesting new candidate relations.

Keywords: Lexical-semantic relations · Word embeddings · Analogies

1 Introduction

When it comes to representing the semantics of a language, two main approaches have been followed: lexical-semantic knowledge bases (LKBs), such as wordnets [3], organise words and their meanings, often connected by relations, such as hypernymy or part-of; distributional models follow the distributional hypothesis [7] and represent words as vectors of numeric features, according to their contexts in large corpora. Despite several models for creating the latter, also known as word embeddings, since 2013, the trend was to use efficient methods for learning dense-vector representations of words, like word2vec [11] or GloVe [12]. Such models have shown very interesting results when it comes to computing word similarity and solving analogies of the kind *"what is to b as a* is to a"*? (e.g., what is to Portugal as Paris is to France?). In fact, the previous task is extensively used for assessing word embeddings in different languages.

An important difference between LKBs and word embeddings is that, in the former, relations are explicit, while in the latter they are implicitly encoded in feature vectors. LKBs are thus more adequate for studying semantic similarity, while distributional models are friendlier for computing semantic relatedness and to be used as the input of neural networks. This motivated the development of word embeddings learned from LKBs [5] and other knowledge bases [14].

© Springer Nature Switzerland AG 2020
P. Quaresma et al. (Eds.): PROPOR 2020, LNAI 12037, pp. 399–405, 2020.
https://doi.org/10.1007/978-3-030-41505-1_38

However, although much knowledge is encoded in the vectors, such knowledge is not easily interpretable. Yet, if, indeed, they capture linguistic regularities, it makes sense to explore feature vectors and try to make some implicit knowledge explicit. Following this idea, several researchers tackled the discovery of relations as an analogy solving task [4], also exploring alternative methods [2].

In this paper, we explore some of those methods while trying to discover lexical-semantic relations in Portuguese word embeddings. Besides (indirectly) assessing the embeddings, newly discovered relations of this kind may be seen as an automatic method for augmenting LKBs. However, with the presented results, human curation is still required before actual integration in the LKB.

2   Related Work

Mikolov et al. [11] proposed word2vec and achieved interesting results in analogy solving (e.g., a is to a^* as b is to b^*) with the vector offset method, later known as 3CosAdd (Eq. 1). Word2vec was assessed in an analogy test that became known as the Google analogy test. It contains 14 categories with 20 to 70 example pairs per category, combined in all possible ways to yield 8,869 semantic and 10,675 syntactic questions. Alternative analogy solving methods [9] include PairDirection (Eq. 2), which assumes that vector distance is not important, only their direction, and 3CosMul (Eq. 3), which attempts at a better balance among the different aspects of similarity.

Interest in relations not covered by the Google test lead to research on automatic labelling the relation of word pairs, based on their vectors [15], and new methods were proposed for this [2], namely 3CosAvg – using the vector with the average offset of a set of relations of the same type (Eq. 4) – and LRCos – applying logistic regression for computing the likelihood of a word belonging to the class of other words in the same argument, in all relations of the same type (Eq. 5). The latter were assessed in BATS [4], an alternative analogy test, balanced across four types of relation – grammatical inflections, word-formation, lexicographical (including hypernymy and meronymy) and world-knowledge relations –, with 50 word pairs per category and 10 categories of each type (overall 2,000 unique word pairs). Other researchers proposed baselines [10] for evaluating word embeddings based on analogies (e.g., SimilarToB, in Eq. 6).

$$b^* = \operatorname*{argmax}_{w \in V} \cos(w, a^* - a + b) \tag{1}$$

$$b^* = \operatorname*{argmax}_{w \in V} \cos(w - b, a^* - a) \tag{2}$$

$$b^* = \operatorname*{argmax}_{w \in V} \cos(w, b^*) * \cos(w, a^*)) / \cos(w, a) \tag{3}$$

$$b^* = \operatorname*{argmax}_{w \in V} \cos(w, b + avg\_offset) \tag{4}$$

$$b^* = \operatorname*{argmax}_{w \in V} P(w \in targetClass) * cos(w, b) \tag{5}$$

$$b^* = \operatorname*{argmax}_{w \in V} \cos(b, w) \tag{6}$$

3   Data and Tools

The first steps for exploring word embeddings involved the selection of a dataset of lexical-semantic relations to use as our "analogies". Although the Google analogy test was translated to Portuguese [13], it does not contain lexical-semantic relations. For this purpose, we looked at the relations extracted from ten lexical resources for Portuguese [6] and selected instances of three types – hypernym-of, part-of and purpose-of – present in at least three resources. Table 1 characterises our dataset with the: minimum number of resources each relation had to be in (the higher, the more consensual it should be); the resulting number of instances; the number of analogy-like questions generated with those instances (e.g., *animal* hypernym-of *dog*, *vehicle* hypernym-of *car* → *what is to vehicle as dog is to animal?*); and examples of instances of each type.

Table 1. Characterisation of the generated lexical-semantic relations test.

Relation	Min.Res.	#Inst.	#Quest.	Example
Hypernymy	5	91	8,190	(*veículo, carro*) (*ave, papagaio*)
Part-of	3	54	3,306	(*núcleo, átomo*) (*minuto, hora*)
Purpose-of	4	13	156	(*escrever, lápis*) (*cozinhar, fogão*)

In our experimentation, we used four models of Portuguese word embeddings: word2vec (CBOW and Skip-Gram) and GloVe models with 300-sized vectors of the NILC embeddings [8]; and the vectors of Portuguese words in the Numberbatch embeddings [14], a different model, learned from several sources, including Open Subtitles and the ConceptNet semantic network, through retrofitting.

The Vecto software package[1] was used to load and process the embeddings, and perform the tests, after converting the relations dataset to a simple compatible format (i.e., a pair of related words in each line).

4   Experimentation

In our first experiment, we used Vecto for running the tests in the created datasets with the six methods described in Sect. 2. For the four embeddings and the three relation types, Table 2 shows the accuracy when solving our tests, for each relation and a macro-average. Since a different relation holds in each direction (e.g., *animal* hypernym-of *dog*, *dog* has-hypernym *animal*), results are presented for the direct (D) and inverse (I) direction.

Accuracies are way under the best for syntactic and semantic analogies using the same embeddings (i.e., between 40 and 60% [8]). Yet, a similar situation happens for English, where using the best method, LRCos, on the BATS

---

[1] https://github.com/vecto-ai (December 2019).

Table 2. Accuracy in the relation tests.

Method	Model	Hypern-of		Part-of		Purpose-of		Macro Avg
		D	I	D	I	D	I	
SimToB	GloVe	2.2%	2.2%	1.9%	3.7%	**23.1%**	15.4%	8.1%
	Word2Vec CB	2.2%	2.2%	1.9%	1.9%	0.0%	0.0%	1.3%
	Word2Vec SG	2.2%	1.1%	1.9%	3.7%	7.7%	0.0%	2.8%
	Numberbatch	1.1%	0.0%	6.5%	2.2%	7.7%	23.1%	6.8%
3CosAdd	GloVe	1.3%	3.4%	2.6%	0.9%	6.4%	19.9%	5.7%
	Word2Vec CB	1.6%	1.8%	1.7%	1.4%	1.9%	2.6%	1.8%
	Word2Vec SG	1.6%	1.8%	2.0%	1.7%	2.6%	10.9%	3.4%
	Numberbatch	0.3%	0.7%	5.3%	2.0%	5.8%	19.9%	5.7%
3CosMul	Glove	0.9%	2.7%	2.3%	0.8%	5.1%	19.2%	5.2%
	Word2Vec CB	1.2%	1.4%	1.5%	1.1%	2.6%	2.6%	1.7%
	Word2Vec SG	1.1%	1.4%	1.8%	1.6%	3.2%	10.9%	3.3%
	Numberbatch	0.3%	1.3%	5.7%	1.5%	7.7%	20.5%	6.2%
PairDir	Glove	0.0%	0.5%	0.5%	0.1%	0.0%	3.2%	0.7%
	Word2Vec CB	0.0%	0.1%	0.3%	0.0%	0.0%	1.3%	0.3%
	Word2Vec SG	0.0%	0.3%	0.5%	0.1%	0.6%	1.3%	0.5%
	Numberbatch	0.0%	0.0%	0.1%	0.1%	0.6%	0.0%	0.1%
3CosAvg	GloVe	2.2%	5.5%	3.7%	3.7%	15.4%	30.8%	10.2%
	Word2Vec CB	2.2%	2.2%	1.9%	1.9%	15.4%	15.4%	6.5%
	Word2Vec SG	2.2%	2.2%	1.9%	1.9%	7.7%	30.8%	7.8%
	Numberbatch	0.0%	0.0%	**13.0%**	2.2%	0.0%	23.1%	6.4%
LRCos	GloVe	0.0%	16.5%	**11.1%**	**5.6%**	15.4%	**53.8%**	**17.1%**
	Word2Vec CB	1.1%	3.3%	3.7%	0.0%	7.7%	23.1%	6.5%
	Word2Vec SG	**3.3%**	**17.6%**	5.6%	0.0%	**23.1%**	30.8%	13.4%
	Numberbatch	1.1%	8.0%	**21.7%**	**10.9%**	7.7%	**53.8%**	**17.2%**

dataset [4], lexical-semantic relations yield accuracies around 20% for different types of hypernymy, and about 17% for part-whole. This is not much different from our results with LRCos for the same relations, and confirms that we face a challenging problem. On the other hand, we get interesting accuracies for purpose-of (>50% for direct), a relation not included in BATS. Though, more purpose-of instances would be required for stronger conclusions.

Overall, the best accuracies are obtained with methods that use all the other relation instances in the dataset, especially LRCos, on GloVe, Numberbatch and, to some extent, Word2Vec-SG. All methods that rely on a single instance achieve very low accuracy and are not suitable for our purpose. The best macro-average is achieved by Numberbatch, by a tiny margin on GloVe. Yet, these results should be looled differently, because ConceptNet was used when learning the former embeddings and not only ConceptNet is structured on semantic relations, including lexical-semantic relations from Princeton WordNet [3], but it was also one of the ten sources of lexical information for our dataset [6].

We also notice that, concerning hypernymy, accuracy is higher for the inverse relation ($\approx$17%), which is explained by the fact that concepts typically have a single hypernym, but many hyponyms, i.e., giving exactly the hyponym in the answer is highly improbable. A similar issue occurs for part-of, with higher accuracy for the direct relation (21% with Numberbatch, $\approx$11% with GloVe), because a concept often has few parts, but it can be part of many concepts. In fact, when looking at the BATS test, more than one answer is possible for the same question, e.g., all possible hyponyms and all inherited hypernyms are accepted. Furthermore, hypernymy relations involving animals are separated from the remaining, making it more adequate for LRCos. Towards the creation of a better relation dataset, all of the previous ideas are worth exploring in the future.

Despite the low accuracy, we used LRCos in GloVe, one of the best configurations, for discovering new instances and confirmed its potential for augmenting LKBs. Although manual curation should still occur, the set of candidates can be substantially narrowed this way, still reducing the time required for this task. This is illustrated in Table 3: for six words b and relations, the first six b^* retrieved are shown. Each b^* word is followed by the number of lexical resources where the relation is in. Apart from incorrect candidates, suggested relations are useful in different ways: those already in several resources confirm that this procedure is working; for those that are in a single resource, confidence could be increased based on this; the remaining ones can be used for augmenting the set of relation instances.

Table 3. Examples of discovered relations with LRCos in GloVe

Word (b)	Relation	Discovered (b^*)
veículo	Hypern-of	~~motorista~~, ~~condutor~~, caminhão(0), caminhonete(1), carro(5), camião(1)
armazém	Hypern-of (I)	edifício, ~~funcionava~~, prédio, local (1), ~~situado~~, ~~num~~
lâmina	Part-of	~~lâminas~~, faca (3), espada (2), ~~corda~~, arma, ~~vidro~~
corpo	Part-of (I)	~~parte~~, músculos (0), peito (3), cérebro (0), físico (1), órgãos (0)
comer	Purp-of	pão (1), pedaço, bolo (1), comida (4), ~~comendo~~, sorvete (1)
lápis	Purp-of (I)	desenhar (3), escrever (3), pintar (1), ler (0), ~~voadores~~, ~~dispôs~~

5   Conclusion

We have explored a set of analogy solving methods for discovering lexical-semantic relations in Portuguese word embeddings. Similarly to English, accuracies in a set of lexical-semantic relations was low. We further discuss noted limitations and present examples that confirm that such an approach is still potentially useful, even if curation is needed.

Lessons learned led to the creation of new test set, dubbed *Teste de Analogias LÉxico-Semânticas* (TALES), more similar to BATS, i.e., it is balanced across relations of more types, and includes exactly 50 instances of each type, selected not only based on the presence in ten lexical resources, but also on the corpus frequency of their arguments. It may also accept more than one

answer for each question. TALES is available from https://github.com/hgoliv/
PT-LexicalSemantics/, for anyone willing to assess their word embeddings.

In the future, we will consider more recent approaches for relation discovery in
word embeddings [1] or combine different methods. We will also explore different
views on the evaluation (e.g., consider the ranking or score of the correct answer)
and make a deeper analysis on the contributions of this kind of approach for
effectively augmenting LKBs.

References

1. Bouraoui, Z., Jameel, S., Schockaert, S.: Relation induction in word embeddings
   revisited. In: Proceedings of the 27th International Conference on Computational
   Linguistics (COLING), pp. 1627–1637. ACL Press (2018)
2. Drozd, A., Gladkova, A., Matsuoka, S.: Word embeddings, analogies, and machine
   learning: beyond king - man + woman = queen. In: Proceedings of the 26th International Conference on Computational Linguistics: Technical Papers, pp. 3519–3530.
   COLING (2016)
3. Fellbaum, C. (ed.): WordNet: An Electronic Lexical Database (Language, Speech,
   and Communication). The MIT Press, Cambridge (1998)
4. Gladkova, A., Drozd, A., Matsuoka, S.: Analogy-based detection of morphological
   and semantic relations with word embeddings: what works and what doesn't. In:
   Proceedings of the NAACL 2016 Student Research Workshop, pp. 8–15. ACL Press,
   June 2016
5. Gonçalo Oliveira, H.: Learning word embeddings from portuguese lexical-semantic
   knowledge bases. In: Villavicencio, A., et al. (eds.) PROPOR 2018. LNCS (LNAI),
   vol. 11122, pp. 265–271. Springer, Cham (2018). https://doi.org/10.1007/978-3-
   319-99722-3_27
6. Gonçalo Oliveira, H.: A survey on Portuguese lexical knowledge bases: contents,
   comparison and combination. Information 9(2), 34 (2018)
7. Harris, Z.: Distributional structure. Word 10(2–3), 146–162 (1954)
8. Hartmann, N.S., Fonseca, E.R., Shulby, C.D., Treviso, M.V., Rodrigues, J.S.,
   Aluísio, S.M.: Portuguese word embeddings: evaluating on word analogies and
   natural language tasks. In: Proceedings of the 11th Brazilian Symposium in Information and Human Language Technology. STIL 2017 (2017)
9. Levy, O., Goldberg, Y.: Linguistic regularities in sparse and explicit word representations. In: Proceedings of the 18th Conference on Computational Natural
   Language Learning, pp. 171–180. ACL Press, June 2014
10. Linzen, T.: Issues in evaluating semantic spaces using word analogies. In: Proceed-
    ings of the 1st Workshop on Evaluating Vector-Space Representations for NLP,
    pp. 13–18. ACL Press (2016)
11. Mikolov, T., Chen, K., Corrado, G., Dean, J.: Efficient estimation of word repre-
    sentations in vector space. In: Proceedings of the Workshop track of International
    Conference on Learning Representations (ICLR) (2013)
12. Pennington, J., Socher, R., Manning, C.D.: GloVe: global vectors for word represen-
    tation. In: Proceedings of the Empirical Methods in Natural Language Processing
    (EMNLP), pp. 1532–1543. ACL Press (2014)
13. Rodrigues, J., Branco, A., Neale, S., Silva, J.: LX-DSemVectors: distributional
    semantics models for portuguese. In: Silva, J., Ribeiro, R., Quaresma, P., Adami,
    A., Branco, A. (eds.) PROPOR 2016. LNCS (LNAI), vol. 9727, pp. 259–270.
    Springer, Cham (2016). https://doi.org/10.1007/978-3-319-41552-9_27

14. Speer, R., Chin, J., Havasi, C.: ConceptNet 5.5: an open multilingual graph of general knowledge. In: Proceedings of the 31st AAAI Conference on Artificial Intelligence, pp. 4444–4451 (2017)
15. Vylomova, E., Rimell, L., Cohn, T., Baldwin, T.: Take and took, gaggle and goose, book and read: evaluating the utility of vector differences for lexical relation learning. In: Proceedings of the 54th Annual Meeting of the Association for Computational Linguistics (Vol 1: Long Papers), pp. 1671–1682. ACL Press (2016)

The ASSIN 2 Shared Task: A Quick Overview

Livy Real[1]([✉]), Erick Fonseca[2,3], and Hugo Gonçalo Oliveira[3] [iD]

[1] B2W Digital/GLiC-USP, São Paulo, Brazil
livyreal@gmail.com
[2] Instituto de Telecomunicações, Lisbon, Portugal
erick.fonseca@lx.it.pt
[3] CISUC, University of Coimbra, Coimbra, Portugal
hroliv@dei.uc.pt

Abstract. This paper offers a brief overview on the ASSIN 2, an evaluation shared task collocated with STIL 2019. ASSIN 2 covered two different but related tasks: Recognizing Textual Entailment (RTE), also known as Natural Language Inference (NLI), and Semantic Textual Similarity (STS). The ASSIN 2 collection was made of pairs of sentences annotated with human judgments for NLI and STS. Participating teams could take part in any of the tasks or both: nine teams participated in the STS task and eight in the NLI task.

Keywords: Shared task · Semantic Textual Similarity · Recognizing Textual Entailment · Natural Language Inference · Portuguese

1 Introduction

ASSIN 2 (Avaliação de Similaridade Semântica e Inferência Textual - Evaluating Semantic Similarity and Textual Entailment) is the second edition of ASSIN, an evaluation shared task in the scope of the computational processing of Portuguese. ASSIN 2 proposed two different tasks: Recognizing Textual Entailment (RTE), recently known as Natural Language Inference (NLI), and Semantic Textual Similarity (STS).

Following the first ASSIN [7], ASSIN 2 was an effort to offer the interested community a new benchmark for computational semantic tasks in Portuguese and thus advancing the state-of-the-art. The shared task was collocated with the Symposium in Information and Human Language Technology (STIL) in Salvador, BA, Brazil, with a workshop held on October, 15th, 2019.

Briefly, as defined in a SemEval 2012 task [1], Semantic Textual Similarity (STS) 'measures the degree of semantic equivalence between two sentences'. Recognising Textual Entailment (RTE), also called Natural Language Inference (NLI), is the task of predicting if a given text (premise) entails (implies) in other text (hypothesis).

© Springer Nature Switzerland AG 2020
P. Quaresma et al. (Eds.): PROPOR 2020, LNAI 12037, pp. 406–412, 2020.
https://doi.org/10.1007/978-3-030-41505-1_39

We follow the tradition of shared tasks for STS and RTE that can be traced back to 2005 with the first Pascal Challenge [4], targeting RTE in a corpus of 1,367 pairs annotated for `entailment` and `non-entailment` relations. In the next Pascal Challenges, different corpora and task designs were tried: paragraphs were used instead of short sentences (Challenge 3); contradictions were added to the data (Challenge 4); non-aligned texts were given to the participants (Challenges 6 and 7) and more recently, the task was presented as multilingual [12,13].

Regarding STS, shared tasks for English go back to SemEval 2012 [1]. Recently, in 2017 [3], Arabic and Spanish were also included. SemEval 2014 included a related task on Compositionality, that put together both Semantic Relatedness and Textual Entailment [10]. The data used, SICK corpus, was the first 'large' dataset the community had, with around 10k pairs of sentences annotated for the two tasks.

In 2015, SLNI, a dataset with >500k pairs annotated for NLI was released [2] and, in 2017, RepEval [11] included the MultiNLI corpus, with >430k pairs annotated for NLI, covering different textual genres.

When it comes to Portuguese processing, data availability and shared tasks on semantic processing are still in their beginning. In 2016, ASSIN [7] was the first shared task for Portuguese STS and NLI. Its dataset included 10k annotated pairs in European and Brazilian Portuguese variants. ASSIN 2 is an effort to continue the goal of ASSIN: offering the community interested in Portuguese processing a new computational semantic benchmark. The present paper offers an overview of the ASSIN 2 task. For more information about the competitor systems and details about the organization, please see the Proceedings of ASSIN 2 [14].

2   Task

When designing the task of ASSIN 2, we considered the previous experience of the first ASSIN (hereafter, ASSIN 1). Its dataset is based on news and it imposes several linguistic challenges, as temporal expressions and reported speech. The NLI task in ASSIN 1 is based on a three-label categorization – `entailment`, `paraphrase` and `neutral` – and, back in 2016, participating systems showed much difficulty to outperform the proposed baselines, which are the same used in ASSIN 2. For example, in the Brazilian Portuguese collection, no participant run did better than the NLI baseline.

Following the ASSIN 1 organizers [7], we decided to have a corpus specifically created for the tasks, as SNLI and MultiNLI, and containing only simple facts, as SICK. Therefore, the ASSIN 2 data was based on SICK-BR [15], a translation and manual adaptation of SICK [10], the corpus used in SemEval 2014, Task 1. SICK is known to have no complex linguistic phenomena, therefore perfect for our purposes.

Another difference from ASSIN 1 is the NLI categorization used. While ASSIN 1 used the `paraphrase` label, we decided to have a two-label categorization, following the earliest tasks for English: `entailment` or `non-entailment`. Firstly, we would like to avoid the use of `paraphrase` as a particular label, since a paraphrase happens when there is a double-entailment, being, somehow, unnecessary to annotate a double-entailment with a third label. Secondly, we would like to have `contradiction` as a third label, following the ideas of Zaenen et al. [16] and recent NLI corpora. However having contradictions soundly annotated in the new corpus would mean much more work than we could do. We would need to correct all the contradiction we already had in SICK, following Kalouli et al. [9]. We also would not have a balanced corpus among the labels, since SICK (and SICK-BR) has less than 1.5k contradictions. Therefore, the fairest corpus we could have for ASSIN 2 was one keeping the same annotation for NLI as the first Pascal Challenges, which, of course, is not a flaw.

Still on data design, as briefly commented above, we wanted to have a balanced corpus. It meant we needed to create and annotate more entailment pairs, the original SICK has around 2.8k entailments. For creating such pairs, we used a semi-automated strategy, taking SICK-BR pairs annotated as entailment and changing some synonyms or removing adverbial or adjectival phrases. All generated pairs were manually revised. We also manually created pairs hoping they would be annotated as entailment, but trying as much as possible not to introduce artifact bias [8].

All the pairs were annotated by at least four native speakers of Brazilian Portuguese with linguistic training. The annotation task was conducted using an online tool prepared for the NLI and STS tasks. For NLI, only pairs annotated the same way by the majority of the annotators were included in the dataset. For STS, the score is the average of scores given by all the annotators. The final result was a dataset with about 10,000 sentence pairs: 6,500 used for training, 500 for validation, and 2,448 for test, now available at https://sites.google.com/view/assin2/. Table 1[1] illustrates the dataset with two annotated pairs.

Table 1. Examples of ASSIN 2 data

Premise	Hypothesis	NLI	STS
Alguns animais estão brincando selvagemente na água	*Alguns animais estão brincando na água*	Entails	4.4
Um avião está voando	*Um cachorro está latindo*	None	1

ASSIN 2 was announced on May 2019, in several NLP mailing lists. Training and validation data were released on 16th June and testing data on 16th September, which also marked the beginning of the evaluation period. The deadline for

---

[1] Examples in English: Some animals are playing wildly in the water `entails` Some animals are playing in the water; A plane is flying `does not entail` A dog is barking.

result submission was 10 days later (26th September) and the official results were announced a few days later. In the NLI task, systems' performance was measured with the F1 of precision and recall as the main metric. In STS, it was measured with the Pearson correlation index between the gold and the submitted scores, with Mean Squared Error (MSE) as a secondary metric[2].

3   Participants and Results

ASSIN 2 had nine participating teams, five from Portugal – CISUC-ASAPPj, CISUC-ASAPPpy, IPR, L2F/INESC, LIACC – and four from Brazil – Deep Learning Brasil, NILC, PUCPR, Stilingue.

The Portuguese processing community is quickly adopting the most recent trends on NLP, with several teams (IPR, Deep Learning Brasil, L2F/INESC and Stilingue), including those with best results, somehow exploring BERT [5] contextual word embeddings, some of which fine-tuned for ASSIN 2. Some teams combined the previous with other features commonly used in STS/RTE, including string similarity measures (e.g., Jaccard similarity of shared tokens, token n-grams and character n-grams), presence of negation, lexical-semantic relations (synonyms and hyponymy) and sentiment, as well as pretrained classic word embeddings (word2vec, GloVe, fastText). Neural architectures, namely LSTM Siamese Networks were also used (PUCPR), while a few teams (ASAPPpy, ASAPPj) followed a more classic machine learning approach, and learned a regressor from some of the previous features. Some teams trained models not only in the ASSIN 2 train collection, but also on data from ASSIN 1.

Best results of each team in the STS and RTE task are shown in Table 2 together with three baselines. The best run in RTE, by Deep Learning Brasil, was based on an ensemble of multilingual BERT, fine-tuned for ASSIN 2, and RoBERTa, fine-tuned for the ASSIN 2 data, after translation to English with Google Translate. To achieve the best ρ in STS, the IPR team also relied on BERT contextual embeddings and used ASSIN 1 data to fine-tune the model.

The word overlap baseline had very competitive results in ASSIN 1. It counts the ratio of overlapping tokens in both the first and second sentence, and trains a logistic/linear regressor (for RTE/STS) with these two features. The second baseline is inspired by Gururangan et al. [8] and trains the same algorithms on bag-of-words features extracted only from the second sentence of each pair. It aims to detect biases in the construction of the dataset. Finally, Infernal [6] is a system with state-of-the-art results on ASSIN 1, based on hand designed features.

---

[2] The evaluation scripts can be found at https://github.com/erickrf/assin.

Table 2. Results of the best run of each team and baselines

Team	STS		RTE	
	ρ	MSE	F1	Accuracy
CISUC-ASAPPj	0.652	0.61	0.606	62.05
CISUC-ASAPPpy	0.740	0.60	0.656	66.67
Deep Learning Brasil	0.785	0.59	**0.883**	**88.32**
IPR	**0.826**	0.52	0.876	87.58
L2F/INESC	0.778	0.52	0.784	78.47
LIACC	0.493	1.08	0.77	77.41
NILC	0.729	0.64	0.871	87.17
PUCPR	0.678	0.85	N/A	N/A
Stilingue	0.817	**0.47**	0.866	86.64
WordOverlap (baseline)	0.577	0.75	0.667	66.71
BoW sentence 2 (baseline)	0.175	1.15	0.557	56.74
Infernal (baseline)	N/A	N/A	0.742	74.18

4 Conclusions

ASSIN 2 was the second edition of ASSIN, a shared task targeting Natural Language Inference and Semantic Textual Similarity in Portuguese. It had 9 participating teams, from Portugal and Brazil, and, differently from the previous ASSIN edition, most of the systems outperformed the proposed baselines. We believe that the effort of having a simpler task in ASSIN 2 was beneficial, not only because systems could do better in this edition, but also because the ASSIN 2 corpus has a sound annotation strategy, comparable with previous shared tasks for English. Looking at the participation, it seems that the Portuguese processing community is now more interested in the proposed tasks.

Considering the results, it is notable that systems based on transfer learning had better results in the competition for both tasks. The Deep Learning Brasil team, the one with the best scores for NLI, had a strategy based on translating the data to English to make possible the use of more robust models. However, it is possible that the nature of the data (a translated corpus) makes this strategy more sound than it would be considering real scenarios. After all, ASSIN 2 results may indicate how the pretrained language models used, namely BERT and RoBERTa, rapidly improved the state-of-the-art of a given task. For the future, we would like to think about new ways of evaluating the generalization power of the proposed systems, since intrinsic metrics, considering only a dataset that follows exactly the same format of the training data, seems nowadays not to be enough to effectively evaluate the systems' performance.

References

1. Agirre, E., Diab, M., Cer, D., Gonzalez-Agirre, A.: SemEval-2012 task 6: a pilot on semantic textual similarity. In: Proceedings of the 1st Joint Conference on Lexical and Computational Semantics-Vol. 1: Proceedings of Main Conference and Shared Task, and, Vol. 2: Proceedings of Sixth International Workshop on Semantic Evaluation, pp. 385–393. ACL Press (2012)
2. Bowman, S.R., Angeli, G., Potts, C., Manning, C.D.: A large annotated corpus for learning natural language inference. In: Proceedings of the 2015 Conference on Empirical Methods in Natural Language Processing, Lisbon, Portugal, pp. 632–642. Association for Computational Linguistics, September 2015
3. Cer, D., Diab, M., Agirre, E., Lopez-Gazpio, I., Specia, L.: Semeval-2017 task 1: semantic textual similarity multilingual and crosslingual focused evaluation. In: Proceedings of the 11th International Workshop on Semantic Evaluation (SemEval 2017), pp. 1–14. ACL Press (2017)
4. Dagan, I., Glickman, O., Magnini, B.: The PASCAL recognising textual entailment challenge. In: Quiñonero-Candela, J., Dagan, I., Magnini, B., d'Alché-Buc, F. (eds.) MLCW 2005. LNCS (LNAI), vol. 3944, pp. 177–190. Springer, Heidelberg (2006). https://doi.org/10.1007/11736790_9
5. Devlin, J., Chang, M.W., Lee, K., Toutanova, K.: BERT: pre-training of deep bidirectional transformers for language understanding. In: Proceedings of the 2019 Conference of the North American Chapter of the Association for Computational Linguistics: Human Language Technologies, Volume 1 (Long and Short Papers), Minneapolis, Minnesota, pp. 4171–4186. ACL Press, June 2019
6. Fonseca, E., Aluísio, S.M.: Syntactic knowledge for natural language inference in portuguese. In: Villavicencio, A., et al. (eds.) PROPOR 2018. LNCS (LNAI), vol. 11122, pp. 242–252. Springer, Cham (2018). https://doi.org/10.1007/978-3-319-99722-3_25
7. Fonseca, E., Santos, L., Criscuolo, M., Aluísio, S.: Visão geral da avaliação de similaridade semântica e inferência textual. Linguamática 8(2), 3–13 (2016)
8. Gururangan, S., Swayamdipta, S., Levy, O., Schwartz, R., Bowman, S., Smith, N.A.: Annotation artifacts in natural language inference data. In: Proceedings of the 2018 Conference of the North American Chapter of the Association for Computational Linguistics: Human Language Technologies, Volume 2 (Short Papers), New Orleans, Louisiana, pp. 107–112. Association for Computational Linguistics, June 2018
9. Kalouli, A.L., Real, L., de Paiva, V.: Correcting contradictions. In: Proceedings of Computing Natural Language Inference (CONLI) Workshop, 19 September 2017 (2017)
10. Marelli, M., Bentivogli, L., Baroni, M., Bernardi, R., Menini, S., Zamparelli, R.: SemEval-2014 task 1: evaluation of compositional distributional semantic models on full sentences through semantic relatedness and textual entailment. In: Proceedings of the 8th International Workshop on Semantic Evaluation (SemEval 2014), Dublin, Ireland, pp. 1–8. ACL Press (2014)
11. Nangia, N., Williams, A., Lazaridou, A., Bowman, S.: The RepEval 2017 shared task: multi-genre natural language inference with sentence representations. In: Proceedings of the 2nd Workshop on Evaluating Vector Space Representations for NLP, Copenhagen, Denmark, pp. 1–10. Association for Computational Linguistics, September 2017

12. Negri, M., Marchetti, A., Mehdad, Y., Bentivogli, L., Giampiccolo, D.: Semeval-2012 task 8: cross-lingual textual entailment for content synchronization. In: Proceedings of *SEM (2012)
13. Negri, M., Marchetti, A., Mehdad, Y., Bentivogli, L., Giampiccolo, D.: Semeval-2013 task 8: cross-lingual textual entailment for content synchronization. In: Proceedings of *SEM (2013)
14. Real, L., Fonseca, E., Oliveira, H.G. (eds.): Proceedings of ASSIN 2. (2020, to be published)
15. Real, L., et al.: SICK-BR: a portuguese corpus for inference. In: Villavicencio, A., et al. (eds.) PROPOR 2018. LNCS (LNAI), vol. 11122, pp. 303–312. Springer, Cham (2018). https://doi.org/10.1007/978-3-319-99722-3_31
16. Zaenen, A., Karttunen, L., Crouch, R.: Local textual inference: can it be defined or circumscribed? In: Proceedings of the ACL Workshop on Empirical Modeling of Semantic Equivalence and Entailment, Ann Arbor, Michigan, pp. 31–36. Association for Computational Linguistics, June 2005. https://www.aclweb.org/anthology/W05-1206

A Multiplayer Voice-Enabled Game Platform for the Elderly

Francisco Oliveira[1,2] (ID), Alberto Abad[1,2(✉)] (ID), and Isabel Trancoso[1,2] (ID)

[1] Instituto Superior Técnico, Av. Rovisco Pais, 1049-001 Lisbon, Portugal
francisco.campos@tecnico.ulisboa.pt
[2] INESC-ID, Rua Alves Redol, 9, 1000-029 Lisbon, Portugal
{alberto.abad,isabel.trancoso}@inesc-id.pt

Abstract. The prevalence of diseases like Dementia is increasing worldwide due to the increase of average lifespan, and consequently, of elderly population. With no cure for dementia, there is a big focus on its early detection, as well as on cognitive stimulation which aims to delay the loss of cognitive abilities. However, there are not yet many technological solutions that allow elders to undergo cognitive stimulation exercises in a group context. This work aims to develop a multiplayer game for European Portuguese to be applied in the context of cognitive stimulation. The game, based on the format of a quiz, serves as a platform for elders to exercise their memory competing with each other, and thus, promoting social interaction which is of major importance for cognitive stimulation. To this end, the game incorporates a virtual gameshow host and speech and language technologies allowing for natural voice interactions. The preliminary results of the user satisfaction survey were generally positive. In particular, the multiplayer component was well received, reinforcing the potential of this type of system.

Keywords: Cognitive stimulation · Games for the elderly · Speech and language technologies · Speech recognition · Virtual agent

1 Introduction

The world's population is ageing. Statistics indicate that currently over 20% of the Portuguese population is elderly, with estimates that in 40 years, elders will comprise over a third of Portugal's overall population [1]. Major advances in medicine in the past decades led not only to there being a greater amount of old aged people, but also to a greater life expectancy. This means mental diseases such as Dementia are increasingly common. Dementia is a type of brain disease, in which there is a gradual deterioration of various mental processes such as memory and thinking, to a point that severely affects everyday activities [2].

This work was supported by national funds through FCT, Fundação para a Ciência e a Tecnologia, under project UIDB/50021/2020 and project BioVisualSpeech (CMUP-ERI/TIC/0033/2014).

© Springer Nature Switzerland AG 2020
P. Quaresma et al. (Eds.): PROPOR 2020, LNAI 12037, pp. 413–419, 2020.
https://doi.org/10.1007/978-3-030-41505-1_40

With no cure in sight, a big effort has been put into the early identification of dementia, as Mild Cognitive Impairment (MCI) can often go unnoticed. MCI is one of the earliest stages of cognitive impairment that does not have noticeable symptoms, making it difficult to diagnose. For this reason, much attention is now focused on not only identifying cognitive impairment, but also on promoting cognitive stimulation as a means to maintain or even improve cognitive capabilities. The main area of application of cognitive stimulation for elders is in the administration of cognitive stimulation therapy (CST). This commonly consists of group sessions where elders discuss past events and play games that stimulate the brain, under the supervision of a therapist.

The need for a computer-based approach to cognitive stimulation has been widely accepted [7]. The gamification of therapy exercises is seen as a more engaging alternative to the repetitive and tedious nature of traditional cognitive exercises [6,13,15,16]. On the other hand, the use of social agents (either virtual or embodied) in computerized therapy has also shown positive reactions of elders in respect to mood and social interactions [5].

There is not yet an easily accessible technological solution that can allow cognitive stimulation exercises to be performed as a group activity. However, studies have shown that this is preferred by patients who suffer from dementia and cognitive impairment [10]. This project aims at developing such a solution by building a baseline system that consists of a multiplayer quiz game to be applied in the context of cognitive stimulation of the elderly population. This project is strongly inspired by VITHEA (Virtual Therapy for Aphasia Treatment) [4,14], a platform designed to act as a virtual therapist for patients that suffer from Aphasia.

Similarly, in the proposed game, a virtual agent–acting in this case as a "virtual host"– presents questions visually and using speech synthesis (TTS), whilst users' answers that are captured with a microphone array are verified using speech recognition (ASR), in a keyword spotting mode. Besides natural voice interactions, participants take their turns using a buzzing device.

2   Multiplayer Quiz Game

2.1   Game Design

The baseline version of our gameshow-like multiplayer quiz game for elderly players was developed in Unity, including simple, general knowledge questions. Two game modes were developed, a *speed* mode where the first player to press a button answers the questions, and a *turns* mode where all players take turns answering questions. All questions had open answers as oppose to multiple choice, so players were forced to provide an answer, using their memory.

In terms of visual design, much attention was given to the intuitiveness of the menus and interactions between the player and the game, as shown in Fig. 1. All the buttons that can be interacted with on-screen mimic the shape and colour of the correspondent button on the BUZZ! controllers used in this project. Figure 1 also shows the incorporation of a virtual agent that acts as a "gameshow host"

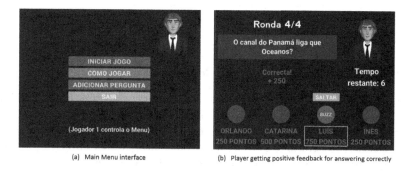

(a) Main Menu interface   (b) Player getting positive feedback for answering correctly

Fig. 1. In-game screenshots.

reading out questions and giving feedback. The game includes a score system, which means that at the end of the game the player that has answered most questions correctly is the winner. This creates objectives and positive feedback for the elders, encouraging them to perform well in the activity.

2.2 System Architecture

The microphone array used to capture the answers of the players was based on the Amazon Echo, state-of-the-art in distant speech. This, along with the Buzz! controllers were used to interact with the game, and connect to a PC that is running the game. The PC connects to a bigger TV screen so that the visual and audio feedback is clearer to the players, who can play at a certain distance from the PC. An internet connection is required for both the speech synthesis

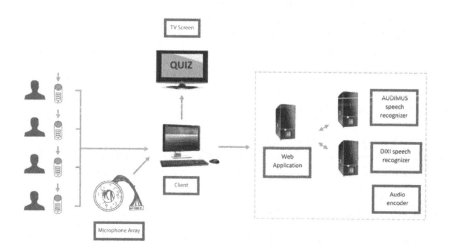

Fig. 2. Illustration of the final system architecture.

used with the virtual character for feedback and the speech recognition used to analyze the players' answers (Fig. 2).

2.3 Speech and Language Technologies

The implementation of the virtual agent in this game, shown in Fig. 1, combines text-to-speech synthesis (TTS) and automatic speech recognition (ASR) technologies, allowing it to take the role of the gameshow host. Speech synthesis is used to ask questions, guide players or give feedback, whilst speech recognition allows to "listen to" users' answers, thus, simulating a two-way interaction aimed at providing a more engaging experience to elder users. The TTS and ASR systems used in this project are AUDIMUS [8] and DIXI [11], respectively, which are in-house web services developed by INESC-ID's Spoken Language Processing Lab (L^2F).

AUDIMUS is a hybrid speech recognizer which follows a connectionist approach [9], and uses a general purpose, gender independent acoustic model that was trained with 57 h of down sampled Broadcast News data and 58 h of mixed fixed-telephone and mobile-telephone data in European Portuguese [3]. AUDIMUS can be used in a keyword spotting mode by incorporating a competing background speech model that is estimated without the need for acoustic model re-training [4]. This feature is used in this game as a manner of identifying if the player has said the correct answer amidst hesitations or long stretches of silence, which are common in elderly speech.

The DIXI speech synthesizer is based on the unit selection synthesis approach trained with an open domain cluster voice for European Portuguese. It serves to generate SAMPA phonemes and their alignment timings, besides the output raw audio signal, which is lossy encoded for usage in the client game. The timing of the phonemes is an essential part of the output of the speech synthesizer, since it serves to determine for how long a viseme should be animated. The 3D character created in the Unity game engine that was used in this project, can take the retrieved phoneme timings and use them to simulate speech by matching the viseme sequence to the audio output.

3 Preliminary Results

The first functional version of the proposed game was tested in home living room environments (group I), as well as in a senior university (group II), with participants consisting of young adult and elderly speakers (Table 1).

3.1 User Satisfaction Surveys

In order to evaluate the user experience, a survey was handed out to all the players with questions relating to the various elements of the game. Generally, the elements that received the best feedback were the virtual agent that acted as the "host" which players found very entertaining, as well as the ease to learn

Table 1. Distribution of participants in the two different age groups.

Group	No. speakers	No. in group I	No. in group II
Young (24–28 years old)	4	4	0
Elder (59–88 years old)	17	9	8

how to navigate the game with the controllers due to the simple game menus. In cases such as the senior university where the internet signal was weak, the excessively long time taken to analyze the players' answers and give feedback was a negative factor, as it slowed down the game considerably.

3.2 Speech Recognition Results

An important component of the game that was evaluated was the speech recognition. The metric used was the Word Verification Rate (WVR) which is the percentage of correct evaluations against total evaluations of players' answers (Table 2).

Table 2. Average WVR for the different categories.

Session category	Average WVR	$T_{positives}$	$T_{negatives}$	$F_{positives}$	$F_{negatives}$
Group I	0.84	82	42	11	12
Group II	0.75	13	17	2	8

As would be expected, elder participants lead to a weaker performance of the speech recognition, due to characteristics of their speech such as pauses and jitter [12]. However, in addition to this, the poor acoustic conditions of the room in the senior university, which had much reverberation and an inconsistent internet connection, meant that the results for that group were significantly lower compared to that of group I.

4   Conclusions and Future Work

This work proposed to develop a multiplayer voice-enabled game platform, to be used for cognitive stimulation of elders. The platform was designed to be as user-friendly and intuitive as possible. It can host a variety of components, such as a virtual host, SLT, Buzz controllers and a microphone array interacting with each other, all in the context of a quiz game.

The evaluation of the game produced quite promising results, with most players enjoying the main aspects of the game, such as the virtual host and the user interface. The main objective of creating a multiplayer experience that encouraged elders to interact with each other was achieved, with many valuing the group experience. A team mode was recently developed as a way to encourage further interaction between players. Recent progress on ASR also allowed further improvements. We plan to add different styles of questions, as opposed to only text-based, such as audio or visual cues in order to make the game more varied. It is also important to test the game in an elderly day care centre with players with early signs of cognitive impairment, as the elders in the senior university were healthy, both physically and mentally.

References

1. World population prospects - population division. https://population.un.org/wpp/. Accessed 28 Aug 2018
2. Dementia. https://www.who.int/en/news-room/fact-sheets/detail/dementia. Accessed 12 June 2018
3. Abad, A., Meinedo, H., Neto, J.: Automatic classification and transcription of telephone speech in radio broadcast data. In: Teixeira, A., de Lima, V.L.S., de Oliveira, L.C., Quaresma, P. (eds.) PROPOR 2008. LNCS (LNAI), vol. 5190, pp. 172–181. Springer, Heidelberg (2008). https://doi.org/10.1007/978-3-540-85980-2_18
4. Abad, A., Pompili, A., Costa, A., Trancoso, I.: Automatic word naming recognition for treatment and assessment of aphasia. In: Thirteenth Annual Conference of the International Speech Communication Association (2012)
5. Broekens, J., Heerink, M., Rosendal, H., et al.: Assistive social robots in elderly care: a review. Gerontechnology 8(2), 94–103 (2009)
6. Goldstein, J., Cajko, L., Oosterbroek, M., Michielsen, M., Van Houten, O., Salverda, F.: Video games and the elderly. Soc. Behav. Personal. Int. J. 25(4), 345–352 (1997)
7. Kueider, A.M., Parisi, J.M., Gross, A.L., Rebok, G.W.: Computerized cognitive training with older adults: a systematic review. PloS One 7(7), e40588 (2012)
8. Meinedo, H., Abad, A., Pellegrini, T., Trancoso, I., Neto, J.: The L^2F Broadcast News Speech Recognition System. In: Proceedings of the Fala 2010 (2010)
9. Morgan, N., Bourlard, H.: An introduction to hybrid HMM/connectionist continuous speech recognition. IEEE Signal Process. Mag. 12(3), 25–42 (1995)
10. Orgeta, V., et al.: Individual cognitive stimulation therapy for dementia: a clinical effectiveness and cost-effectiveness pragmatic, multicentre, randomised controlled trial. Health Technol. Assess. 19(64), 1–108 (2015)
11. Paulo, S., et al.: DIXI – A generic Text-to-Speech system for European Portuguese. In: Teixeira, A., de Lima, V.L.S., de Oliveira, L.C., Quaresma, P. (eds.) PROPOR 2008. LNCS (LNAI), vol. 5190, pp. 91–100. Springer, Heidelberg (2008). https://doi.org/10.1007/978-3-540-85980-2_10
12. Pellegrini, T., et al.: A corpus-based study of elderly and young speakers of European Portuguese: acoustic correlates and their impact on speech recognition performance. In: INTERSPEECH, pp. 852–856 (2013)
13. Peretz, C., Korczyn, A.D., Shatil, E., Aharonson, V., Birnboim, S., Giladi, N.: Computer-based, personalized cognitive training versus classical computer games: a randomized double-blind prospective trial of cognitive stimulation. Neuroepidemiology 36(2), 91–99 (2011)

14. Pompili, A., Amorim, C., Abad, A., Trancoso, I.: Speech and language technologies for the automatic monitoring and training of cognitive functions. In: Proceedings of SLPAT 2015: 6th Workshop on Speech and Language Processing for Assistive Technologies, pp. 103–109 (2015)
15. Torres, A.C.S.: Cognitive effects of video games on old people. Int. J. Disabil. Hum. Dev. **10**(1), 55–58 (2011)
16. Vasconcelos, A., Silva, P.A., Caseiro, J., Nunes, F., Teixeira, L.F.: Designing tablet-based games for seniors: the example of CogniPlay, a cognitive gaming platform. In: Proceedings of the 4th International Conference on Fun and Games, pp. 1–10. ACM (2012)

Towards a Conversational Agent
with "Character"

Gonçalo Melo[(✉)] and Luísa Coheur

Instituto Superior Técnico/INESC-ID, Lisbon, Portugal
goncalo.de.melo@tecnico.ulisboa.pt, luisa.coheur@l2f.inesc-id.pt

Abstract. We present a simple approach to create a "persona" conversational agent. First, we take advantage of a large collection of subtitles to train a generative model based on neural networks. Second, we manually handcraft a small corpus of interactions that specify our character (from now on the "persona corpus"). Third, we enrich a retrieval based engine with this corpus. Finally, we combine both into a single agent. A preliminary evaluation shows that the generative model can hardly implement a coherent "persona, but can successfully complement the retrieval model.

Keywords: Conversational agents · Generative and retrieval-based models · Persona bot

1 Introduction

Due to the release of large collections of movies' subtitles it is now possible to build data-driven conversational agents. However, despite the considerable success achieved in training NLP data-driven models, these models still have many downsides. An interaction with one of these agents quickly exposes its shortcomings, being their inability to display a consistent "persona" during a conversation a major issue [3]. The examples from Table 1 (taken from [3]) illustrate this problem.

Table 1. Examples demonstrating the consistency problem.

message Where do you live now?	message How old are you?
response I live in Los Angeles	response 16 and you?
message In which city do you live now?	message What's your age?
response I live in Madrid	response 18

If the target is to create a specific character such as a movie star or a book character, some interactions, defining the "persona" characteristics (*e.g. What is your name?, How old are you?, Are you evil?*), need to be provided. These

© Springer Nature Switzerland AG 2020
P. Quaresma et al. (Eds.): PROPOR 2020, LNAI 12037, pp. 420–424, 2020.
https://doi.org/10.1007/978-3-030-41505-1_41

usually are handcrafted and, thus, not in enough quantity to be used in a data-driven approach. Thus, a question arises: how can we create a "persona" bot and, at the same time, take advantage of existing large amounts of dialogues? In this work, we show how we have combined a data-driven approach with a retrieval-based one, being the latter based on a small corpus defining a "persona". We built a conversational agent that represents a book character: Carlos da Maia, from the Portuguese writer Eça de Queirós book, "Os Maias". We start by collecting a subtitles' corpus, which is used to train a generative model based on a Sequence-to-Sequence (seq2seq) model with an attention mechanism [6]. After that, we define the "persona corpus" that characterize the agent. This corpus is used as the knowledge base of Say Something Smart (SSS) [1], a retrieval-based dialogue engine. Finally, we combine both models into a single agent. When the conversational agent is queried, it will search for a suitable answer using SSS. If no suitable answer is found, it will use the generative model to generate an answer.

This paper is organized as follows: in Sect. 2 we describe the used datasets, and, in Sect. 3 we detail our model. In Sect. 4 we show the results of our experiments, and, finally, in Sect. 5 we present the main conclusions and point to future work.

2 Datasets

Our work is based in two corpora in Portuguese. The first is constituted of subtitles and is used to train the generative model; the second is handcrafted and "defines" Carlos da Maia. We used the OpenSubtitles dataset [4][1], which is publicly available (the Portuguese dataset contains subtitles of 96711 movies). Then, as many subtitles are badly ranked, some contain profanity words, etc., we have filtered the original corpus, by taking advantage of the B-Subtle [8] tool. B-Subtle allows to create corpora according to many different filtering options. The applied filters were: (a) Audience Adult: false; (b) Subtitle Rating Minimum: 5.0. Then, the data goes through a trimming and filtering process where we remove interactions: (a) with infrequent words (count < 3); (b) with sentences of length superior to a determined threshold (length > 10).

In what concerns the Carlos da Maia dataset, we have built the persona corpus. It has 71 interactions, such as (Onde estudaste? (Where did you go to college?), Estudei em Coimbra (In Coimbra.)).

3 Model

The proposed system includes a generative model based on a seq2seq model, and the retrieval-based engine SSS. Given a user query, we start by calling an instance of SSS, which retrieves an answer from its knowledge base corpus. If the selected answer does not have a score above a certain threshold, the generative model is called upon, generating a new answer (as represented in Fig. 1).

---

[1] http://opus.nlpl.eu.

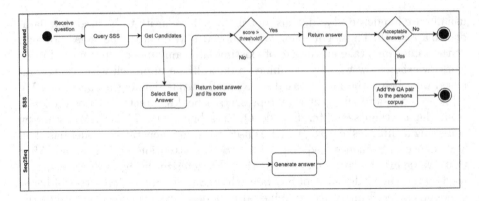

Fig. 1. Activity Diagram of the proposed architecture.

3.1 Generative Model

In the generative part of our agent the encoder uses the bidirectional variant of the Gate Recurrent Unit (GRU) [2]. We also implement the attention mechanism described in [6]. The loss function used for training the model calculates the average negative log likelihood of the elements of the sentence. During training we use teacher forcing with a ratio of 0.5. Another mechanism used to aid in convergence is gradient clipping. We use 50 as the max value for gradients. The model was trained for ten thousand iterations over the dataset defined in the previous section.

3.2 The Retrieval-Based Module

Upon receiving a query, the SSS engine retrieves an answer from a set of question/answer pairs that define the agent "persona" by using Lucene[2]. The selection of the best answer is made according to a set of weighted criteria, whose weights were previously defined [1,7]. In our model we use the following criterion to select the correct answer: (a) Answer Similarity To User Question (weight = 25); (b) Question Similarity To User Question (weight = 50); (c) Simple Conversation Context (weight = 25). To measure the similarity between the utterances (for the criterion used) we used the following measures: (a) Dice (weight = 25); (b) Jaccard (weight = 25); (c) Edit Distance (weight = 50).

4   Evaluation

Since automated metrics are sub-optimal for evaluating dialogues [5], we perform a human evaluation. We asked 10 people (from 20 to 53 years old, with different backgrounds) to chat with two chatbots (a simple Seq2Seq model as described and the composed model) as if they were meeting someone new; then

---

[2] http://lucene.apache.org.

they are asked to fill a questionnaire about their experience. The questionnaire is composed of 3 statements about the bots and the user must give a score from 1 to 5 (1 meaning "completely disagree" and 5 meaning "completely agree"). The statements are: (a) The bot's answers were satisfying; (b) The bot seemed to maintain a coherent personality; (c) The interaction with the bot felt natural. Figure 2 shows the obtained results (average).

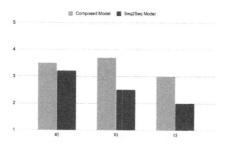

Fig. 2. Results from the human evaluation.

Table 2 shows examples of interactions. In the first the user request was in the "persona corpus"; in the second a similar question was in the "persona corpus"; in the third interaction the answer was obtained with the generative model. Thus, the first two questions were answered by SSS and the third by the generative model.

Table 2. Samples of the conversations that occurred during evaluation.

Human - Como te chamas?	What is your name?
Machine (Retrieval model) - Chamo-me Carlos da Maia	My name is Carlos da Maia
Human - E vives no Ramalhete?	And do you live in Ramalhete?
Machine (Retrieval model) - N'O Ramalhete	At Ramalhete
Human - Sabes se és real?	Do you know if you are real?
Machine (Generative model) - Não sei	I don't know

As in [9], we assume that each line of dialogue corresponds to a full speaker turn; also we assume that two consecutive utterances belong to the same conversation; in addition, the subtitles' dataset is large, open-domain and noisy, and it does not specify which character speaks in each line of dialogue. Considering this, a certain level of noise is introduced in our training, since consecutive lines may not be part of the same conversation or even the same scene and might even be spoken by the same character. In what respects the "persona corpus", even though we attempted to add as many paraphrases as possible to each question, these are virtually never-ending, which means that the generative model will be used to generate a new answer when confronted with a new formulation, potentially answering in an inconsistent way.

5   Conclusions and Future Work

In this work we have explored a simple approach to create a "persona" conversational agent, in Portuguese, taking advantage of recent trends in the field. The suggested model allowed us to create an agent that is able to remain consistent (to some degree) when answering personal questions and still flexible enough to answer questions not answered in the "persona corpus". Our results are encouraging, indicating that this approach is able to achieve a smoother interaction and overall more pleasant experience for humans when using chatbots.

Future work includes exploring more refined tactics, and take advantage of the Internet Movie Script Database, which identifies which character speaks each line of the script, although not much data is available for Portuguese.

References

1. Ameixa, D., Coheur, L., Fialho, P., Quaresma, P.: Luke, I am your father: dealing with out-of-domain requests by using movies subtitles. In: Bickmore, T., Marsella, S., Sidner, C. (eds.) IVA 2014. LNCS (LNAI), vol. 8637, pp. 13–21. Springer, Cham (2014). https://doi.org/10.1007/978-3-319-09767-1_2
2. Cho, K., et al.: Learning phrase representations using RNN encoder-decoder for statistical machine translation. In: Proceedings of the 2014 Conference on Empirical Methods in Natural Language Processing (EMNLP), pp. 1724–1734, Doha, Qatar. Association for Computational Linguistics, (Oct 2014). https://doi.org/10.3115/v1/D14-1179, https://www.aclweb.org/anthology/D14-1179
3. Li, J., Galley, M., Brockett, C., Spithourakis, G., Gao, J., Dolan, B.: A persona-based neural conversation model. In: Proceedings of the 54th Annual Meeting of the Association for Computational Linguistics (Volume 1: Long Papers), pp. 994–1003, Berlin, Germany. Association for Computational Linguistics (Aug 2016). https://doi.org/10.18653/v1/P16-1094, https://www.aclweb.org/anthology/P16-1094
4. Lison, P., Tiedemann, J., Kouylekov, M.: OpenSubtitles2018: statistical rescoring of sentence alignments in large, noisy parallel corpora. In: Proceedings of the Eleventh International Conference on Language Resources and Evaluation (LREC-2018), Miyazaki, Japan. European Languages Resources Association (ELRA) (May 2018)
5. Liu, C.W., Lowe, R., Serban, I., Noseworthy, M., Charlin, L., Pineau, J.: How NOT to evaluate your dialogue system: an empirical study of unsupervised evaluation metrics for dialogue response generation. In: Proceedings of the 2016 Conference on Empirical Methods in Natural Language Processing, pp. 2122–2132, Austin, Texas. Association for Computational Linguistics (Nov 2016). https://doi.org/10.18653/v1/D16-1230, https://www.aclweb.org/anthology/D16-1230
6. Luong, M.T., Pham, H., Manning, C.D.: Effective approaches to attention-based neural machine translation. arXiv preprint arXiv:1508.04025 (2015)
7. Mendonça, V., Melo, F.S., Coheur, L., Sardinha, A.: A conversational agent powered by online learning. In: Proceedings of the 16th Conference on Autonomous Agents and MultiAgent Systems, AAMAS 2017, pp. 1637–1639. International Foundation for Autonomous Agents and Multiagent Systems, Richland, SC (2017). http://dl.acm.org/citation.cfm?id=3091282.3091388
8. Ventura, M.: One Million Agents Speaking All the Languages in the World. Master's thesis, Instituto Superior Técnico, Universidade de Lisboa, Lisbon, Portugal (2018)
9. Vinyals, O., Le, Q.: A neural conversational model. arXiv preprint arXiv:1506.05869 (2015)

Author Index

Printed in the United States
By Bookmasters